Capital Ships of the Imperial Japanese Navy 1868–1945

Ironclads, Battleships & Battle Cruisers:

An Outline History of Their Design, Construction and Operations

Volume III

The *Yamato* Class and Subsequent Planning

With 87 photos, 202 figures/drawings, 15 maps/track charts, 60 tables

Hans Lengerer & Lars Ahlberg

*N*imble Books LLC

NIMBLE BOOKS LLC

Nimble Books LLC

Ann Arbor, MI, USA
http://www.NimbleBooks.com
wfz@nimblebooks.com

Copyright 2021 Hans Lengerer and Lars Ahlberg
Printed in the United States of America
ISBN-13: **9781608882328**

∞ The paper used in print versions of this publication meets the minimum requirements of the American National Standard for Information Sciences—Permanence of Paper for Printed Library Materials, ANSI Z39.48-1992. The paper is acid-free and lignin-free.

TABLE OF CONTENTS

Introduction 1
Part I: Technical Section 17
    Chapter 1—Design History and General Description 19
    Chapter 2–Outline Description of the Main Armament 147
    Chapter 3–Fire Control System 195
    Chapter 4–Bridge Structure 233
    Chapter 5–Additional Notes on the Armor Protection 267
    Chapter 6–Detailed Description of the Main Gun Turret
Part II: Operational Section 369
    Chapter 7—Operational Histories 371
    Chapter 8—Loss of the *Musashi* 415
    Chapter 1—Loss of the *Yamato* 457
Part III: Subsequent Planning Section 527
    Chapter 10—Incomplete Sisters and the Never-Built
    Super *Yamato* Class 529
Select Bibliography 543

NIMBLE BOOKS LLC

PREFACE

This is the third volume of a trilogy dealing with the history of the Japanese capital ships (armorclads, battleships and battle cruisers) from the introduction of the first armorclad in the early Meiji era until the definite end of the battleship era, coinciding with the end of World War II.

Volume One will deal with the foreign built armorclads and battleships from *Fusō* (I) to *Kongō* (II), in company with the Chinese (1895) and Russian war prizes (1905), incorporated in the register of Imperial Japanese Navy (IJN) warships as either second class or first class battleships, and the first domestic built forerunners of the battle cruiser and pre- and semi-dreadnoughts, the latter built in a period dominated by the British *Dreadnought* and hence already outdated when commissioned. Irrespective of this fate, design and construction of these ships, less than forty years after the Meiji Restoration, was a milestone in the history of Japanese warship construction and proof of the breath-taking tempo of Japan's struggle to become a world naval power. The building of two sisters of the battle cruisers of the *Kongō* class in civilian shipyards meant the preliminary completion of the military-industrial complex. During this period of time the foremost imaginary enemy, against which the naval armament was directed, changed from Russia to China in 1882 and back again to Russia in 1895 before, in 1907, the United States was included in the list of imaginary enemies, but considered a budgetary enemy rather than an actual one.

Volume Two will be dedicated to the super-dreadnought type battleships designed and built within the scope of Japan's famous Eight-Eight Fleet (in 1918 expanded to the Eight-Eight-Eight Fleet). Both plans came to an abrupt end with the Washington Arms Limitation Treaty in 1922. Even though the conclusion unburdened the national budget and permitted the reduction of the naval organisation, including the military-industrial complex, the ratio, decided by the treaty on the basis of the existing capital ship tonnage, caused consternation. Forced to revise the strategic and tactical planning against the primary hypothetical enemy (which had been the United States since 1918), the Naval General Staff conceived countermeasures, which strongly influenced shipbuilding policy and affected the modernization of the capital ships, particularly those built before the lessons of the Jutland sea battle in 1916 were known and applied to newly built ships. The London Arms Limitation Treaty in 1930 imposed further restrictions upon the IJN. These referred primarily to ship types not considered in the former treaty and also caused the conversion of the battleship *Hiei* into a training ship. These changes reinforced the effects already exerted by the first treaty and the military order made efforts to invent unconventional countermeasures and upgrade the fighting power of the existing capital ships on the basis of a revised operational planning.

Acknowledgements from Hans Lengerer

In compiling the material for this monograph I depended heavily upon the extraordinary kind assistance and generous support of many individuals, besides those to whose memory this book is dedicated. The help of these individuals and others mentioned later was not, of course, limited to the *Yamato* class, and, as a matter of fact, some of them never supplied information about these giants. Instead they shared parts of their special interests in the Meiji and Taishō eras war vessels and their immense knowledge of Japanese naval history in general with me. For instance, Professor Takahashi Shigeo, who spoke and wrote German, was instrumental in writing a manuscript on the Meiji navy, former Rear-Admiral Takasu Kōichi, who studied weapon technology at the Tōkyō University in 1943, promoted my understanding in this particular field and Dr. Itani Jirō, a naval chemist, provided documents, literature, and insightful advice. In doing so they provided invaluable help and one part of the fruits of their efforts will be expressed in volumes I and II of this trilogy. It is for this reason that this volume also is dedicated to them. Among Japanese individuals I am especially thankful to (in alphabetical order) Messrs. Endō Akira, Fujita Takashi, Hayashi Yoshikazu, Kamakura Takumi, Kimata Jirō, Kitagawa Ken'ichi, Kitamura Kunio, Koike Naohiko, Maejima Hajime, Mizutani Kiyotaka, Dr. Morino Tetsuo, Naitō Hatsuho (via Dr. Itani) and Tamura Toshio.

Special thanks go to Messrs. Izumi Kōzō and Tsukamoto Hideki. It was by the good offices of Mr. Tsukamoto that Mr. Izumi permitted the use of some of his very fine drawings. Mr. Tsukamoto has already been introduced in the book *BC Kongō Class–CV Unryū Class*[1] and Mr. Izumi, one of Japan's leading model builders, if not the leading model builder, requires no introduction to scholars of Japanese naval history. Model builders and readers will surely enjoy the reproduction of more of his drawings in volumes I and II.

The generous use of photographs from the well-known Fukui Shizuo Collection, which is now in the possession of the Kure Maritime Museum, was permitted by Messrs. Todaka Kazushige, the director of the *Yamato* Museum,

---

[1] Katowice: Model Hobby, 2010, www.modelhobby.pl

and Tsuda Fumio, the head of the Curator Service of the Museum, for which I would like to express my utmost thanks once again. Photos from this outstanding collection have been published, in the previously mentioned book about the *Kongō* and *Unryū* classes as well as in *Japanese Hybrid Warships*.[2]

The descriptions of the last operations of *Yamato* and *Musashi*, ending with their total loss, depend very much upon the Japanese official war history, compiled in 102 volumes. Written permission for the use of selected volumes including track charts, maps, cruising dispositions and other illustrations was obtained, besides others, by the good offices of Dr. Itani, who visited what was then called the Historical Branch at the end of the 1980s. Copies of track charts etc. as drawn in the detailed action reports (DARs) or redrawn on their basis are reprinted for their value as documentary material.

Even with such support I am sure that owing to my amateurish knowledge and understanding, errors of fact or interpretation will be discovered and I wish to point out that I alone am responsible for such errors in the Introduction and chapters 1–6 and 8–10.

Hans Lengerer
Birkenhard, Germany
14 June 2014

---

[2] Katowice: Model Hobby, 2009.

Acknowledgements from Lars Ahlberg

Over the years several individuals have supplied me with information about the Imperial Japanese Navy.

I would particularly like to mention Messrs. Ishibashi Takao, an excellent draughtsman and a noted authority on the IJN (his recent book *Senkan • Junyōsenkan* is highly recommended[3]), who has not only answered my questions but also gave me permission to use some drawings; Nakagawa Tsutomu, author of numerous articles for the well-known journal *Sekai no Kansen*; Takagi Hiroshi, an expert on propulsion systems who also gained me permission to use drawings from *Sekai no Kansen* and *Maru* (Ushioshobō-Kōjinsha Co., Ltd.); the late Rear-Admiral Takasu Kōichi, who has already been introduced above; and Iwasaki Yutaka, a naval architect who has also checked and re-checked many Japanese expressions.

For the operational section of this book Messrs. Robert Hackett and Sander Kingsepp have kindly permitted me to use the Tabular Records of Movement (TROMs) as published on the Internet site *Senkan! Stories and Battle Histories of the IJN's Battleships*.[4]

Mr. Nathan Okun, a leading authority on guns and armor, has read parts of an early draft of the armor and armament sections and his expert knowledge is greatly appreciated. Several remarks made by him are included in the presented text. Mr. Richard Worth, an excellent naval historian and author, has generously answered numerous questions.

Without the assistance of all these individuals it would have been much more difficult to write this story about the *Yamato* class battleships and any merit this work possesses is in large part attributable to their generosity. I therefore express my warmest thanks to them all. Any errors and omissions are, however, my own responsibility.

Lars Ahlberg
Halmstad, Sweden
14 June 2014

---

[3] Tōkyō: Namiki Shobō, 2007.
[4] http://www.combinedfleet.com/senkan.htm

NIMBLE BOOKS LLC

Introduction

The design and construction of the 70,000-ton "mammoth" battleships *Yamato* and *Musashi*, armed with the largest guns ever mounted on modern battleships and protected by the thickest and newest types of armor, were the zenith of Japanese warship building and the pride of both Japanese naval architects and Japanese tacticians. The former were proud to have accomplished an unprecedented task by not only expanding former examples but by incorporating novel features in a new class of battleships, which, according to the intention of the tacticians, should turn the tide by one stroke and secure the IJN's supremacy in the Western Pacific. Responding both to the accomplishment of a technical masterpiece and to the consequent pursuance and development of strategical planning to exploit these valuable assets, there exists a wealth of literature in Japan about this class describing all conceivable aspects. To treat all of this material would mean the inclusion of trivial items and would also require an unacceptable volume for general readers. In view of this aspect the description has been limited to the principal characteristics of these battleships, supplemented by some data of general nature.

The design of this class was begun in 1934 or roughly sixty years after the establishment of the Navy Ministry in April 1872. This was almost 17 years after the forceful opening of the "closed country" Japan by Commodore M. C. Perry's "black ships" in July 1853. At that time Japan was still a medieval country with feudal structure; the central government formed by the Tokugawa Shogunate and about 250 fiefs ruled by Daimyōs, and a population divided into four classes. There was no industrial production but only handicraft manufacturing. As Japan had been practising the seclusion policy since the beginning of the 17th Century, there existed no navy worthy of the name. Coastal forts armed with various types of guns had been erected in several strategic positions but neither these nor the small, wooden vessels propelled by oars and sails, were capable of opposing the two American (Western type) steamships and the two sailing ships.

The warnings about the dangers of the seclusion policy in a world experiencing the effects of the industrial revolution and the advice the Bakufu, as the government of the Shogun was called, received in 1844 and afterwards via the Dutch merchant house at Deshima were ignored even though they were strongly underlined by Commodore J. Biddle's arrival at Uraga in 1846. Even when the Bakufu received all available information about the American expedition to Japan via the Dutch, nothing was done and the Bakufu was thrown into confusion by the appearance of the American ships in Edo (Tōkyō) Bay. The power of the Bakufu, already waning before the arrival of the "black ships," declined rapidly thereafter. Treaties were concluded with an increasing number of foreign countries, ports were forced to open to settlement by foreigners, anti-foreign outbursts were punished by expeditions of Allied forces, and interior rivalries accelerated before the feudal regime collapsed under pressure and was relieved by a new government in 1868.

Before its collapse the Bakufu had made some important steps indispensable for the build-up of a navy, such as establishment of schools and training centres based upon Dutch advice; the invitation of naval missions from abroad (Holland and Britain and practical instructions by a few Frenchmen); dispatch of students to abroad to study naval techniques and tactics; adoption of Western sciences and technologyp[5] domestic construction of "Western type" ships, followed by purchase from abroad when the insufficient technical level in Japan was recognised; organisation of a coastal navy; reformation of domestic shipyards; and the design and construction of iron works (actually shipyards) with the hiring of foreign instructors.

The leaders of the new Meiji government clearly recognised that Japan would become a member of the world community having equal rights only by modernization, that is, the revision of not only the state structure but also the daily life of the people. Education by the adoption of Western science and learning was the key for the transformation of a feudal society into a modern community and the oligarchs made utmost efforts in this direction so that they could be freed from the unequal treaties the Bakufu had been forced to sign under the pressure of shipboard guns. To achieve this final goal setting-up of a parliamentary form of government, solution of fiscal problems, resumption of foreign relations, encouragement of industry and commerce, build-up of infrastructure, establishment of military forces to prevent the fate from becoming a colony etc., all were recognised as necessary. In short: A complete transformation of almost every aspect of national life had to be accomplished.

---

[5] The Bakufu supported and expanded the original Dutch School (*Rangaku* = the scholars who now were informed about developments outside Japan by reading Dutch books and experienced, sometimes, suppression when progressive ideas were discussed or warnings given.) into the Office for the Study of Barbarian Writings (*Bansho Torishirabesho*) in 1856.

Sixty years later Japan would design the world's largest battleships. The pride many Japanese still feel in having made such a phenomenal development in such a short time may be understandable.

Turning to the naval aspect only it must be considered a big stroke of luck that, in general, the new government continued the previously outlined naval policy of the Tokugawa Shogunate. It adopted a new defense structure incorporating the newest developments taken over from the model which, since 1870, was Britain's Royal Navy, by Imperial rescript. The Douglas mission, coming to Japan in 1873, taught the British naval way, and students were dispatched to England and the United States for studies. Yokosuka shipyard, built under French supervision, was still under French command until the end of 1875 and here the building of wooden sailing ships with steam propulsion as auxiliary means was begun. Hampered by serious financial problems the build-up of the IJN was very slow. Only one armored frigate and two belted corvettes of composite construction were built in British shipyards for the IJN in the 1870s.[6] In 1883 an expansion was announced under the stimulus of a tense situation in Korea, and worsened relations with China caused the shift of the hypothetical enemy to China from Russia. The 1880s were characterized by the quick transformation from wood to steel as construction material, via the "intermediate types" of domestically built ships, requiring both revisions of shipyard facilities and training of workers, while modern protected cruisers and unique coast defense ships were ordered from Britain and France. With the hiring of the eminent French naval architect L. E. Bertin as adviser of the Navy Ministry, from 1886 to 1890, French influence dominated naval policy, warship design and construction techniques for a short time before the British style finally gained the upper hand in the 1890s.[7]

As a consequence the Sino-Japanese War 1894–95 was fought almost entirely with foreign-built warships, as was the Russo-Japanese War in 1904–05. Stimulated by the victory in the Sino-Japanese War and the recognition of the value of the navy within the national defense structure, the major part of the huge Chinese war indemnity was used for the tremendous expansion of the

---

[6] For more on this see *Contributions to the History of Imperial Japanese Warships*, papers I–III, written by Hans Lengerer and edited by Lars Ahlberg. These papers can be ordered from Lars Ahlberg (e-mail: lars.ahlberg@halmstad.mail.postnet.se) or Hans Lengerer (e-mail: hans.lengerer@gmx.de).

[7] See also *Contributions to the History of Imperial Japanese Warships*, papers V & VI, and "Louis Emile Bertin and the Imperial Japanese Navy" (*The Mariner's Mirror*, vol. 93, no. 4, November 2007).

IJN and the build-up of the military-industrial complex, supplemented by the promotion of merchant shipbuilding and shipping by subvention laws. These steps were also furthered by the so-called Triple Intervention (of Russia, France and Germany) immediately after signing the peace treaty to end the Sino-Japanese War. Under the leadership of Russia, Japan was forced to cede the Liaodong Peninsula to China, while Russia leased Port Arthur and Dalian (Liaodong Peninsula) and increased the tempo of its advance to the south; France leased territory in South China; and Germany occupied and then leased Quingdao. Britain leased Weihai (Shandong Peninsula) after the Japanese troops retreated. Russia's advance was recognised as the biggest threat to Japanese interests and caused the shift of the hypothetical enemy back to Russia. To oppose the Russian Pacific Fleet a two-stage naval expansion programme was worked out, with the so-called Six-Six Fleet (six battleships and six armored cruisers) as the centrepiece. All the battleships and four of the six armored cruisers were ordered from British shipyards. The co-operation between Japanese naval architects, naval engineers and weapon production officers and their British counterparts in the design of the most modern large warships, and the dispatch of the former as supervisors when the ships were under construction, deepened the theoretical and practical basis of Japanese naval shipbuilding and paved the way for domestic design and building of many ship types. The British-Japanese Alliance, concluded in January 1902, was not only a diplomatic masterpiece to prevent another Triple intervention, but also a mechanism for obtaining confidential information from the Royal Navy. During the Russo-Japanese War the ingenious *Tsukuba* class,[8] the prototype of the later battle cruiser, and the *Satsuma* class, then the largest pre-dreadnought type battleships, were laid down in Kure Navy Yard and Yokosuka Navy Yard, respectively, in 1905.

In order to learn the newest design and building techniques the battle cruiser *Kongō* (II) was ordered from Britain in 1910. By the dispatch of more than 200 employees to Vickers this order also enabled the two largest private shipyards, Kawasaki Kōbe and Mitsubishi Nagasaki, to be part of the construction of the largest warships.[9]

---

[8] See *Contributions to the History of Imperial Japanese Warships*, papers VII & VIII, and "Japan's Proto-Battlecruisers: The *Tsukuba* and *Kurama* Classes" (*Warship 1992*).

[9] See "The Battlecruisers of the *Kongō* Class" (*Warship 2012*).

Like other navies the IJN had recognised the armorclad and then, from 1890 when the first British standard type battleship appeared, the battleship as the centre of the fleet. Efforts to order armorclads comparable with foreign counterparts from abroad had been in vain up to 1890 due to financial reasons, and were then postponed by serious controversies between the newly established Diet and the government, very worsened relations with China and the Emperor's urging caused the passing of a programme including two of the later "Six" battleships, referred to above.

After the victory in the Russo-Japanese War the principles of the national defense were worked out and adopted by the Emperor in April 1907. For the IJN the so-called Eight-Eight Fleet was considered the minimum necessary force. The core of this fleet was eight battleships and eight armored cruisers (later battle cruisers) of less than eight years of age. The Eight-Eight Fleet was the IJN's most ambitious programme and required tremendous expenditures due to the expansion and completion of the military-industrial complex, spiralling building expenses during World War I and thereafter, material shortages and so on. However, it took time before the construction of this fleet was begun. Before, Russian war prizes were repaired, sometimes after salvage, and included in the warship register, among them six as battleships. However, their relative fighting value as pre-dreadnought ships was already considerably reduced before commissioning by the appearance of the "all-big-gun" British battleship *Dreadnought*. This was a fate shared with the domestically built battleships and armored cruisers mentioned above and also with the later built semi-dreadnoughts *Kawachi* and *Settsu*. One cannot but state that the leaders of the IJN must have suffered from a remarkable lack of farsightedness when taking these measures, which also included permission to mount guns of different length on the same ship, with the result that battleships that would otherwise have been dreadnoughts were degraded to semi-dreadnoughts.

These errors were corrected in the design and construction of the domestically built battleships *Fusō* (II) and *Yamashiro* and their improved "quasi sisters" *Ise* and *Hyūga*. After the extensive practical preparation by the building of the battle cruisers of the *Kongō* (II) class, these battleships were designed and built without foreign assistance in the large navy yards and the two large civilian shipyards. Armed with the same calibre guns as the *Kongō* (II) class—

14"/35.56-cm—they were called "Ultra *Do*" class in Japan.[10] With the adoption of this calibre on the battle cruiser *Kongō* (II) the IJN preceded the United States Navy and when the next generation of battleships (the *Nagato* class) was designed with 16"/40.6-cm guns, the IJN again preceded the USN and expressed her belief that future sea battles would be decided by the power of the main guns, as in the past. The 33,800-ton battleship *Nagato* was completed in Kure Navy Yard in 1920 as the biggest battleship and was also recognised as the most powerful one. This was approximately 14 years after the completion of the armored cruiser (later battle cruiser) *Tsukuba* by the same navy yard with a displacement of about 41% and a broadside weight of approximately 15% of the later ship. For the construction of *Tsukuba* steel material imported from the United States and other countries had to be used, but for the construction of *Nagato* almost everything was produced in Japan, apart from some fittings and equipments. This is evidence of the very quick development and the almost independent warship technology the Japanese had attained at the end of World War I. It also underlines the unique forerunner role of the shipbuilding industry in the industrialization process of Japan. With the passing of the Eight-Four Fleet Preparation Programme (eight battleships and four battle cruisers) in 1916, the Eight-Four Fleet Completion Programme in 1917, the Eight-Six Fleet Programme in 1918 and, finally, the Eight-Eight Fleet Programme in 1920, the IJN aimed at the possession of three fleets at the end of fiscal year (FY) 1927 (31 March 1928). Each fleet should be composed of eight of the newest battleships and eight of the newest battle cruisers. Another fleet should consist of older capital ships, including dreadnoughts and semi-dreadnoughts. The latter was outside the Eight-Eight Fleet for ships in these fleets had to be younger than eight years after completion. Even though the minimum necessary force had to be expanded to an Eight-Eight-Eight Fleet at the revision of the national defense policy in 1918, the building of a third fleet, that should consist of eight of the most modern battleships was probably never seriously considered according to a statement made by the Navy Minister to the Diet. The Navy's view was to concentrate upon the Eight-Eight Fleet goal for the time being. These capital ships fleets required a large number of support and escort ships, plus logistics vessels, and many auxiliary warship types

---

[10] *Do* = *Dreadnought*, ultra because the calibre exceeded the 12"/30.48-cm calibre guns of the *Dreadnought*.

were needed for the defense of naval ports and facilities within each naval region. These additional ships required a further expansion of the military-industrial complex and their maintenance would puff up the naval budget still more. Every responsible statesman had to recognise that the national finances would collapse under this heavy burden, which was accentuated by the depression period after the World War. The tempo of the naval competition had accelerated after the American Josephus Daniels' Three-Year Plan of 1916, as shown by the quick passage of the Japanese naval expansion programmes.

Before financial collapse ensued, the conclusion of the Washington Arms Limitation Treaty in February 1922 ended the naval race. After the end of World War I, Japan had advanced to the third position among the world naval powers, when counting number and displacement of capital ships. This advance was caused more by the annihilation of the Imperial German Navy, the quasi impotence of the former Imperial Russian Navy and the reduction of the French Navy than by the addition of new capital ships. Therefore the IJN had a considerable number of pre-dreadnought, semi-dreadnought and dreadnought type ships when the famous 5: 5: 3 ratio (USA, Britain, Japan) for modern capital ships was accompanied by the abolishment of the earlier types. The "naval holidays" (ten-year building stop of capital ships) and the scrapping of many old capital ships meant a big reduction of the naval budget, but the ratio was recognised as alarming in view of the national defense and caused uneasiness within the population.

With battleships, battle cruisers and aircraft carriers (collectively known as capital ships) limited, the naval race shifted to auxiliary ship types, foremost among them were cruisers and destroyers, whose possession had not been regulated by the Washington Treaty. But the quantitative inferiority was expanded upon these types and also submarines by the conclusion of the London Arms Limitation Treaty in April 1930. The acceptance of the ratios for these ship types in that treaty brought about the biggest crisis of the IJN. Plotted by "hawks" in the Naval General Staff it ended with a great reshuffle of officers in the highest positions of the Navy Ministry and the Naval General Staff and new rules for the co-operation between the highest administrative and the highest military order organs of the IJN–the hawks won.

During the remaining period of arms limitation, and also before and after, the modernization conversion of the battleships, aircraft carriers and heavy cruisers was carried out and concealed ship types were built to bring particular attack weapons into action. The latter were part of a revised strategy, which had to be adapted to the new situation after the conclusion of the London Arms Limitation Treaty. Besides midget submarines, heavy torpedo ships (converted light cruisers) were also intended to play an important role. The improvement of the aircraft and aircraft carriers was realised as a requirement but their role as an auxiliary force did not change. The seclusion of the military-industrial complex relative to other organisations, and the excessive use of military secrecy, prevented the inclusion of private and public scientific and research organisations for technical development and the transformation of the results of scientific researches into practical applications. On the other hand some critics contend that responsible persons often lacked the capability to make use of technical innovations for military purposes and this critique refers to both technicians and tacticians. In his "Notes on Warships" (*Kansen Nōto*), p. 10, the well-known naval architect (and later Dr.) Makino Shigeru states that the construction of *Yamato* and *Musashi* "forced us to make technically strenuous efforts but it also forced us to maintain a very strict secrecy" and he believes that "much was lost because the latter prevented the application of complete wisdom."

Among the countermeasures newly adopted or intensified with the goal to eliminate the quantitative inferiority embedded in the naval arms limitation schemes were the principles of "superior quality of each ship" and "outranging firing." The value of the battleship was determined by the combination of the following three elements:

- *Adequate fire power.* The capability to deal destructive blows within the shortest time.
- *Strong armor protection.* The ability to take a beating without losing fighting capability.
- *Mobility.* The ability to attain high speeds and have good manoeuvrability and also sufficient range.

These principles first appeared as dominant features of the modern naval landscape during the American Civil War in the 1860s. The Battle of the Yellow Sea (Yalu) on 17 September 1894 and the Battle in the Japan Sea (Tsushima) on 27–28 May 1905 verified these combinations in a new form. The effect of the large calibre gun and the value of strong protection were confirmed, again, in the Jutland sea battle on 31 May – 1 June 1916.

The IJN, which was faced with the responsibility of annihilating a numerically superior force with the much inferior Six-Four Fleet (Six-Three Fleet after the conclusion of the London Treaty),[11] concluded that she had to adopt the "outranging method" to attack and sink or, at least, damage the enemy outside the firing range of his guns. The 16" (40.6-cm) gun with a maximum firing range of 37,900 m could not win against the 18.1" (46-cm) gun, whose projectile bridged 40,800 m. This was the basic principle underlying the construction of the super-battleships of the *Yamato* class. But with an attack range of 40 km no battleship could defeat an aircraft carrier when the planes of the latter attacked from a distance of 200 km or even more. The problem at that time was the unreliability of the calculation of the number of planes necessary to defeat a battleship.

In the 1930s the the IJN assumed the maximum bomb load of an enemy bomber to be less than one ton when attacking a Japanese battleship. The penetrating power of the bomb was less than the 40-cm armor-piercing (AP) projectile; the effect of the detonation in the water corresponded to about that of a torpedo. If the battleship had a complete underwater protection and a vertical and horizontal protection designed against the super large calibre AP projectiles (40-cm), it should be practically invulnerable to air attacks. Therefore, one had not to bother much about air attacks; a completely protected battleship could not be sunk by aircraft.

Previously collected experiences and statistical data about hitting rates proved that only a few percent of the fired projectiles and launched torpedoes would hit and the same was true with regard to the released bombs. However, these 1930s calculations totally neglected industrial productivity. Small planes could be produced in enormous numbers and could attack a battleship with numerous torpedoes and bombs. If the attacks were well coordinated or, simply, the number of torpedoes and bombs was overwhelming, the battleship

---

[11] The principles for the national defence were revised in June 1936, in expectation of the lapse of the treaties and in response to the international situation. The minimum necessary forces were newly defined and the main battle force was decided to be twelve battleships. This means that this goal was attained with the reconstruction of the training battleship *Hiei* and the building of the two super-battleships *Yamato* and *Musashi*. It will be explained later that the IJN was forced to expand this number considerably under the impact of the huge naval expansion programmes of the USN, but since there was no revision of the national defence principles after 1936 the plan for these twelve battleships was the last official statement.

would have no chance of surviving, and this was demonstrated by the sinking of both super-battleships by air attacks.[12]

The opportunity for which the super-battleships were built–the use of their artillery at long range–occurred only once, on 25 October 1944 near Samar Island. The battle of the battleships *Yamato*, *Nagato*, *Kongō* and *Haruna* against American escort carriers protected by destroyer escorts began from a range of 32 km, but after about one hour only one escort carrier had been sunk. Even though, according to Mr. Robert Lundgren's recent findings,[13] *Yamato's* firing was considerably more effective than hitherto acknowledged in published sources it can still be recognised as an example of the inferiority of a conventional (mechanical-optical) fire control system compared with a progressive radar-directed system. This example demonstrates that (1) the mounting of super large guns, with a firing range exceeding those of the guns mounted by

---

[12] Former Tech. Captain Makino Shigeru describes on p. 57 in his "Notes on Warships" that, then Tech. Captain, Fukuda Keiji forwarded the critique made by, then Rear-Admiral, Yamamoto Isoroku at the Higher Technical Conference about the fundamental design of the *Yamato* class. Speaking at a Higher Technical Conference, Yamomoto offered his view, which was that under an ever increasing air threat the building of these super battleships, designed for long-range gunnery engagements, must be useless and not more than an inexcusable waste of building capacity and expenses, "but nobody believed his arguments."Yamamoto's biographer, Agawa Hiroyuki, summarised Yamamoto's arguments (in the translation by John Bester) as follows: "However big the battleship, it could never be unsinkable. The attacking power of the planes of the future would increase enormously, making it possible to destroy vessels from the sky before they ever fired a gun at each other. Thus super battleships would inevitably, sooner or later, become white elephants."(p. 92). On p. 93 remarks made directly to Fukuda are paraphrased along these lines: "… I'm afraid you'll be out of work before long. From now on, aircraft are going to be the most important thing in the navy; big ships and guns will become obsolete."

According to Makino Captain Fukuda seemed to be satisfied with the fact that the American and British battleships had no other particular planning principle (such as the long-range gunnery engagement). He also believed that Fukuda considered the sinking of both battleships as quite natural in view of that (1) the intensity of the aerial attacks was beyond imagination and (2) the damage control system was calculated for 'only' three torpedo hits, because the attack of so many planes could not be foreseen at the time of the design. It is said that Tech. Vice-Admiral Fukuda never expressed his true feelings about the sinking of "his masterpieces"but it is incontestable that both ships sank only after receiving torpedo and bomb hits far exceeding the designed resistance. Therefore Fukuda's satisfaction may be true from this point of view and it is also in line with his counter arguments to Yamamoto's, see above, to which he replied: "… We're going to produce a ship that's–I don't say absolutely impossible, but–extremely difficult to sink. We're taking every eventuality into account when designing it."

[13] Robert Lundgren, *The World Wonder'd: What Really Happened off Samar*, Ann Arbor: Nimble Books, 2014. An optical system can, e.g., be seriously hampered by weather conditions and visibility.

enemy ships, in order to exercise the outranging tactics was almost meaningless if the fire control system did not keep pace with the increased ranges,[14] and (2) the transformation of technical innovations into practical applications was a very difficult process in the IJN[15] and was considerably retarded by the military secrecy, as stated above. Finally, but with certain restrictions, it may be regarded as a failed adaptation of the strategy to the technical stage or, conversely, the inability to develop a technical product to the perfection required by the strategic premise and, hence, secure the success of the outranging tactics.

With the appearance of radar the conditions presupposed for the night battle, which the IJN pinned its hopes on, changed fundamentally and its execution became very, very difficult. The backwardness of Japan with regard to the development of radar has to be recognised as a very great deficit. Another deficit can be seen in the many examples of failures or breakdowns of radio communications in the Pacific War. Even though the use of the newly invent-

---

[14] Simply expressed by "a chain is only as strong as its weakest link."

[15] A rather harsh critique (for Japanese conditions) made by Makino Shigeru can be found in his "Notes on Warships" (*Kansen Nōto*), p. 123: "... in the IJN there was a tendency that the ideas which abolished the former example could not be executed easily. Of course, the lack of creativity must have been one reason ..."Beside others he refers to the much-delayed adoption of the unit arrangement of boiler room-engine room-boiler room-engine room in the destroyer escorts of the *Matsu* and *Tachibana* classes–the advantages of this style had been shown already by lessons in World War I! Another example, given on p. 53, makes plain this tendency still more. The second funnel of the destroyers of the *Hatsuharu* class was placed a little to starboard, outside the centreline, which may be taken as representation of the flexibility shown by Captain and– naval architect –Fujimoto Kikuo, was the responsible designer of this class and the head of the Fundamental Design Section in the Fourth Division of the Navy Technical Department at that time.). This innovation was seriously criticised by Fujimoto's predecessor, Vice-Admiral Hiraga Yuzuru, as a "violation of warship dignity". In other words: An advantageous technical solution should not be practised; a "ceremonial" reason was more appreciated. There are many other examples how traditionalism and conservatism influenced warship construction. Two of them brought about the biggest constructive defects of the super battleships: the extreme shortness of the citadel, combined with too thin bulkheads in the spaces outside the vital part and the design of the underwater longitudinal bulkhead against the Type 91 AP projectile, with underwater trajectory capability. American capital ships, instead, used an effective multi-layer system to protect against torpedo attack. The multi-layer system's superiority had been demonstrated by trials made under Fujimoto's direction. Another example, also referring to the super-battleships, is an argument by Yamamoto Isoroku to Kuwabara Torao when the latter visited him in his office in the Navy Air Technical Department, it is quoted on p. 94 in the biography by Agawa Hiroyuki: "... They've decided to build both the *Yamato* and the *Musashi*. *They're the kind of old men who believe there's only one way of doing things—the traditional way.* [Authors' italics] There's nothing a younger man can do against them."

ed wireless communication system in the Russo-Japanese War was a great success and demonstrated its practical value, the development afterwards did not respond to its importance in modern sea warfare and gives the impression that "hardware" was favored and "software" was badly neglected.

As shown in the examples of the warship purchases and dispatch of supervisors and other staff to foreign countries, the goal was the import of advanced technologies to put Japanese naval architects in a position to produce warships of equal or even better quality at home. Copying a model or prototype and improving it to be suited for the fastidious nature of the Japanese was a matter of course. When after about fifty years a certain technical level, recognised as almost equal to the European countries and the United States, was attained and an equal qualitative product or a slightly improved variant could be built now and again, it was reported as "first class" or as "an achievement unsurpassed by any nation." Examples before the Pacific War are reports about the battleships of the *Nagato* class, the heavy cruisers of the *Myōkō* class or the destroyers of the *Fubuki* class, while after that the war-built battleships of the *Yamato* class took the first place. But the actual "products" did not deserve these superlatives in their true meaning, and with regard to the *Yamato* class various misgivings must be voiced. Before the war, the scientific-technical level was not as high (and the basis also rather narrow) and the industrial development not as progressed as was expressed in the exaggerated eulogies for the super-battleships. Design and production of a new product required utmost efforts. Quality was considerably overrated relative to quantity[16] and the "quality first" principle—applied to the *Yamato* class with the goal to absolutely overpower its American counterparts—was the counter-current to the production technique that modern warfare required—mass production. When applied under the pressure of the worsened war situation, Japanese designers and constructors were surprised that their fear that "mass production

---

[16] As an example the tactical requirements for the torpedo boats of the *Chidori* class may be mentioned. The efforts of the technicians to fulfil them gave the very light vessels an extreme fighting power, but caused the "*Tomozuru* Incident" in 1934 (see 'The *Tomozuru* Incident' in *Warship 2011*). Another example is the "Fourth Fleet Incident" (dealt with in *Warship 2013*) in 1935, which was caused in the end by the then not up-to-date level of the theoretical shipbuilding. On the other hand, the actual level of the theoretical shipbuilding and the inalterability of physical laws were recognised. From this point of view it is not too much to state that these :incidents" affected even the design and construction of heavy ships advantageously.

= bad quality" was not true and their own results sometimes proved the contrary.

The "quality first" principle was the expression of the basic rule that Japan must defeat a numerically superior foe with an force of lesser size. This rule had governed operations in both the Sino-Japanese War and in the Russo-Japanese War, and its importance was enhanced by the stipulations of the arms limitation treaty system that established the inferior ratio of the IJN, and also by reduced naval budgets. In this situation the compensation for the numerical inferiority by ships and weapons of superior quality was recognised as an appropriate solution and the example of the *Yamato* class makes obvious how much efforts, time and money were concentrated to attain this goal. Novel features were for instance:

- The mounting of 45-cal 18.1" (46-cm) guns in newly developed triple mounts, which were decisively different in various respects from the British Vickers type generally adopted.
- The introduction of turbo-hydraulic machinery for the operation of the main guns.
- The huge bulbous bow to decrease resistance and save horsepower.[17]
- The introduction of honeycomb armor instead of coaming armor, and the revision of production processes in company with qualitative improvements to solve the problem of producing huge amounts of armor in a rather short time.
- The compact foremast.
- The arrangement of the hangar for the ship's boats and aircraft just below the weather deck.
- The introduction of air-conditioning in one part of the living compartments.
- The use of turbo-driven coolers.

---

[17] This was quite necessary for tacticians of the Naval General Staff worried much about the low speed of the *Yamato* class. In this respect the use of the same turbine sets as fitted in the destroyers of the *Hatsuharu* class but with the output reduced by 2,250 shp per set and shaft, a total of 9,000 shp, may be criticised. The reason–caution to prevent any disturbance of the turbines, which were mounted below the 200-mm thick protective deck and, hence, very difficult, if not impossible, to replace–may be comprehensible but reflects a comparatively low state of engineering. Generally speaking, it is often said that among the three principal technical divisions of warship construction–*zōsen* (shipbuilding), *zōki* (machinery) and *zōhei* (shipboard weapons)–the second was the weakest one.

- The inclusion of a damage control system in the design, whose performance in war surpassed the pre-war assumption of how many torpedo hits a ship would receive, together with the fitting of well-devised valves etc.
- The simplification of the fittings for storerooms.

These were all results of the efforts to produce a "superior" battleship.

On the other hand, the efforts to suppress from public knowledge the increase of dimensions and displacement brought about significant disadvantages, the most serious ones being the overly concentrated protection system of the citadel and the use of very thin lateral and longitudinal bulkheads outside the citadel. Severe restrictions on electric welding, implemented under the influence of the "Fourth Fleet Incident" and the very conservative opinion of former Tech. Vice-Admiral Hiraga Yuzuru and, as a consequence, the expanded application of riveting, influenced watertightness disadvantageously besides of lengthening the building time.

The actual technical level which—contrary to belief—was lower than in European countries, like Britain and Germany, and the United States prevented, for instance, the mounting of 50-cal main guns. Similarly, the connection of the belt armor with the underwater longitudinal armor bulkhead which he designers wanted, could not be made due to fabrication problems. This had serious consequences.

In the end *Yamato* and *Musashi* may be recognised as unique battleships embodying the essence of the Japanese naval technique with the goal to completely overpower their American counterparts. However, they suffered from design errors, defects based upon Japan's scientific-technical leveland overlooked shortcomings like the protection of the secondary gun mounts. As pointed out by Makino Shigeru, who was involved in the design and construction, the extreme military secrecy prevented the collection of the wisdom by which disadvantages might have been eliminated or mitigated and more powerful and better protected ships have been generated. However, this is pure speculation and even with their inherent defects *Yamato* and *Musashi* were masterpieces and demonstrate the surprisingly high level the Japanese naval technology had attained in less than seventy years, after the first efforts to transfer a medieval country into a modern community and building-up an industry.

From the strategic point of view some readers may have got the impression that the building of these ships was a dramatic error, but such a judgement is based upon present knowledge. Yamamoto Isoroku, an advocate of air power, using detailed figures, sought to demonstrate that the fighting power of the IJN would be improved immeasurably if the budget for these "mammoths" would be used for improving and strengthening naval aviation. He was proven correct that, overwhelmed by air power, battleships would become superfluous, but at the time decisions were made Yamamoto could not provide the proof. The battleships sunk by air attacks as victims of the Washington Arms Limitation System in defenseless and immobilised condition were often outdated ships lacking post-Jutland protection and, hence, were unacceptable as proof of the superiority of the aircraft. After the termination of that treaty system all large naval powers–the United States, Britain, France, Italy and also Germany–again started the naval race with battleships and the tacticians of these navies still believed the battleship to be the ruler of the sea and the champion of sea battles. There were strong advocates of air power in these navies but all were in almost the same situation as the Japanese counterparts–the battleship had proven its fighting power; the superiority of air power was theory and lacked proofs. Therefore, the building of these Japanese battleships should not be criticised as lack of farsightedness; the IJN simply did the same as other naval powers did[18] and the majority of the strategists in these navies were, in the mid-1930s, in conformity of the value of the battleship.

---

[18] What should be criticised is the persistence the IJN showed after proving the superiority of air power against both immobilised and navigating battleships during the first days of the Pacific War at Pearl Harbor and off Malaya. It was only in February 1944 that the battleship force was degraded to an auxiliary force with the main purpose to support the operations of the mobile force–the aircraft carriers.

Part I–Technical Section

Chapter 1–Design History and General Description

Summary

The battleships *Yamato* and *Musashi* were the culmination of the Imperial Japanese Navy's "quality first" policy and "outranging" tactics. Because of Japan's enormous inferiority in relation to the industrial and economical potential of the USA, quality would have to offset, or even surpass, the quantitative disadvantage. The properties of the new battleship type should bring about a fundamental change in fighting power and cause a sudden turn of the present 60% ratio of the USA to Japan's favor.

Staff officers of the Japanese Naval General Staff (*Kaigun Gunreibu*) believed, in 1933, that two capital ships of the new type were sufficient to turn the scale in favor of the Japanese main fleet in the decisive battle and end it with a victory like the one won at Tsushima.[19] The new capital ships were to form the main power for the defense of the country and guarantee Japan's superiority in terms of main gun calibre for about ten years.[20]

After preliminary investigations in the Naval General Staff and the Navy Technical Department (*Kaigun Kansei Honbu*), resulting in a tentative design by Rear-Admiral Fujimoto Kikuo mounting 20" (50.8-cm) guns, the Naval General Staff officially required the construction of a high-speed new battleship type armed with 18" (45.7-cm)[21] guns in October 1934.

The Navy Technical Department immediately commenced works on the fundamental design and arrived at a rough conclusion in the autumn of 1935, when the "Fourth Fleet Incident" occurred, which for a while interrupted the study. The final design was submitted to the Higher Technical Conference in July 1936 and was adopted as originally planned. The chosen design was propelled by a combination of turbines and diesel engines.

---

[19] One of these was Commander Matsuda Chiaki who later became the 2nd commanding officer of the *Yamato*.

[20] For details readers should refer to "The Japanese Super Battleship Strategy" in *Warship* #25, pp. 30–39; #26, pp. 88–96; #27, pp. 161–169.

[21] Later changed to 18.1" (46-cm) by the First Division of the Navy Technical Department.

Photo 1-1: *Yamato* during trials off Sukumo on 30 October 1941 (Authors' collections)

Meanwhile, the building facilities in the Kure Navy Yard and Mitsubishi's Nagasaki Shipyard were enlarged in preparation for the construction of the giants. Many machines and machine tools were bought, and Kure's Steel Division was expanded by the Third Work to produce specially developed armor types and shapes, as well as the steel for the 46-cm guns. The extension of the building dock in Kure and the #2 gantry crane berth in Nagasaki were truly both time- and money-consuming works.

In March 1937, immediately before laying down #1 ship in Kure, the design was changed in haste to a turbine-only propulsion system. This required the lengthening of the hull, and the redesigning of the propulsion plant and the machinery spaces, affecting the general arrangement.

The fundamental design period lasted until March 1937, a period of two years and five months, and during this time 24 designs were worked out and seriously considered.[22]

Many experiments to reduce hull resistance were carried out by the Navy Technical Research Institute to save required engine power and, hence, weight. Trial firings against the new armor types were executed at Kamegakubi Proving Ground. The former ended with an appreciated result, the latter revealed a fatal defect of the connection of the upper (belt) and the lower (underwater) armor, which, for reasons hard to explain, was not corrected.[23]

Because the superiority of the new type was based primarily upon the main gun calibre, maintenance of secrecy was of the utmost importance. On the other hand, even Japanese authors grant in post-war comments that the extreme "hush-hush" brought about immeasurable troubles, which, in the end, proved disadvantageous rather than advantageous.

Besides some weak design points or even failures, there were defects in workmanship and quality control. Even so, the "products" that were released in December 1941 and August 1942 as *Yamato* and *Musashi*, respectively, must be acknowledged as outstanding achievements of Japanese naval architects and shipbuilders.

A neutral observer should always consider that (1) the start of a modern shipbuilding industry in Japan was commenced in the 1870s, when Japan still had a feudal structure, (2) a capital ship was ordered from Britain in 1910 to import the latest design and construction techniques, (3) independence from abroad was only attained at the end of the 1910s, (4) the Arms Limitation Treaty System prevented the realization of the IJN's "dream fleet" and (5) the "Naval Holidays" stopped design and construction of capital ships for several years.

What should be criticised most is the Naval General Staff's obsession with the decisive gun battle that resulted in the design of the underwater protection being focused against the "underwater trajectory" Type 91 AP shell, rather than the torpedo. The lack of farsightedness with regard to the development of aircraft and submarines belongs to the same category.

---

[22] According to Fukui Shizuo in *Kaigun Hōjutsu-shi*, p. 163, "… After all a few dozen plans of design A 140 were studied and among them more than 20 were substantially studied …"

[23] The type of joint wanted by the designers was too difficult for the producers.

Before both ships were sunk by aircraft they were hit by one torpedo each fired from American submarines, and these hits revealed defects in both cases: *Yamato* in the joint of the upper and lower armor, *Musashi* in the extensive flooding of the watertight compartments in the unprotected fore part. The latter proved that the bulkheads were made too thin in order to save weight. Eight months later *Musashi* sank with the whole unprotected fore part flooded and the flying deck awash. This was after a number of torpedo and bomb hits and near misses for which her defense (protection) system was not designed. Four months after that *Yamato* showed almost the same resistance against torpedo and bomb hits, even though in her case concentration of the attack upon one hull side accelerated the loss of buoyancy and stability.

The members of the United States Naval Technical Mission to Japan who investigated the hull design of surface warships (Report S-01-3) characterized the battleships of the *Yamato* class as "the largest in size, the most heavily gunned, and the most heavily protected class of its type in the world" (p. 43). Adding that the poor strategical and tactical handling "should be no discredit to their designers," they did not forget to mention some deficiencies in the design, namely:

- Lack of depth of the underwater protection system.
- Connection between the upper and lower side armor (p. 44).

Because a full description would require too much space only a rough outline of the design can be given here, focusing upon the main guns and turrets, main gun fire control system and armor protection. In the framework of the latter the noted deficiencies in the protective system, which were truly the Achilles heel for these vessels, will be pointed out in some detail.

Requirements and Design

The designing of the new battleships began at the end of 1934 following Japan's decision to denounce the arms limitation treaty system on 8 July 1934. The treaty system was judged extremely disadvantageous for Japan's security because it kept the IJN in imbalanced inferiority. The requirement for the new design was worked out by the Naval General Staff on the basis of Japan's fundamental strategy for war against the United States. The requirements did not consider any restrictions by the treaty. The fighting power was calculated as what was necessary for victory in the "decisive battle under the controlled air space" and the possession of two ships was, at first, considered sufficient to attain victory.

The specifications called for a new type of ship armed with more than eight 18" guns, four 15.5-cm triple guns or four 20-cm twin guns, more than 30 knots speed, endurance of 8,000 nautical miles at 16 knots, and protection against 18" shells fired from 20,000 m to 35,000 m distance. The Navy Technical Department was officially informed at a conference in October 1934.

The displacement, which was a common part of an official requirement, was omitted because so big a ship was without precedent. Any figure provided a priori would be an insubstantial supposition, so the Naval General Staff preferred to wait for the result of the comparative investigation of various tentative designs.

The AP projectiles of 18" calibre must be able to penetrate the armor of future American battleships, with increased protection, at any range. This would increase the probability of success of the outranging tactic. The requirements for the secondary guns were an economy measure enabled by the planned dismounting of the 15.5-cm guns of the light cruisers of the *Mogami* class and their replacement by 20-cm guns. The mounting of new 15.5-cm guns was also considered, should these light cruisers retain their original main armament. Instead of the 15.5-cm guns the larger calibre of 20-cm, the main armament of the 10,000-ton heavy cruisers, should be used, depending on the situation.[24].

Speed of more than 30 knots was required because the future battleships were to operate along with "Treaty heavy cruisers," modern aircraft carriers, and the high-speed battleships of the *Kongō* class. However, it is uncertain whether it was intended that the new type would operate in combined task forces with such vessels.

The deck armor should resist the impact of 46-cm AP projectiles hitting at a steep angle of fall after their trajectory of 35,000 m, while the hull side armor should prevent the piercing by shells fired from 20,000 m distance. Protection against torpedoes and bombs had to be considered and embraced.

---

[24] It deserves attention that the mounting of secondary guns (either 15.5-cm or 20-cm) was even maintained in the 51-cm-gunned battleship designed later as A 150.

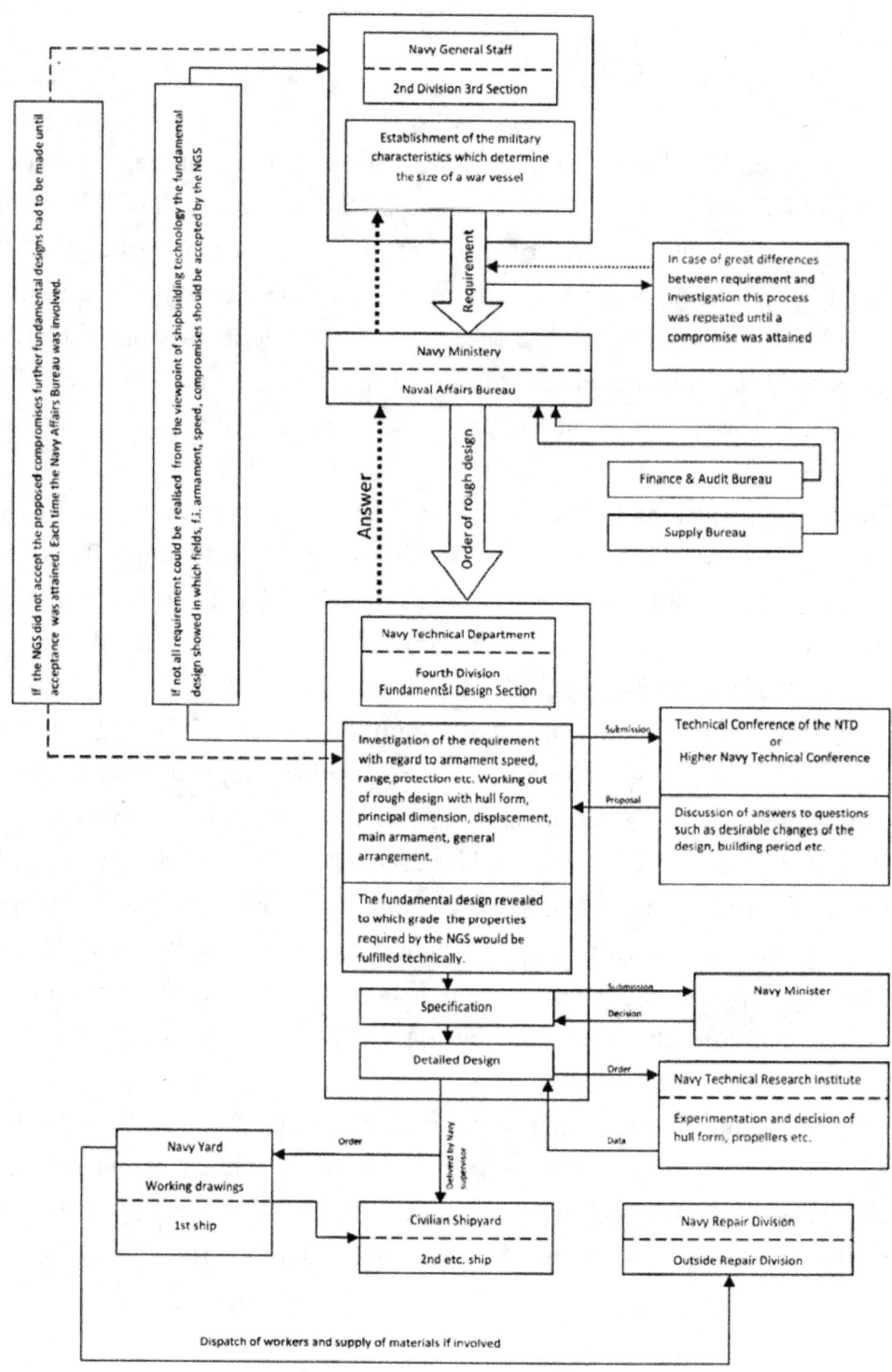

Figure 1-1: Warship design procedure within the IJN (Hans Lengerer)

Photo 1-2: Constructor Fukuda Keiji (1890–1964) was the person mainly responsible for the design of the *Yamato* class (*Sekai no Kansen*)

Immediately after receiving the official information the Navy Technical Department began the fundamental design. The chief was Admiral Nakamura Ryōzō. The head of the Fourth Division, in charge of the design, was Vice-

Admiral Yamamoto Mikinosuke, and the person mainly responsible for the fundamental design was Captain Fukuda Keiji, the successor of Rear-Admiral Fujimoto Kikuo. Among his team must particularly be mentioned then-Lieutenant Matsumoto Kitarō, who first described the *Yamato* class in the magazine *Shizen* in 1950, then in a comparatively small booklet in 1952, and finally in a much expanded book version in 1961. The general arrangement (the inside of the hull as well as placement of the superstructures) was mainly done by the first class naval engineer Okamura Hiroshi. He was very skilled, with experience in both the capital ship types of the "Eight-Eight Fleet" and Fujimoto's *Kongō* replacement design. A top member of Fukuda's team was Ezaki Iwakichi, and when Fukuda was promoted to the head of the Fourth Division on 15 October 1940 Ezaki took over the post of *Keikaku Shunin* (the official responsible for the fundamental design). The chief of the First Division, in charge of guns and armor, was Rear-Admiral Tanimura Toyotarō, but the actual work on the *Yamato* design was carried out by then-Captain (weapon constructor) Hishikawa Mansaburō and the famous naval engineer Hata Chiyokichi. In the Fifth Division (Machinery) Rear-Admiral (Eng.) Shibuya Ryūtarō was in charge of the propulsion system.

In addition, the former Vice-Admiral Dr. Hiraga Yuzuru who, as adviser of the Navy Ministry, was in charge of the technical direction of ship properties improvement measures after the *Tomozuru* Incident was shifted to the Navy Technical Department as adviser and directed the fundamental design "from behind." He definitively influenced the design. The design principles of Fukuda were all along the lines of Hiraga, and this makes it evident that the new type battleship was designed practically according to Hiraga's ideas, as expressed in his private *Kongō* replacement design. Consequently Hiraga's design is illustrated below and outlined with some technical data.[25] But Fukuda was not the only "disciple" of Hiraga. For example, the latter was also much respected by Rear-Admiral Tanimura who, like Hiraga, was also a Professor at Tōkyō Imperial University, and they were good friends.[26]

---

[25] The designs of the *Kongō* replacement ships by the Navy Technical Department (Fujimoto) and Hiraga will be discussed in volume II of this series.

[26] Private relations played a remarkable role. Also, the Japanese custom to establish consent of the participants to a design before convening an official conference (e.g. the Higher Technical Conference) prevented contrary discussions before decisions were made.

Table 1-1: Hiraga's design for a *Kongō* replacement 1928

Standard displacement	35,000 tons
Trial displacement	39,200 tons
Operational displacement	44,000 tons
Tons per inch immersion	129.6
Length (over all)	768 ft
Length (waterline)	760 ft
Beam (max)	110 ft
Draught	30 ft 6 in
Freeboard	27 ft 6 in (forward)
	30 ft 6 in (amidships)
	23 ft 6 in (aft)
Armor	Belt 15 in at waterline, reducing to 13.8 in at lower edge; 13.2 in upper belt; 7.2 in lower belt; torpedo bulkhead 4 in at top, 3.5 in at bottom; 9.4 in middle deck on flat, 11.75 in middle deck on slope (inclined at 20°); 19 in turrets above roller path, 17 in below roller path; 10.6 in upper funnel protection, 14–17 in lower funnel protection; 3 in (roof) and 5 in (sides) steering compartment; 19 in conning tower
Immunity zone	17,000–28,000 m
Length of citadel	321 ft
Width of citadel	50 ft 3 in
Height of side armor	5 ft 9 in
Height of deck armor	13 ft (forward), 11 ft (midships), 13 ft (aft)
Main armament	10 x 16-in (2 × 2, 2 × 3)
Secondary armament	16 x 6-in (8 × 1, 4 × 2)
Anti-aircraft armament	8 x 4.7-in (4 × 2)
Torpedo tubes	2 x 24-in
Main machinery	4 shaft geared turbines; 4 boilers of 12,500 hp each and 4 boilers of 7,500 hp each; 80,000 shp = 26.3 kts
Auxiliary machinery	4 x 500 kW turbo generators, 2 x 250kW diesel dynamos

Photo 1-3: Constructor Hishikawa Mansaburō (1888–1973) (Gakken)

Photo 1-4: Of all the Imperial Japanese Navy's constructors Hiraga Yuzuru (1878–1943) is probably the most well-known and perhaps also the most influential (Authors' collections)

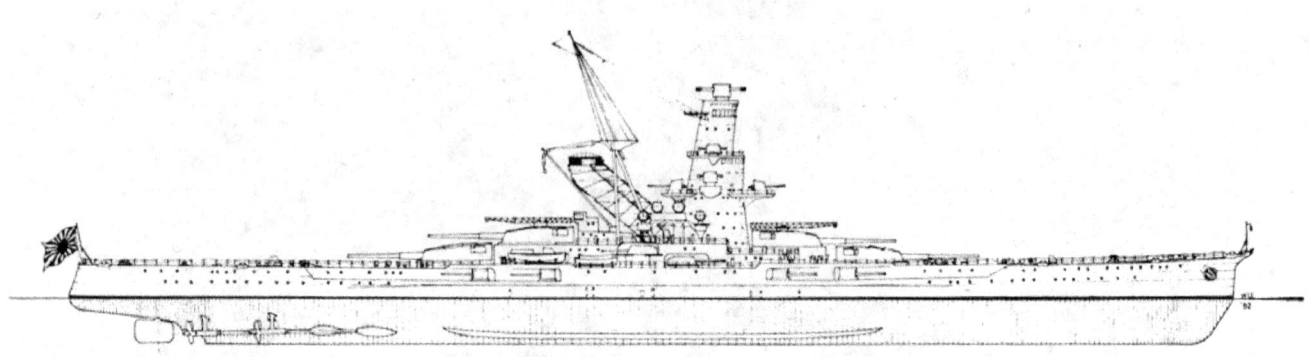

Figure 1-2: Hiraga's design for a *Kongō* replacement (1928)–external profile (Michael Wünschmann)

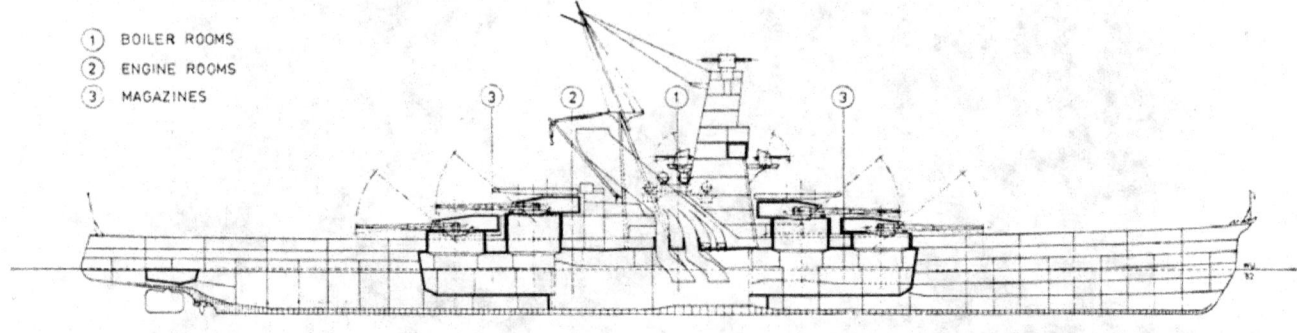

Figure 1-3: Hiraga's design for a *Kongō* replacement (1928)–longitudinal section and armor layout (Michael Wünschmann)

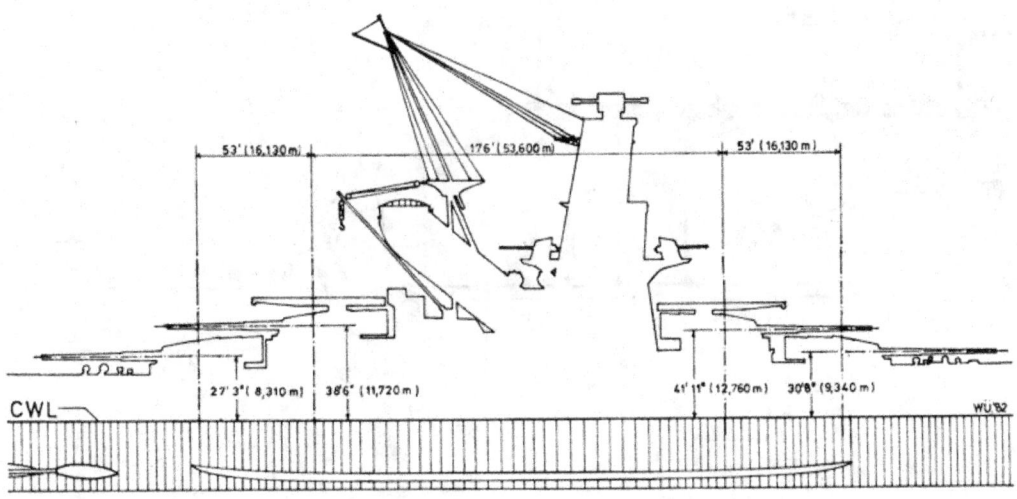

Figure 1-4: Hiraga's design for a *Kongō* replacement (1928)–arrangement of main gun turrets (Michael Wünschmann)

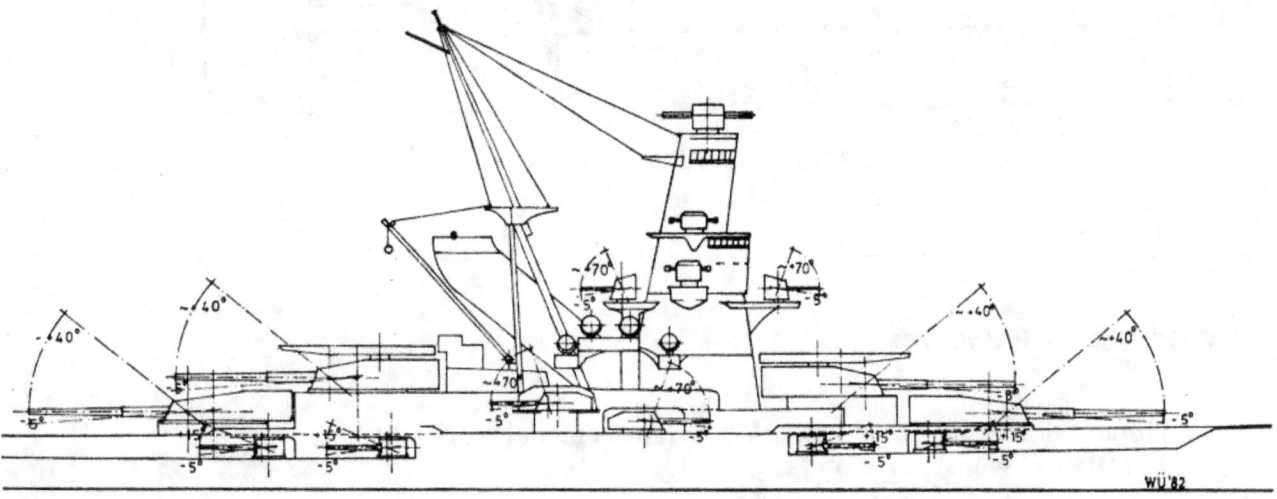

Figure 1-5: Hiraga's design for a *Kongō* replacement (1928)–gun elevation profile (Michael Wünschmann)

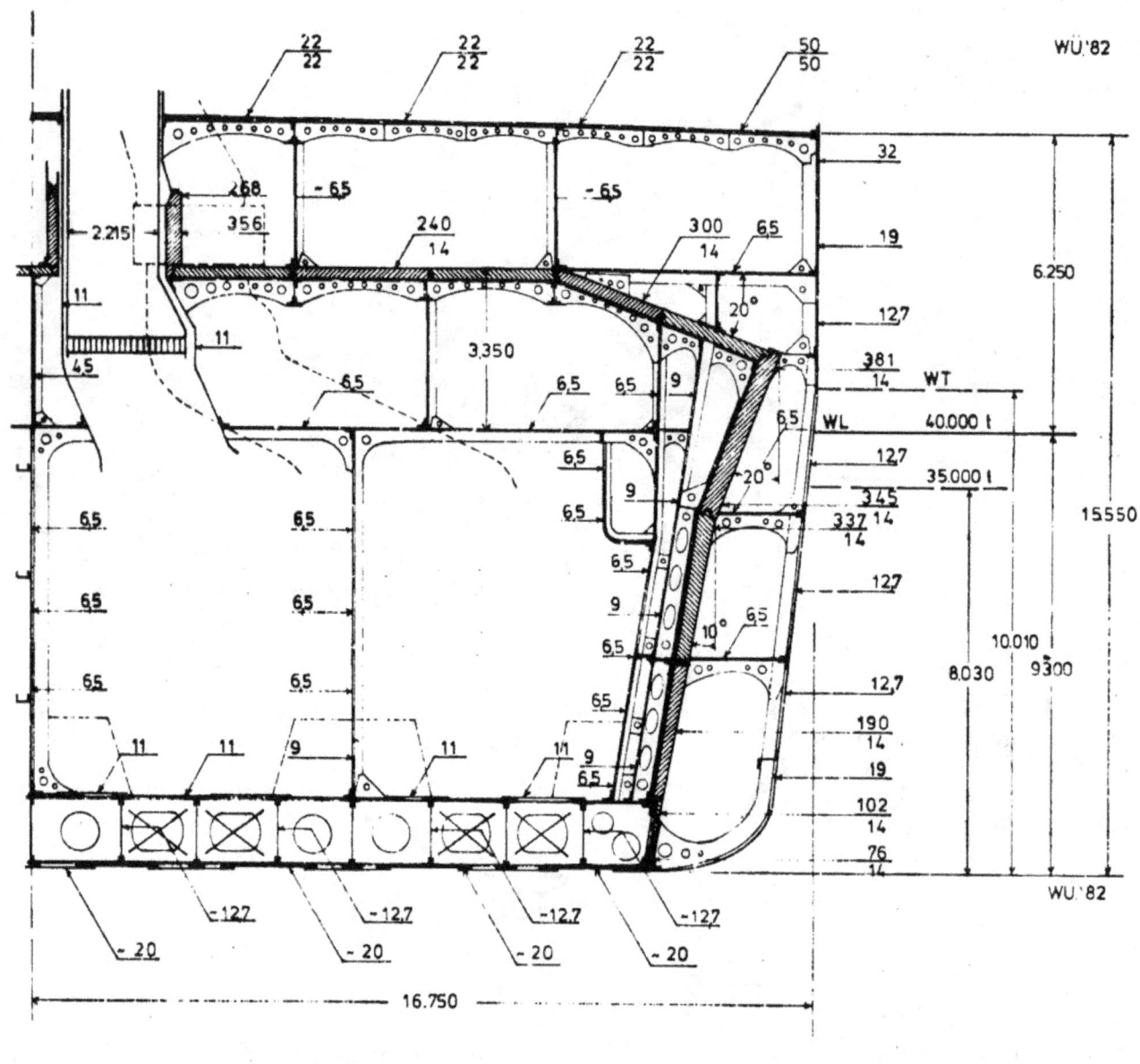

Figure 1-6: Hiraga's design for a *Kongō* replacement (1928)–midships section (Michael Wünschmann)

Technical references were made to (1) the fundamental design of the last high-speed capital ships of the Eight-Eight Fleet armed with 18" (45.7-cm) guns in 1921 subsequent to that of the *Kii* class in the previous year, (2) the results of the demolition experiments with the incomplete battleship *Tosa* in

1924, by which many valuable data were obtained,[27] (3) the lessons of the First World War and the study of overseas information on the construction of the new 35,000-ton 16" (40.6-cm) gun armed battleships of the Royal Navy and the US Navy, (4) the fundamental design of the treaty type battleships of 35,000 tons armed with 16" (40.6-cm) guns[28], and (5) lessons learned in shipbuilding technologies from the conversion of the existing capital ships and the construction of new heavy cruisers.[29]

The fundamental design number for the *Yamato* class was A 140.[30] The *Kaga* class had been designed as A 127 and this makes evident that after the capital ships of the Eight-Eight Fleet and including the official *Kongō* replacement design there had been twelve intermediate designs studied. None was realized due to the "Naval Holidays."

Matsumoto lists 23 alternative designs before the decision of the entirely turbine-propelled ship was made. The length of waterline was from 221 m to 294 m, maximum beam from 36.0 m to 41.2 m, draught from 10.1 m to 10.4 m and the trial displacement from 50,095 tonnes to 69,500 tonnes. The speed varied from 24 knots to 31 knots and the number of 46-cm main guns ranged from eight to ten, in triple or triple and twin mounts combined and either concentrated in front of the bridge or distributed forward and aft. Some designs mounting 40-cm guns were also made but they were not earnestly considered. The 40-cm gunned ships were to be protected against projectiles of the same calibre, while the protection of the designs mounting 46-cm guns should prevent the penetration of AP shells fired from distances of 20,000 m to 27,000 m or 30,000 m.

The following table and figures illustrate some "substantial designs" and variations mainly referring to the armament. They were completed on 1 April 1935 as alternatives to design A 140, finished 21 days before, and submitted to the Higher Technical Conference, but found not to satisfy the requirements. The designs completed in May, July and August shared their fate.

---

[27] This series was set forth with various experiments on armor and underwater protection in preparation for the building of the replacement.

[28] The Hiraga design just outlined had to be cancelled because of the prolongation of the building holiday following the conclusion of the London Treaty in April 1930.

[29] Summing up, the IJN, like other navies, made great efforts after the conclusion of the Washington Treaty to preserve the ability of constructing capital ships.

[30] A stood for battleship, B for battle cruiser, C for cruiser, F for destroyer, and so on, and the number indicated the 140th battleship designed by the IJN.

Table 1-2: Fukuda's battleship plans, proposed on 1 April 1935.

	A 140-A	A 140-B	A 140-C	A 140-D	A 140 A 1	A 2	B 1	B 2
DIMENSIONS								
Displacement (tons)	68,000	60,000	58,000	55,000	68,000	68,000	60,000	60,000
Length at waterline (m)	277	247	247	247	277	277	247	247
Beam at waterline (m)	40.4	40.4	40.4	40.4	40.4	40.4	40.4	40.4
Draught, trials (m)	10.4	10.3	10.2	10.1	10.4	10.4	10.3	10.3
MACHINERY								
hp (diesel)	68,000	140,000	105,000	140,000	68,000	68,000	140,000	140,000
hp (turbines)	132,000	-	-	-	132,000	132,000	-	-
hp (total)	200,000	140,000	105,000	140,000	200,000	200,000	140,000	140,000
Speed (kts)	30	28	26	29	30	30	28	28
Endurance (nm/kts)	9,200 / 18	9,200 / 18	9,200 / 18	9,200 / 18	9,200 / 18	9,200 / 18	9,200 / 18	9,200 / 18
Boilers	8	2 aux	2 aux	2 aux	8	8	2 aux	2 aux
ARMOR (length in m)								
Aft magazine	6.5	6.5	6.5	6.5	43	45	42.5	44.5
Engine room	67.2	53	50	53	67.2	67.2	53	53
Forward magazine	63	63	63	63	39	34	34	32
Total	136.7	122.5	119.5	122.5	144.2	144.2	129.5	129.5
Total on wl	142.7	128.5	125.5	128.5	150.2	150.2	135.5	138.5
ARMOR (height, ft-in)								
Side (at 25°)	17-6	17-6	17-6	15-5	17-6	17-6	17-6	17-6
Side (at 17.5°)	14-0	14-0	14-0	12-5	14-0	14-0	14-0	14-0
ARMOR (thickness - in)								
Deck	9-5	9-5	9-5	8-5	9-5	9-5	9-5	9-5
Turret roofs and conning tower	23	23	23	18	23	23	23	23
Lower deck fore and aft	3	3	3	3	3	3	3	3
ARMAMENT								
Main armament arrangement	3 × 3 for'd	3 × 3 for'd	3 × 3 for'd	3 × 3 for'd	2 × 3 for'd, 1 × 3 aft	2 × 2 for'd, 2 × 2 aft	2 × 3 for'd, 1 × 3 aft	2 × 2 for'd, 2 × 2 aft
Main armament	9 x 46-cm	9 x 46-cm	9 x 46-cm	9 x 46-cm	9 x 46-cm	8 x 46-cm	9 x 46-cm	8 x 46-cm
Secondary armament	12 x 15.5-cm (4 × 3)–all designs							
Anti-aircraft (AA) armament	12x 12.7-cm AA (6 × 2)–all designs							
AMMUNITION STOWAGE (rounds per gun)								
Main	130 - all designs							
Secondary	200/150 – all designs							
Anti-aircraft	200 – all designs							
STABILITY DATA								
KG (m)	12.5 – all designs							

YAMATO CLASS

	A 140-A	A 140-B	A 140-C	A 140-D	A 140 A 1	A 2	B 1	B 2
GM (m)	2.9 – all designs							
OG (m)	2.0 – all designs							
Angle of maximum stability	67° – all designs							
Rolling period	16s – all designs							
WEIGHTS (tons)								
Hull	18,000	16,100	15,600	14,700	18,000	18,000	16,100	16,100
Fittings	2,150	1,900	1,850	1,750	2,150	2,150	1,900	1,900
Permanent equipment	680	570	520	460	680	680	570	570
Consumable equipment	820	730	460	555	820	820	730	730
Armor	24,340	21,300	20,800	18,085	25,340	26,587	22,320	23,547
Guns	11,900	11,900	11,900	11,900	11,900	11,161.5	11,900	11,161.5
Torpedoes	60	50	50	50	60	60	50	50
Electrics	880	700	680	650	880	880	700	700
Aircraft	90	90	90	90	90	90	90	90
Machinery	5,580	4,300	3,750	4,300	5,580	5,580	4,300	4,300
Fuel	3,650	2,600	2,550	2,500	3,650	3,650	2,600	2,600
Water	180	25	25	25	25	180	25	25
Water in hydraulic system	150	150	150	150	150	150	150	150
Reserve	200	200	200	200	200	200	200	200
Total	68,680	60,615	58,800	55,395	69,200	70,188.5	61,635	62,123.5

WEIGHT DISTRIBUTION OF GUN TURRETS (tons)

Type	Triple turrets in designs A, B, C, D, A 1 & B 1	Twin turrets in designs A 2 & B 2
Turrets	2,654.5 × 3 = 7,963.5	1,869 × 4 = 7,426
Ammunition	753 × 3 = 2,259	502 × 4 = 2,008
Others	1,677.5	1,677.5
Total	11,900	11,161.6

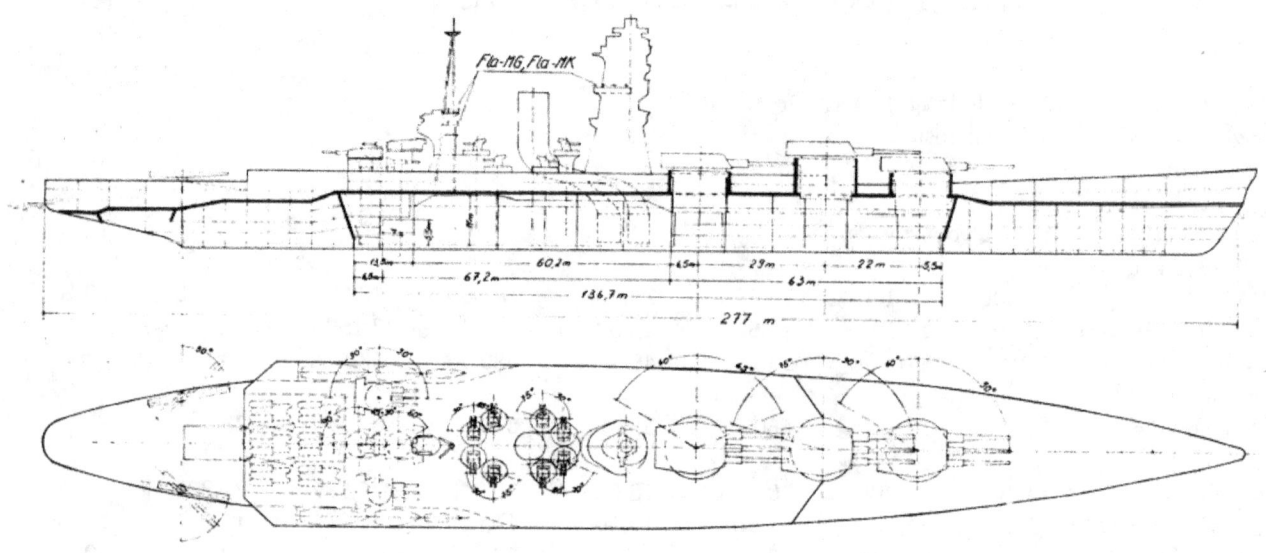

Sketch design A140/A.

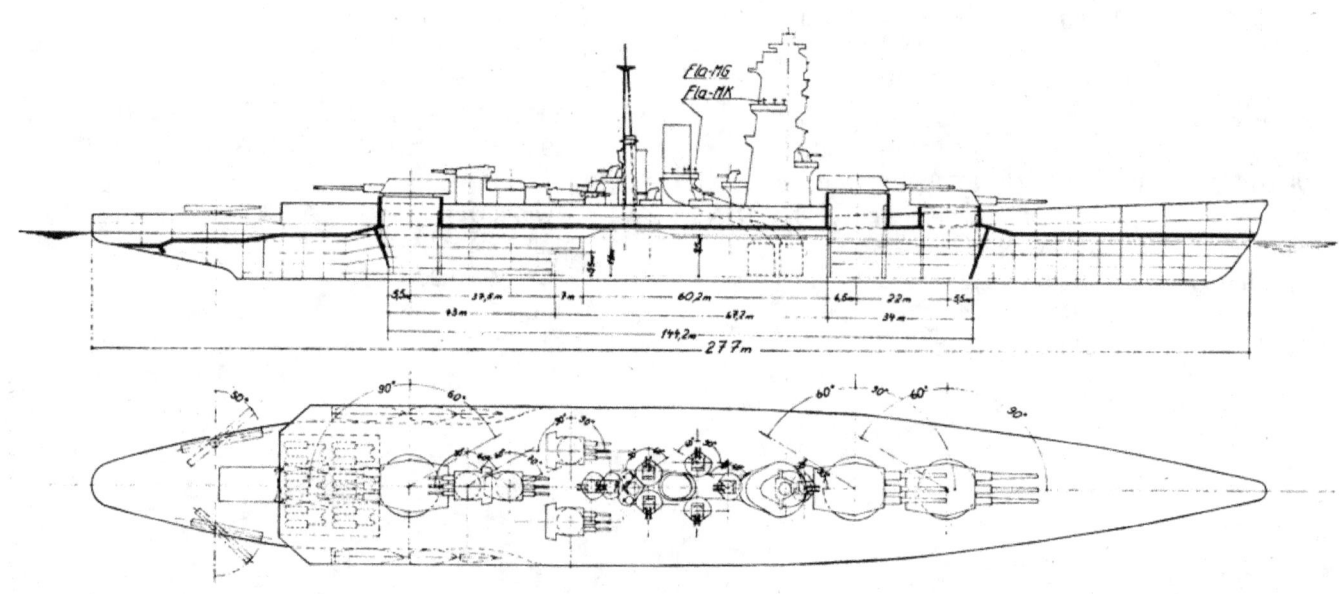

Sketch design A140/A1.

Figures 1-7 and 1-8: Sketches for designs A 140/A and A 140/A1 (Hans Lengerer)

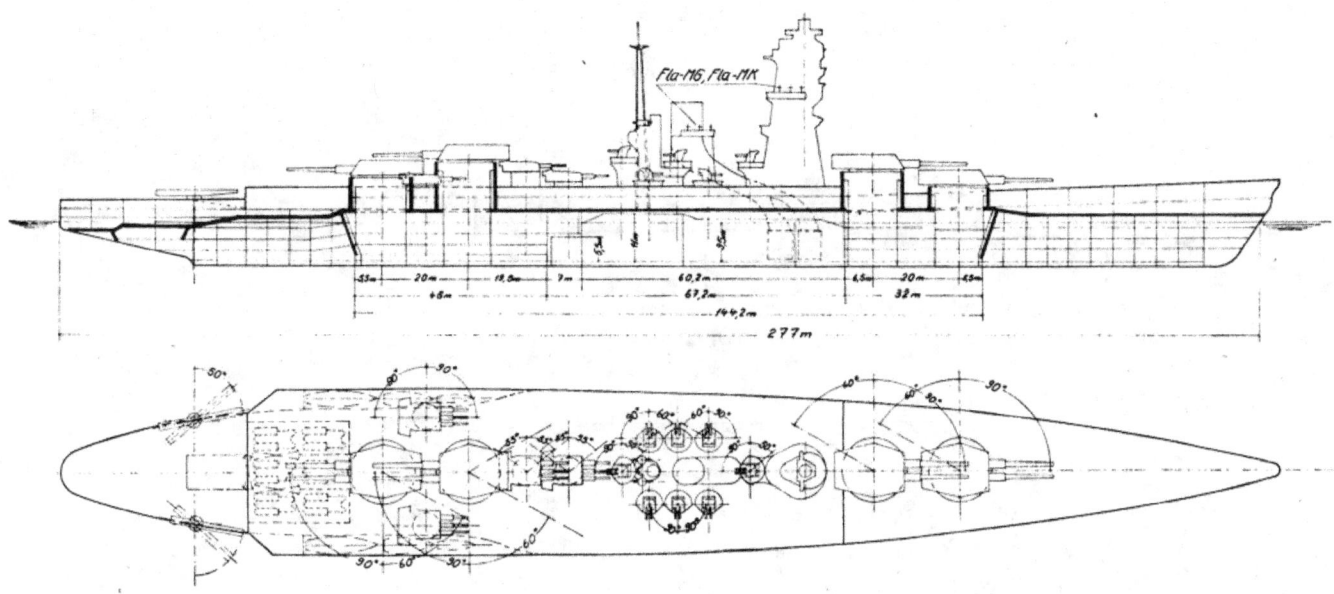

Sketch design A140/A2.

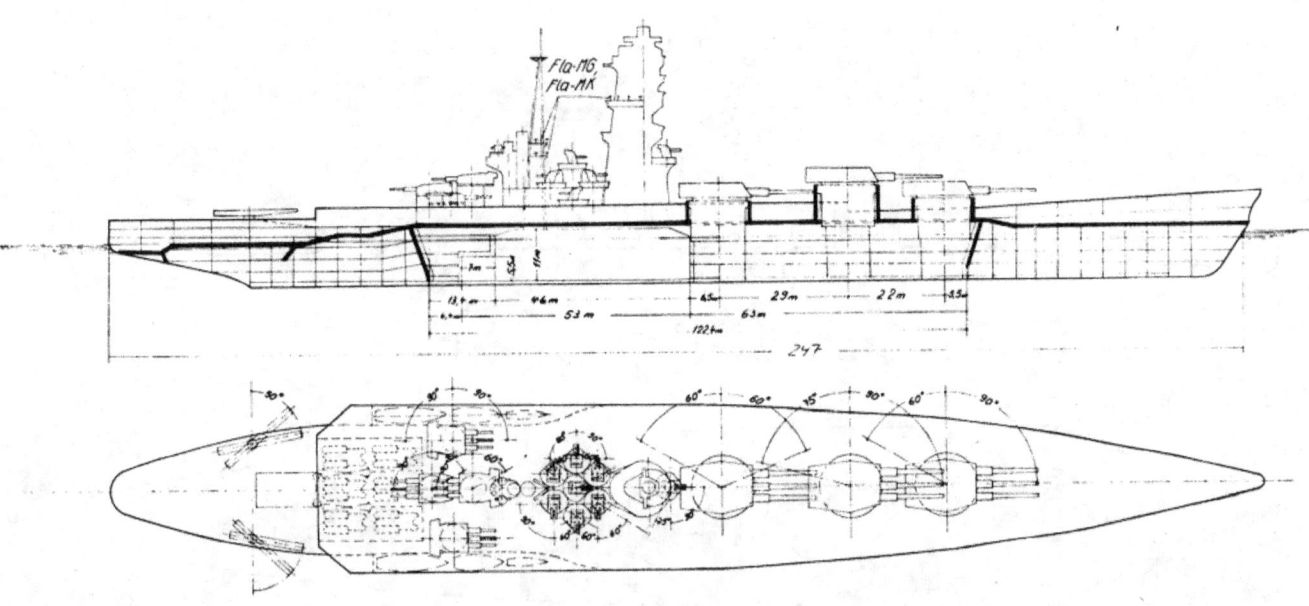

Sketch design A140/B.

Figures 1-9 and 1-10: Sketches for designs A 140/A2 and A 140/B (Hans Lengerer)

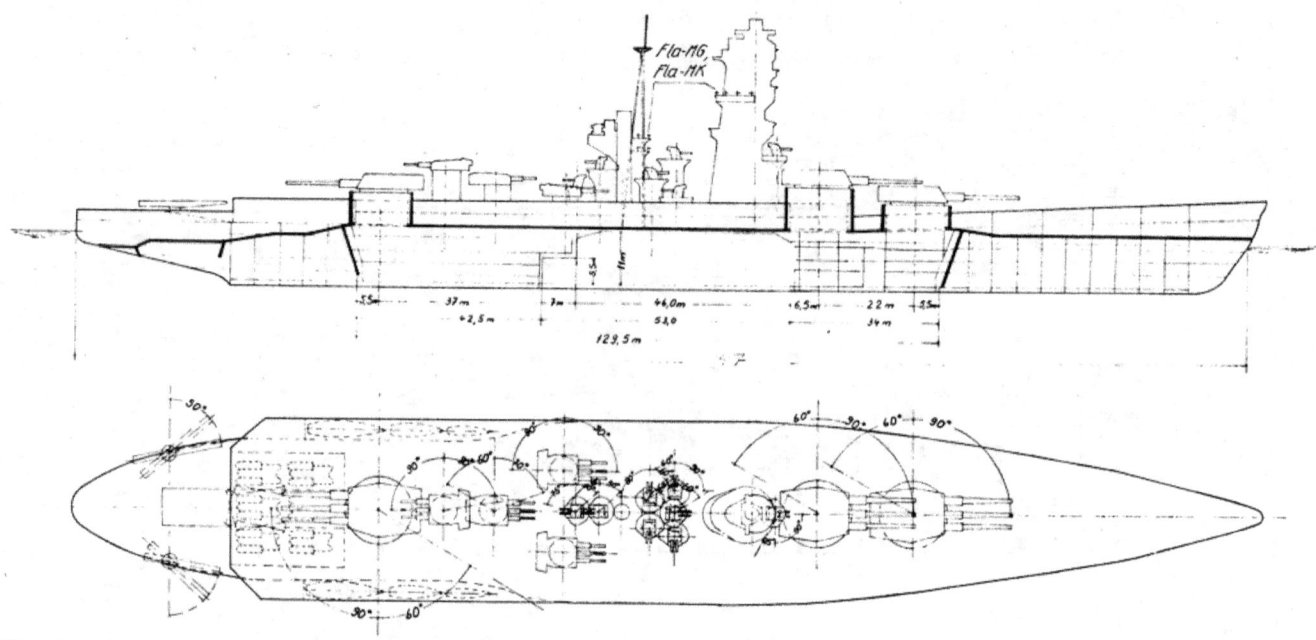

Sketch design A140/B1.

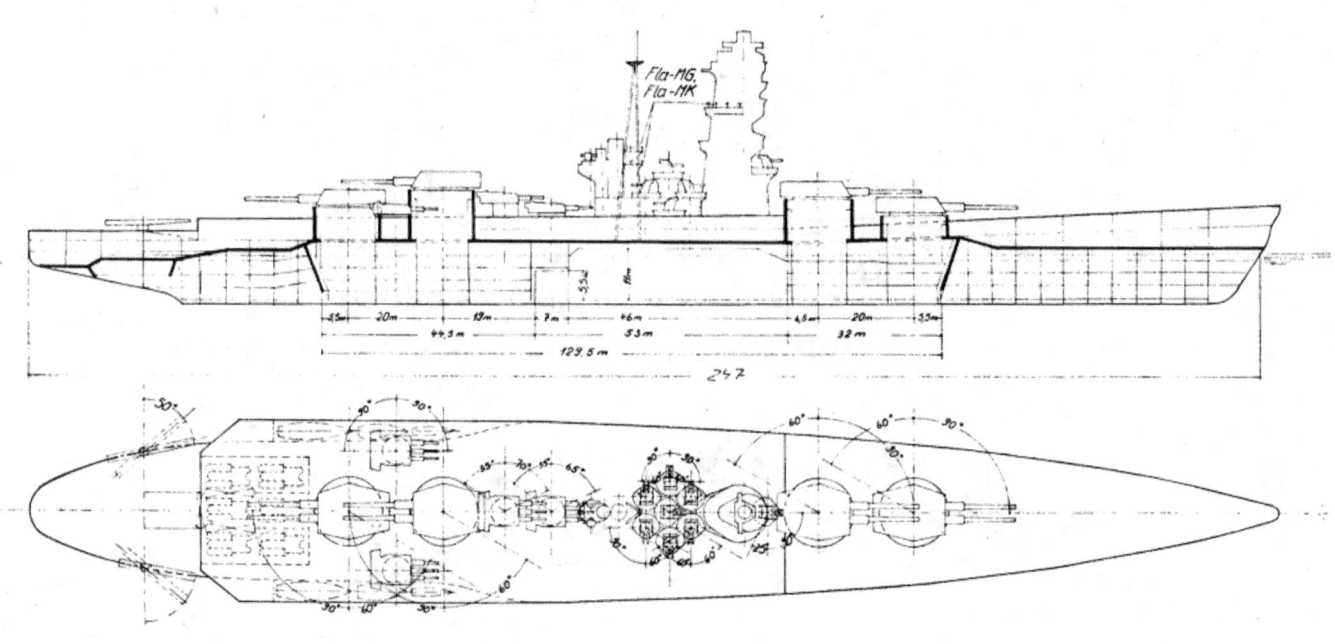

Sketch design A140/B2.

Figures 1-11 and 1-12: Sketches for designs A 140/B1 and A 140/B2 (Hans Lengerer)

On 26 September 1935 the so-called Fourth Fleet Incident occurred and about one month later the Higher Technical Conference adopted design A 140-F4, completed on 5 October, as being the most suitable.[31]

The following table shows the principal particulars of designs A 140 and A 140-F4.

Table 1-3: Particulars of designs A 140 and A140-F4.

Item / Design	A 140	A 140-F4
Trial displacement	69,500 tonnes	62,545 tonnes
Length	294 m	248 m
Beam	41.2 m	38.9 m
Draught	10.4 m	10.4 m
Main guns	Three 18" triple turrets (arranged forward depending upon the demand of the NGS)	Three 18" triple turrets (two forward, one aft)
Secondary guns	Four 15.5-cm triple turrets	Four 15.5-cm triple turrets
Speed	31 knots	27 knots
Engine output	200,000 shp	75,000 shp (turbine) 60,000 bhp (diesel)
Protection	Resistant to 18" projectiles fired from 20,000 to 30,000 m	Resistant to 18" projectiles fired from 20,000 to 30,000 m
Range	18 knots/8,000 nm	18 knots/7,200 nm

Notes:

- NGS = Naval General Staff.
- Besides dimensions, the principal differences were main gun arrangement, speed and engines. The size of A 140 was recognised as being too huge. The system of using two shafts each of diesel and turbine, combined in order to make the ship smaller, and to sacrificing speed was strongly supported as a prototype.
- The concentration of the turrets in front of the bridge, as in the Royal Navy's *Nelson* class, was not as advantageous because of the position of the magazines, sight angle and weight distribution. Hiraga's proposal of

---

[31] According to Naitō Hatsuho, in the "The Construction of the 'Musashi': A Portrait of the Yamato-Class Battleships," the members of the Higher Technical Conference agreed upon the design, but Vice-Admiral Nakamura refused to comment. The identity of Nakamura is uncertain; it was either Kamezaburō, of the Naval General Staff, or Ryōzō, of the Navy Technical Department.

a mixed type (ten guns mounted in two twin and two triple turrets) was difficult to design, as time was important. Three triple turrets divided two forward and one aft was in the end considered to be best.

- Speeds of 30 knots or more required 200,000 shp, making the displacement excessively large. The reduction of protection was out of the question so 27 knots with 135,000 shp (turbine and diesel mixed) was finally accepted.[32] The adoption of diesel engines would cause some vibrations, increase engine weight and floor space but was remarkably advantageous as to fuel consumption. The displacement could be decreased (due to the reduction of fuel), and the danger of boiler explosion was reduced. The mounting of boilers was necessary for the operation of the gun turrets so that the mixed use of both was considered better. The adoption of diesel engines on a battleship was a very courageous step, but it was finally abandoned because the reliability of the diesel was insufficient. The inner two shafts were to be driven by 75,000-shp turbines and the outer two shafts by four large-sized two-cycle double-acting diesels each, exerting a total power of 60,000 bhp by Vulcan gear.

A 140-F4 was given to every division (of the Navy Technical Department) and related boards for investigation and comment, and on 2 November Vice-Admiral Nakamura Ryōzō gave detailed instructions to all division chiefs.[33]

On 15 January 1936 the Japanese delegation left the preparatory conference for the renewal of the Washington Treaty, and after the "2-26 Rebellion" and the formation of the Hirota Cabinet, which succeeded the dissolved Okada

---

[32] The reduction of the speed caused dissatisfaction within the Naval General Staff. E.g. Commander Nakazawa who had succeeded Commander Matsuda Chiaki, as responsible for armament in the Naval General Staff, considered it meaningless for the envisaged operations. He protested to Vice-Admiral Nakamura Kamezaburō, the chief of the First Division of the Naval General Staff, and wanted to be transferred to another position. Others argued likewise, and it is said that Nakamura intended to alter the requirements. Very unfortunately the authors are lacking certain data, for it would be very interesting to know Nakamura's plan, if there was a somewhat substantial one.

[33] He complained about the loss of opportunities to refine the technologies due to the "Naval Holidays" and appealed to everyone to make utmost effort to attain technical perfection and leave other nations behind. An unrivalled capital ship should be created. He stressed the need for accurate planning and mutual communication to avoid waste of time and imbalance, creativeness to achieve maximum power with minimum weight, and consideration of the rough handling likely in actual use. Referring to the design as the "fundamental model" of the characteristic military forces required by Japan's strategic situation he emphasised secrecy, efforts against espionage and pointed out the extreme danger by unconscious, careless words.

Cabinet, Japan drifted quickly to military fascism. Tension heightened and the realization of the new battleships was accelerated. On 27 June four million yen were prepared as special expenses, and on 20 July A 140-F5 was adopted[34] as the final design. The trial displacement increased by 2,655 tonnes to 65,200 (standard displacement by 4,055 to 62,315 tons), and the length at the waterline by 5 m to 253 m. According to Matsumoto, the first design period of the overall process ended with its approval. Since the official requirements of the Naval General Staff were presented, about 20 months had passed.

On 25 November the top secret paper "Proposal about the Building Order of A 140" (*Kampon Kimitsu 1 Gō 185*),[35] written by Vice-Admiral Sawamoto Yorio, was transmitted to the chiefs of the divisions and to Kure Naval Station. The Kure Navy Yard had been chosen for the construction of the first ship. On 26 December Vice-Admiral Ueda Muneshige[36] invited the director of the Mitsubishi Heavy Industry Head Office to visit him, and, after stressing utmost secrecy, showed the outline and gave him the internal order for building the second ship. On the same day the 70th session of the Diet was opened. The Third Naval Replenishment Programme (the so-called *Maru San Keikaku*) passed the Lower House on 8 March 1937 and the Upper House on 29 March, after considerable irritation about the huge budget. (On the 31st the Diet was forcefully dissolved.) At that time the building preparations were nearing completions and it seemed that the combined turbine-diesel A 140-F5 design would be realized, for the order to Mitsubishi included diesel engines (two units of *13 Gō 10 Gata* [*48 Gata*]) to be delivered in August 1940. However, their mounting was stopped "suddenly and surprisingly." It is said that the decision for sole turbine propulsion was made at the end of March, but the official mechamism of decision is still uncertain.[37] It is well known that the

---

[34] It must be considered a fact that the Higher Technical Conference approved this design, but according to the most recent published books no documents have yet been found.

[35] Mainly maintenance of secrecy, supervision, faultless production and products and short building period.

[36] He had succeeded Hyakutake Gengo on 1 December 1936 who in turn had relieved Nakamura Ryōzō as chief of the Navy Technical Department on 16 March 1936.

[37] Naitō quotes a statement made by then Commander Kondō Ichirō (later rear-admiral) of the Fifth Division, and responsible for diesel engines, to Commander Kubota Yoshio, in charge of the budget, that the reason for stopping the diesel use was "the lack of real application," i.e. insufficient experience and, hence, fear of troubles. The replacement of the engines in a heavily protected ship

high-powered two-cycle double-acting diesel engines (*11 Gō 10 Gata*) of the submarine tender *Taigei*, serving as an experimental ship for diesel propulsion, disclosed fundamental defects during the trials (in September 1934 they developed 18,254 bhp instead of 32,000 bhp). After commissioning *Taigei* served as a training ship, but her diesels continued to have serious troubles. She was classified as a reserve ship in November 1935, and in February 1936 the order to change the main engines was given. The problem of the reliability of the diesel engine was made a theme after the beginning of the exact fundamental design of A 140-F5 from the end of November 1935 to January 1936, and the reason for making the decision at the "last moment" must have been that the Navy Technical Department wanted to see whether the investigations and land experiments with the single-cylinder trial diesel would bring about satisfactory results. The mounting of unreliable engines in a heavily armored ship, which was considered a decisive trump-card, would have been inexcusable, and the 144 hours continuous running without troubles of the trial engine was not considered sufficient basis for a sound decision.[38]

The decision to drop the diesels meant a big change of design A 140-F5 and the redesign had to be executed quickly for any delay would influence the scheduled completion dates. The machinery spaces had to be completely modified, and this also affected the general arrangement within the hull. The fuel capacity had to be increased to maintain the range and the doubling of the boilers (uptakes, protection, funnel) also influenced superstructures. Principal dimensions were also changed. The length at the waterline was increased to 256 m from 253 m and the trial displacement rose by 3,000 to 68,200 tonnes. The engine power increased with roughly 11% to 150,000 shp but the speed remained unchanged because of the increased weight. The change of the weight distribution is shown in the next table. The increase in hull weight resulted in a displacement of 69,100 tons at final trials.

---

like *Yamato* is almost impossible after putting the armor deck overhead. It was an extremely important problem calling for a quick decision.

[38] After the war this decision was sometimes criticised very much, particularly by Shibuya Ryūtarō, and more mildly by Kondō Ichirō. However, smoke in the exhaust, breaking of pistons, and friction in the cylinders were defects that could not be overlooked, and despite the self-confidence of the engineers responsible that these shortcomings could be rapidly overcome, there was no experience to prove that this would occur. This was a wise decision. Hans Lengerer has to confess to having argued differently in *Warship* but deeper studies in the course of writing the present work have caused him to change his point of view.

Table 1-4: Comparison between designs A 140-F5 and A 140-F6.

Item / Design	A 140-F5	A 140-F6 (final design)	Yamato as completed
Hull	17,600	18,600	20,226
Fittings	1,850	1,930	1,970
Armor	22,492	21,727	21,310
Protection	Included in figures provided for armor	1,765	1,620
Permanent equipment	460	440	415
Consumable equipment	577	600	608
Guns	11,832	11,802	11,930
Torpedo	132	112	80
Electric	1,140	1,140	1,094 (+ 62 W/T)
Nautical instruments	Included in?	Included in?	38
Aviation	148	109	113
Machinery	5,430	5,043	5,083
Fuel	2,961	4,330	4,200
Light oil (gasoline)	22	22	13
Lubrication oil	175	80	59 (+ 2 L.O.)
Reserve feed water	125	200	200
Margin	258	300	100
Total (tonnes)	65,200	68,200	69,134

Sources:
Matsumoto Kitarō, "Design and Construction of the *Yamato* and *Musashi*", p. 151, Fukuda Keiji, "Outline of the Fundamental Design of Warships", p. 37 (for final design and as completed).

Because the *Yamato* class was a completely new design, the designers had to address several grave challenges, some of which may be outlined as follows:

- *Reduction of the main dimensions of the hull, length of the vital spaces, and displacement.* The key for the success of the design was the reduction of the length[39] for if this was not realized the area that had to be directly protected would become very large. The increase of the armor weight would cause the displacement to rise, which in turn required an increase

---

[39] See for example the 294 m in design A 140 and the 290 m in the tentative Fujimoto design, the latter mentioned under the headline "Armament."

of the engine power to keep the speed, and finally the ship would become too heavy. Together with the ship's length, the vital spaces also had to be made as short as possible. The extremely concentrated protection limited the ratio of length of the vital spaces to 53.5%. There had been warnings that air attacks would be inevitable and that the large unprotected forward and after parts were too weak, but it was finally recognised as justified because, according to the calculations, the heavily protected part could maintain stability and buoyancy in case of damage. In the end, these reductions and weight savings all over the ship kept her within the predetermined weight limitation. The principal dimensions also had to be kept as small as possible with regard to the existing building and production facilities and the budget. Immediately before the execution of the design the shipyards had been investigated as for the maximum size and launching weight. The results were a standard displacement of 55,000 tons and a launching weight of 35,000 tons. Many facilities, already expanded in view of the construction of the 47,500-tonners of the Eight-Eight Fleet, could be used up to 65,000 tons standard (70,000 tonnes trial) and the launching weight regulated by suitable measures. But if this displacement would be exceeded enormous difficulties would occur in terms of the dimensions of docks and building slips, water depths in ports, navigation in narrow straits and so on. For example the width of the dock in Kure Navy Yard imposed a limit on the beam unless a large-scale revision of the dock was to be undertaken. Similarly, it was found that the maximum draught should be about 12 m considering the depth of the ports, the dry dock and the piers. These limitations restricted the displacement to about 65,000 tonnes in trial condition.

- *Mounting of main guns of unprecedentedly large calibre.* The ruling factors were that (1) the armor thicknesses of the new American battleships would be so great that the penetration by 41-cm shells was difficult, (2) initiatives to adopt larger calibre guns had been taken by both the IJN and the United States Navy in the past, so that the possibility of the US Navy adopting 18" guns was fairly great, which would leave the IJN far behind, (3) the weight limit of the American battleships was estimated as being about 45,000 tons standard considering the necessity of passing the Panama Canal, (4) this displacement did not allow the mounting of 18" guns as these required about 60,000-ton ships (5) the IJN could be at an advantage for several years to come when it went secretly ahead, and (6) because Japan could never outnumber the USA in the battleship competition, it was thought necessary to out-range the opponent.

- *Complete armor protection of the vital spaces with minimum possible weight.* In order to attain this goal several new ideas were tried and various materials for armor plates and their production investigated in parallel. An outline is given under the headline "Protection." For more data refer to chapter 5.
- *Combined use of turbines and diesel engines as main machinery.* The intention was to save fuel and increase endurance. Damage control aspects played a subsidiary role. Diesel engines were already used in the 10,000-ton class submarine tenders *Taigei* and the *Tsurugizaki* class but adoption for capital ships deserved attention. The effort for the *Yamato* class finally failed because of technical difficulties.
- *Keeping the secret.* The adoption of 46-cm guns was to be kept an absolute secret. Any information about the calibre and any dimensions that might enable specialists to know the calibre, such as diameter of turret ring bulkhead, displacement, or beam of the hull, were classified as highest military secrets. This resulted in a heavy burden on the personnel related to design and construction, as well as adding many inconveniences to assessments and discussions.

Table 1-5: Principal particulars of the *Yamato* class as completed.

Item / Ship		Yamato	Musashi
Dimensions			
Displacement (tons)	Standard (*kijun haisuiryō*) (T)	65,000	
	Trial (*kōshi jōtai*) (t)	69,100	69,935
	Full load (*mansai jōtai*) (t)	72,809	
Length (m)	Over all	263.0	
	Waterline	256.0	
	Perpendiculars	244.0	
Beam (m)	Max	38.9	
	Waterline	36.9	
	Below water	38.9	
Depth (m)	Uppermost deck (*saijō kanpan*)	18.915	
Freeboard (m)	Bow	10.00	
	Amidships	8.667	
	Stern	6.40	

Item / Ship		Yamato	Musashi
Draught (m)	Bow	10.40	10.38
	Amidships	10.40	
	Stern	10.40	10.76
	Mean	10.40	10.57
	Mean at full load	10.86	
Machinery			
Main machinery	Type	Kampon geared turbines	
	Number of engines	4	
	Floor area (m²)	640	
Design	Power ahead (shp)	150,000	
	Power astern (shp)	44,000	
	Speed (knots)	27.0	
	Rpm	225	
Trial results	Power (shp)	151,707	154,470
	Speed (knots)	27.3	27.61
	Rpm on trial	223.2	224.9
Propellers	Number of shafts	4	
	Diameter (m)	5.00	
	Number of blades	3	
Boilers	Type	Kampon *Ro Gō*	
	Number of boilers	12	
	Temperature (°C)	325	
	Pressure (kg/cm²)	25	
	Floor area (m²)	798	
Bunkerage (max) (t)	Oil	6,300	
	Range (knots–nm)	16–7,200	
Rudders	Main + Auxiliary	2	
Generators	Turbo type	4 × 600-kW	
	Diesel type	4 × 600-kW	
Electricity	Power	4,800-kW/225V DC	
Armament			
Artillery	Main guns	9 × 45 calibre Type 94 40-cm guns (460 mm) in three Type 94 46-cm triple turrets; 100 rpg	
	Secondary guns	12 × 60 calibre 3 year Type 15.5-cm guns in four 3 year Type triple turrets; 150 rpg	
	Anti-aircraft guns	12 × 40 calibre Type 89 12.7-cm high-angle guns in six twin mounts (A₁ Modification); 300 rpg	
	Anti-aircraft machine-guns	24 × Type 96 25-mm machine-guns (L/60) in eight Type 96 25-mm triple machine-gun mounts	

Item / Ship		*Yamato*	*Musashi*
		4 × Type 93 13-mm machine-guns (L/75) in two Type 93 13-mm twin machine-gun mounts	
Fire control	Main guns	2 × Type 98 directors Modification 1	
	Secondary guns	4 × Type 98 directors	
	Anti-aircraft guns	2 × Type 94 high-angle firing systems	
	Anti-aircraft machine-guns	4 × Type 95 machine-gun firing systems	
Underwater weapons	Paravanes	2	
	Depth charges	10	
Aeronautics	Aircraft	7	
	Catapults	2 × Kure Type Number 2 Model 5	
Searchlights	Searchlights	8 × 150-mm Type 96	
	Controllers	8	
Boats		14	
Complement *	Officers	150	
	Petty officers and men	2,150	
Armor (mm)			
Sides	Main belt	410–200 VH	
Armored transverse bulkheads	Middle deck (*chû kanpan*) forward	340 MNC	
	Lower deck (*ka kanpan*) forward	300 VH	
	Middle deck aft	340 MNC	
	Lower deck aft	350 VH	
Decks	Middle deck	200–230 MNC	
	Uppermost deck (*saijō kanpan*)	50–35 CNC	
Below waterline	Torpedo bulkhead	200–50 NVNC–CNC	
Magazines	Deck flat	200–230 MNC	
	Deck slope	230 MNC	
	Side	270–100 VH	
	Floor	50–80 CNC	
Conning tower	Side	500–380 VH	
	Roof	200 MNC	
	Floor	75 CNC	
	Communication tube	300 MNC	
Main armament gun houses	Front	660 VH	
	Side	250 VH	
	Rear	190 NVNC	
	Roof	270 MNC	
	Barbette	560–380 VH	

Item / Ship		Yamato	Musashi
Secondary armament	Shield	25 HT	
gun houses	Barbette	25 DuCol Steel (DS) + 50 CNC	
Steering gear	Top	200 MNC	
	Side	360–350 VC	
Funnel	Tube	380 MNC (50 CNC)	

Main sources for this table are: *Senkan • Jun-yōsenkan* ("Battleships & Battle Cruisers") by Ishibashi Takao and *Senkan* Yamato • Musashi *Sekkei to Kenzō* ("Design and Construction of the *Yamato* and *Musashi*") by Matsumoto Kitarō.

Notes:

T = British long tons (1,016 kg); t = Metric tons (1,000 kg).

* No certain data could be obtained. 2,500 officers and men are an oft-stated number at the time of completion. The rough number at completion as stated in *Senkan • Jun-yōsenkan* is 2,300 (150 officers and 2,150 petty officers and men) and the figures at the time of loss are 2,397 for the *Musashi* and 2,774 for the *Yamato*.[40]

Table 1-6: Comparison of the A 140 series. Tables 1-6 through 1-9 compiled by Takagi Hiroshi.

Plan no.	Lwl (m)	B (m)	D (m)	Displ (T)	46-cm guns Aft	46-cm guns Fore	Speed (kt)	Hp Turbine	Hp Diesel	Hp Total	Radius (kt/nm)	Fuel (t)	Date planned
A 140	294	41.2	10.4	69,500	0	3+3+3	31.0	200,000	0	200,000	18/8,000		35-03-10
-A	277	40.4	10.3	68,000	0	3+3+3	30.0	132,000	68,000	200,000	18/9,200		35-04-01
-B2	247	40.4	10.3	62,000	2+2	2+2	27.5	0	140,000	140,000	18/9,200		do.
-G	273	37.7	10.4	65,883	0	3+3+3	28,0	70,000	70,000	140,000	18/9,000		35-05-25
-G1-A	244	38.9	10.4	61,600	0	3+3+3	26.0	45,000	70,000	115,000	16/6,600		35-07-30
-I	268	38.9	10.4	65,050	2+3	3+2	28.0	73,000	70,000	143,000	16/6,600		do.
-F	247	38.9	10.4	60,350	3	3+2	27.0	65,000	65,000	130,000	16/7,200		35-08-14
-G0-A	268	38.9	10.4	65,450	0	3+3+3	28.0	75,000	70,000	145,000	16/7,200		do.
-G2-A	262	38.9	10.4	63,450	0	3+3+3	28.0	73,000	70,000	143,000	16/7,200		do.
-K	221	36.0	10.1	50,059	0	3+3+2	24.0	40,000	40,000	80,000	16/6,600		do.
-F3	246	38.9	10.4	61,000	3	3+3	27.0	75,000	60,000	135,000	16/4,900		35-10-05
-F4	248	38.9	10.4	62,545	3	3+3	27.0	75,000	60,000	135,000	16/7,200		do.
-F5	253	38.9	10.4	65,200	3	3+3	27.0	75,000	60,000	135,000	16/7,200		36-07-20
Final	256	38.9	10.4	68,200	3	3+3	27.0	150,000	0	150,000	16/7,200	6,300	37/3/E

Note: Takagi Hiroshi has stated that the original designs of A-140 and A-140-A, both with 200,000 hp, must have shown six shafts (not four shafts). The evidence for this appears in A 140-A in which the power of the turbine sets was around twice the diesel sets. Therefore, it is most likely that the two wing shafts were driven by the diesels and the four inner shafts by the turbines.

---

[40] The authors appeal to readers who do know (apparently) exact data to share their knowledge with them.

Table 1-7. Comparison of A 140-G1-A with all-turbine and combined turbine-diesel machinery

Hp			Machinery weight (T)	Floor surface (ft²)	Hp/ft²	Fuel needed for 8,000 nm at 18 kt	Fuel needed for 1 nm at 18 kt	Ratio (%)
Turbine	Diesel	Total						
115,000	0	115,000	4,008	15,033	7.65	8,400	1.05	100
45,000	70,000	115,000	4,253	16,429	7.00	5,700	0.71	68

Table 1-8. Differences between A 140 and A 140-A.

Plan no.	Lwl (m)	B (m)	D (m)	Displ (T)	46-cm guns Aft	Fore	Speed (kt)	Hp Turbine	Diesel	Total	Radius (kt/nm)	Fuel (%)	Date planned
A 140	294	41.2	10.4	69,500	0	3+3+3	31.0	200,000	0	200,000	18/8,000	100	35-03-10
-A	277	40.4	10.3	68,000	0	3+3+3	30.0	132,000	68,000	200,000	18/9,200	100	35-04-01
Difference	-17	-0.8	-0.1	-1,500	0	0	-1	-68,000	+68,000	0	+1,200	0	3 weeks

Table 1-9. Difference between A 140-F3 and A 140-F4.

Plan no.	Lwl (m)	B (m)	D (m)	Displ (T)	46-cm guns Aft	Fore	Speed (kt)	Hp Turbine	Diesel	Total	Radius (kt/nm)	Fuel (%)	Date planned
-F3	246	38.9	10.4	61,000	3	3+3	27.0	75,000	60,000	135,000	16/4,900	100	35-10-05
-F4	248	38.9	10.4	62,545	3	3+3	27.0	75,000	60,000	135,000	16/7,200	147	35-10-05.
Difference	+2	0	0	+1,545	0	0	0	0	0	0	+2,300	+47	0

The detailed design was generally assigned to the builder and executed in close co-operation between the Naval Technical Department and the Navy Yard. The Navy Yard was ordered to perform the construction as shown in the figure. The working drawings were made by the builder.

Construction

Yamato was built in #4 building dock of Kure Navy Yard, *Musashi* on #2 berth of Mitsubishi Nagasaki. The construction of the former was ordered in August 1937 and she was laid down in November of the same year. The work proceeded smoothly, but after the launching in August 1940 orders were issued for the acceleration of effort.

Many upgrades were required to the existing facilities for construction of these huge vessels. At Kure Navy Yard there was an enlargement of the drydock, strengthening of gantry cranes, raising of a roof over the dock for concealment, providing storage space for working drawings, expanding the drawing room for armor, building of a new steel factory, increase of pontoon bridges for fittings, preparation of a summarised factory for fittings, and an increase of the capacity of floating cranes to 300 tons. Among many improvements at Nagasaki Shipyard were the enlargement and strengthening of the berth, a newly installed gantry crane, space for working drawings, a wood workshop, fitting factory, machinery factories, enlargements of iron workshops for shipbuilding, construction of fitting pier, and building of 150-ton crane ship and tug boats. A self-propelled ship of 350 tons for loading the turrets was built by the IJN in Ishikawajima Shipyard and lent to Mitsubishi.

The success of *Musashi*'s construction depended on her launching. Therefore, the Navy Technical Department first conducted the launching calculations and then committed further studies to Mitsubishi. The launching weight amounted to more than 35,000 tons and her launching was carefully calculated and prepared. The expansion of the berth was begun in June 1939. The official order was given in 1937 after which the building was prepared by the instruction of the Kure Navy Yard. The contract was concluded in February 1938 and the keel was laid in March. She was launched on 1 November 1940, towed to Sasebo Navy Yard in July 1941 for docking, returned to Nagasaki in August, and left for Kure Navy Yard in May 1942, where the rest of the works was completed and the official trials held in August of the same year.

Her construction also had to be accelerated. It was much more troublesome than in case of *Yamato*. The main difficulties were (1) the distance between the gantry cranes and the hull was very narrow, (2) the compartments above the middle deck could not be completely fixed because most of the middle deck armor plates were to be fitted after the launching, (3) the measures for not making the launching weight excessive greatly slowed progress, and (4) the complicated procedure that was required with towing the ship to Sasebo to carry out the first outfit in the dock for about one month, followed a cruise under her own power to a second docking at Kure Navy Yard.

Difficulties were encountered in the fixing of the vertical and horizontal armor as well as large castings and forgings, the riveting of 40-mm rivets and the ring bulkhead and its lower structure (ring support), the latter being made a cylinder of CNC armor supported down to the propellant magazine floor. Riveting formed the main connection method with total 6,153,030 rivets including the principal longitudinal strength members, DS steel and the armor.

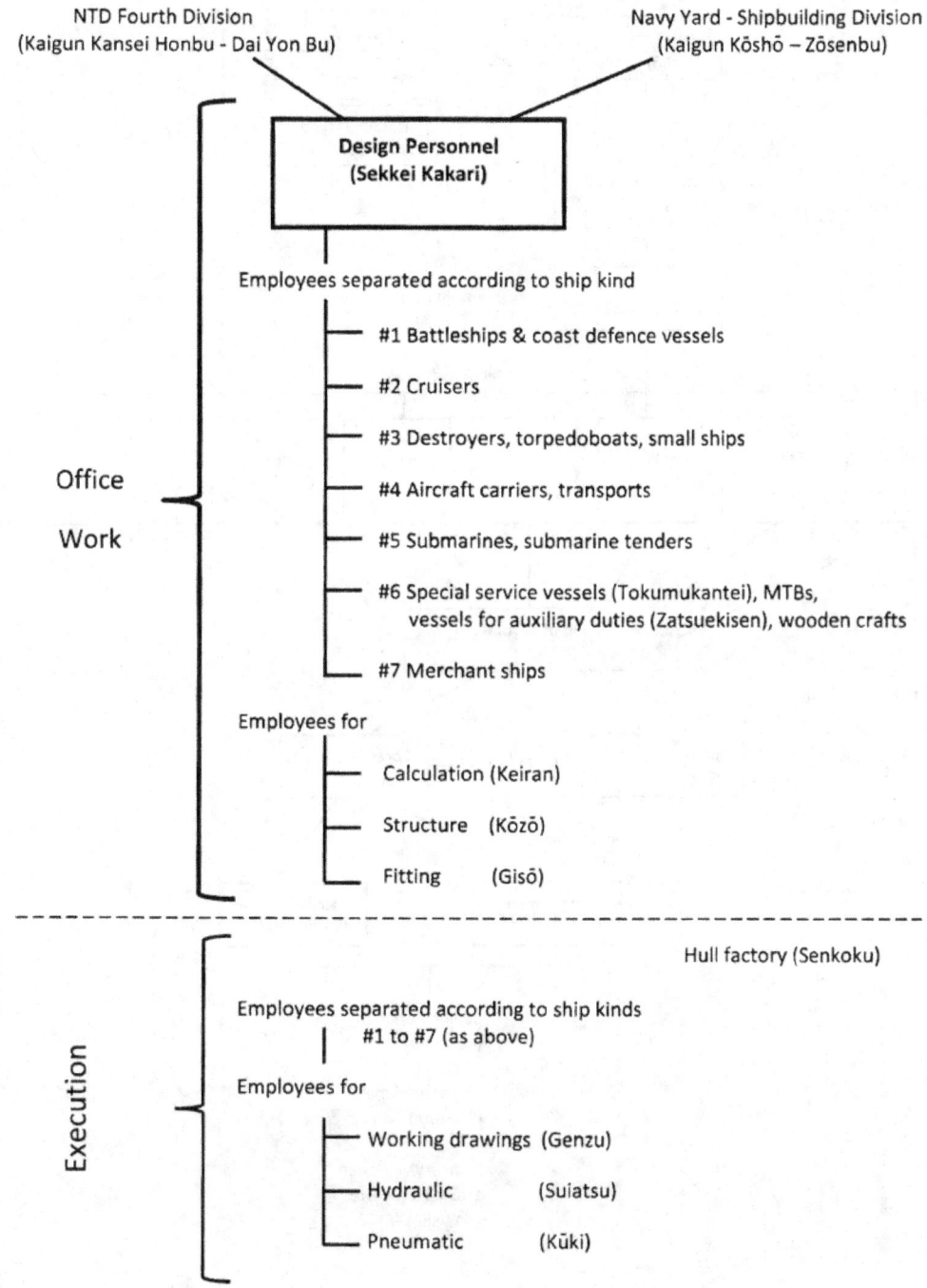

Figure 1-13: Comparison of the Detailed Design Section of the Navy Technical Department and a Navy Yard (Hans Lengerer)

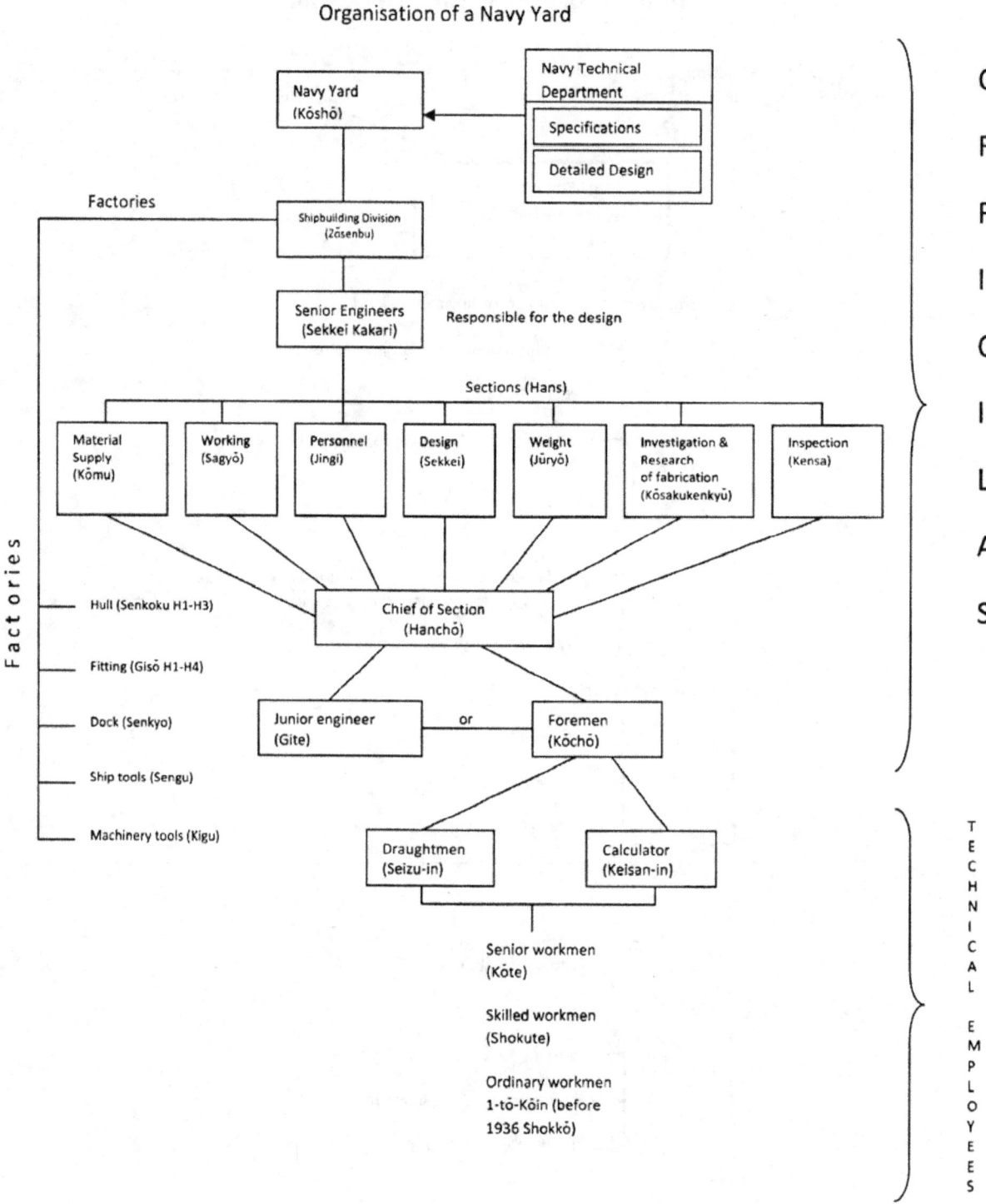

Figure 1-14: Organisation of a Navy Yard (Hans Lengerer)

Electric welding was applied for lateral compartments and constructions forward and aft and for the superstructures as much as possible (total 463,784 meters using 7,507,536 rods). The longitudinal strength and rigidity were enhanced by making the central vertical keels double-lined box type girder at the interval of one meter and mounting two longitudinal central bulkheads in the engine rooms with an interval of 600 mm from the double bottom up to the middle deck, which, simultaneously, had the function to support this deck. The additional bulkheads on both sides were made continuous at the upper end as well as aft and forward.

Effort was also made to maintain the continuity of both ends of the hull armor of the vital spaces. Her curved flush deck from bow to stern was copied from the heavy cruisers and used for the same purpose: to make the longitudinal strength members continuous, which was the most effective design and saved structural weight.

Authors like Fukui Shizuo and Makino Shigeru state that the great effort involved in keeping the project top secret was more troublesome than the construction itself.

Table 1-10: Abbreviated building schedule of the *Yamato* (as described by the Kure N.Y. in October 1941)

Item	Scheduled date	Actual date
Laying down	4 November 1937	4 November 1937
Launching	August 1940	8 August 1940
Mounting of main engines	September–November 1939	Coincides
Mounting of boilers	May–October 1939	Coincides
Mounting of main guns	May–October 1941	March–May 1941
Preparatory trial runs	December 1941–January 1942	16–18 October 1941
Trial runs	January–February 1942	22–30 October 1941
End of the first period fitting out work	Beginning of May 1942	November 1941
End of the second period fitting out work	Beginning of June 1942	10 December 1941
Delivery	15 June 1942	16 December 1941

Source: *Kenkan Hiwa* (Niwata).

Note: Pay attention to the fact that her delivery was eventually advanced by seven months by the three advance requirements/orders.

Table 1-11: Summary history.

Name and (Prov. #)	Builder	Laid down	Launched	Completed	Lost	Removed from list
Yamato (1)	Kure N.Y.	4 Nov 1937	8 Aug 1940	16 Dec 1941	7 Apr 1945 (Aircraft)	31 Aug 1945
Musashi (2)	Mitsubishi Nagasaki	29 Mar 1938	1 Nov 1940	5 Aug 1941	24 Oct 1944 (Aircraft)	31 Aug 1945

Photo 1-5: Launching ceremony of the *Yamato* at Kure on 8 August 1940. To the left can be seen part of the sisal rope curtain fitted to hide the ship during construction. The bow of the ship is to the left, just outside the photograph (Kure Maritime Museum)

Photo 1-6: *Yamato* fitting out at Kure on 20 September 1941. The aircraft carrier on the right is *Hōshō* and in the background are two heavy cruisers, *Kinugasa* and *Aoba*, and the supply ship *Mamiya* (Authors' collections)

Individuals Involved in Yamato's Construction

In *Kenkan Hiwa* ("Secret Stories about Warships") Vice-Admiral Niwata Shōzō states the principal individuals involved in the building as follows:

Yamato was laid down on 4 November 1937, was launched on 8 August 1940 and was completed on 16 November 1941. It took four years and one month to build her and during this period of time the Chief of the Shipbuilding Division (*Zōsenbuchō*) changed three times; from Rear-Admiral Kuwabara Shigeharu to Rear-Admiral Masaki Nobutsune and then to Rear-Admiral Niwata Shōzō, but I was the most fortunate as I was involved from the launching to the completion. The following naval architects were also in charge of her construction:
  Chief of works (*Sagyō shunin*): Captain Yoshii Kazuo
  Chief of detailed design (*Sekkei shunin*): Commander Makino Shigeru

Chief of hull construction (*Senka kōjō shunin*)[41] Commander Nishijima Ryōji

Staff in charge (*Tantō-buin*): Captain Kurata Masahiko

Electric welding (*Denki yōsetsu*): Engineer Tsuji Kageo

Inside and outside work (*Nagaigyō*): Engineer Naeka Kōichi

Chief of fitting out (*Gisō kōjō shunin*): Commander Fukui Matasuke

Staff in charge (*Tantō-buin*): Lieutenant-Commander Hirohata Masuya

Finishing everything (*Shiage-naigaigyō*)[42] Engineer Oda Morikichi

The personnel consisted of 23 officers, 13 engineers (*gishi*) and 6,606 workmen. The latter were divided as follows:

Male workers: 6,233

Apprentice workers: 358

Female workers: 15

In the same work Niwata Shōzō also provides interesting anecdotes about the hull construction:

> I remember mainly about the armor below the protective deck. But it was fitted before I came to Kure N.Y. and I can tell only a few stories after I arrived on duty.
>
> One of the most difficult items in the hull construction was the ring bulkhead of the main gun turrets (barbettes). As described by Engineer Shimomura of the Gunnery Division of Kure N.Y. it was, in the magazines, a round-shaped wall upon which the roller path, for the training of the turret, was placed. The ring bulkhead was made to support the weight of the rotating part of the main gun turret directly and it had to be resistant to shock and firing, so this part was extending from the hull bottom to the upper part, penetrating each deck. The top of the ring bulkhead had to form a perfect circle and had to be completely horizontal. In *Yamato*'s case the diameter of the ring bulkhead exceeded twelve meters and to make this structure a perfect circle and also exactly horizontal was a difficult task causing much trouble and requiring considerable measuring. The thickness of the plates of the ring bulkhead was 40 mm and the big circle was formed by many plates that were adjusted exactly by using the large-sized ring before being riveted together with rivets 40 mm in diameter.
>
> It was found that the armor of one turret[43] (I forgot which one) deviated a little so that on one side the reduction in height was too much, and it was feared that the head of the rivets would be sheared off, but we could not replace the ring by a higher one. To rectify this defect a special type rivet was made and accepted by the Gunnery Division.
>
> The fitting of a perfect ring using the "circle gear" and other tools and the finishing were all troublesome works, but the result was really satisfactory

---

[41] His function is not absolutely clear.

[42] Refers to outside and inside.

[43] This was probably turret No. 2. See *Senkan* Yamato *Kenzō Hiroku*, p. 257, Kure report No. 1.

with very minor errors, which could be categorized as miscellaneous ones. (I was impressed by the excellent techniques used by the workmen of Kure N.Y. and I felt very pleased.)

The next trouble was the fitting operation of the side armor. The VC armor plates were 410 mm thick with a height of 5.9 m, a width of 3.6 m and a weight of 68.5 tons. But *Yamato* was built in the building dock that had a length of 335 m and a width of 43 m. This dock was enlarged after the construction of the battleship *Nagato* and when the battle cruiser *Akagi* was under construction the length and width were expanded, expecting a further increase of capital ship dimensions, but the depth remained the same. Therefore, when building the *Yamato* the depth was inadequate and the bottom of the dock was deepened by about one meter. With launching at full tide the draught would be just seven meters, but if the belt armor was fitted before launching the draught would increase to more than eight meters. The fitting of the belt armor had to be stopped at the top of the bulges, and the fitting of the remaining part should be done after launching. The draught was decided to be 6.5 m. The fitted weight was controlled to prevent an excess of this value and the fitting work of the armor became remarkably difficult.

After launching the hull of the *Yamato* was not brought to the fitting out pier of the yard, instead it was moored to a bridge made of two large-sized pontoons (length 150 m, width 20 m, newly constructed). However, the fitting of the armor was very troublesome because the sides were inclined and the plates had to be fitted very tightly to each other to prevent defects in resistance. If the hull was in the dock the fitting of the armor plates could be made by using many cranes of 100 or 30 tons, but at sea only one 30-ton moving crane was on the pontoon and it was thus insufficient to carry an armor plate. Therefore, we were forced to use the 300-ton crane ship of Kure N.Y.'s Gunnery Division (*Hōkōbu*) equipped with one 100-ton crane. In addition a lighter for scaffolding had to be built. In this way, considerable preparations had to be carried out.

One more trouble was the gradual increase of the draught. List and trim had to be controlled because of the increase of the draught calculated before the beginning of the fitting work. We decided to fit the armor plates from amidships alternately to both sides forward and aft and to adjust the draught in this way. *Yamato*'s beam was almost 39 m so the 300-ton floating crane could not reach the opposite hull side and it had to be moved constantly to the opposite side.[44]

---

[44] By the way the Shipbuilding Division of the Kure N.Y. had a bad experience of dismantling armor plates at sea. It was in 1922 at the disassembly of the armor of the abolished ship *Suō* with a 200-ton crane when the ropes ripped and the approximately 40 ton heavy plate fell into the sea. It made a staggering movement, caused perhaps by the condition of the plate, and hit the hull near the bottom and penetrated it. Because it was an abolished ship the watertight compartments lacked watertightness and the ship flooded slowly until it capsized (or was run aground). The responsible engineer, Yamagata, was punished.

Niwata Shōzō then writes about the acceleration of construction and trials:

The building schedule of *Yamato* was decided at Kure N.Y. in October 1937. The keel was to be laid down in November 1937, the hull to be launched at the beginning of August 1940 and the trials should be executed in January 1942. Afterwards the end of the first period fitting out works, namely the armament, was to be at the beginning of May followed by the trial firing of the weapons and tests of other weapons. All works were to be completed at the beginning of June, which was also the end of the second period fitting out works. The date of delivery was to be 15 June 1942.

The construction went very smoothly according to this schedule and the hull was launched on 8 August 1940. Afterwards the work proceeded at the particular fitting out pier. During this time the relations between Japan and the United States of America worsened gradually and we had an emergency. In this situation the acceleration of the construction of *Yamato* in order to complete her as early as possible became rather natural. In October 1940 the Navy Technical Department dispatched an officer to investigate the possibility to advance the completion date. A secret conference was held and it ended with the result that the ship was to be delivered two and a half months earlier, that is at the end of March 1942 with the advance of the gunnery trials to the beginning of February 1942.

However, in March 1941 the navy minister demanded the work to be hastened and it was almost an order that the ship should be completed two months earlier. At an urgent conference the very urgent construction by speedy work and night work was decided in order to complete her at the end of January 1942. The very pressing situation was explained to the workmen and they were requested to work around the clock in three shifts.[45]

But in June 1941 the Kure N.Y. was ordered to complete *Yamato* within this year. In this situation the completion date was advanced to the middle of December 1941 by focusing upon her and use as many skilled workers as possible.[46] The result was impressive and *Yamato* appeared off Tosa on 18 October 1941 to make her trial. On that day the sea was rough and a strong wind of 20m/s from the southeast. Three submarine chasers that accompanied her dropped out of formation and proceeded to port to avoid the bad weather. But the huge ship of 70,000 tons did not roll at all and attained 27.4 (27.46) knots with 153,000 (153,550) shp; an excellent achievement beyond imagination.

After that the "equipment trials" (mainly adjustment) of the main guns, secondary guns, high-angle guns and machine-guns were made and from the end of November the gunnery trials were begun. The trial firing of the main guns was performed in the Suō Nada in the Inland Sea on 7 December 1941. The outer sea was avoided and the Inland Sea was chosen because of the

---

[45] Tech. Vice-Admiral Niwata describes his impression of the great spiritual power and the very rigid procedures involved in this work.

[46] Tech. Vice-Admiral Niwata points out the extreme efforts of the workers during the very hot summer of 1941 and again describes his impression.

mounting of the 18" guns, which was the most secret property of this ship. The range was decided to be 20,000 m and the salvo was fired from the rear to Tokuyama Bay with an excellent result. She was "certified to have sufficient quality as the strongest battleship in the world."[47]

Photo 1-7: Constructor Niwata Shōzō (1889–1980) (*Sekai no Kansen*)

Building Expenses and Man-Days

Both themes can be treated in only a rudimentary fashion because no correct data are left. Matsumoto Kitarō regrets (on p. 272) that "this kind of documents were all reduced to ashes," Niwata Shōzō estimates the expenses to approximately ¥150,000,000, Fukui Shizuo to about ¥160,000,000 and the tables in *Shōwa Zōsen-shi* are the official budgets. As far as man-days the situation is slightly better because some statistics of Kure N.Y. are left. Despite these shortcomings it may be interesting to estimate how many man-days were nec-

---

[47] Tech. Vice-Admiral Niwata notes that he later heard that the Tokuyama citizens heard a loud noise, like a far off remote thunder. On that day Niwata was in the foremast near the turrets to measure the influence of the blast upon the hull by a blast meter. He states that the design proved its excellence also in this respect, compared with the past battleships, because nothing was situated on the upper deck, with the ship's boats and aircraft all placed in the hangars at the stern below the uppermost deck. According to him no damage was reported even after salvo firing, which was a rare case.

essary to complete such a "historical construction." The expenses today would surely be regarded as an astronomical sum.

Photo 1-8: Yoshii Kazuo (1919–2002) was *sagyō shunin* during the construction of the Yamato (Authors' collections)

To conceal the true displacement, which would have permitted the conclusion that the new ship would mount guns exceeding the calibre of 41 cm, the budgets submitted to the Diet for the Third Replenishment Programme in 1937 and the Fourth Completion Programme in 1939 were simply wrong both in the total and in the costs per ton. One part of the expenses was hidden in budgets of "ghost ships", also included in the budget but never intended to be built. When these expenses are added the sum is still short of the total estimate of ¥150,000,000 and more, as stated above. However, "balancing" had a tradition in the IJN–as in today's budgets–and to conceal fictitious expenses became easier the darker the war clouds became and control by the Diet diminished.

The "official" budgets per ship are shown in the next table.

Table 1-12: Official budgets per ship.

Programme	Standard displacement	Expenses per ton (¥)	Total expenses (¥)	Notes
Maru San	35,000	2,800	98,000,000	First budget calculation
Maru San	35,000	3,083	107,933,075	Corrected budget
Maru Yon	40,000	3,250	130,000,000	
Maru Go	Not stated	5,221	281,536,000	*Yamato* type, drafts dated 19 July 1941
Maru Go	Not stated	3,973	214,062,000	New type, 50-cm guns, draft as above

Sources: For the *Maru San* and *Maru Yon* Programmes *Shōwa Zōsen-shi*, *Nihon no Gunkan* (Fukui), etc. For the *Maru Go* Programme *Kaigun Zōsen Gijutsu Gaiyō*, vol. 7, p. 1598, *Nihon Kaigun Nyūmon* ("The Imperial Japanese Navy"), p. 151.

With reference to the *Maru San Keikaku* the formal budget request to the Finance Ministry was ¥104,405,000 on 2 June 1936. The next table shows the first budget calculation and the actual calculated expenses.

Table 1-13. Official budget and actual calculated expenses.

Item	Official budget data	Actual calculated expenses	Note
Hull	37,596,430	50,000,000	Shipbuilding
Machinery	14,305,011	22,156,000	Expenses
Gunnery	32,200,207	46,714,000	Weapon
Torpedo	703,765	852,000	
Navigation	833,450	1,044,000	Production
Electric	9,318,577	13,355,000	
Aviation	1,246,325	1,334,000	Expenses
Supervision & transportation	1,646,235	2,347,000	
Total	98,000,000	*137,802,000	

* Niwata, op. cit. p. 54, states ¥137,000,000 in round numbers (apparently referring to this calculation).

According to Matsumoto the calculated total building expenses amounted to ¥142,877,000, which apparently appears realistic in view of the estimates by Niwata and Fukui. The inflation between 1936 and 1941 was 1.758[48] and if the calculated total of ¥150,000,000 is multiplied by the inflation factor it becomes ¥263,700,000, which is only short by approx. ¥18,000,000 from the calculation in 1941. On the other hand, when the budget calculated in 1941 (¥281,536,000) is divided by the inflation factor (1.758) the result is ¥160,145,620 and this coincides with Fukui's data.

In Gakken's *Nihon Kaigun Nyūmon*, p. 150, a table with the inflation rates from 1936 (= 1) till 1945 (= 3.5) and 2006 (= 1,787) are given. When the calculation in 1941 is taken as "correct" the building expenses of the *Yamato* in 2006 would amount to ¥286,180,222,980 (¥281,536,000 : 1.758 × 1,787) or about the annual GNP of a small-size industrialized country.

Matsumoto, op. cit., p. 272, estimates the total number of man-days (per 8.5 working hours) necessary to build the *Yamato* to more than 15,000,000, including civilian companies for finished and semi-products. What is most interesting in this respect is the comparison of the construction amount between *Yamato* and the considerably smaller *Mutsu*, given as follows:

Table 1-14. Construction costs of *Yamato* v. *Mutsu*.

Item	Yamato	Mutsu
Hull (apparently including drawings & wood works)	999,000	872,000
Fitting (Niwata & *Shōwa Zōsen-shi* state 595,000 & 594,108 for fitting)	696,000	868,000
Total	1,695,000	1,740,000

Sources: Matsumoto, op. cit., p. 272, a breakdown of the man-days for the hull structure can be found on p. 273.

Notes: The explanation in parenthesis in the hull item was added on the basis of the statistics used by Niwata, op. cit. p. 54. As for fitting no reliable explanation for the differences was found.

According to Matsumoto the schedule in the hull factory was 1,474,000 man-days on the basis of improved efficiency but the actual result was reduced to 68% of the schedule. The reasons are analysed as:

---

[48] Gakken, *Nihon Kaigun Nyūmon* ("The Imperial Japanese Navy"), p. 150.

- Much better mechanization of the facilities.
- Many workers recruited in 1932–1935 reached their peak in skill.
- More than half of the foremen had experience of more than 20 years and they always gave appropriate instructions to the workmen.
- High spirit of all labourers.

Matsumoto estimates the total number of man-days for the entire construction to a little less than 4,700,000 on the basis of the man-days of shipbuilding.

The following two tables represent statistics of Kure N.Y.'s Shipbuilding Division and show some details of weight, man-days and expenses.

Table 1-15. Weight, man-days, and expenses.

Item	Planned weight (tons)	Actual weight (tons)	Man-days (8.5 hours)
Hull	16,600	21,063	908,440
Armor & protection	23,492	22,895	79,164
Fitting	1,930	1,749	594,108
Fixed equipment	440	413	11,358
Drawings & records			278,801
Wood work for hull			38,809
Testing			59,018
Miscellaneous			40,989
Total	44,462	46,120 (+ 1,658 tons)	2,010,682

Table 1-16: Expenses by item.

Item	Expenses (¥)	Note
Hull	4,506,351	The average wage of a worker slightly exceeded ¥2/day
Material	11,744,136	Includes ¥1,540,928 for orders outside the N.Y.
Furniture and architecture	6,210,562	The authors do not know what the item architecture includes
Total	22,461,049	

General Arrangement

The general arrangement is shown sufficiently in the figures made for Report S-01-3 "Surface Warship Hull Design" of the US Naval Technical Mission to Japan.

Like the vital spaces the superstructures were also extremely concentrated. Forward of the fore mast were two main gun turrets superimposed by one secondary gun turret, and aft of the after mast there was another superimposed secondary gun turret followed by the third main gun turret. Between the masts, with the funnel in between, were the two side secondary gun turrets, six 12.7-cm twin high-angle guns, eight 25-mm triple machine-guns, eight 150-cm searchlights and their directing equipment, piled up like a pyramid almost symmetrically. They were arranged with extreme care to avoid the influence of blast.

The masts were simplified according to the newly specified standard and the real sized model of the foremast was inspected from the standpoints of arrangements and equipment. It became relatively small and was of almost the same size as that of a smaller battleship, in spite of the functional upgrading. The fore and after masts were equipped with, respectively, one 15-m and one 10-m rangefinder. The height of the foremast was planned on the requirement of 34-m eye-level for the 15-m rangefinder to cope with long distance firing, and the double bridge system was adopted for day and night battles. The conning tower below the night battle bridge was heavily protected and functionally divided into steering centre, command and control centres for the reserve fire control systems of the main and secondary guns and also for damage control. The direct passage system from the conning tower to the lower conning tower through the communication tube was the same as that executed in earlier capital ships.

The fore mast was constructed as a double cylindrical structure and the inner tube was protected against strafing of large calibre airplane machine-guns. The inside of the inner tube was protected against poison gases and the elevator was fitted to connect the fighting and communication centres. The fitting of two lines of staircases, each consisting of up and down stairs, proved very successful for quickly manning the battle stations by many people.

The vital spaces contained the machinery spaces in the centre and the main and secondary gun magazines forward and aft and on the sides. Four parallel shaft lines of three boiler rooms and one engine room each shortened the length of the vital spaces. The evaporators were placed behind the engine room of the inboard shafts; while the electric power rooms, the magazines for the side secondary guns, the hydraulic machines and coolers were arranged between the engine room and boiler room of the outboard shafts.

Four turbo and diesel generators of 600kW each were installed in eight generator rooms surrounded by the control board rooms, the transformers, the ring main and the secondary batteries.

Other rooms for auxiliary machinery contained four hydraulic pumps (for the operation of the main gun turrets with one pump in reserve) and four large capacity cooling machines (for magazines and living compartments etc.). Included in the vital spaces were many other rooms like lower conning tower, mother compass room, control rooms for the main and secondary guns (mainly the computers and transmission gears), power rooms for the remote controlled machine-guns, wireless rooms, emergency pump rooms for damage control and their control stations, and so on.

The aviation gasoline tanks, the refrigerators and the ice-producing facilities were placed aft, below the waterline but outside the vital spaces. The spacious command facilities were located on the central upper deck, which was convenient to communicate with the masts, around which living compartments for officers, the communication control room and communication rooms were distributed. The living compartments were placed on the upper and middle decks as well as on the lower deck forward and aft. For sleeping these had numerous beds instead of hammocks.

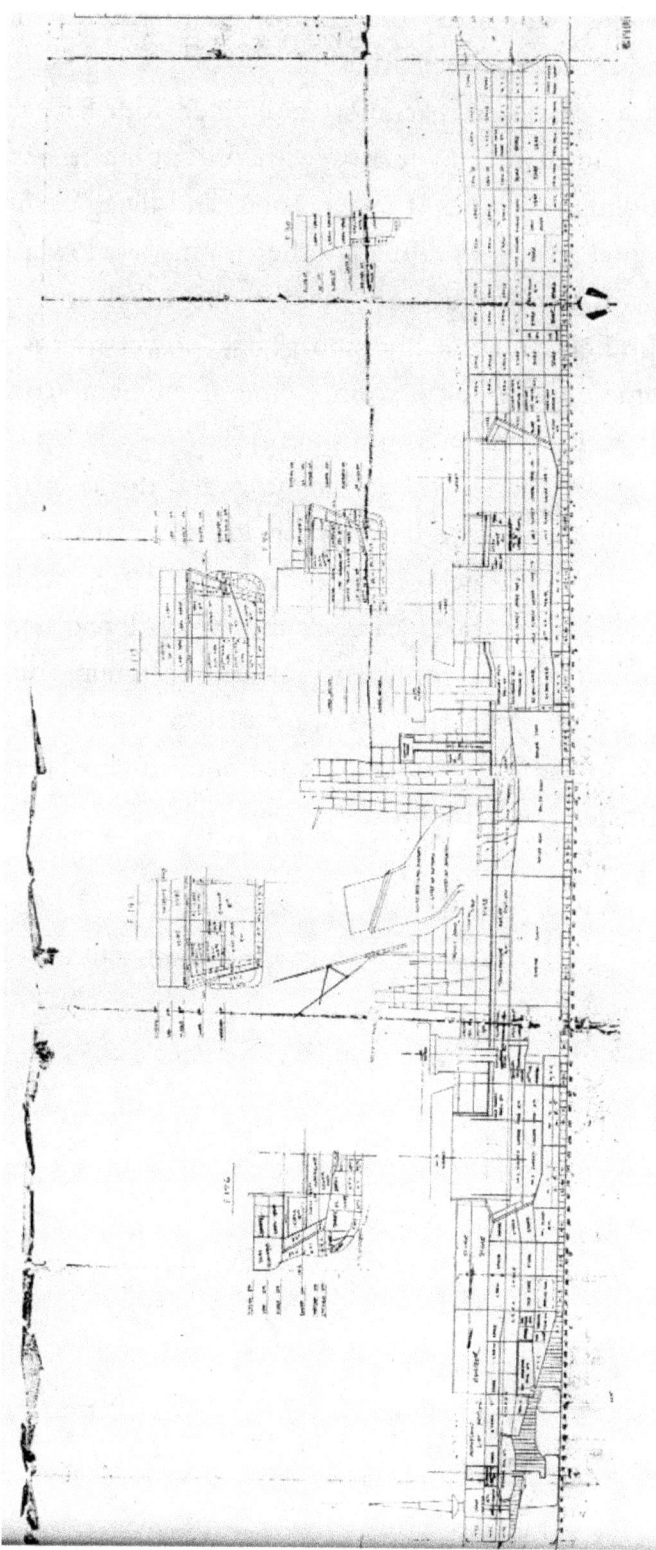

Figure 1-15: General arrangement (profile section) of *Yamato* (US Naval Technical Mission to Japan, Report S-01-3, Enclosure 3)

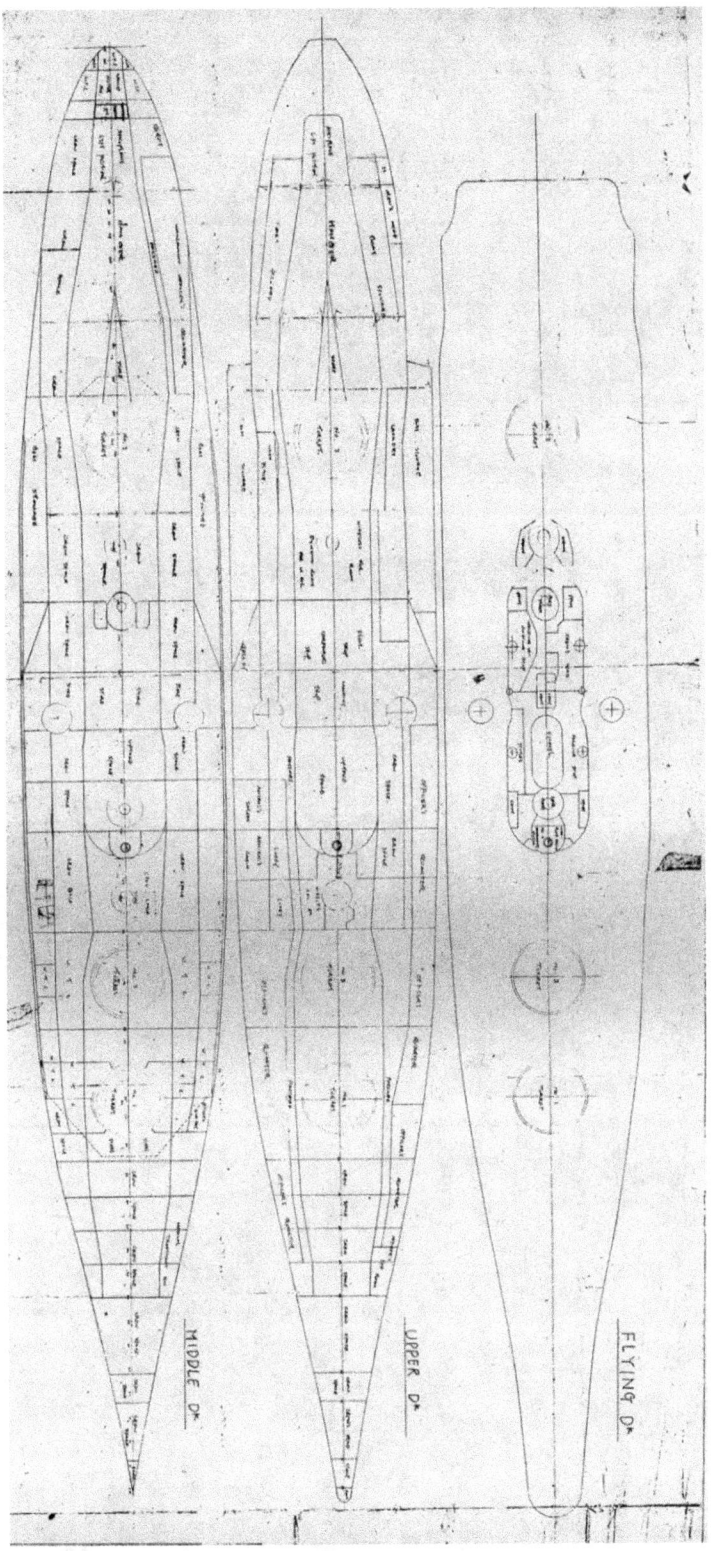

Figure 1-16: General arrangement (flying deck, upper deck, middle deck) of *Yamato* (US Naval Technical Mission to Japan, Report S-01-3, Enclosure 4)

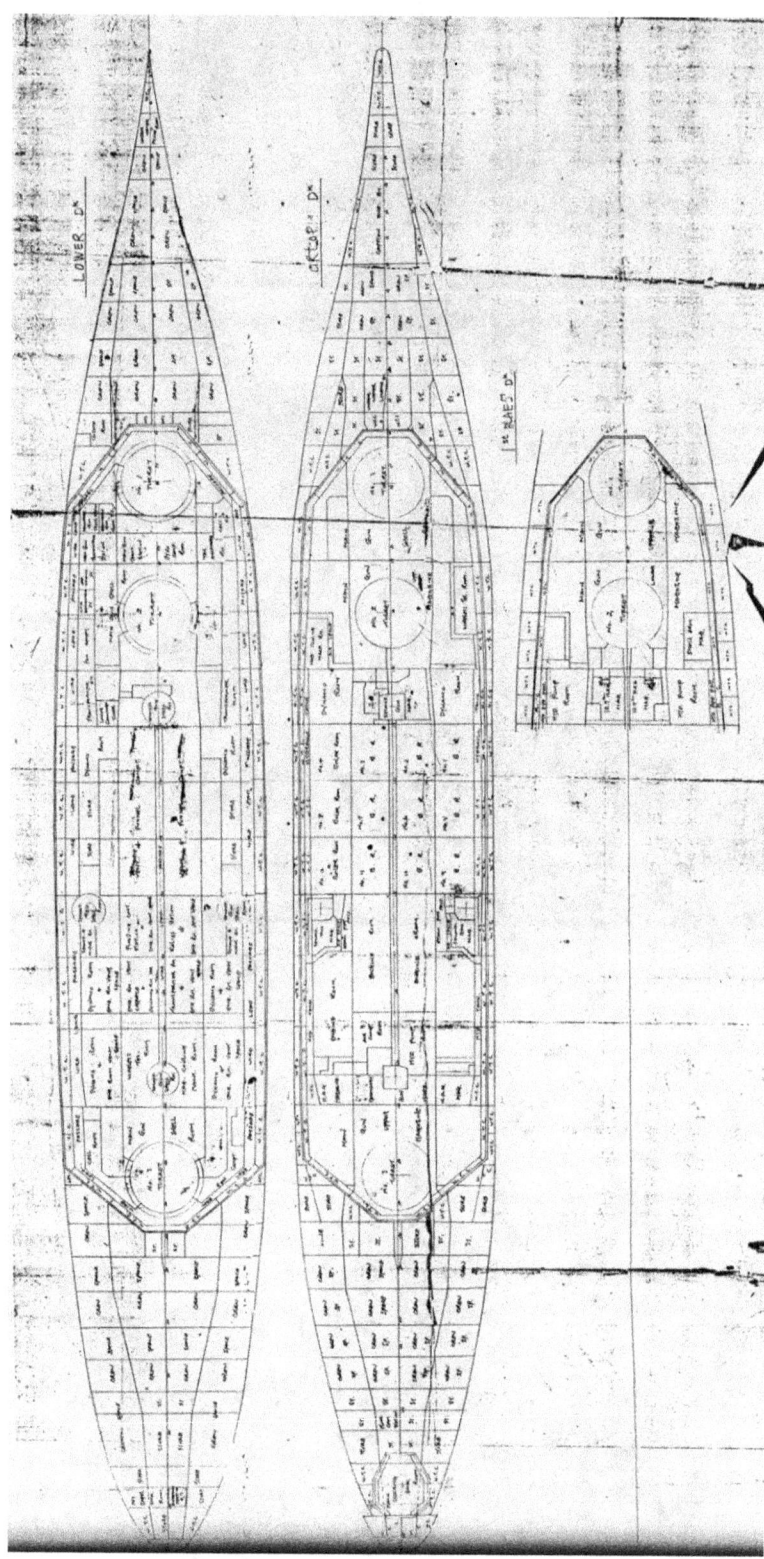

Figure 1-17: General arrangement (lower deck, orlop deck, 1st platform deck) of *Yamato* (US Naval Technical Mission to Japan, Report S-01-3, Enclosure 5)

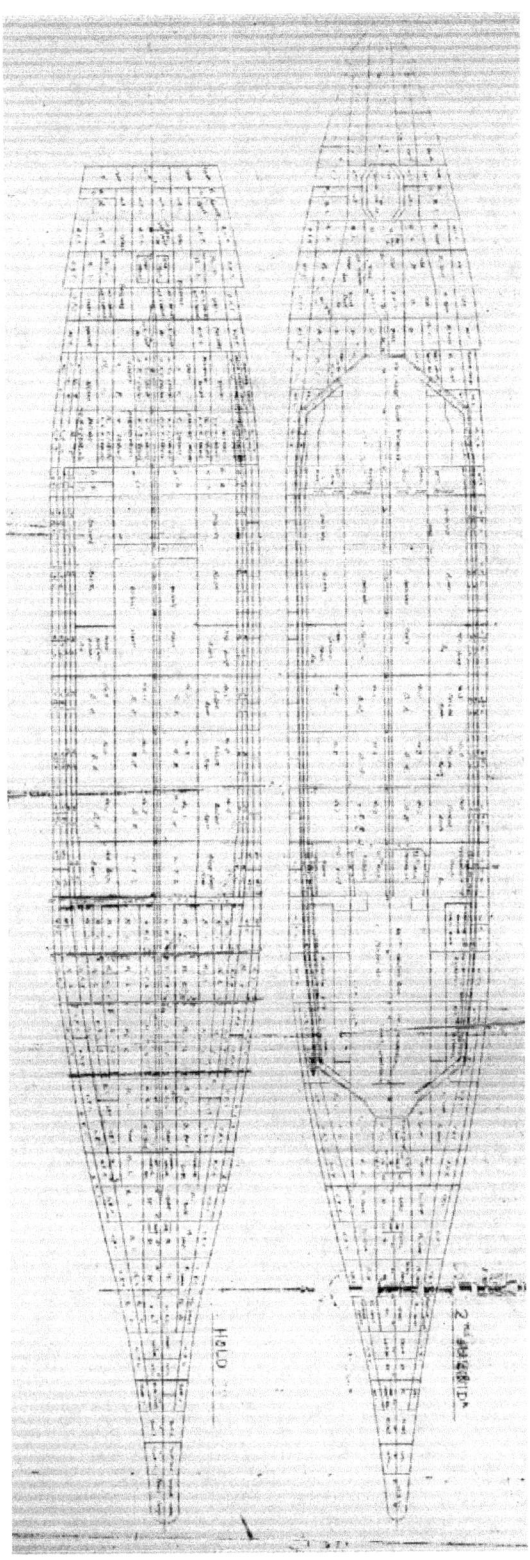

Figure 1-18: General arrangement (2nd platform deck, hold) of *Yamato* (US Naval Technical Mission to Japan, Report S-01-3, Enclosure 6)

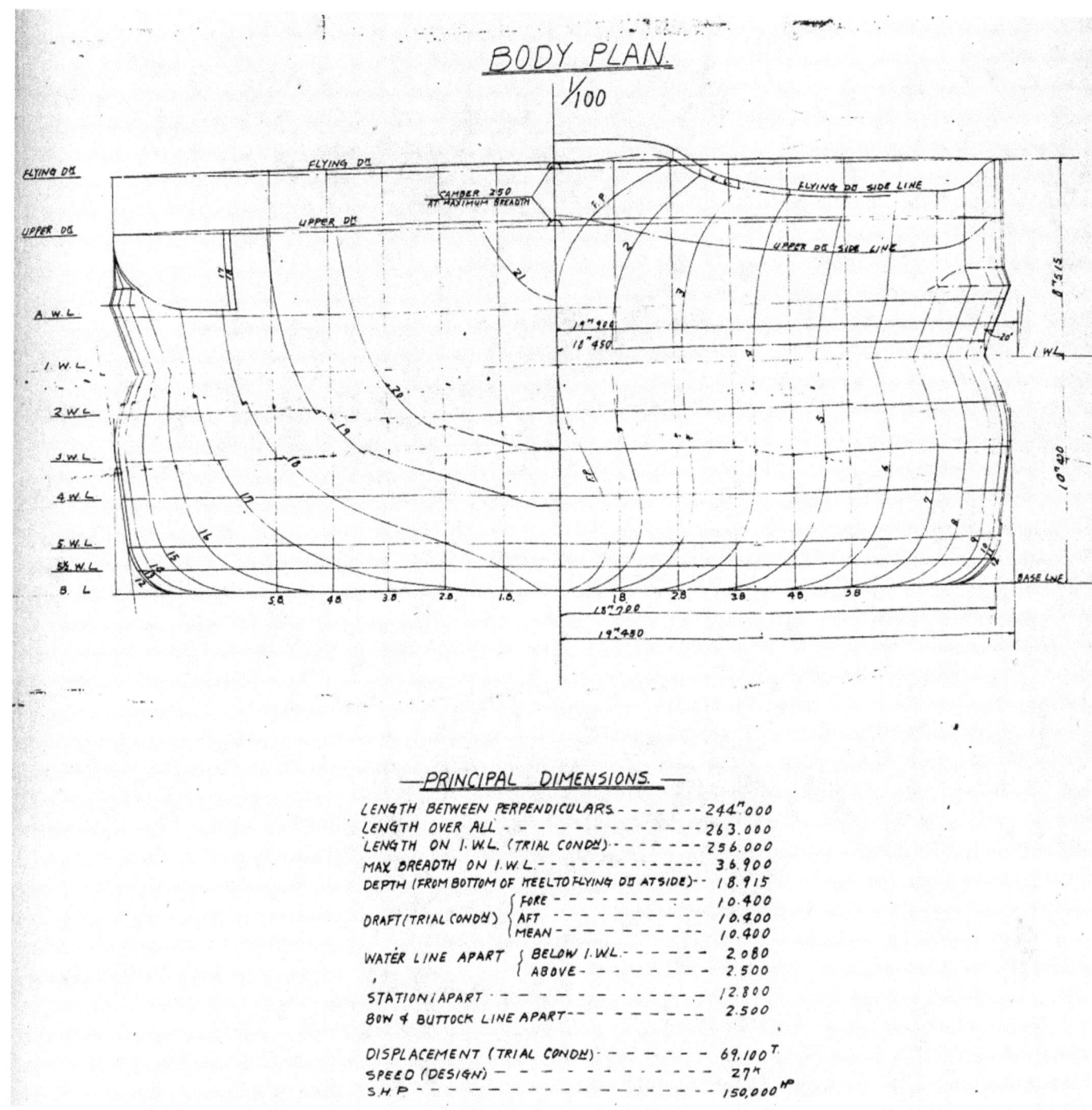

Figure 1-19: Body plan of *Yamato* (US Naval Technical Mission to Japan, Report S-01-3, Enclosure 9A)

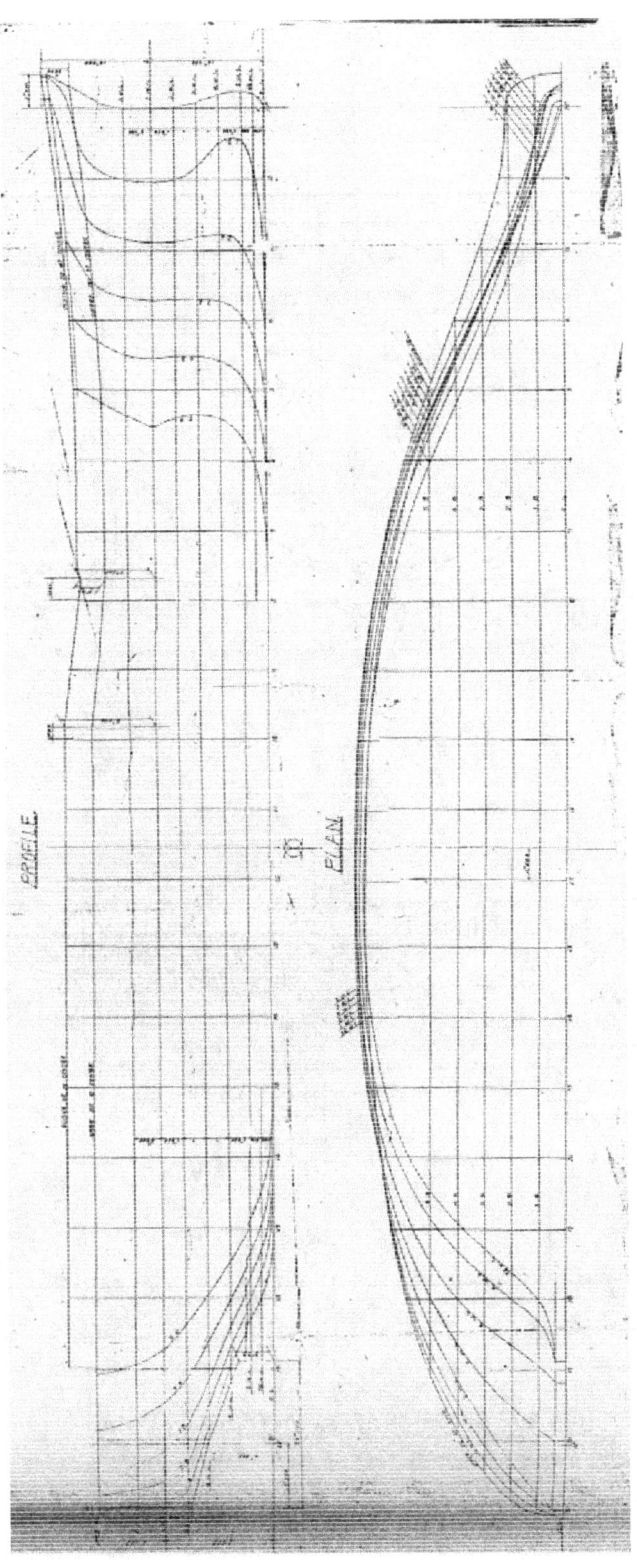

Figure 1-20: Lines of *Yamato* (US Naval Technical Mission to Japan, Report S-01-3, Enclosure 9A)

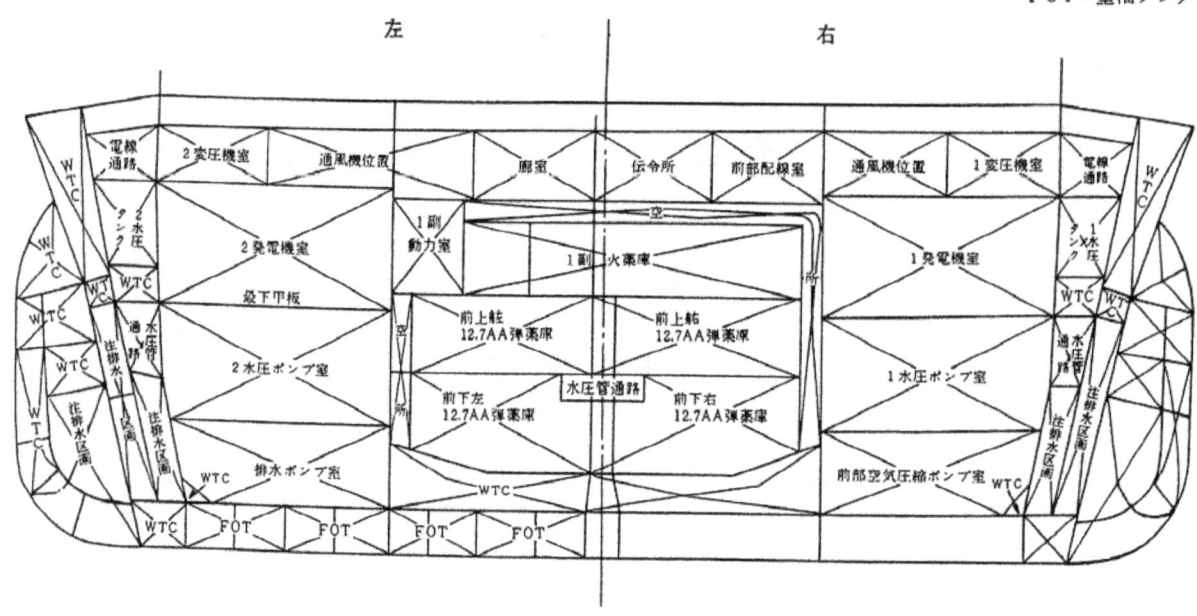

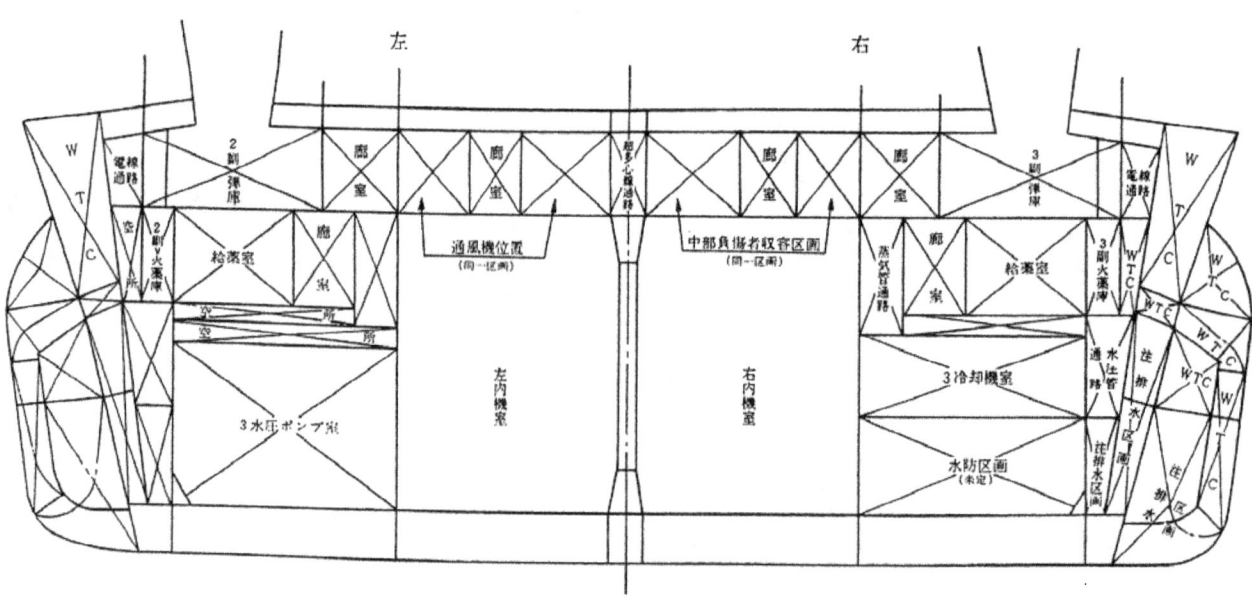

Figures 1-21–22: Frames 107 & 138 of *Musashi* (*Senkan* Yamato • Musashi *Sekkei to Kenzō*)

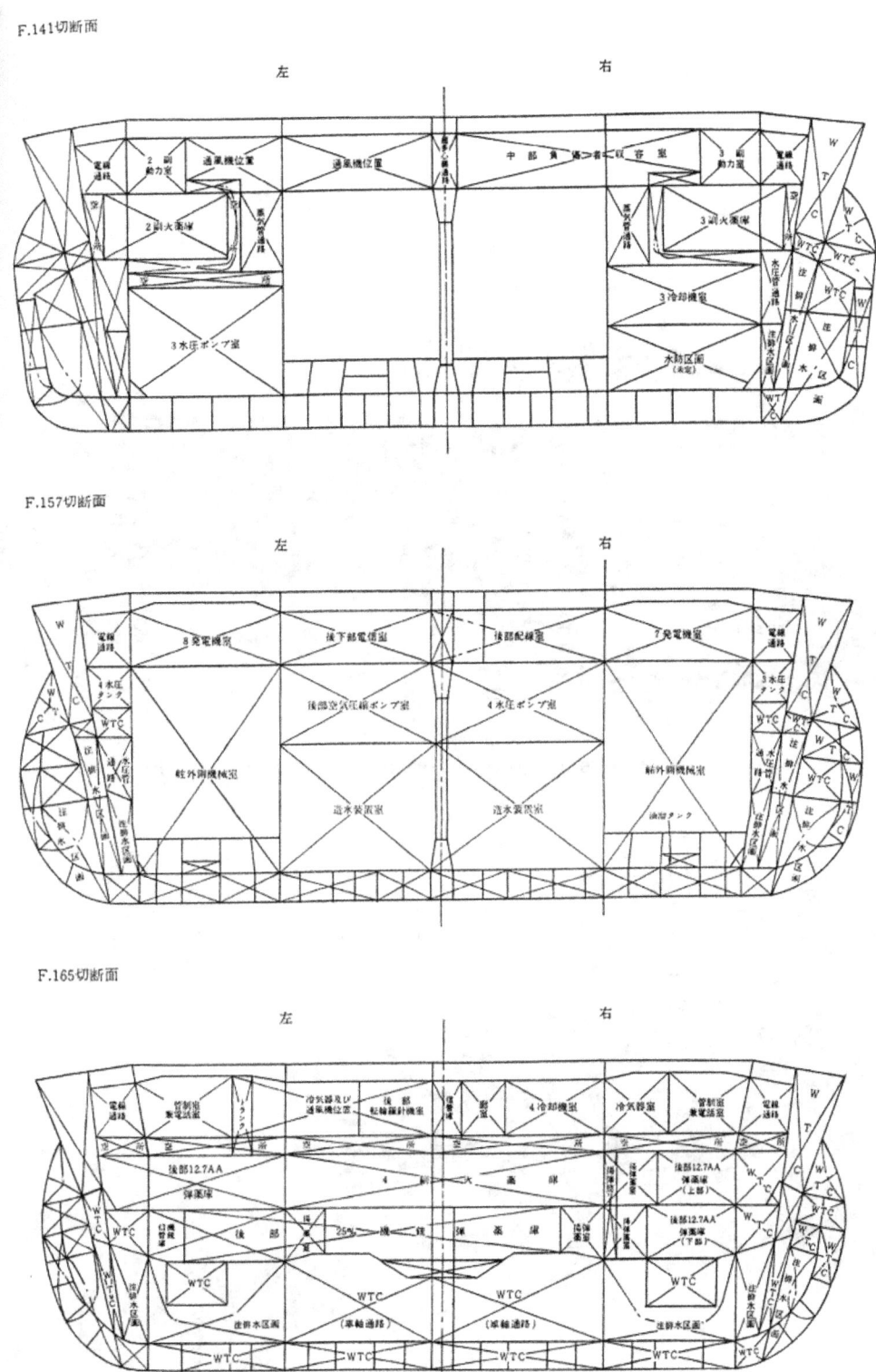

Figures 1-23–25: Frames 141, 157 & 165 of *Musashi* (*Senkan* Yamato • Musashi *Sekkei to Kenzō*)

Photo 1-9: *Yamato* during trials off Sukumo on 30 October 1941 (Authors' collections)

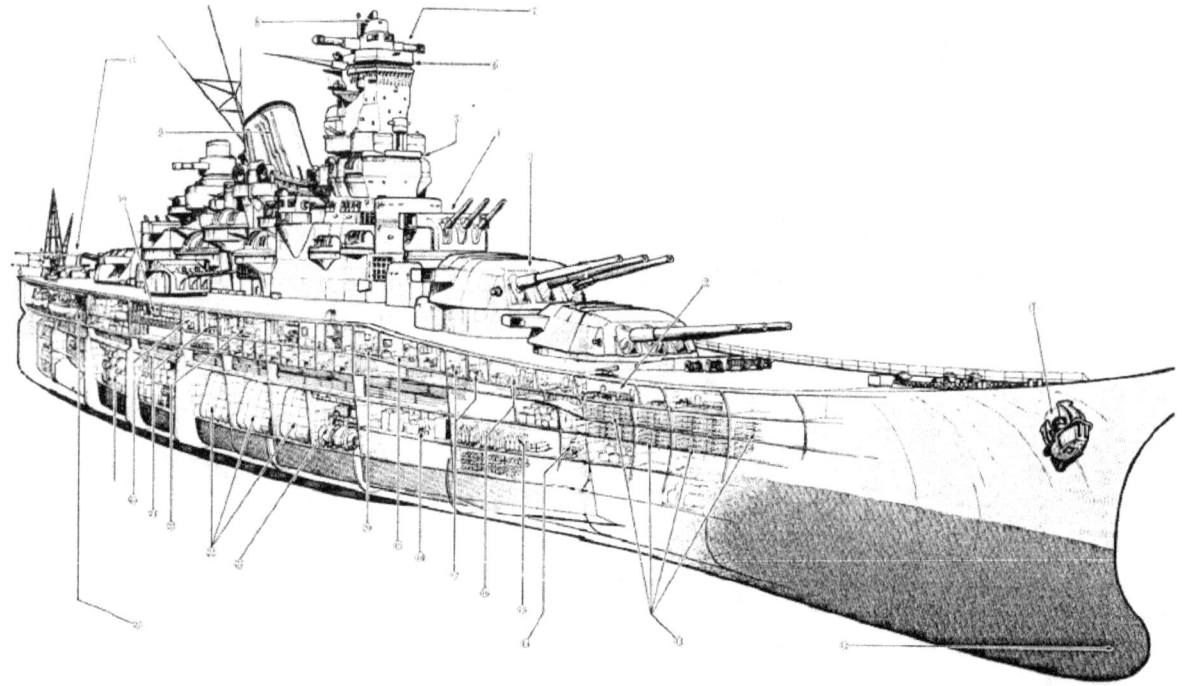

Figure 1-26: Perspective view of *Yamato* (*Teikoku Kaigun: Kyū Nippon Kaigun Kanzen Gaido* via Kitamura Kunio)

Key to Figure 1-26:

(1) Main anchor
(2) Living space for division chiefs (*buntaichō*)
(3) 46-cm main gun triple turret
(4) 15.5-cm secondary triple gun turret
(5) Lower bridge (upper lookout station)
(6) Upper bridge
(7) 15-m triple rangefinder
(8) Main gun fire director tower
(9) Funnel
(10) Galley
(11) Type 0 seaplane
(12) Bulbous bow
(13) Crew spaces
(14) *Sake* store
(15) Main gun shell magazine
(16) Officers' living spaces
(17) Staff officers' room (*sanbō shitsu*)
(18) Forward lower information room
(19) Fleet staff officer's room (*bakuryō shitsu*)
(20) Captain's room
(21) Generator room
(22) Boilers
(23) Captain's auxiliary room
(24) Toilet and bath room
(25) Executive officer's room
(26) Main engines (turbines)
(27) Ship's boats hangar

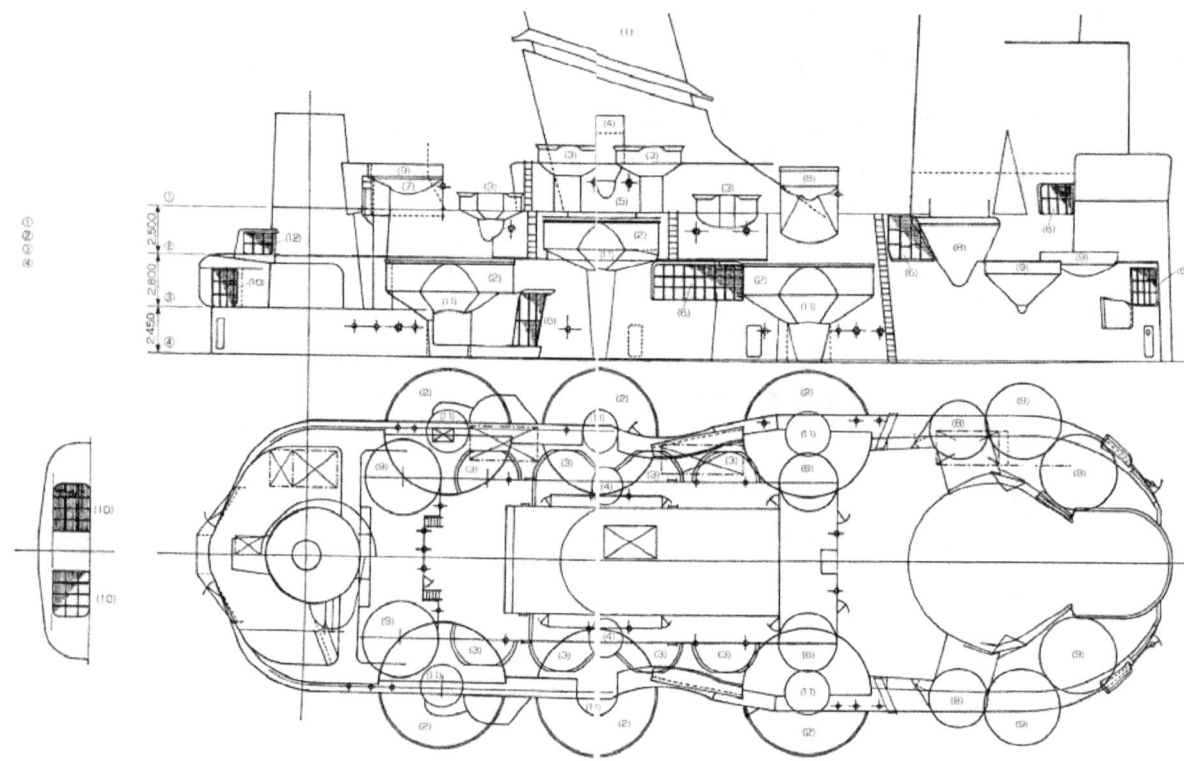

Figure 1-27: Superstructure of the *Musashi*. This drawing shows the appearance at the time of completion. Drawn are the sponsons for the 40 cal. Type 89 12.7-cm twin high-angle guns, the Type 96 25-mm triple machine-guns, the machine-gun fire director and the Type 96 150-cm searchlights and passageways (***Nihon no Senkan***)

Key to Figure 1-27:

    (1) Lower searchlight deck (*Kabu tanshōtō kanpan*)

    (2) Upper high-angle gun deck (*Jōbu kōkakuhō kanpan*)

    (3) Lower high-angle gun deck (*Kabu kōkakuhō kanpan*)

    (4) Uppermost deck (*Saijō kanpan*)

    (1) Funnel (*Entotsu*)

    (2) Twin high-angle gun flat (*Rensō kōkakuhō furatto* [flat])

    (3) 150-cm searchlight flat (*150 senchi tanshōtō furatto*)

    (4) 25-mm machine-gun fire control system sponson (*25 miru kijū shagekisōchi-dai*)

    (5) Passageway (*Tsūro*)

    (6) Ventilation trunk (*Kyūkiro*)

    (7) Machine-gun ammunition supply position (*Kijū danyaku kyūdansho*)

    (8) 4.5-m rangefinder sponson (*4.5 mētoru sokkyogi-dai*)

(9) Type 96 25-mm triple machine-gun flat/sponson *(96 Shiki 25 miru 3 rensō kijū-dai)*

(10) The Japanese original states "Rangefinder flat" *(Sokkyogi furatto)* but this must be a misprint because the line points upon the position of the mouth of the exhaust trunk and no rangefinder was situated there. Therefore, it must be assumed that (10) is identical to (12).

(11) Base of 12.7-cm twin high-angle gun *(12.7 senchi rensō kōkakuhō-dai)*

(12) Mouth of exhaust trunk *(Haikikō)*

Photo 1-10: In the foreground is one of *Musashi*'s 12.7-cm high-angle guns in June–July 1942. The deck was covered with unpainted Japanese cypress (*hinoki*) (Kure Maritime Museum)

Figure 1-28: 3-D sectional drawing of *Yamato*'s foremast (*Sekai no Kansen*)

Figure 1-29: 3-D drawing of *Yamato*'s foremast (*Sekai no Kansen*)

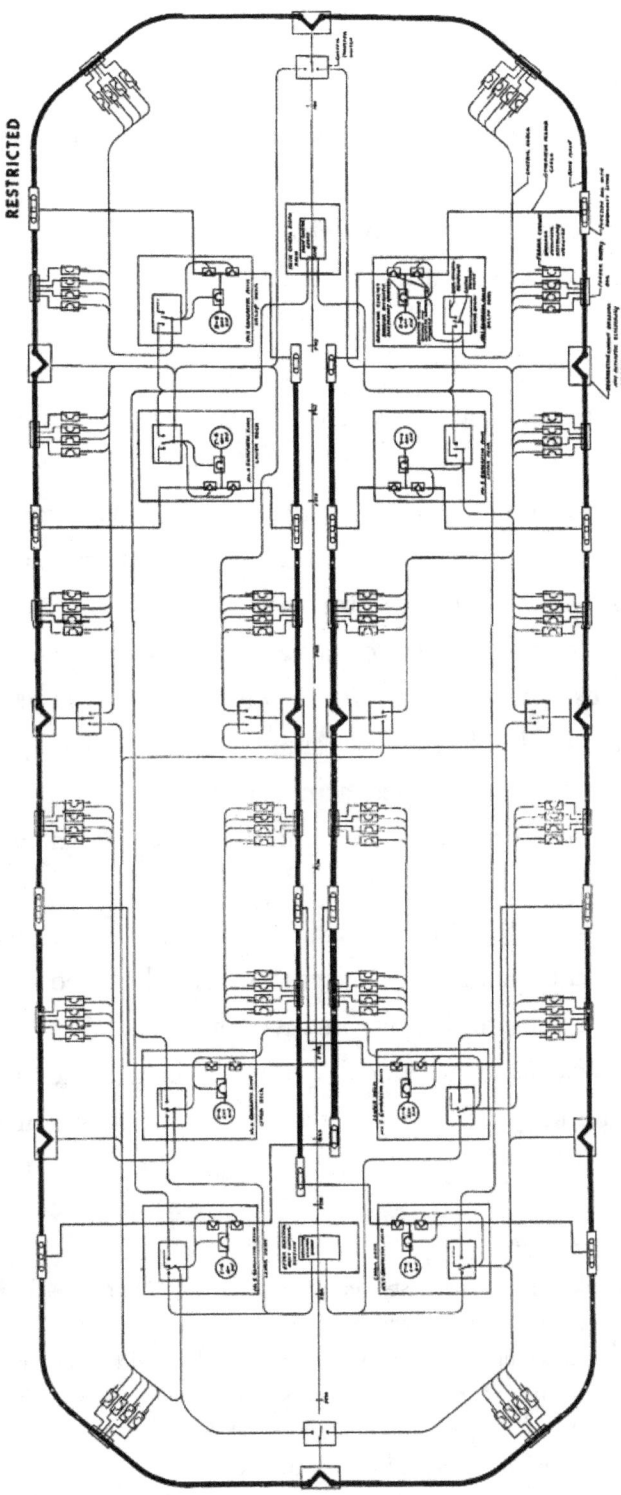

Figure 1-30: Plan showing the electric ring main distribution system, including control system, of the *Yamato* (US Naval Technical Mission to Japan, Report S-01-5)

Protection

Direct Protection

The protection arrangement is shown in the protection drawings (from Report S-01-3, US Naval Technical Mission to Japan, and "Design and Construction of the *Yamato* and *Musashi*" (*Senkan* Yamato • Musashi *Sekkei to Kenzō*), Matsumoto Kitarō & Chihaya Masataka) and the midships sections (same sources).

The basic principle was to have protection against the power of the ship's own Type 91 46-cm AP shell fired from a 45 calibre gun at distances from 20,000 to 30,000 m. The planning was made on the basis of experiments and their analysis. Data about the effect of the Type 91 AP projectile against VC and NVNC armors were available for the calibres 36 cm and 41 cm, but to obtain all the ballistic data necessary for working-out range tables, experiments with 46 cm shells were necessary to gather the practical effect at various distances. For these tests, the 48-cm gun, developed as a trial gun for the 46-cm guns to be mounted on the last four capital ships of the Eight-Eight Fleet, was used[49] against the newly developed armor (VH compared to KC and KNC but also MNC) and these data became the basis for the calculation of the armor thicknesses.[50]

The area between the forward and after magazines was considered the main protection area, i.e. the vital spaces. It was protected by the waterline belt (upper armor) and the longitudinal protective bulkhead (lower armor) on the sides, the middle deck (as armor deck) from above and thick transverse armor bulkheads forward and aft. Below the magazines a bottom protective layer of

---

[49] This gun had been damaged when test-fired in December 1920 and was repaired in 1934 (there is also one source stating the time of repair to have been at the end of the *Taishō* period, but for reasons that will be explained in volume II the authors regard the 1934 time as more likely) and two projectiles were also produced. The trial firing was successful–the gun withstood the pressure. After that it was used for determination of the blast and the trial firing of the test armor plates at the Kamegakubi range without incident. The effect was two-fold: It enabled not only the determination of the armor but also increased the self-confidence of the main persons responsible for the successful design and production of the "smaller" 46-cm calibre gun. See also footnote 84 in chapter 2.

[50] The test results on the armor plates using the completed 46-cm gun later indicated that an armor thickness of 400 mm, instead of 410 mm, was sufficient for the belt, 190 mm instead of 200 mm for the armor deck and 540 mm instead of 560 mm for the main gun barbettes.

thin armor was applied for the first time. This was the so-called citadel or raft body system.

The citadel was to be immune against hits of projectiles, bombs, torpedoes and mines. It was to remain intact to secure buoyancy and stability and maintain mobility, even if the forward and after parts (which could be considered as "floats") were damaged and flooded. The arrangement of the armor, particularly its inclination, differed according to the most probable hitting angles and the thicknesses were calculated accordingly.

The following objects were also heavily protected, like the vital spaces: (1) gun houses and barbettes of the main guns turrets, (2) conning tower and its substructure down to the armor deck, (3) main steering machinery room.[51]

The waterline belt had an inclination of 20°. A shell fired from a distance of 20,000 m hit with 26°30' angle of fall and its kinetic energy was insufficient to penetrate 410-mm thick VH armor.

The transverse armor bulkheads consisted of 300-mm thick VH plates in the middle part. For the obliquely arranged side parts 350-mm thickness were chosen.

The horizontal (deck) armor was made of 200-mm thick MNC plates. Effective against a shell fired from a distance of 30,000 m and hitting with 59° angle of fall. The thickness of its slopes and the sloping part between the barbettes were increased to 230 mm and 340 mm, respectively.

The barbette of the main guns were made of 560-mm thick VH armor considering the effect upon the cylinder at the hitting angle of 16°30'. This was the second largest thickness after the 660-mm used for the front shield of main gun houses.[52]

Before the demolition experiments with the stricken battleship *Tosa* underwater protection was made against underwater weapons, such as torpedoes and mines, and the "underwater trajectory projectile" was not considered. But in the case of the *Yamato* class the underwater protection of the vital spaces

---

[51] The protection of the auxiliary steering engine room was slightly reduced.

[52] All Japanese sources, with two exceptions, used by the authors state that the front shield was 650 mm thick. The exceptions are *Shōwa Zōsen-shi* ("History of Shipbuilding in the Shōwa Era"), 660 mm VH, p. 701, and Ishibashi Takao's *Senkan • Jun-yōsenkan* ("Battleships & Battle Cruisers"), 660 mm VH, pp. 383, 392 and 432. See also Nathan Okun's 660 mm in the chapter on armor. The authors are of the opinion that 660 mm is the correct figure regardless of what has been published in most Japanese sources and elsewhere. Some figures from Japanese sources used in this book still show 650 mm.

was designed in accordance with the results of the *Tosa* experiments, and the thickness so calculated that it could not be penetrated by a 46-cm AP shell.[53] A longitudinal tapered NVNC armor bulkhead (lower armor) was directly connected to the lower side of the waterline belt and it descended until the inner bottom along the machinery spaces at 14° inclination, being 200 mm thick at the upper and 75 mm thick at the lower end. The arrangement was in three layers. Along the ammunition magazines the inclination was increased to 25° and the thickness to 270 mm at the upper end and 100 mm at the lower one. The remarkably greater thickness was necessary because only two layers were used. The lower end was not connected to the inner bottom but to the bottom NVNC armor of the magazines, which had a thickness of 80 mm to 50 mm (see figures 1-34–35). This was sufficient to resist the detonation of 200 kg of explosives directly on the bottom. In company with the double bottom, the three-layer arrangement provided so strong a protection that it was also sufficient for the later-appearing magnetic mine. On the other hand, the large spaces below the magazine floors were without protection.

The lower armor had also the function of a longitudinal torpedo bulkhead.

At the early period of the fundamental design, the advantages of the liquid layer for underwater protection were known by the results of the experiments[54] and the use of fuel tanks was designed. But irrespective of this result,

---

[53] In *Kaigun Zōsen Gijutsu Gaiyō*, vol. 1, written by Tech. Vice-Admiral Fukuda Keiji and devoted to the *Yamato* class, the principle of the underwater protection in the fundamental design is explained. The outline is as follows: "The goal of the design of the underwater protection of the vital spaces … was to stop the flooding sufficiently at the detonation of 350 kg of explosives. The underwater protection outside the vital spaces depended on the watertight subdivision being attentively designed. As for the ship's bottom, protection was given to the floor of the magazines, even though this could not be given to the machinery spaces. However, it should be remembered that the *Yamato* was the first battleship of the world that adopted the ship's bottom protection to any extreme degree.

The hull sides along the machinery spaces were protected by the armor descending to the bottom, gradually decreasing the thickness. This was made for the protection against underwater shells."

It should be noted that figures 1-34–35 are studies only. They show the principles but do not show the actual armor thicknesses of the *Yamato*.

[54] During the design of the battleship *Nagato*, comparative experiments with reduced scale models were executed comparing the system devised by Hiraga Yuzuru (curved longitudinal bulkhead from the lower end of the belt armor to the bottom composed of three plate layers with the air layer in front, which was very difficult to produce) and that adopted in US battleships (three layers of longitudinal bulkheads jointly using liquid layers). Hiraga adopted his system for all capital ships and heavy cruisers designed by him, stating that the experiments had proven its superiority. But Fujimoto Kikuo, who succeeded him as *Keikaku Shunin*, afterwards doubted the effect of this system. In preparation for

the final decision was that the liquid layer was unnecessary because the armor against the underwater AP projectile would provide sufficient protection also against torpedoes etc. This decision, based upon the overestimated effect of the lower armor, was fateful for it could never bring about the effect of the multiple liquid layers. Consequently, the supposed amount of flooding was about twice that calculated for the system of the US battleships, with the corresponding bigger destruction area.

A system using no liquid but only air layers needed much depth (footnote 54 item [2] and also footnote 15 in the Introduction) but, irrespective of the great hull beam, sufficient depth could not be provided. On the back of the upper and lower armor were placed a 16-mm DS[55] backing plate and the 14-mm thick longitudinal DS splinter bulkhead, and further inside there was a 9-mm thick watertight bulkhead, forming the wall of the outer boiler rooms amidships. All the joints of these bulkheads, belonging to the protective structure, were riveted because electric welding was not permitted.

The distance between the skin of the bulge and the lower armor was only 2.78 m at the depth of six meters[56] because the bulge roughly followed the inclination of the lower armor. This distance was much too narrow for any real reduction of the force of the torpedo warhead's detonation gases as they expanded, and would allow a large backward distortion of the nearby supporting structure and armor with its depth depending on the position of the torpedo detonation. Ironically, this defect was the result of an advantage that will be mentioned under the headline "Machinery." In short: By placing the four main turbines and four boilers each transversely in parallel, to connect with three boilers each and one turbine set in line to one shaft, a width of 27.8 m was

---

the design of the new capital ships many experiments with regard to the underwater protection were carried out and the utilisation of the liquid layer proved to be superior. As advantages the following effects were confirmed: (1) Obstruction of the penetration of protective bulkheads by fragments of the ship's structure caused by a torpedo detonation (the water had the effect of a brake and annihilated much of the kinetic energy), (2) distribution of the detonation gas pressure as water pressure upon the whole area of the protective bulkhead (therefore the force of the detonation effected upon a much larger area than in case of an air space, in which only the distance to the detonation point reduced the force of the expanding gases), (3) reduction of the flooding in the protective compartments (by offering more resistance) and reduction of the total amount of flooding by putting more transverse bulkheads (the water of the layers was already in the ship and considered in the calculations and transverse bulkheads limited flooding in the longitudinal direction).

[55] British design by Mr. David Colville for an extra-high-strength construction steel.

[56] This depth could be expected as setting on a torpedo against as large a ship as the *Yamato*.

necessary, while the maximum beam at the skin of the bulges amidships was 38.9 m.

Also, along the magazines only the longitudinal splinter protection bulkhead on the back of the armor was fitted because of the decreased beam of the hull and the large space needed for the magazines. On the back of the bottom armor of the magazines neither a splinter protection nor a watertight flat was provided.

This and insufficient depth were not the only disadvantages. Because of the necessity to adopt a very concentrated protection system, the length of the upper armor was shortened to 53.5% of the length of waterline. Furthermore, the bottom armor of the magazines was recognised as necessary to prevent flooding, and so the necessity of underwater protection on the hull below that armor was denied. As a result, the portion of the lower armor that went down to the hull bottom (and only this can be recognised as complete underwater protection) was reduced to the length of the machinery spaces i.e., 60 m or 22.7% of the total length. This was only about 60% of the length of the previous battleships.

In addition, there was a weakness in the supporting structure of the armor at the joint between the upper (VH main waterline belt) and lower (NVNC underwater protective bulkhead) armor. The stacked plates were not joined together by interlocking shape (as the turret armor plates were at their edges) or by keying (steel strips wedged into notches or grooves in both mated edges to lock them in place), and were only held together by their common hull back supports. If a torpedo hit the upper part of the lower armor, that plate would be pushed inward, crushing those back supports and tearing free from its weak joint with the upper armor, causing the flooding of the outer boiler rooms and, hence, the failure of the reserve buoyancy calculations (for stability and trim) in riddled (all hull areas outside the armor flooded) condition. This was demonstrated by the torpedo hit.

It seems as if the fixation upon defense against the underwater trajectory shell (the Type 91 AP shell) and the resulting application of the lower armor may have prevented the IJN from studying underwater protection requirements from different angles and this caused defects which otherwise might have been eliminated. These defects were: (1) underwater protection by the lower armor down to the bottom was only provided along the machinery spaces; (2) the bottom armor of the magazines was placed very high up in the hull, and because the lower armor was connected to this bottom armor at its lower edge, the lower armor's depth was much reduced compared with (1)–the cause of this was the necessity to save armor weight; and (3) the bottom armor protected the magazines, but created large unprotected spaces below it due to defect (2), above. These unprotected bottom spaces were subdivided by longitudinal and lateral bulkheads (considered to belong to the indirect protected area), but were not useful for underwater protection. The comparatively wide space between these thin vertical bulkheads made the limitation of flooding doubtful and in case of damage by a torpedo hit extensive flooding, and a consequent increase of list, could be expected underneath the magazines.

The VH upper armor plates were conveniently fixed to the hull plates of the ship's structure by means of armor bolts. The upper edge of the VH armor was very strongly and tightly connected to the MNC armor deck edge by dove-tail junction (the kind of locking joint missing at the lower edge). The lower edge of the VH armor also required strong support and in order to avoid a backward rotation tearing the plates free due to the impact of a heavy projectile, the connection between the VH and lower NVNC armor plates and the supporting structure was deeply considered. At the beginning of the design the arrangement of the upper and lower armor joint supporting structure on one level by adopting a cross form had been proposed, but rejected because of the very difficult fabrication. The actual executed joint, whose effectiveness was calculated as 50%,[57] is shown in figures 1-38–40 (inboard is on the left).

DS plates 28-mm thick and about 1.6 m in width were made as the basis structure (as rack plate) and the upper and lower support materials were fixed to it. The lower support material was fastened to the basis structure by, mainly, three-ply rivets, while in case of the upper support material tap rivets were primarily used. The diameter of the rivets was 28 mm and many were conveniently located. But the resisting forces of both support materials against the powerful pressure from the outside in the transverse direction (shell or torpedo hits) depended primarily on the shearing strength of these rivets. The basis structure had an inclination of 10°, so that the inner side was higher. It resulted in a little increased resistance of the upper support by the wedge effect of

---

[57] Efficiency greater than 50% was aspired to. According to the calculations the resistance was sufficient to withstand a detonation of 520kg of explosives in the machinery spaces, and at least 350kg in the area of the ammunition magazines. Because no water layer was applied, the bulge could be completely used for flooding and counterflooding, but this was a dangerous method.

the inclination, but brought about the converse effect to the lower support, which could more easily be driven into the hull.[58]

Yamato was torpedoed by USS *Skate* (SS-305) on 25 December 1943. One torpedo (of four) struck her at about F 168 as she was steaming 180 nm north of Truk Atoll (10°05'N/150°32'E). On the bridge they felt a very slight impact but one escorting destroyer reported a water column starboard aft. After searching for damage, the flooding of the upper magazine of #3 main guns turret became known. *Yamato* entered Truk and divers investigated the damage from the outside. One hole, about 5 m in depth and 10 m in length with cracks stretching between F 151 and F 173, was found. The upper armor inside the bulge apparently did not have any abnormality. Then Tech. Sub-Lieutenant Nishijima Teruhiko from the repair ship *Akashi* dove into the flooded magazine. He discovered small holes in line over the length of several frames at the starboard longitudinal bulkhead. It was seen from the outside of the hull that the lower end of the lower bracket of the web frames, which reinforced the plate behind the armor, resembled the toe part of a shoe. He recognised the breaking of the 14-mm DS longitudinal splinter bulkhead behind the armor by the edge of these toes, and reported that these web frames after being pushed in and, after breaking the bulkhead, returned to their original position by their elasticity, so that no change was observed behind the armor.

The centre of the detonation was only about 1.2 m below the waterline and, hence, about the same distance above the joint between the upper and lower armor. This was an extraordinary shallow depth for torpedoing a battleship but despite this, water flooded into the citadel[59] and the total amount of water that poured into the ship was beyond imagination. An interesting conclusion is made in the Report S-06-2 "Reports of Damage Japanese Warships–Article 2

---

[58] Because the junction of the armor plates and the supporting structure are very important for the effectiveness of the armor protection, firing tests were conducted at the Kamegakubi range using a full-size model. The model was fired at using the repaired 48-cm gun at a distance corresponding to the effect of a 46-cm AP shell fired from 20,000 m. The result was disappointing: The protective effect of the armor was sufficient, but the lower part of the armor plates was pushed in several metres. Thus it became obvious that the supporting structure did not fulfil its purpose. As countermeasure a "limitation bulkhead" (wing passage bulkhead) was additionally built to restrict flooding. This small, and in fact insufficient, countermeasure was the only one undertaken to remove this dangerously weak spot.

[59] Flooding into the citadel offset all stability and trim calculations which were made–of course–on the assumption that the watertightness of the vital spaces would be maintained.

Yamato (BB), *Musashi* (BB), *Taiho* (CV), *Shinano* (CV)" of the US Naval Technical Mission to Japan, p. 9, by stating:

> The connection joining the upper main belt [upper armor] to the lower section [lower armor] undoubtedly would be ruptured somewhat liberally, the seriousness of the rupture increasing with proximity to the joint. Thus, within reasonable limits, a deeper hit can be expected to cause a much more serious rupture of the joint than did this shallow hit.
>
> The first bulkhead inboard of the armored bulkhead [lower armor] would be ruptured—the extent of the rupture depending on the distance inboard which either the top edge of the lower armor moves or the distance inboard which the bottom of the main belt [upper armor] moves.

Nishijima's observations were confirmed by the investigation in Kure Navy Yard where the repair was made. The wedge effect did not work and the rivets fixing the 28-mm thick base plate were broken. The fact that only one torpedo hit caused the flooding of about 3,000 tons of water into the ship, of which a considerable amount was inside the citadel, shocked the personnel in charge and made them realize this grave defect. But no fundamental countermeasures were taken because reinforcement of the supporting structure was impossible. The only measure was the fitting of a 45° sloping 6-mm thick DS plate across the corner of the upper void, between the two inboard bulkheads along the machinery spaces.[60] The avowed purpose was to maintain watertightness of the void between the two bulkheads. However, one has to agree to the opinion expressed in the same US Naval Technical Mission to Japan report (p. 10) that this measure seems hopelessly inadequate and the former Tech. Rear-Admiral Fukuda is quoted "that it could not have been of any possible value." A critique the former Tech. Captain Makino Shigeru agrees to in his dissertation:

> The pressure (caused by the underwater detonation of a torpedo or impact of a shell) affected the upper and lower armor. The nearer the centre was to the joint the more pressure was affected upon the edges of the armor

---

[60] According to Naitō the upper parts of the magazines of #1 and #2 main gun turrets had one more longitudinal watertight bulkhead inside the splinter bulkhead (as countermeasure against flooding) but the upper magazine of #3 main gun turret lacked this protection only at the damaged part. Thus the torpedo hit at the weakest point accidentally. However, this must not be taken as excuse of the fundamental weakness of the armor joint. By the way, the (useless) DS plate was fitted to only *Yamato*. *Musashi* remained as she was.

and consequently upon the supporting material and, hence, resistance of the rivets against the pressure. As shown by this hit, the supporting material did not have a sufficient structure to withstand such an underwater detonation. Entire rivets sheared off for a certain length and the armor was pushed in together with the support material. The loss of the battleship *Musashi* and the aircraft carrier *Shinano* manifested this structural defect and confirmed the deadly consequences for the ships.

As stated before, the initial (cross type) supporting structure of the joint between the upper and lower armor could not be applied because the Armor Manufacturing Division of the Kure Navy Yard considered the structure to be too complicated. Then, the structures chosen because of this inability were not successful and left the fatal weak points in the protection of the vital spaces. Here Makino makes an interesting supposition: If the liquid layer had been placed in the bulge the detonation pressure would have been distributed over the whole surface of the lower armor[61] resulting, very probably, in the compensation of the weak point of the fixed (supporting) structure of the upper part (of the lower armor).

With regard to horizontal protection, the "roof" of the vital spaces was a 200-mm thick MNC armor placed on the middle deck, sufficient to resist the impact of 800-kg bombs released from horizontal bombers from 4,000 m altitude. For the junctions of the armor plates either dove-tails or double buttstraps were used. Firing tests using full-size models and 48-cm projectiles corresponding to the effect of 46-cm shells fired from 30,000 m range confirmed that the designed resistance was obtained.

The support of the middle deck armor was made by box type girders (beams). Below them at 800 mm distance 9-mm thick DS plates were fitted as splinter protection.

The areas forward and aft of the vital spaces were protected by 55 mm to 35-mm thick CNC armor, offering sufficient protection against 250-kg bombs. This measure was taken to avoid the loss of buoyancy of these areas. The part of the sloped funnel that was directly above the honeycomb funnel uptake armor, was protected by 50-mm thick CNC armor reaching high into the superstructure in order to cause the detonation of bombs on this elevated plating and avoid direct bomb hits on the armor grating, which might cause blast damage to the boilers through the holes in that plate.

---

[61] See footnote 54 and footnote 15 in the Introduction.

One more weak point of the protective system was the secondary guns. In contrast to the main gun turrets, which, like the vital spaces, had very strong protection, the lightly-protected 15.5-cm triple-gun turrets, removed from the light cruisers of the *Mogami* class when they were converted into heavy 20.3-cm twin-gun turret cruisers, were mounted unchanged. At the openings for the 15.5-cm shell and powder hoists through the MNC middle deck, coaming armor was used to deflect shell and bomb hits. Fire was to be extinguished by a fire fighting system designed to stop a fire from reaching the magazines. But the powder magazines of the secondary guns placed on the centreline forward and aft (#1 and #4 that were on tall barbettes so that they could super-fire over the forward and after main turrets) were too near to those of the main guns, so that a reinforcement of this area was urgently required. Therefore, the thickness of the barbettes for 15.5-cm mounts #1 and #4 were doubled to be able to resist 800-kg bombs released by horizontal bombers, as well as 250-kg bombs dropped by dive bombers, and the openings in the middle deck for shell and powder lifts were further strengthened by splinter and flame protection. The fire fighting equipment of these parts was generally improved. The battleship *Musashi* incorporated these improvements prior to her delivery, *Yamato* after completion only. They were only makeshift measures for perfect reinforcement would have required a considerable change of the fundamental armament plan.

Much more could be said about the direct protection system but let's close with a word about the resistance effect of the armor. The maximum value was only attained at the central part of an armor plate, and it was taken for a fact that some decline of the resistance against a projectile at the edges of the armor, as far as to a distance of 2.5 times the calibre, was inevitable. Therefore, the larger the area of an armor plate, the larger the part offering maximum resistance. On the other hand, the weight of an armor plate was inevitably restricted by the production facilities, etc. The plates of the upper VH side armor were 3.6 m wide and 5.9 m high. Therefore, the central part occupied not more than 22% of the whole area of 21.34 m² and about 78% belonged to the weaker part, which surrounded the centre with 1.15 m width. The reduction of the resistance could be compensated partly by the inclination, but in case of the horizontal armor no countermeasure existed. The production facilities of the Kure Navy Yard Steel Production Division were enlarged for the production of armor plates weighting 100 tons. These plates were used for the slopes of the armor deck, while for the flat central part standard 70-ton plates were applied. By the way, the mosaic fitting of horizontal armor plates was not an easy work and the fixing of the upper and lower belt armor to their backing plates and the supporting structures also required considerable efforts, and a good deal of tools.[62]

Photo 1-11: Battleships *Musashi* and *Yamashiro* photographed in June 1943 (Kure Maritime Museum)

---

[62] The reduction of armor plate resistance at its edges is minor if the plate edge is supported properly (such as the upper edge of the VH belt armor was buttressed by the thick MNC deck edge locked to its back). Only if the edge is not supported properly or, in a face-hardened plate, there is no other heavy steel plate to absorb the shell impact shockwave moving toward that edge (so that the shockwave reflects at that edge, doubling the force on the edge and possibly cracking the face-hardened plate there, which could result in a chunk of armor breaking off) does hitting close to an edge cause a significant loss in plate resistance. [Nathan Okun]

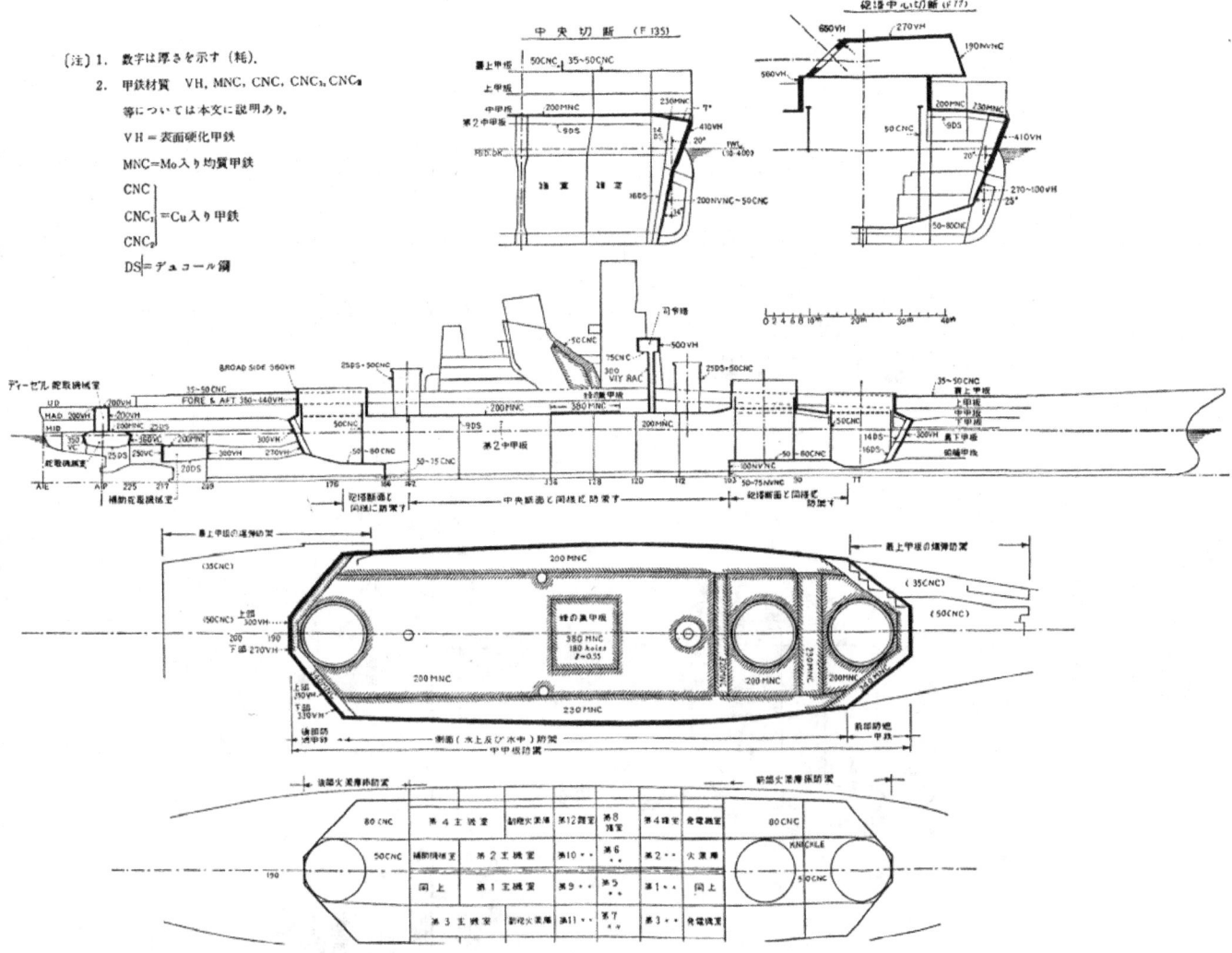

Figure 1-31: Armor arrangement of the *Yamato* (*Senkan* Yamato • Musashi *Sekkei to Kenzō*)

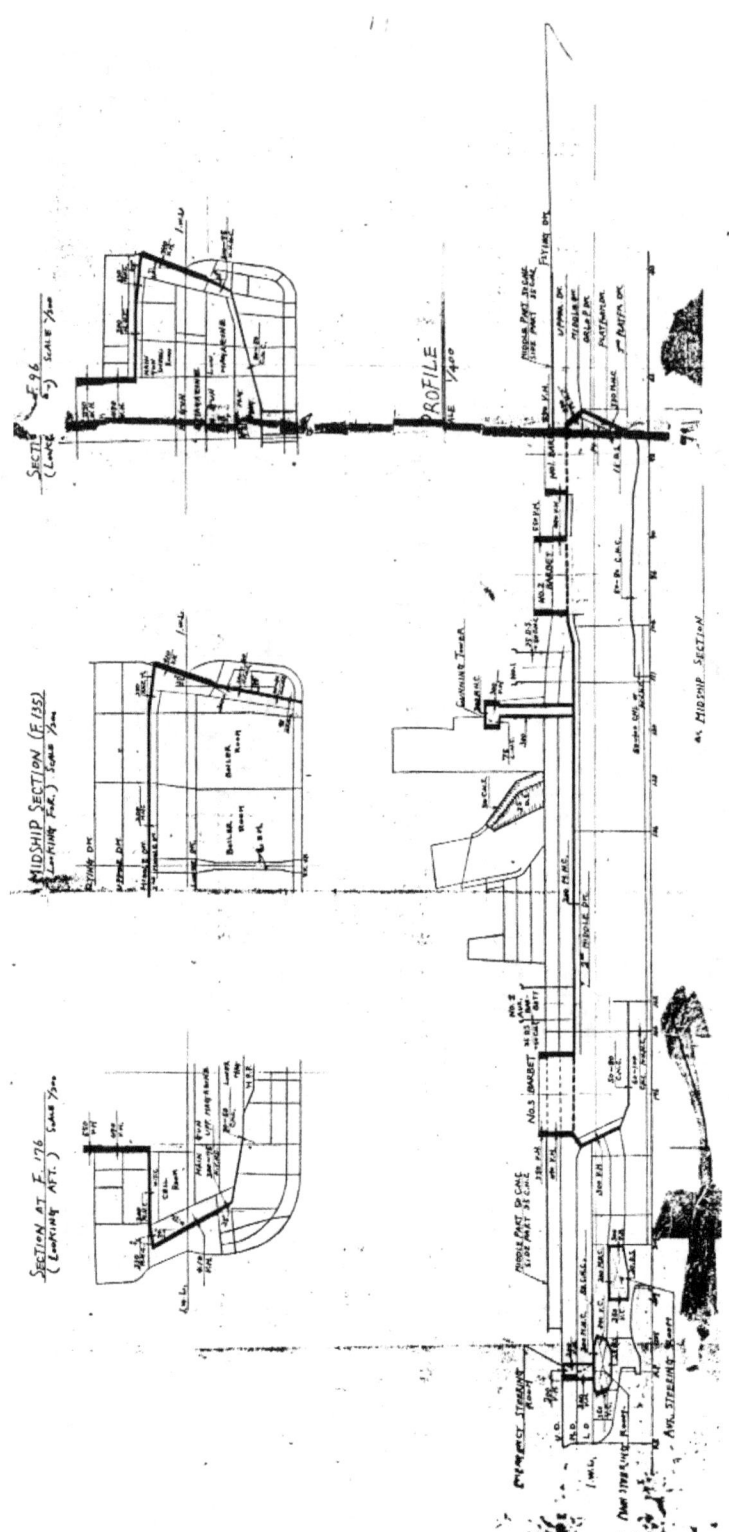

Figure 1-32: Armor arrangement of *Yamato* (US Naval Technical Mission to Japan, Report S-01-3, Enclosure 9)

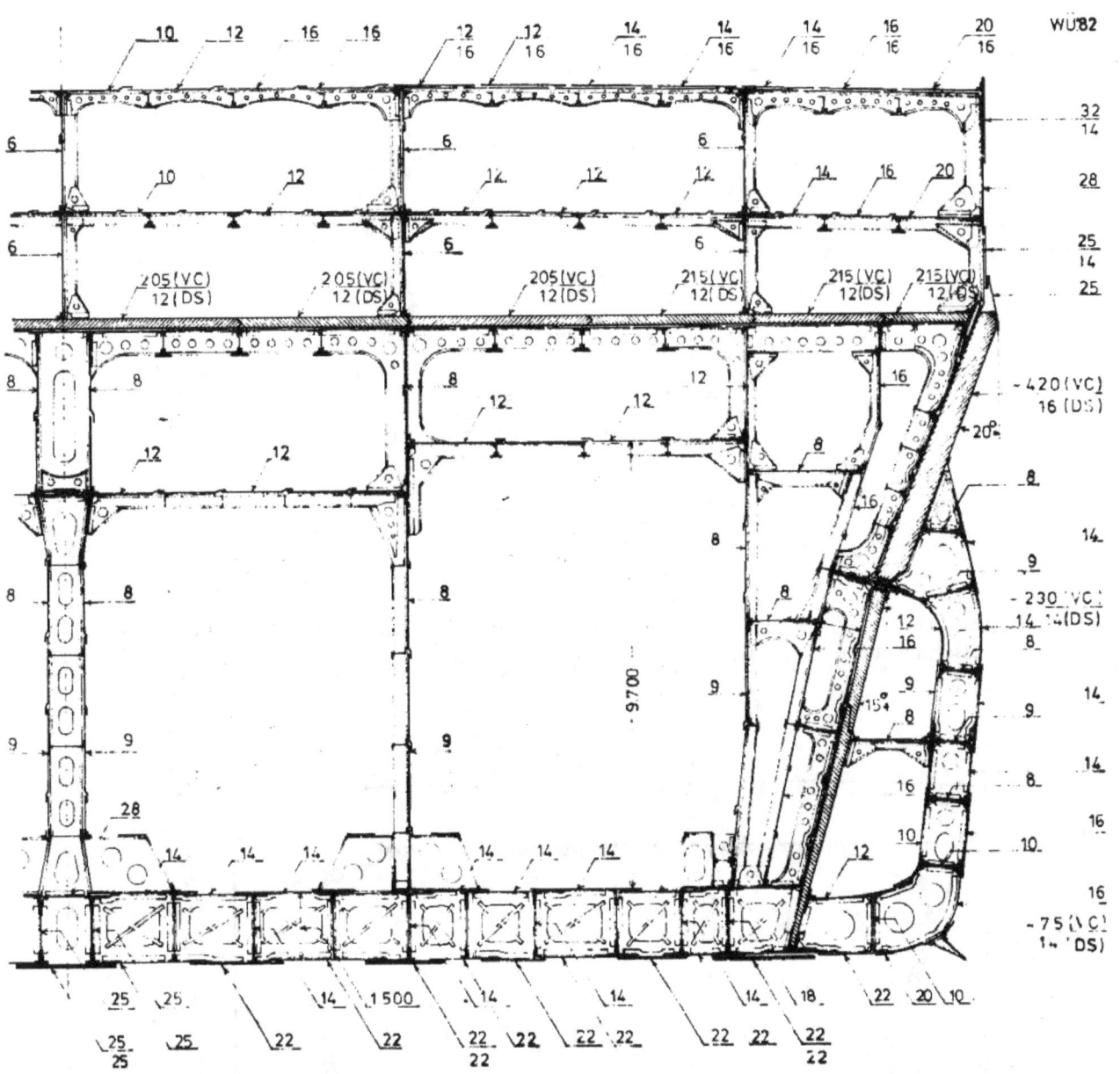

Figure 1-33: Midships section of the *Yamato* design (9 March 1936) showing thickness' of plating in mm (Michael Wünschmann)

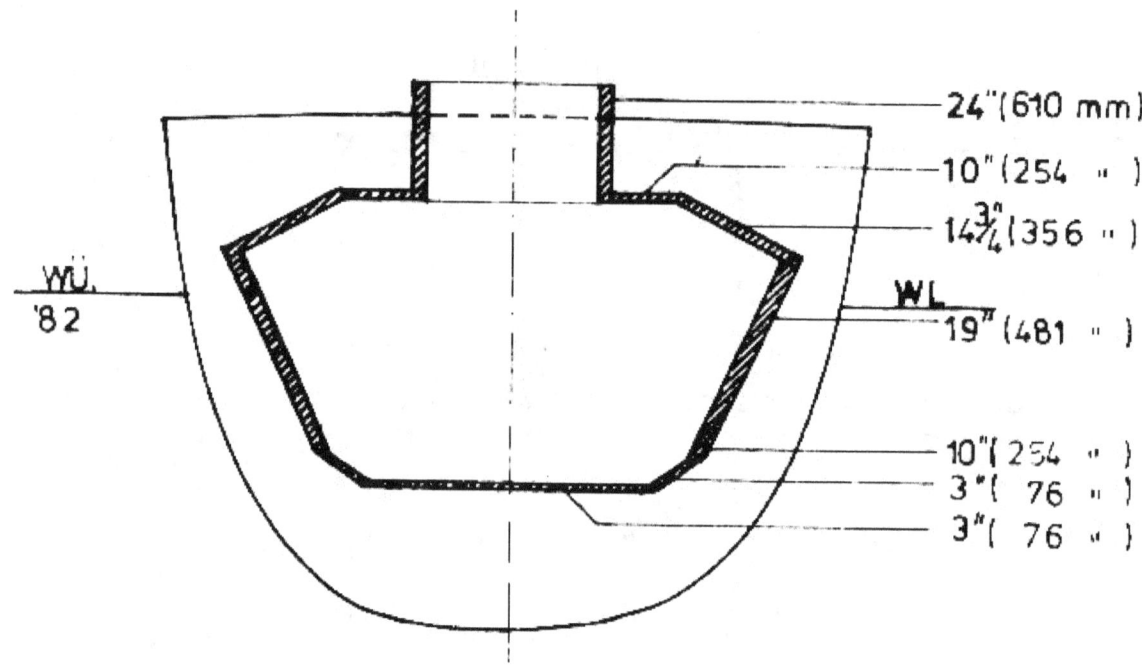

Figure 1-34: Principle and thickness of armor around shell and powder magazines (Michael Wünschmann)

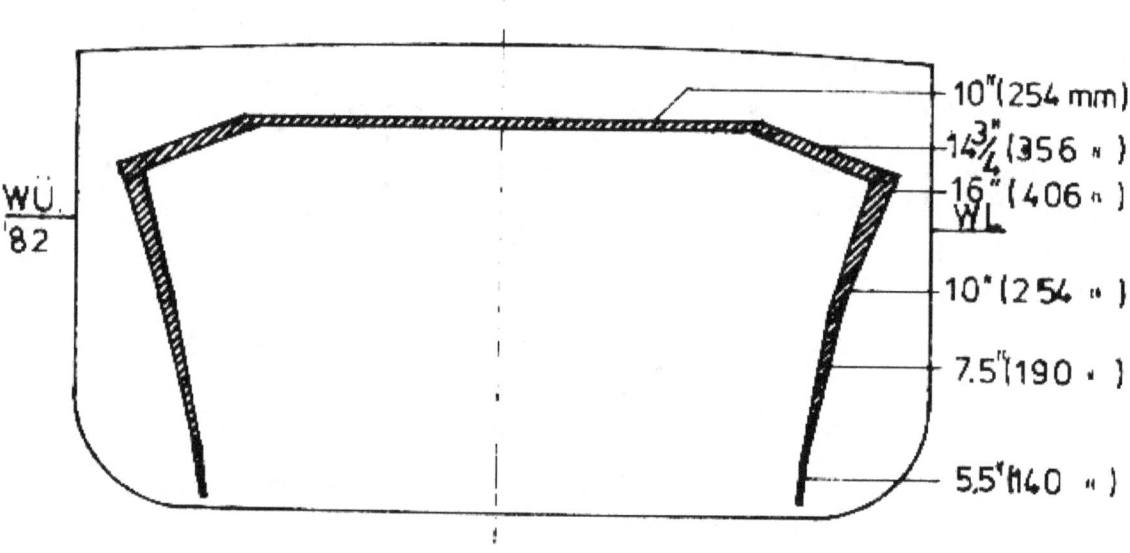

Figure 1-35: Principle and thickness of armor of boiler and engine compartments (Michael Wünschmann)

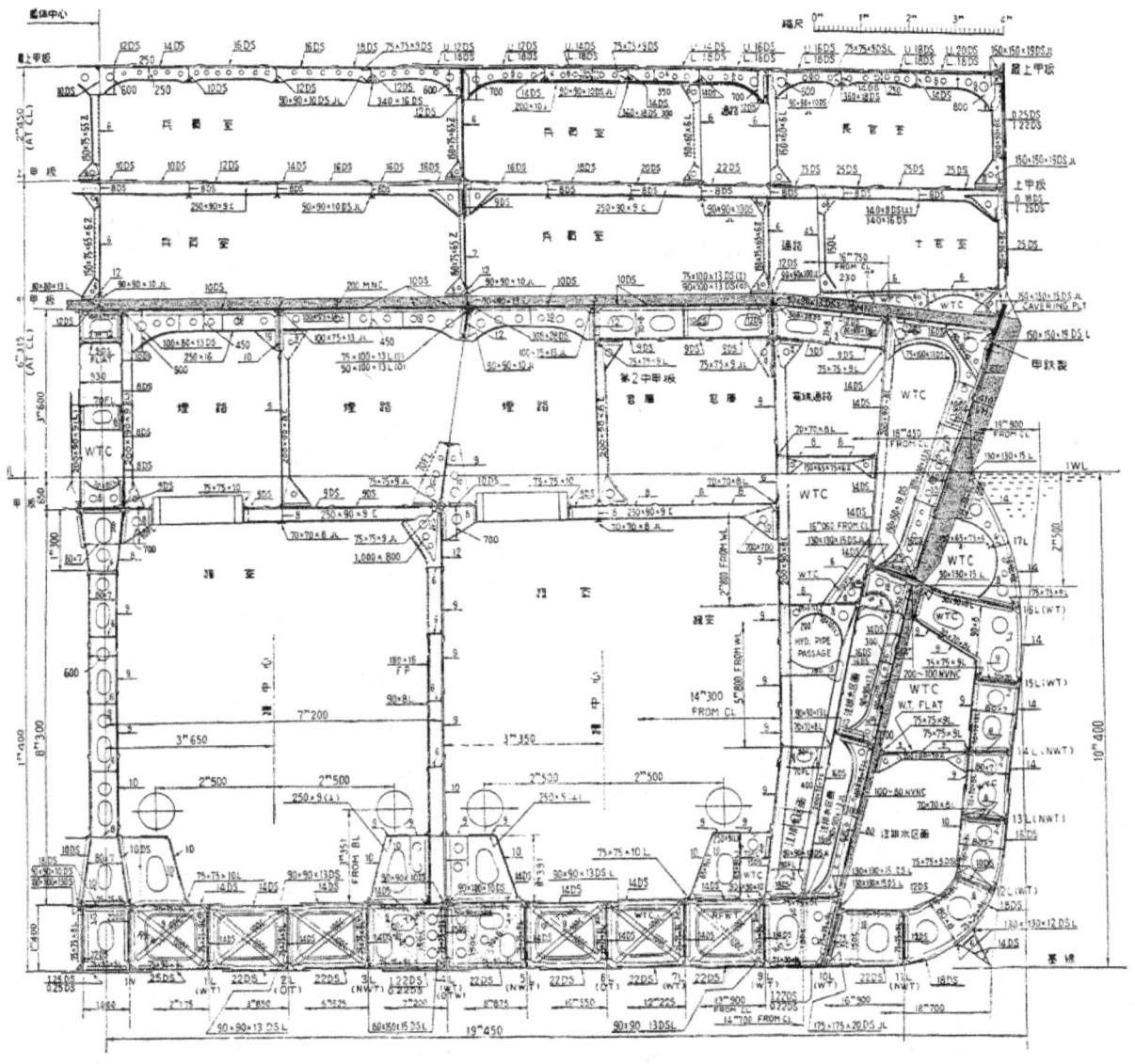

Figure 1-36: Midships section of the *Yamato* (*Senkan* Yamato • Musashi *Sekkei to Kenzō*)

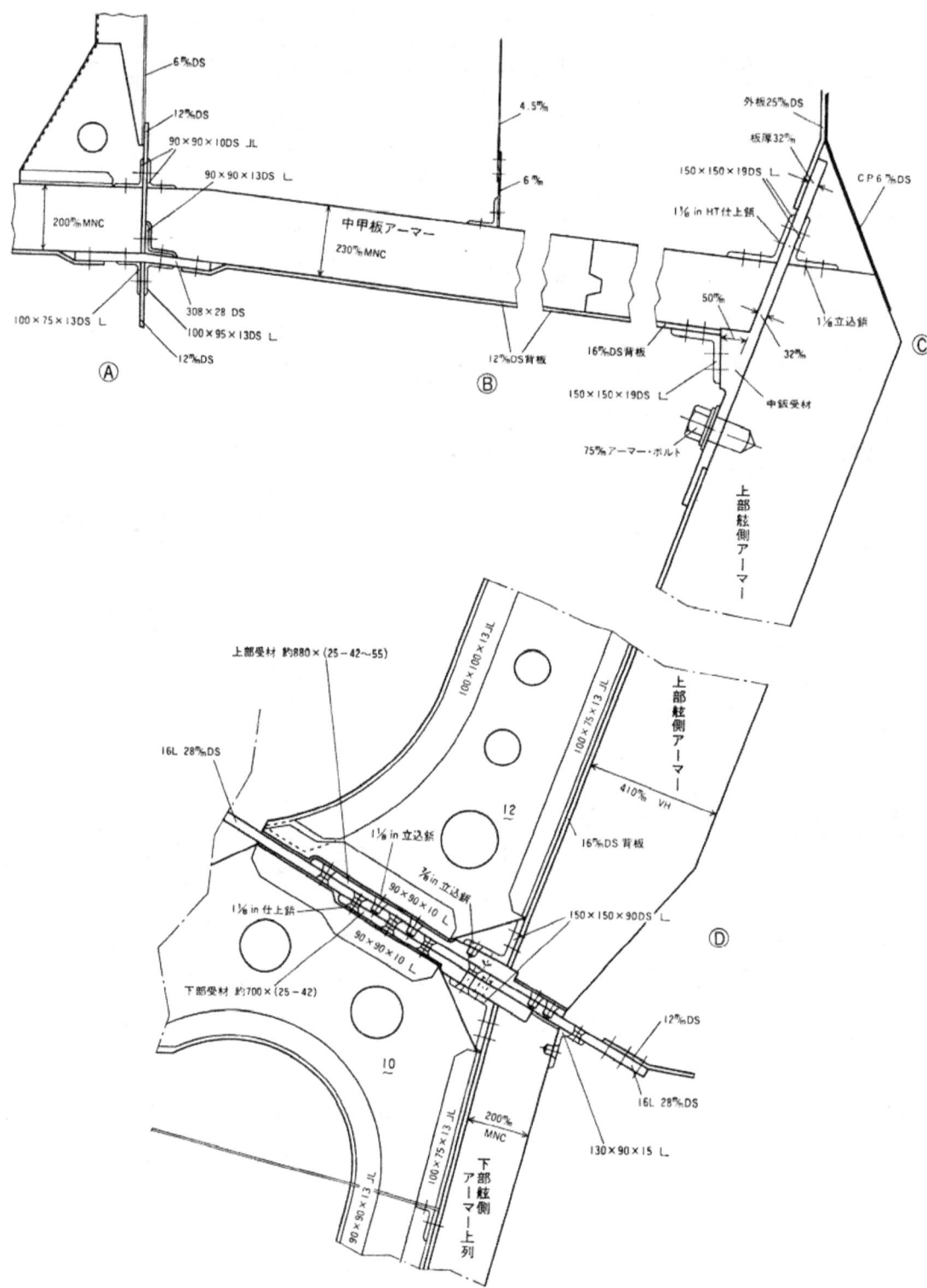

Figures 1-37–38: (top drawing) Joint of vertical (side) and horizontal (deck) armor and (bottom drawing) joint of 410-mm VH armor and 200-mm NVNC underwater protective bulkhead (*Senkan* Musashi *Kenzō Kiroku*)

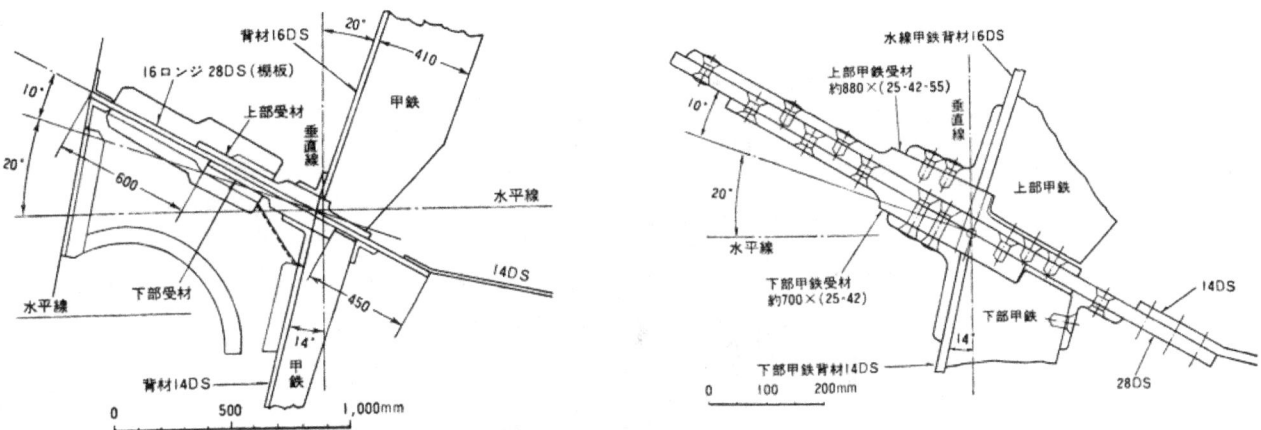

Figures 1-39–40: Joint of 410-mm VH armor and 200-mm NVNC underwater protective bulkhead (*Senkan* Musashi *Kenzō Kiroku*)

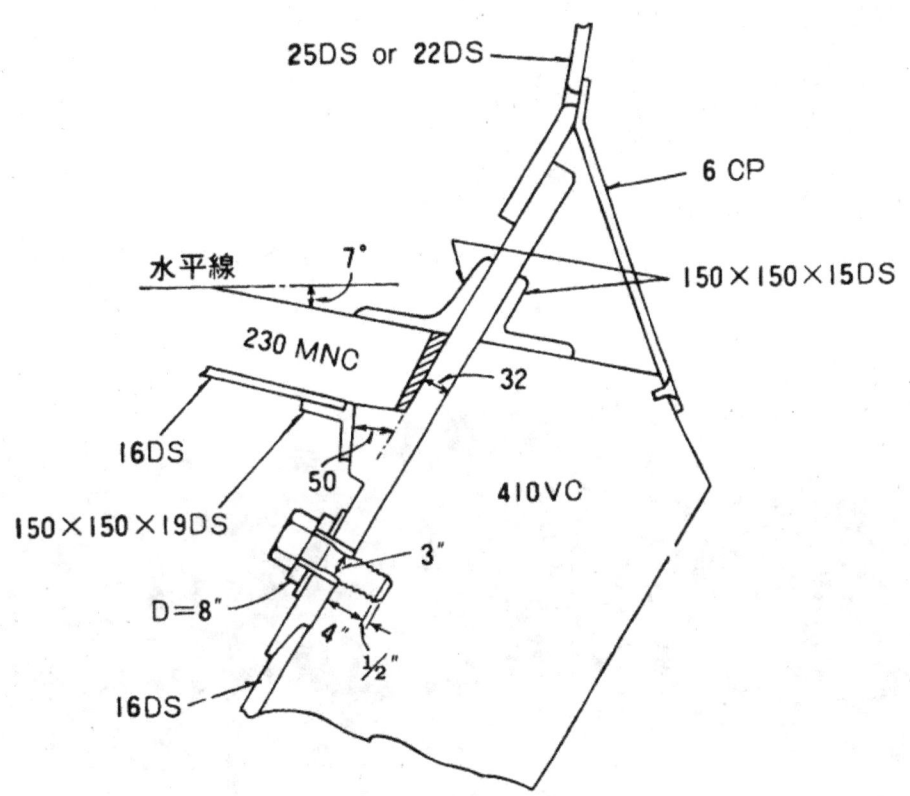

Figure 1-41: Joint of vertical (side) and horizontal (deck) armor (*Senkan* Musashi *Kenzō Kiroku*)

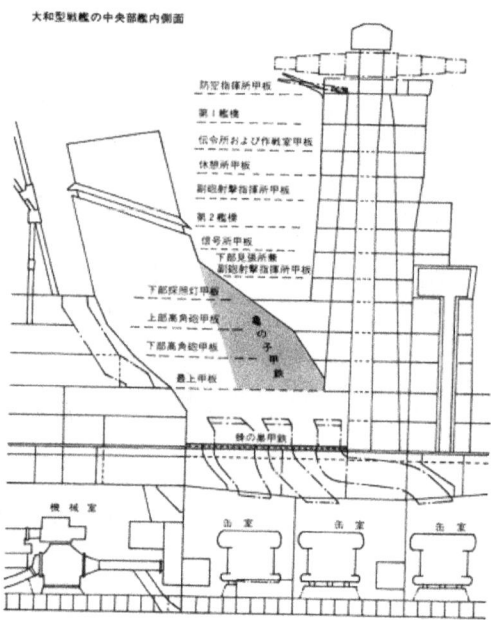

Figure 1-42: The dark area on this drawing is the 50-mm thick funnel uptake armor (*Sekai no Kansen*)

Photo 1-12: *Yamato* during trials off Sukumo on 30 October 1941 (Authors' collections)

Indirect Protection

The areas forward and aft of the citadel were indirectly protected by watertight compartments. However, because of the short length of the citadel, the length of these parts was about 51 m forward and 26 m aft. To these, the voluminous unprotected spaces below the magazine bottom armor must be added. The distances between the thin lateral bulkheads increased near the ends of the forward and after parts. In case of the detonation of one or more submarine or airplane torpedo hits these bulkheads would crack or even collapse,[63] and the same condition could also be expected for the bulkheads below the magazines. The gradual increase of the flooding, and consequently the list, in the cases of *Musashi*, *Shinano* and *Yamato* until their capsize prove these effects. The counterflooding even into the engine room of the opposite side as executed in *Yamato*'s case, i.e. into the citadel, showed only a temporary effect, and one has to agree with the statement in the aforementioned report that too much reliance was placed in counterflooding.

Damage Control and Stability

The number of watertight compartments was increased to a total of 1,147 compared with 1,086 in *Nagato* and 737 in *Yamashiro*. Among them 1,065 were below the protective deck compared with 865 and 574, respectively, in the other two ships taken as a comparison. Those located above that deck were only 82 compared with 224 and 163, respectively. The reason for the decrease is given by Matsumoto Kitarō (p. 189) as the comparative high position of this deck above the waterline, so that "the arrangement of more watertight compartments was considered technically unnecessary." He points out (p. 188) the remarkable comparative increase of the watertight compartments below the protective deck. But when the indirect protected volumes are considered it be-

---

[63] *Musashi* was hit by one torpedo fired from USS *Tunny* (SS-282) on the port side forward when she navigated off Palao (07°30'N/134°30'E) on 29 March 1944. The detonation caused a big hole with the length of about 12 m and a height of about 10 m from the waterline to the bottom. The centre was at the forward capstan room, and most compartments between F 12 and F 40 were flooded. The total amount of water was estimated to be 2,620 tons. Of course, flooding was unavoidable but the amount was very large and caused fears about the indirect protection by watertight subdivision outside the citadel. Weight considerations had prevented thicker bulkheads and also influenced narrowness.

comes evident, that the number should have been more than twice that of the *Yamashiro*, namely around 1,600.

According to Matsumoto (p. 192) and Fukuda (p. 32) the height of the freeboard was 10.0 m (7.90 m in *Nagato*) forward, 6.40 m (5.00 m) amidships and 6.60 m (4.85 m) aft, and the reserve buoyancy at trial condition was calculated as 57,450 tonnes or 80% of the trial displacement (29,292 tonnes; 67.6%). Stability and trim in case of damage were carefully considered and in riddled condition, i.e. all watertight compartments outside the vital spaces flooded, she could maintain stability until her list reached 20°. This range dropped to 18° because of the weight increase at completion.[64] As for the trim the calculations indicated that the freeboard forward would decrease to 4.5 m from 10.0 m; the aft one to 3.8 m from 6.4 m. But many conditions had to be considered and because of the uncertainty of several criteria the final conclusion seems to be doubtful.

The basis of the calculation was always one or two torpedo hits (each with 300 kg explosive and each causing a hole of about 30 m in length and 10 m in height) on one side, with the assumed amount of flooding water and assumed damage control measures.[65] The fundamental requirements for the emergency flooding and counterflooding system, as this damage control system was called by the IJN, were (1) the first hit is treated by the rapid counterflooding system to obtain the standard condition[66] within five minutes[67] after the order to operate the valves, and (2) the second hit on the same side is treated by the ordinary counterflooding system and the standard condition has to be obtained within 30 minutes. After correcting list and/or trim the loss of reserve buoyancy may not exceed 35% of the total buoyancy up to the upper deck.

The rapid flooding compartments amounted to 64 on one hull side for 2,173 tons of water and was sufficient to correct a list of 9.8°. Ordinary compartments were 39 on one side for 1,650 tons of water to adjust a list of 4°. The total number amounted to 103 for 3,823 tons to correct a list of 13.8°.

---

[64] The calculations were made with 65,200 tonnes. Therefore, the number of oil tanks within the vital spaces was reduced to increase the range of stability.

[65] See e.g. Matsumoto, p. 224.

[66] Determined as a list of about 4°, trim difference of 2.3 m between the bow and the stern. This condition was considered to have no influence upon the fighting properties.

[67] Discharging was to be within 30 minutes.

Furthermore, the shifting of oil to the opposite tanks could correct a list of 4.5°. Therefore, a list of up to 18.3° could be corrected.

The damage control system required extensive piping and a considerable amount of pumps (see also under "Machinery") to shift the heavy oil for heel or trim correction were necessary; e.g., 20 pumps of 100 tons/hour capacity were fitted in the forward and aft pump rooms, and each room was connected to one oil pipe of 230-mm diameter on both sides and distributor lines to each allotted tank. The valves, etc., were remote controlled and the control rooms placed inside the vital spaces. This system was also applied to the "water system" with the difference that the rapid flooding compartments were charged by the natural water head, while for the ordinary compartments ten bilge pumps of 100 tons/hour each were used. Remotely readable meters were equipped to the tanks and the valves were pneumatically operated.

This system was the best one among the Japanese battleships and despite of the previously stated uncertainty of several criteria in the calculations, the actual performance was greater than calculated as will be shown at the loss of the *Musashi*.

Photo 1-13: *Yamato* during trials off Sukumo on 30 October 1941 (Authors' collections)

Machinery [68]

Main Engines and Boilers and their Arrangement

The type of main engine changed from the sole use of diesel engines to the combined mounting of diesel engines and steam turbines, but finally propulsion by only turbines was decided on. The reasons were grave doubts on the reliability of the high-powered DA diesels but considerations as to the necessity of large amounts of steam for the hydraulic power system also played a role, albeit a subsidiary one.

As turbine ships, the *Yamato* class had 12 boilers in 12 boiler rooms and four turbine sets in four engine rooms, designed to generate 150,000 shp for 27 knots at 68,200 tonnes trial displacement (62,315 tons standard). This means that each boiler generated high-pressure high-temperature (HPHT) steam of 25kg/cm² and 325°C for 12,500 shp. At that time the use of HPHT steam of 30kg/cm² and 350°C for 20,000 shp was the rule in aircraft carriers, heavy cruisers and light cruisers. The performance of the boilers experimentally adopted for the destroyer *Shimakaze* (II) exceeded these values with 40kg/cm², 400°C and 25,000 shp per boiler.

The Kampon #2 Model T 1 turbine was the same type as those mounted on the destroyers of the *Hatsuharu* class, designed in 1931.[69] Each main unit consisted of two high-pressure turbines (HPT) and two low-pressure turbines (LPT) operating in parallel and connected to one shaft via the Kampon #1 A model 1 reduction gear.[70] One turbine set (i.e. one HPT and one LPT) developed 21,000 shp in the destroyers but in the *Yamato* class the output was re-

---

[68] For the material in this section, the authors have mainly relied upon chapter 4 of "The Construction of the 'Musashi': A Portrait of the Yamato-Class Battleships" by the Editorial Committee of the "Musashi" (the members of the committee are stated on p. 28 of the book). Hans Lengerer is very much indebted to the late Dr. Itani Jirō who dealt with this theme with the editorial committee member Naitō Hatsuho while the latter was hospitalised. Some tables and one drawing were taken from this book.

[69] The shape of the turbine blades was changed for at that time countermeasures against turbine blade vibrations were investigated (the so-called Turbine Blade Incident in some destroyers of the *Asashio* class) and studies about the "replacement" turbine were carried out.

[70] According to Mr. Takagi Hiroshi this type of "twin turbine" configuration was first introduced in the *Amagi* class battle cruisers (16,400 shp per turbine set and 32,800 shp per shaft) of the "Eight-Eight Fleet", and then applied in the treaty cruisers of the *Myōkō* and *Takao* classes (16,250 shp per turbine set and 32,500 shp per shaft).

duced to 18,750 shp per set (-10.7%)[71] and 37,500 shp per shaft.[72] This type of turbine was popular, but the use of the conventional type turbine as main engine and the reduction of the performance were also criticised by users, and some tacticians complained seriously about the slow speed. The reason was the extremely cautious construction of this class in order to avoid failures and to maintain mobility even in case of damage, by limiting the influence upon the propulsion system.

The latter consideration was mainly expressed in the distribution of one boiler in each boiler room and one main engine unit in each engine room, and the arrangement side by side athwartships of four boiler rooms each in three rows in the forward and aft direction, with the engine rooms behind. This arrangement permitted the connection of one main engine unit to the three boilers forward of it into one system,[73] i.e. each group of three boilers supplied the main engine unit immediately aft of it. The outer groups supplied the outboard shafts and the inner the inboard shafts. Cross-connecting lines were provided in the forward end of the machinery spaces but aft of the bulkhead stops. This arrangement afforded the maximum amount of protection for the two inboard shafts, their engine rooms and the three boilers supplying each of them.

Also, the length of the machinery spaces became relatively short and this was advantageous for limiting the length of the vital spaces to save armor weight.

A cross-connection between main steam lines was provided just aft of the boiler room bulkhead, while a cross-connection to the auxiliary steam line was arranged in each engine room. The cross-connection valves were operable from both sides of the fore and aft bulkhead. Space does not permit to mention auxiliary steam lines, auxiliary exhaust lines, boiler feed system, etc. but it

---

[71] According to the "Specifications of Engines for Ship #1" (Navy Technical Department, 1937) "the main engine must be able to bear an overload of 10%," but this overload was the common power of these turbines.

[72] In the IJN, when turbines designed for the supporting (non-capital) ships, including aircraft carriers, were applied to capital ships (i.e. battleships and battle cruisers), it was necessary to "de-rate" for the sake of long-term reliability. For example, in the *Kongō* class during their 2nd rebuilding, four turbine sets for the *Mogami* class cruisers were adopted with 10% de-rating from 38,000 shp to 34,000 shp per set. [Takagi Hiroshi]

[73] The "Specifications ..." stipulated "... it is planned to make four independent battle compartments by arranging three boilers to one shaft."

may be pointed out that the members of the US Naval Technical Mission to Japan who investigated surface warship machinery design (Report S-01-2) found the arrangement in the *Yamato* class "particularly good as concerns protection," but they at the same time criticised it because "this protection was obtained at the expense of a listing movement created in case the outboard firerooms on one side became flooded as the result of the rupture of the torpedo defense system."

The arrangement of boilers and turbines is outlined in the figure 1-43. The two LPTs with the astern turbines housed in their casings were placed forward, the two HPTs aft of the main reduction gear and the Kampon #2 A model 1 cruising turbine was connected to the inboard HPT through a Kampon #1 A model 1 reduction gear and claw clutch (see figure 1-44). The exhaust was led to first stage of the same HPT. The cruising turbines were used at up to 21 knots and then de-clutched. One HPT and one LPT were used at up to about 25 knots. At this speed the other HPT and LPT were brought into operation. Cooling steam was not admitted to the idling turbines below this speed. Provision for use of auxiliary exhaust steam in the LPT was made.

Table 1-17: Principal turbine particulars

Item / Turbine	HPT	LPT	AST	CRT
Total power (shp)		150,000	44,000	30,000/42,000
One main set (shp)		37,500	11,000	7,500/10,500
Propeller rpm		225	150	138/146
Main rotor rpm	3,298	2,135	1,423	7,560/?
Stages (bucket wheels with rows of blades)	1 with 2 rows 4 with 1 row	5 with 1 row	1 with 3 rows	1 with 2 rows 2 with 1 row
Pitch circumference diameter (mm)	900–1,000	1,740–1,640	1,350	500–460
Shaft bearing interval (mm)	1,570		2,780	760
Steam consumption (kg/shp/h)		4.1		4.5
Designed weight (tons)	12.0		36.0	3.0

Source: *Senkan* Musashi *Kenzō Kiroku* ("Construction of the *Musashi*"), p. 92.
Note: The specified power of the cruising turbine and the specified rpm of the main shaft were (1) cruising power: 22,000 shp, 116rpm; (2) total in excess of cruising power: 30,000 shp, 130 rpm; (3) maximum permitted cruising power: 42,000 shp, 146 rpm.

Table 1-18: Principal particulars of the reduction gears

Gear	Main reduction gear			Cruising reduction gear	
	Main wheel	HP pinion	LP pinion	Main wheel	Pinion
Pitch circumference diameter (mm)	3,723.92	254.04	392.60	513.27	137.40
No. of teeth	645	44	68	127	34
Bearing length (mm)		2 × 525			2 × 290
Helical angle (°)		30° 0' 0.6"			30° 0' 2.2"
Gear type		M5			M3.5
Designed weight (tons)		92.0			3.5

Source: *Senkan* Musashi *Kenzō Kiroku* ("Construction of the *Musashi*"), p. 92.

The single-pass type condensers were mounted under each LPT and the following auxiliary machines fitted: eight main condensate pumps (axial flow type connected to turbine speed reduction gear), 16 main water feed pumps (centrifugal type connected to turbine speed reduction gear) and eight air ejectors (two-step, triplex steam ejector type).

The 12 *Ro Gō* Kampon type heavy oil-burning boilers were fitted with superheaters and air preheaters. Their main specified characteristics were: 27 kg/cm² pressure in the steam drum, 25kg/cm² pressure on the superheater outlet, 325°C steam temperature on superheater outlet (at combustion rate 4.44 kg/m²), specified rate of combustion 5.6 kg/m² (but capable of being used safely up to 8.0 kg/m²), heating surface area (one boiler) 1,060 m² including superheater,[74] area of air preheater pipes 432 m², volume of the combustion room 35 m³. The nine burners were of Kampon Type 15 Model 5 (capacity 800 kg/hour) and seven of the atomisers belonged to Kampon Type 16

---

[74] Area of evaporator tubes was 895 m² and that of the superheater tubes 165 m².

Model 3; other two to the same type but of Model 5. The weight per boiler was 77 tons so that steam for 162 shp was generated per ton of weight.[75]

Matsumoto explains the progress in engineering by pointing out the developed shp per m² of the machinery spaces in comparison with other capital ships. The following data, excerpted from Fukuda's "Outline of the Fundamental Design of Warships" p. 147, evidence that the length of the machinery spaces was really short (this was also the result of the extreme beam) but the already stated "caution" prevented the adoption of a powerful plant and, e.g., the battleship *Kongō*'s plant developed more shp/m² than the ships of the *Yamato* class.

Table 1-19: Principal conditions of boilers

Item / Condition	Official	Battle	Designed
Steam temperature (superheater outlet) (°C)	325	335	340
Steam consumption per boiler (kg/h)	59,420	64,160	74,000
Water temperature (preheater) (°C)	90	90	90
Boiler efficiency (estimated) (%)	80.5	80	79
Fuel consumption per boiler (kg/h)	4,600	5,060	5,930
Fuel consumption per boiler (kg/cm²/h)	4.34	4.77	5.60

Source: *Senkan* Musashi *Kenzō Kiroku* ('Construction of the *Musashi*'), p. 93.

---

[75] The boiler was much criticised by the investigation team of the US Naval Technical Mission to Japan in their Report S-01-12 "Characteristics of Japanese Naval Vessels Article 12–Boilers and Machinery" pp. 17–20. When this type is compared with the same Kampon *Ro Gō* type installed in the aircraft carrier *Shōkaku*, completed earlier than *Yamato*, the reason becomes evident. One boiler of *Shōkaku* generated steam for 20,000 shp (instead of 12,500), its weight was 67.5 tons (instead of 77) and the shp per ton of weight was 296 (instead of 162). This was the price paid for "caution" by mounting a boiler that had proven its reliability in the destroyers of the *Hatsuharu* class, but was far from including the progress in engineering the Fifth Division of the *Kaigun Kansei Honbu* had made in the past six to seven years. By the way, the efficiency of the burners is also dealt with in this report. The authors cannot but highly recommend the reading of this report for readers interested in this subject for feed water is also treated etc.

Table 1-20: Comparison of engines and boilers between *Yamato* and *Kongō* classes

	Yamato class		**Kongō after second refitting**	
	Engine rooms	Boiler rooms	Engine rooms	Boiler rooms
L × B × H × number (m)	22.8 × 6.85 × ? × 2 = 842 m² 22.9 × 7.2 × ? × 2 = 763 m²	9.5 × 7.1 × ? × 6 9.5 × 7.2 × ? × 6 = 814.5 m²	29.87 × 20.12 × 10.21 = 594.6 m²	39.014 × 16.052 × 8.077 = 624.22 m²
Shp per m²	197	185	228.7	217.9
Shp per total m²		95.1		112

Note: L = Length; B = Beam; H = Height.

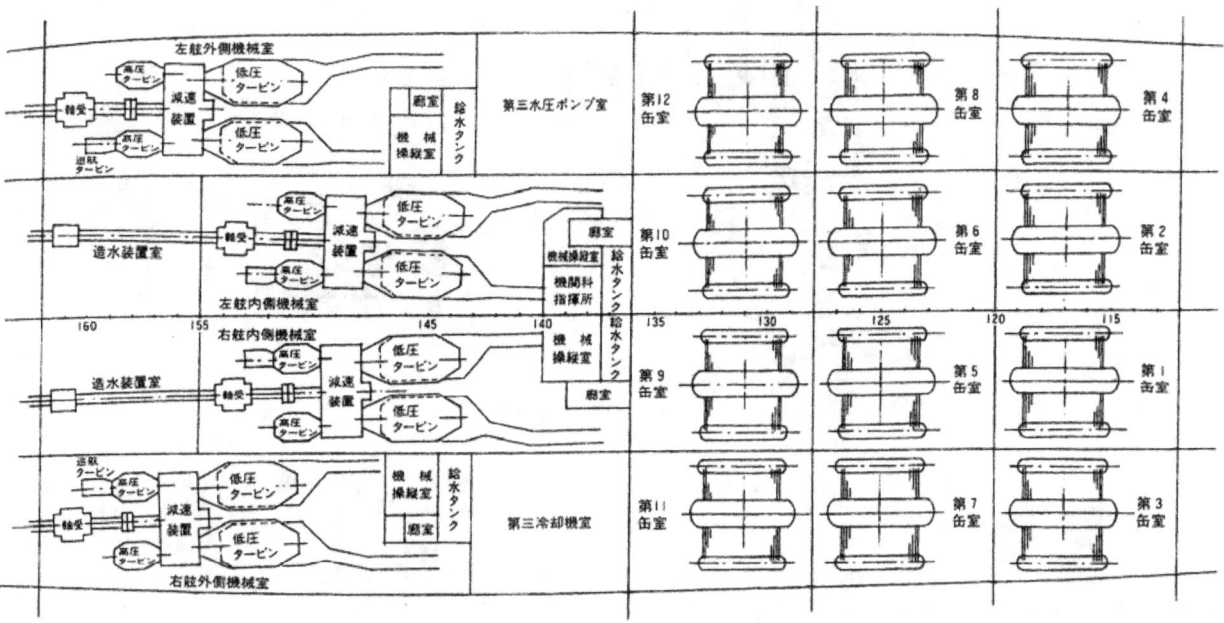

Figure 1-43: Turbines and boilers arrangement (*Senkan* Musashi *Kenzō Kiroku*)

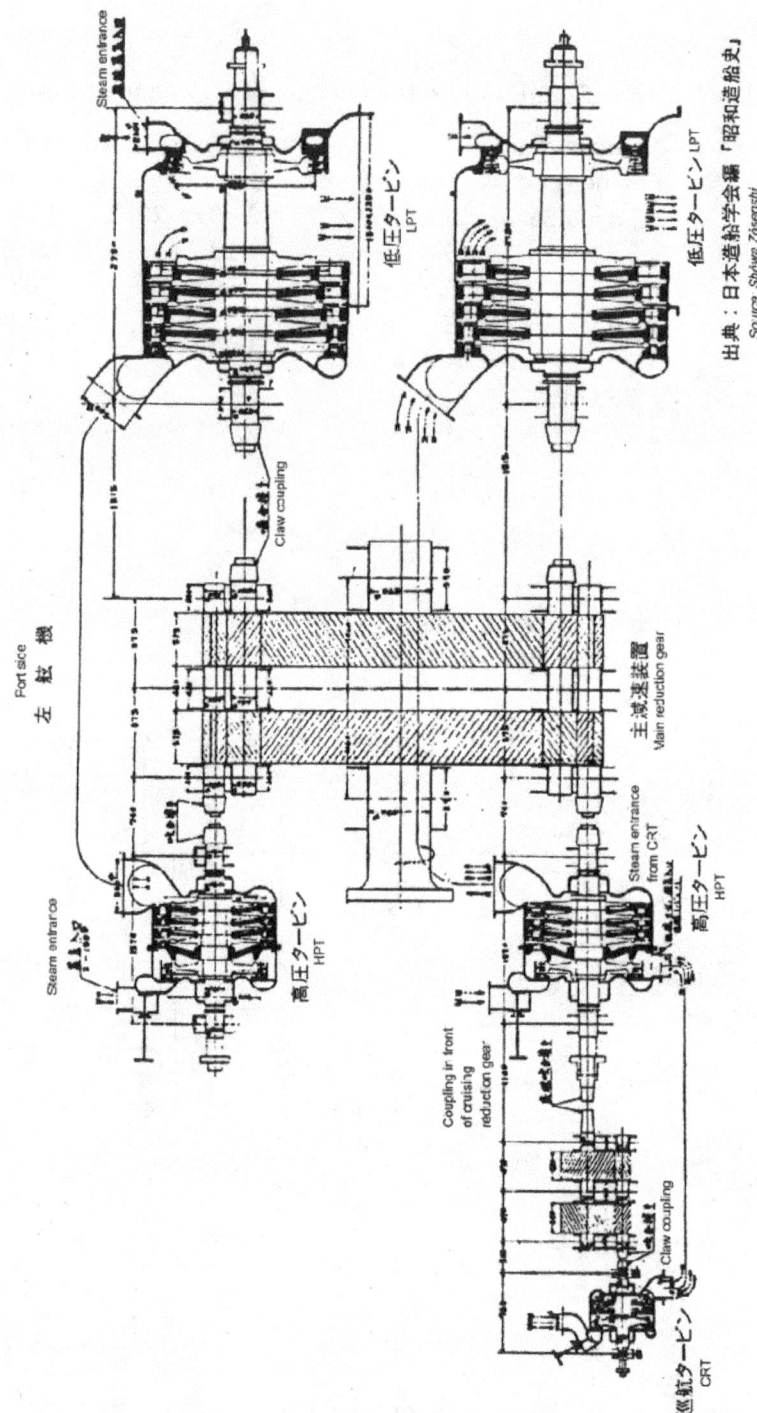

Figure 1-44: *Yamato* class port side turbine set. The arrows indicate steam conditions (*Shōwa Zōsen-shi*)

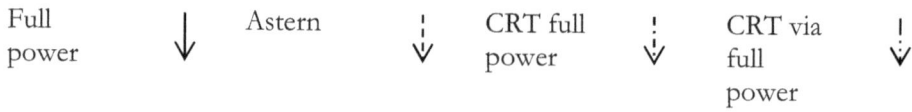

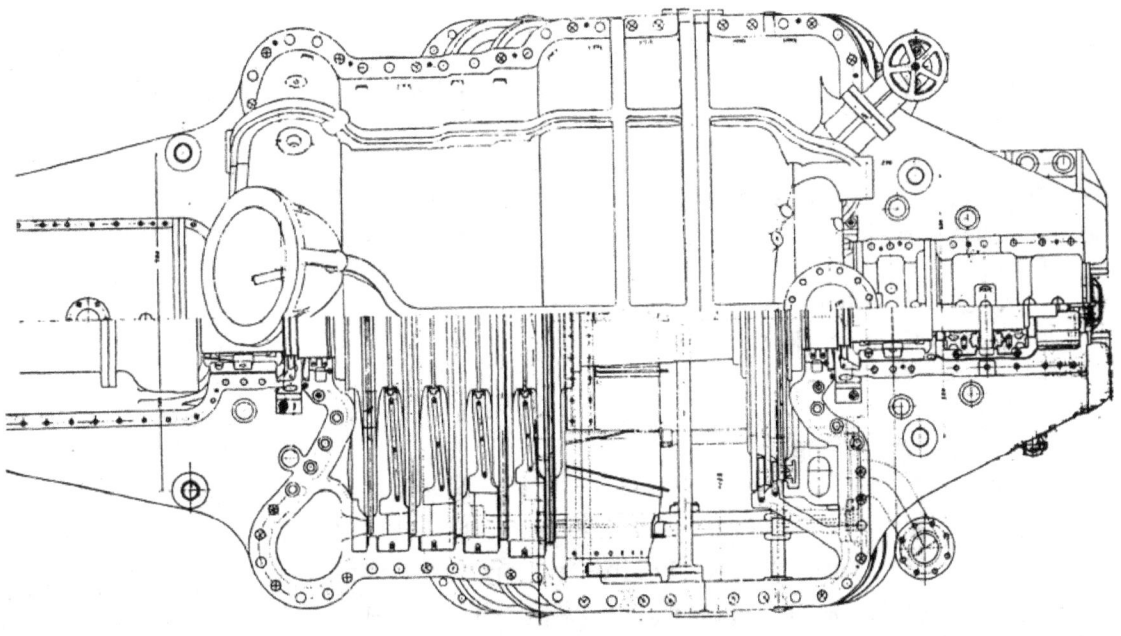

Figure 1-45: Nagasaki-built LPT (*Senkan* Musashi *Kenzō Kiroku*)

Photo 1-14: *Yamato* during trials off Sukumo on 26 October 1941. She is making economical speed of 15.91 knots with 17,432 shp (Authors' collections)

Machinery Weight and Trial Results

Table 1-21: Weight of the machinery

Item / Condition	First Design	Modified Design	Actual Weight
Main engines (tonnes)	1,028	1,085	1,085/1,085
Shafting and propellers	589	589	589/615
Auxiliary machines	480	480	480/654
Boilers	918	918	925/925
Uptakes and funnel	320	300	300/300
Pipes, valves and cocks	640	640	600/600
Miscellaneous	388	388	350/358
Water	450	450	450/546
Hydraulic pumps (engines)	230	230	230/----
Total	5,043	5,080	5,035/5,083

Source: *Senkan* Musashi *Kenzō Kiroku* ('Construction of the *Musashi*'), p. 91.
Notes: In the column "actual weight" the first values are for *Musashi*, the second ones for *Yamato*. In *Yamato*'s case the weight of the hydraulic pumps is included in auxiliary machines and the amount of water also includes oil. The weight excluding water and oil was 4,537 tonnes in her case.

Table 1-22: Trial results of the battleship *Yamato* (October 1941 at 69,100 tonnes displacement)

Item /Condition	Full overload power	Official trial power	Cruising maximum speed	Cruising full speed	Standard speed	Full astern speed
Speed (knots)	27.68	27.30	21.54	19.23	15.91	17.2
Power (shp)	166,120	151,707	44,790	30,739	17,432	44,370
Propeller rpm	228.6	223.2	156.7	138.8	115.4	155.3
Steam consumption (t/h)	62.7	57.2	20.5	14.0	7.71	42.0
Fuel consumption (kg/shp/h)	0.378	0.377	?	0.455	0.449	?
Steam pressure on turbine chamber (kg/cm^2)	18.95	1936	19.68 (CRT) 14.95 (HPT)	19.83	16.05	15.33
Steam temperature (°C)	323	319	229 (CRT) 260 (HPT)	298	257	277
Condenser vacuum (mm)	709	712	726	735	738	718

Note: The IJN began with the design of the so-called cruising overload power (*junkō kyoyō zenryoku*) in 1931 and adopted the following standard for battleships: 14 knots standard speed, 16 knots cruising full speed, and 20 knots cruising overload speed. The standard speed was increased to 16 knots for all ships of the Third Fleet Replenishment Programme and the cruising overload speed was set at 21.3 knots for the *Yamato* class. In company with these changes the term changed to cruising maximum speed (*junkō saidai sokuryoku*) because of the high rpm of the turbines. In this condition the main engine got steam and CRT and one part of the main engines worked in combination.

Table 1-23: Trial results of the battleship *Musashi*

Item / Condition	Full overload power	Official trial power	Maximum cruising power	Cruising full power	Standard speed	Official trial power (end)
Displacement (tonnes)	70,358	70,433	70,302	70,328	70,342	70,638
Speed (knots)	28.05	27.61	21.69	19.36	16.16	27.62
Power (shp)	167,310	154,470	44,560	30,341	17,527	153,930
Propeller rpm	230.0	224.9	156.4	139.1	115.9	224.3
Fuel consumption (kg/shp/h)	0.354	0.359	0.399	0.432	0.455	0.395
Fuel consumption (kg/cm²) heating surface/h	4.66	4.36	2.80	3.09	1.85	4.29
Cruising per tonnes fuel (nm)	0.473	0.498	1.22	1.48	2.03	0.506
Cruising distance (nm)	2,366	2,493	6,095	7,392	10,141	2,530

Note: Cruising trials were carried out on 25 June, full overload and official full power on 22 June and official full power (end) on 24 June 1942, all at Sada-misaki pylon.

These speeds only became possible by the remarkable reduction of propulsion resistance of the hull form as shallow draught and very fat was extremely disadvantageous for resistance. More than 50 models were studied in the model basin of the Navy Technical Research Institute to cope with the problem and the huge bulb stretching 3 m forward was finally adopted and, in company with the improved fitting method of bilge keels and shaft struts, was successful to reduce resistance with 8.2% at full speed, and obtain a propulsion efficiency of 50% at full power and 58.7% at standard speed, which were rare cases among IJN warships.

Photo 1-15: *Yamato* during trials off Sukumo on 20 October 1941 (Authors' collections)

Photo 1-16: *Musashi*'s forecastle when the ship undertook final tests in June–July 1942 in the Western Inland Sea (Kure Maritime Museum)

Funnel

The uptakes (smoke passages) penetrated the lower, the middle, the upper, and the uppermost decks from each boiler. They were fitted with a drain elimination system and assembled into one funnel whose top was 29.6 m above the waterline. The sectional area of the uptakes was calculated 0.38 m² per 1,000 kg/hour fuel; 2.25 m² per boiler and 27 m² per 12 boilers.

It is interesting to note the stipulation in the "Engine Specifications" that the single funnel "must be constructed so as to have sufficient strength to resist bomb attacks and the effects of bomb blast."

The number of valves (and weight) was as follows: Boiler rooms 2,616 (72,268 kg), engine rooms 2,568 (116,157 kg) and others 820 (25,176 kg) making a total of 6,000 (213,619 kg).

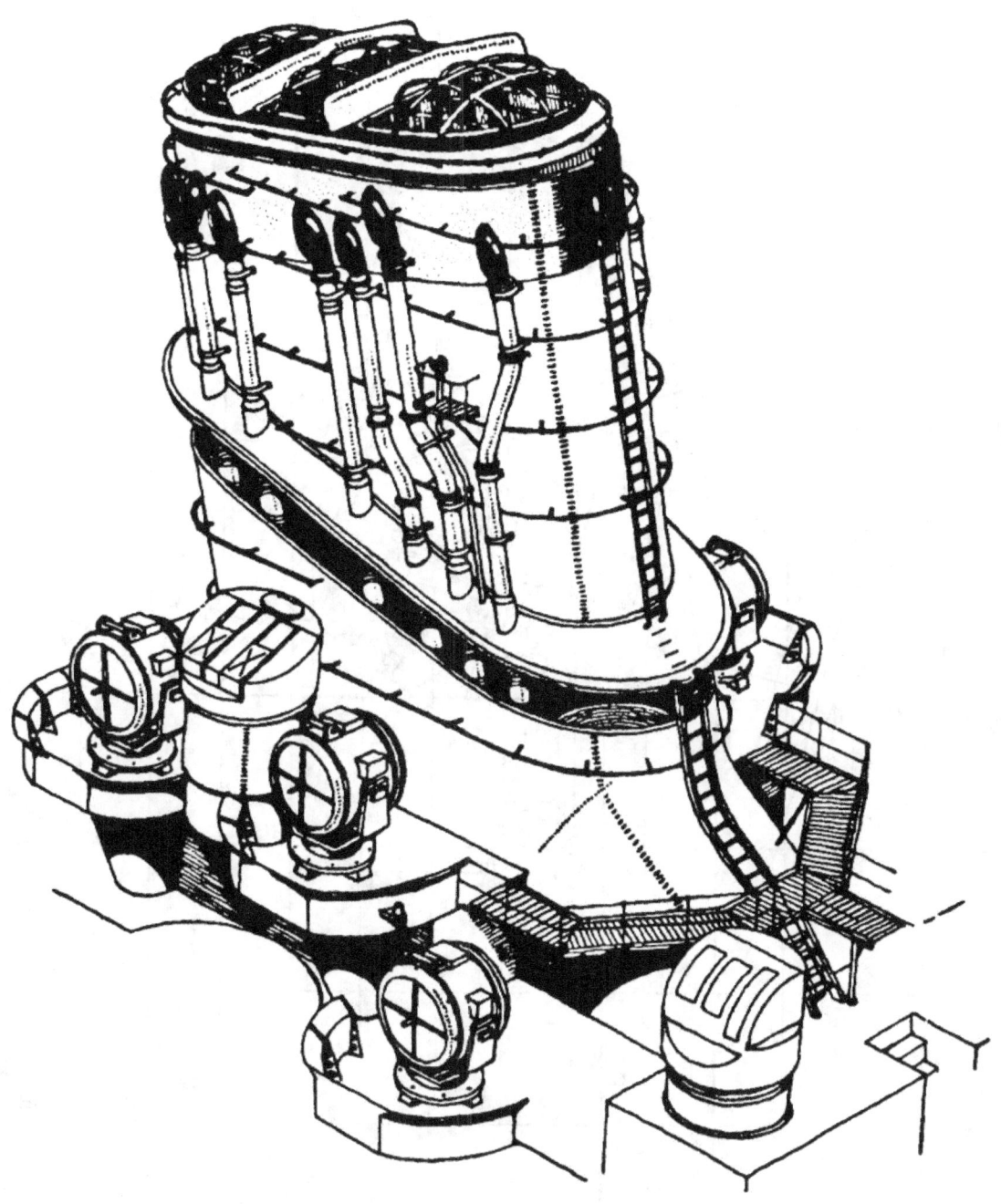

Figure 1-46: Oblique bird's eye perspective of *Yamato*'s funnel and environment. Visible are the funnel grating (for canvas cover), the rain cover plates with gutter, various steam pipes, the ladder, the lower rain cover cap, 50-mm armor plate casing below the lower forward part, 25-mm machine-gun fire control system, 150-cm searchlights and the lower passageway (*Nihon no Senkan*)

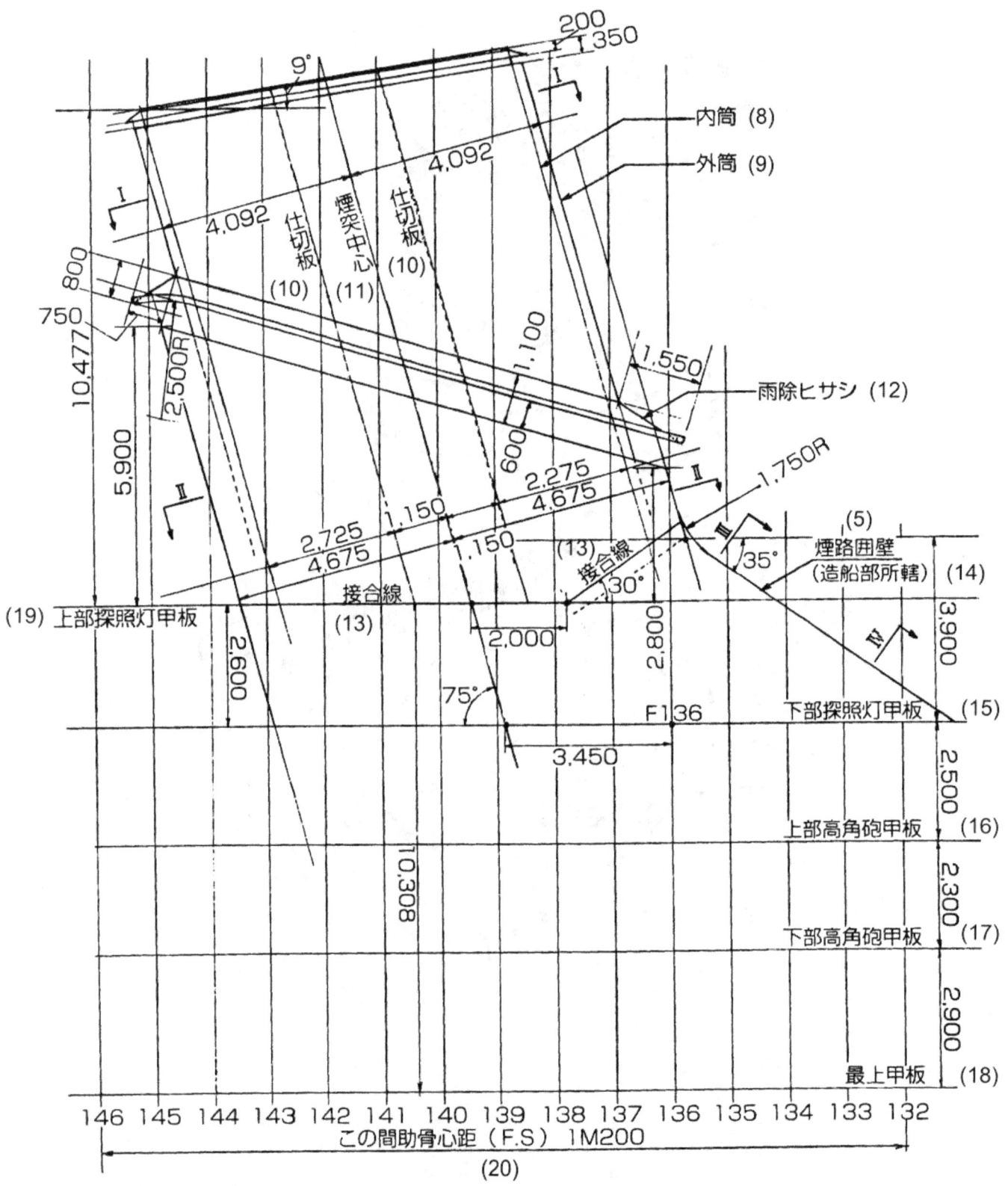

Figure 1-47: Drawings of *Yamato*'s funnel has often been published. Provided here are simplified views of *Musashi*'s funnel based on working drawings (in scales 1:50, 1:25, 1:20, 1:10 and 1:5). The drawings presented here are "not to scale."

Key to Figure 1-47:

Main part of *Musashi*'s funnel showing its basic form with dimensions. The dimensions are the original ones in mm and were duplicated from the structure plan of the working drawings. The connection line (*setsugō-sen*) is the borderline between the lower end of the funnel and the upper end of the uptakes between the funnel and the uppermost (superstructure) deck [*Nihon no Senkan*]

- (1) Plate thickness (mm) of outer tube
- (2) Plate thickness (mm) of inner tube
- (3) (Outside dimension)
- (4) (Plate thickness included)
- (5) Casing
- (6) Outer tube
- (7) Inner tube
- (8) See (7)
- (9) See (6)
- (10) Separation plate
- (11) Centreline of funnel
- (12) Rain cover canopy
- (13) Connection line
- (14) (Belongs to the shipbuilding division)
- (15) Lower searchlight deck
- (16) Upper high-angle gun deck
- (17) Lower high-angle gun deck
- (18) Uppermost deck
- (19) Lower lookout deck
- (20) Frame space 1.20 m

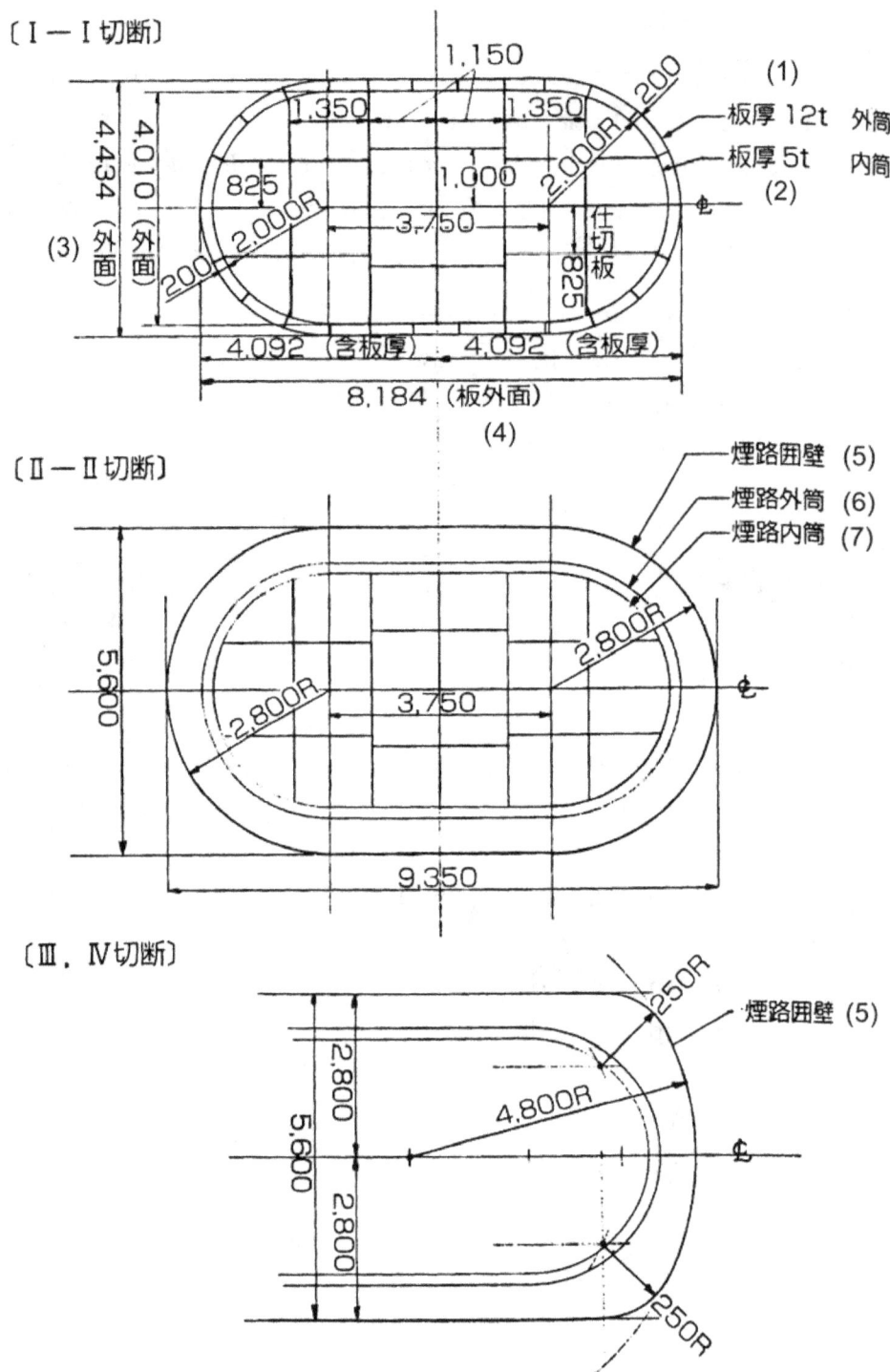

Figures 1-48–50: The dimensions are the original (real) ones expressed in mm. Plan views of the positions are shown in the side section (figure 1-47) as (I–I), (II–II), (III, IV). The casing outer tube, inner tube and the separation plates inside the funnel are drawn. For numbered items see figure 1-51–53 (*Nihon no Senkan*)

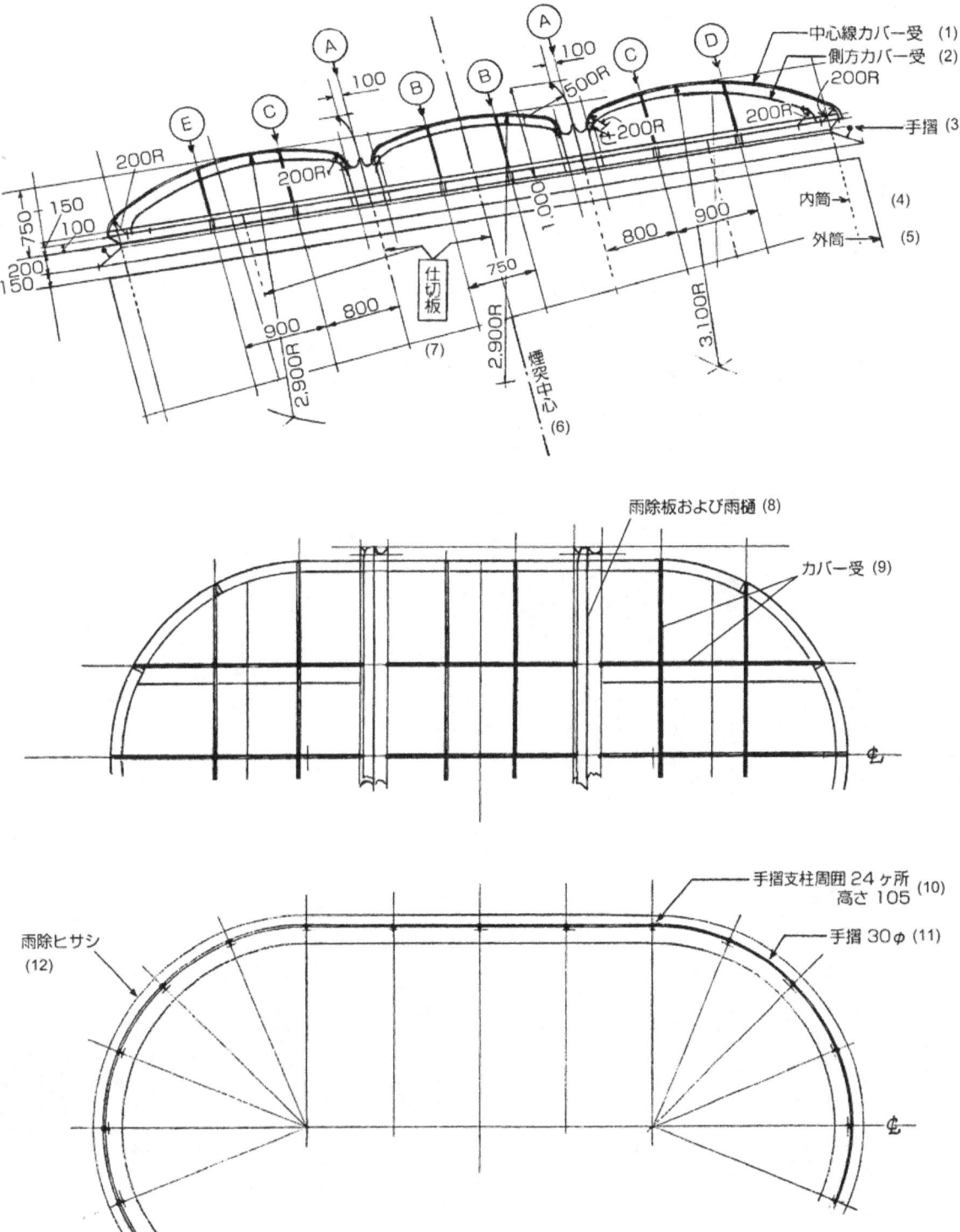

Figures 1-51–53: Detailed drawings of *Musashi*'s funnel top. One side view (grating for central and side covers, rain cover cap with stanchions for jackstay) and two plan views (rain cover plate with gutter and rain cover with stanchions for jackstay) are shown. For mounting the jackstay (handrail) 24 stanchions were fixed near the circumference of the rain cover cap. Letters A to E in the side view mark the views shown in the next drawings (figures 1-54–59) (*Nihon no Senkan*)

Key to Figures 1-51-53:

(1) Rain cover cap frame (centre)
(2) Rain cover cap frame (side)
(3) Jackstay
(4) Inner tube
(5) Outer tube
(6) Centre of funnel
(7) Separation plate (inside the rectangle)
(8) Rain cover plate with gutter
(9) Rain cover cap frame (transverse)
(10) 24 jackstay stanchions of 1.05 m length each
(11) Jackstay of 30 cm diameter
(12) Rain cover

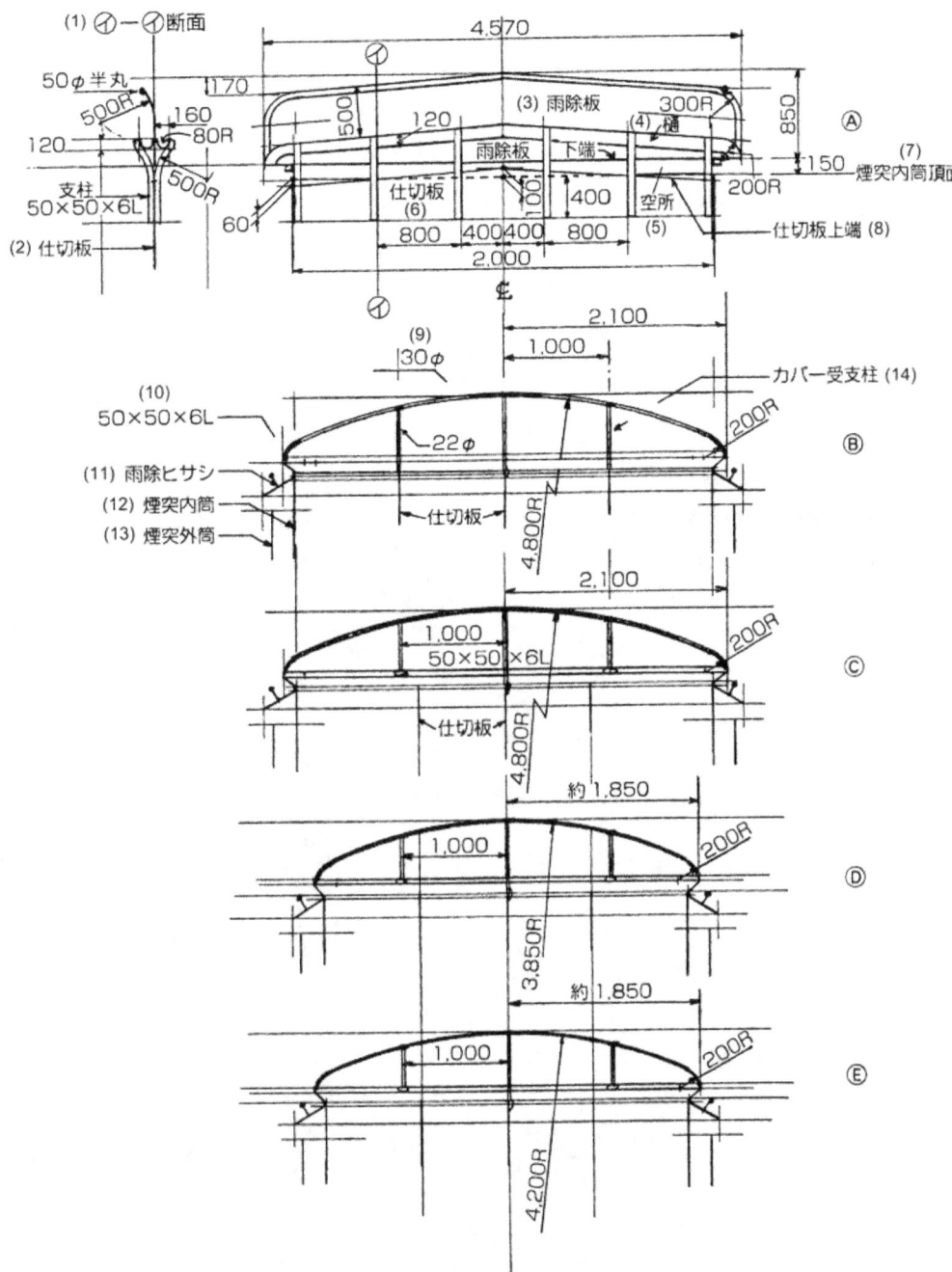

Figures 1-54–59: Detailed drawings of the grating and the rain cover plates with gutter for the funnel top cap. Five sections of the funnel top are shown. At sections B to E the (upper) rain cover cap is drawn. This cap served as cover to prevent the immersion of rain between the funnel's outer and inner tubes. The space between these two tubes was used for the flow of heated air, which came out at the distance between the upper end of the outer tube and the underside of the (upper) rain cover cap. On the upper side of the cap the jackstay (visible are the stanchions; the black circle at the upper end indicates the jackstay made of pipes with a diameter of 30 mm) for the fitting of the rain cap (*Nihon no Senkan*)

Key to Figures 1-54 – 1-59:

(1) (I)–(I) section
(2) Separation plate of inner tube
(3) Rain cover plate
(4) Gutter (channel)
(5) Opening
(6) See (2)
(7) Top of funnel inner tube
(8) Top of separation plate of inner tube
(9) Round bar of 30 mm diameter
(10) L-shaped angle bar with a flange size 50 × 50 mm and 6 mm thick
(11) Upper rain cover canopy
(12) Funnel inner tube
(13) Funnel outer tube
(14) Rain cover cap support rods

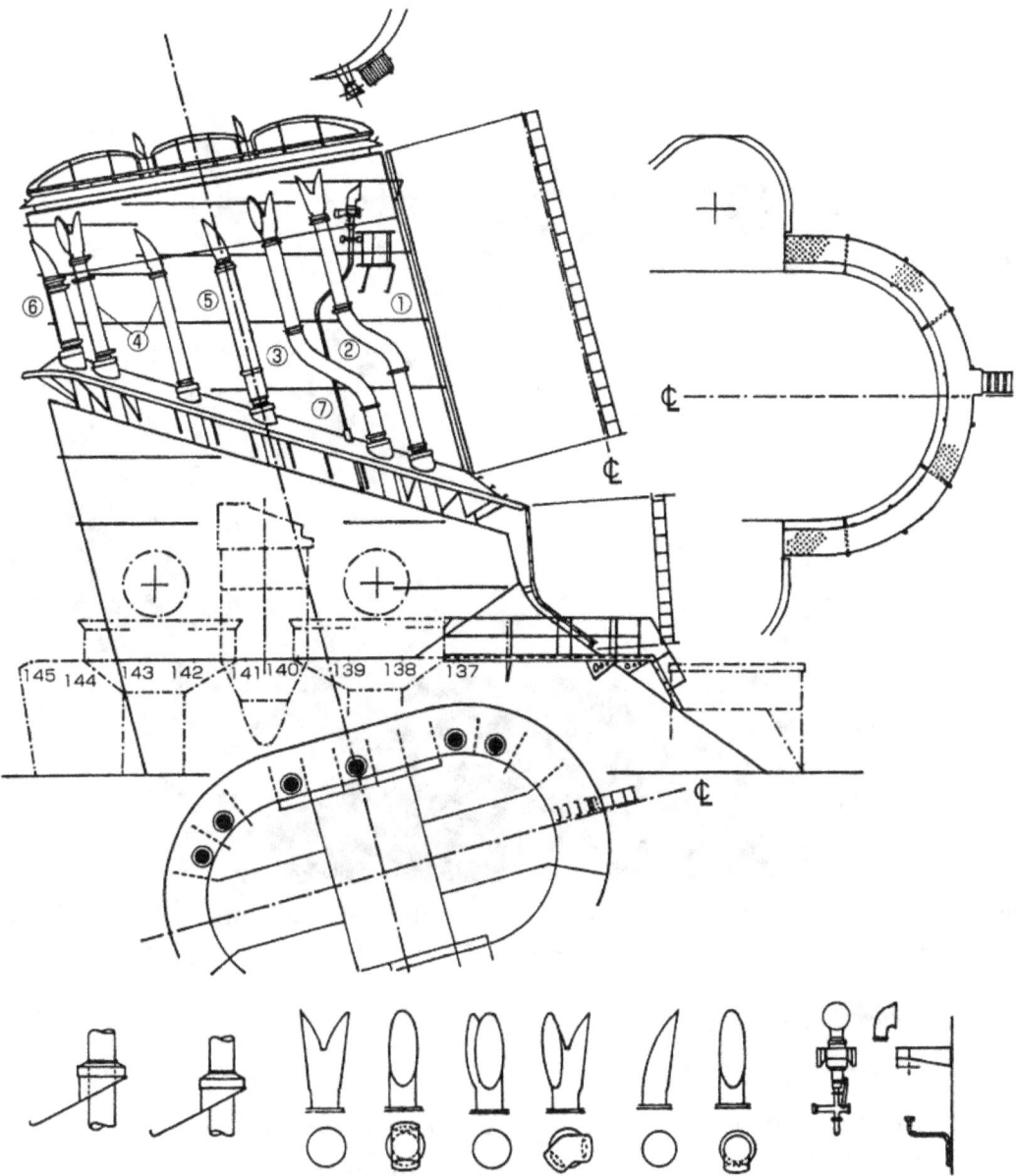

Figures 1-60–62: Starboard side view (figure 1-60) of *Musashi*'s funnel as completed shows various steam pipes, ladder, lower passageway and passage of the pipes through the lower rain cover. The pipes are: (1) Siren and grating platform, (2) to (4) steam exhaust pipes, (5) and (6) exhaust pipes for generators, (7) steam pipe for siren. On the right side of the side view the ladder and the lower passageway are drawn. The ladder was fixed to the front side of the funnel with its right side along the centerline, as shown in the drawings. Above the funnel top drawing the siren and the grating platform are drawn separately. To illustrate the passages of the steam pipes etc. a plan of the lower rain cover cap is placed below the side view (figure 1-61). Further below are front views of the upper portions of the steam pipes (figure 1-62). The siren and the grating platform are to the right. The pipes with two openings were for steam exhaust. On the left vents near the top of the pipes are drawn. The lower rain cover cap was supported by 26 brackets, as shown in the side view and as dotted lines in the plan view (*Nihon no Senkan*)

Photo 1-17: A view looking aft over the funnel and through the main mast of the *Musashi* in June–July 1942 (Kure Maritime Museum)

Shafts, Rudders, Steering Gear and some Noteworthy Auxiliaries

The shafts consisted of thrust shaft, intermediate shafts, stern tube shaft (585 mm outer diameter/340, 440 mm inner diameter) and propeller shafts (630–628 mm/200–420–470 mm). The outboard shafts had three intermediate shafts (585 mm/440 mm) and the inner shafts had five (same diameters) each. Aside from the thrust bearing, all bearings were self-lubricating. Shaft bearing pressures were 1.5 kg/cm² on the intermediate shafts, 1.05–1.06 kg/cm² on the tube shaft ring and 1.39 kg/cm² on the projected ring bearing. The thrust bearings were of Mitchel type and the specifications stipulated that the thrust should not exceed 20 kg/cm² on the white alloy pad.

The four propellers were made of manganese bronze with a diameter of 5.00 m and a pitch of 4.80 m.

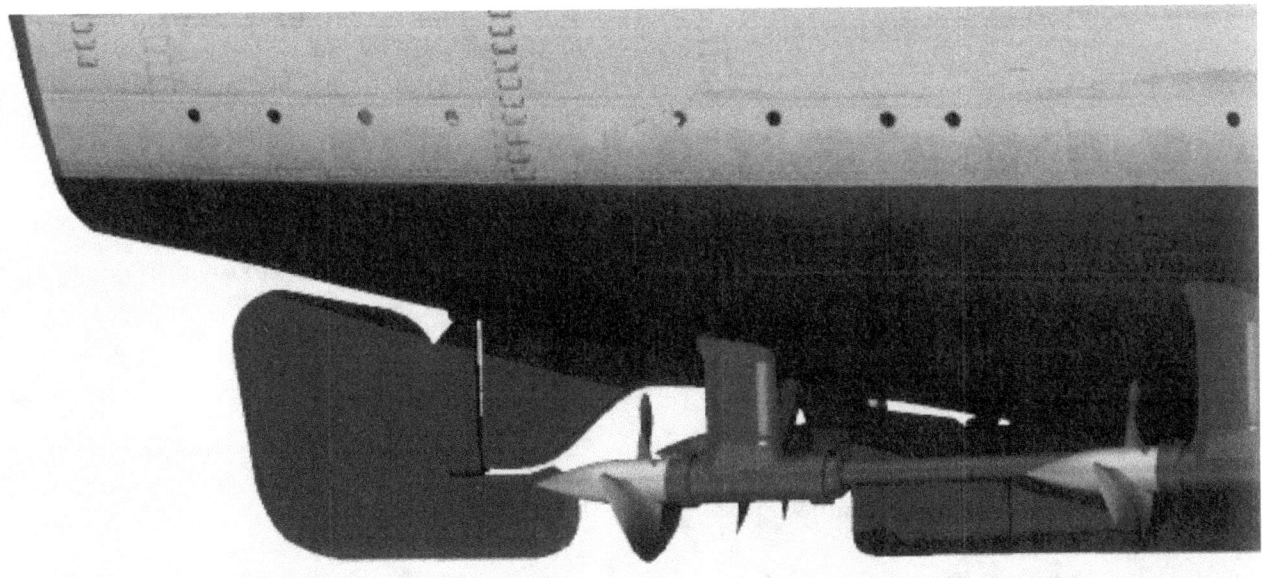

Figure 1-63: Rudder and propeller arrangement (*Sekai no Kansen*)

Two rudders were fitted: the main and the auxiliary rudder, located in front of the former. The steering gears were of the electrically operated, hydraulic plunger type. The main steering gear was equipped with a reserve diesel engine electric generator to be prepared for the destruction of the electric line. The secondary steering gear was fitted with a manually operated hydraulic pump enabling to switch to the main room.

Table 1-24: Principal particulars of the rudder

Item / Gear	Main steering gear	Auxiliary steering gear
Type	Model D (Lapson slide)	Type A (jointed bars)
Forward full speed maximum torque moment (t-m)	358.1	123.2
Astern full speed maximum torque moment (t-m)	235.8	69.3
Complete turn from full starboard to full port	70° in 30s	70° in 30s
Distance between centre of plungers (mm)	1,000	-------
Diameter of plungers (mm)	450	375
Radius of steering handle (mm)	-------	750
Stroke—maximum common rudder angle 70° (mm)	1,400.4	860.4
—maximum stop rudder angle 74°	1,507.2	902.7

Motor		
Type	All closed, self-ventilation Model *Otsu* (B)	All closed, self-ventilation Model B
Size no.	K-30	K-29
No. of units	4	2
Power (kW–French unit)	90	75
Electric pressure	DC 220V	DC 220V
rpm	500	600
Super load (%/minutes)	100/30	100/30
Start (rotating) power (%)	200	200
Hydraulic pump		
Type	Janney Model 24	Janney Model 12
No. of units	4	2
Diameter of piston (mm)	54	42
No. of pistons	11	11
Diameter of pump plungers (mm)	248	195
Angle of plate (°)	10	15
Piston movement (litres/min)	595	497
Oil pressure/designed/safety valve control pressure/maximum (kg/cm²)	120/125/140	120/125/140
Manual pump		
Type and units	-------	Vertical, twin tube × 2
Plunger diameter and stroke (mm)	-------	80 × 130
Oil pressure tube		
Main oil pressure tube diameter and length	-------	60–7
Manual pump oil pressure tube diameter and length	-------	40–5.5

Source: *Senkan* Musashi *Kenzō Kiroku* ("Construction of the 'Musashi'"), p. 94.

The anchor windlass was electrically operated and capable of raising 94 tonnes at a speed of 9m/min.

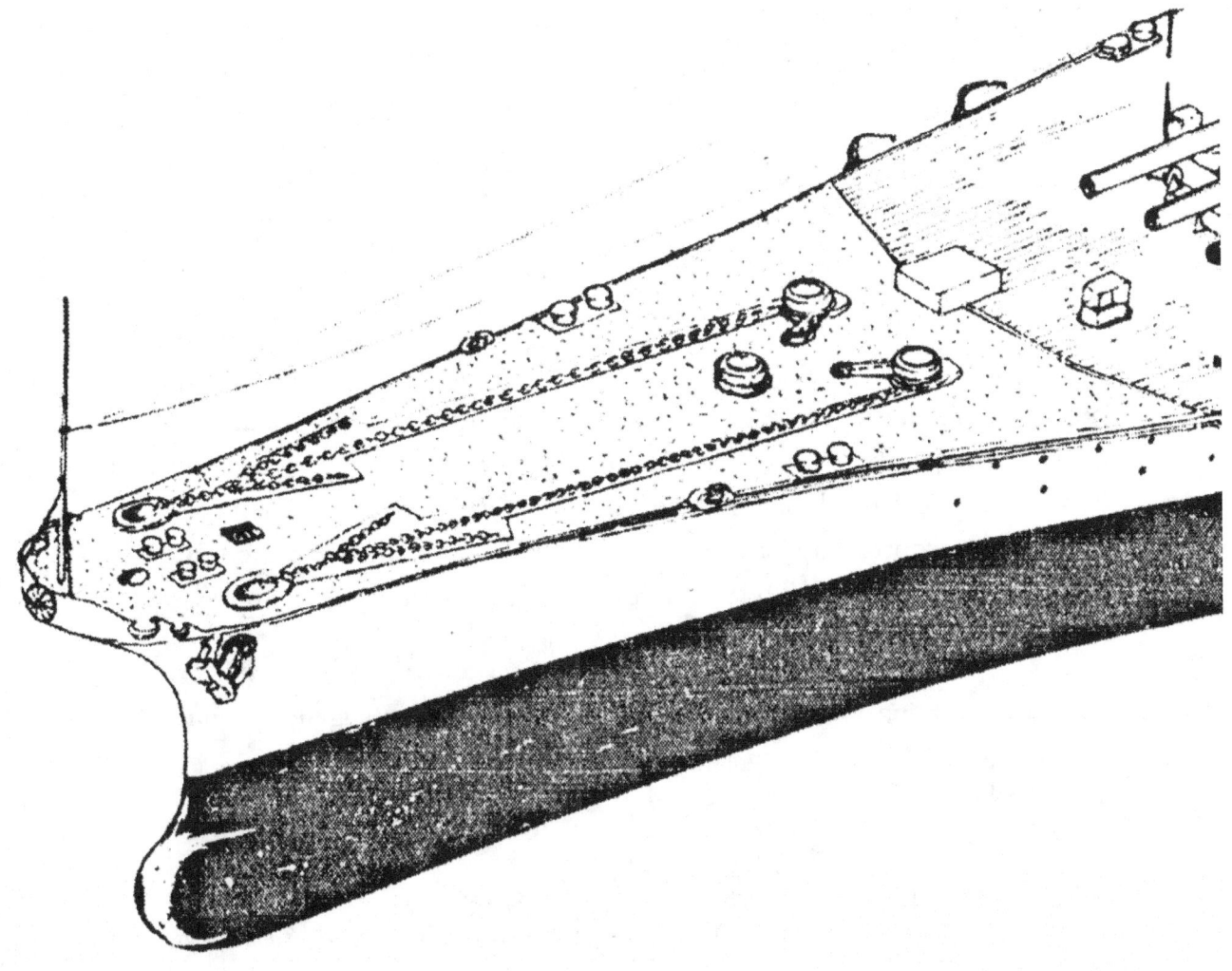

Figure 1-64: Bulbous bow, anchor equipment, etc. (*Nihon no Meikan* via Kitamura Kunio)

It deserves attention that 20 electric gear fuel oil transfer pumps were particularly specified for emergency correction of list or trim, while an additional four pumps were for general use.

Also, the hydraulic pumps for the operation of the main gun turrets were also specified as a total of four pumps, three main and one reserve[76] with turbines directly connected to the centrifugal pumps. Each turbine had an independent water condenser. The capacity of each pump was (1) specified 800

---

[76] According to the Engine Specifications "the intention is to use two pumps with a capacity of 400 m³/h" but this was not realised and all pumps were of the same type.

m³/hour with a pressure of 70 kg/cm², (2) overload 1,100 m³/hour with a pressure of 60 kg/cm².

A large size steam ejector was developed for pumping water from the engine rooms and two of 500 t/hour capacity were fitted in each engine room, one in each boiler room; and one of 250 t/hour in the auxiliary machine rooms.

Turning Ability

The Second Investigation Committee, established after the loss of the torpedo boat *Tomozuru*,[77] worked out not only stability standards but also turning circle standards, because of the effect of the heel angle upon stability and, hence, safety of the ship. This angle also influenced fighting capability (particularly fire control) and manoeuvrability of a force and was therefore important and well worth to be standardised. The values decided by the committee are stated in the next table:

Table 1-25. Turning ability values specified by the Second Investigation Committee

Ship type	Relation DA/Lwl	Relation DT/Lwl	Heel angle (°)
Battleship	3/4.5	3/4.5	7/5
Heavy cruiser	4/5	3.5/7	13/10
Light cruiser	5/5.5	4/7	13/10
Destroyer, torpedo boat	6/6	4.5/9	15/12

Sources: Fukuda, op. cit., p.124, Matsumoto, op. cit., p. 214, *Shōwa Zōsen-shi*, vol. 1, op. cit., p. 638 etc.

Notes:

(1) DA (Advance) is the distance the ship continues in the former direction until turned 90° to it. The centrifugal force generated during the turning causes the ship to heel outwards.

(2) DT (Tactical diameter) is the diameter the ship needs to reverse the course (that is 180°).

(3) Lwl is the length of the hull measured at the waterline.

(4) Values in front of the oblique stroke should be attained with the helm laid to 35° and 8/10 full speed. The values behind the oblique stroke referred to a helm angle of 15°.

---

[77] During an exercise she capsized on 12 March 1934 in what became known as the *Tomozuru* Incident. For more on this see "The *Tomozuru* Incident" in *Warship 2011*, pp. 148–164.

The decision of these values meant that the rudder (or rudders) had to be designed according to these standards.

The actual values of the *Yamato* are shown in the next table in comparison with other Japanese battleships. The table shows that she fell short of the standard, except in case of the heel angle, and that she had better values than the other battleships.

Table 1-26: Turning ability values for *Yamato*

Name	Displ.	Speed	Helm (°)	Am/A	DA	DT	DA/Lwl	DT/Lwl	Heel (°)
Yamato	69,500	26.0	35	49.1	589	640	2.3	2.5	9.0
Nagato	43,861	24.0	35	34.9	631	531	2.87	2.4	10.5
Yamashiro	39,053	23.85	35	36.4	615	593	3.07	2.89	10.0
Kirishima	36,703	28.56	30	36.68	871	826	3.84	3.73	11.5
Haruna	35,921	29.6	30	36.0	820	953	3.71	3.80	9.5
Ise	40,514	24.4	35	36.28	---	---	---	3.35	10.4

Source: Matsumoto, op. cit., p. 214, Fukuda, op. cit., p. 124 (sometimes slightly different data!).

Notes:

(1) Speed refers to that run with 8/10 full power at the official turning trial.

(2) Am is the hull area below the waterline, A is the rudder area. All ships were fitted with two rudders; so A means the total area of both rudders.

(3) The small heel angle was attained with the rather big metacentre (GM) of 2.6 m in trial condition.

(4) The values given from *Nagato* to *Ise* were attained after the modernization conversion.

When the fundamental design of the *Yamato* class was made the Naval General Staff strongly demanded a better turning ability to evade bombs and torpedoes. Several studies were made and numerous model experiments carried out but everything ended in failure and, after all, the past type half-balanced rudder type was again used. As for the shape of the rudder experiments had already been executed with light cruisers and aircraft carriers and these confirmed that the half-balanced rudder had less effect for its area. The Navy Technical Department received the information that the new battleships of the US Navy used a half-balanced rudder type and was very much concerned. It was not recognised as the new Mariner type rudder and the Navy Technical Department arrived at the conclusion that it was of the past type.

Because the *Yamato* class were extraordinary big ships with heavy main gun turrets and armor weights the momentum increased remarkably. To overcome it and to reduce the time for the change of the helm angle to become effective, an increase of the rudder area was the natural countermeasure. But the big increase of the rudder area could not be done. After all, the rudder effect could not be improved because the effect upon the heel angle was already in excess of the standard.

The *Yamato* class was fitted with one main and one auxiliary rudder as a countermeasure to rudder damage. In contrast to the former capital ships, which had two rudders arranged in parallel behind the propellers and inclined outwards, the *Yamato* class had them placed in line, 15 m apart. In the former case both rudders could be put out of action by a direct torpedo hit, or damage of the steering engine by a hit in that room. While the steering engine room was protected by armor, this was impossible in case of the rudders. Therefore, the designers choose the method to use two rudders placed apart as much as possible, to minimise the danger of simultaneous loss.[78] Each of them should be capable to maintain steering. A_m/A was 1:65 for the main rudder located aft and 1:200 for the auxiliary rudder situated 15 m forward of it. The ratio of the total area of both rudders against the area of the underwater hull was 1:49.1.

The auxiliary rudder was of the ordinary type and was located just aft of the cut up. Its effect was unsatisfactory. At the trial it took a very long time after putting the helm over before the turn began (DA = advance) and after turning it took even longer to resume the original course–if at all. The inertia of the ship to continue the advancement on the altered course was bigger than the force generated by the turning of the auxiliary rudder. The design was intended to be used for steering in case of damage to the main rudder, but the trials proved that it could be used only in combination with the latter. Even though both rudders were used it took some time until the turning force was effective. After details of the loss of the German battleship *Bismarck* and the battleship

---

[78] The types of rudders and their arrangement resembled that of the British battle cruiser *Hood*, the world's largest super-dreadnought at the end of World War I.

Hiei became known[79] the requirement to improve the effect of the auxiliary rudder was recognised as urgent in order to completely fulfil its reserve function for steering. According to Matsumoto, op. cit., pp. 216–17, a design was worked out after research[80] but not executed "due to the change of the war situation."

It may be of some interest to add that before the arrangement of the rudders in the way described above had been decided it had been planned to fit one rudder in the conventional way at the stern and another one at the bow; each capable of steering the ship. Model experiments were carried out but no favorable effect was attained. So the designers were forced to adopt the use of one main and one auxiliary rudder and locate them at the stern rather far apart.

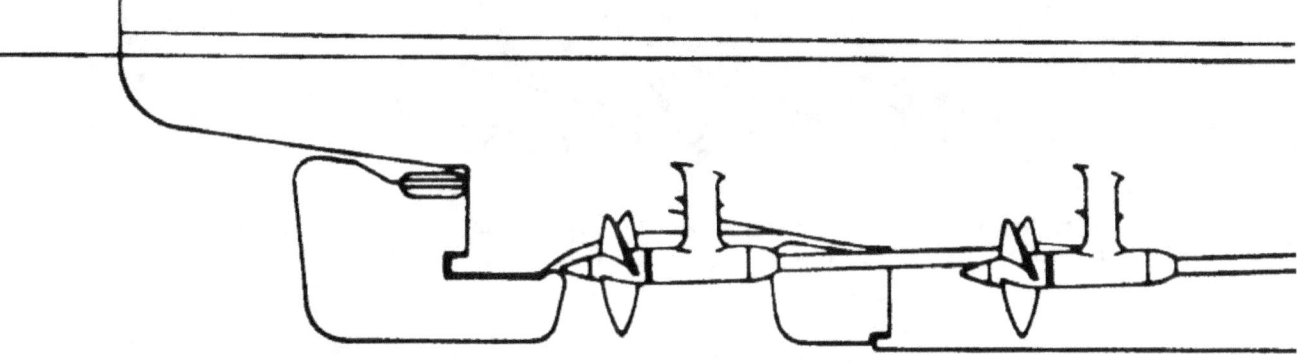

Figure 1-65: Rudder arrangement (*Senkan* Musashi *Kenzō Kiroku*)

---

[79] The former lost steering due to damage to the rudder, the latter due to damage of the steering engine room. In both cases the ships became immobilised and in this condition they became easy preys to enemy forces. The loss of steering was the indirect cause of the loss and proved how important the maintenance of steering was. In his "A Comparative Study of Japanese and U.S. Battleships" Makino Shigeru also mentions a "rudder disaster" of the battleship *Kirishima* and refers to *Yamato*'s shift to the operation of the diesel-driven hydraulic pump, just above the main steering gear room (fitted just after completion), after the damage of electric cables to maintain the function of the main rudder. Even though she escaped the crisis temporarily on her last cruise to Okinawa it was of no use after all.

[80] His statement "conducted with some success" indicates that the goal was not attained. Unfortunately, he does not refer to the nature of the research nor do the authors of the other sources.

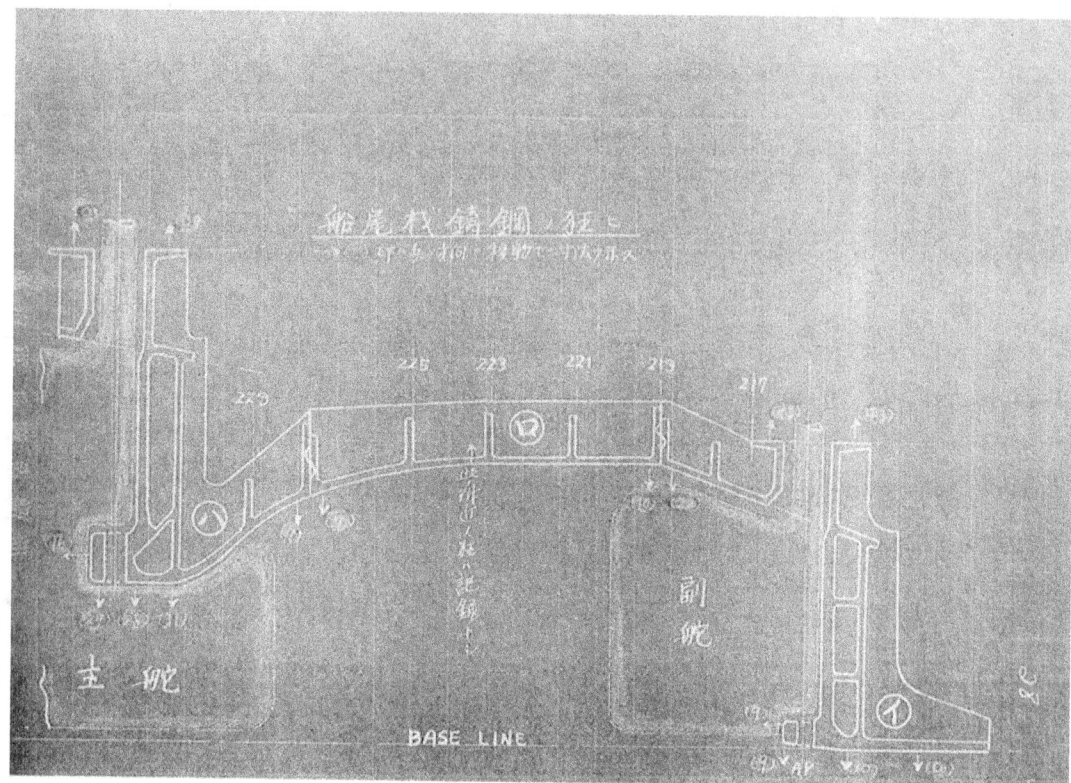

Figure 1-66: Deviation of cast steel sternpost. The auxiliary rudder to the right and part of the main rudder to the left (*Senkan* Yamato *Kenzō Hiroku*)

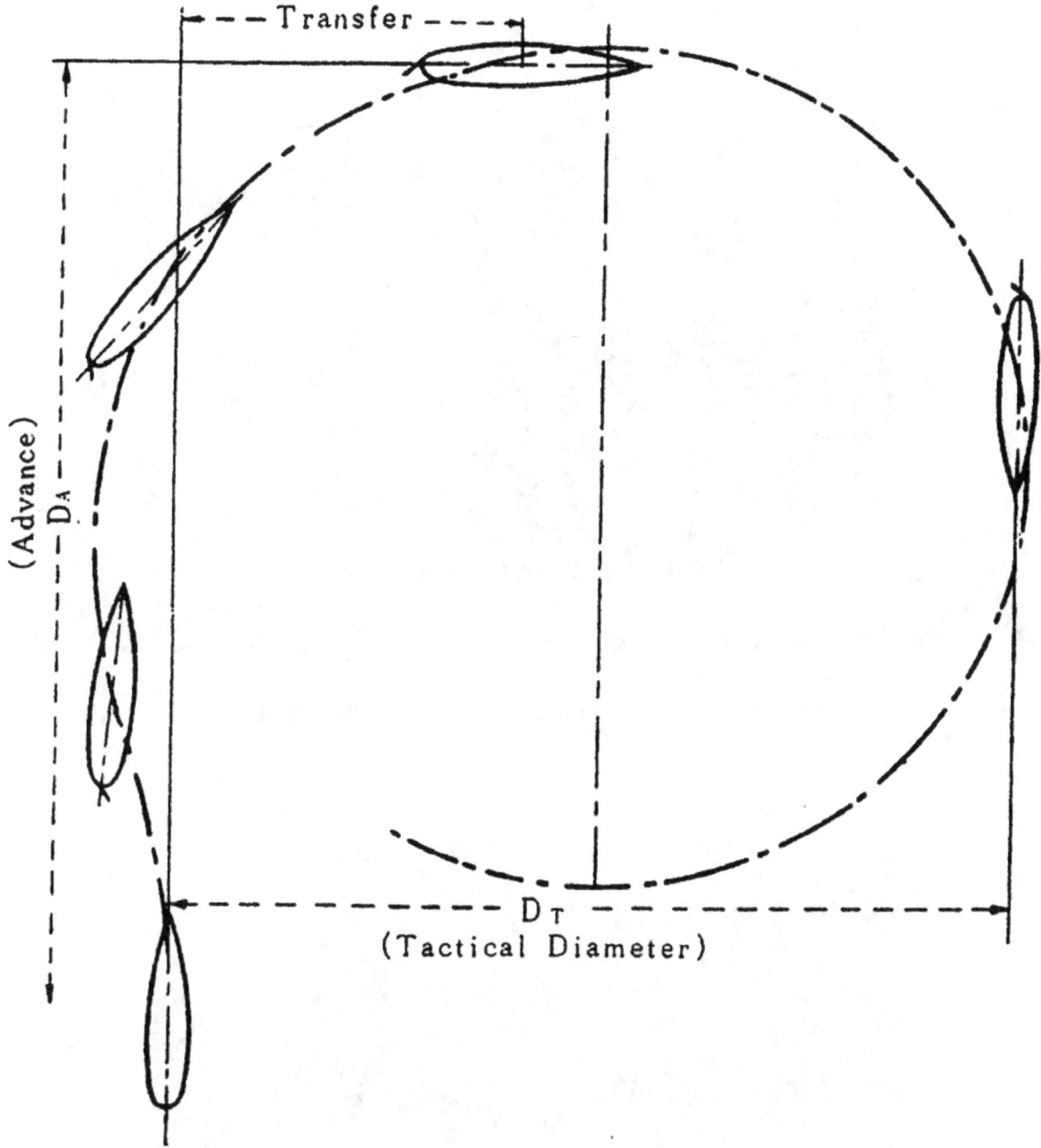

Figure 1-67: Turning circle of the *Yamato*. See table 1-25 for explanations (*Senkan Yamato • Musashi Sekkei to Kenzō*)

Photo 1-18: *Musashi* maneuvers at 27 knots on 30 October 1942 (Kure Maritime Museum)

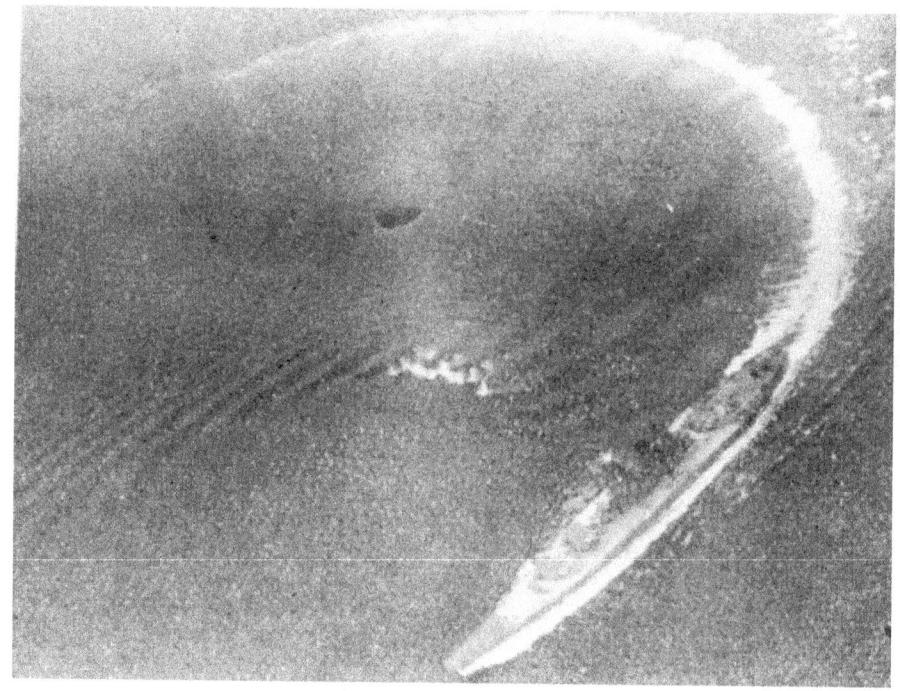

Photo 1-19: Another photo of *Musashi* maneuvering on 30 October 1942. Here she is making 20 knots (Kure Maritime Museum)

Chapter 2–Outline Description of the Main Armament

Decision of the Main Gun Calibre: 45.7-cm or 50.8-cm?

After the London Treaty the power of the "fleet faction" was strengthened and the leaders of the "treaty faction" dispelled. The position of the Naval General Staff vs. the Navy Ministry was much strengthened and the organisation expanded. The extension of the "inferiority ratio" upon auxiliary ships and the prolongation of the "naval holidays" stimulated the outranging tactics to an extreme degree. In view of the planned notice to terminate the Washington Treaty the Naval General Staff investigated the construction of a new type battleship in 1933. The investigation was executed by Lieutenant-Commander (promoted to commander on 5 November 1933) Matsuda Chiaki (operation planning) and Commander Ishikawa Shingo[81] (armament planning)[82] and the latter summarised the result on 21 October 1933 with the proposal of an "incomparably dimensioned new type battleship," with the following principal particulars: (1) Displacement about 50,000 tons, (2) speed > 30 knots, (3) main guns near 20" × 9, (4) protection safe against 40-cm projectiles fired from 20,000 m to 38,000 m and safe against 10 torpedo hits of 500 kg of explosives each. Two ships were to be built with expenses of ¥25,000,000 each, the preparations completed until the end of 1936.

---

[81] According to Admiral and Navy Councillor Katō Hiroharu's (Kanji's) diary Ishikawa rather often visited him, so that the exchange of opinions on the new battleship type is highly probable. See also Katō's "Private Idea About the Disarmament of the Ages to Come–1933, 1934." Prof. Asada Sadao points out in his *From Mahan to Pearl Harbor*, p. 206, the five *Yamato* class ships mounting 20" guns were wanted by Ishikawa. Readers interested in other opinions than those of the "fleet faction" should read the very condensed statements of some influential advocates of the "aircraft first" policy in this book.

[82] At that time Prince Fushimi Hiroyasu was Chief of the Naval General Staff, Rear-Admiral (later admiral and navy minister) Shimada Shigetarō directed the Operation Division (#1 *bu*) and Rear-Admiral Koga Mineichi (later admiral and Commander-in-Chief Combined Fleet) headed the War Armament Division (#2 *bu*).

The new concept was studied in the Navy Technical Department and the following tentative design was presented to the Second Armament Limitation Investigation Committee (*Gunbi Seigen Kenkyū Iinkai*) by Rear-Admiral Fujimoto (promoted 15 November 1933) on 21 March 1934.

Table 2-1: Tentative design of new type battleship

Displacement	**50,000 tons standard > 60,000 tonnes trial**
Length × Beam × Draught	290 m (wl) × 38 m (wl) × 9.8 m (trial)
Main guns	12 50.8-cm (20") guns mounted in four triple turrets
Other guns	16 15.5-cm (6.1"), 8 to 10 12.7-cm HAGs, some MGs, 3 aircraft and 3 catapults
Horizontal protection	280 mm (11") to resist 41-cm AP projectiles fired from < 38,000 m
Vertical protection	406 mm (16") 17.5° inclined to resist 41-cm AP projectiles fired from > 20,000 m
Speed	30 knots
Machinery	Diesel engines performing 140,000 bhp
Endurance	> 12,000 nm at 16 knots

The features were (1) sole mounting of diesel engines to increase endurance, (2) long length of waterline to attain high speed with moderate bhp, (3) heavy protection, (4) mounting of twelve 51-cm guns in four triple turrets.

Aside from the fact that these features could not have been realized within 50,000 tons standard, only the calibre of the main guns, even a little larger ones were selected than the proposed "about 20"", will be considered.

Table 2-2: Comparison of gun particulars

Item / Calibre	36 cm	41 cm	41 cm	46 cm	48 cm	51 cm
Barrel length (calibres)	45	45	52.5	50	47	50
Barrel weight (tons)	85	102	123	170	150	240
Total weight of guns (tons)	187	268	442	437/623/824	?	661/940/1,246
Turret weight (tons), twin	700	1,060	---	1,850	?	2,780
, triple	---	---	1,730	2,570	?	3,790
, quadruple	---	---	---	3,350	---	4,900
Notes	Mounted on the battleships of the *Ise* class etc.	Mounted on the battleships of the *Nagato* class	Scheduled for the *Kongō* replacement ship	Under study	Test produced	Under study

The 50-cal 46-cm and the 50-cal 51-cm guns were under study at that time. The larger calibre was chosen for Fujimoto's tentative design and was to have the following characteristics:

Table 2-3: Characteristics of 50-cal guns.

Calibre Item / Date	50-cal 46-cm February 1934	50-cal 51-cm February 1934	50-cal 51-cm July 1934
Actual calibre	460 mm	510 mm	508 mm
Barrel length	23.62 m (51.38 cal)	26.185 m (51.34 cal)	26.084 m (51.35 cal)
Barrel weight	170 tons	240 tons	242 tons
Bore pressure	29.0 kg/mm²	?	29.2 kg/mm²
Muzzle velocity	835 m/s	?	835 m/s
Structure, 1 A	25 tons (ingot 125 tons)	35 tons (ingot 175 tons)	75.6 tons
, 2 A	37 tons (185 tons)	53 tons (265 tons)	52.8 tons*
, 4 A	46 tons (230 tons)	65 tons (325 tons)	60.3 tons*
, 4 B	18 tons (90 tons)	26 tons (130 tons)	25.4 tons

Notes:

* Scheduled to be divided into two parts.

(1) The 508-mm gun (July investigation) was to fire a projectile of 1,965 kg weight using 480 kg of propellant powder filled in eight bags of 60 kg each.

(2) All guns were wire-wound over their full length (3 A and 3 B layers), as actually executed in the 45-cal 46-cm guns of the battleships of the *Yamato* class.

(3) The weight difference between the summarised weight of the tubes and the barrel weight is made up by the weight of the gun wire and the breech.

The First Division of the Navy Technical Department, in charge of guns, armor etc., was cautious about the production of the 51-cm gun. Therefore, Captain Soma Rokurō, who represented this division, proposed to the aforementioned committee that "… because of the change of the situation compared with that before the London Conference and the shift of the competition upon the application of the most modern techniques, the tentative construction of the 50-cal 18" gun should be started immediately and finished as quickly as possible in order to confirm the technical realization. In addition, the necessary production works should be established urgently and the expansion of other facilities carried out in order to begin the investigation of the 20" gun, in parallel with the successful testing of the 18" gun, and in preparation for the future shipbuilding competition …"

It is said that the order for the tentative production of the 18" gun[83] was given to the Kure Navy Yard from the Navy Ministry in July 1934, after the Ōkada Cabinet had decided to wreck the Second London Conference on 8 July, and the information of the Navy Councillors about the principles on 16 July.

The design was based largely on the experience with the 18.9" (48-cm) gun of the Eight-Eight Fleet age.[84] In order to keep the calibre secret and give the impression that the 41-cm gun of the battleships of the *Nagato* class was to be progressed, or a gun of this calibre newly to be designed, the term Type 94 (corresponding to 1934[85]) 40-cm gun was chosen.

As for the structure of the barrel three studies were investigated, namely:

(1) Half wire-wound, five layers.
(2) Wire-wound (3 A and 3 B), four layers (by removing 4 A tube); weight of the barrel 177 tons.
(3) Half wire-wound (2 A), four layers (3 B wire-wound in [2] was abolished); weight of the barrel 167 tons.

In March 1935 the following outline was decided:

---

[83] 18" corresponds to 45.72 cm but the calibre was decided to be exactly 46 cm (18.1").

[84] The design of this gun was begun in 1916 and test firings took place in November and December 1920 on the Kamegakubi range. When the ninth projectile was fired in December the breechblock etc. was heavily damaged. The investigation concluded that it was due to "insufficient dimensions and, hence, strength," i.e. construction failure. Before that corner ghosts had been discovered in the 1 A tube and on 27 June 1919, at the finishing of tubes 2 A, 2 B, 2 C and 2 D, very small (microscopic) cracks were found on the outsides. They must have appeared during the heat treatment of these parts (this phenomenon was later called "temper brittleness"). After replacing the damaged parts by wire winding the trial took place with the result stated above. At that time arms limitation was already being discussed so the gun was not repaired but left as it was. The repair was made in 1934 and used for the purposes stated under the headline "Protection."

[85] The IJN did not formally adopt a gun as a weapon before the practical tests had been executed. Also, the designing team of the hull had to consider the ballistic data obtained by the trial firing. This procedure was recognised as an absolute necessity to avoid failures such as the Royal Navy had experienced with the mounting of a single 35-cal 45.7-cm gun on the large light cruiser *Furious*. When this gun was fired very strong vibrations of the hull were generated. The second gun was not mounted, the mounted one was later landed and *Furious* was converted into an aircraft carrier.

(1) 2 A tube has to be made as one unit (in above [3] 2 A tube was divided into the wire-wound part as the forward half and the steel-made 2 B as the after half). The use of 1 A inner tube (radially expanded liner for quick re-lining) and 2 A tube is permitted. The background was to prevent the damage of the barrel.

(2) The weight of the ingot for 2 A tube is scheduled to be 130 tons with the finished weight of one-fifth, e.g. 26 tons. 1 A inner tube is to be made thinner (than 2 A) and prepared for (easy) re-lining after being worn out.

(3) The muzzle is of the two layer type composed of 1 A and 2 A tubes and the third layer should be suitably divided.

(4) The after half of the barrel should be made wire-wound to the degree of the 5th Year 36-cm gun.

(5) The weight of the ingot of the fifth layer is scheduled to be 130 tons with the same finished weight as stated in (2).

(6) The bore pressure should be made the same as in the 36-cm and 41-cm guns with 30kg/mm². In case of using the strong propellant the pressure may not exceed 36 kg/mm².

(7) The muzzle velocity of the 50-cal gun, with barrel weight from 186 tons to 205 tons, should be 830 m/s, that of the 45-cal gun, with barrel weight 160 tons to 177 tons, should be 770 m/s.

As seen from (7) above the length of the gun, either 50-cal or 45-cal, was not yet decided at that time. Since the time of mounting 50-cal 12" (304.8-mm) guns in the forward and after centreline twin main gun turrets of the battleships *Kawachi* and *Settsu*, and 45-cal guns of the same calibre in the side twin turrets, the IJN was reluctant to use the longer length because the 50-cal guns obtained fewer hits, in comparative trials, than the 45-cal ones.[86] On the other hand, experiments with an experimentally produced 50-cal 36-cm gun had proven an increase of the muzzle velocity with around 30 m/s, with all other factors, particularly weight and type of propellant and bore pressure, unchanged. Progress in gun construction and projectile shape might also

---

[86] The longer the length of a wire-wound gun the bigger the droop and the vibrations of the muzzle.

attribute to minimise the droop of the barrel and vibrations of the muzzle, so that the results of the 1910s were not considered to be transferable, at least fully, to the conditions in the middle of the 1930s. This made the former theory doubtful and reduced the cause to a pure construction matter.

The calculation of the properties of the 45-cal and the 50-cal guns resulted in the following characteristics:

Table 2-4: Comparison of 45-cal and 50-cal guns

Length of the gun	45-cal	50-cal
Projectile weight	1,460 kg	1,460 kg
Muzzle velocity	780 m/s	820 m/s
Maximum range	41,400 m	44,000 m
Elevation angle for 20,000 m (30,000 m)	12°43' (23°12')	11°21' (20°26')
Angle of fall at 20,000 m (30,000 m)	16°31' (31°21')	14°44' (28°08')
Striking velocity at 20,000 m (30,000 m)	522 m/s (475m/s)	551 m/s (491 m/s)
Flight time for 20,000 m	32.5 s	30.6 s
Armor balance thickness, vertical	566 mm (417 mm)	605 mm (465 mm)
, horizontal	168 mm (231 mm)	208 mm (249 mm)

Notes:

(1) Striking velocity means the (remaining) speed of the projectile with which it hits the enemy ship at the given distance.

(2) Balance thickness means the armor thickness that cannot be penetrated at the given distance. All armor thicknesses below of the balance thickness will be penetrated, those above will resist the impact of the projectile.

With 40 m/s higher muzzle velocity, 2,600 m longer maximum range and about 10% more penetrative power the 50-cal gun had remarkably better properties than the 45-cal one. On the other hand there were several minus factors of the 50-cal gun; such as the increase of the weight of the barrels and turrets, which, in turn, would cause a raise of the displacement. The size of the ingots would become larger and production tools would require adjustments, etc., so that a direct advance from the 45-cal 41-cm gun to the 50-cal 46-cm gun was judged to cause difficult technical problems. After considering all pros and cons the conclusion was that the intended goal could be attained with the 45-cal gun and its adoption was decided.

In company with the decision of the barrel length the structure of the barrel was decided to be a wire-wound five layer type composed of 1 A inner tube, 2 A tube, 3 A tube, gun wire and 5 A tube, and to mount three guns in one turret, as will be described later.

The fundamental design was made in the First Division of the Navy Technical Department by a design team headed by the excellent naval engineer Hata Chiyokichi, who was the designer of most of the IJN's guns and turrets from the 1920s onwards and became particularly famous for the design of these guns. He died in 1943 and could not be interrogated by the members of the US Naval Technical Mission to Japan. It is supposed that he would have supplied many precious data about the IJN's guns, data that must now be considered lost forever. The detailed design was practised in the Gunnery Division of the Kure Navy Yard and this was usual practice.

Two guns and one turret were ordered to be test produced. The Gunnery Division was in charge. The first gun was completed in March 1938 and in the following year the second one and the turret were ready. The earlier completed gun was test-fired at Kamegakubi Proving Ground in 1938 and after the completion of the test-production several more trial firings were conducted. Numerous tests and experiments followed with improvements or modifications executed before the practically operable gun and gun mount could be produced.

The construction of the gun barrel was a combination of old and new methods, namely wire-winding and radial expansion. It was built-up of the 1 A inner tube as liner and the 2 A tube, which ran the full length of the barrel. Over the latter the 3 A tube, which extended for about 3/5 of the length from the breech, was shrunk and these two were wire-wound in the conventional way over the full length. Upon the wire layers 4 A and 5 B tubes were shrunk with the former one covering about 2/3 of the length, and the latter one the breech and the after part of the powder chamber. Belleville springs made of silicon steel and called "cunnular rings" by the IJN, were fitted in the angles where the tubes changed diameter in order to take part of the stress caused by thermal expansion while firing. The 1 A inner tube, as the liner was called by the IJN, was inserted last and was then radially expanded into place with hydraulic pressure. The length of the bore was divided into three sections of which the after one was given maximum expansion.

Table 2-5: Principal particulars of 45-cal Type 94 40-cm[87] gun

Item / Type	45-cal Type 94 40-cm
Calibre, nominal/actual	40 cm/460 mm (18.11")
Barrel length, breech face to muzzle	21,300 mm
overall/in calibres	21,130 mm/45.94
Weight including breech mechanism	167.000 tons (165.760 plus breech plug of 1.240 tons)†††
Construction	wire-wound, liner radially expanded, four layers at the muzzle and five layers at the breech
Breech	Interrupted screw
No of grooves/depth and width	72/4.06 mm ×?
Twist (rifling)	uniform (1-in 28-cal)
Length of rifling	approx. 18,000 mm
Bore cross section	1,698 cm²
Chamber, length	?
volume	480 litres
Powder container	6 bags of 60 kg each
Muzzle velocity; designed/actual	780 m/s; 785 m/s*; 805 m/s in case of CS and IS
Maximum bore pressure	30 to 32 bar
Muzzle pressure	32 mm²
Projectile weight	1,460 kg (Type 91 AP, TS)** 1,360 kg (CS, IS)
Charge weight	360 kg ***
Ignition weight	2.5 kg
Projectile travel	17.590 m (Type 91 AP shell)
Point of complete combustion	?
Maximum ranges, horizontal/vertical	42,007 m††/12,064 m
Approximate life	200†

Notes: * The muzzle velocity depended on the weight of the projectile and charge. Also, it changed considerably during the service life. 785 m/s are given in *Kaigun Hōjutsu-shi*, p. 21. However, most other sources state 780m/s.

** AP = armor piercing, TS = target practice shell; CS = common shell; IC = incendiary shell.

*** Three types of charges were used, namely: Full (4/4), reduced (3/4), and weak (2/4). There was also a strong charge (full + up to 20%) but it was used only for trial purposes.

---

[87] This was actually designated a "40-cm" gun although the real diameter was 46 cm.

† The service life was not definitively determined, but was estimated at about 200 projectiles. The IJN calculated the service life by the number of rounds fired with full charge (4/4). When a strong charge was fired, it was calculated as if two projectiles had been discharged. A reduced charge was calculated as ½ projectile fired and a weak one as 1/16. This calculation gives an impression of the different grades of the abrasion by thermal influences and pressure inside of the liner.

†† In Japanese sources 41,400–42,800 m are stated as the maximum firing range.

††† According to the original Kure drawing (see figure 2-1).

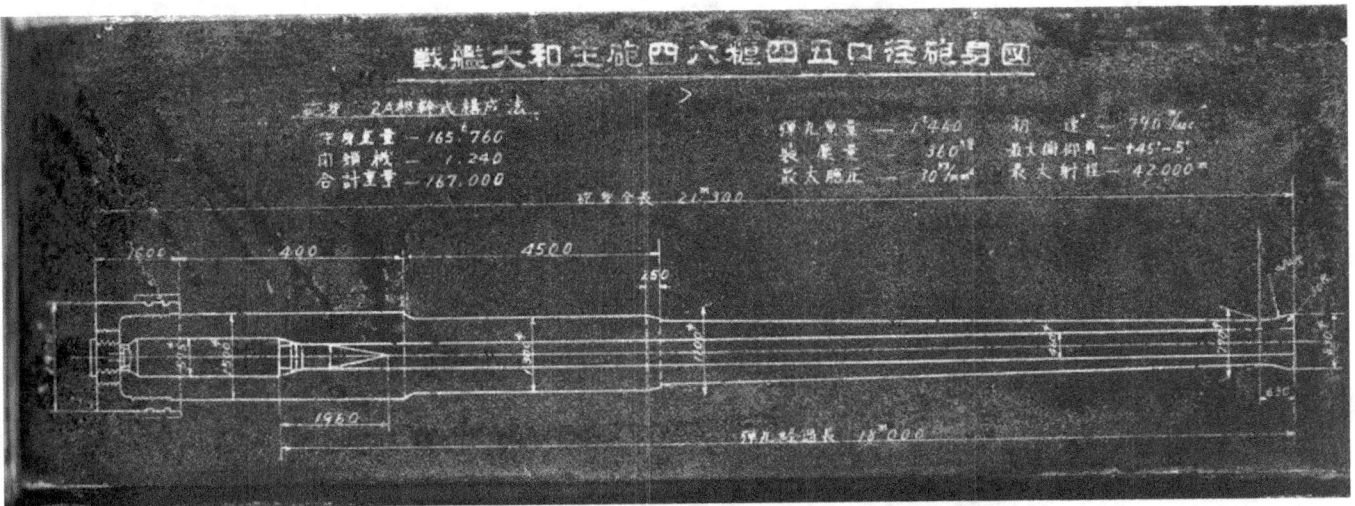

Figure 2-1: Original Kure drawing of the 46-cm barrel (Gakken #20)

Photo 2-1: 46-cm gun at Kamegakubi, balance weights not fitted (*Senkan* Yamato *Kenzō Kiroku*)

Photo 2-2: Same gun as in 2-1 (*Senkan* Yamato *Kenzō Kiroku*)

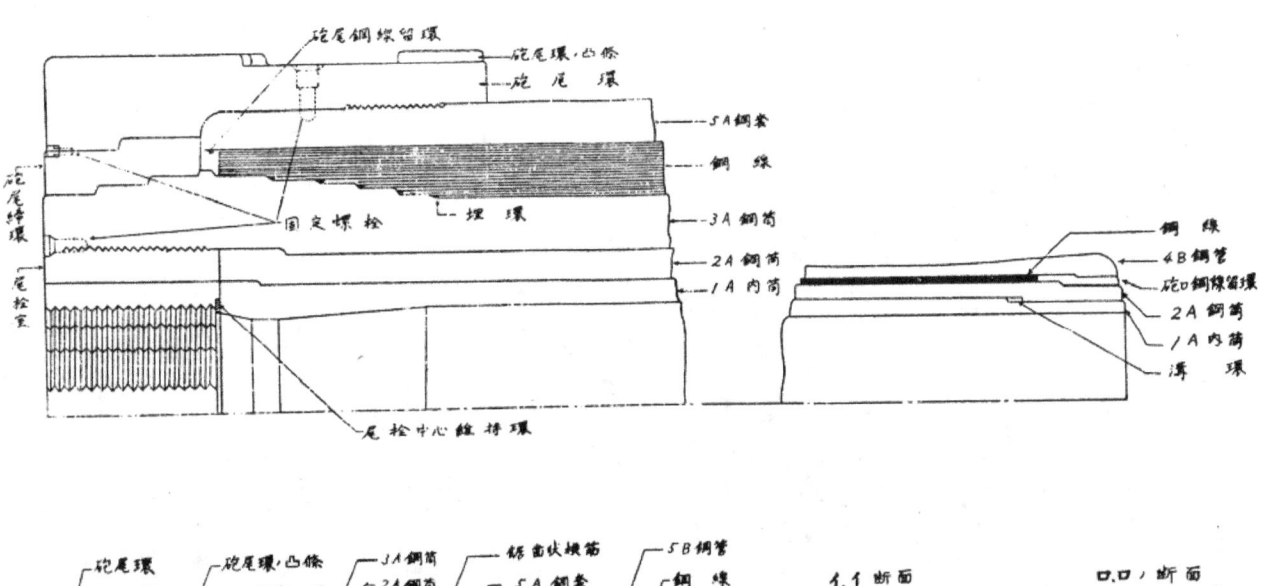
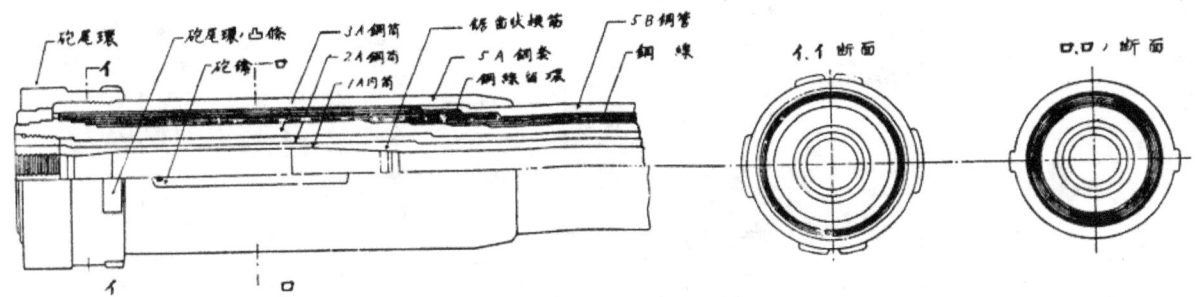

Figures 2-2–6: Build-up of the gun barrel. The lower left drawing (figure 2-4) shows the rear cylinder of the 46-cm gun barrel and the two right hand drawings (figures 2-5–6) are cross sections (at イ and ロ). The upper left drawing (figure 2-2) is a detail of the rear cylinder. Note the positions of the 1 A inner tube and the 2 A, 3 A and 5 A steel tubes. The gun wire is between the 3 A and 5 A tubes. The upper right drawing (figure 2-3) is a detail of the bell muzzle showing (from bottom to top) the gutter (shape) ring, 1 A inner tube, 2 A steel tube, muzzle gun wire stop ring, 4 B steel tube and gun wire (*Kessen Senkan* Yamato *no Zenbō*)

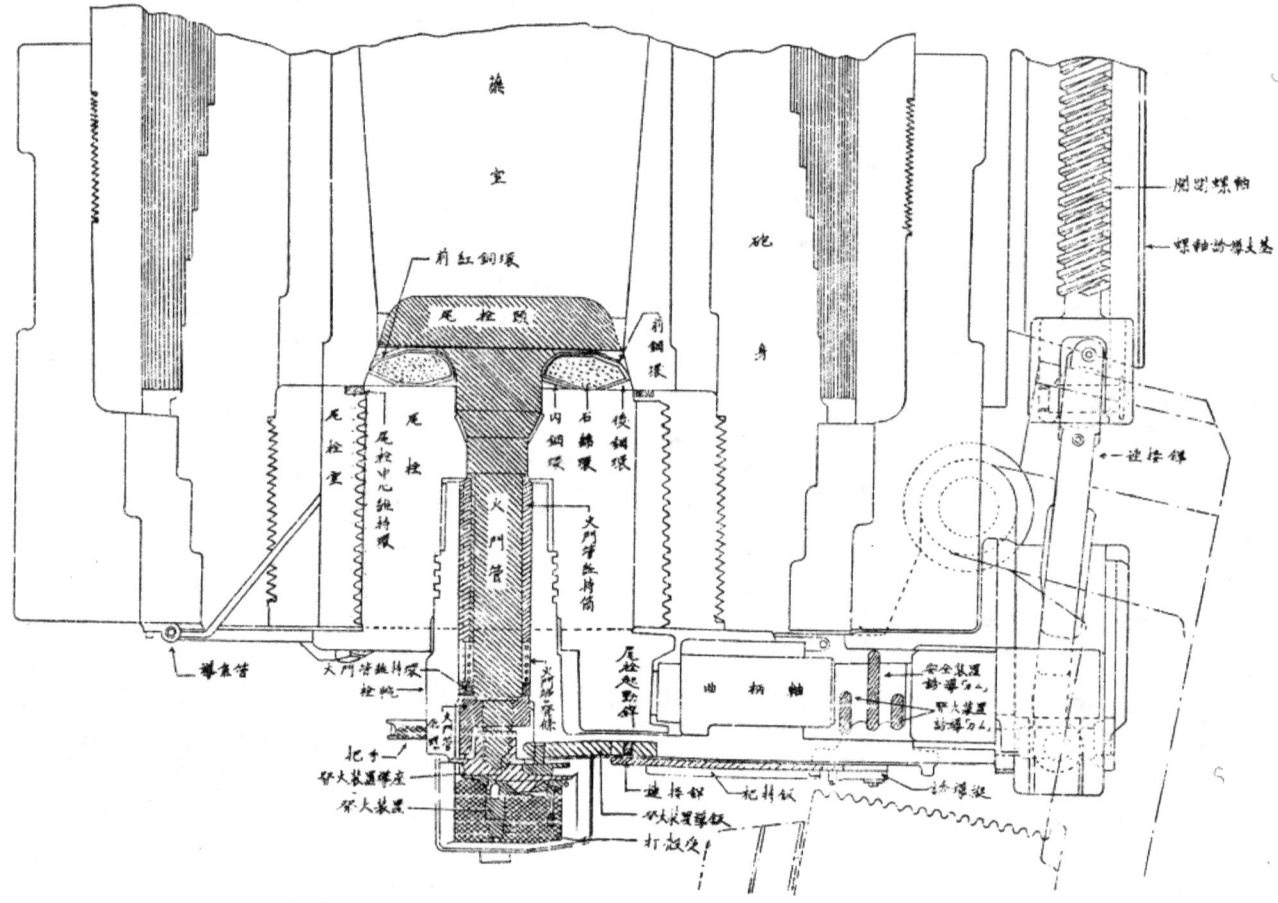

Figure 2-7: Build-up of the gun barrel and breech mechanism (*Kessen Senkan Yamato no Zenbō*)

The goal of the adoption of the 1 A inner tube was of course easy relining when this liner was worn out. As described before, the liner was simply to be removed by hydraulic pressure (after cooling the liner and heating covering tubes) and then a new liner would be inserted. However, the Report O-45 (N) "Japanese 18"-Gun Mounts" of the US Naval Technical Mission to Japan, p. 16, describes that the liner could only be removed by machining out, e.g. the process which should be avoided by the adoption of the 1 A inner tube, and that this process was so expensive in practice "that it was considered more practical to discard the gun without relining." No data could be found in the Japanese sources the authors were able to consult.

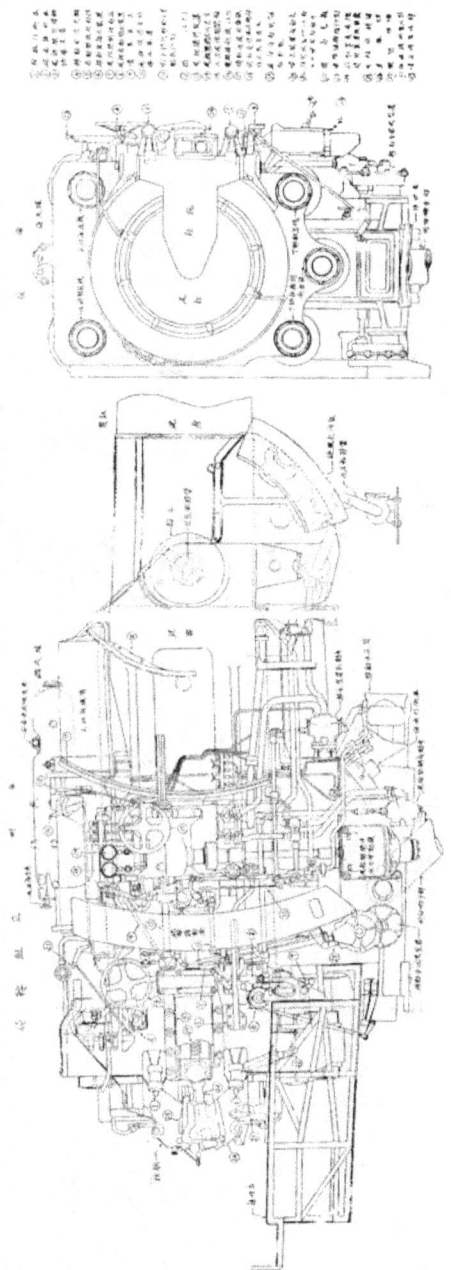

Figure 2-8–9: Gun cradle with breech mechanism (left) and rear view of the gun cradle (right). Note the four (circular) recoil cylinders and the run-out cylinder between the two lower recoil cylinders. The elevating cylinder is the circular object below the run-out cylinder (right figure) (*Kessen Senkan* Yamato *no Zenbō*)

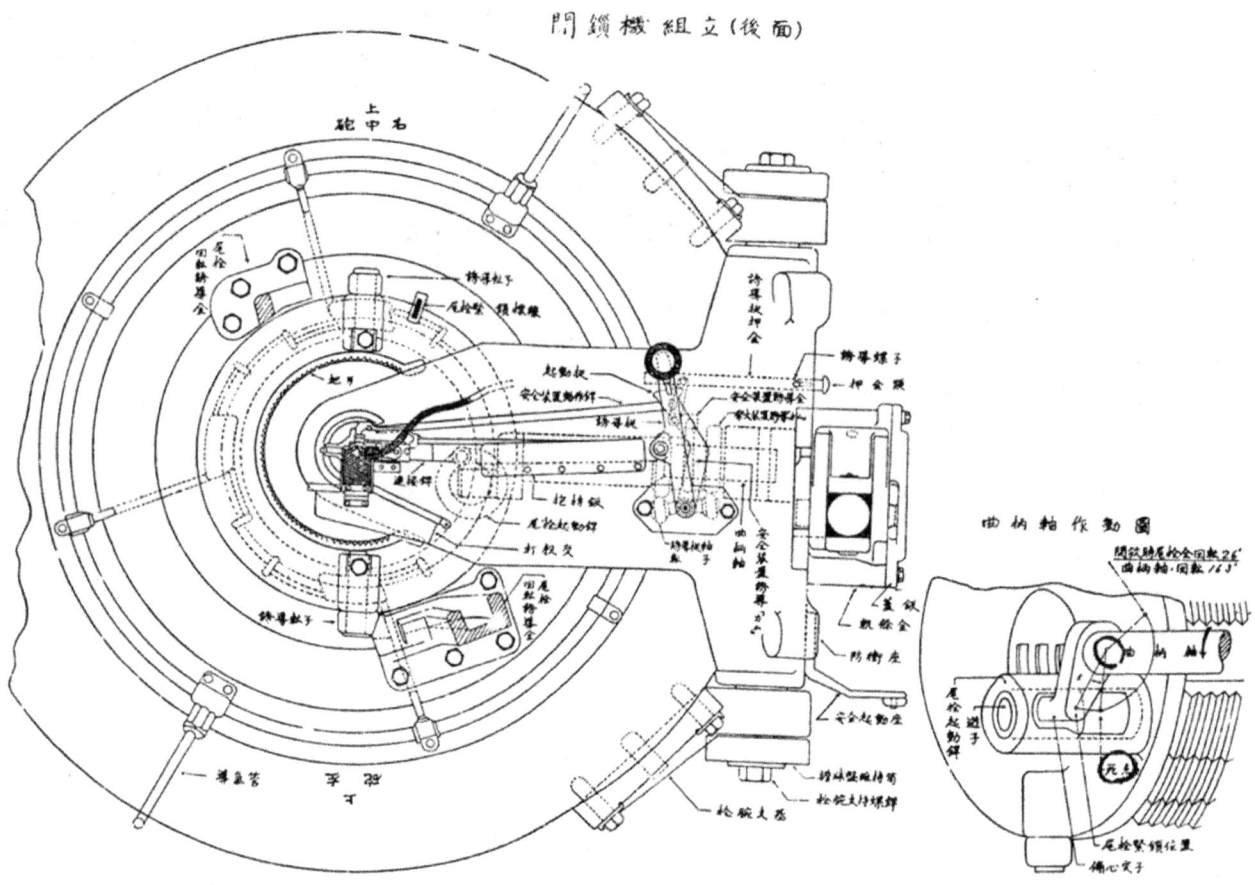

Figure 2-10: Breech mechanism (*Kessen Senkan* Yamato *no Zenbō*)

Armor-Piercing Projectile and Ballistic Properties

With regard to exterior ballistics *Kaigun Hōjutsu-shi*, p. 21, gives the following data at a range of 30,000 m: Elevation angle 23°12', angle of fall 31°21', striking velocity 474 m/s, penetrative power vertical 416.6 mm, horizontal 231.1 mm. These data do correspond with the calculated ones shown above.

In the Report O-45 (N), p. 17, the following data can be found:

Table 2-6: Ballistic properties for the 46-cm cannon

Elevation angle	Range	Time of flight	Note
10°	16,827 m	26.05 s	
20°	27,740 m	49.21 s	
30°	35,810 m	70.27 s	
40°	40,682 m	89.42 s	Slight increase of range between 30° and 40°
45°	42,007 m	98.60 s	Maximum elevation in gun mount
48°	42,090 m	104 s	Maximum range. Theoretical elevation
50°	41,852 m	106.66 s	Note reduction in range. Maximum theoretical elevation

The rough structure of the 46-cm shell is shown in figure 2-15 and the principal parts are similar to the previous AP shell. The particular property of the 46-cm AP shell is shown in the detail drawing of section A in figure 2-14. This structure was not used only for the 46-cm shell but for all AP shells from 20-cm upwards. The principal particulars of this AP shell are as follows:[88]

(1) Shell body or case (*dantai*). After penetrating the hard, strong steel plate the main parts of the projectile (*dangan*) detonated and caused extensive damage by the blast (detonation gases) and splinters (the main parts were the tip and the head part).

(2) Cap (*hibō*). If the projectile hit the armor the cap protected the tip of the shell body and effected the penetration of the armor. In order to support the penetrative power the cap was soldered to the shell case.

---

[88] This section is mostly based upon "Secret Weapons of the IJN" (*Kimitsu Heiki no Zenbō*), pp. 245–256. This rare book (published in 1952) was once referred to as volume II of the first edition of Fukui Shizuo's "Japanese Warships" (*Nihon no Gunkan*).

(3) Cap-head (*hibōtō*). This part was completely hardened and destroyed the surface of the armor plate.

(4) Windshield (*fūbō*). The windshield was fitted in order to reduce air resistance and had no relation to the shells armor-piercing properties.

(5) Base plug (*sokora*). This was the after cover of the explosive room (*dankō* = projectile plug; *sakuyaku* = explosive; *shitsu* = room) screwed into the shell body. It did protect the explosive against the pressure (of the gases) at the moment of firing and also acted to increase the damage.

(6) Fuse adapter (*fuku sokora*). The fuse adapter was screwed into the base plug and protected the fuse. For the storage of the shells in the magazine of a warship a plug/stopper (cork) was fitted instead of the fuse in peacetime. Immediately before a battle the fuse adapter was unscrewed, the cork removed and the fuse inserted.

(7) Copper gas-check rings and copper caulking (*tenjūdō*). At the moment of firing powder gases could pass through very small slits in the threads of the base plug and fuse adapter and actuate the fuse. This is called premature burst (*tō-hatsu*). By this the gun was largely destroyed and in addition extensive damage could be caused inside the turret. There were some cases in the IJN, as that of the battle cruiser *Haruna* and the heavy cruiser *Ashigara*. In order to avoid such cases copper gas check rings were inserted and caulked to obtain gas tightness. This process was called *tenjūdō*.

(8) Guiding rings (*dōkan*). These rings are also called rotating (driving) bands. There were a forward and an after band; both together formed one pair. They were made of copper. At the moment of firing the rifles inside the barrel were pressed into the bands and caused a rotation of the shell body. At the same time they avoided the passing of powder gases along the shell body to the muzzle.

(9) See number 8.

(10) Trinitroanisol filler *(sakuyaku* = explosive). The shaped explosive was filled in greased paper with the fore part melted according to the shape of the powder tube (*dankō*). In contrast to this the explosive was directly melted into the powder tube in case of common shells or bombs (*bakudan*), etc.

(11) Fuse (*shinkan*). This was a time delay fuse and was actuated by the impact when the shell hit the target. After a determined time (in sec-

onds) the ignition was caused via the tube (*kan*) hat (*bō*) powder (*yaku*). The fuse had several safety devices to avoid premature firing or any other failure. The first step was to not be ignited by the shock of the firing or to be fitted with a device that prevented the firing of the shell until it had obtained a determined rotation speed.

The particulars of the structure were as follows:

(1) The fore part (cap head) (vide figure 2-15) was pointed and this shape was favorable for the piercing property. The British type AP shell had the structure that the cap and cap-head were combined (fitted together), as shown in figure 2-14. If an AP shell with this structure hit the water surface it either ricocheted (*chōdan* = hopping shell) back into the air or dived at high speed into the water. It is like a stone being thrown into the water at a very small angle upon a calm surface; it skips several times before diving (same effect as skip-bombing). In contrast, the *saitō-dan* (flat-head shell) had a flat head and continued into the water straightaway, if it hit the water surface. In other words: There was no effect in case of the pointed shell (*senei-dan*) if it did not hit the target, while the *saitō-dan* had the advantage to hit the comparatively thin underwater part of the enemy ship if it struck the water near the target.

Therefore, the production of an AP shell was required that fulfilled both conditions stated above. In response the 46-cm shell was so constructed that it functioned like a *saitō-dan* in case of hitting the water surface.

Figure 2-14 shows the part A–A of figure 2-15. Unlike the previous AP shell items (3) and (4) were produced as separate parts and combined at the position C. In the part B of (4) a nut was grooved on the whole circumference. The thinnest part was about 1 mm thick. Therefore, if the projectile hit the water surface part B and ④ (windshield) were removed together with (3) (cap-head). In this way the *saitō-dan* was created with the flat head. This type of AP shell was nonexistent in the navies of the world powers and the Japanese were very proud of it.

(2) The self-explosion prevention fitting (*sakuyaku* = explosive; *jibaku* = self-explosion; *bōshi* = prevention; *sōchi* = gear, apparatus, fitting,

etc.). The explosion was comparatively safe in case of the common shock. However, if the AP shell hit the armor plate the shock was enormous and the explosive exploded sometimes prior to the action of the fuse. Therefore, the function and goal of the time delay fuse was nullified and in order to avoid a self detonation a damper, consisting mainly of pulp, was filled in front of and behind the explosive.

The principal particulars of the 46-cm AP shell and its piercing power against the protective armor are shown in table 2-8 and in figures 2-16–17.

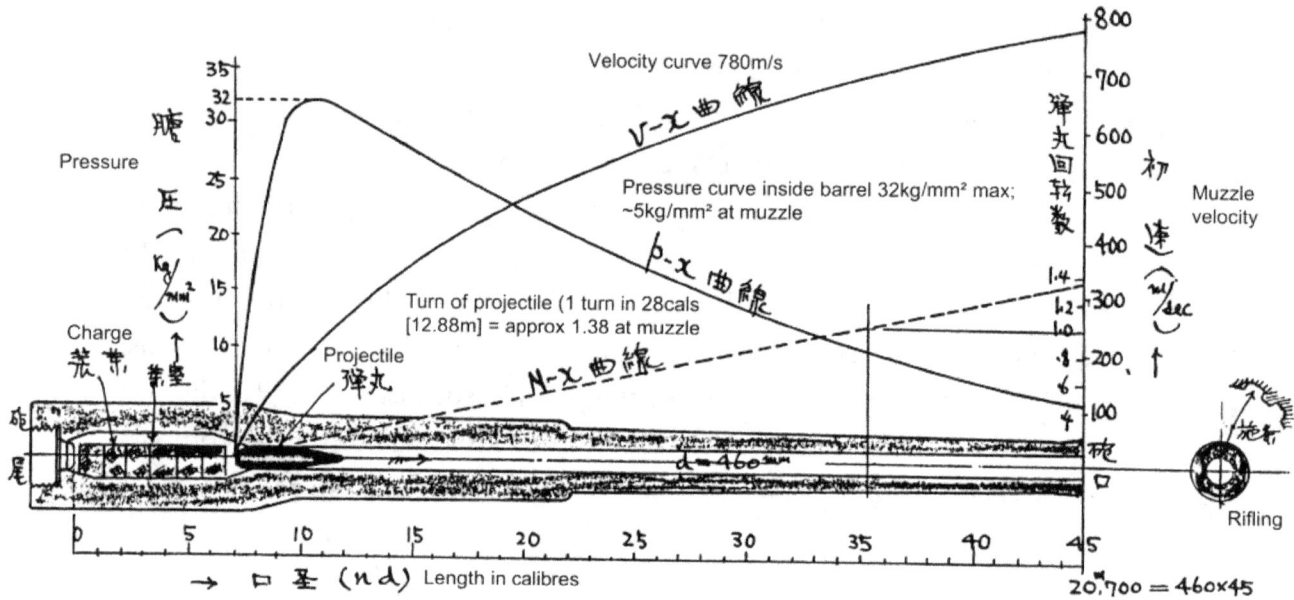

Figure 2-11: Ballistic properties of the 46-cm 45-cal gun (*Senkan* Yamato *Kenzō Hiroku*)

Table 2-7. Shell comparison

Item	Unit	Value	40-cm shell comparison	20-cm shell comparison	50 calibre 12.7-cm shell comparison
Diameter of shell	mm	459	-	-	-
Length of shell	mm	1,953.9	1.1 times	2.2 times	4.5 times
Weight of shell	kg	1,460	1.4 times	11.7 times	63.5 times
Weight of filler	kg	33.85	2.3 times	10.9 times	18.5 times
Relation filler/shell weight		2.3%			
Range	m	40,800	1.1 times	1.4 times	2.2 times

Source: *Kimitsu Heiki no Zenbō*, p. 248.

Table 2-8. Armor penetration capacity

Calibre	46 cm	40 cm	36 cm	20 cm (II)	15.5 cm
Diameter of shell (mm)	459	409	354.7	202.3	154.2
Length of shell (mm)	1,953.5	1,738.5	1,524.7	906.2	677.8
Weight of shell (kg)	1,460	1,020	673.5	125.85	55.87
Weight of filler (kg)	33.85	14.888	11.102	3.106	1.152
Muzzle velocity (m/s)	780	780	770	835	920
Base fuze type	13 *Shiki* 5 *Gō*	13 *Shiki* 5 *Gō* cap change	13 *Shiki* 5 *Gō* cap change	13 *Shiki* 4 *Gō* 1 *Kai*	13 *Shiki* 3 *Gō*
Maximum range (m)	40,800	38,300	35,450	28,800	27,400
Piercing power					
Armor type	VH	VC	VH	NVNC	NVNC
Thickness (mm)	560	459	410	165	100
Striking velocity (m/s)	555.8	490.1	537.6	474.4	677.9
Striking angle (°)	16.5	22	16.5	30	60

Source: *Kampō Shageki no Rekishi* ("History of Naval Guns and Fire Control Systems") by Mayuzumi Haruo, pp. 296–297.

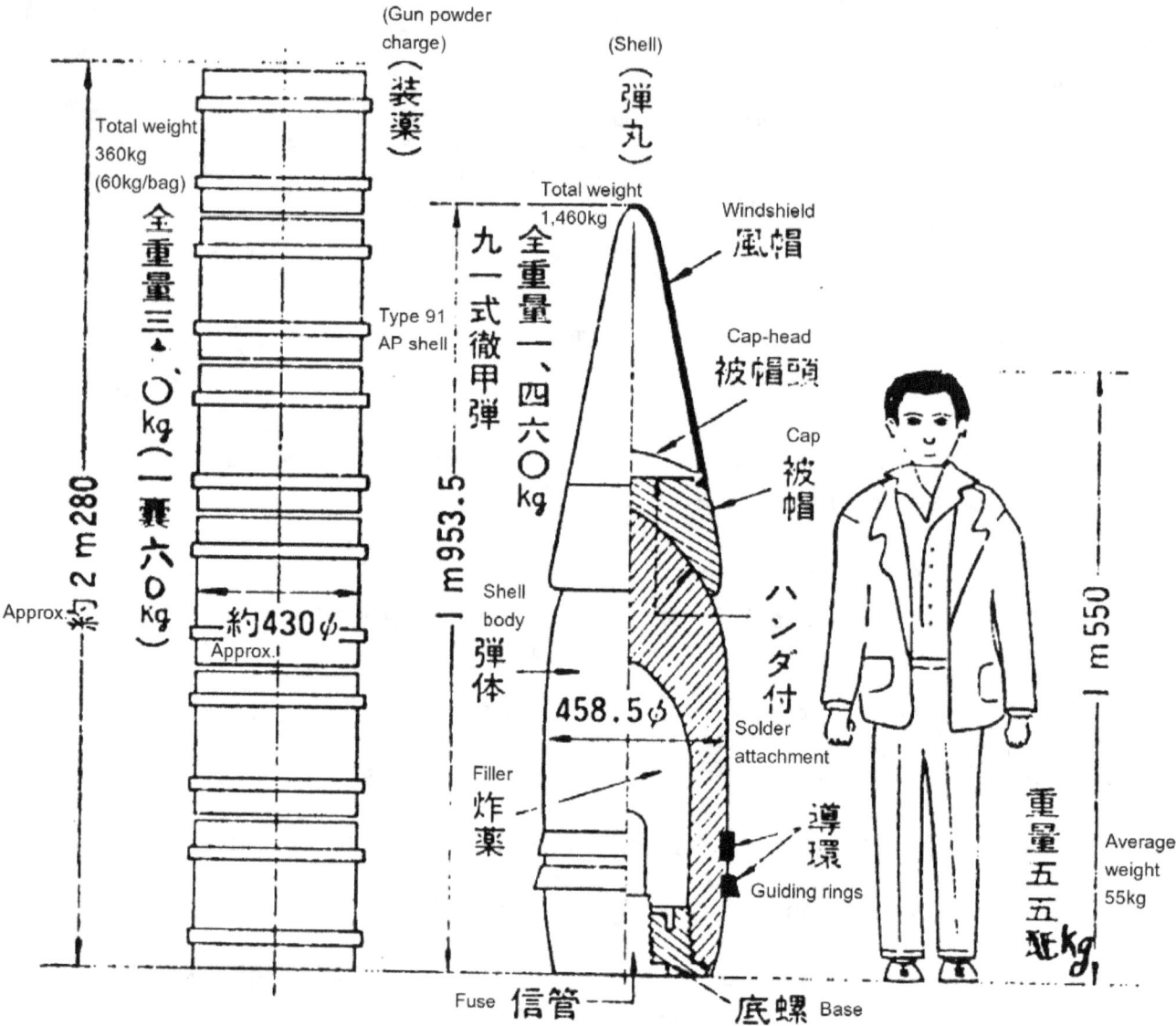

Figure 2-12: Comparison of the propellant powder bags (6 × 60 kg = 360 kg), the 46-cm Type 91 AP projectile (1,460 kg) and a Japanese man of medium-height. Note that in the identical figure originally published in *Kaigun Hōjutsu-shi* the propellant weight is given as 6 × 55 kg = 330 kg. See table 2-11 for more on this weight difference (*Kampō Shageki no Rekishi*)

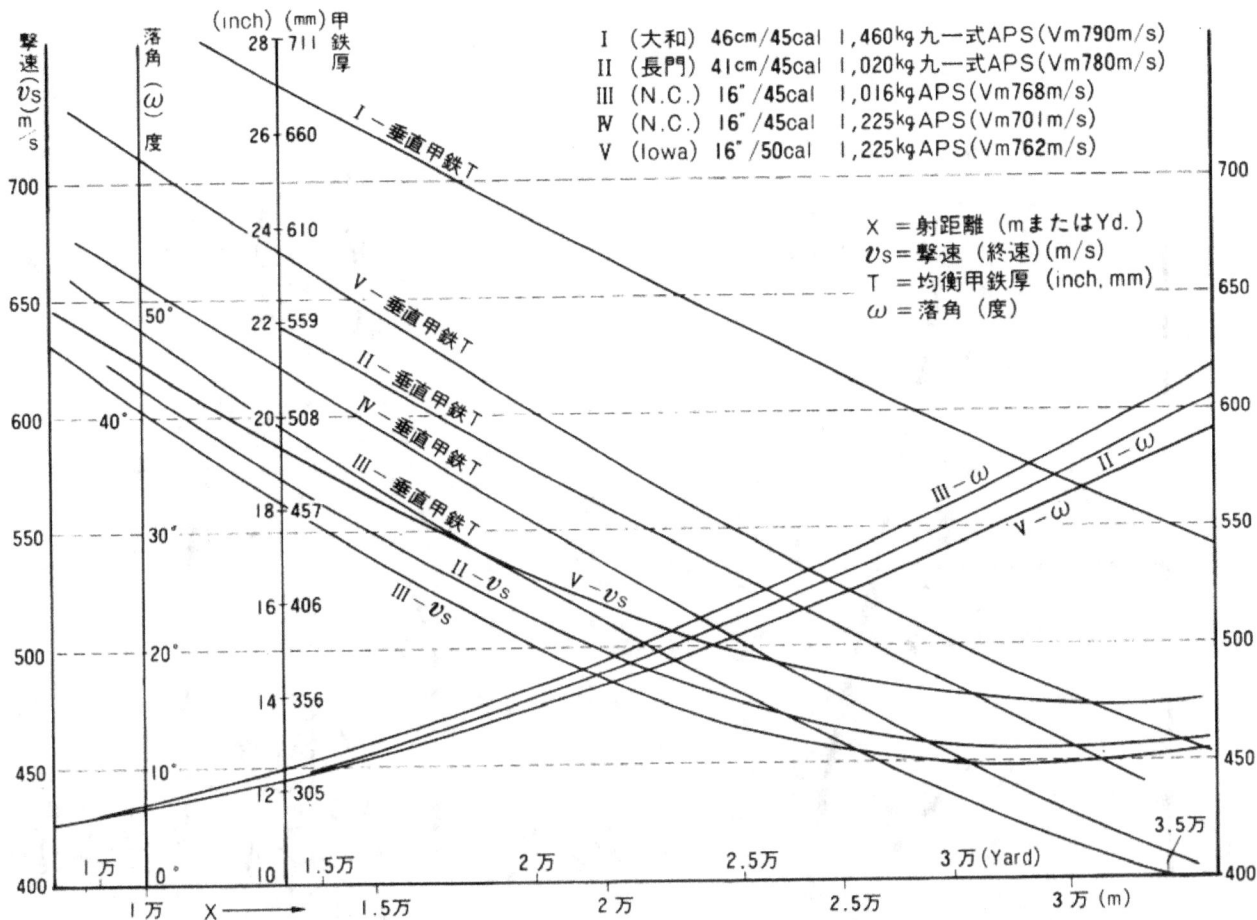

Figure 2-13: Interesting graph comparing the performance data of *Yamato*'s and *Nagato*'s guns with the American modern 16" guns (*Senkan* Musashi *Kenzō Kiroku*)

Note: X = range; v_s = muzzle velocity; T = penetrative power; ω = angle of impact (°)

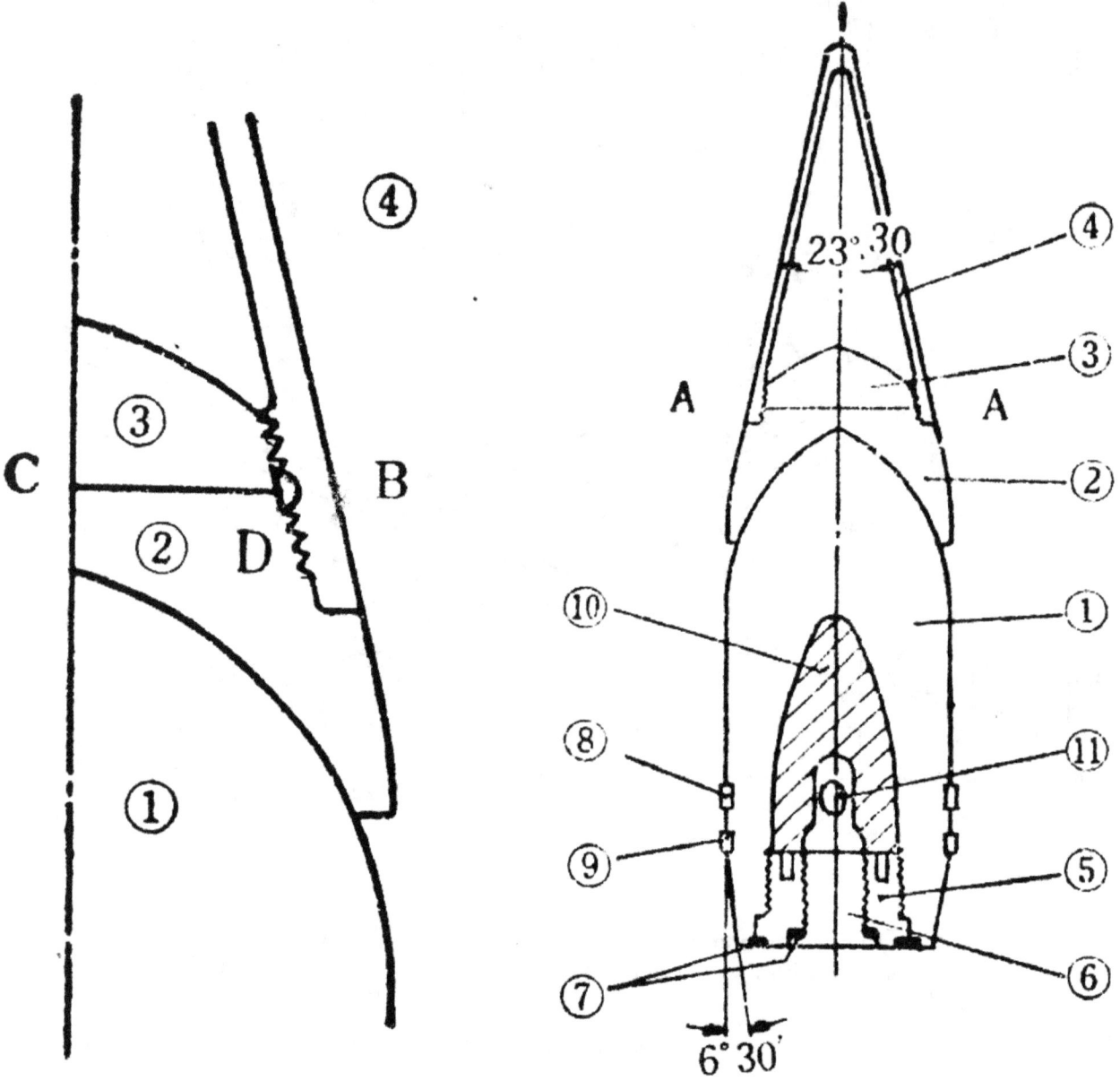

Figure 2-14–15: Structure of the 46-cm shell (*Kimitsu Heiki no Zenbō*)

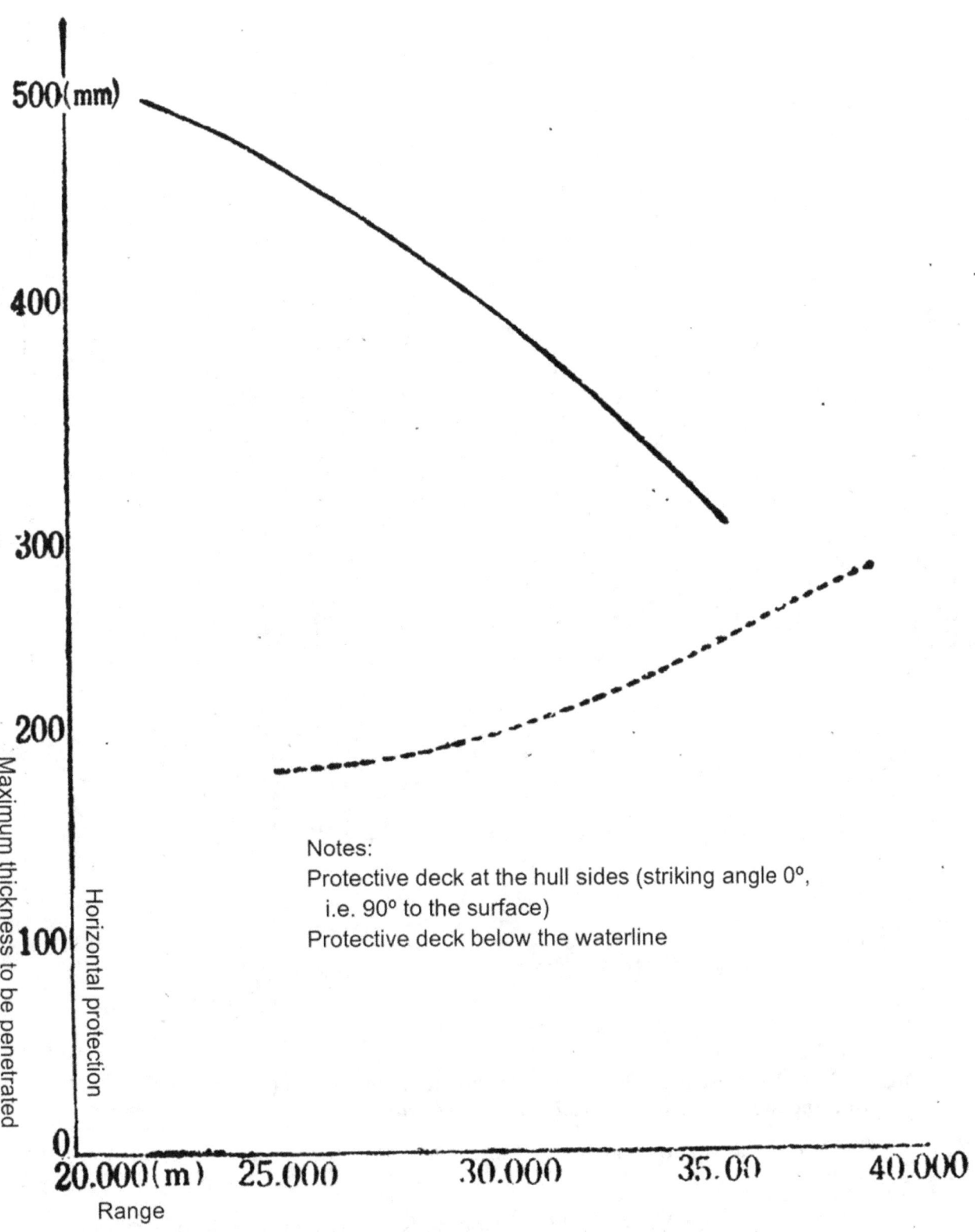

Figure 2-16 (*Kimitsu Heiki no Zenbō*)

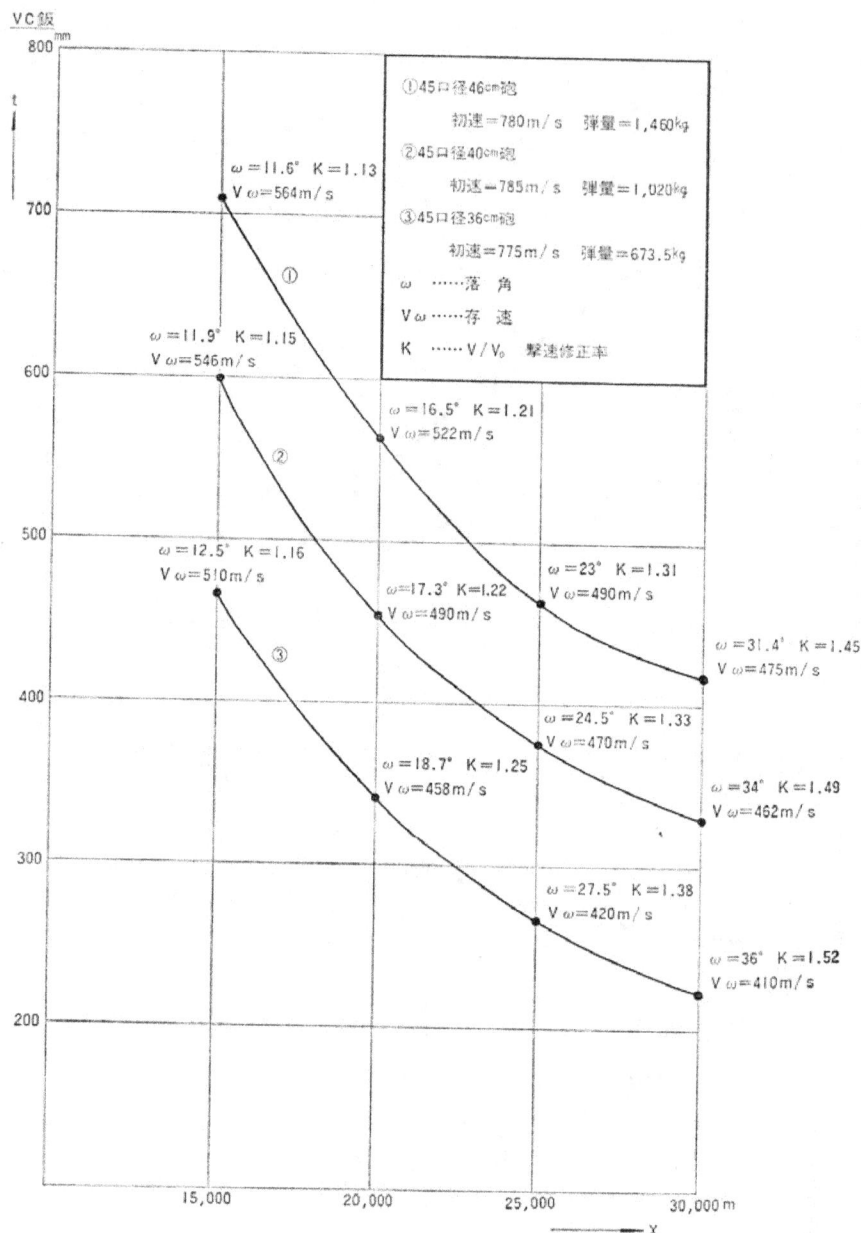

Figure 2-17: Penetration curve of 46-cm (1), 40-cm (2) and 36-cm (3) Type 91 AP projectiles against VC armor (*Kaigun Hōjutsu-shi*)

The vertical axis shows armor thickness and the horizontal axis the firing range

ω = Striking angle; Vω = Striking velocity; K = Correction rate of striking velocity

Table 2-9. Ballistic properties of the 46-cm projectile

Elevation (°)	10	20	34	40	50
Range (m)	16,887	28,005	35,945	40,836	42,005
Time of flight (s)	26.05	49.21	70.27	89.42	106.66

Source: *Kimitsu Heiki no Zenbō*, p. 245.

Note: Difference in range compared with, e.g., tables 2-6–8.

If the bottom of the shell was made thinner, like the stern of a ship, the firing range became larger due to the decrease of the air resistance. This shape was called boat-tail and the IJN adopted this shape in about 1935. However, if the boat-tail was adopted a disadvantage was the reduction of hit probability. The cause of the decrease was uncertain but it was supposed that a streaming-mechanical force was generated at the bottom part of the shell if the pressure of the powder gases, which hit the bottom part of the shell at the moment of passing the muzzle, was not distributed equally and effected vertical to the flight direction of the shell. The French Army in small calibre projectiles first used the boat-tail.

The IJN, like the Royal Navy (RN), considered the hitting probability more important than the loss of range, so the boat-tail was not at first adopted. However, as a result of the Washington Arms Limitation treaty the number of capital ships was restricted so that the IJN was "forced" to adopt the boat-tail for the large calibre shells in order to improve the quality of its capital ships. The range of the 36-cm shell could by this adoption be increased by approx. 1,500 m to 35,000 m.

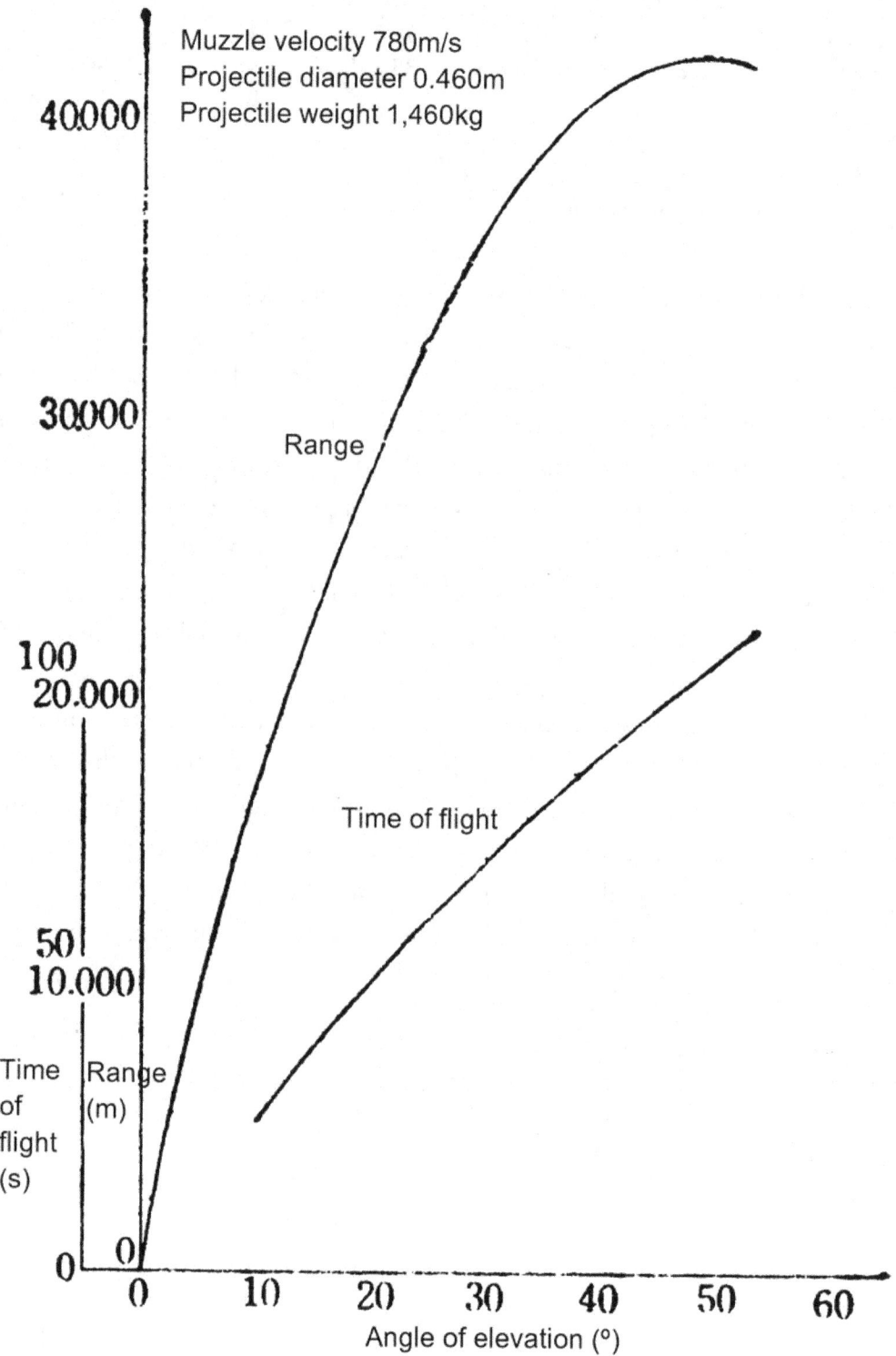

Figure 2-18: Ballistic properties of the 46-cm projectile (*Kimitsu Heiki no Zenbō*)

Because the shells with a boat-tail were longer compared with the older AP shell types its adoption required a conversion of various parts of the main gun turrets of the capital ships. Of course, all projectiles were changed into this type and the old type shells were abandoned. However, it was these old type projectiles that were most effectively used in the Pacific War and this fact was a truly ironical result. Also, the IJN, which had planned for a decisive battle between capital ships and had trained hard for such an engagement, had no opportunity for such an action during the Pacific War. The particularly improved most modern type AP shell ended its story without being effectively used in battle; a treasure worth nothing!

Main Gun Turrets

After the decision of the calibre and the length of the gun, the next problem the designers faced was the number of guns per turret. The Navy General Staff had required the mounting of more than eight main guns because of the convenience of fire control. Therefore, the designers had to arrange more than eight guns in the most effective manner, to suit both construction and gunnery points of view and to create a highly efficient battleship. In response, twin and triple turrets, varieties of arrangement and effects upon protection and weights of various types were investigated and they concluded that the adoption of triple turrets, as intended for the *Kongō* replacement ship[89] and "tried" in the light cruisers of the *Mogami* class, was advantageous from the viewpoint of weight, protection and number of guns.

---

[89] This 52.5-cal 40-cm gun is described in paper I of the *Contributions to the History of Imperial Japanese Warships* under the headline "The New 16" (406 mm) Gun Designed for the so-called *Kongō* Replacement." This paper can be ordered from Lars Ahlberg (e-mail: lars.ake.ahlberg@telia.com) or Hans Lengerer (e-mail: milanovich@t-online.de).

Photo 2-3: Turrets #1 and #2 of *Musashi* in June–July 1942. Note the exceptional size of the ship (Kure Maritime Museum)

From the point of view of the naval architects the symmetrical distribution of one twin and one triple turret forward and aft, respectively, as proposed in Vice-Admiral Hiraga's "private" *Kongō* replacement design, and also in one of the alternate designs for the new battleship class, was the best design. The advantages would be:

(1) evenly distributed weight forward and aft, therefore, balanced weight arrangement
(2) one more main gun to oppose the new American battleships, most probably equipped with nine main guns
(3) small and, hence, acceptable weight increase
(4) the twin turrets arranged forward and aft, in front of the triple ones, required only one deck height for the magazines (triple turrets needed two heights) so bottom protection was better
(5) therefore, the height of the main guns above the waterline could be lowered compared with the triple turrets and the protective weight could be reduced correspondingly
(6) this, in turn, would influence the position of the centre of gravity that would also be lowered

But the realization would require the production of two turret types that, in turn, might retard both the scheduled laying down and completion dates of the ships. Therefore, it was not adopted.

With regard to the triple turret the Naval General Staff demanded the placement in the fore part, like the British *Nelson* class, and it was studied comparatively. The concentration had advantages as for the protective weight of the main guns. However, it was disadvantageous in view of location and ammunition supply. Also, the magazines of the secondary guns and the high-angle guns, which had to be placed aft in this case, had also to be protected. So, in the end, the saving of weight was only minimal. In addition, the position of the tower bridge came close to amidships if the turrets were concentrated forward.

There were many more items to be considered, but finally the arrangement of two triple turrets forward and one triple turret aft was decided upon.

In determining the height of the guns above the waterline, which is one of the most important problems when designing capital ships because of the influence these big masses of weight execute upon the centre of gravity, the height of the first turret was made as low as possible and the difference of the height between the first and the second turret[90] was minimised.[91] As for the height of the third turret, under which the four propeller shafts passed, special considerations were necessary not to place the centre of the turbines too low. However, such special considerations are outside the scope of this outline.

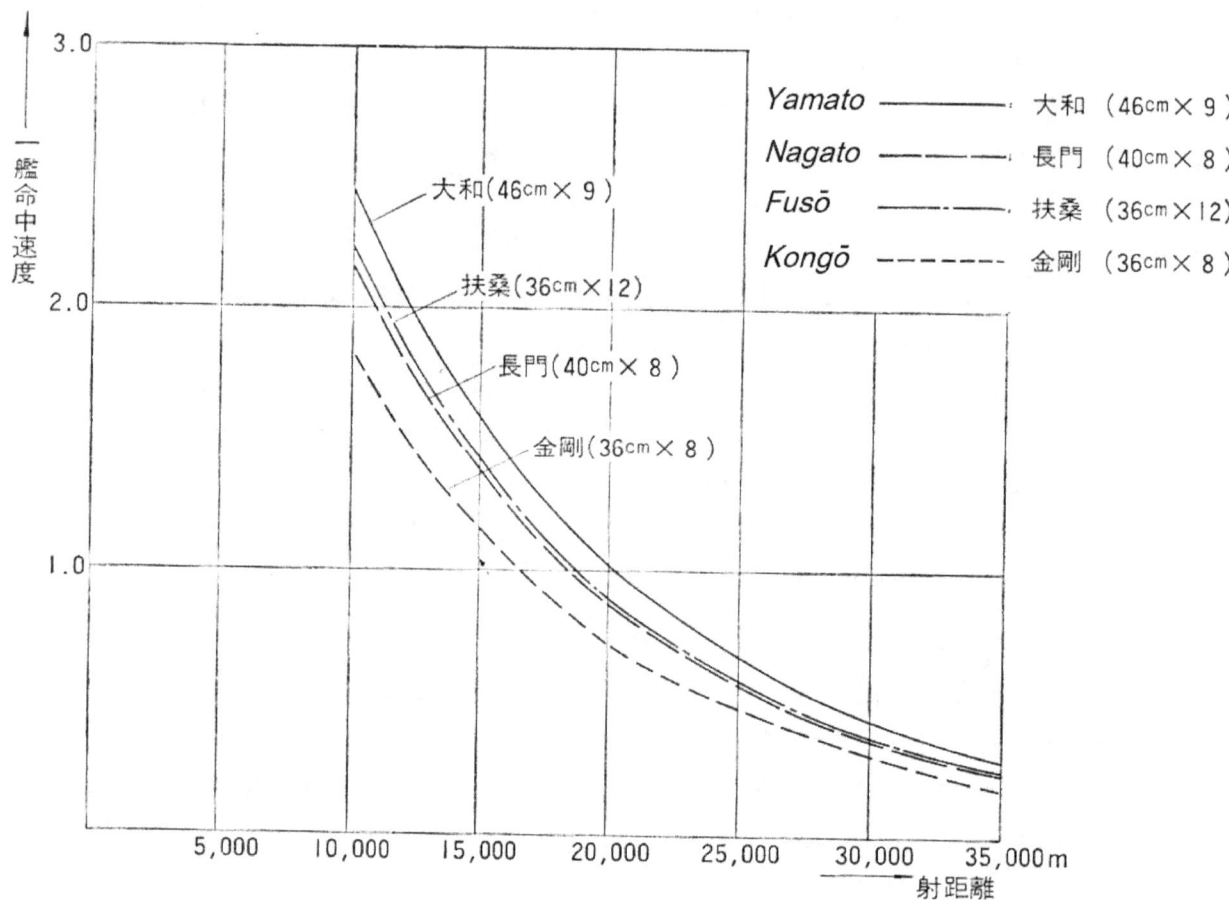

Figure 2-19: Curve of hitting rate with all guns firing. Vertical axis shows hitting rate per minute and the horizontal axis shows the firing range (*Kaigun Hōjutsu-shi*)

---

[90] The height of the second turret was decided with reference to the height of the first one, and then the height of the secondary guns, conning tower and the high-angle guns were decided. This makes obvious the big influence upon the centre of gravity of the ship.

[91] For this purpose the guns of the second turret had to have about 10° elevation when trained in normal position.

The fundamental requirements for the design and construction of the main gun turrets were as follows:

(1) The armor thicknesses have to provide protection against 46-cm AP projectiles fired from the same distances as in case of hull armor, e.g. vertical from 20,000 m upwards, horizontal up to 30,000 m. Therefore, protection cannot be penetrated if the fighting takes place at ranges between 20,000 m and 30,000 m and this means that the ship was immune within this zone. The roof may not be penetrated by the impact of a 250-kg general-purpose (GP) bomb released from 1,000 m height.

(2) The ammunition transport from the magazines deep in the hull to the guns should be quickly made by motor drive even if the ship rolls and pitches heavily. Continuous salvo firing may not be influenced by ammunition transport.

(3) Within the powder magazine mechanical transport using a motor is prohibited.[92]

(4) The training part has to be divided into effective flame protection areas. If there is a fire in one position inside of this part it shall not spread to other areas.

(5) Even if the ship is maneuvering at high speed and is rolling and pitching in a direction different from that of the target, the training of the main gun turrets and the elevation of the main guns have to be quick and accurate in order to open fire as soon as the firing values are transmitted.

(6) If the barbette and roller path have large diameters the beam of the hull may have to be increased, therefore the diameters have to be kept as small as possible. Also the dimensions of the gun house have to be decided after considering this requirement.

(7) As it is a triple turret the distance between the guns may not fall short of a determined value. If the distance is too small, the projectiles will

---

[92] This was the biggest reason why the rate of fire could not be improved. For firing one projectile 360 kg of propellant powder was necessary, and this weight was divided by six to have six bags of 60 kg each. This was the upper limit for manual transport. If the total amount would have been divided by eight the time for loading would increase by one-fourth; therefore the distribution into six bags was decided upon. However, much effort was made to reduce the time for the execution of the other processes.

interfere with each other in case of salvo firing, to bring about differences in ballistic. However, the requirement stated earlier has to be considered when deciding the distance.

(8) The openings in the front shield for the guns have to be made as small as possible.

(9) In order to not reduce the rate of fire the various operation processes have to be checked from every angle and their functions have to be well conceived.[93]

(10) The strength of the turret is decided by the training part. If a salvo is fired the strength has to be sufficient to take up all the stresses without any deformation in any part. In order to obtain the required strength the distance between the centre of the roller part and the trunnions of the guns in horizontal position should be made as small as possible.

(11) The various divisions of the main gun turret should be controlled by "instruction devices" (*shiji sōchi*), so that either electrical or mechanical control (*sōra*; also steering) or instruction (*shiji*), transmitting (*tsūshin*) devices (*sōchi*) have to be mounted at each function position. In addition, so-called "failure proof devices" (safety gears) have to be installed in the control circuits to avoid any malfunction. No process may be executed on the basis of faulty information.

(12) In case of damage or disorder of the principal equipment inside the turret the firing of the main guns should be continued. Therefore, this equipment should be duplicated by reserve ones.

(13) The elevation/depression movement of the three guns should be executed independently from each other.

(14) The total weight of the gun turret should be kept to a minimum.

(15) The recoil distance should be about three times the calibre. However, the time necessary for recoiling and running-out should always be the same, irrespective of the elevation angle of the guns. In order to increase the rate of fire by the reduction of the time necessary for the movement of the barrels the recoil distance should be made as short as possible.

---

[93] In other words: New approaches had to be found.

(16) If the turret is trained to the target the area of the front shield, directed towards the target, should be as small as possible with a favorable inclination for protection against projectiles.

These requirements were considered and applied in the design of the new turret whenever possible and the result was a turret whose principal dimensions, weights and capabilities are shown in the next table. The fundamental structure was a mixture of the turret mounted on the British-built battle cruiser *Kongō* (ordered in 1910 from Vickers and delivered in 1913) and that of the 20.3-cm main gun turrets of the heavy cruisers, but there were numerous novel items in detail so that the Type 94 40-cm turret, as it was officially called, should be classified as *Nihon Kaigun shiki hōtō*, i.e. Japanese Navy main gun turret type, designed roughly 20 years after those made for the battleships of the *Nagato* class, which were replicas of the Vickers type turret.

Table 2-10. Summarised explanations of the motion actions of the 46-cm triple turret

Item	Explanation
Type of gun turret	Type 94 triple turret; three guns per turret
Calibre and barrel length	45 calibre 46-cm (bore of gun 46-cm × calibre length = 46-cm × 45 = 20.70 m)
Elevation and depression	+45°/−5°
Operation	Turbo-hydraulic pump using water and mineral oil ("congolene oil") with 70 kg/cm² pressure. Pump running with 3,700–4,000 rpm and developing 3,600 hp normal and 5,000 hp overload (for details see separate table). Training by two separate 500 hp hydraulic pumps of which only one was in operation and supported by a 100 hp electric motor (for details see separate tables)
Power supply	Via ring main; one turbine pump per turret in operation and one pump for three turrets in reserve
(1) Gun cradle and slide	
Recoil	After firing the gun recoils with the slide; this movement is stopped by two recoil cylinders (*chūtai-ki*; also called firing liquid resistance brakes [*ekitai kōryoku*]) using glycerine and water
Opening and closing of breech	For opening of the breech (*bisen*) at the end of the recoil and closing after reloading a 100 hp hydraulic motor is used
Run-out	After stopping at the end of the recoil motion the gun is run out to its former position by two

	pneumatic run-out cylinders (*suishin-ki* or HP air tubes) with initial pressure of 90kg/cm². The run-out speed is controlled by a hydraulic cylinder using glycerine and water
(2) Loading process	
Loading angle	For loading the shell and the propellant powder bags the gun is fixed at 3° elevation (fixed loading angle)
Loading (*sōten-ban* = loading platform)	Separate hoists for transport of shells ("pusher type" hoist transporting the shell in a vertical position until tilting it into the tilting bucket in the gun house) and propellant powder cage (wire type hoist operated by a hydraulic winch mechanism transporting the powder cage from the lower (for centre gun) and upper (for outer guns) handing rooms to gun house behind the breech
Fuse setting	Manual either in shell handing room (fuse protectors were used to prevent damage) or on waiting tray in gun house
Ramming (*sōten-ki* = loading machine)	Separate, hydraulic motor operated gun house rammers were used for ramming shell and powder bags (six one-sixth charges) by a single rammer stroke
(3) Elevation and depression of guns	
Vertical angle type (*fugyō-yōshiki*)	Each gun can be laid separately
Power source (*fugyō-doryoku*)	One hydraulic piston and cylinder is connected to each gun and the gun is laid using the trunnion (*mimi-jiki*) as centre. The connection of the piston rod to the gun slide is moveable longitudinally along the gun
(4) Ammunition supply	
Shell supply hoist (*yōdan*) type (*yōshiki*)	Each gun is continuously supplied by one (pair) of pusher type shell hoists (*yōdan-ki*) from the shell handing room (*kyūdan-shitsu*) to a position behind the breech
Power (*dōryoku*)	The shells are transported step by step using hydraulic power
Shifting of the shell (*dangan-idō*)	For the transport of the shell in the shell rooms (magazines) and handing rooms hydraulic power is used
Powder supply hoist type (*yōyaku yōshiki*)	Six one-sixth powder bags are loaded into one cage and each gun is supplied directly, either from the upper (outer guns) or lower (centre

	gun) handing room to a position behind the breech and are ready for ramming
Powder supply hoist power(*dōryoku*)	Wire type hoists operated by a hydraulic (piston and cylinder) winch mechanism
Reserve equipment (*yobi sōchi*)	Considering the breakdown of the main power of the shell (*dangan*) or powder (*sōyaku*) supply hoists a hydraulic motor (pump) (*suiryoku-gendōki*) is fitted additionally
(5) Targeting	
Fire director targeting (*hōiban shōjun*)	Targeting is executed by the fire director located atop the foremast (main) or after mast (secondary). The guns in the turrets are laid according to the transmitted firing data (TT & TE) from the computer (calculation device [*keiki*]) to the turrets via a three-phase selsyn "follow-the-pointer" system and are fired by the layer in the fire director (for details see the chapter on fire control)
Safety arrangement (for firing)	Only the guns that are laid and trained correctly (i.e. the red base pointer [*kishin*] and the white chasing pointer [*tsuishin*] coincides) by the fire director can be fired; otherwise the electric circuit is interrupted
Turret targeting (*hōsoku shōjun*)	In case of not using fire director targeting the guns are laid by targeting at the gun side using the telescopes fitted in the turret
Targeting telescope (*hōsoku shōjun yo-bōenkyō*)	Three 10-cm targeting telescopes (*shōjun-kyō*, one per gun) of periscope type (*senbokyō shiki*) are fitted in each gun turret. They can be elevated/depressed + 10° to –10° and trained freely 160 mils right and 130 mils left. These telescopes are fitted near the front shield. In addition a 6.5-cm type is situated aft and is used for cross-levelling. Others are for training (at the centre gun) and elevation (both left and right guns)
15-m rangefinder (*15-m-yō sokkyogi*)	Rangefinders of 15 m base length are fitted in the turrets and atop the foremast (the latter a triple type). They measure the range to the target and deliver the data to the computer
(6) Ventilation	
Fresh air (*kyūki*)	Three 2.5-hp electric fans (*dendō kyūkiki*) are used for supplying of fresh air
Exhaust (*haiki*)	Three 5-hp electric exhaust fans (*dendō haikiki*) are fitted to transport the consumed air outside (Report O-45 (N) says <u>five</u> exhaust fans)
(7) Training	
Training type (*senkai yōshiki*)	The turret is trained to left and right by a training

		rack fixed to the ring bulkhead and a straight-toothed (training) pinion fitted to the rotating part of the turret
Hydraulic motor (*suiryoku-gendōki*)		The training gear is operated by two special 500-hp vertical swashplate (hydraulic) engines of which only one is used at a time; the other being in reserve
Starter motor (*kidō-gendōki*)		At the beginning of the training and the reversion of the turning direction the 500-hp hydraulic motor is helped by the use of 100-hp Williams-Janney (the IJN said only Janney or "Johnny") variable speed gear and motor (known as "special No. 20 type oil pressure controller")

Table 2-11. Some principal dimensions, weights and capacities of the 46-cm triple turret

Item	Dimension	Explanation
(8) Principal dimensions		
Gun house front shield	660-mm VH	According to *Shōwa Zōsen-shi*, vol. 1, p. 701 (650-mm VH are shown in the protection drawing)
Gun house sides	250-mm MNC	According to *Shōwa Zōsen-shi*, vol. 1, p. 701 (as vertical armor should have been NVNC)
Gun house rear	190-mm NVNC	According to protection drawing
Gun house roof	270-mm MNC	NVNC according to the protection drawing but supposed to be MNC on basis of various Japanese sources (see footnote 18 in chapter 5)
Roller path diameter	12,274 mm	This is the diameter measured from the vertical centreline of a roller to that of the roller on the opposite side. The internal diameter is 11,500 mm, the external diameter 13,050 mm. The revolving part of the turret turned upon the roller path situated on top of the ring bulkhead
Height from centre of roller path to longitudinal bore axis	5,250 mm	This is the height measured from the centre of the roller path to the centre line of gun if laid horizontally ($\pm 0°$). (Given as 4,400 mm in Report O-45 (N) but four Japanese sources state this value)

Distance from centre of rotation to trunnions	3,250 mm	Measured in the fore and aft line from the turret centreline to the vertical centre of the trunnions
Distance between centrelines of guns	3,050 mm	Three guns are mounted in one turret and this marks the distance between the longitudinal axis of two guns
Length of recoil	1,430 mm	The gun recoils when fired by the pressure of the decomposition of the propellant powder and the length of recoil is the motion the gun and slide make respective to the cradle
(9) Various capacities/performances		
Elevation and depression speed	8°/s	The gun turns around the trunnion either upwards (elevation) or downwards depression)
Training speed	2°/s	The turret turns either to the right or to the left with the vertical axis of the turret as centre
Shell and powder supply rate	3 shells/2 × 6 powder bags per minute	The time necessary for the transport of the powder cage from the handing room (shell from the shell handing room) to behind the breech
Firing rate and retardation of firing the centre gun	One round in 40 s	Each of the three guns of one turret are capable of firing one round every 40 seconds. This means that three rounds could be fired in two minutes at maximum elevation. In case of salvo firing the centre gun fired with a delay of 0.3 seconds to preclude the projectiles from intervening with each other during the flight *
(10) Weights		
Guns (including breech)	495 tons	The weight of one gun amounts to 165 tons and three guns amount to 495 tons (3 × 165 tons)
Elevation and depression parts (excluding guns)	228 tons	The weight of one gun carriage (cradle and slide) is 76 tons (3 × 76 = 228 tons)
Turntable (excluding guns, elevating parts and armor)	350 tons	Including trunnion brackets and (supposedly) gun turret frame
Remainder of training	647 tons **	Including the hydraulic power

parts below turntable		system and HP air system
Gun house armor	790 tons	
Total weight	2,510 tons ***	Revolving part plus a number of shells stored in this part. Three turrets mounted per ship. The total weight amounts to 7,530 tons
Weight of shell	1,460 kg	Type 91 AP
Weight of propellant powder per round	360kg ****	Service (common) charge. The propellant powder for one shell is divided into six silk-made bags, of 60kg each, in order to enable manual transport

(11) Fundamental ballistic data

Muzzle velocity	780 m/s	Obtained with service (common) charge. For testing the strength of the gun a "strong" charge is used. There is also "reduced" and "weak" charges
Maximum firing range	42,025 m	This range is obtained at 45° maximum elevation angle. The theoretical maximum firing range (said to be 42,108 m) would be obtained with an elevation angle of 48° *****
Time of flight	98.6 s	At 40,836 m (corresponding to 40° elevation angle) it is 89.42s

(12) General judgement of performance and problems

Performance	Almost satisfactory. Blast at firing was very severe and particularly troublesome in the area of the tower bridge
Problems	Biggest problem was the great consumption of lubricating oil for training and propellant hoist gears, followed by the leakage of water from the pipes. The latter was a common problem of all turrets of the IJN.
	There were also complaints about the noise generated by the rollers in the "coaster" (training) gear and "difficulties" in hoisting projectiles at more than 5° rolling. However, the latter was neither specified in the reports nor mentioned in the Japanese sources consulted. The later fitted reinforcements often lacked the blast shields because these were not available in time. To protect the gunners simple steel shelters of 5.5-mm or 6-mm MS were given, to offer an imperfect protection, at least.

> But some of them were useless and depending on the direction of firing of the main guns, these weapons could not be manned and it is said that some were blown off the deck.
>
> In contrast, Mr. Kozuka Sansaku, once layer (*shashu*) of *Musashi*'s #2 main gun, and also other gunners, stated that the noise inside the gun house was remarkably low even when a salvo was fired. However, the air pressure in the gun house suddenly and tremendously changed (as a reaction of the firing) and this was the cause of impairment of hearing of several gunners

Notes:

* Fukada Masao in "Story of the Development of Warship Mechanisms". This is in striking contrast to the 0.08 s given in Report O-45 (N). However, Fukada explains that 0.1 s was applied to the 15.5-cm secondary guns and it gradually increased to 0.3 s in the *Yamato* class. In case of 0.3 s the shells fired from the right and left guns were approx. 230 m in front of the gun mouths. The Type 98 firing time retarding device (*98 Shiki happō chiensōchi*) was also known as Type 98 firing delay system. The urgent necessity to develop this system was recognised because intervening had been ascertained as the largest cause of the wide dispersion of salvos fired from the 20-cm (actually 20.32-cm) guns of the heavy cruisers. Afterwards dispersion was remarkably reduced. For the *Yamato* class 450 m to 500 m at maximum firing range are stated and in the Battle of Samar the exceptionally small dispersion is pointed out in American records.

** Below the turntable were two shell supply (handing) rooms in which 180 shells were stored vertically. These rooms belonged to the rotating part of the turret. Consequently the weight of these projectiles (262.8 tons) must be included in that weight.

*** Figures on turret weight are contradicting. In *Kimitsu Heiki no Zenbō* ("Secret Weapons of the IJN") these figures can be found:

- Guns (3 units) 495 tons (1 gun 165 tons)
- Cradle and accessories (3 units) 228 tons (1 gun 65 tons)
- Turntable 350 tons
- Remainder of revolving part below the turntable 647 tons (would mean ~263 tons, including shells)
- Gun house armor   790 tons

- Total   2,510 tons

Kaigun Hōjutsu-shi ("History of Naval Gunnery") says 2,565 tons, pp. 21–22, 2,510 tons, pp. 21 & 25, and 2,200 tons, p. 661. On p. 114 it is said that the revolving part weighed 2,265 tons. It is also noted that half the number of shells (180 = approx. 260 tons) were stored in the revolving part because shell supply during the training of the turret "becomes a little difficult". "The total weight of the revolving part during the early stage of an engagement was approx. 2,700 tons ..." but the author does not say anything about the written calculation that 2,265 plus approx. 260 tons (2,525) is approx. 2,700 tons. *Shōwa Zōsen-shi* ("History of Shipbuilding in the Shōwa Era") says 2,265 tons for the revolving part only, p. 701, and 2,500 tons as a round figure. *Senkan* Yamato • Musashi *Sekkei to Kenzō* ("Design and Construction of the *Yamato* and *Musashi*") says 2,774 tons, p. 156. Fukuda Keiji's *Gunkan Kihon Keikaku Shiryō* ("Outline of the Fundamental Design of Warships") has several figures (45-cm 45-cal 2,354 tons [left column], 2,630 tons and 2,573.51 tons [right column–different designs?]), p. 157, and *Nihon Kaigun Kansai Heiki Daizukan* ("All about Japanese Naval Shipboard Weapons") says 2,510 tons, p. 47. Matsumoto Kitarō (*Senkan* Yamato • Musashi *Sekkei to Kenzō*) was a naval architect and not a gunnery specialist and the authors do believe his turret weight figures to be incorrect. Fukuda's data cannot be identified as he refers, apparently, to designs. The authors have decided to use 2,510 tons for the revolving part.

****As for the weight of the charge—360 kg (6 × 60 kg) or 330 kg (6 × 55 kg)—sources are in disagreement. 330 kg has been stated in, i.e., *Maru*, #400, (by Engineer Ōtani Toyokichi), *Senkan* Yamato *Kenzō Hiroku* ("All about super-battleship *Yamato*"), p. 64, *Kaigun Hōjutsu-shi*, p. 25, *Senkan* Yamato • Musashi *Sekkei to Kenzō*, p. 156, Report O-45 (N) "Japanese 18" Gun Mounts", p. 16, and by the late Rear-Admiral Takasu Kōichi. 360 kg can be found in, i.e., *Kaigun Hōjutsu-shi* ("History of Naval Gunnery"), p 21, *Senkan* • *Jun-yōsenkan* ("Battleships & Battle Cruisers"), p. 412, *Umi to Sora* ("Sea and Sky"), 6/1958, p. 51 (the sixth part of a contribution about the development of naval guns and gunnery in Japan), and in the Kure drawing (see figure 2-1).

Tech. Vice-Admiral Shimizu Fumio[94] and Tech. Rear-Admiral Sendō Michizō[95] wrote the part on the *Yamato* class in *Kimitsu Heiki no Zenbō* and they firmly stated 360 kg (6 × 60 kg). Both Shimizu and Sendō were ordnance experts and the authors trust that their figure is the correct one.

***** It is said that with the theoretical elevation angle of 50° the range was 42,005 m and the time of flight 106.66 s. As maximum range was with 48° it had to be shorter at 50° and the time of flight longer due to the higher maximum trajectory.

Table 2-12. Table showing the gradual increase of range with the same type of powder

	36-cm	41-cm	46-cm
Propellant weight (kg)	142.8/100% (132/100%)	219/153.36% (224/169.70%)	360/252.10% (330/250.00%)
Projectile weight (kg)	673.5/100% (635/100%)	1,020/151.45% (1,000/157.48%)	1,460/216.78% (1,460/229.92%)
Maximum range (m)	34,450/100% (same)	38,300/111.18% (same)	42,000/121.92% (same)

Source: *Shōwa Zōsen-shi*, p. 701.

Note: From the above table 360 kg appears more probable because the same type of powder was used.

Table 2-13. Comparison of main gun properties of the battleships of the *Yamato* and *Nagato* classes

Item	Yamato class	Nagato class
Calibre (cm)	46	41
Length of barrel (m)	20.7 (45-cal)	18.4 (45-cal)

---

[94] Vice-Admiral Shimizu Fumio (1894–1965). Graduated in 1917 from the Engineering Faculty, University of Tōkyō, and was in the same year promoted to *kaigun zōhei chūgishi* (ordnance/sub-lieutenant). He was supervisor for ordnance (*zōhei kantokukan*) in Britain in 1922–1924. In 1941 (as rear-admiral) he became chief of the Gunnery Division at Kure N.Y. (*Kure Kaigun Kōshō Hōshō buchō*) and one year later he became chief of the No. 1 Bureau of the Navy Technical Department (*Kansei Honbu Dai Ichi buchō*) and ended the war as vice-admiral and director of Toyokawa N.Y. (*Toyokawa kōshōchō*). A navy yard actually specialised in ordnance production.

[95] Rear-Admiral Sendō Michizō (1895–1969). Graduated in 1920 from the Powder Department, Engineering Faculty, University of Tōkyō, and was during the same year promoted to *kaigun zōhei chūi* (ordnance/sub-lieutenant). He travelled to Europe and the USA in 1925–1926. In 1941, as captain, he became chief of the No. 2 Powder Yard Research Division (*Dai Ni Kayakushō Kenkyū buchō*). He ended the war as a rear-admiral and professor at the University of Tōkyō.

Weight of shell (kg)	1,460	1,020
Type of powder	DC$_1$ (Ø 11 mm)	DC$_1$ (Ø 10.2 mm)
Amount of powder (1 round) (kg)	360	216
Muzzle velocity (m/s)	780	780
Maximum barrel pressure (kg/cm²)	3,100–3,200	3,080
Maximum firing distance (m)	41,000	37,700

Sources: (1) "Secret Weapons of the IJN" (*Kimitsu Heiki no Zenbō*), p. 286, composition of powder, same source, p. 287; (2) "History of Naval Gunnery" (*Kaigun Hōjutsu-shi*), p. 72; (3) Unpublished manuscript "Japanese Naval Powder" by Hans Lengerer, pp. 12–16.

Notes:

(1) The so-called non-volatile solvent powder was invented in Germany in 1912.

(2) After the end of World War One a Japanese delegation, headed by then Vice-Admiral Katō Hiroharu (Kanji) and Rear-Admiral Gotō Tatsuo, visited Germany to inspect the military industry. After obtaining information the manufacturing equipment for this type of powder was purchased and the Köln-Rottweil Powder Company granted the manufacture and utilisation rights. Four German engineers were hired.

(3) Research in Japan was undertaken at Hiratsuka Naval Powder Factory by a Joint Research Committee (the IJN and the IJA) in 1920. Experimental production began in July 1921 followed by "real" production in April 1922 and the adoption of the IJN's first non-volatile solvent powder (Type 13 powder) in December 1924.

(4) On 12 May 1933, the Type 93. No. 1 smokeless powder (abbreviated DC$_1$/DT$_1$, composed of 41% nitroglycerine, 51.8% mixed nitrocellulose, 4.5% centralite [biphenyl-diethyl urea], 2% OTU [orthotolylurethane] and 0.7% other, mostly inorganic components) was adopted, particularly for the 40-cm-gunned[96] battleships and later also for the 46-cm-gunned battleships *Yamato* and *Musashi*.

---

[96] The actual calibre was 41-cm but the official classification was changed to 40-cm gun.

The background was as follows: Compared with the volatile solvent powder of the Two-Year-Type, which used strong gun cotton, the new powder was weaker. This, of course, could be compensated by using a larger amount of Type 13 powder but there were narrow limitations. E.g. the powder hoists and powder bag containers for the 41-cm guns of the battleships *Nagato* and *Mutsu*, designed for the use of the Two-Year-Type powder, were not suitable for the new powder when the same trajectory was to be obtained. In view of the outranging strategy of the IJN, both in terms of guns and torpedoes, it was deemed absolutely necessary to maintain the same trajectory as that obtained with the Two-Year-Type powder. This led to the introduction of the Type 93 powder series.

(5) In case of the 40-cm guns of the *Nagato* class 110 C_2 powder (Ø 11.06 mm, length 450 mm) and 102 DC_1 (Ø 10.20 mm, length 370 mm) were used; 219 kg when firing Type 91 AP shells and 224 kg when using Type 88 AP shells (*Kaigun Hōjutsu-shi*, p. 70). However, in the *Yamato* class this was avoided and only one type and one weight were used.

(6) The guns of the *Yamato* class were the culmination point of the outranging strategy as far as gunnery is concerned and the powder had to be chosen very carefully in order to obtain a range superseding that of all enemy ship guns. The main problem was the diameter of the powder cords. During firing trials with the test-produced 48-cm gun and the 40-cm gun the trajectory calculations—performed by Iso Megumi of the First Division of the Navy Technical Department—were found to be correct and the powder was decided after one experimental series. It was the 110 DC_1 powder with a diameter of 11.0 mm and a length of 370 mm.

(7) The powder was produced by the Hiratsuka Powder Factory and 360 kg, containing six powder bags of 60 kg each, were used for a full charge.

Countermeasures Against Blast

Utmost efforts had to be made for countermeasures against the immense blast. Experiments at the Kamegakubi range were conducted with real size and actually fitted models to observe the blast pressure (7.0 kg/cm² at a point

15 m in front of the muzzle; this was twice as much as that of the 41-cm guns of the *Nagato* class) and the strength of the structures. As a result, most of the objects usually mounted on the uppermost (weather) deck had to be shifted to inside the hull and the rest, including high-angle guns and anti-aircraft machine-guns, were given blast resistant shields. The ventilator heads were assembled into rigid big structures, resulting in a very clean upper deck, and the doors and covers were reinforced. The planes were stored in the hangar in the central part, just below the after upper deck, and the shipborne torpedo boats, the boat for the Commander-in-Chief, the launches and cutters, in the boat hangars on both sides at the stern, just below the same deck, and the hangars were closed by solid doors as protection from blast.

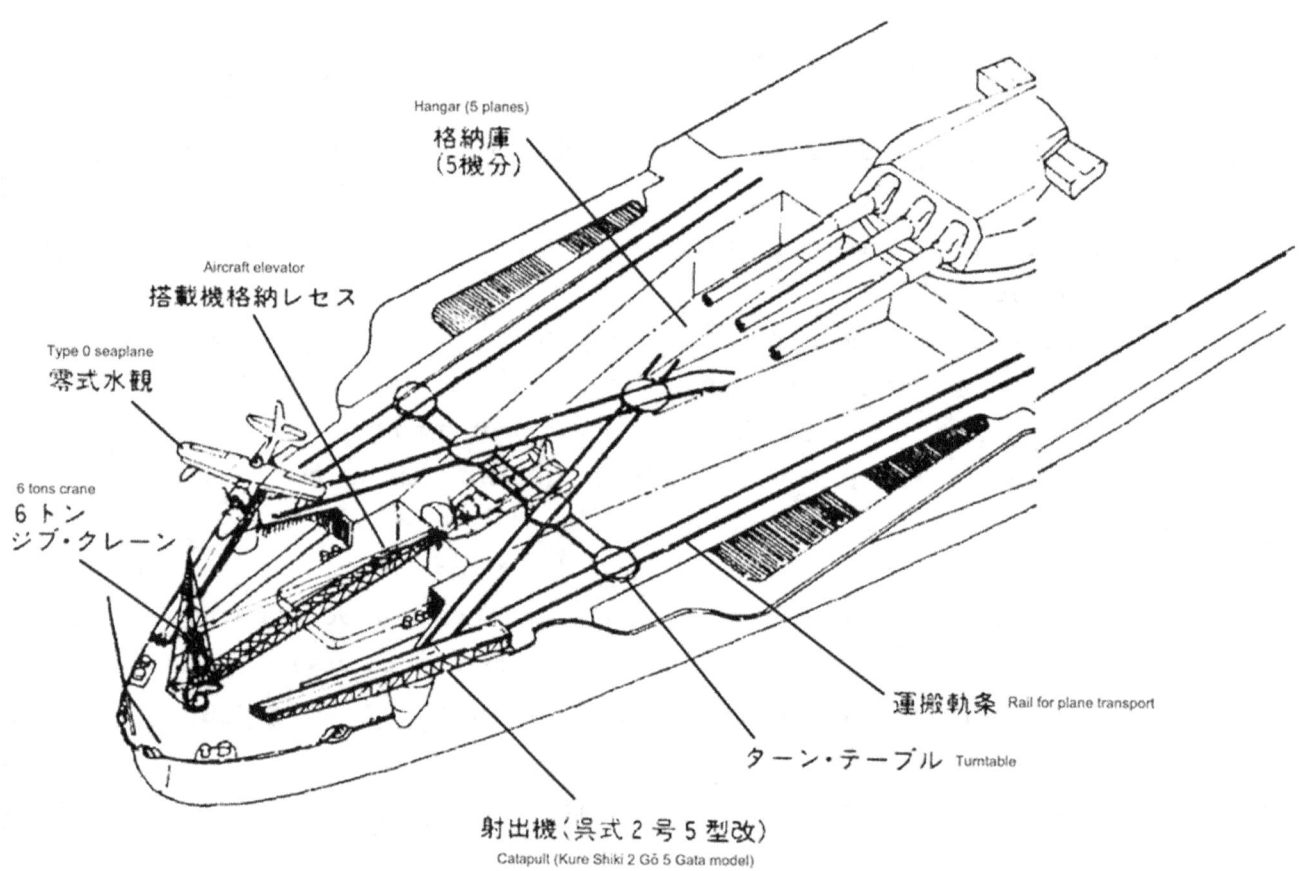

Figure 2-20: Aircraft installations on the quarter deck (*Nihon no Meikan* via Kitamura Kunio)

Increase of Anti-Aircraft Weapons

The secondary gun mounts on both sides amidships were removed early in 1944 in order to obtain space for the increase of AA weapons. When designed the danger of air attacks was greatly underestimated and only six 40-cal Type 89 12.7-cm twin high-angle guns and eight Type 96 25-mm triple machine-guns were conveniently distributed amidships. For the defense against strafing fighters two Type 93 13-mm twin machine-guns were mounted on the bridge tower. The success of the air forces in the first operational phase made the real danger potential of the aircraft evident and the close range AA armament of *Musashi* was strengthened by four shielded 25-mm triple mounts forward and aft of #2 and #3 secondary gun turrets in the first decade of July 1942.[97] In preparation for *A Gō Sakusen* (known as the Mariana Sea Battle) the AA armament was greatly increased according to a design made by the Kure Navy Yard and it was approved on 7 February 1944. On this basis the aforementioned secondary gun turrets were landed and *Yamato* was equipped with six more 12.7-cm twin high-angle guns. For their control two more Type 94 high-angle gun fire control systems were mounted, to make a total of four units. The high-angle guns for *Musashi* were not available in time so six 25-mm triple machine-guns, without blast protection shields, were mounted instead. The close range weapons were increased to a total of 23 (*Musashi* had 29 units but only six 12.7-cm twin high-angle guns) 25-mm triple mounts, and the number of Type 95 machine-gun fire directors to remotely control the fire of one group (usually three mounts) was doubled to 12. In addition, *Yamato* and *Musashi* mounted 26 and 25 single 25-mm machine-guns, respectively. *Yamato* retained the same number of 13-mm machine-guns but according to Naitō Hatsuho *Musashi* had a total of 18 instead of four.

The Mariana Sea Battle ended with disastrous results. The carrier force was destroyed and the ships had to fight under absolute enemy air supremacy. Therefore the Navy Ministry ordered the Navy Technical Department to further reinforce the AA armament. On the basis of plans again worked out by the Kure Navy Yard, and approved on 14 July 1944, five more 25-mm triple machine-guns were mounted to increase the total to 113 in *Yamato* and 130 in *Musashi*. According to the same source the 13-mm machine-guns of the latter

---

[97] Date according to Naitō Hatsuho, who also states that spare machine-guns were mounted at the same time. The authors are lacking the date these machine-guns were mounted on *Yamato*.

were reduced to four in two twin mounts, as in the *Yamato*.[98] According to Ishibashi Takao[99] and several other Japanese sources the *Yamato* had 50 triple and two single 25-mm machine-guns as well as two double 13-mm guns when she departed for her final mission.

The later fitted reinforcements often lacked the blast shields because these were not available in time. To protect the gunners simple steel shelters of 5.5-mm or 6-mm MS were given, to offer an imperfect protection, at least. But some of them were useless and depending on the direction of firing of the main guns, these weapons could not be manned and it is said that some were blown off the deck.

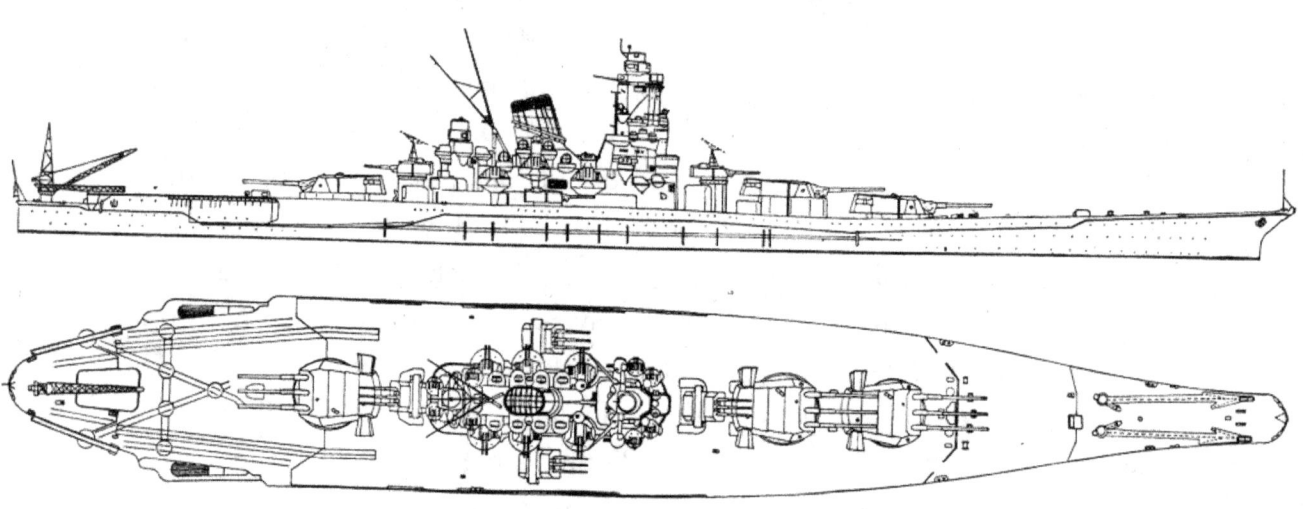

Figure 2-21: *Yamato* as completed in 1941 (*Nihon no Senkan*)

---

[98] These data coincide with table 3 in Fukui's "Japanese Naval Vessels Illustrated, 1869–1945," vol. 1, "Battleships & Battle Cruisers," p. 424.

[99] Ishibashi Takao, *Senkan • Jun-yōsenkan* ("Battleships & Battle Cruisers"), p. 385.

YAMATO CLASS

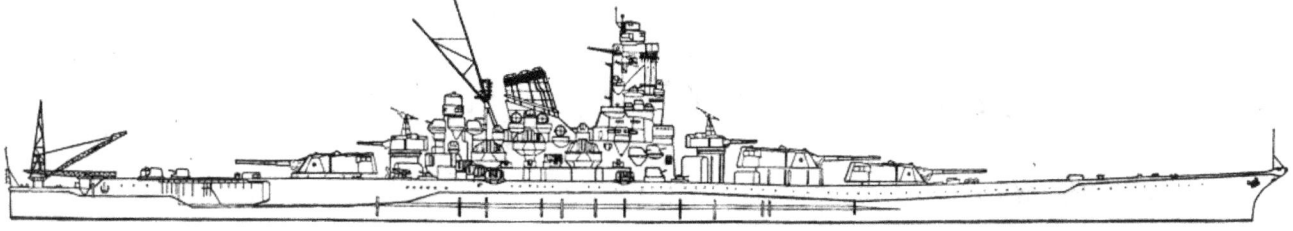

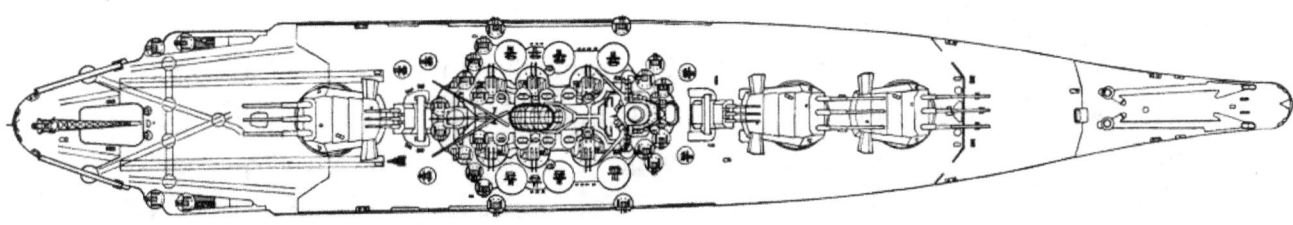

Figure 2-22: *Musashi* in 1944 just prior to Leyte Gulf. Her wing 15.5-cm turrets have been landed but note that she did not sport any extra 12.7-cm high-angle guns (*Nihon no Senkan*)

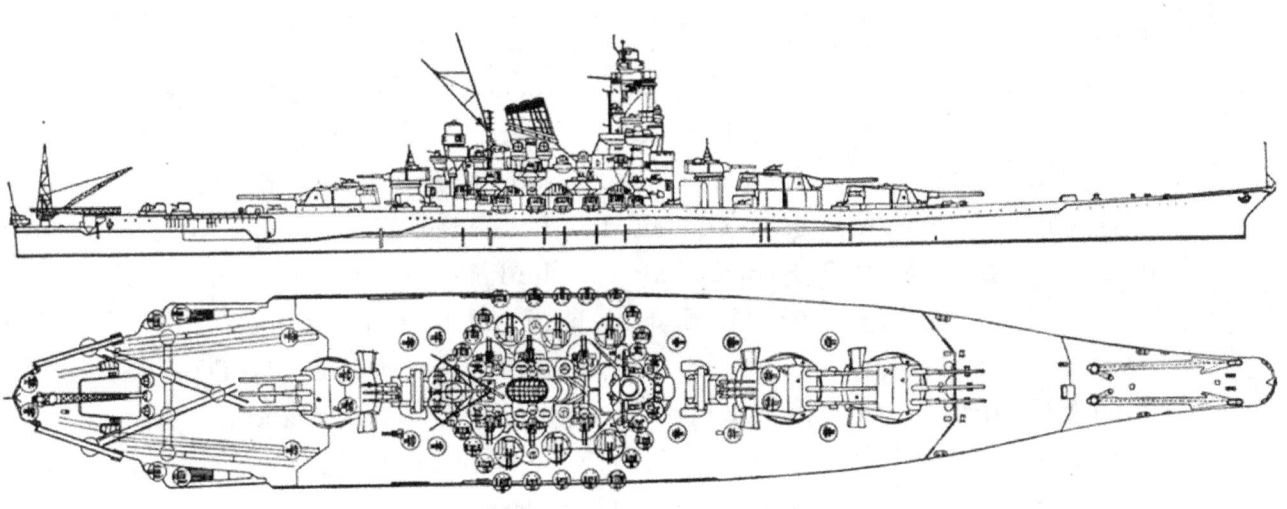

Figure 2-23: *Yamato* in 1945 with a substantially increased AA outfit (*Nihon no Senkan*)

Chapter 3 – Fire Control System

The Type 98 Fire Control System

Aiming at and firing on a target with a gun stationed on land is relatively simple but if executed from aboard a ship, which is maneuvering, rolling and pitching on the sea, on a target that is also moving and making, perhaps, evasive maneuvers, it becomes a complicated process providing a high grade of technical difficulties.

In order to obtain the maximum hit probability many factors have to be considered before a gun on sea can be fired. These factors form the basis for the calculation of the firing elements, which have to be calculated very quickly, and also accurately, for some of the factors change continuously. Most of these factors have to be estimated or measured immediately before firing. Among them only the outer and inner ballistics are known by pre-calculated tables and all the other ones have to be measured and calculated to the firing elements. Therefore, the shipboard gun fire control system (*kanpō shageki shiki sōchi*) is very complicated and multiple functional devices requiring exact technical solutions of numerous mathematical problems basing upon the most recent scientific findings. In other words, the fire control system represents the most precise instrument among the gunnery weapons.

In a gunnery duel ship versus ship the destruction of the enemy by making full use of dominance was an absolute condition. The following conditions were considered to be the fundamental pre-requisitions to attain this goal:[100] (1) How quickly can the target be detected and aimed at? (2) How quickly can the shells hit the target? (3) How quickly can the fighting power of the enemy be destroyed? In other words: "Hit first, hit hard and continue hitting."

The principal components of the fire control system were: (1) Type 98 Model 1 fire director (*hōiban*), (2) Type 98 computer (*shagekiban*) and (3) Type 98 target speed and bearing panel (*sokutekiban*). They were all newly designed for this class of battleships and represented the latest ideas, expressed in some

---

[100] From the Sino-Japanese War until 1944 the principal strategy of the Imperial Japanese Navy (IJN) was the decisive battle of the fleet (*kantai kessen*). The large calibre main guns of the capital ships were to play the main role and the 46-cm guns were the culmination of this strategy

novel parts such as: (a) Periscope-type optics with movable prism; addition of high-angle (HA) telescope for anti-aircraft firing and use of an improved spotting telescope in the fire director, (b) division into two principal independent systems, namely calculation and transmitting parts, use of electro-mechanical follow-ups and use of free gyro in the computer (c) use of an optical system instead of mechanical gears for providing target course and speed; (d) input of data from the fire director by power selsyn and (e) transmitting the solutions by selsyn to the computer. The triple type rangefinder (*sokkyogi*) had 15-m base length and combined the advantages of three different systems to improve measuring and reading. Like the other components it was also adopted for the first time for this ultimate battleship type.

If the gunnery armament (*hōkō heiki*) of a warship is compared with the human body the fire director (*hōiban* = bearing panel, *shōjun* = aiming; *sōchi* = equipment/device) and the rangefinder (*sokkyogi*) represent the eyes, the computer (*shagekiban*) is comparable to the brain and the guns correspond to the hands and legs (of a boxer to deliver blows). The fire control system (*shageki shiki sōchi*) is the combination of the eyes and the brain.

The firepower of the 45-cal Type 94 46-cm gun was considered to be second to none. To utilise it most effectively an excellent brain, sensitive nerves and strong hands and legs were necessary and these attributes were represented by the technical level of the fire control system and the abilities and experiences of its operators.

The fire director was placed high in the foremast and here was also the position of the gunnery officer who executed gunfire control. It represented the brain in the technical meaning but the gunnery officer was the real head. The rangefinder and the target speed and bearing panel (*sokutekiban*) were situated directly below the fire director and all three were connected to the computer and range-averager in the fire control station below the protective deck. Between the stations continuous data transmission took place using often separate electrical circuits. The latter represented the nerves (in the comparison with a human body) and combined the brain with the executive (the guns).

Figure 3-2 indicates the general arrangement of the main gun fire control system.

Rough Survey of the General Functions of the Fire Control System

(1) When the position of the enemy was roughly known through incoming information and verified by reconnaissance etc. the ship advanced

to the appropriate spot and was prepared for battle by the order "Clear for action!"

(2) If a target appeared, the layer and trainer in the fire director moved their periscopes until the aiming point (e.g. the lower part of the foremast or midships, near the waterline) was exactly in the centre of the cross-hairs. The training angle (*senkaikaku*) and the elevation angle (*fugyōkaku*) were transmitted to the calculation device[101] (*keisan-sōchi*) in the control room (*hatsureijo*).

(3) At the same time the distance to the target, called range, was measured by the rangefinders (*sokkyogi*), situated just below the main and reserve fire director stations and in the main gun turrets. The measured values were transmitted to the range-averager (*sokkyo heikinban*), in the fire control room, which averaged them and excluded obviously wrong values before sending them to the computer.

(4) The target speed and bearing panel (*sokutekiban*) received data from the computer and solved the equations for target course and target speed optically before transmitting the values to the computer.

(5) The computer processed these data together with some other inputs, calculated the corrections to the training and elevation angles transmitted from the fire director and added them to obtain total training and total elevation.

(6) These angles were transmitted via the information lines (*tsūshin-kairo*; the "nerves") to the main gun turrets and the fire director by angle communicators etc. using separate circuits.

(7) The trainer and the gun layers in the main gun turret actuated their handles for the hydraulic valves to train the turret and to elevate the guns to the ordered angles shown on their "follow the pointer" system receivers, see figure 3-3.

(8) If all the guns were correctly laid (visible in the fire command station) the gunnery officer ordered "Fire!" and the layer (who was also the firing hand–*shashu*) of the fire director pulled the trigger.

(9) The guns were fired electrically and the gunnery officer observed the positions of the splashes relative to the target through his spotting telescope and ordered corrections depending on his judgement.

---

[101] This is, of course, the computer (*shagekiban*).

(10) Corrections were transmitted to the computer and calculated to angle corrections, which were transmitted to the gun turrets where the necessary corrections in laying or training or both were executed before the next salvo.

(11) Aside from the previously mentioned angle communicators (*kakudo tsūshin*) several other means for information transmitting in the fire control circuits [such as signal lamps, bells, loud speaking telephones (*kōsei denwa*)[102] etc.] were used.

---

[102] Of sturdy construction and producing only few errors in distribution this particular telephone was often used in warships.

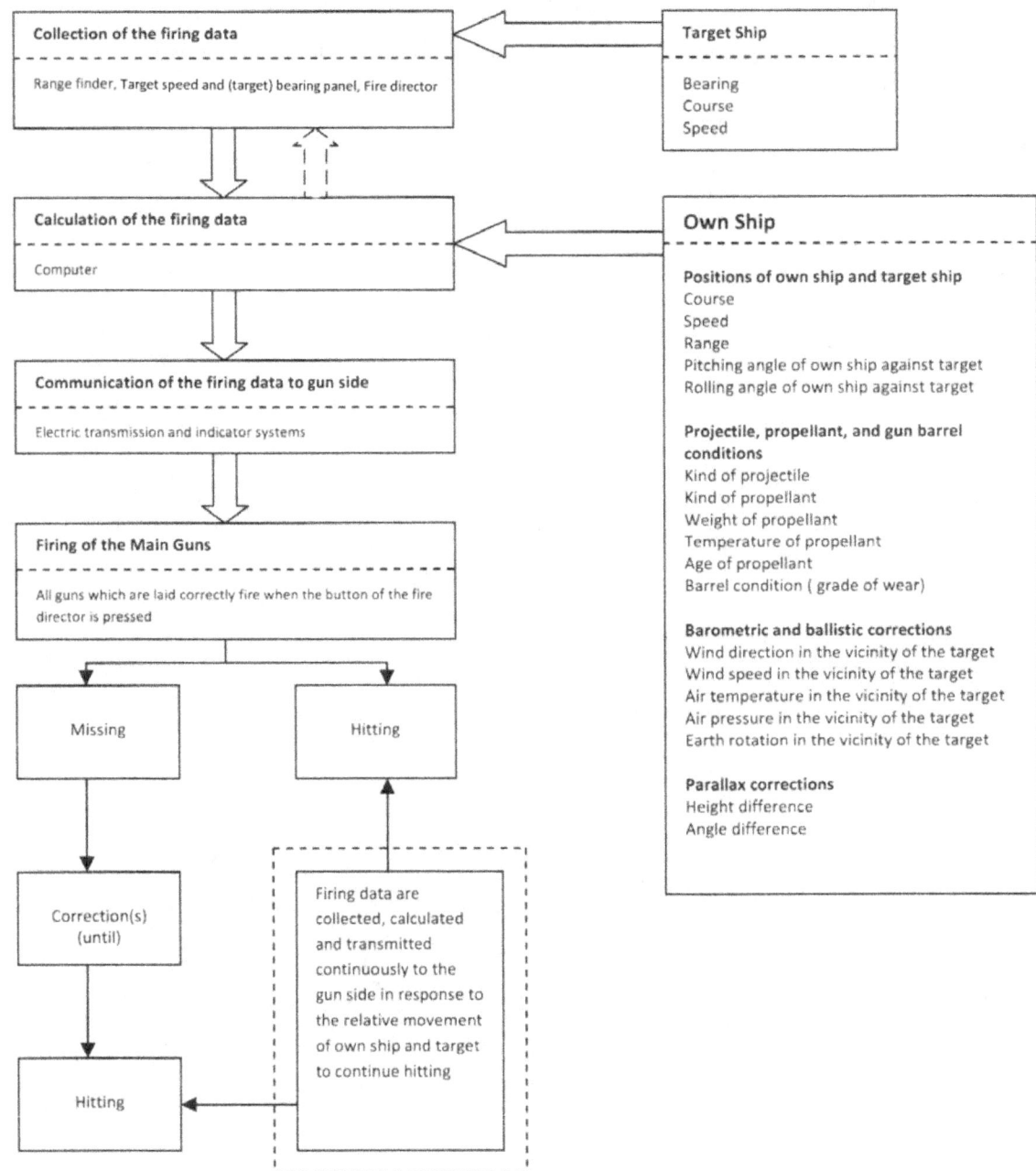

Figure 3-1: Rough scheme of fire control (Hans Lengerer)

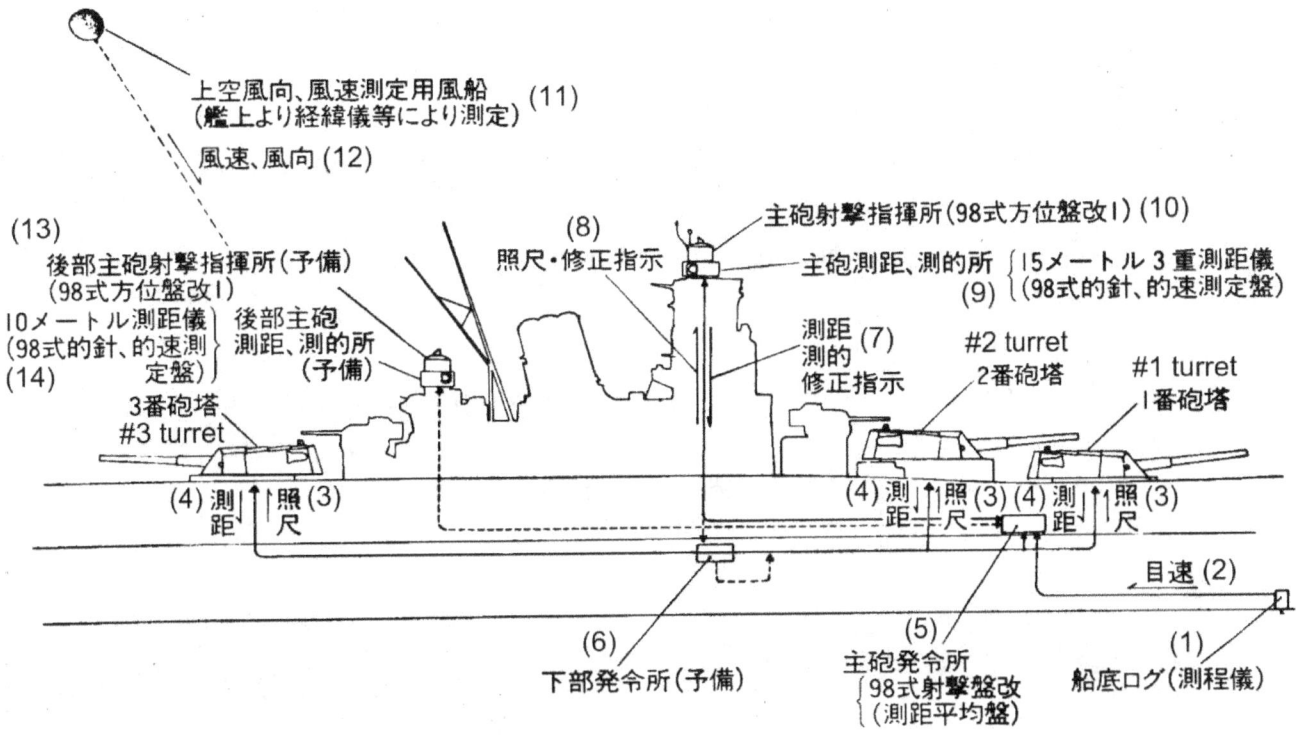

Figure 3-2: Fire control arrangement (*Maru*, #420, by permission of Ishibashi Takao)

Key to Figure 3-2:

(1) Ship's bottom log (*sokuteigi*) (measures own speed)

(2) Transmission of own speed to computer

(3) Input of TT and TE (scale = *shōsaku* = gun sight angle meaning both elevation and training) to turret indicators

(4) Range (*sokkyo*); measured by all rangefinders and delivered to range-averaging panel

(5) Main gun control station (*shuhō hatsureijo*) including a Type 98 Model 1 computer (*98 Shiki shagekiban Kai 1*) and range-averaging panel (*sokkyo heikinban*)

(6) Lower control station (reserve)

(7) Range and target bearing correction values (*sokkyo; sokuteki; shūsei shiji*) from fire director to control station

(8) Scale correction values (*shōshaku shūsei shiji*) from control station to fire director

(9) Main gun range and target speed and bearing measurement station (*sokkyo sokutekijo*) including the 15-m triple rangefinder (*hikari 48*

kanamono) and a Type 98 target speed and bearing panel (*98 Shiki tekishin tekisoku sokutekiban*)

(10) Main gun fire command station (*shagekishikijo*) with a Type 98 Model 1 fire director (*98 Shiki hōiban Kai 1*)

(11) Balloon for measuring wind direction, wind speed, air pressure (measured by shipboard instruments)

(12) Wind speed, wind direction transmission to ship

(13) After main gun fire command station (reserve) with a Type 98 Model 1 fire director

(14) After main gun range and target speed and bearing measurement station (reserve) with a 10-m triple rangefinder (*hikari 43 kanamono*) and a Type 98 target speed and bearing panel

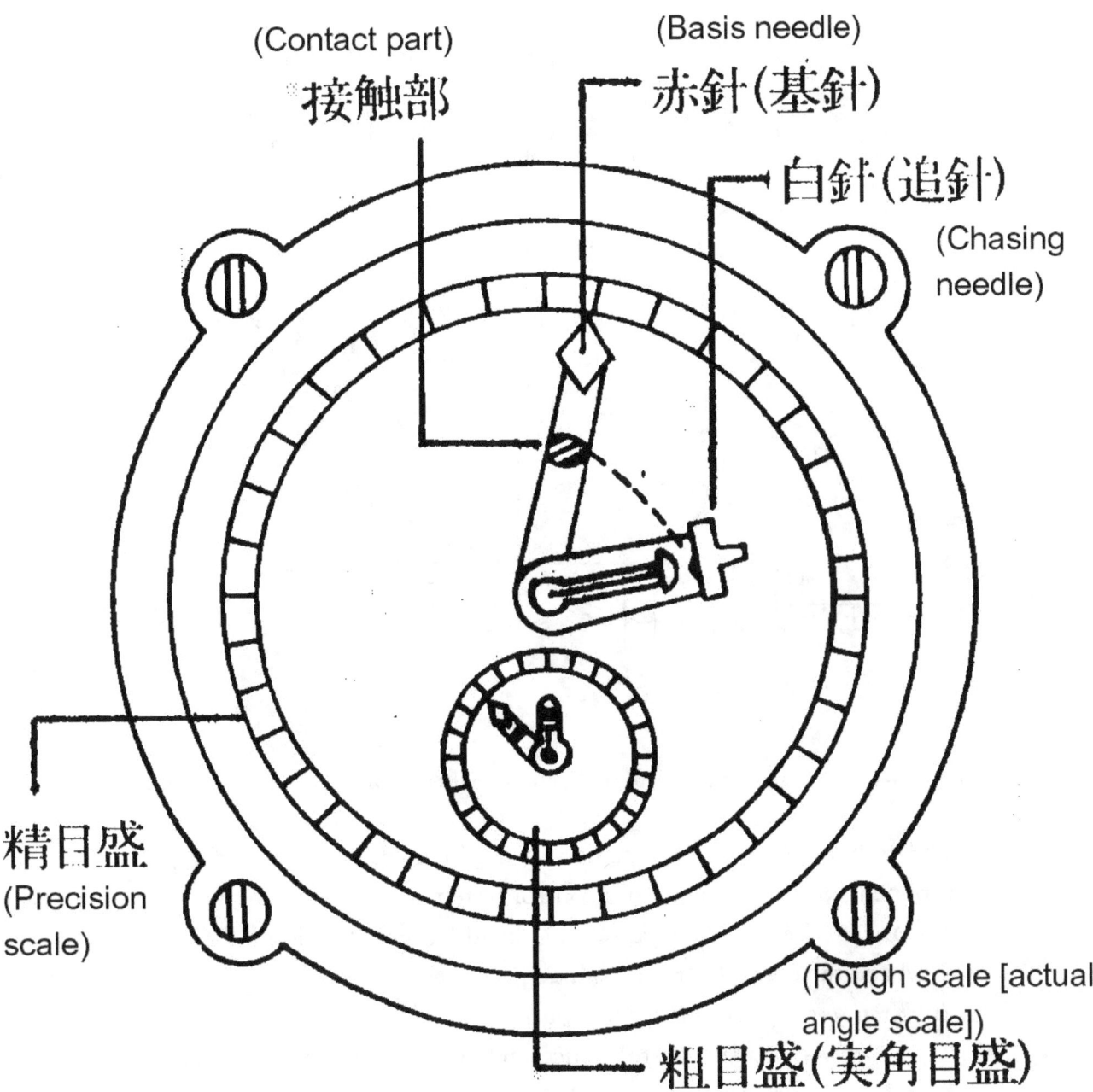

Figure 3-3: Training angle and elevation angle receiver [Gakken, #11]

201

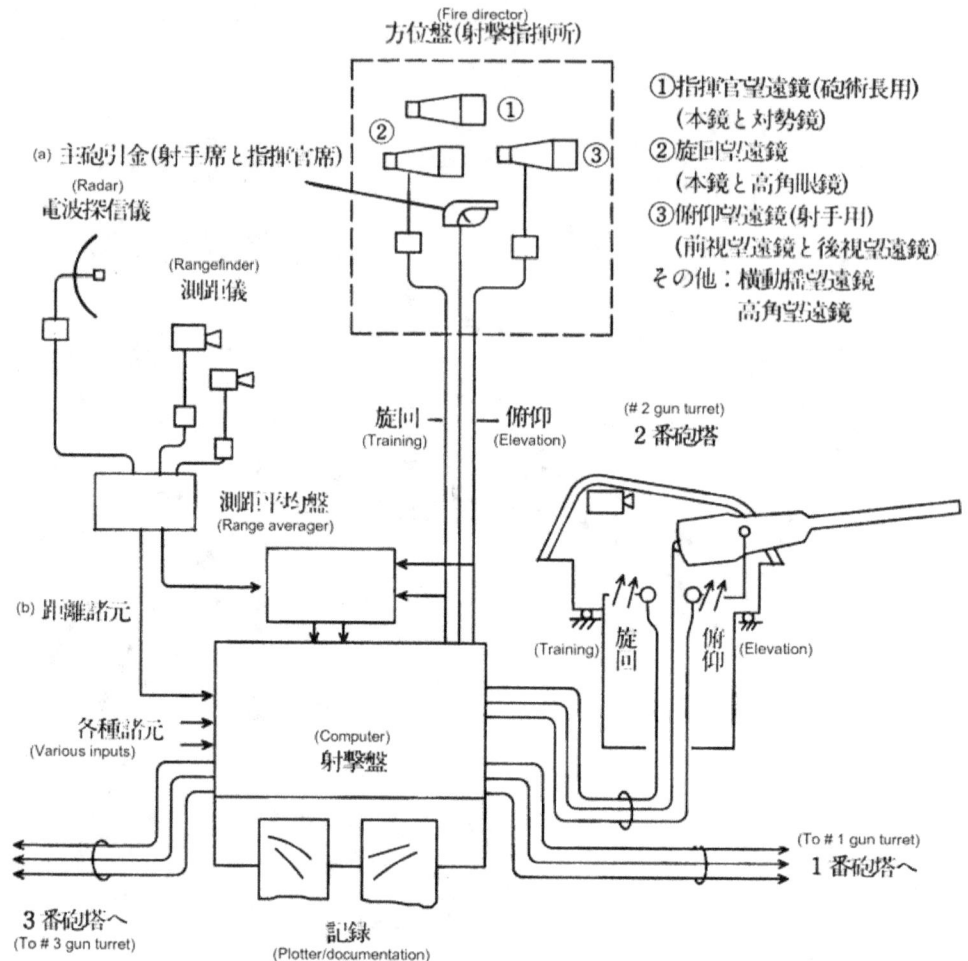

Figure 3-4: Fire control command main components (*shageki shiki keitō yōryōzu*) (Gakken, #11)

Figure 3-4 is a rough explanation of the interaction between the principal components of the main gun fire control system.

(a) *Shuhō-hikigane* (main gun firing hand [layer]) (Station of firing hand [*shashu*] and the control officer [*shikikan*])

(b) *Kyori shogen* (averaged range input)

(1) *Shikikan-bōenkyō* (control officer binoculars) (to chief gunnery officer [*hōjutsuchō*]) (panorama view)

(2) *Senkai-bōenkyō* (trainer binoculars) (main binoculars and pitching glasses [*kōkaku-gankyō*])

(3) *Fugyō-bōenkyō* (for layer [firing hand, *shashu*]) (*zenshi-bōenkyō* [fore horizon sight binoculars] and *kōshi-bōenkyō* [rear horizon sight binoculars])

Others: *Yoko-dōyō-bōenkyō* (rolling binoculars), *kōkaku-bōenkyō* (pitching binoculars), *sokkyo-heikinban* (range-averager)

The Type 98 Fire Director

The Type 98 fire director (*hōiban*) was the centre of the main gun fire control system and it was located atop of the foremast. It was completely enclosed by a cylindrical hood (or tower)–3 m in diameter and 2.4 m in height. Its purpose was to protect the operators, not only from weather influences and blast of the main guns but also from machine-gun bullets from strafing fighters. Therefore, special steel was used and the thickness was calculated to resist 13-mm (i.e. 12.7-mm = 0.5") armor-piercing bullets fired from 200 m. The optics for the operators was of periscope type (*senbōkyō*) and was combined in the "director head", a column (0.8 m in height and 0.6 m in diameter) protruding through the roof of the hood. Since the periscopes were rigidly fixed only the prisms could be moved, from $-12°$ to $+45°$. The objectives were about 40 m above the waterline and the horizon could be seen to about 32,000 m.

There were a total of four operators, namely control officer, layer, trainer and cross-leveller. Their telescopes were of periscope (*senbōkyō gata sōgan-kyō*) type, as stated before, and had the light through the windows and prisms atop. That of the control officer was of panorama type and could be trained independently from the training direction of the fire director to search the horizon all-round and make it possible to estimate the complete tactical situation. The magnifying power of the periscopes was from 10 times to 20 times and the diameter of the lenses either 6-cm or 12-cm, and 15-cm in case of the control officer's one. With them (1) the control officer trained the fire director in the direction of the target, (2) the cross-leveller (*dōyōshu*)[103] stabilised the periscopes by adjusting the horizon on the target, (3) the trainer (*senkaishu*) chased the horizontal movement of the target and kept it on the vertical line of his periscope (searcher sight), and (4) the layer (*fugyōshu*) chased the vertical movement (i.e. approaching or opening) of the target and kept it on the horizontal line of his periscope. He operated a "fore horizon periscope" (*zenshin bōenkyō*) and a "back horizon periscope" (*kōshin bōenkyō*), both with searcher sight. Besides of the periscope type telescopes there were also binoculars with large magnification enabling an all-round view by five openings in the hood.

---

[103] His periscope was called "left/right" (*yoko-dōyō*) and "up/down" (*kōkaku*) periscope (*bōenkyō*).

Even though the *Yamato* class had large dimensions and a huge displacement the hull rolled and pitched depending on the weather conditions. The biggest vibrations were at 8/10 full speed (*zensoku*). Therefore, the pedestal of the fire director, whose total weight amounted to 3.5 tonnes, was mounted upon a vibration damper equipment (*bōshin kadai*), whose base plate was connected to the mast. The damper used the oscillation difference of springs (*hatsujō*) and the hull and also the effect of a liquid buffer. Above the damping device there were rollers for the training of the fire director according to the movement of the steering handle of the control officer. In bad weather conditions and at high speed rolling and pitching were very severe and to keep the target in the cross-hairs of the periscopes, with the high magnifying power from the top of the mast 40 m above the waterline, was very difficult and required much training.

Selsyn was the trade name of the American General Electric Company and the IJN called it angle data transmission gear (*kakudo tsūshinki*) and used it for the transmission of elevation angle (*fugyōkaku*) and training angle (*senkaikaku*) between the fire director (*hōiban*) and main gun turrets (and also other gun turrets). Transmitter and receiver were some kind of small AC electric motors and both had an identical structure. If the rotor of the transmitter began to rotate, the rotor of the receiver followed the rotation to the same angle and the pointer of the receiver scale indicated the angle. The precision of the receiver was very important for the angle transmission. The first class products of the IJN (white mark) had a deflection within $\pm$ 0.8° at 360° rotation (1/450th of 360°).

When used for the main gun fire control systems a gear increased the number of revolutions of the transmitter so that one rotation (360°) indicated a real angle of 6°, that is 60° rotation of the rotor means 1°. At the receiver this 1° was indicated with the deflection of $\pm$ 0.013°.

The handles of the trainer and layer were each connected to one angle transmitter (*kakudo hasshinki*) of selsyn principle and the chasing movement of the target, namely in case of the trainer the angle between the direction of the fire director and the horizontal movement of the target (*senkai kaku* = bearing) and in case of the layer the vertical movement (approaching or opening) of the target (*fugyō kaku* = elevation angle), were electrically transmitted to the computer.

The layer was also the firing hand (*shashu*). If the target was caught in the sights of the periscopes, i.e. the three operators (except the control officer), he pulled the trigger and the ready guns fired.

One more fire director was placed on the after mast and if the main fire director failed all the functions were switched to the reserve director.

In addition, a fire director with the functions limited to training was mounted in the conning tower.

Photo 3-1: The Type 92 computer (*shagekiban*) aboard the surrendered battleship *Nagato* photographed on 31 May 1946. The computer is partly dismantled but it gives an impression of how complex these analogue mechanical computers were (Gakken, #15)

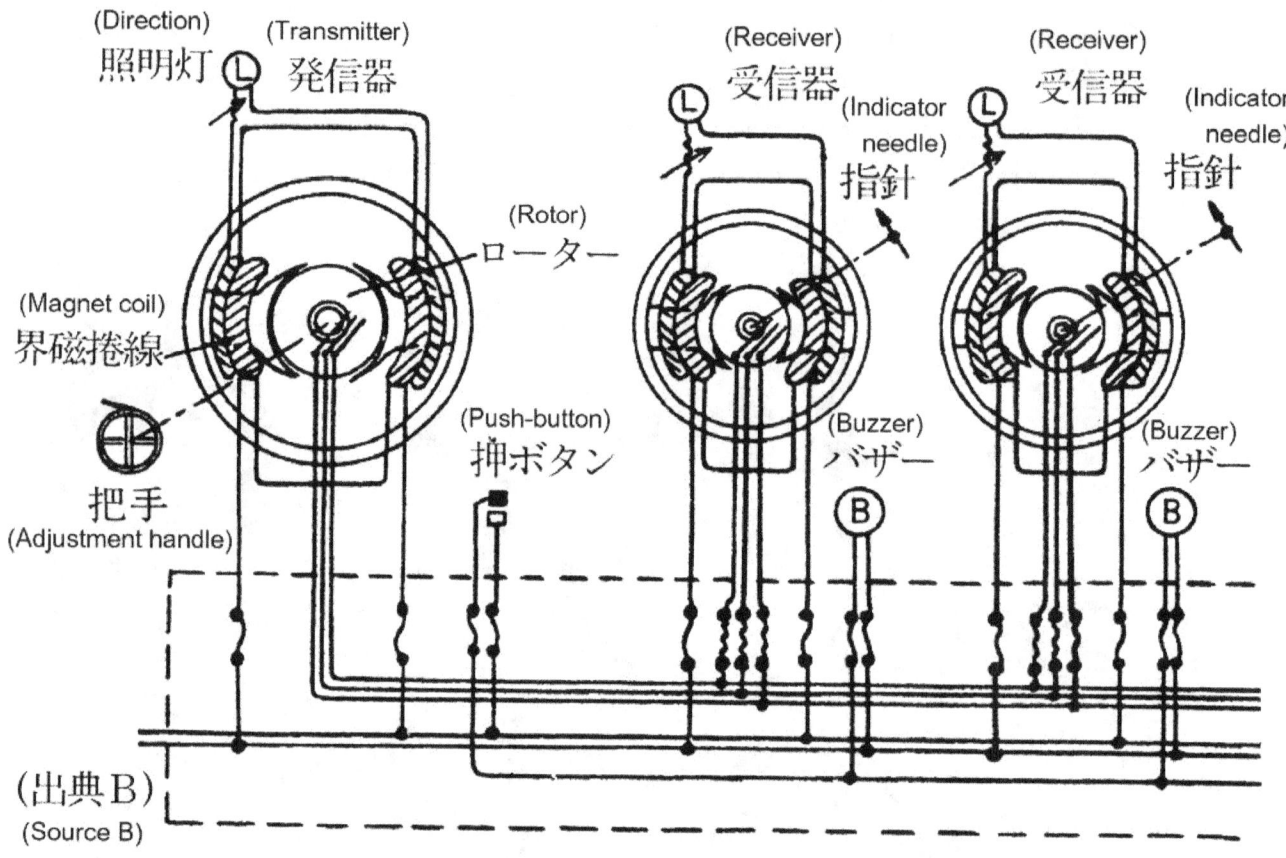

Figure 3-5: Angle Data Transmission Gear–selsyn (Gakken, #11)

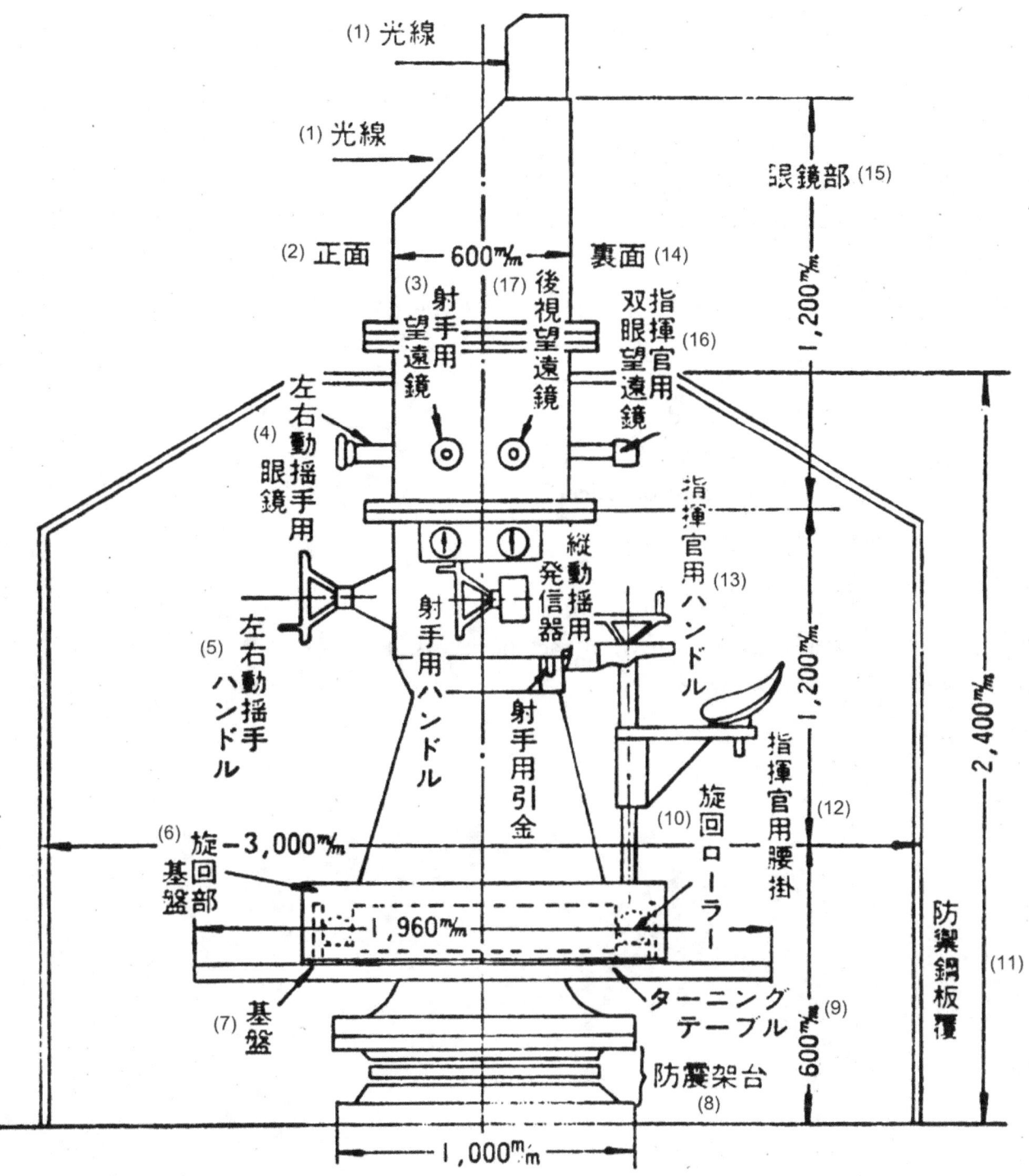

Figure 3-6: Type 98 fire director (*hōiban*) (*Kaigun Hōjutsu-shi*)

Key to Figure 3-6

    (1) Daylight (windows for periscopes)
    (2) Front
    (3) Layer's (*shashu*) periscope
    (4) Cross-leveller's (*sayūdōyōshu*) periscope
    (5) Cross-leveller's handle
    (6) Base plate of the rotating part
    (7) Base plate
    (8) Vibration damper equipment (*bōshin kadai*)
    (9) Turntable (training platform)
    (10) Training roller
    (11) Protective hood
    (12) Chair for control officer (*shikikan*)
    (13) Handle for control officer
    (14) Backside
    (15) Optic part
    (16) Periscope for control officer
    (17) Periscope for rear view (back horizon sight)

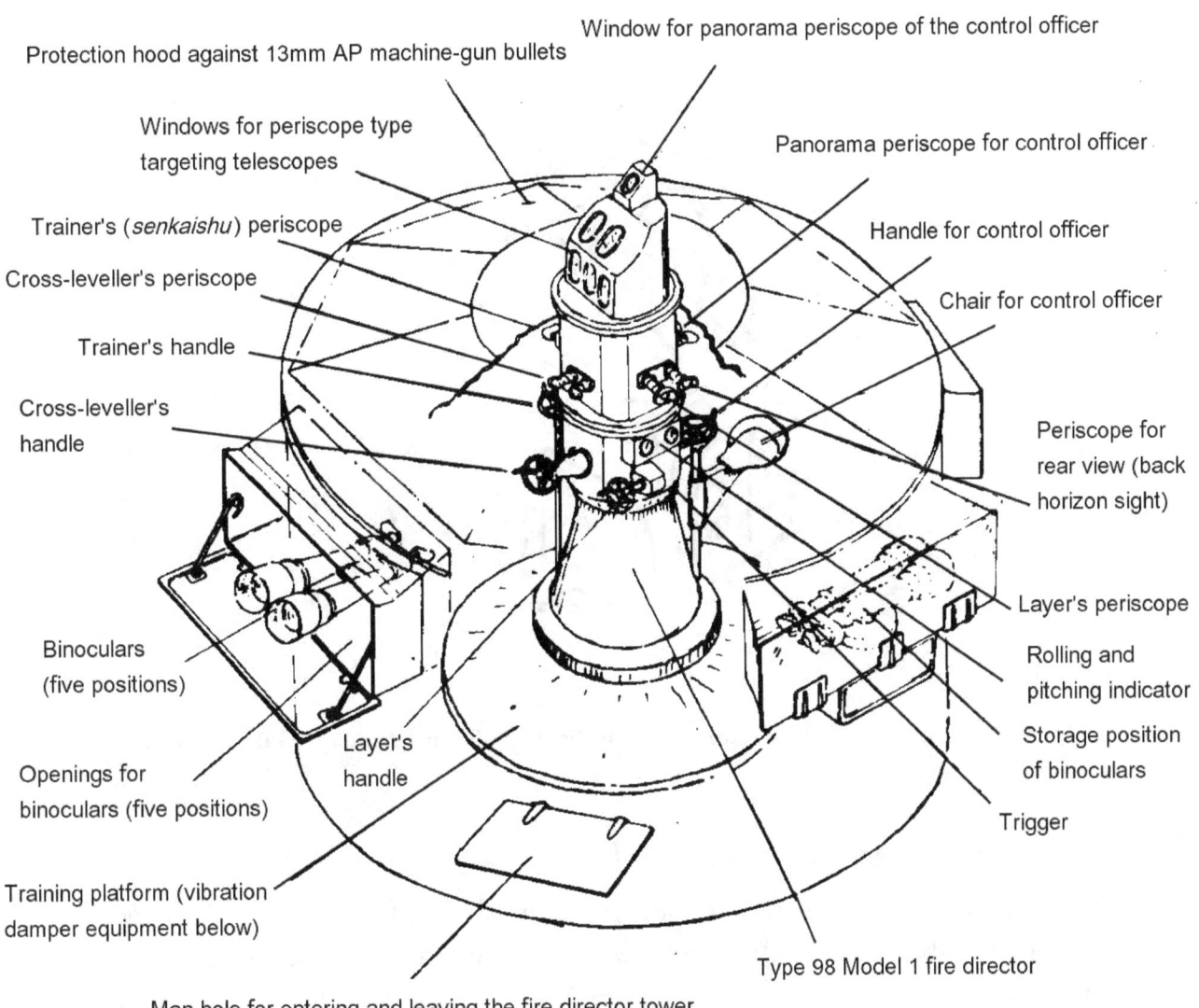

Figure 3-7: Type 98 fire director (*hōiban*) (*Maru*, #420, by permission of Ishibashi Takao)

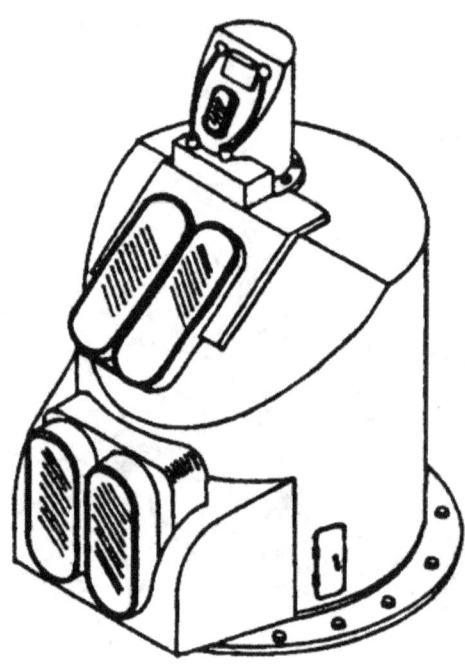

Figure 3-8: Shape of the "director head" of the Type 98 fire director (Gakken, #11)

The Type 98 Target Speed and Bearing Panel (Sokutekiban)

Among the instruments for solving the problems of fire control the target speed and bearing panel (*sokutekiban*) was the only one developed independently by the IJN and it had no equivalent in the US Navy or the Royal Navy fire control equipment. This instrument was designed to provide transmission of target course (bearing) and target speed to the computer. In the former fire control system it resembled a fire director in appearance but in the Type 98 fire control system it was rather more of an appendage to the computer than a sort of fire director. It received data from the director and transmitted the aforementioned values to the computer after calculation.

The past target speed and bearing panels had solved the equations for target speed and target inclination by a mechanical system, but for the new type an optical calculation system was developed in company with the so-called speed vector method. The background of the introduction was to eliminate errors inherent in a mechanical system by friction, clearances, deformation, wear and tear, etc. However, as seen in figure 3-10, a mechanical gear system was used for the transmission of the vector to a value.

The target speed and bearing panel was mounted in the target speed and bearing measurement station directly below the main gun fire director station and on the same level as the 15-m triple rangefinder as shown in figure 3-8.

The equations and method of solving are described in Report O-31, p. 39, from which the optical arrangement, shown as figure 3-11, was taken.

The principal designers were Engineer Sugi Yutaka of Japan Optical Works at Mizonokuchi,[104] assisted by his colleague Engineer Sarata. In the First Division of the Navy Technical Department Nakajima and Tokugawa were in charge.

All inputs were by power selsyn and the transmissions of target speed and target inclination were made by selsyn to the computer. The performance of this type was judged as excellent and in *Kaigun Hōjutsu-shi*, p. 109, it is considered a product "to be proud of in the world."

---

[104] The Nippon Kōgaku Kabushiki Kaisha was originally established at Ōi (Tōkyō) and the later added work at Mizonokuchi, just outside Tōkyō, was completed shortly before the outbreak of the Pacific War. The Japan Optical Works must be considered to have been the second largest producer of fire control systems for the IJN. By the way, Sugi later became president of the company.

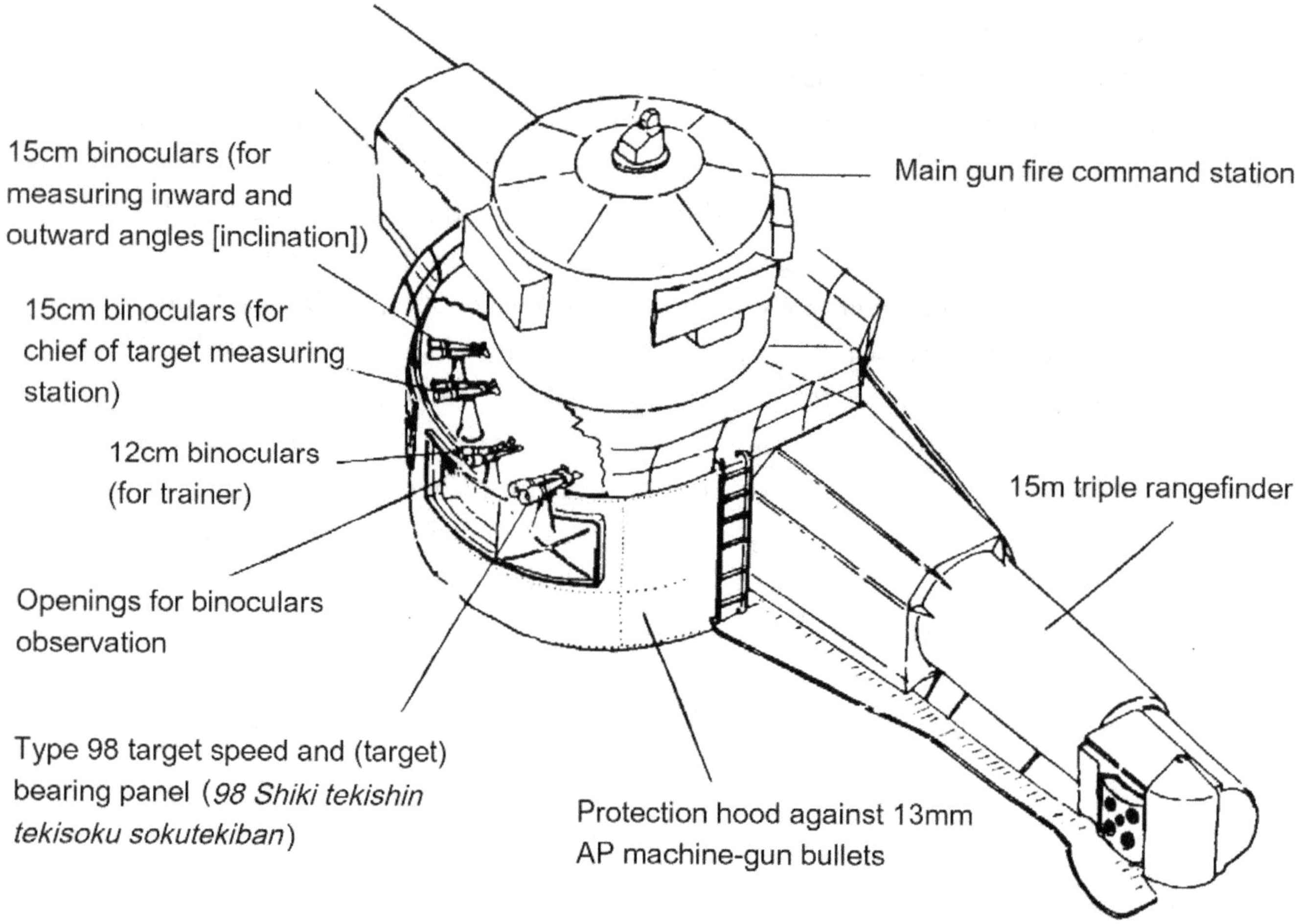

- 15cm binoculars (for measuring inward and outward angles [inclination])
- 15cm binoculars (for chief of target measuring station)
- 12cm binoculars (for trainer)
- Openings for binoculars observation
- Type 98 target speed and (target) bearing panel (*98 Shiki tekishin tekisoku sokutekiban*)
- Main gun fire command station
- 15m triple rangefinder
- Protection hood against 13mm AP machine-gun bullets

Figure 3-9: Main gun range and target speed and bearing measurement station (*shuhō sokkyo sokutekisho*) (*Maru*, #420, by permission of Ishibashi Takao)

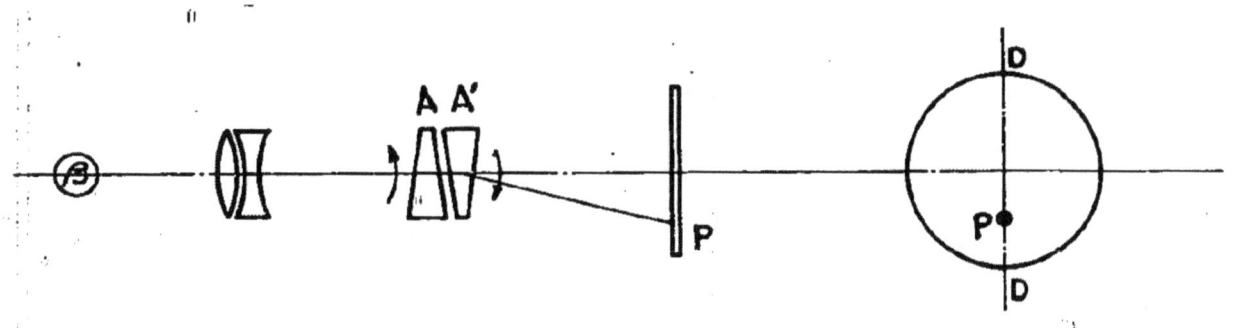

Figure 3-11: Type 98 *sokutekiban* optical arrangement (US Naval Technical Mission to Japan, Report O-31)

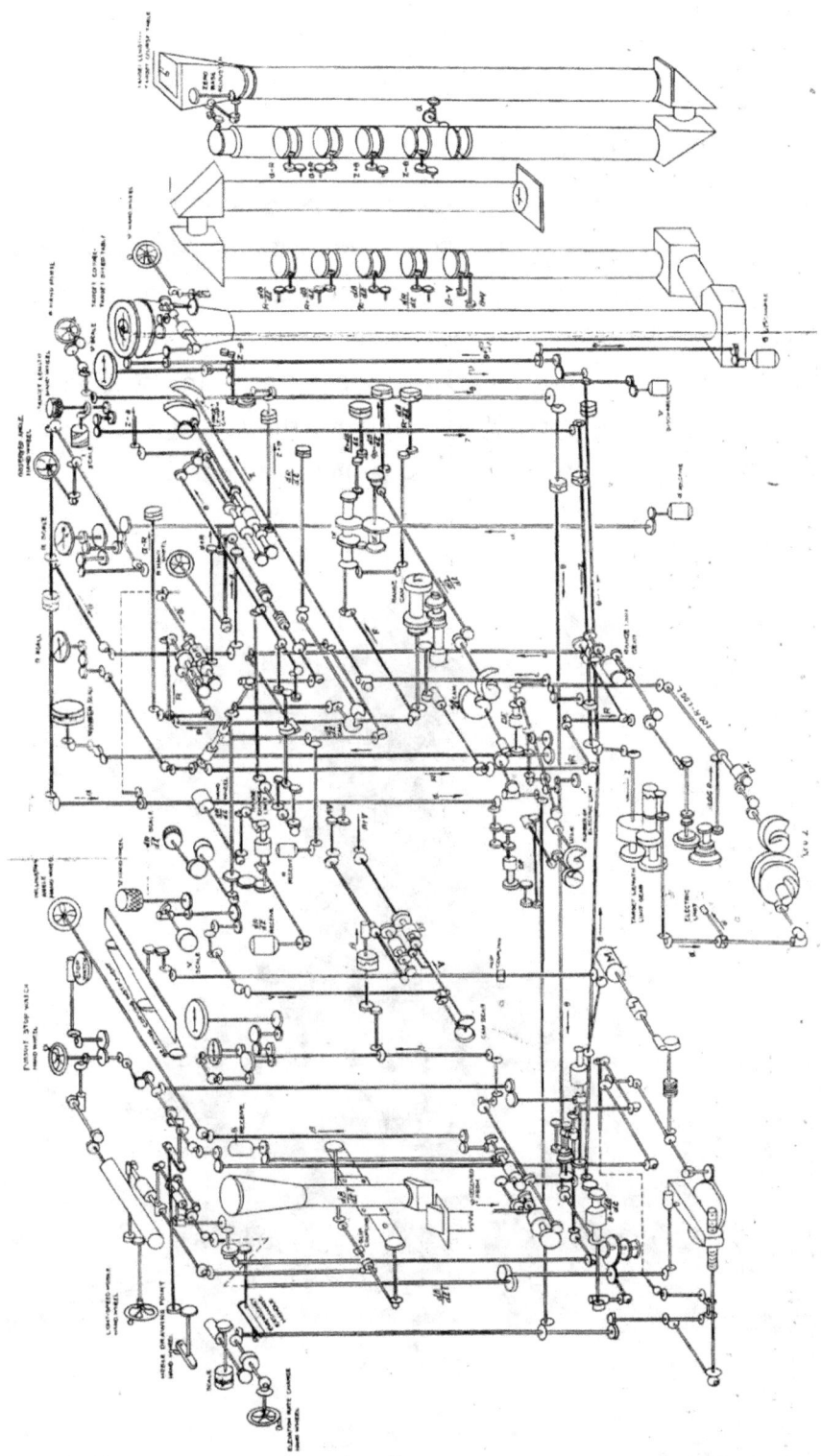

Figure 3-10: Type 98 *sokutekiban* diagram (US Naval Technical Mission to Japan, Report O-31)

The 15-m Triple Type Rangefinder (Sanjū Sokkyogi)

The accuracy of the rangefinder (*sokkyogi*, formerly also called *kyorikei* [range measuring instrument]) for measuring the distance to the target (range) is the better the longer the base length (*kisen-chō*). This does correspond to the eyes of a human being, i.e. the distance between the left and right objective. Also the higher the position the earlier the range can be measured. In the *Yamato* class the fire director was placed atop of foremast, i.e. the highest position in the ship, and the trainable 15-m rangefinder was located directly below. Like the fire director it was mounted inside a tower and was also protected from strafing but the difference was that both the tower and the rangefinder were trained together. The weight of the rangefinder was 4.5 tons.

Photo 3-2: The 15-m rangefinder on the tower mast is particularly conspicuous in this photo of the *Musashi* from June–July 1942 (Authors' collections)

The main gun turrets were also equipped with the same type 15-m rangefinder and below the after reserve fire director a 10-m rangefinder was mounted.

The particular designations were "*hikari 48 kanamono*" for the tower mast rangefinder, "*hikari 43 kanamono*" for the after rangefinder and "*hikari 39 kanamono*" for the turret rangefinders. See also figure 3-2. The Type 98 rangefinder Model 1 was used for the turrets, Model 2 for the forward tower mast and Model 3 was the rangefinder with 10 m base length. All models had the same design.

The main reason for the increase of the base length was to improve the accuracy but also other, less important, reasons existed. The width of the triple turrets was remarkably wider than that of the past twin turrets and, in addition, the undisturbed measuring with the rangefinder mounted in the after part of the #2 turret had to be considered when the guns of #1 turret were at maximum elevation.

The inner tubes of the rangefinders were of cast steel and they were surrounded by steel tubes with a diameter of 600 mm. Also, the outer tube was covered by an aluminium tube at some distance for protection against heat. Inside the tubes there were actually three rangefinders, hence the designation triple type rangefinder. Two rangefinders were of the vertical coincidence type, i.e. the vision was separated into an upper and a lower image and for reading the range the two images had to be brought in coincidence by moving the prism (zone dividing type [*taibunzō gatchi shiki sokkyogi*]), and one rangefinder was of the vertical stereo type (the patent of the German Carl Zeiss Company) (*seibunzō rittaishi shiki sokkyogi*) and could also be used for high-angle measuring.[105]

In order to keep the interior of the casing dry, and to avoid the prisms, lenses, etc. getting covered with damp, there was a particular drying device, i.e. dry and warm air was blown into the casing from both ends. For cleaning the objectives there was a fresh water spray device (*seisui funsha sōchi*) controlled from the centre of the objectives.

---

[105] The accuracy of range measuring was considered 1.6 times better compared with the British coincidence type and the reading of the range was also simpler and more accurate. Therefore, the IJN decided to import and adopt this system in order to exactly find the target at the horizon and to improve the measuring of the range for the 46-cm guns.

There were three range takers (*sokkyo-shu*), one trainer and one layer (pointer) and the rangefinder was gyro-stabilised.[106]

One rangefinder supplied three range data and these were transmitted by selsyn to the range-averaging panel (*sokkyo-heikinban*) in the control station (*hatsureijo*) where the data transmitted from all rangefinders were averaged and corrected before the average range was used in the computer calculations.

In 1944 the conversion of #22 radar (*dempa tanshingi*) for fire control was ordered and also executed but it ended with an unsatisfactory result. The lack of fire control radar was a serious setback compared with the fire control systems used by the US Navy and the Royal Navy. Consequently, the superiority in the hitting rate that the IJN was so proud of before the outbreak of the war was lost already in the first war year.[107]

The trial production of the double type rangefinder of vertical stereo type was begun early in 1937. It was based on the 6-m type bought from the Zeiss company and for trials it was fitted on the battleship *Yamashiro*. The upper step was left as a vertical stereo type and the lower step was altered to a zone dividing type and these combined produced the triple rangefinder. The design was made in the Optical Experimental Division (*Kōgaku Jikkenjo*) of the Yokosuka Navy Yard and it was completed in June 1937. The construction was charged to Japan Optical Company (Nihon Kōgaku Kōgyō KK).

---

[106] There are also sources disputing the presence of a layer.

[107] If the fire control radar had functioned as intended it could have replaced the bearing angle transmitted from the fire director and the range measured by the rangefinders, or their data could have been added to those measured by the radar. In addition, the firing of the main guns in mist or at night (without utilising searchlights or illumination shells) would have been possible, as executed by the Americans.

Photo 3-3: Turrets 1 and 2 and the tower mast of the *Musashi* in June–July 1942. The 15-m turret rangefinder in the foreground has been closed with a sliding steel screen (Kure Maritime Museum)

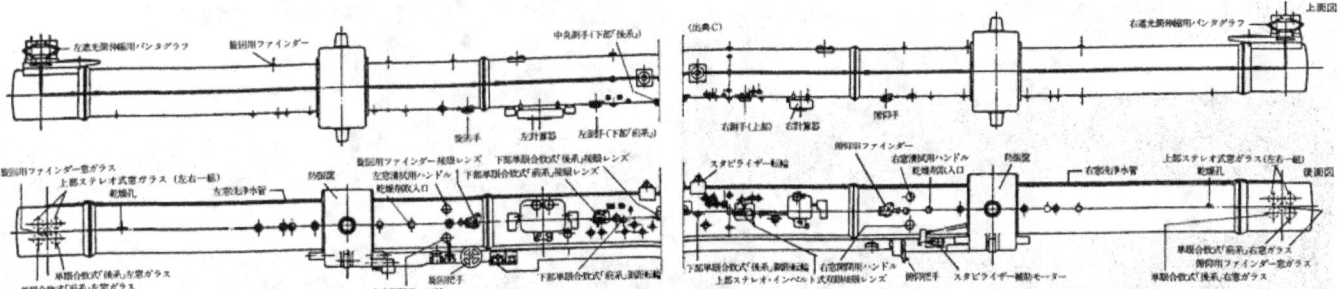

Figure 3-12: 15-m triple type rangefinder (Gakken, #11)

Figure 3-13: Combination of fire director (*hōiban*) and rangefinder (*sokkyo*) (Gakken, #11)

Key to Figure 3-13

    (1) Fire director (*hōiban*)
    (2) Range-finding room (*sokkyo shitsu*)
    (3) Radar room (*dentan shitsu*)
    (4) Air defense control station (*bōkū shikisho*)
    (5) #1 bridge (*dai 1 kankyō*)
    (6) Binoculars (*sōgan bōenkyō*)
    (7) 15-m (triple) rangefinder (*sokkyogi*)
    (8) #21 radar (*2 Gō 1 Gata dentan*)
    (9) #22 radar (*2 Gō 2 Gata dentan*)
    (10) E 27 electronic countermeasure (ECM) (*E 27 gyakutan*)

*The Type 98 Model 1 Computer (*Shagekiban*) and the Range-Averaging Panel (*Sokkyo Heikinban*)*

The Type 98 Model 1 computer was the modified version of the experimentally produced Type 98 computer completed in 1938 for the 36-cm main guns of the battleship *Hiei*.[108] This ship had to be converted into a training battleship (*renshū senkan*) under the terms of the first (1930) London Arms Limitation Treaty and was under reconstruction to a high speed battleship at that time, as both treaties (Washington and London) had lost their effects at the end of 1936. Designed with the intention to be mounted on the *Yamato* class battleships some improvements were carried out after extensive experiments aboard the *Hiei*. The modified type was mounted on the battleships *Yamato* and *Musashi*.

Both versions were produced by the Aichi Clock and Electrical Instrument Manufacturing Company, Ltd. (Aichi Dokei Denki KK) at Nagoya. This company, founded in 1899, was involved in the production of fire control equipment since the start of the domestic production and it developed into Japan's largest civilian manufacturer with a specialised fire-control plant that averaged about 600 employees. Detailed design and production in Aichi Clock company were carried out under the leadership of engineers Tsuda Takashi, Mita and Tsuchida (Type 98) and Tsuda, Oshima Torasaburō and Tsuchida (Type 98 Model 1), while in the First Division of the Navy Technical Department Tokugawa and Nakayama (Type 98) with the addition of Commander Suganuma Yoshikato, in case Type 98 Model 1, were in charge of the fundamental design, planning and other administrative tasks. Among them Tsuda played the leading role and Japanese authors attribute this "excellent product" to his efforts.

Figure 3-14 is a top-plan view of the computer and may, in company with the enumeration of the firing factors following later, make obvious how complicated the structure of this mechanical analog computer was. As the computer was constructed of steel made rods, various types of gears, also made of steel, and several kinds of cams and steel plates it was a product of considerable weight and volume. The weight amounted to 4 tons[109] and the principal

---

[108] It was developed on the basis of the results with the Type 92 computer as a much improved type (see photo 3-1).

[109] In Report O-31, p. 37, an incorrect figure (7.5 tons) is used.

dimensions are given in figure 3-14, which does also show that the computer was made in three main sections; two calculation sections and one plotting and transmitting section in between.

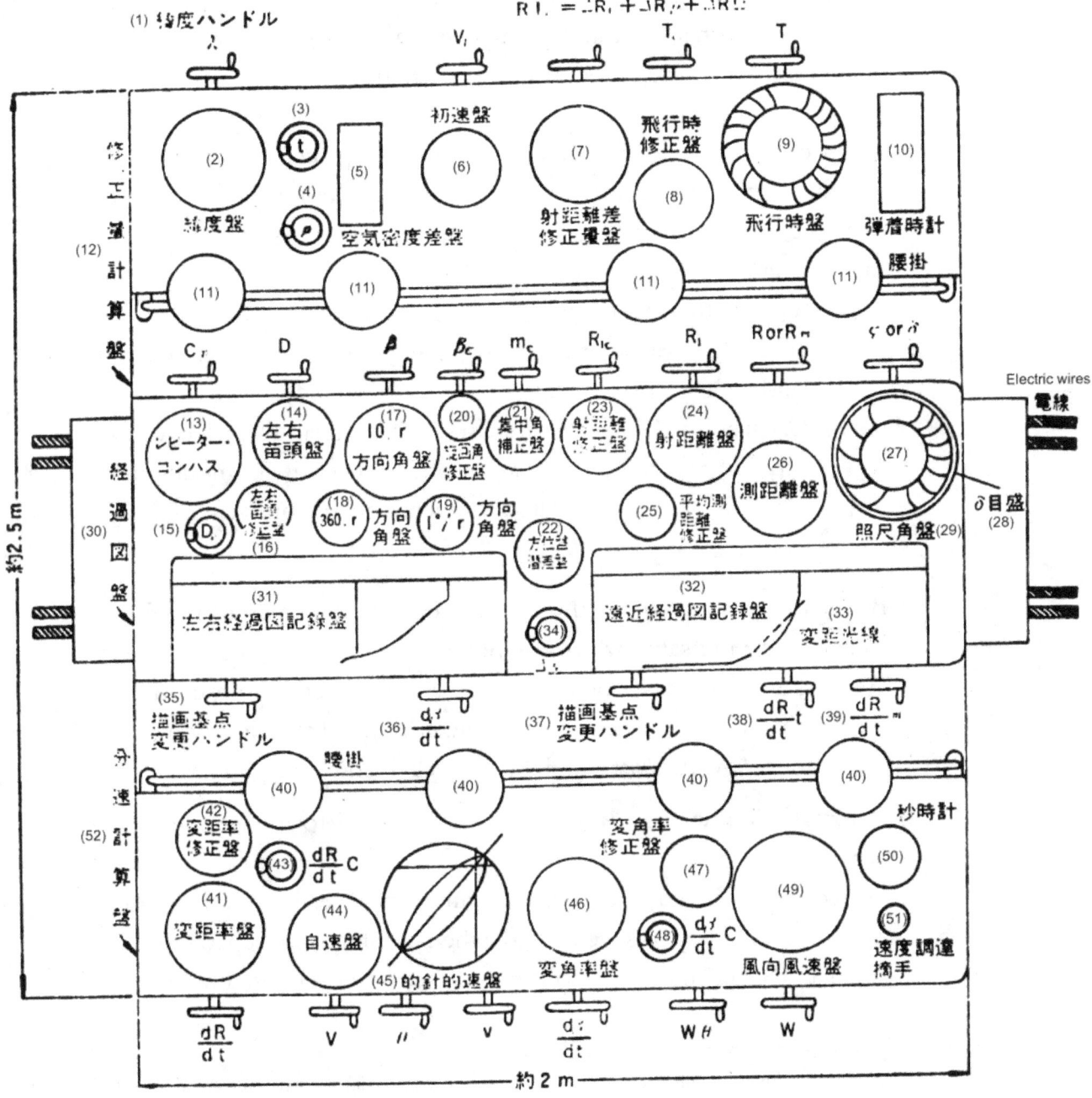

Figure 3-14: Type 98 Model 1 computer (*shagekiban*) (*Kaigun Hōjutsu-shi*)

The division of the computer into three main sections had much to do with one of the features that the designers incorporated in order to improve the properties. Generally speaking, electrical equipment was used as much as possible to reduce the number of operators and simplify the mechanical parts. The following items were particularly considered in the course of the design and several problems were solved; so they may be identified as the features:

(1) The use of mechanical calculation gears was the cause of small errors (generated by clearances, deflection of shafts, friction of disks, etc.) and the problem of all computers that could not be avoided as long as no change in the mechanical system took place. In the Type 98 computer the designers tried to solve this problem, or at least to reduce the grade, by dividing the mechanical gear series into two separated systems, namely:

  a) Transmitting (*hasshinki*) system—This system required absolute accuracy because any error of the adjusted real angle caused problems (errors).

  b) Calculation (*keisankikō*) system—In this system the effect of the error of the real angle was secondary even if it amounted to 1°; in fact errors generated by such a deflection were often ignored.

By the use of two systems the accuracy of the calculation of the firing values, using the same factors as before, was improved. The highest grade of accuracy was required for the values directly introduced into the training angle transmitter (*senkai hasshinki*) and the elevation angle transmitter (*fugyō hasshinki*) and, hence, delivered to the gun side.

(2) Automatic follow-ups (*jidō tsuibi sōchi*) were used to reduce the number of operators.[110]

(3) The contact points of the electric circuit sometimes became the cause of disorders by sparks generated when closing and separating the contact. This problem was solved and the defect removed by the ap-

---

[110] In Report O-31 "Japanese Surface and General Fire Control," p. 35, only the automatic follow-ups are mentioned as the special features of this computer "which, up until the time of its design, had been lacking in nearly all Japanese fire control." It is fully described in one of the enclosures of the report.

plication of the epicyclical curve invented by the Aichi Clock company.[111]

(4) For the first time the free gyro, developed by Tōkyō Kiki, was fitted for use at indirect firing.[112]

(5) As the motors and transmitters were fitted inside the casing of the computer the temperature rose tremendously but this problem was solved by better ventilation.

The input and chasing operations were made by operators using the handles distributed around the computer.

For the calculation of total training (TT) and total elevation (TE), as the product of the solution of several arithmetical problems,[113] three calculation methods were used in combination, namely mechanical (*kikai shiki*), electrical (*denki shiki*) and electro-mechanical (*denki-kikai shiki*). In case of the mechanical calculation very precise cams and gears were combined and operated either manually or electrically.

The electrical calculation method used the combination of voltage, current and phases in order to execute the training angles of the selsyns. This method was used as much as possible in order to reduce the mechanical parts and also the number of operators.

The reliability of the vacuum tube left much to be desired at that time so the electronic calculation method (*denshi shiki*) could not be applied. If the vacuum tube could have been used, accuracy must have improved and the structure most probably been simplified.

The computer was mounted in the main gun #1 control station (*hatsureijo*), below the protective deck, together with the range-averaging panel. The physical dimensions were about 2.5 m in length (3.5 m maximum), 2 m in width and 1 m in height.

---

[111] It deserves attention that this defect was already discovered when the computer of the British Barr & Stroud company was imported and it was described as "errors by the melting of the contact point of electric circuit (*denro*) change over/reverse (*tenkan*) apparatus (*ki*)."

[112] Before the repeater of the Anschutz gyrocompass for navigation had been utilized for the computer but this solution did not satisfy the users.

[113] In Report O-31, pp. 35 and 37, the principal equations are stated. See also explanations to figure 3-14.

Table 3-1: Limits of the fire control system

Maximum range	50,000 m	Range rate	Far and near: 80 knots
Firing range	40,000 m	Own ship's speed	35 knots
Flight time	90 s	Target ship's speed	40 knots
Maximum deflection	Left 160; Right 130 mils	Wind speed	40 m/s
Deflection in azimuth, i.e. angle changing rate	Left and right 500 mils/min	Latitude of the earth	North latitude 55° South latitude 20°

Source: *Kaigun Hōjutsu-shi*, p. 104. In Report O-31, p. 37, firing range is given as 41,300 m.

As shown in figure 3-14 the Type 98 Model 1 computer was divided into three sections; two calculation and one transmission and plotting section in between. The inputs were as follows:

A) Correction calculation section (wind speed resolver, deflection and range difference calculator in Report O-31) (#12 on the drawing)

#	Item	Japanese	O-31
1	Handle for latitude input		L
2	Latitude dial		
3	Temperature dial	t	t
4	Humidity	p	p
5	Air density difference dial		
6	Initial velocity	Vt	Vt
7	Range difference correction dial	Rd	Rd
8	Time of flight correction dial	Tc	
9	Time of flight dial	T	T
10	Time of flight clock		Sp
11	Chair		

B) Plotting and transmission section (tangent elevation, parallax correction calculator, range and bearing plots, training and elevation transmissions in O-31) (#30 on the drawing)

#	Item	Japanese	O-31
13	Azimuth correction	C1	Bc
14	Lateral deflection (*byōdō*)	D	DT
15	Right hand lateral difference dial	Dc	
16	Left hand lateral difference dial	bc	
17	Target bearing (*hōkōkaku*) dial (10°/r)	ß	B or ß
18	Target bearing (*hōkōkaku*) dial (360°/r)		
19	Target bearing (*hōkōkaku*) dial (1°/r)		
20	Training angle (*senkaikaku*) correction dial	ßc	
21	Parallax (*shūchūkaku*) correction dial (lateral)	mc	
22	Parallax (*senra*) correction dial (vertical) (*hōiban taisa ban*)		
23	Future range correction dial	R1c	Ro

24	Future range (*shakyori*)		R1	R1
25	Mean present range correction			Rmo
26	Range dial (*sokkyori*)		R or Rm	
27	Target angle dial (*shōshakukaku*)			TE
28	Scale			TE scale
29	Scale			
30	Plotting part			
31	Bearing plotter			
32	Range plotter			
33	Range rate difference line			
34	TE correction			
35	Handle for changing the start of plotting			
36	Bearing rate		dß/dt	
37	Handle for changing the start of plotting			
38	Range rate (in time t)		dR/dt.t	
39	Average range rate		dR/dt.m	
40	Chair			

C) Speed calculation section (own ship's and target speed resolvers and bearing rate calculator in O-31) (#51 on the drawing)

41	Range rate dial	dR/dt	
42	Range rate correction dial		
43	Range spotting and correction	dR/dt. C	Ro
44	Own ship's speed dial (*jisokuban*)	V	V
45	Target bearing and target speed dial	, v	Ta (,v)
46	Bearing rate dial	dß/dt	dß/dt
47	Bearing rate correction dial		
48	Bearing rate correction	dß/dt.C	
49	Wind direction and speed dial	W	W
50	Stop watch		
51	Speed resolver		

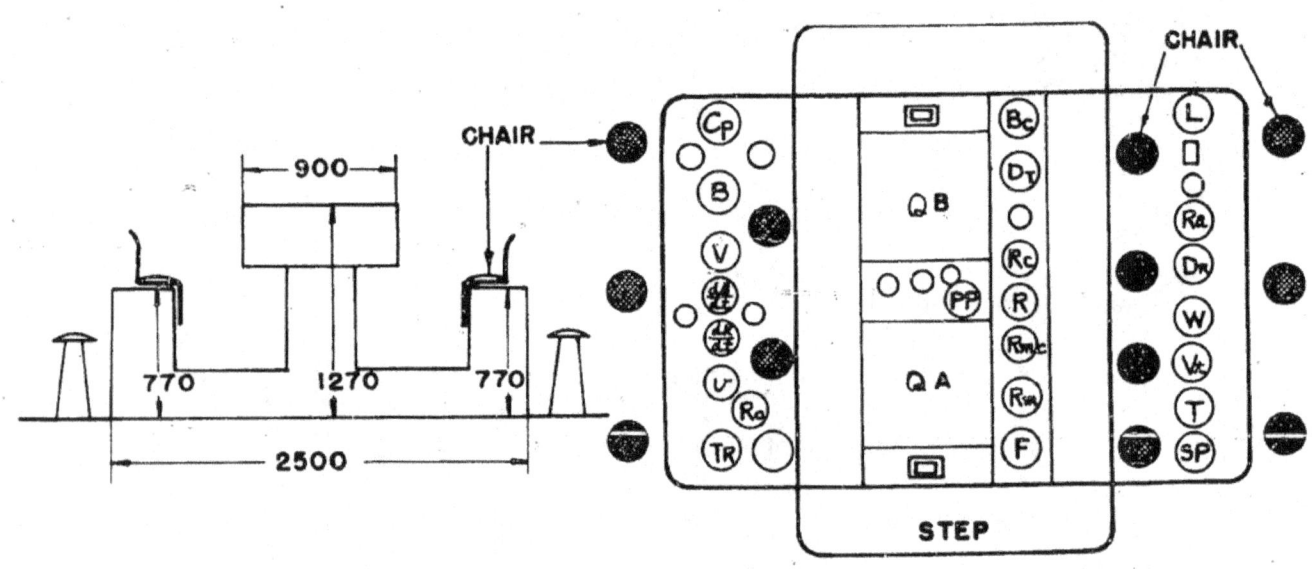

Figure 3-15: Type 98 Model 1 computer (*shagekiban*) (US Naval Technical Mission to Japan, Report O-31)

The Factors for the Calculation of TT and TE

It was quite evident that no projectile would hit the target if the angles measured by the fire director would be directly transmitted to the gun turrets and the guns be laid accordingly because the target, as well as the own ship, were moving and the shells needed some time of flight to reach the target. Therefore, the future position of the target (i.e. the hitting point of the shells) had to be calculated and the guns had to be laid according to total training and total elevation. The calculation of the corrective angles and their addition to those transmitted by the fire director was the main task of the computer.

The factors for the calculation may roughly be classified into those referring to (1) positions of own ship and target ship, (2) projectile, propellant and gun barrel conditions, (3) barometric and ballistic corrections, (4) positions of the main gun turrets and the fire director (parallax corrections).

If these groups are more specified the following items belong to (1):

1	Own course	*jishin*	Measured and transmitted by gyro. North is '0'.
2	Own speed	*jisoku*	Measured and transmitted by the ship's bottom log (*sokuteigi*).
3	Range	*kyori*	Measured by the 15-m rangefinder in the main gun rangefinder station (*shuhō sokkyosho*) and the 15-m rangefinder in each

			turret. Transmitted to the range-averaging panel for correction and calculation of average range.
4	Target bearing (also relative bearing)	hōkōkaku	This is the angle between the direction of the bow, i.e. own course, and the line of sight, i.e. the targeting line, clockwise. Measured by the Type 98 Model 1 fire director fitted in the main gunfire director station. Also known as direction angle and bearing angle.
5	Target course	tekishin	North is '0'. Measured and transmitted by the Type 98 target speed and bearing panel (sokutekiban) fitted in the main gun range and target speed and bearing measurement station (shuhō sokkyo sokutekisho).
6	Target speed	tekisoku	Also measured and transmitted by the Type 98 target speed and bearing panel. The continuous measuring of 'relative bearing' and 'range' in determined time intervals shows any change of bearing and range and if these values are calculated with own course and own speed the course and speed of the target are obtained.
7	Pitching angle of own ship against target	senkaikaku (tatedōyō)	If the target is kept in the vertical line of the trainer's periscope (senkai bōenkyō) in the main gunfire command station the relative bearing angle is obtained. By following the left and right movement of the target from the vertical line the fire director pitching angle is obtained as the fire director training angle (hōiban senkaikaku).
8	Rolling angle of own ship against target	fugyōkaku (seiyudōyō)	If the target is kept in the centre of the horizontal line of the layer's telescope (fugyō bōenkyō) in the main gun fire command station, the angle relative to the horizontal line as seen from the height of the fire director to the target is obtained. By chasing the up and down movement of the target from the horizontal line the fire director listing (rolling) angle is obtained as fire director elevation (hōiban fugyōkaku).

Notes:

(1) 1 and 2 are known values; 3 to 8 are obtained by measuring after picking up the target.

(2) 7 and 8 are continuously changing depending upon the movement of the own ship.

(3) 1 to 8 are the basic values for the calculation of the elevation angle (*fugyōkaku*) that corresponds to range, to which a correction for the future position of the target (and hence the laying of the guns) has been added.

The enumeration of projectile, propellant and interior ballistic conditions provides the following list:

9	Type of shell	*danshu*	Depending on the kind (APS, CS, ICS) shapes and weights are different and influence muzzle velocity (V_0) and ballistic curve.
10	Type of propellant	*yakushu*	A known factor and not changing after loading ammunition.
11	Weight of propellant	*yakuryō*	Depends on the type ordered by the chief gunnery officer, i.e. common (standard), weak, etc.
12	Propellant temperature	*yakuon*	Exerts influence upon burning properties, particularly speed, which in turn has influence upon the time when the maximum gas pressure is generated.
13	Age of propellant	*yakurei*	The properties may be influenced by the time of storage due to chemical processes.
14	Barrel condition	*hōrei*	This means the condition at the time of firing. Each time a shell was fired the interior of the inner A tube was exposed to wear and tear and the life of the 45-cal 46-cm gun barrel was given as being about 200 rounds (but there are big differences depending upon the type and the weight of powder). Exerts influence upon muzzle velocity, ballistics and firing range.

Note: These factors do consider the change of range caused by the difference of muzzle velocity, depending on the conditions of projectiles and propellants, which may differ from the calculated standard conditions. The effect of the barrel erosion can be taken from the trajectory table.

As for the barometric and ballistic (*dandō*) (outer ballistic) corrections the follow items must be included in the calculations:

15	Wind direction in the vicinity of the trajectory	*fūkō*	May be measured by meteorological instruments in a balloon and transmitted to the ship.
16	Wind speed in the vicinity of the trajectory	*fūsoku*	Same as above.
17	Air temperature in the vicinity of the trajectory	*ondo*	Same as above.
18	Air humidity in the vicinity of the trajectory	*shitsudo*	Same as above.
19	Earth rotation in the vicinity of the trajectory		Depends on the degree of latitude.

Note: The time of flight of the shell to reach a target at 40,000 m was about 90 seconds and the maximum height of trajectory was about 12,000 m. The shell rotated very quickly (about 3,600 1/min) around its longitudinal axis, i.e. it had the properties of a gyroscope so that the earth rotation had some influence upon its direction. These factors influenced range and flight direction of the shell and required the addition of corrections to TT and TE.

Most of the factors listed from 9 to 19 are so-called "correction of the day" (*tōshitsu shūseiryo*) values.

The differences between the position of the fire director and the gun turrets required the following parallax corrections:

| 20 | Height difference | *senra* | Height differences between the fire director and each turret. |
| 21 | Angle difference | *shūchūkaku* | Horizontal differences between the fire director and each turret. |

Note: The arrangement of the fire director and the main gun turrets indicate that corrections had to be made both in the vertical and the horizontal direction because the difference in height between the fire director, atop of the foremast, and the lowest gun turret was more than 30 m. Horizontally the distance to the forward #1 gun turret was about 60 m and to the after #3 turret about 65 m.

The aforementioned data were either set before or were continuously transmitted electrically to the computer (*shagekiban*) and set either automatically or mechanically by manual handling of the operators. The computer calculated TE and TT and transmitted them to the fire director and each main gun turret via selsyn. In addition, it generated continuously a graph showing the position of the own ship relative to the target ship and another one showing the result of the firings (i.e. the situation of the hitting points relative to the target).

The Range-Averager (Sokkyo Heikinban)

As a separate but integral part of the computer the range-averager (*sokkyo heikinban*[114]) was also produced by Aichi Dokei Denki Co. It weighted roughly 1 ton or ¼ of the weight of the computer and the main dimensions were, of course, also smaller in about this relation. The officers in charge and the designers were the same as in case of the computer. The *Yamato* class was equipped with four rangefinders of 15 m base length, each one capable of

---

[114] It may deserve attention that the range-averaging panel is not mentioned in Report O-31 and it is also seldom mentioned in Japanese sources, although the mechanism was mounted in a separate casing.

making three range measurements, i.e. twelve ranges (or 15 if the 10-m rangefinder was included) could be measured at one time, and all were transmitted to the range-averager. It calculated the average of these ranges to secure the highest possible accuracy of the range input used by computer for calculation. If the error of a rangefinder (by reading or any other reason) became too big it was excluded from the calculation and corrections were transmitted to the rangefinder.

Interlude photo: *Musashi* in the Inland Sea in June–July 1942 (Kure Maritime Museum)

NIMBLE BOOKS LLC

CHAPTER 4–BRIDGE STRUCTURE

Introduction

The tower bridge of the battleships of the *Yamato* class was the final stage in the development of the foremast. Here all conning and control centres and most of the communication facilities were concentrated. The function was comparable to the human brain and the numerous connections to transmitters and receivers distributed in the entire ship may be considered as nerves. As command centre it was of particular importance for the functions of the ship.

The structure should satisfy the following requirements:

(1) The functions should be maintained even in case of being hit by enemy projectiles causing considerable damage.
(2) It should be very solid and rigid to withstand impacts from many sources.[115] It should particularly be immune from vibrations by which the presetting of optical instruments, fire control system, etc. would be impaired and, probably, cause a fatal result.
(3) No influence of funnel smoke and hot gases.

But it is very doubtful if a completely satisfactory foremast to these requirements ever existed.[116] However, much effort was devoted to seeking an ideal condition.

The Tower Mast of the Yamato Class

According to Matsumoto Kitarō, op. cit., pp. 218–20, the aforementioned standard was decided after several investigations with the following principal details:

(1) Daytime battle bridge (#1 bridge). Should be about 34 m above the waterline and be protected against large calibre machine-gun bullets. From

---

[115] Including hitting and detonation of projectiles and bombs nearby, shock waves by torpedo detonations and influence of the blast of the ship's own main guns.

[116] An oft chosen example is the confusion and breakdown of the most important functions in the battleship *Hiei*'s foremast caused by hits of medium calibre shells during her last battle.

this height an enemy battleship of the same size could be detected at up to 45,000 m.

(2) Night battle bridge (#2 bridge). Should be placed near the conning tower.

(3) Main gun fire control station. The height should permit the sighting of an enemy battleship of the same size at the own maximum firing range and the station has to be completely protected against large calibre machine-gun bullets.

(4) Secondary gun fire control station. Should be completely protected against large calibre machine-gun bullets.

Other items referred to the operations room, conning tower, target speed and bearing measuring station, high-angle gun fire control station, air defense command station, searchlight command station, order rooms (bridges, operations room, conning tower etc.), lookout stations (upper, lower, lookout command), signal command station, signal observation posts, flag signal station, hand flag post, etc.

In contrast to the carrier structure of the former masts (tripods or multi-post) the structure of the foremast of the *Yamato* class was made double cylindrical to prevent it from collapsing after some shell or bomb hits, to reduce vibrations to a minimum and to avoid the influence of the extremely large blast of the main guns, capable of killing and hurting persons and damage precision instruments and other bridge equipment. The inner tube was made of 20-mm thick DS and had a diameter of 1.5 m. The thickness was sufficient for protection against large calibre machine-gun bullets and splinters. The upper end of this tube formed the support of the main gun command station with the 15-m triple rangefinder in the after half and the main gunfire director atop. Inside the tube there were electric wire passages and various pipes. The rooms arranged on the various levels between the inner and outer cylinders were connected by an elevator from the upper deck level to that of the operations room, just below the daytime (#1) bridge. Its transport capacity was four men. Besides of it there were ladders inside and, in the upper half, also outside in order to pass from one level to another. Outside the outer cylinder some stations for targeting and directing were positioned. Similar to the most important rooms inside they were also constructed airtight to prevent the killing of personnel by poison gas.

The conning tower was protected against hits of 46-cm AP projectiles. Inside the steering and defense command stations were arranged forward and the main gun reserve command station aft. For communication between the conning tower and each command station within the vital part a cylinder passed through. With an outer diameter of 1,000 mm and an inner diameter of 500 mm the electric wires running inside were very well protected.

The private and official rooms of the commanding officer and his staff as well as the flagship accommodations were situated directly below the bridge.

The next table (4-1), taken from Matsumoto, op. cit., p. 220, shows the projected areas of the foremast (and also main masts) of three classes of battleships and makes plain that, irrespective of the almost double displacement, the tower masts of the *Yamato* class had a compact structure. Japanese authors proudly state that it was attained without impairing the properties and most of them claim that they were even better.

Table 4-1: Foremast areas of *Yamato, Nagato,* and *Fusō* class battleships.

Ship	Forward tower mast		After tower mast (main mast)	
	Front	Side	Front	Side
Yamato	159	310	59	98
Nagato	162	371	61.3	97.1
Fusō	150	351	68.5	135.3

Notes:

(1) Pay attention to the much different sizes of the foremasts and the main masts.
(2) The principal rooms in the after tower mast were the reserve fire control and command stations for the main and secondary guns and also the high-angle guns for reserve and supporting purposes and command centres.

Photo 4-1: *Musashi*'s massive tower mast in June–July 1942. In the foreground is part of turret no. 2's 15-m rangefinder (Kure Maritime Museum)

Foremast Structure[117]

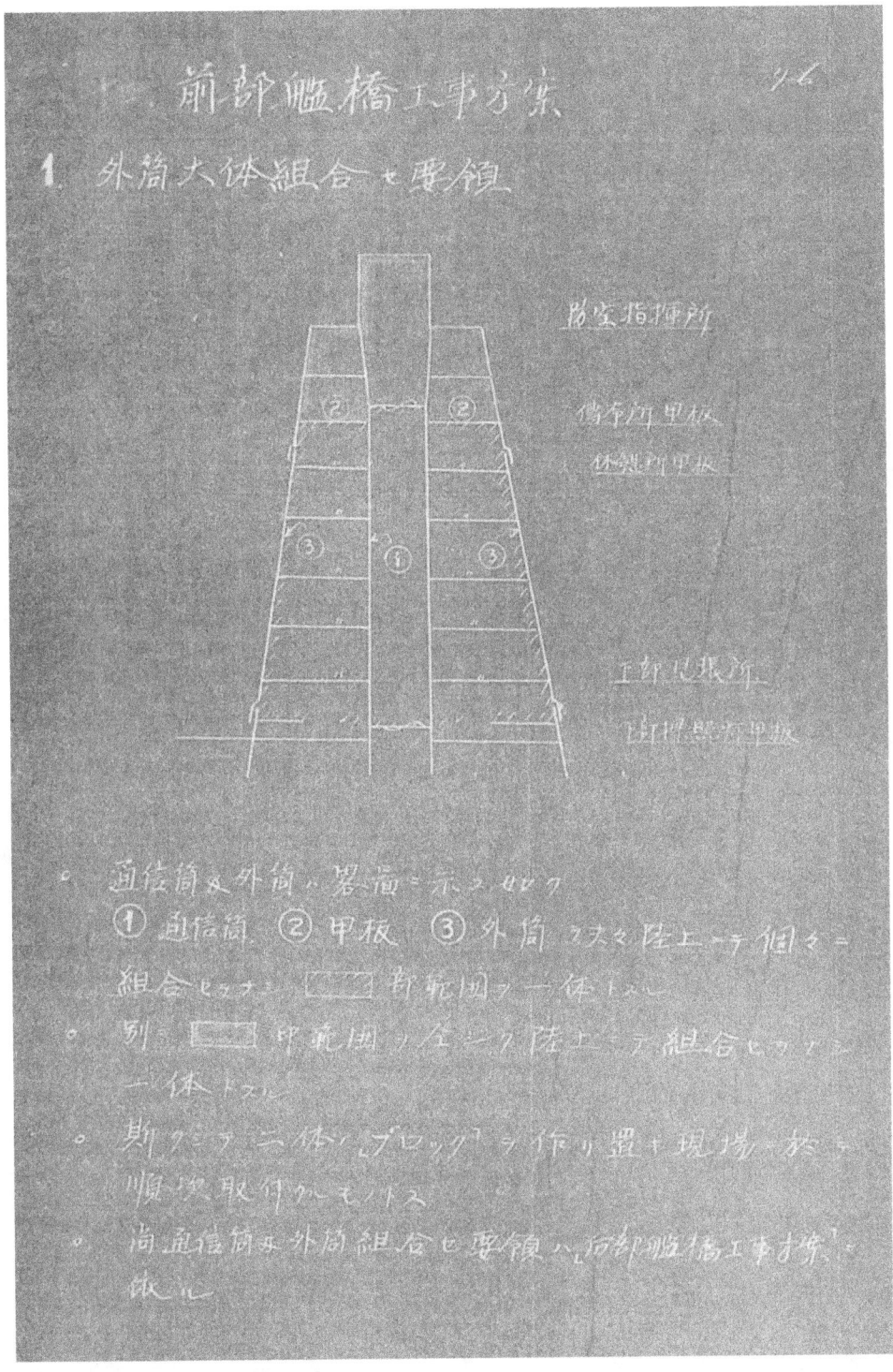

---

[117] From Kure Navy Yard Shipbuilding Division: "Building Report of #1 Ship–#3 General Construction."

Figure 4-1: D–Section

Decks from top:

- Air defense control station
- Rest/recreation deck
- Lower lookout station
- Lower searchlight deck

The foremast was about 32 m tall and was constructed upon the uppermost deck by means of a 100-ton crane with two block structures, which were prefabricated in the shipyard. The order of construction was:

(1) Fabricate according to each deck
(2) Construct in order (1) to (8) fitting the outer frame together
(3) Build two structures (A) and (B) and fix them in order of (B) and (A)

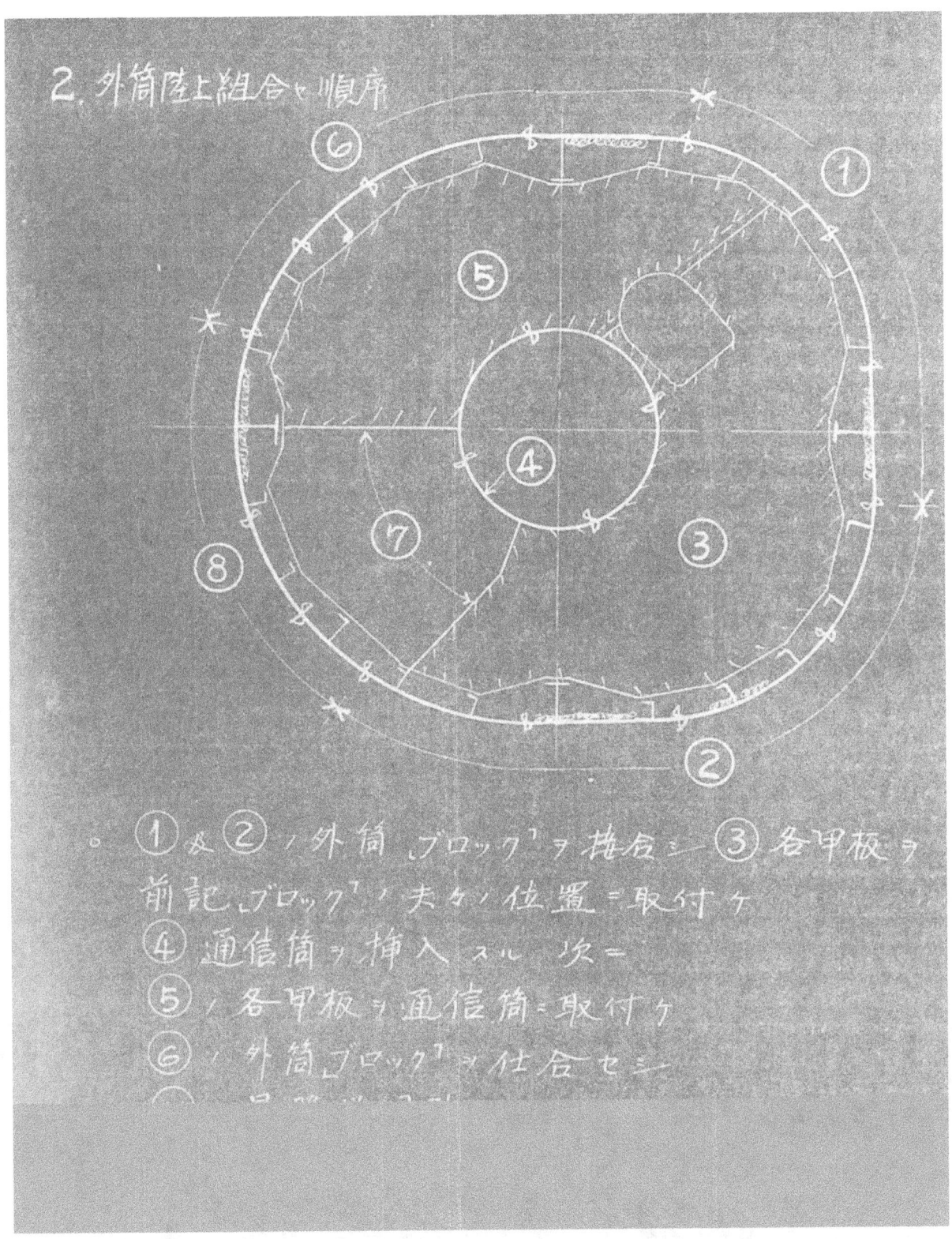

Figure 4-2: B–Order of frame construction

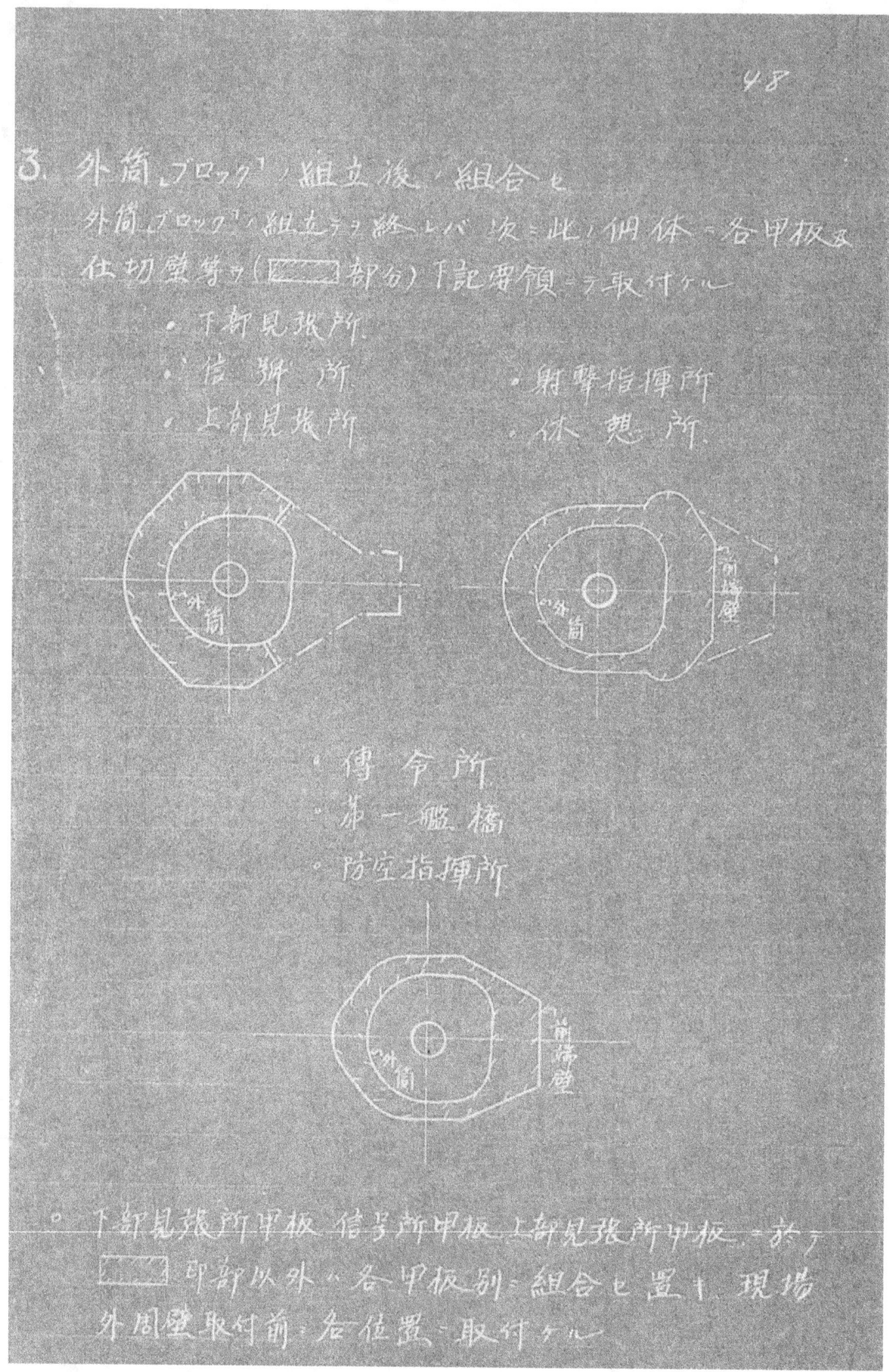

Figure 4-3: A–Plan of foremast–arrows indicate direction to forward bulkhead

Top left:

- Lower lookout station
- Signal bridge
- Upper lookout station

Top right:

- Fire director deck
- Rest/recreation deck

Bottom:

- Orderly (messenger) station
- First bridge
- Air defense control station

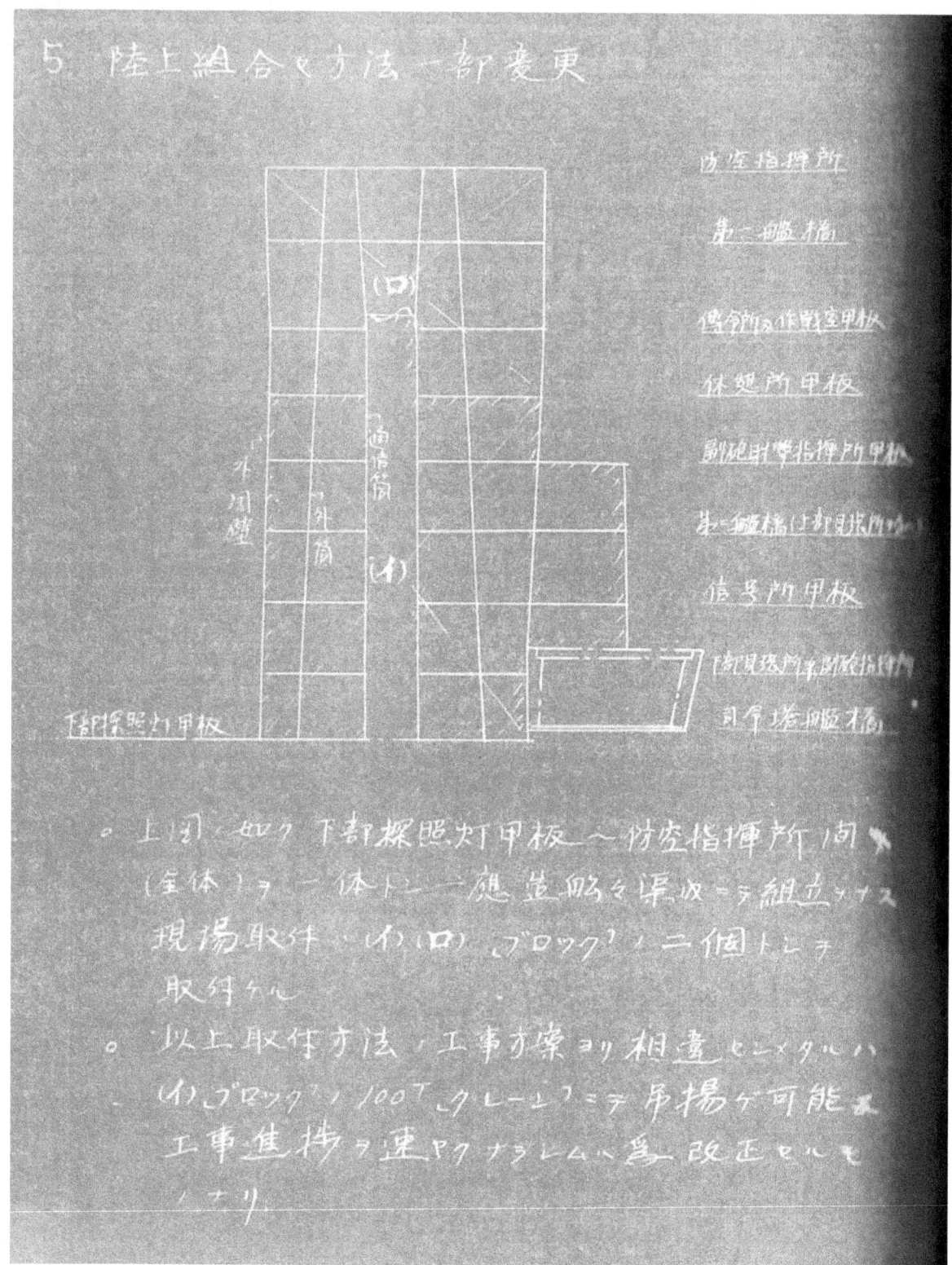

Figure 4-4: C–Section–side view

Decks from top:

(B or 口 [*ro*])

- Air defense control station
- First bridge
- Orderly (messenger) station, operation room
- Rest/recreation deck

(A or イ [*i*])

- Secondary gun fire director and control deck
- Second bridge (upper lookout station)
- Signal bridge
- Lower lookout station and secondary gun fire director deck
- Lower searchlight deck and conning tower deck

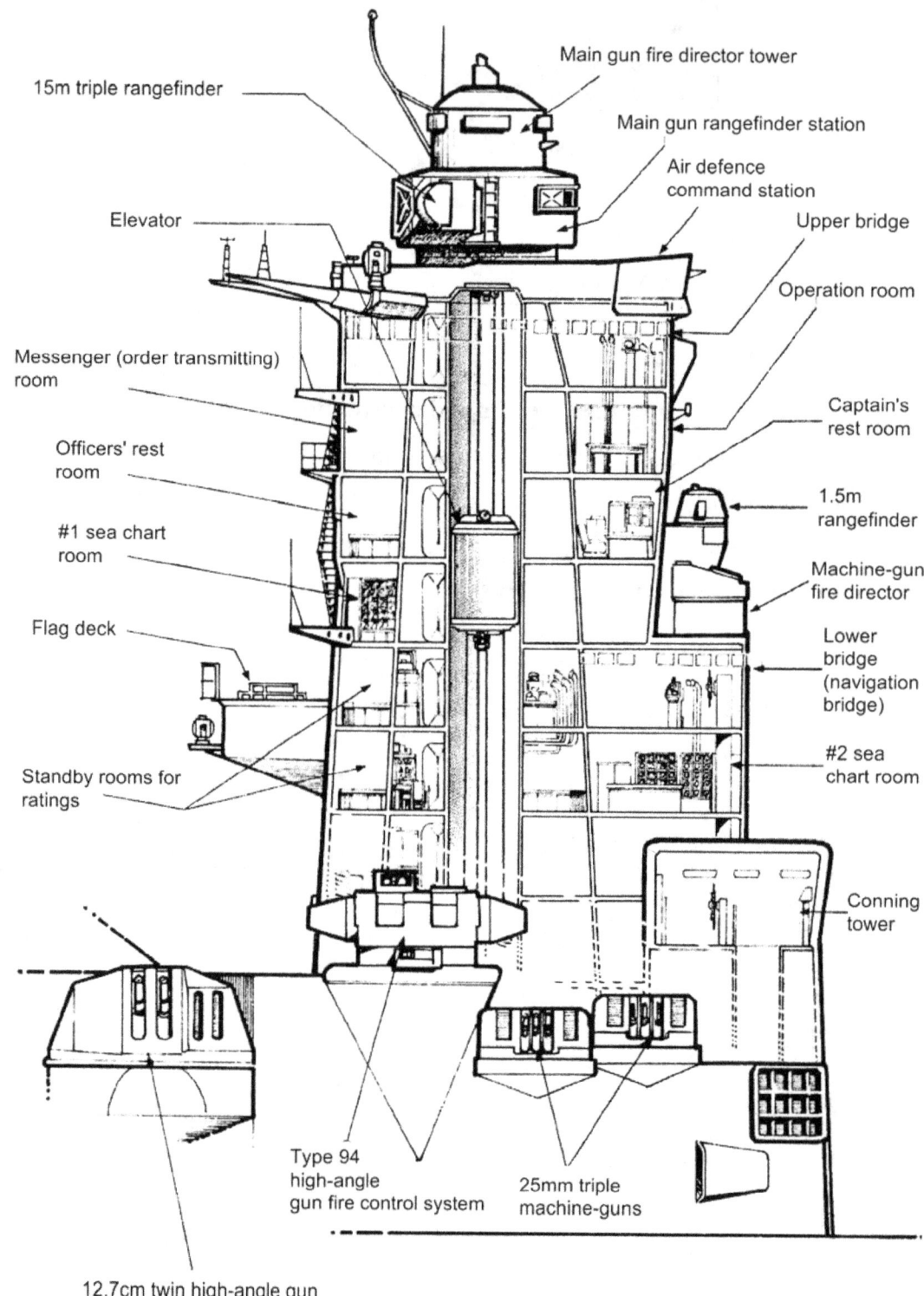

Figure 4-5: Sectional drawing of *Yamato*'s foremast (*Teikoku Kaigun: Kyū Nippon Kaigun Kanzen Gaido* via Kitamura Kunio)

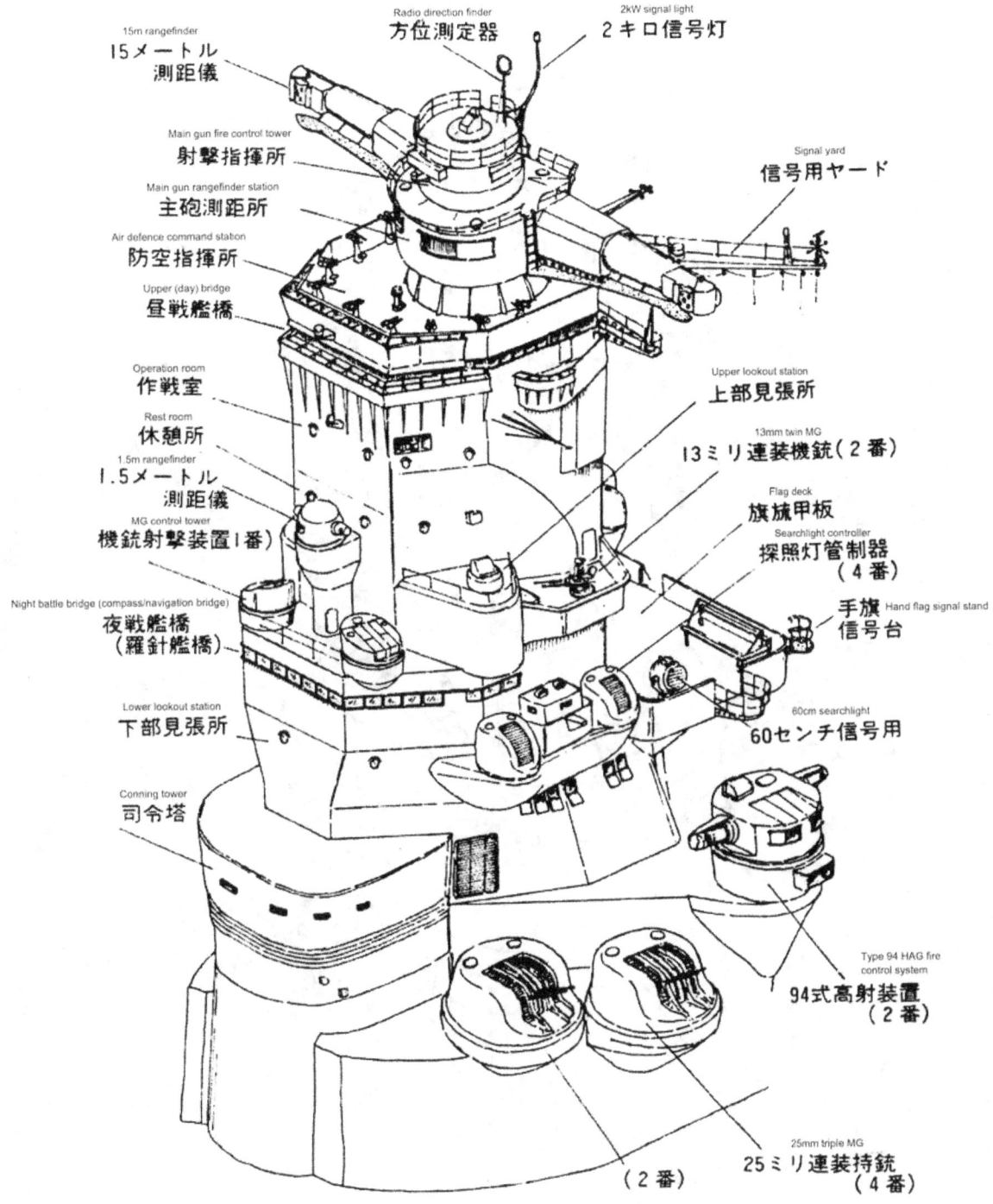

Figure 4-6: Perspective view of *Musashi*'s foremast–front view (*Nihon no Meikan* via Kitamura Kunio)

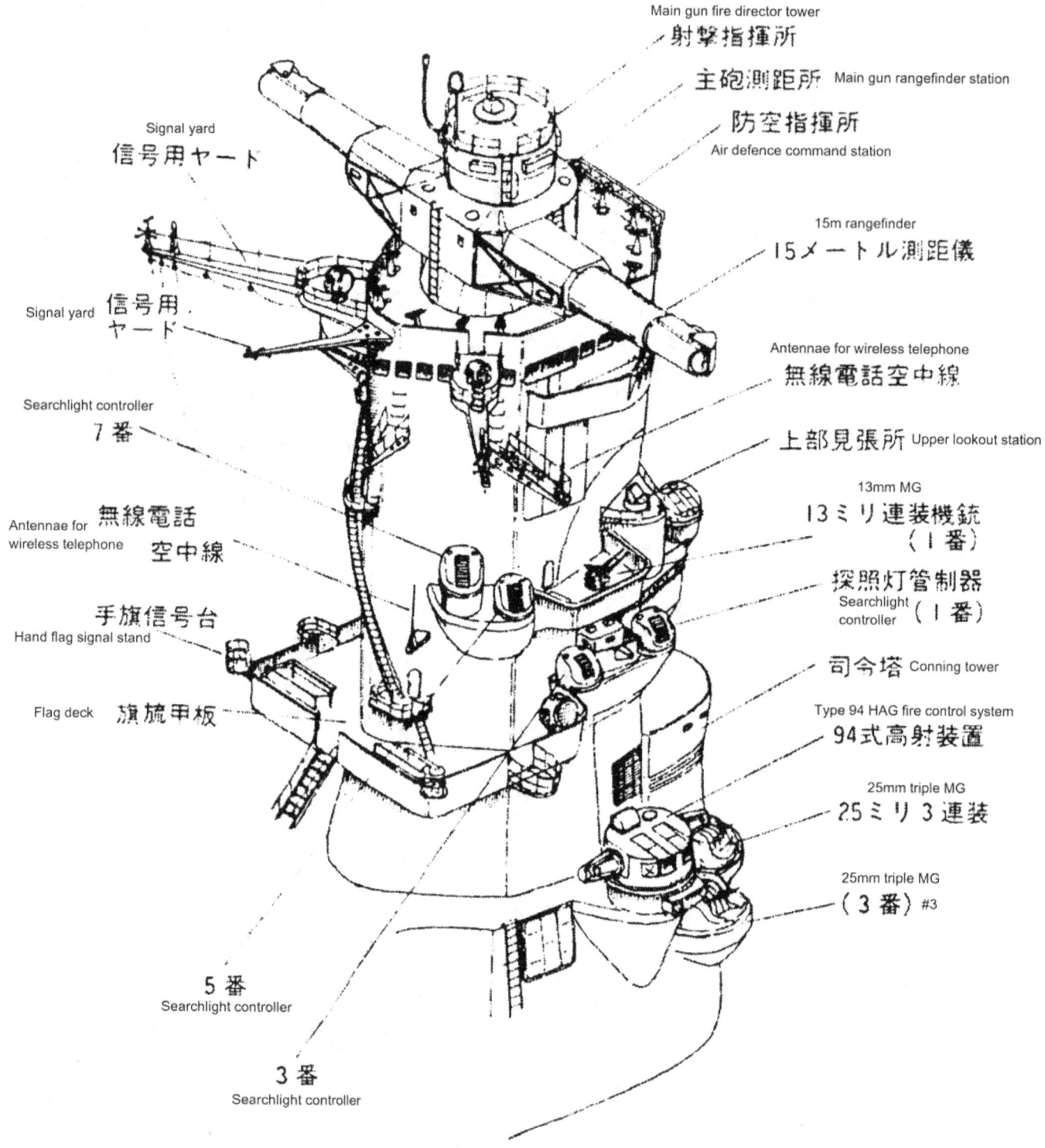

Figure 4-7: Perspective view of *Musashi*'s foremast–rear view (*Nihon no Meikan* via Kitamura Kunio)

In *Kenkan Hiwa* ("Secret Stories about Warships") Vice-Admiral Niwata Shōzō has described the construction of the foremast of the *Yamato*:

> The foremast was constructed after launching the ship but the central tube, prefabricated on land, stood on the deck. The structures around the central tube were prefabricated in blocks and were mounted one by one. But the central tube was a very high structure with 13 levels from the middle deck, which was the base, to the floor of the large AA command station. The height was 31 m with a diameter of 12 m at the base part and reduced to 10 m atop.
>
> The erection of the scaffold and the mounting of the ladders to construct this structure were very troublesome. The construction was made from the bottom to the top in sections and each time the scaffold and the ladders had to be positioned. The elevator inside the central tube was completed as early as possible, to be used to move the principal engineers, but it was only shortly before the completion of the construction and earlier these men had to use the 100 steps from the uppermost deck to the top of the bridge.

Height from the waterline to the top of the rangefinder	40 m
Height from the uppermost deck to the AA command station, 11 floors:	26 m
Height from the uppermost deck to the upper bridge, 10 floors:	approx. 24 m
Diameter of the central tube at the base:	12 m
Diameter of the central tube atop:	10 m

> The staircases for going up and down were separated and at the after outside of the tower type foremast the inclined ladders were separately fitted. These ladders were differently placed in *Yamato* and *Musashi* and were an identification mark of the ships. Fukuda Keiji told me this. *Yamato* had the inclined ladder made in four parts of 12 steps each and between each part was a resting place. This ladder went up 19 m from the lower searchlight deck to the upper bridge, bridging a total of seven levels. *Musashi*'s ladder had only one resting place with 12 steps at the upper part and 40 steps at the lower one; a long spiralled ladder to go down without any resting place.
>
> The design of the foremast was a most troublesome item by the newly established standard of mast facilities and a committee was secretly organised to decide the shape. It was to be inspected and decided by using a full-scale model. However, we had no proper space to put such a full-scale model secretly and, therefore, we decided to place it at the upper floor of the wood shop of the fitting factory and to shut off the traffic. The model of the bridge

was built in three sections but it was too big and we were confused about the arrangement left and right, upper and lower and were unable to form any conception of how to place the instruments etc. Then a 1:50 scale model of the bridge structure was constructed. We had five conferences to decide every detail. After deciding the places requiring extensions the dimensions were determined and then the positions of the measuring instruments and other fittings were decided, mostly using the originals.

Photo 4-2: This is *Musashi* in September 1942 and we can see the Type 21 radar on top of the 15-m rangefinder. Two 150-cm searchlights can be seen on her funnel. Note the shape of the ladder on the tower mast (Kure Maritime Museum)

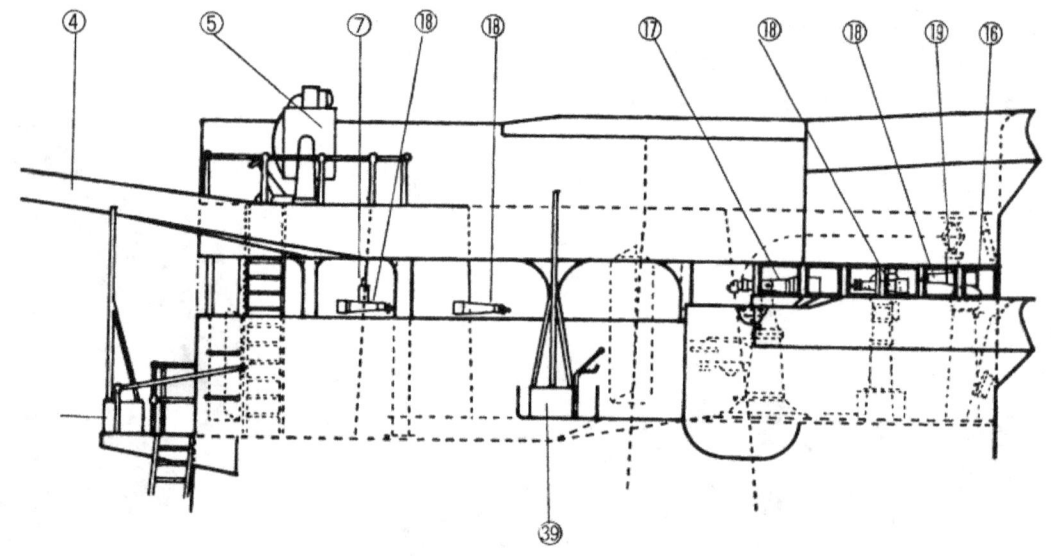
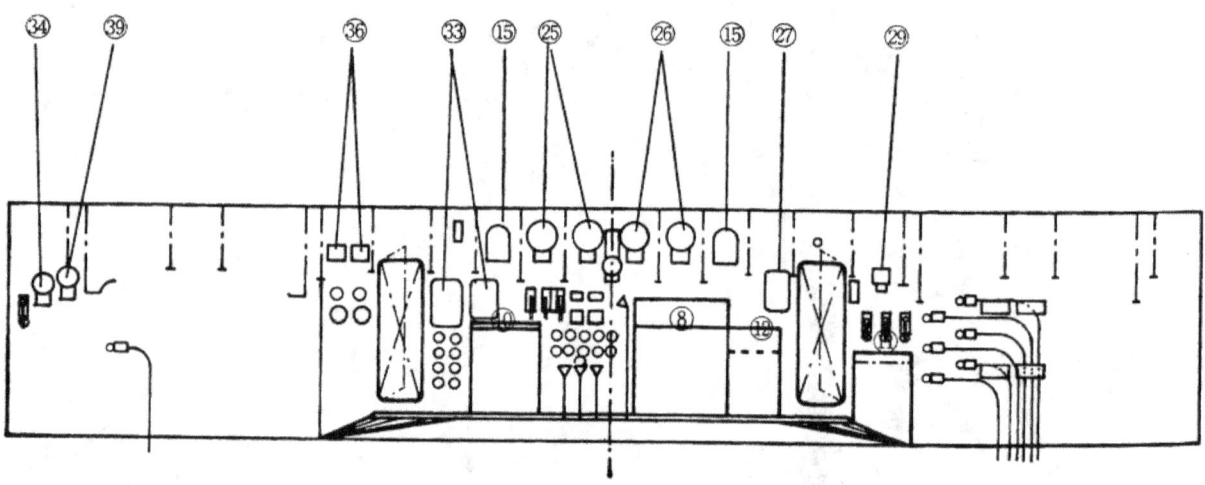

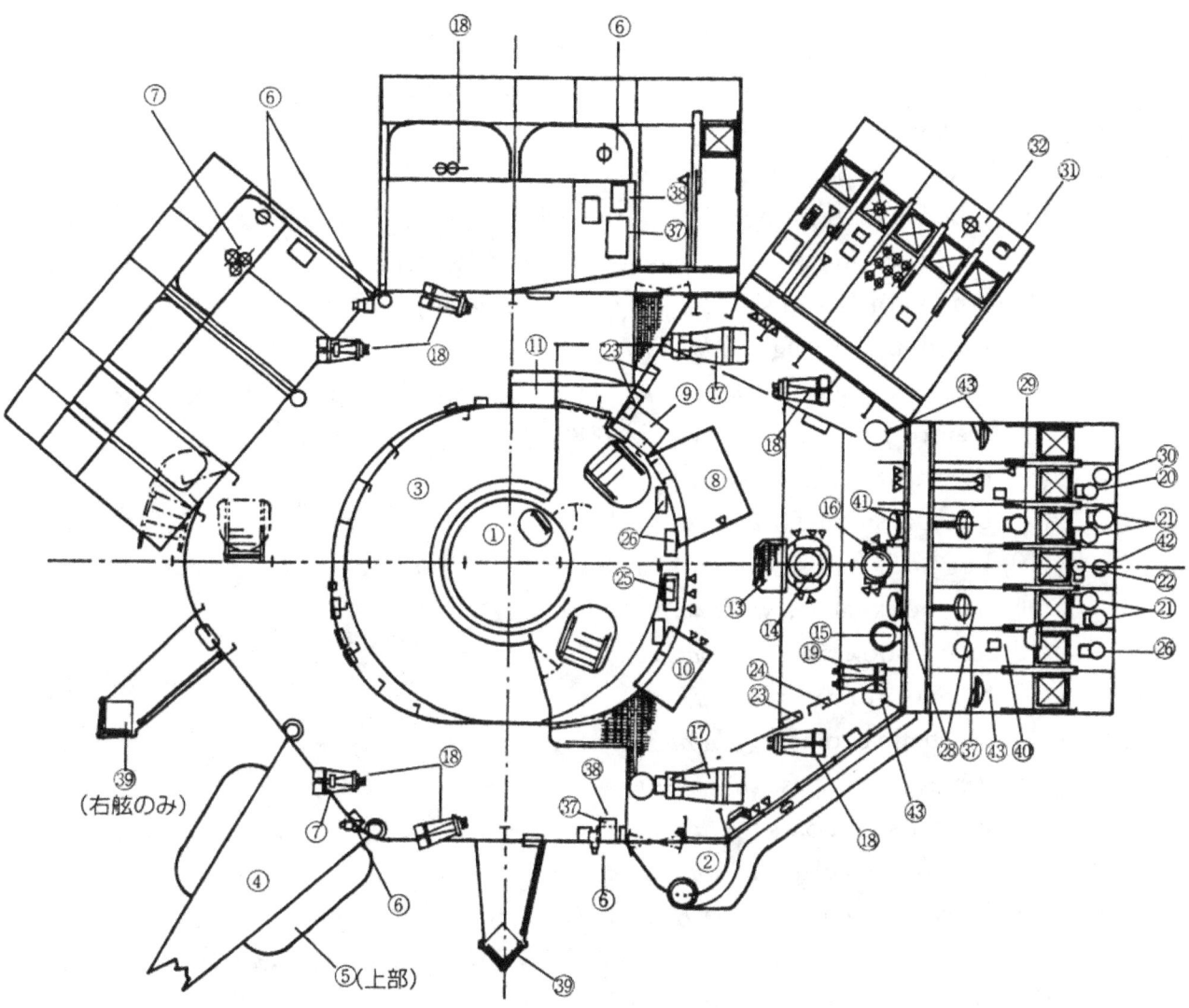

Figures 4-8–10: 1st vessel, 1st bridge equipment (*Dai 1 Gō kan Dai 1 kankyō sōchi*) (*Nihon no Senkan*)

(Note: *Yamato* was the 1st vessel and *Musashi* the 2nd)

(1) Direction finding room (*Hōi sokuteishitsu*) (Received data from D/F revolving loop antennae)

(2) Air lookout post (*Jōkū kansokujo*)

(3) Upper electric wiring room of the bridge (*Kankyō jōbu haisenshitsu*)

(4) Antennae yard as well as signal yard (*Kūchūsen keta ken shingō keta*)

(5) Position of 60-cm signal light (*60 senchi shingōtō*)

(6) Direction signal light (*Hōkō shingōtō*)

(7) Yamakawa light (*Yamakawa-tō*) (This was an infrared light connected to a pair of 12-cm binoculars, viz. (18))

(8) Sea chart table (*Kaizu-dai*)

(9) Sea chart storage (*Kaizu-bako*)

(10) Log book and signal book table (*Nisshi-dai ken shingōsho-dai*)

(11) Log book table (*Nisshi-dai*)

(12) Signal book table (*Shingōsho-dai*)

(13) Step/platform (*Fumi-dai*)

(14) Magnetic compass (*Jiki-rashingi*)

(15) Repeater compass (*Jū-rashingi*)

(16) Repeater compass (*Jū-rashingi*)

(17) 18-cm binoculars (*18 senchi sōgan-bōenkyō*)

(18) 12-cm binoculars (*12 senchi sōgan-bōenkyō*)

(19) Hanging type 12-cm binoculars (*Kensuishiki 12 senchi sōgan-bōenkyō*)

(20) Screw rpm receiver (*Kaiten jushinki*)

(21) Voltage type speed indicator (*Denatsu shiki sokudokei*)

(22) Rudder angle receiver (*Dakaku jushinki*)

(23) Change of range receiver (*Henkyo jushinki*)

(24) Target bearing and target speed receiver (*Tekishin tekisoku jushinki*)

(25) Range-taking receiver (main) (*Sokkyo jushinki (shu)*)

(26) Range-taking receiver (auxiliary) (*Sokkyo jushinki (fuku)*)

(27) Loud voice order transmitter (*Kōsei reitatsuki*)

(28) Engine telegraph (*Sokuryoku shijiki*)

(29) Rhumb receiver (*Kōtei jushinki*)

(30) Speed receiver (*Sokudo jushinki*)

(31) Wind intensity receiver (*Fūsoku jushinki*)

(32) Wind direction receiver (*Fūkō jushinki*)

(33) Blinking signal alarm transmitter (*Tenmetsu hōchiki*) (used if distance[s] became too small)
(34) Firing command order transmitter (*Shashitsu gōrei hatsureiki*)
(35) Firing preparation receiver (*Shashitsu seibi jushinki*)
(36) Distribution box (*Haiden-bako*)
(37) Change-over switch (*Tenkanki*)
(38) Telegraph key Type 3 (*Denken 3 Gata*)
(39) Type 90 wireless telephone transmitter (*90 Shiki musendenwa sōwaki*)
(40) Repeater compass connection box (*Jū-rashingi setsuzoku-bako*)
(41) Engine telegraph (*Sokuryoku shijiki*)
(42) Clock (*Tokei*)
(43) Stool (*Koshikake*)

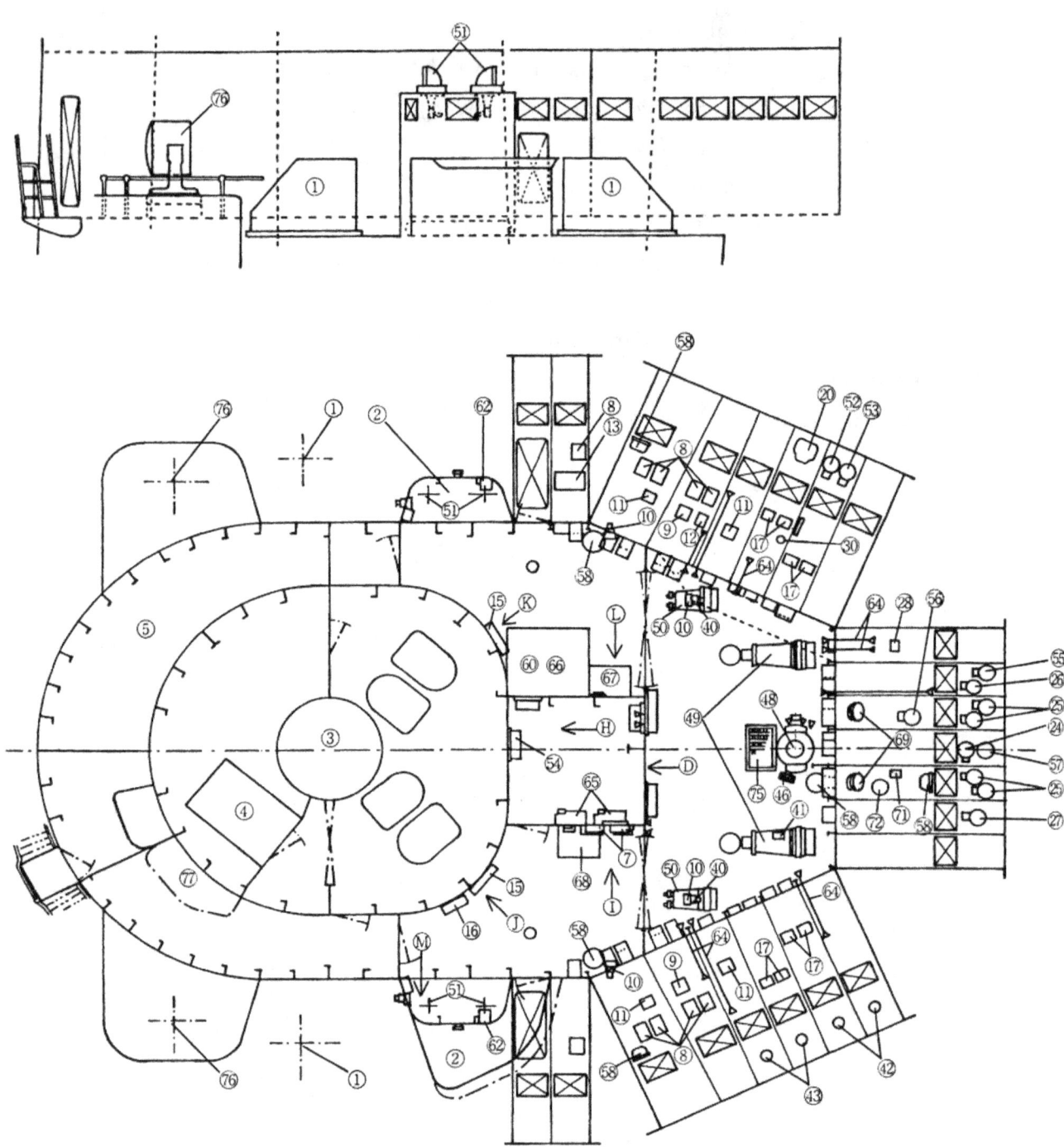

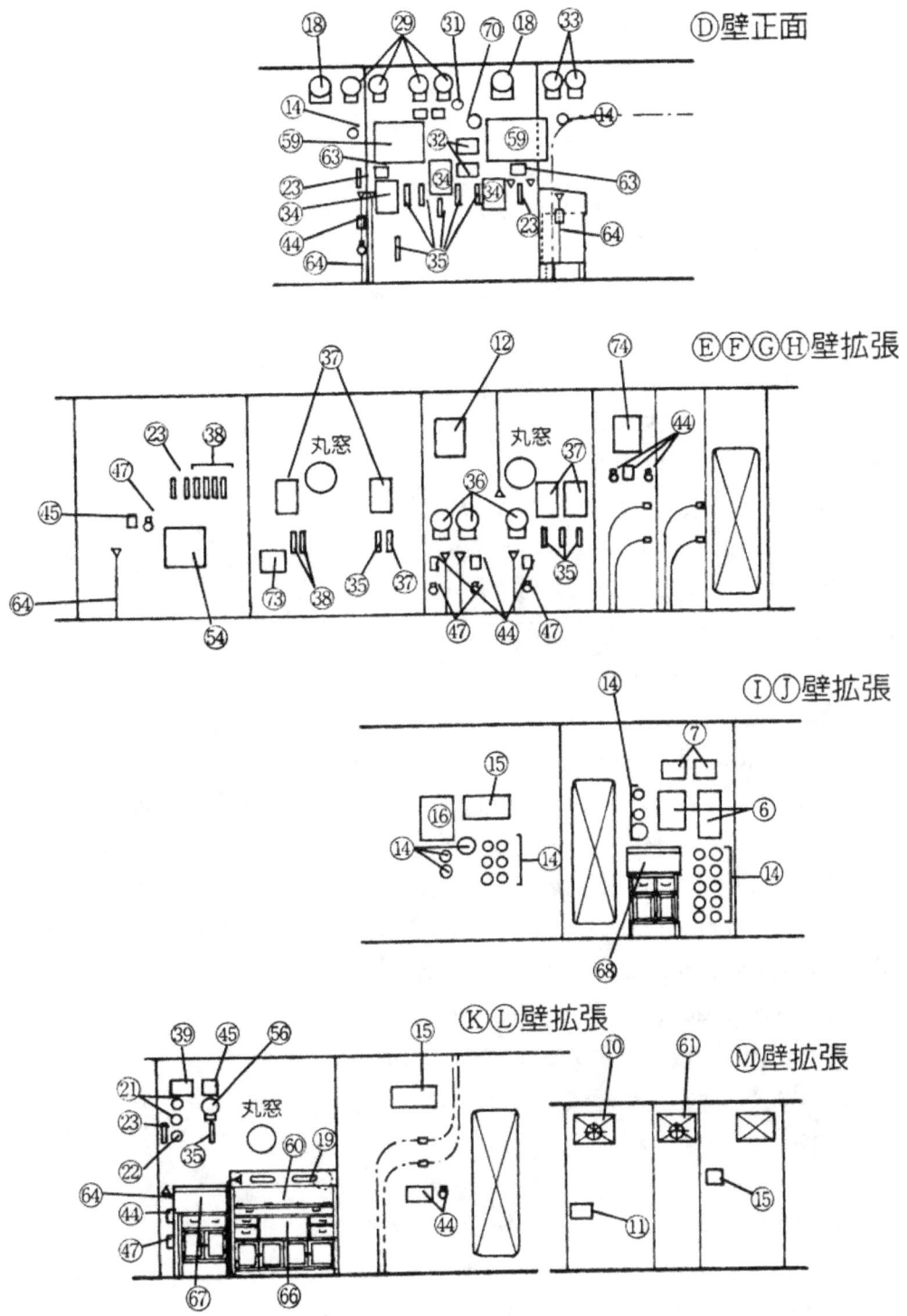

Figures 4-11–16: 1st vessel, 2nd bridge equipment (*Dai 1 Gō kan Dai 2 kankyō sōchi*) (*Nihon no Senkan*)

(D) = Front wall; (E) to (M) = Wall expansions

(1) Searchlight controller (*Tanshōtō kanseiki*)
(2) Air lookout post (*Jōkū kansokujo*)
(3) Communication tube (*Tsūshintō*)
(4) Elevator (*Shōkōki*)
(5) Stand-by room for watch (*Heiin taikisho*)
(6) Blinking signal alarm (*Tenmetsu hōchiki*)
(7) Distribution box (*Haiden-bako*)
(8) Telegraph key Type 3 (*Denken 3 Gata*)
(9) Change-over switch (*Tenkanki*)
(10) Direction signal light (*Hōkō shingōtō*)
(11) Connection box (*Setsuzokuza-bako*)
(12) Resistance regulator (*Teikō kagenki*)
(13) Change-over switch (*Tenkanki*)
(14) Contact breaker (*Setsudanki*)
(15) Controller (*Kanseiki*)
(16) Distribution box (*Haiden-bako*)
(17) Indicator light for wireless telephone (*Musendenwa yō shijitō*)
(18) Echo sounder repeater (*Jū-tanshingi*)
(19) Sounding receiver (*Sokushin jushinki*)
(20) Sonar direction angle receiver (*Suichū chōonki kakudo jushinki*)
(21) Sonar contact position (Suichū chōonki juchōki setsuzokuza)
(22) Echo sounder sound listener socket (*Tanshingi juchōki setsuzokuza*)
(23) Direct dialling telephone (*Chokutsū denwa*)
(24) Rudder angle receiver (*Dakaku jushinki*)
(25) Speed receiver (*Sokudo jushinki*)
(26) Screw rpm receiver (*Kaiten jushinki*)
(27) Rangefinder data receiver (*Sokkyo jushinki*)
(28) Rudder angle change transmitter (*Tenda hasshinki*)
(29) Rangefinder data receiver (*Sokkyo jushinki*)
(30) Rescue call button (*Kyūnan oshibotan*)
(31) Emergency alert receiver (*Hijō jushinki*)
(32) Lookout call button (*Mihariyō oshibotan*)
(33) Change of range receiver (*Henkyo jushinki*)

(34) Type 92 telephone exchanger (*92 Shiki tokushu kōkanki*)
(35) Type 92 loud speaking telephone (*92 Shiki kōsei denwaki*)
(36) Order transmitter (*Gōrei hasshinki*)
(37) Type 92 telephone exchanger (*92 Shiki tokushu kōkanki*)
(38) Type 92 loud voice telephone (*92 Shiki kōsei denwaki*)
(39) Loud voice order transmitter (*Kōsei reitatsu hasshinki*)
(40) Direction order transmitter (*Hōkō hasshinki*)
(41) Rudder angle indicator light (*Sōkaji hyōjitō*)
(42) Target bearing and target speed receiver (*Tekishin tekisoku jushinki*)
(43) Change of range receiver (*Henkyo jushinki*)
(44) Indicator button (*Shijiki oshibotan*)
(45) Transmitter for smoke screen (*Baienmaku hasshinki*)
(46) Rudder angle telegraph (*Sōda tsūshinki*)
(47) Electric bells (*Denshō*)
(48) Type 93 magnetic compass (*93 Shiki jiki-rashingi*)
(49) 18-cm binoculars *(18 senchi sōgan-bōenkyō)*
(50) 12-cm binoculars (*12 senchi sōgan-bōenkyō*)
(51) L-shaped 12-cm binoculars (*L gata 12 senchi sōgan-bōenkyō*)
(52) Wind direction receiver (*Fūkō jushinki*)
(53) Wind intensity receiver (*Fūsoku jushinki*)
(54) Course and rhumb transmitter (*Shinro kōtei hasshinki*)
(55) Speed receiver (*Sokudo jushinki*)
(56) Rhumb receiver (*Kōtei jushinki*)
(57) Clock (*Tokei*)
(58) Repeater compass (*Jū-rashingi*)
(59) Elevation and training angle receiver (*Fugyō senkai kakudo jushinki*)
(60) Ship's track tracer panel (*Jigaban*)
(61) Light box for Yamakawa light (*Yamakawa tōbako*)
(62) Controller (*Kanseiki*)
(63) Push button (*Oshibotan*)
(64) Voice-pipe (*Denseikan*)
(65) Air pressure chute (*Kūki densōkan*) (For transmitting paper messages)
(66) Sea chart storage (*Kaizu-bako*)
(67) War diary table (*Nisshi-dai*)
(68) Signal book table (*Shingōsho-dai*)
(69) Indicator to engine telegraph (*Sokuryoku tsūshinki shijiki*) (pair)

(70) Inclinometer (*Keishakei*)
(71) Electric circuit connection box (*Denro setsuzokuza-bako*)
(72) Control panel/switchboard (*Denro tenkanki*)
(73) Voltage resistance box (*Kōatsu teikōki-bako*)
(74) Resistance regulator (*Teikō kagenki*)
(75) Step/platform (*Fumi-dai*)
(76) Position of 60-cm signal light (*60 senchi shingōtō*)
(77) Weapon (weather measuring instrument) (*Kishō-heiki sōbi ichi*)

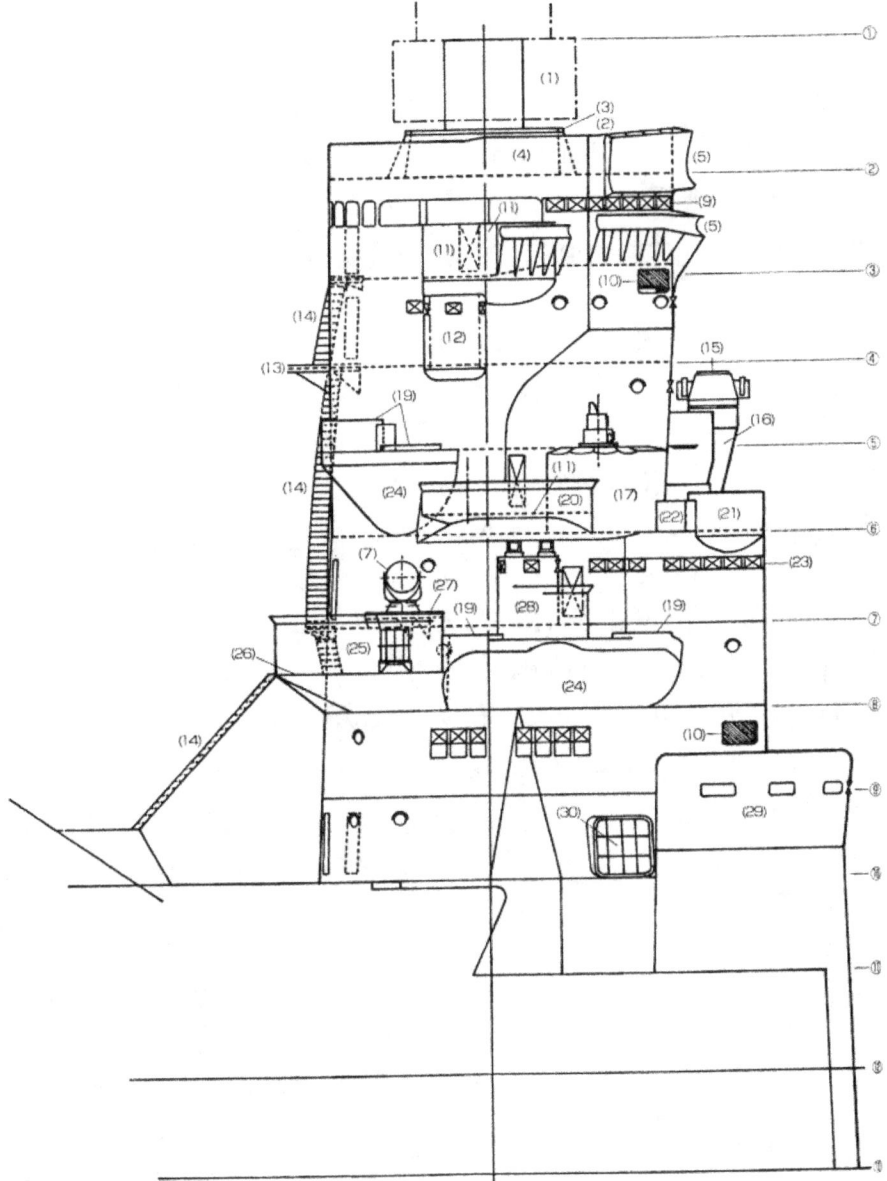

Figure 4-17: This and the following two drawings (4-18 & 4-19) differ from the hitherto published exterior views of the *Musashi*'s foremast and it may be of interest to compare the differences. The positions are: (1) The projecting platforms (sponsons) on both sides of the 1st bridge, (2) the projecting platforms (sponsons) of the signal command post on both sides of the operation room, (3) the 60-cm signal light sponsons, (4) signal post, (5) sponsons for the searchlight controller. However, with the order for fitting No. 22 radar (Navy Technical Department secret order No. 2549 dated 15 June 1943–*Kanpon kimitsu 2549 Gō*) the disassembly of the 60-cm signal light sponsons was ordered (*Nihon no Senkan*)

The decks (figures 4-17–19):

(1) Forward rangefinder tower (*Zenbu sokkyotō*)
(2) Air defense command station deck (*Bōkūshikisho kanpan*)
(3) 1st bridge deck (battle bridge) (*Dai ichi kankyō kanpan*)
(4) Order transmitting, operation room deck (*Denreisho, sakusenshikisho kanpan*)
(5) Rest room deck (*Kyūkeisho kanpan*)
(6) Secondary gun fire command station deck (*Fukuhō shagekishikisho kanpan*)
(7) 2nd bridge deck (*Dai ni kankyō kanpan*)
(8) Signal post deck (*Shigōsho kanpan*)
(9) Lower lookout deck (*Kabu miharijo kanpan*)
(10) Lower searchlight deck (*Kabu tanshōtō kanpan*)
(11) Upper high-angle gun deck (*Jōbu kōkakuhō kanpan*)
(12) Lower high-angle gun deck (*Kabu kōkakuhō kanpan*)
(13) Uppermost deck (*Saijō kanpan*)

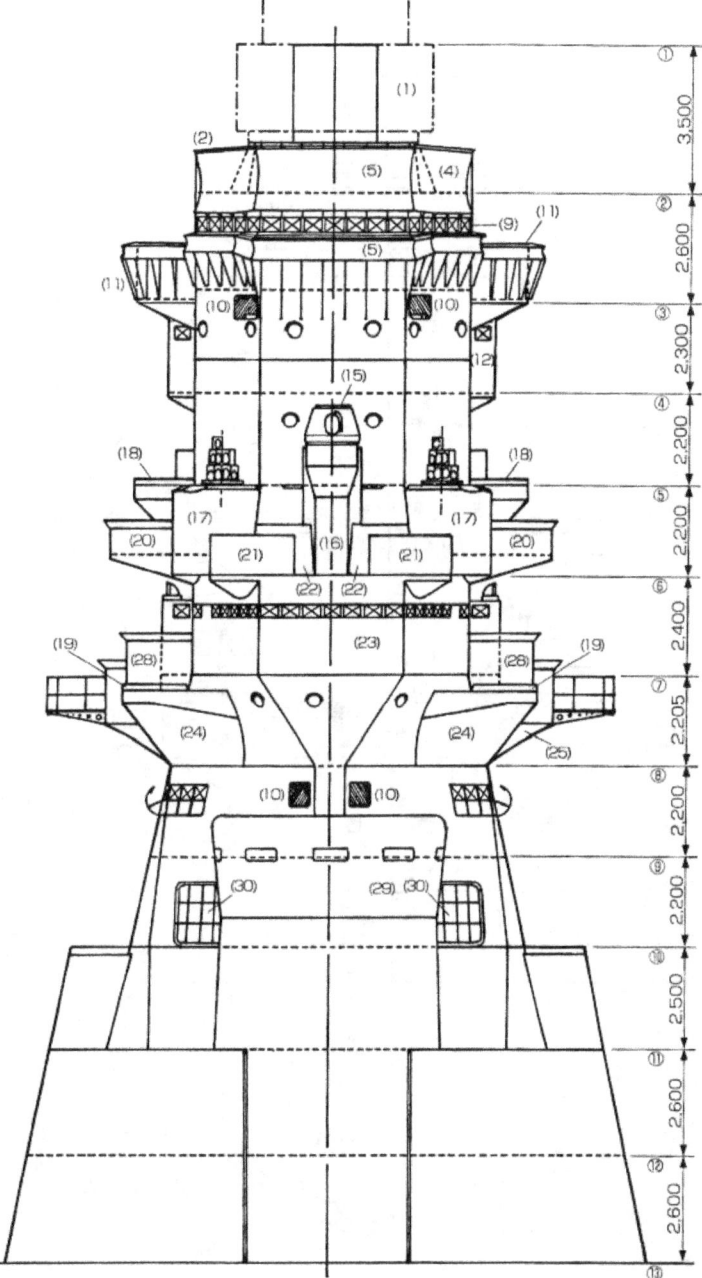

Figure 4-18: Pay attention to the structure of the decks, the connection between the 25-mm machine-gun fire control systems on both sides on the front of the secondary gunfire command station deck and the support of the 1.5-m rangefinder (*sokkyogi*). This is also explained as a passageway but it was actually the motor room for the training of the 25-mm machine-gun fire control system tower. The four black windows on the front of the foremast, two each below the 1st bridge and the signal post deck, mark the positions where the temporarily called Type 0 12-cm binoculars (retractable) were fitted (*Nihon no Senkan*)

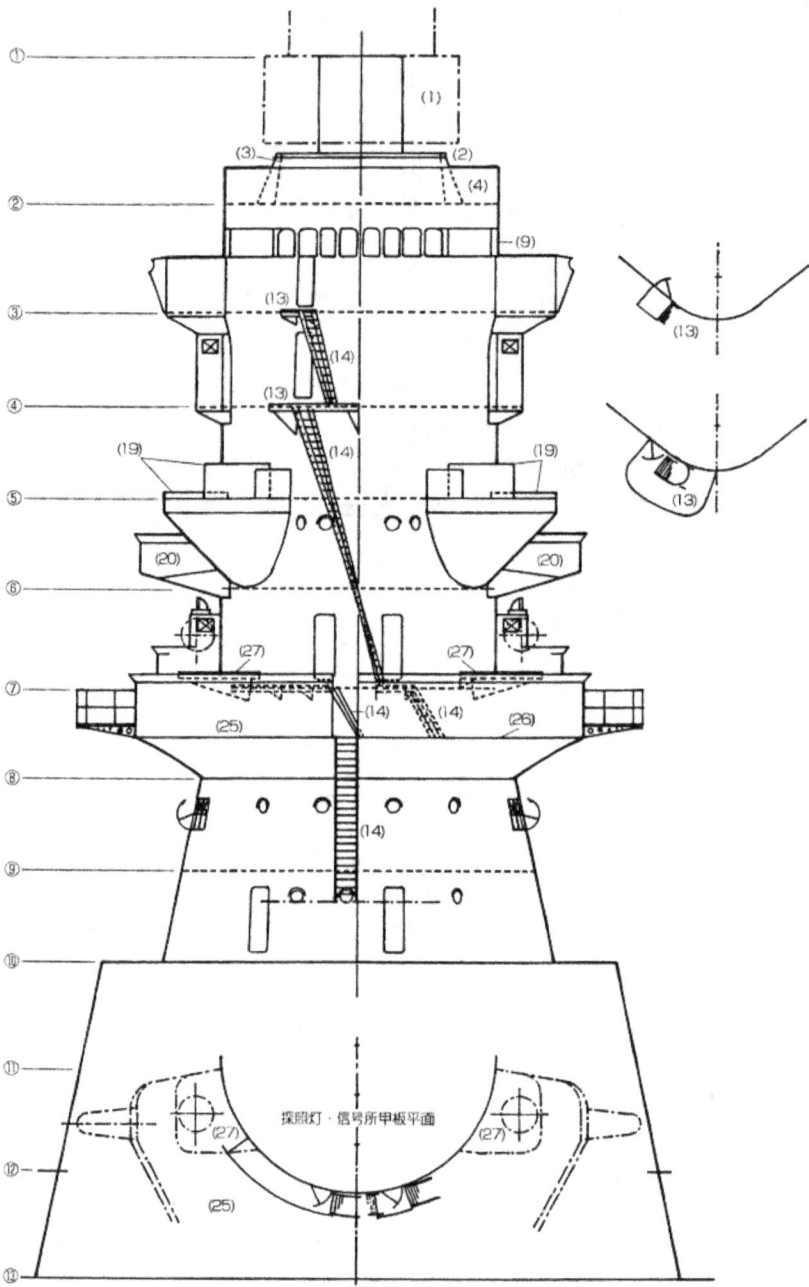

Figure 4-19: Note the ladder on the rear of the foremast. *Musashi* lacked one rest place compared with the *Yamato*. The shapes of the rest places were also different and this was an identification mark (viz. the recollections of Vice-Admiral Niwata Shōzō in this book). With the Navy Technical Department secret order No. 2549, dated 15 June 1943, the revision of the sponson of the 60-cm signal light and the signal post was ordered (*Nihon no Senkan*)

(1) Type 39 15-m rangefinder (*39 Shiki 15 mētoru sokkyogi*)
(2) Target speed and (target) bearing measurement station (*Sokutekisho*)
(3) Order transmitting station (*Denreisho*)
(4) Air defense command station (*Bōkūshikisho*)
(5) Wind baffle (*Kazeyoke*)
(6) Signal yard (*Shingō keta*)
(7) 60-cm signal light sponson (*60 senchi shingōtō-dai*)
(8) 2-kW signal light (*2-kW shingōtō*)
(9) 1st bridge (battle bridge) (*Dai ichi kankyō*)
(10) Type 0 12-cm binoculars (*Rei Shiki 12 senchi sōgan-bōenkyō*)
(11) Air lookout station (*Jōkū miharijo*)
(12) Signal order station sponson (*Shingō shikisho haridashi*)
(13) Ladder rest place (*Shōkō furatto* [flat])
(14) Ladder (*Shōkō hashigo*)
(15) 1.5m rangefinder (*1.5 mētoru sokkyogi*)
(16) 1.5m rangefinder sponson/support (*1.5 mētoru sokkyogi-dai*)
(17) Type 98 secondary gun fire control system (*Fukuhō 98 Shiki hōiban shōjun sōchi*)
(18) 13-mm machine-gun flat (*13 miru kijū furatto*)
(19) Searchlight controller sponson (*Tanshōtō kanseiki-dai*)
(20) 13-mm twin machine-gun sponson (*13 miru rensō kijū-dai*)
(21) 25-mm machine-gun fire control system (*25 miru kijū shagekisōchi-dai*)
(22) 25-mm machine-gun fire director tower training equipment (*25 miru kijū shagekitō senkaisōchi*)
(23) 2nd bridge (*Dai ni kankyō*)
(24) Searchlight flat (*Tanshōtō torisuke furatto*)
(25) Lower lookout station deck, light signal flat (*Kabu miharijo kanpan, shingōtō furatto*)
(26) Searchlight and signal station ddeck (*Tanshōtō, shingōjo kanpan*)
(27) Searchlight flat (*Tanshōtō torisuke furatto*)
(28) 2nd bridge sponsons, air lookout posts (*Dai ni kankyō gensoku haridashi, jōkū kansokujo*)
(29) Conning tower (*Shireitō*)
(30) Mouth of ventilation trunk (*Kyūkiro*)

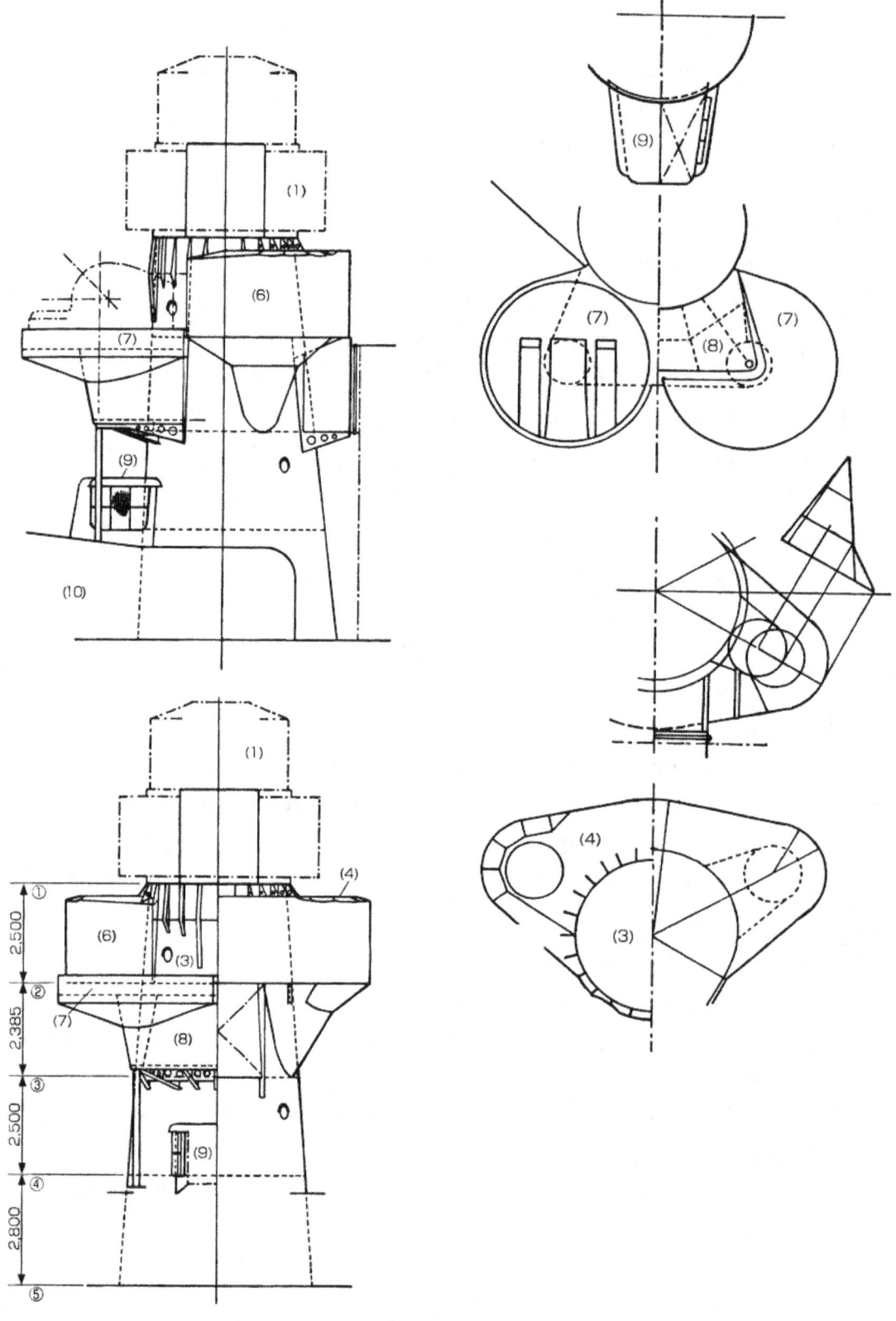

Figure 4-20–24: After bridge of the *Musashi* (*Nihon no Senkan*)

(1) After rangefinder tower (*Kōbu sokkyotō*)

(2) After secondary gun fire command station (*Fukuhō kōbu shagekishikisho*)

(3) Lower searchlight deck (*Kabu tanshōtō kanpan*)

(4) Upper high-angle gun deck (*Jōbu kōkakuhō kanpan*)

(5) Lower high-angle gun deck (*Kabu kōkakuhō kanpan*)

(1) Type 39 10-m rangefinder (*39 Shiki 10 mētoru sokkyogi*)

(2) 25-mm machine-gun fire control system sponson (*25 miru kijū shagekisōchi-dai*) (not visible on drawing)

(3) After main gun fire command station (*Kōbu shuhō shagekishikisho*)

(4) Roof of after secondary gun fire command station (*Fukuhō kōbu shagekishikisho tengai*)

(5) After secondary gun fire command station (*Fukuhō kōbu shagekishikisho*)

(6) Secondary gun Type 98 fire control system (*Fukuhō 98 Shiki hōiban shōjunsōchi*)

(7) Type 96 25-mm triple machine-gun sponson (*96 Shiki 25 miru 3 rensō kijū-dai*)

(8) Machine-gun ammunition supply position (*Kijū danyaku kyūdansho*)

(9) Mouth of exhaust trunk (*Haikikō*)

(10) Ventilation trunk (*Kyūkiro*)

NIMBLE BOOKS LLC

Chapter 5—Additional Notes on the Armor Protection

Some General Remarks about Warship Protection

The IJN divided the protection of a warship into (1) armor and (2) protective material. The latter term was generally used for a material thickness of 25.4 mm or less. In the weight classification scheme, valid since the termination of the arms limitation treaties, armor belonged to group 30, protective material to group 40. Generally speaking, items proper to the constructor were included in these groups while, e.g., gun house armor belonged to the armament group, strength members among the elements of the protective deck and non-armored bulkheads to the hull group.

Fundamentally, all elements had the same purpose and the terms "protection" or "protective arrangement" refer to both systems.

Protective arrangements had to prevent or limit the extent of damage in order to enable a warship to continue its primary function: to fight the enemy. This function means the maintenance of fighting power and mobility when under enemy attack. To respond to these requirements the vital parts, such as machinery spaces, projectile and powder magazines, steering engine room (including cross-head room), conning tower, uptakes and ventilation openings, attack weapons, etc., and their service personnel should be protected.

The methods of attack that a warship may have to withstand changed according to the progress of shipbuilding, weapon and engine development. At first, protection was developed along the line of a gunnery engagement between warships and it mainly consisted of a waterline belt and side armor. Following lessons learned during the Russo-Japanese War and World War I the underwater protection against mines and torpedoes and the radical increase of the horizontal protection against projectiles, hitting at steep angles, and later also bombs became important elements of the protection. Between the two world wars the utilisation of chemical weapons was considered and it brought about several protection methods. From the middle of World War II rockets were used by aircraft but their power was inferior compared with known weapons and required no additional protective methods.

In case of special ships, such as submarines, special weapons, like depth charges, were made necessary, as was the adoption of special protective measures.

The danger of fire generated by hits of each of these weapons required measures to limit the probability of fire and to fight it effectively when the former method was ineffective. Besides of the fire main system the drainage system, flooding and sprinkling systems, special fire fighting systems in aircraft carriers, anti-poison gas systems, damage control by counterflooding, etc. belonged to the protective measures to limit and compensate damages to some degree. Another indirect protection method was the rational subdivision of the hull into watertight compartments to limit the degree of damage. In case of submarines the reduction of own ship's noise also belonged to the protective methods.

Owing to the limited weight and size of a warship, complete protection against all kinds of attack was impossible. Therefore, the degree of protection mainly depended upon type, duty and size of the own ship and most the probable types of enemy attacks. Also, within a protective system, the importance of each protected part for the maintenance of fighting power and mobility, as well as the kind and degree of the enemy's destructive power to which it most probably would be exposed, had to be considered very thoroughly in order to select the most suitable defense.

The methods of defending the own ship against the enemy's destructive power were (1) direct protection, (2) indirect protection and (3) supplementary protective methods.

Direct protection meant the armor fitted to stop the intrusion of projectiles, torpedoes, bombs, etc. into the vital parts. This armor was directly exposed to the enemy's weapon effect and it consisted of all kinds of vertical and horizontal armor.

Behind this "outer" armor the "inner" protective material was fitted at some distance. It was arranged to protect the vital parts against splinters, armor bolts, rivet heads, etc. and consisted mainly of thin bulkheads behind the side armor and a "second" deck underneath the armored one.

The chemical and physical properties of these materials differed depending upon their purpose.[118]

Ships too small for direct protection, were given indirect protection and this meant the rational subdivision of the hull into watertight compartments in order to minimise damage and, hence, the range of flooding to prevent the loss of buoyancy. In case of large ships, such as battleships, aircraft carriers and heavy cruisers, both direct and indirect protection were used to various degrees, while light cruisers (when smaller than heavy cruisers, which was not always the case) only had much restricted direct protection. Destroyers had only very limited indirect protection.

With the application of protective measures the designers also intended to maintain reserve buoyancy and stability.

---

[118] The very heavy side armor of large warships designed to stand up against enemy gunfire required extreme hardness on the surface and sufficient toughness behind this layer; while in case of the protective material high elastic limit and tensile strength were required, primarily. This armor was termed "face-hardened" armor and was designed to stop an enemy weapon "in its tracks" or to so damage it as to limit its effectiveness if it does penetrate this outer armor layer.

The thinner plating designed to stop smaller, less penetrative weapons is usually kept soft and tough throughout its volume, termed "homogeneous", ductile armor. It resists by its ability to deform and absorb the impact gradually with minimal tearing until the last possible moment. Toughness (crack resistance) is equally required in addition to strength and hardness, so this kind of armor sometimes uses less strong materials that can stretch more easily. This is especially true for armor for use against fragments and blast, including underwater blast. It has included true armor steels like US Navy Special Treatment Steel (STS) used extensively for light armor and thinner portions of the heavy armor in large warships after about 1905, but also sometimes high-strength construction steels like British HT, US Navy HTS, and later British, Japanese, and Italian DuCol ("D") steels used both for light armor and construction purposes ("killing two birds with one stone," as it were).

Armor designed to deflect, rather than stop, an enemy weapon hitting at a highly oblique angle, such as the thicker armored decks and turret roofs, also uses the homogeneous, ductile armor type, but in this case highest strength is also needed, so such armor designed to resist the direct hits from large AP projectiles of battleships is invariably a material like US Navy Class "B" armor or STS or equivalent (British NCA, German Wh, Japanese NVNC, CNC, or MNC, etc.). This material is usually an alloy or alloys that are rather similar to the face-hardened armor type(s) used by that same country at the same time, though minor details in these alloys will be different to optimise their individual properties. Note that face-hardened armors usually have poor performance compared to an equal weight of homogeneous armor against such highly oblique impacts, since the hard face of the face-hardened armor may deflect the projectile, but be punched out like a cue ball (the projectile) hitting a group of billiard balls (the armor plate) at an angle, bouncing off, but throwing some balls out the far side (armor chunks going into the ship)–this is obviously not desired! [Nathan Okun]

Supplementary protective measures were the introduction of various equipment in double and triple quantity, such as the adoption of a steering engine for each of the main and auxiliary rudders of the *Yamato* class and the aircraft carrier *Taihō*, the utilisation of double (later triple) telemotors for each steering engine of the *Yamato* class, double fire fighting systems (CO_2 and foam) in aircraft carriers, installation of both sprinkler and flooding systems in ammunition magazines, etc., in order to ensure the ship's function in case of damage. Efficient damage control equipment in double quantity also belonged to this category. Similar to the indirect protection, supplementary protective measures could be realized comparatively easy in large ships but hardly in classes below heavy cruisers.

As long as the warships were built abroad, mostly in Britain, the IJN adopted British designs. With the planning of the capital ships of the "Eight-Eight Fleet" the IJN designs became more independent and, as far as the underwater protection is concerned, a new Japanese style was created.

Until the construction of the first class cruisers (later battle cruisers) of the *Tsukuba* class the IJN imported armor plates and steel for armor from abroad, but for these ships domestically produced armor was partly used.

The history of armor and armor protection is the adoption of foreign techniques for the first period of about 35 years, while the following period may be characterized by continuous progress, independence from abroad and efforts to attain a high state of development. This eventually culminated in the protection designs of the battleships of the *Yamato* class, the heavy cruisers of the *Tone* class and the aircraft carrier *Taihō*, which introduced some novel features but also showed fatal defects and weak points in design and fabrication.

Basic Considerations for New Armor Types

After the building of the battleships *Nagato* and *Mutsu* the production of thick armor plates stopped[119] as a result of the so-called Naval Holidays, but study and research were continued and intensified in preparation for the construction of the WWII super-battleships. In his "Recollection about Ship Armors and Special Steel Production" the former Technical Rear-Admiral Dr. (Eng.) Sasagawa Kiyoshi evaluated the protective power as "the key point of the design" of the *Yamato* class and emphasised that "the essence of our steel technology was concentrated" on it.

The requirement of the tacticians to make the *Yamato* class safe against 46-cm projectiles fired from 45-cal guns at distances from 20,000 m to 30,000 m could not be fulfilled with the hitherto applied armor, because the kinetic energy of the 46-cm projectile necessitated unprecedented armor thicknesses for the direct protection of the vital parts. Thickness meant weight, but its increase could be avoided with better quality. Refined methods would permit the production of tremendous amounts in time and the use of raw materials available in Japan decreased the dependence from abroad. Therefore, the following basic considerations were considered when developing new armor types:

(1) In case of the thick armor the protective power against the impact of large calibre AP projectiles (*taidan kōryoku*) decreases with the increase of the thickness. This effect must be, at least, stopped and efforts be made to reverse it. In other words: The quantitative increase should be accompanied by qualitative and also structural improvements.[120]

(2) The larger the fighting distance the larger the elevation angle of the gun and the angle of fall of the projectile. The kinetic energy of a 1,460-kg heavy 46-cm shell hitting with a velocity of about 500 m/s far surpasses that of the hitherto mounted gun calibres. The shock upon an armor plate caused by the impact of the projectile is so big that the probability of its destruction is likewise big. In order to avoid penetration by an enemy shell, when the armor is thinner than the calibre of the gun, it is

---

[119] The belt armor of heavy cruisers had a maximum thickness of 127 mm.

[120] This is called "Scaling" and it has more or less effects, depending on the structural properties needed by the material to do its job as the size of the mass being used increases. Here, the purpose is to stop larger and larger enemy projectiles with thicker and thicker plates. [Nathan Okun]

absolutely necessary to destroy the strong head by increasing the thickness of the very hard layer on the armor plate surface and to improve the toughness of the back. In other words: The enemy projectile should be broken and the armor plate remain intact.[121]

(3) The thickness of the deck armor must be about half the calibre and withstand the impact of flat-headed capped AP shells hitting at steep angles of fall–as well as bombs. The mounting of a horizontal splinter deck is desirable.

(4) In order to produce large quantities of armor plates the production time must be shortened, the production capacity increased and the expenses saved. Because Japan is poor in natural resources the production of armor using material available in Japan is necessary.

(5) The warships have limited displacement. Therefore, all unnecessary weight must be avoided even in the armor. To obtain this goal, the most suitable forms, improvement of joint efficiency, fitting methods and the concept of using of as much armor as possible also for increasing the structural strength of the hull must be investigated.

This resulted in the invention of new types of armor material called NVNC, VH, MNC and CNC (CNC_1 and CNC_2), the extension of the application of tapered armor and the adoption of honeycomb armor instead of coaming armor.[122]

---

[121] This is <u>only</u> for impacts where stopping the projectile, rather than deflecting it, is primary the method of achieving the desired protection and projectile nose breakage reduces the projectile's ability to punch through the plate hit. A broken projectile may throw pieces of itself through a hole made in an armour plate, where an intact projectile will bounce off in one piece with rather little damage other than to the armour plate hit, which is what an armour plate is designed to accept, after all. Also, a broken projectile does not ricochet well, since an upward force on the nose no longer pulls the rest of the projectile along with it if the nose ricochets. For both reasons, breakage of a projectile at high obliquity impacts is therefore something to be avoided. [Nathan Okun]

[122] New Vickers Non-Cemented (NVNC) and Vickers Hardened (VH) use the same high-carbon-content steel, the former a homogeneous, ductile armor and the latter the same armor with a thick hard face quenched into it. NVNC was used in several up-armored battleships and in the *Yamato* class for all homogeneous, ductile heavy armor except the main armored deck. Molybdenum Non-Cemented (MNC) is an improved alloy similar to NVNC, but with less carbon, giving increased toughness (crack resistance), and using the alloy element molybdenum to increase the ability to strengthen the steel during manufacture (British and German post-WWI armor steels used this element extensively in their armor steels, while the US WWII naval armor manufacturers only used it for some thicknesses of homogeneous Class "B" naval armor, avoiding this element otherwise). VH for

Vickers Hardened Armor (VH)

VH plates were used for the (1) 410-mm thick hull side armor, (2) 660-mm thick front shield of the main gun turrets and (3) 560-mm thick upper part of the main gun barbettes.

The biggest features were (1) to stop the surface carbonisation of the V(ickers) C(emented) armor and (2) to improve the toughness of the back plate.[123] These goals were attained by the adoption of a special production

---

the thick side armor and MNC for the heavy 20–23-cm main deck armor were only used in the *Yamato* class battleships. Copper Non-Cemented (CNC) was only for homogeneous armors up to 10 cm thick, or even less in some cases, in either of its two grades (thicker plates did not pass the minimum acceptance tests; another scaling effect) and used copper to replace a significant amount of the nickel used in the other armor steels mentioned above–this was to save expensive, hard-to-get-in-Japan nickel for more important uses. CNC plates were by far the most widely used armor plates in very many Japanese WWII warships, including all cruisers, so the saving in nickel was considerable. [Nathan Okun]

[123] The face layer back to the point where the face completely ends and the back layer starts, in all Japanese face-hardened armor plates, VC or VH, was exactly 35%, which is what the face thickness was for the original German Krupp Company "Krupp Cemented" (KC) armor developed in 1894 and retained by Krupp through 1918 (called "KC a/A" later to differentiate it from the later "KC n/A" used in the pocket battleship turret faces and, in an improved alloy, in the *Scharnhorst* and *Bismarck* class warships of WWII). It was later licensed to all other manufacturers as the only kind of side armor by 1905, who used it as-is or who modified it considerably, with varying results. This was also the face thickness of the British KC armor that Vickers used circa 1912 when the IJN *Kongō* was made in Britain and later three copies made in Japan. See US Naval Technical Mission to Japan, Report O-16, page 15, figure 3. Indeed, Japanese high quality control meant that their VC and VH armors had plate-to-plate differences in their face layer properties that were less than any other manufacturers through the end of WWII. Standard production VH plates of all thicknesses made for *Shinano*–not experimental plates–tested by the US Navy after WWII had almost perfect 35% faces no matter how they might vary (not much) in other properties. During the 1930's, using improved metallurgy and a better understanding of the effects of scaling than most other manufacturers, it seems, all British naval CA (KC-type "Cemented Armor") manufacturers reduced the face layer thickness to circa 25% of the plate without any loss in resistance, making the plates about the best in WWII against large-calibre projectiles due to minimum scaling from the thin face layer. Tests showed that this thinner face layer lost none of its projectile-breaking properties, as tests with British, American and German projectiles (the latter after WWII) showed. Just before and during WWII, the US Navy Class "A" (face-hardened) armor specification added a stupid [*sic*] requirement that the armor cause a certain amount of nose damage to US late-model AP projectiles–not that the shells be damaged to the point that they would not explode properly (be no longer "effective"–"fit to burst" in British nomenclature) but just that the nose be broken, for some dumb reason. To meet this part of the spec, the armor manufacturers had to use a very thick 55% face layer and by the end of WWII, US AP projectiles were so good, even that no longer worked, but that thick face caused a large scaling effect that reduced the resistance of the heaviest US Class "A" armor to large-calibre shells even though the steel quality and all other parameters were second to none. By keeping their face thickness at 35%, the Japanese avoided most

method that became a secret patent of the IJN. Roughly speaking the principles were the application of the then world's biggest hydraulic press, the change of the heat treatment and the introduction of a particular method for the investigation of the physical properties. An outline of the process follows.

Melting and Ingot Practice

All armor steel was made in the acid open hearth (AOH) process. For the production of the large quantity the Third Steel Work (Seikō Kōjō) was established in Kure Navy Yard and four new acid open hearth furnaces of 70 tons each were installed. In the charges about 35% pig iron (mainly from Korea [Kenjuko] or Kamaishi [Iwate Prefecture]) and 65% scrap were used. The heats of three furnaces were necessary to fill up one mould in order to get one ingot of approximately 200 tons.[124]

Rolling and Forging

The steel ingot was roughly forged to approximately half of reduction and then rolled. Forging was accomplished by a very large hydraulic press,[125] roll-

---

of the problems, as that face thickness is a good all-round value, as Krupp had found out. [Nathan Okun]

Comment to the above footnote regarding Mr. Okun's statement that "... all Japanese face-hardened armor plates, ..., was exactly 35%, ...": Figure 5-3 clearly shows approx. 1/5 (the 60 mm shown in figure 5-6) for VC and for VH the 135 mm in figure 5-5 and the about 140 mm mentioned under the headline "Face-Hardening," do not correspond with exactly 35%, which would be 143.5 mm. See also the comments to figures 5-5 and 5-6 under the same headline. Consequently the authors do not agree with Mr. Okun's statement.

[124] The ingot for one 410-mm VH plate had the following details: (1) Top pouring mould, big end up, (2) rectangular section with rounded corners and a slight taper, (3) approximate dimensions in cm:

Item	Height	Width	Thickness
Hot top	132	272	190
Body	363	292/286	190

(4) Weight 175 tons.

[125] This hydraulic press (*suiatsu-ki*) was then the largest in the world. Before its purchase the thickness of the armor plates had been finished by the rolling mill. This method affected the front and rear layers but left the central layers untouched. The Steel Division of Kure Navy Yard declined any responsibility for the production without the new hydraulic press for neither the thicknesses could be finished nor the structure of the central layers be affected. This turned the scale and a very big expense of ¥3,955,734 for the order of a 15,000-ton press (The 50,000 tons stated in the US Naval Technical Mission to Japan, Report O-16, p. 12, are definitively wrong.) to the German Hydraulik

ing by either the British made (Davy Bros., bought in 1904) or Japanese-made mill (using the Davy Bros. unit as a model, built in 1921) with rolls of 1.21 m in diameter in both cases and 3.61 m long in case of the former, 6.27 m long in the latter. Reciprocating steam engines of 12,000 hp drove both.[126]

Taking a 420-mm thick VH plate with the approximate dimensions 1,900-mm gauge, width 2,850 mm and length 2,160 mm (the latter was also the forging direction) and a weight after cropping of about 100 tons as an example the process of rolling and forging was as follows:

(1) Heat in a producer-gas fired furnace (used for all sequences) in 32 hours to 1,200°C, hold 10 to 15 hours.
(2) Press from 1,900 mm to 1,550 mm. Then second press to 1,340 mm.
(3) Heat to 1,200°C in 25 hours, hold 8 to 10 hours.
(4) Press to 1,100 mm.
(5) Heat to 1,200°C in 25 hours, hold 8 hours.
(6) Roll to 850 mm (4,090 mm width).
(7) Re-roll to 600 mm (width unchanged).
(8) Relief heat to 650°C in 28 hours, hold 32 hours, air cool. Then reheat to 650°C in 28 hours, hold 30 hours, air cool.
(9) Scale and scarf.
(10) Heat to 1,200°C in 25 hours, hold 8 hours.
(11) Roll to 420 mm (still 4,090 mm wide and 6,500 mm long).

Company was permitted. It was the biggest one produced by this company. Because of the capacity of the cranes in Japan the weight of the parts had to be kept below 100 tons, as an example the upper frame was divided into three, the lower one into seven parts. The parts were to be assembled in Japan under the supervision of two German engineers. These arrived somewhat late and were surprised to see that the Steel Division had the press already assembled on the basis of the German drawings. Therefore, they concentrated upon the adjustment of the press, the training of the operators and the initial operations. According to a fine contribution of the former Technical Captain Iki Tsuneo in *Suikō*, within the scope the series "History of Naval Techniques" (*Kaigun Gijutsu Monogatari*, numbers 39–41 and 45–46), "both engineers were very eager and experienced, and the press worked without trouble from the very beginning." The press was classified a "military secret" (*gunki*) and no people of the Steel Division, except those persons directly belonging to it, were permitted to enter the area of the Third Steel Work. Iki, who worked in the Steel Division, points out that assembly and operation of the press under the strict secret was very troublesome and caused numerous problems.

[126] Data according to *Kaigun Hōjutsu-shi*. In the US Naval Technical Mission to Japan, Report O-16, 9,000 hp is stated, but this is believed to be wrong.

(12) Relief heat to 650°C in 20 hours, hold 20 hours, air cool.[127]

Face-Hardening

While VC plates were carbonised ("cemented") to obtain a thin super-hard surface layer,[128] VH plates were face-hardened to attain a hardened layer of about 140 mm thickness in case of the 410 mm armor. This was accomplished by the following method:

(1) The plate was placed, face up, on a bed of wet sand of about the same thickness as the plate. The edges of the sand and the plate were insulated by firebrick. The whole assembly was supported on two layers of steel plates between 76 and 102 mm thick.

(2) One Pt-Pt/Rd thermocouple was secured to the face of the plate; another inserted into a hole through the back of the plate and extended through 70% of the plate thickness.[129]

(3) A Siemens type reverberatory furnace, with recuperator equipment, fired with producer gas was brought to 1,100 to 1,150°C and the assembly then charged into the furnace to heat the plate from the surface as rapidly as possible

---

[127] Data according to US Naval Technical Mission to Japan, Report O-16, p. 12. The data given in *Kaigun Hōjutsu-shi* etc. are much more general.

[128] About 1.25–2.5-cm thick (on the thin side compared to most other KC-type armors), circa 650 Brinell Hardness, with a circa-500 Brinell Hardness face layer just behind the cemented skin, dropping more-or-less smoothly down to circa 200 Brinell about 35% of the total plate thickness back from the face surface, forming a tough, elastic back layer, and stayed at close 200 Brinell Hardness to the plate back surface. The cementing process requires about two weeks per plate in a special cementing oven, which is obviously a significant expense and delay. This was quite conventional for KC-type armor, using the existing metallurgical skills of circa-1912. By using a tempering process to toughen the steel, which Krupp itself did not use for its KC a/A armor, British KC-type armors and, by inheritance, VC armor was slightly superior to the original KC a/A. In fact, just after *Kongō* was made, British manufacturers seem to have discovered an improved tempering process that improved their KC-type armors noticeably, something few manufacturers of the time were able to beat and which took the greatly improved skills of the mid-1930s to finally make generally better. VC armor did not get that improved technique, however, from what test results exist. VC armor had rather a high carbon content compared to most, which used 0.2–0.35% carbon (this was retained by the later VH and NVNC armors, causing brittleness problems with NVNC). [Nathan Okun]

[129] The use of two Pt-Pt/Rd thermocouples was necessary because the workers were comparatively unskilled and the process required exact temperatures. Without the adoption of this method the limitation of the surface-hardening layer to about 1/3 of the total thickness of the plate would have been impossible and even so it was difficult to obtain plates of uniform quality.

(4) The plate was removed when the interior thermocouple registered about 730°C (face had reached at least 850°C) and immediately water-sprayed at the front and back.

(5) The plate was charged with a concave curve so that the quench resulted in a more or less flat plate. However, when necessary plates were rectified at about 150°C to relieve stress.[130]

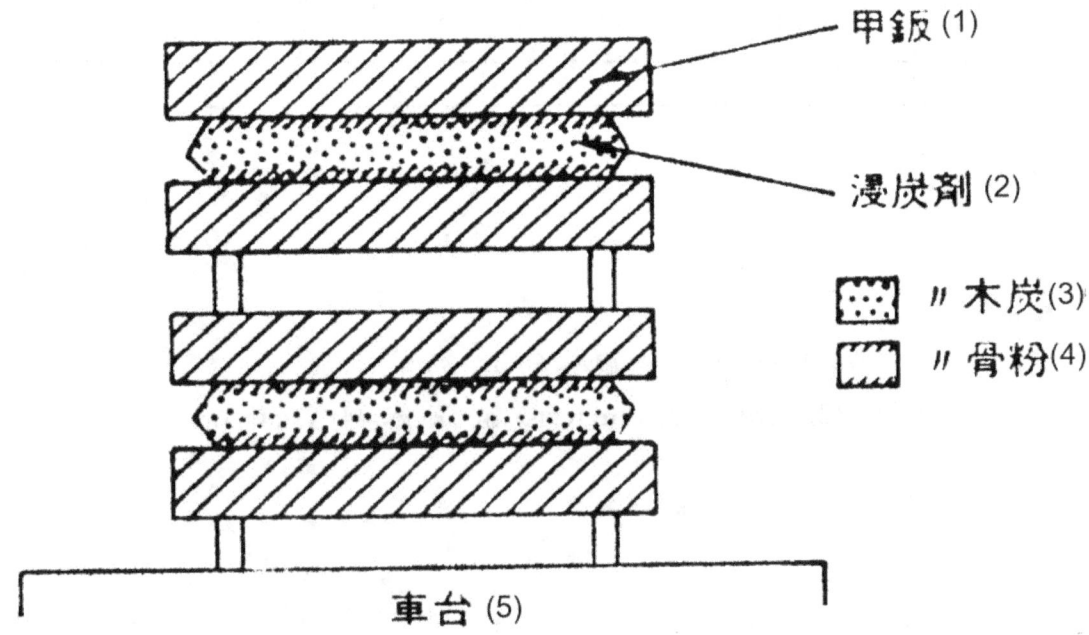

Figure 5-1: Carbonisation method (*Kaigun Hōjutsu-shi*)

(1) Armor; (2) Carbonisation chemical; (3) Charcoal; (4) Bone powder; (5) Platform

---

[130] Before the war, plates were weathered for six months before mounted on the ships to determine whether they would crack under average conditions but this was impossible in case of the plates for the *Yamato* class.

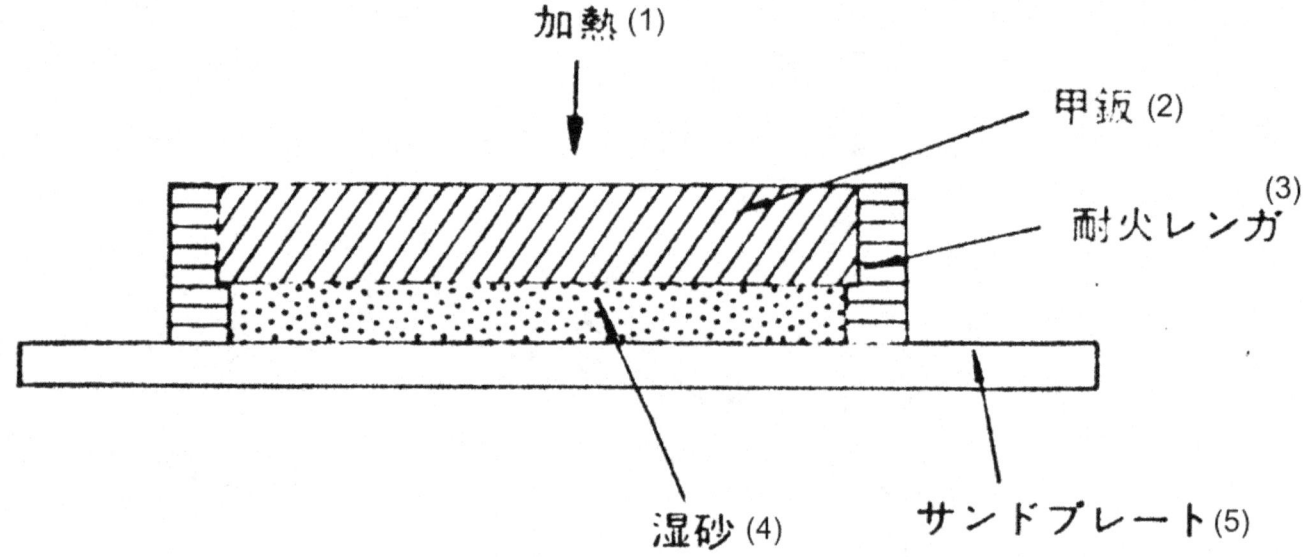

Figure 5-2: Surface hardening (*Kaigun Hōjutsu-shi*)

(1) Heating; (2) Armor; (3) Fire resistant bricks; (4) Wet sand; (5) Sand plate

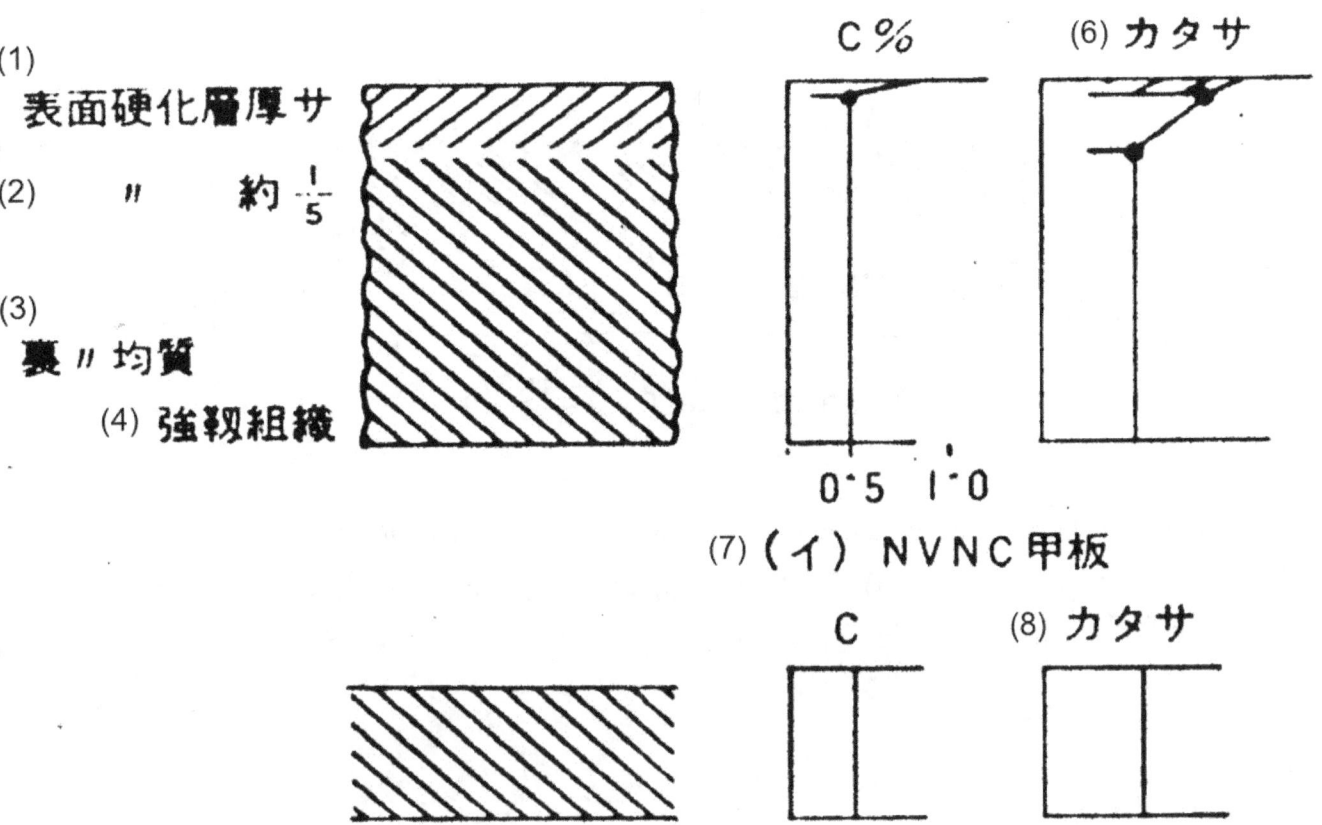

Figure 5-3: Armor, carbon content and hardness section (*Kaigun Hōjutsu-shi*)

(1) Hardened layer; (2) Thickness of hardened layer approx. 1/5; (3) Inner uniform part; (4) Tough composition; (5) (a) VC armor; (6) Hardness; (7) (b) NVNC armor; (8) Hardness

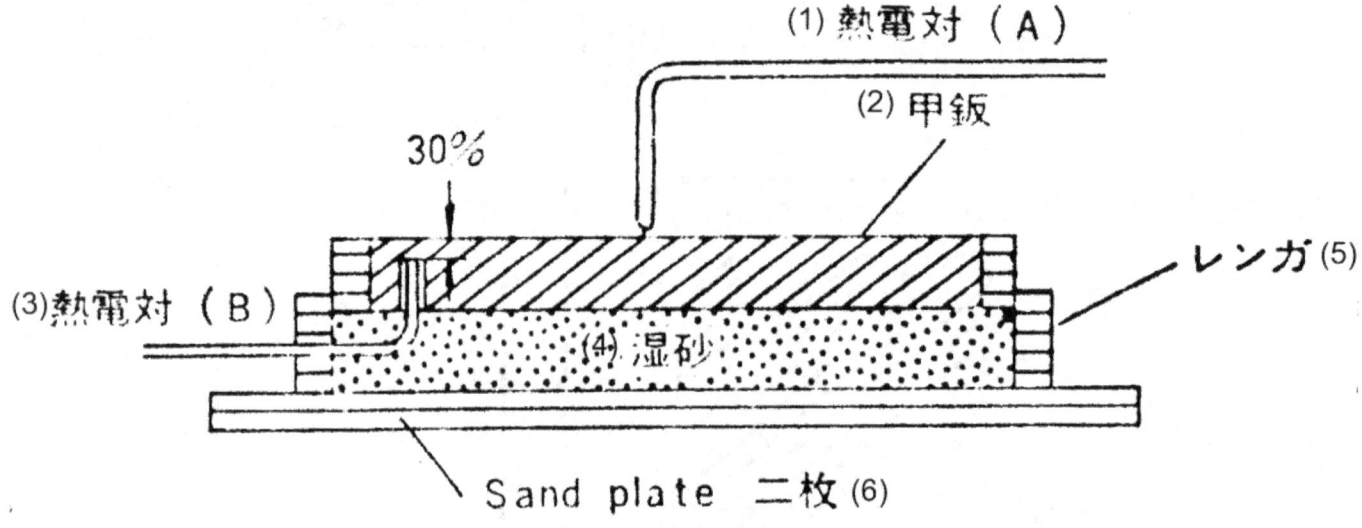

Figure 5-4: Surface heating method of armor (*Kaigun Hōjutsu-shi*)

(1) Thermocouple (A); (2) Armor; (3) Thermocouple (B); (4) Wet sand; (5) Bricks; (6) Two layers

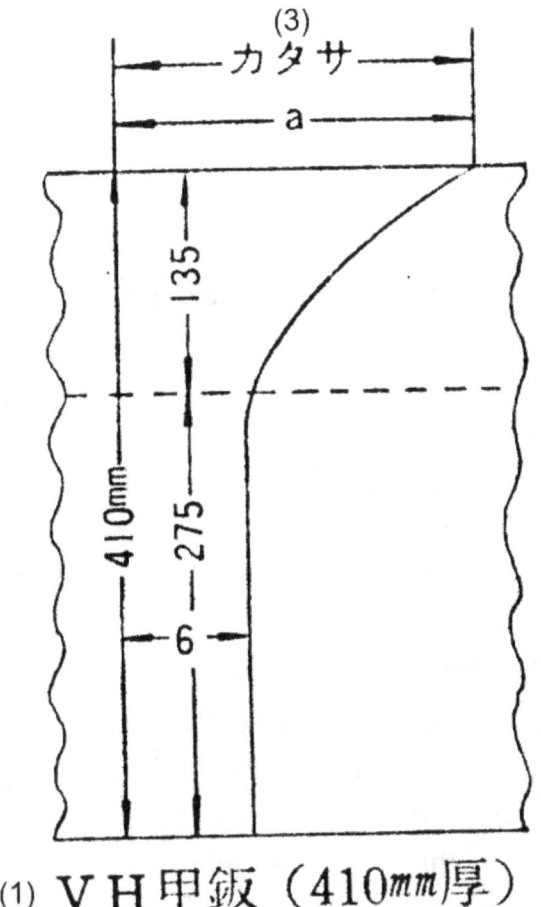
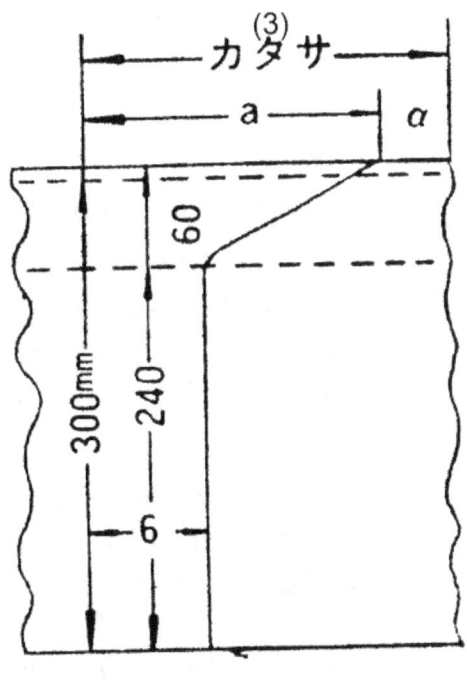

Figures 5-5-6: Comparison between VH armor (*Yamato*) and VC armor (older battleships) and experimental plate (*Kaigun Hōjutsu-shi*)

(1) VH armor (410 mm thick); (2) VC armor (300 mm thick); (3) Hardness

Figures 5-5-6 shows the comparison between VH and VC armor in relation to the thickness of the hardened part (about 1/5 in the VC and 1/3 in the VH plate).

The face-hardening process resulted in almost uniform material structure from the front to the back including the centre layers, disappearance of the so-called Krupp disease (called temper brittleness by the Japanese) and other irregularities, increase of impenetrability and reduction of the production process to about 2/3 compared with VC armor.[131]

Tests

Structural tests were conducted frequently at various processes of melting, casting, pressing, rolling, heating, quenching, etc. In none of these process cracking, webbing, strains, "ghosts", etc. were permitted if they would affect the impenetrability of the finished plate. The carbon-gradient analysis (composition test) after the heat treatment in six depths was a special test of the VH plate. The main physical tests were (1) blow-bend fracture, (2) tensile strength, (3) Izod impact and (4) Charpy shock. After these tests and the measurement of dimensions, weight and, if need be, taper and curvature a few plates underwent ballistic tests.

VH Adoption for Economical Rather than Ballistic Reasons

Before the adoption of VH armor extensive ballistic tests were conducted, which indicated only a slight superiority[132] of the VH compared with the VC in gauges from 330 mm to 430 mm, while thin plates, for example of 152 mm thickness, had even occasional inferior results. But this was meaningless for the IJN did not intend to use such thin face-hardened armor and although plates of 183 mm thickness were produced they served only for experimental purposes or projectile tests.

---

[131] The Japanese concept of "temper brittleness" was not the same as other manufacturers, as mentioned in Report O-16, page 14, since they were talking about brittle behaviour due to improper quench hardening of the middle of plates over 43-cm thick (brittle "upper bainite" crystals formed), while others were talking about tempering that failed to add toughness after quenching was over due to incorrect temperatures being used (fixing the true temper kind of temper brittleness was done by most armor manufacturers by the mid-1930s, but not by the Japanese, and fixing the thickest-plates quenching problem was eventually done, but after VH armor ceased to be made for actual ships). [Nathan Okun]

[132] According to the contemporary (1939) document "Reports On Armour Ballistic Tests". This is in contrast to the "excellent" and "much better properties" stated by Sasagawa, Matsumoto, Fukui, Makino, Niwata, etc. but they mostly refer to Sasagawa. However, in aspects other than ballistic the attributes used by these Japanese authors are surely correct. The standard penetration formula was the de Marre equation but this theme is too specialised to be discussed here.

When VH armor was finally adopted to replace VC it was for a number of economic reasons rather than ballistic ones :[133]

(1) To decrease the time cycle for production and, hence, increase the manufacturing capacity (It took about one month to produce one VC armor plate and this time was shortened to about half in case of VH armor. Thus, about twice as many armor plates could be produced with the same equipment and the costs decreased remarkably.).

(2) To eliminate carbonisation materials and fuel consumption in the carbonisation process (mainly time and cost saving).

(3) To be able to re-roll plates with certain types of defects, for example flaking, into thinner homogenous NVNC plates if necessary (NVNC and VH plates had the same analysis so that a VH plate could be changed at any time during or even after the processing [a very important economical factor]).

The maximum dimensions (l × w × thickness in mm) were 11,000 × 4,500 × 660 with a weight of 99.8 tons and those of a 410-mm side armor plate of the *Yamato* class 5,900 × 3,600 and weight 68.5 tons.

The front shield of the main gun turrets provided particular problems. It consisted of four plates of which the two sheets at the centre (between the two outer guns) had a narrow width of only 2.5 calibres. It was supposed, that the huge capped AP projectiles would destroy these plates when hitting at about 0°. There existed no method to increase the thickness of the armor or to adopt a special shape to stop the projectile. Finally, the purpose could be attained with VH armor and the maximum possible production thickness of 660 mm.[134]

---

[133] The reason that VH had no cemented layer is that it was determined by tests with hard-capped AP projectiles that the cap destroyed the thin cemented layer on impact and thus that layer had virtually no effect on the resistance to such modern anti-ship projectiles, so this expensive process was wasting time and money. This was confirmed by US tests, where the best medium-thickness US Navy Class "A" plate ever tested was an experimental Carnegie-Illinois non-cemented plate and by Krupp itself whose armor design personnel stated that they only kept cementing the plates due to "tradition" (!). Only the Japanese "put their money where their mouth was" and changed this, of all modern armor manufacturers. [Nathan Okun]

[134] The turret faceplate of *Shinano* tested by the US Navy after WWII (right side outer plate) was exactly 660-mm thick, not 650-mm thick. I do not think that the armor in *Yamato* and *Musashi* was thinner than *Shinano* here. The necessary resistance was obtained by sloping the plates back at 45 degrees, so that a right-angle impact would only occur at a very long range where the chance of hitting is

Molybdenum Non-Cemented Armor (MNC)

In 1939 the protection of the aircraft carriers became a problem when the IJN wanted to build the *Taihō* with a heavily protected flightdeck.[135] It was decided to purchase several armor types from Germany while Kure Navy Yard Steel Division developed MNC homogenous armor. First tested at Kashima proving ground against 250-kg bombs and then at Kamegakubi proving ground against large calibre projectiles, in comparison with the armor plates bought from Germany, the properties of the MNC armor were found to be slightly superior, and the IJN decided to entirely use it for horizontal protection.

Before the adoption of the 46-cm gun NVNC and VNC armor was used for horizontal protection. This armor was not cemented and therefore comparatively tough all through its thickness. This property was thought to offer maximum resistance against projectiles hitting not with its head but with its shoulder. But the research of the piercing power of the 46-cm shell ended with the recognition that a more flexible and tough armor plate than NVNC was necessary to stop a projectile hitting at an angle of fall of up to 55° and avoid the breaking of the plate. This shell would hit the armor a flat-headed type (with the ballistic wind shield and the secondary cap broken off) with so large a kinetic energy that only the flexible reaction of the armor material upon the impact would prevent piercing and breaking.

MNC was a specially heated molybdenum steel with nickel and chrome additions to obtain a very flexible and tough (crack resistant) armor plate. It was found less susceptible to a grain fracture under severe impact conditions and, according to Japanese personnel interrogated after the Pacific War, MNC had superior ballistic resistance for shock or high obliquity impacts and these advantages, particularly in case of large calibre shells and heavy bombs, are also pointed out by Sasagawa. It could be used interchangeably with NVNC but

---

small compared to the turret roof and the striking velocity much reduced from close range velocities. The 2700-lb US 16" Mk 8 MOD 6 AP tests at right angles showed that the plate was indeed somewhat brittle and split in two on impact, but that its resistance was just about the same as the thinner VH plates at a quality about midway between the original KC a/A plate and a perfect WWII KC plate with a 35% face. Japanese manufacturing processes did not change as much as British, German and US manufacturers did (attempts to make the 46-cm Type 91 satisfy a higher obliquity spec did not meet with much success and the other AP projectiles still used the old tests verbatim). [Nathan Okun]

[135] For the story of this ship see the authors' work *Taihō* in two volumes (AJ-Press, 2004 & 2008).

was preferred especially when large thickness was required. MNC was mainly used for the middle deck and the roof of the main gun houses[136] of the *Yamato*

---

[136] While the protective plans of the *Yamato* class indicate the roof protection to have been 270-mm thick VH armor, Rear-Admiral Dr (Eng.) Sasagawa writes in his recollections, under the headline "Armor Plates – The Pride of the IJN and the Special Way of Domestic Steel Production", in the section referring to the invention of MNC armor: "… the NiCr steel with molybdenum with the special heat treatment. This plate was very flexible and powerful … mainly used for the middle deck and the roof of the gun houses … [the plate] showed the new power not only against the large calibre shells but also against the large size bombs."

Tech. Captain Iki Tsuneo writes in his contribution "Establishment and End of Steel Production Techniques in Japan" to *Suiko* in the fifth part (chapter VIII "The Building of the Large Battleships of the *Yamato* Class and the Steel Production") that "MNC (molybdenum non-carbonised – *mushintan*)" was used for "horizontal protection". With reference to VH he states "gun turrets, barbettes, hull sides". In dealing with NVNC he mentions "inclined armor at the lower part of the hull sides" but not the back and sides of the main gun turrets, which were of NVNC armor, according to the armor plan. Therefore, his "gun turrets" as VH is too simplified, at best, and it can be supposed that he would not have mentioned particularly MNC in the gun turrets (while he admits the exclusive use of MNC for horizontal protection). His sole "VH" indicates that he took the front plate (with the excessive thickness pointed out by everybody) as the decisive factor.

In their "Notes of the History of the Former Military Steel Technology" Dr (Eng.) Horikawa Kazuo and Dr (Eng.) Onodera Shinsaku (of Nippon Kōkan Co., and Nippon Seikōsho, respectively) omit the turret armor of the *Yamato* class, while explaining MNC as the armor of the middle deck, VH as belt armor and NVNC as underwater protection.

Matsumoto Kitarō refers in his 1961 version to the adoption of new armor plates in part 2, chapter 10, and points out Rear-Admiral Sasagawa as the inventor. While describing the properties etc. no reference is made to its detailed distribution.

In *Sekai no Kansen*, #5–7/1982, an interesting contribution on the *Yamato* class written by Naitō Hatsuho was published (and also included in an expanded form in the book *Senkan Musashi Kenzō Kiroku*). In the third continuation Naitō refers to Vice-Admiral (*Chūjō* – An error as the correct rank was rear-admiral, which Sasagawa became on 1st May 1944) Sasagawa Kiyoshi as the inventor of VH and MNC armor etc. and explains: "In case of the MNC armor molybdenum was added. A homogenous structure and, hence, equal quality all through the thickness was obtained. This armor was particularly suited for horizontal protection and was used for the middle deck and the roof of the gun houses. Also, the quality of the honeycomb type armor increased remarkably."

The statement by Matsumoto, the career of Dr Sasagawa (graduated 1921 *Tōdai Kōgaku-bu Tetsu-chikin-Gakuka* Dr Eng., rear-admiral at the end of the Pacific War – Chief of the Special Material Division (*Rinji Shizai Buchō*) of the Navy Technical Department and Chief of the Material Research Division (*Zairyō Kenkyū Buchō*) of the Navy Technical Research Institute in personal union. In between he was Weapon Supervisor (*Zōhei Kantokukan*) in France (mainly the French University), member of the Steel Production Division (*Seikōbu*) and Steel Experimental Division (*Jikkenbu*) of the Kure Navy Yard, later Chief of the Steel Production Division and the generalisation of Iki (graduated from the Tōkyō University – metallurgy course – in 1928 and worked [mostly?] in the Kure Navy Yard's Steel Production Division) give rise to the supposition that MNC instead of VH was used as roof armor. All authors admit that MNC was better suited as horizontal protection; why, then, should the IJN have used the less suited VH to protect something regarded as a "decisive weapon"? In addition, why class and the maximum thickness was 340 mm for the front and after slope of the armored deck.

The mass production was begun early in 1940–just in time to be used on the *Yamato* class.

Copper Non-Cemented Armor (CNC)

In 1931 CNC experimental armor plates were produced in five different thicknesses to conserve the nickel supply and instead use more copper. The gauges up to 100 mm showed ballistic qualities equivalent to NVNC armor but the thickest plate (215 mm) was inferior in resistance. Therefore, the CNC analysis was adopted for armor gauges below 75 mm. The limitation to ¾ of the thickness, which was recognised as equal to NVNC armor, was to provide some margin of safety. CNC armor was used interchangeably with NVNC, but was preferred for horizontal protection. The background of the study and experimental production of CNC was the high nickel content in NVNC. This metal was not produced in Japan and had to be imported under unfavorable conditions. Resistance against penetration by a flat-headed shell was insufficient. Improvement of the elastic limit was proposed by mixing copper and remarkably reduce the high nickel content in NVNC (4%). This became quite necessary when large quantities of this armor were required.

About ten years later the CNC analysis was reinvestigated and modified to further reduce the nickel content but contain the ballistic quality. CNC_1 and CNC_2 plates were studied with the following results:

(1) The already known fact that no CNC armor gave satisfactory results in plate thicknesses of more than 102 mm again became evident.
(2) The ballistic quality of CNC_1 armor plates of 36, 50 and 100 mm thickness was equivalent to CNC plates of the same gauges.
(3) The ballistic quality of CNC_2 plates of 25 mm and 50 mm thicknesses was equivalent, but 100-mm thick plates were inferior to CNC plates of the same thickness.

---

should the inventor err on the application? The protective plan is no original but was reconstructed after the termination of the Pacific War, thus an error cannot be denied. On the other hand, the true sense of Japanese sentences is often hard to grasp and sentences are by no way unambiguous. Therefore, the authors hesitate to state frankly that the protective drawing is wrong but they suppose an error in this respect and are inclined to believe Dr (Eng.) Sasagawa's information.

Based upon these data the IJN decided to adopt the (1) CNC_1 analysis for gauges from 38 to 100 mm, (2) CNC_2 analysis for gauges from 25 to 37 mm and continue with the use of MNC or NVNC for plates thicker than 102 mm.

In short: The armor containing copper as replacement of nickel was a secret patent of the IJN and the composition was changed depending on the plate thickness according to the rule that the thinner the armor the less its content of nickel. The elastic limit was heightened and resistance against deshaping and penetration improved.

The following two tables enable the comparison of the chemical standard composition analysis and physical properties of past and new armor materials.

Table 5-1: Metal composition of armor types

Type/Contents	C	Si	Mn	P	S	Ni	Cr	Cu	Mo	Note
VC, VH, NVNC	0.43–0.53	0.05–0.25	0.30–0.45	<0.035	<0.035	3.7–4.2	1.8–2.2	<0.20	-----	1, 2
MNC	0.30–0.38	same as above	same as above	same as above	same as above	3.3–3.8	same as above	<0.25	0.25–0.40	3
CNC	0.38–0.46	same as above	same as above	same as above	same as above	2.5–3.0	0.8–1.3	0.9–1.3	-----	4
CNC_1	same as above	same as above	same as above	same as above	same as above	1.8–2.8	1.5–2.0	0.6–1.0	0.10–0.20	5
CNC_2	same as above	same as above	same as above	same as above	same as above	1.3–1.8	same as above	same as above	same as above	6

Notes:

(1) VC and VH were used for vertical protection of more than 150 mm thickness.

(2) NVNC was used for vertical protection of less than 200 mm thickness and for horizontal protection requiring thicknesses from 75 mm to 180 mm.

(3) MNC was used for horizontal protection of more than 180 mm thickness.

(4) CNC was used for armor plates of less than 75 mm thickness.

(5) CNC_1 was used for armor requiring thicknesses from 38 mm to 100 mm.

(6) CNC_2 was used for thicknesses of less than 37 mm.

Table 5-2: Specifications of armor types

Specification /Type	Thickness (mm)	Elastic limit (kg/mm²)	Tensile strength (kg/mm²)	Elongation (%)	Impact value /ft-lb) Minimum	Maximum
VC	> 150	> 40	75 ± 10	> 20	> 28	-----
VH	> 180	> 40	75 ± 10	> 20	> 30	35
NVNC	> 180	> 40	75 ± 10	> 20	> 30	35
	180–75	> 45	80 ± 8	> 19	> 28	35
MNC	> 180	> 40	75 ± 10	> 28	> 35	40
CNC	75–50	> 60	85 ± 6	> 19	> 30	-----
CNC$_1$	< 50	> 60	80–90	> 19	> 30	-----
CNC$_2$	< 25	> 60	80–90	> 19	> 30	-----

Notes:

(1) Contraction of the section (reduction in area) for all types of armor was 40% or more.

(2) VC = Vickers Cemented = surface carbonised face-hardened armor.

(3) VH = Vickers Hardened = surface not carbonised face-hardened armor.

(4) NVNC = New Vickers Non-Cemented armor, MNC, CNC and variations = homogenous armors (no carbonised surface = not face-hardened).

(5) The term "non-cemented" to mean "homogeneous, ductile" comes from British practice, where their homogeneous naval armor–turret roofs and so forth–after adopting Krupp KC nickel-chromium armor steel was merely KC without the hardening applied, so "non-cemented" (British KNC, VNC and eventually just "NC Armor" or NCA).

(6) Note how much better MNC is than any of the other armors in many properties related to toughness.

Particular Armor Shapes

In addition to the outline of new armor material it may be of some interest to mention two particular shapes, either especially introduced for the *Yamato* class or whose application was expanded extensively.

<u>Honeycomb Armor</u>

Before the construction of the *Yamato* class coaming armor had been used for the protection of holes in the armor deck. But jointly with the increase of the fighting distance and the development of aircraft the angles of fall increased remarkably to require an increase of the height of the coaming armor, and still it was nearly useless against bombs. Particularly the openings for the funnel uptakes could not be protected. This led to the idea of the honeycomb armor invented by Matsumoto Kitarō. This kind of armor had many holes of 120 mm and 180 mm in diameter to be convenient for ventilation and to effectively avoid penetration by a projectile or bomb. The percentage of the holes on the total area amounted to 55% and the thickness of the 'holed part' was increased to 380 mm compared with the surrounding 200 mm in order to provide the same resistance against piercing. According to Sasagawa the armor material should be "extremely strong" and this goal was "fortunately" attained by "MNC armor and the improvement of the heat treatment" and it "was also a big achievement of the Japanese shipbuilders."[137]

Tapered Armor

The production of tapered armor had been investigated since 1912 but it was stopped because no plates with the required dimensions could be produced. When, in 1921, the Japanese rolling mill was completed this theme was taken up again and satisfactory results were attained in 1928. The IJN wanted the application of tapered armor plates in order to decrease and properly distribute the weight. This meant an adjustment of the armor thickness to the actual probability grade of damage and, concretely, the upper part of the hull side armor should be thicker than the lower one where the destructive power of the projectile had already been limited by structures such as bulges etc. In this way, removing unnecessary parts without reduction of the protective power could decrease the weight of the ship. At first the armor plate was produced in uniform thickness and then the unnecessary part was removed mechanically by planing, but this method was disadvantageous from the viewpoints of man-days, expenses and machines. In order to remove these defects and accelerate production remarkably special equipment[138] was fitted to the

---

[137] Very thick solid plates with holes punched/bored through them for funnel uptakes, called "gratings" even though they no longer were made of criss-cross steel bars forming a horizontal fence, was used in all post-1930 US Navy battleships. They looked virtually identical to the *Yamato* class uptake gratings. US ballistic tests showed that they were equivalent in protection to a solid plate of the same material 40% as thick (152-mm solid MNC plate for a 380-mm MNC grating). [Nathan Okun]

[138] The upper roll was given an inclination and the lower roll remained unchanged. Owing to the different distance between the rolls the thickness of the armor plates decreased gradually from top to bottom. This method was successful and by the combined rolling and pressing procedure the plates

"old" rolling mill (the Davy Bros. product bought in 1904) to produce tapered armor plates without the additional metal-cutting process.

According to Sasagawa, it was a "really advantageous epoch-making armor production."

---

became a flat surface despite the variation of the thickness. The production of tapered armor plates with this method was registered later as a secret patent (*kimitsu tokkyo*) of the IJN. Besides the saving of time and expenses the yield quality of the plates was improved by the combined production method.

CHAPTER 6–DETAILED DESCRIPTION OF THE MAIN GUN TURRET

Introduction

The fundamental requirements for the design and construction of the main gun turrets have been described before, and the fact of an independently developed product have been pointed out. Against this background some additional data about this noteworthy turret will be provided. The sources are those mentioned before but are here supplemented by descriptions from Gakken, *Maru, Sekai no Kansen* ("Ships of the World") and some more books by Japanese authors.

Features of the Turret

The design team led by naval engineer Hata Chiyokichi introduced so many novel items and noteworthy details that even the members of the US Naval Technical Mission to Japan, who investigated the 46-cm gun and the mount, appreciated the construction in general aside from criticising "an unduly large factor of safety … in the design of the turret machinery as a whole, resulting in a very heavy mount …:"

They pointed out as the most interesting features:

(1) The method of stowing and moving shells about the shell and shell-handing rooms using a fairly simple, but bulky and heavy mechanism.
(2) The powder cage and rammer, designed to enable a full charge to be loaded by a single rammer stroke.
(3) The attachment of the elevating piston rod to the slide which was designed to avoid the necessity for a complicated slide locking gear, and to reduce the loading cycle time by cutting out the time usually required for locking and unlocking the slide.

As particular mechanisms of interest the members noted:

(1) The powder bogie and mechanism for transferring powder from the fixed to the moving structure.
(2) The gun house shell bogie and rammer.

(3) The wormless training gear, with its "coaster" gear substitute for the normal friction discs.

(4) The electric cable leading-in gear.

The general arrangement of the Type 94 46-cm triple gun mount installed in battleships of the *Yamato* class is illustrated in figures 6-1 to 6-4.

The turret was built-up in five distinctive sections, which from above to below were:

(1) Gun house (formed by the armor).
(2) Turntable with gun house deck and trunnion brackets.
(3) Upper and lower projectile handing rooms (the shell stowage rooms around the lower projectile handing room were not part of the turret).
(4) Upper and lower propellant handing rooms (the adjacent magazines were not part of the turret).
(5) Centre pivot with hydraulic pressure, high pressure air and cable lead-in arrangements.

The turret was composed of the rotating and the fixed structures, each consisting of several parts. Among the former ones the turntable was the central part with the guns and the gun house above and below, connected to the upper and lower rotating projectile and propellant supply rooms and the centre pivot.

The gun house was the part above the barbette and it was formed of very thick special armor plates to protect the gunners, guns and all the mechanisms necessary for their handling. At the after end of the gun house there was the rangefinder compartment for the rangefinder of 15 m base length and one of the four periscopes.[139]

---

[139] The earlier capital ships had the holes cut in the roof plates for the targeting telescopes but the *Yamato* class used periscopes to reduce the diameter to only 1/16th of the holes in order to provide better protection.

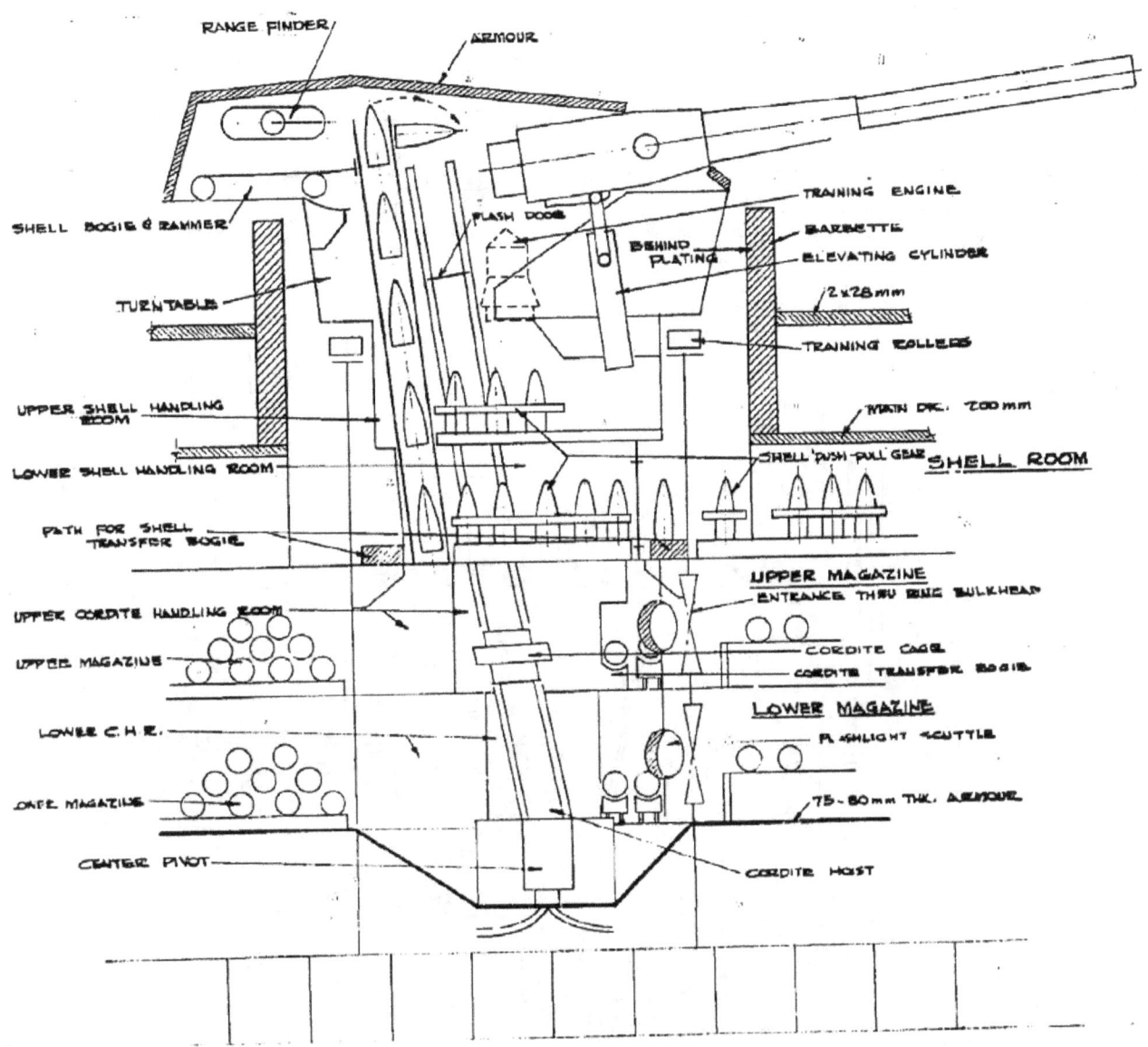

Figure 6-1: Side view of Type 94 46-cm triple gun mount (US Naval Technical Mission to Japan, Report O-45 (N))

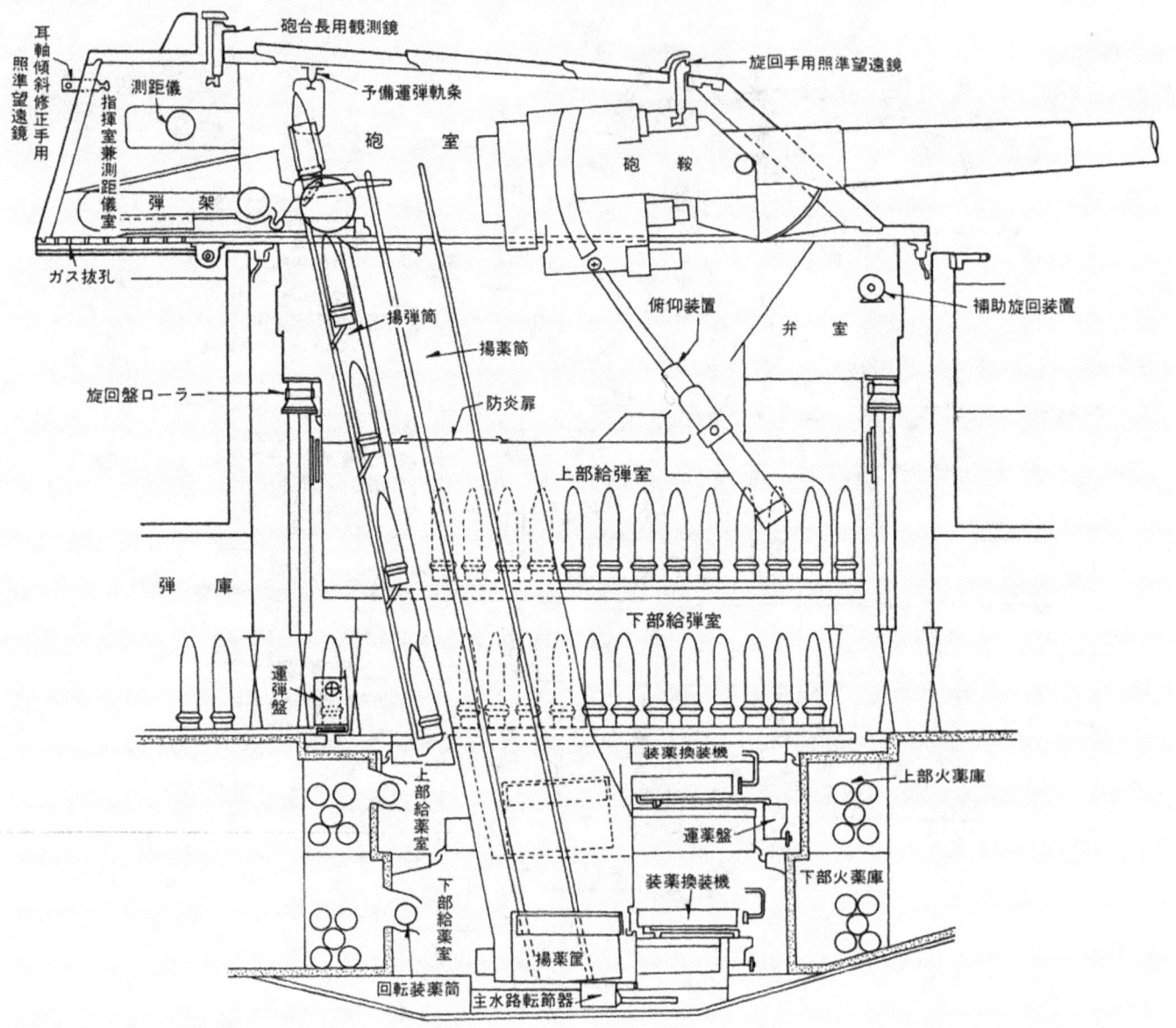

Figure 6-2: Side view of Type 94 46-cm triple gun mount (*Sekai no Kansen*)

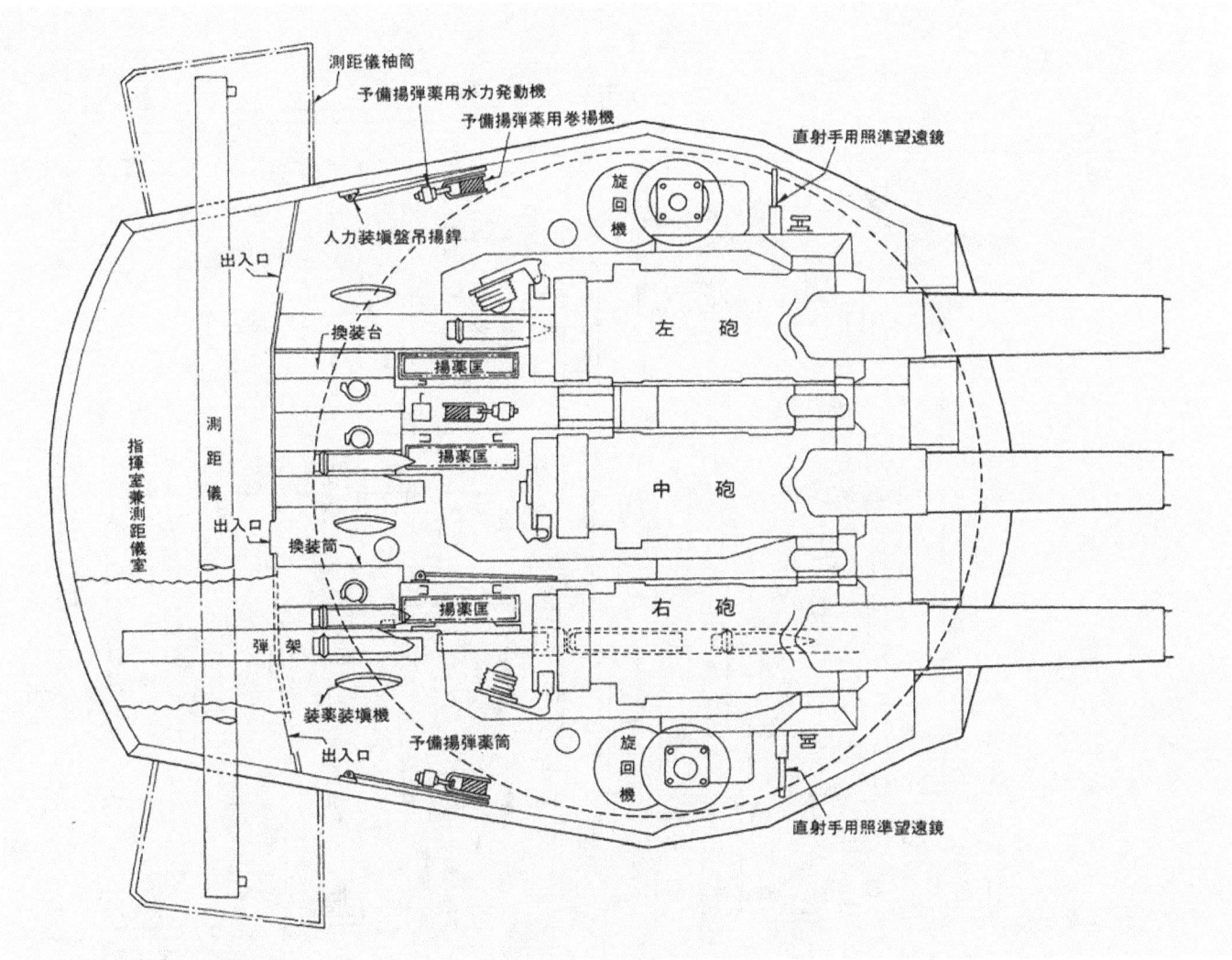

Figure 6-3: Plan view of Type 94 46-cm triple gun mount (*Sekai no Kansen*)

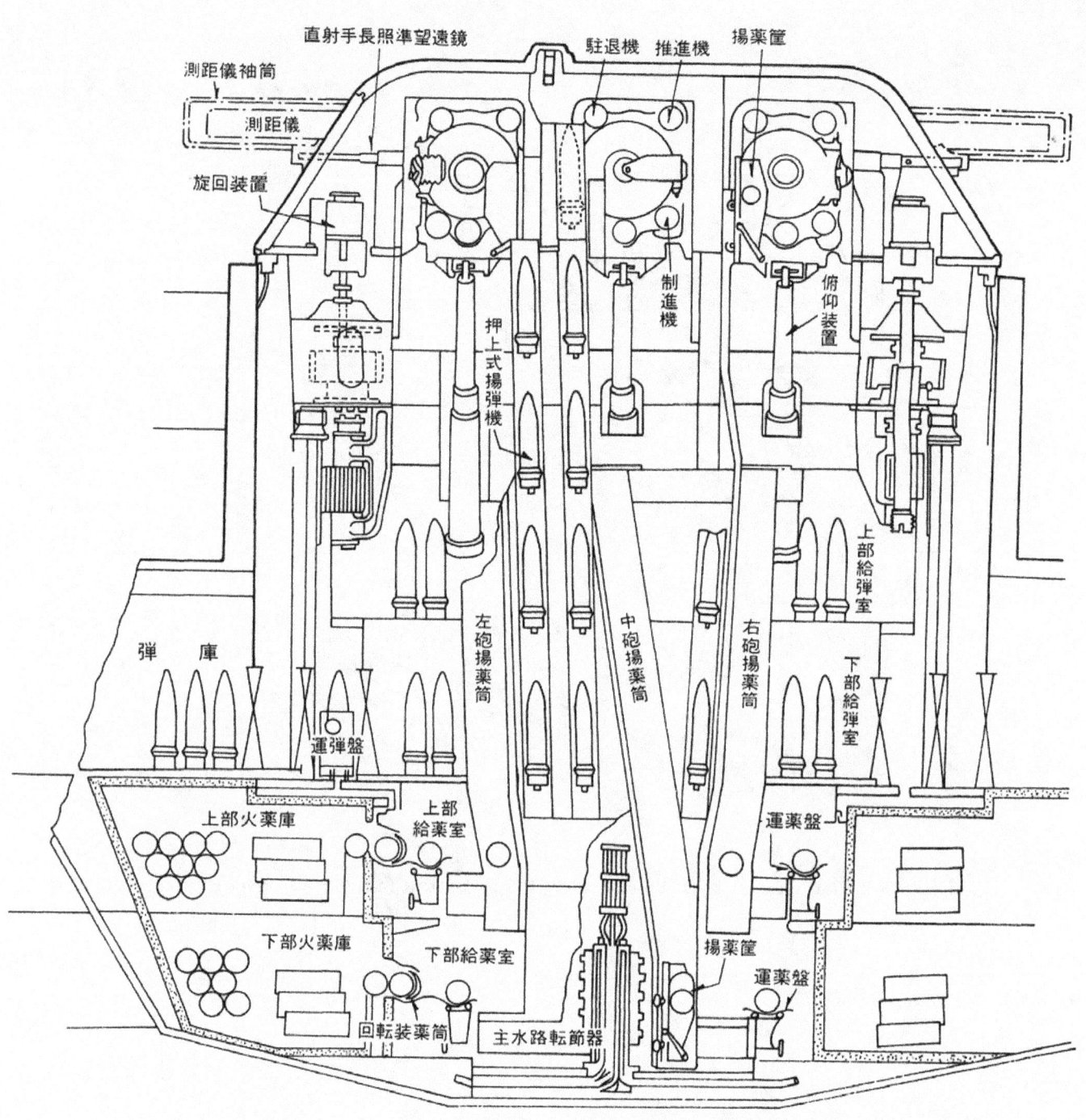

Figure 6-4: Rear view of Type 94 46-cm triple gun mount (*Sekai no Kansen*)

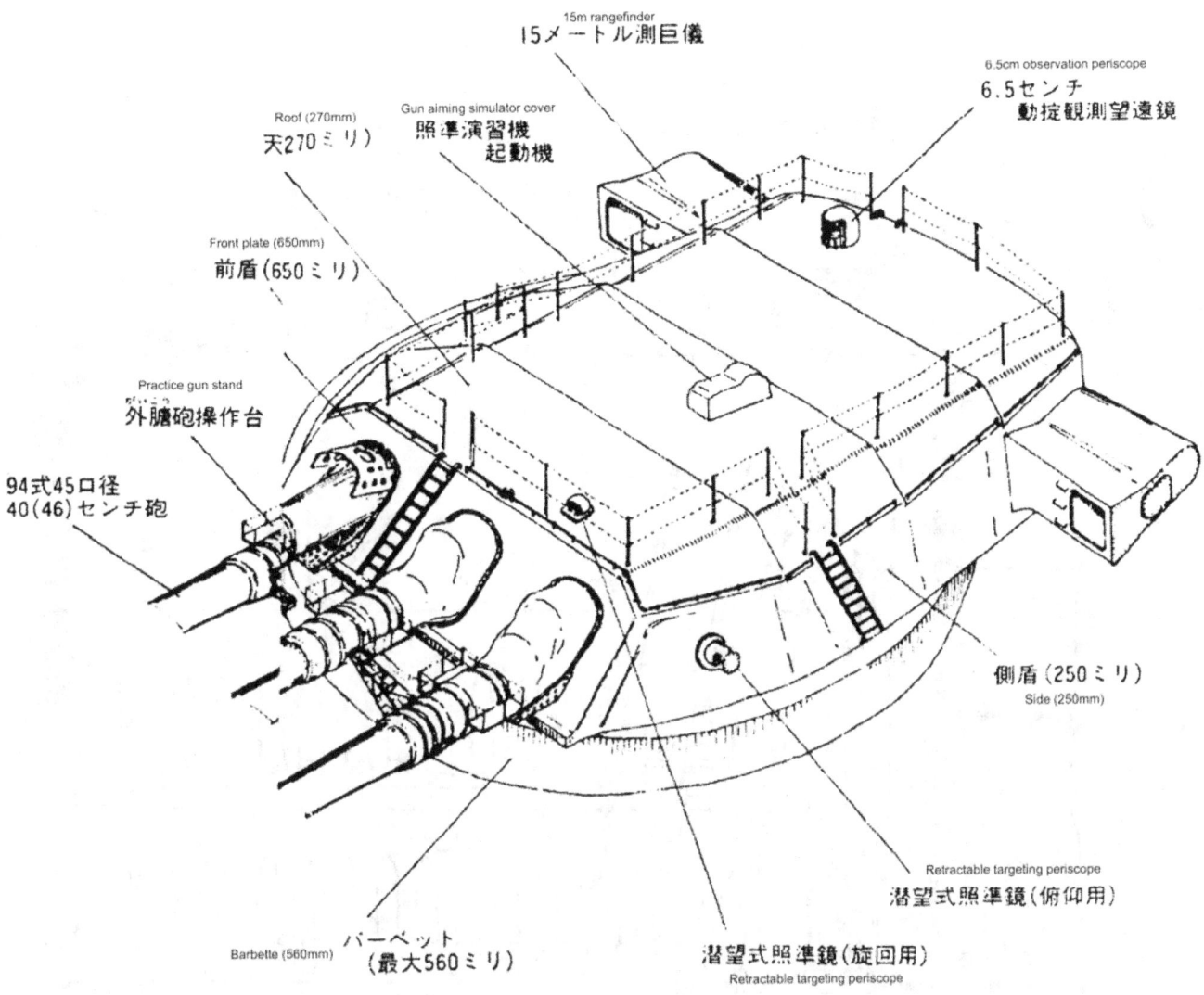

Figure 6-5: Perspective view of main gun turret. Note that the front plate was actually 660 mm and not 650 mm (*Nihon no Meikan* via Kitamura Kunio)

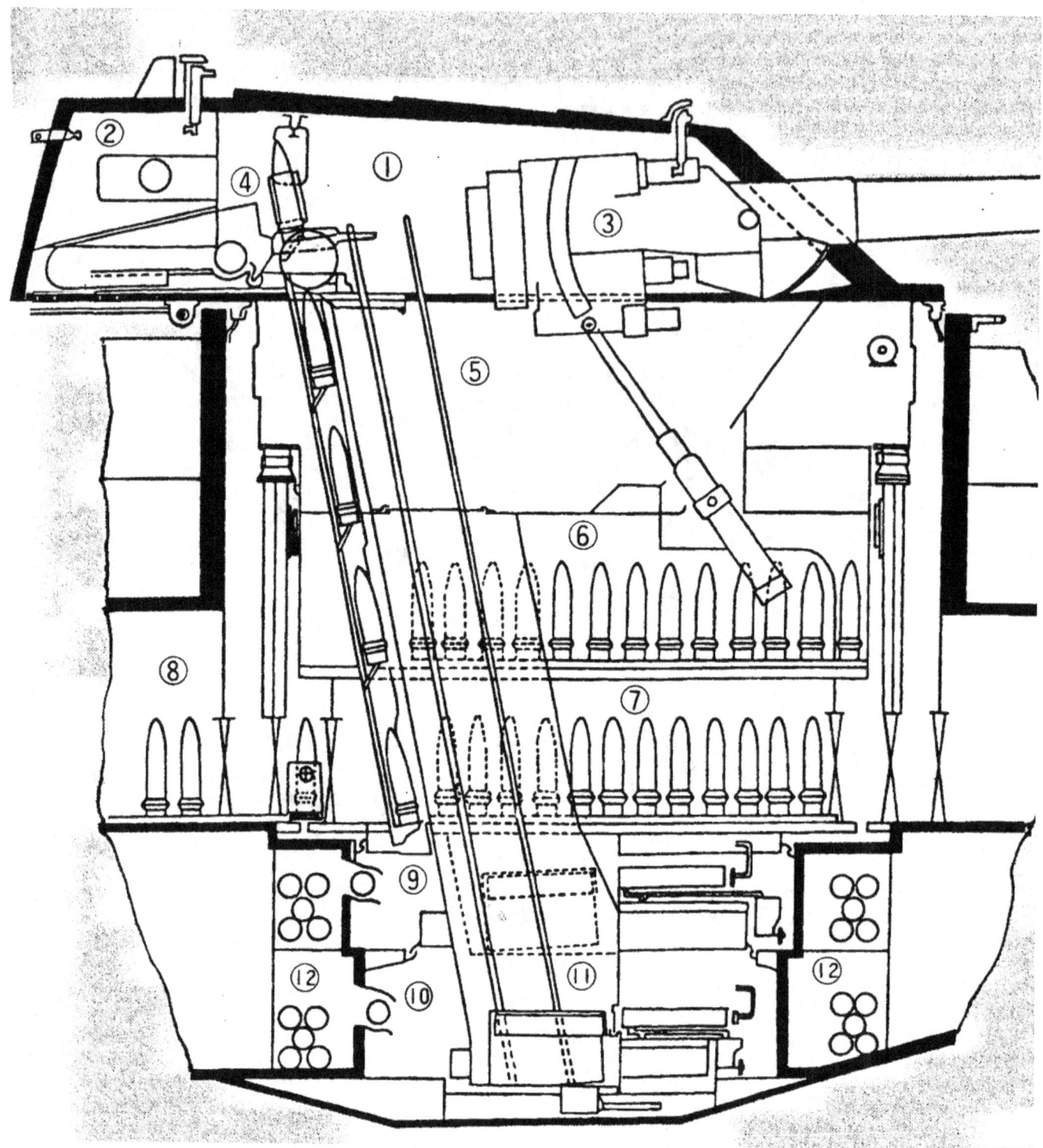

Figure 6-6: This view, like, the earlier ones, shows that the term "gun turret" includes all rotating and fixed structures. (Gakken, #11)

Key to Figure 6-6

(1) *Hō-shitsu* — Gun house
(2) *Sokkyo-shitsu* — Rangefinder room
(3) *Hōkura* — Gun cradle
(4) *Hōdan sōtenki* — Shell rammer
(5) *Yōdan-tō* — Projectile hoist tube
(6) *Jōbu kyūdan-shitsu* — Upper projectile supply room
(7) *Kabu kyūdan-shitsu* — Lower projectile supply room
(8) *Danko* — Projectile magazine
(9) *Jōbu kyūyaku-shitsu* — Upper propellant supply room
(10) *Kabu kyūyaku-shitsu* — Lower propellant supply room
(11) *Yōyaku bakō* — Propellant hoist cage
(12) *Kayakuko* — Propellant magazine

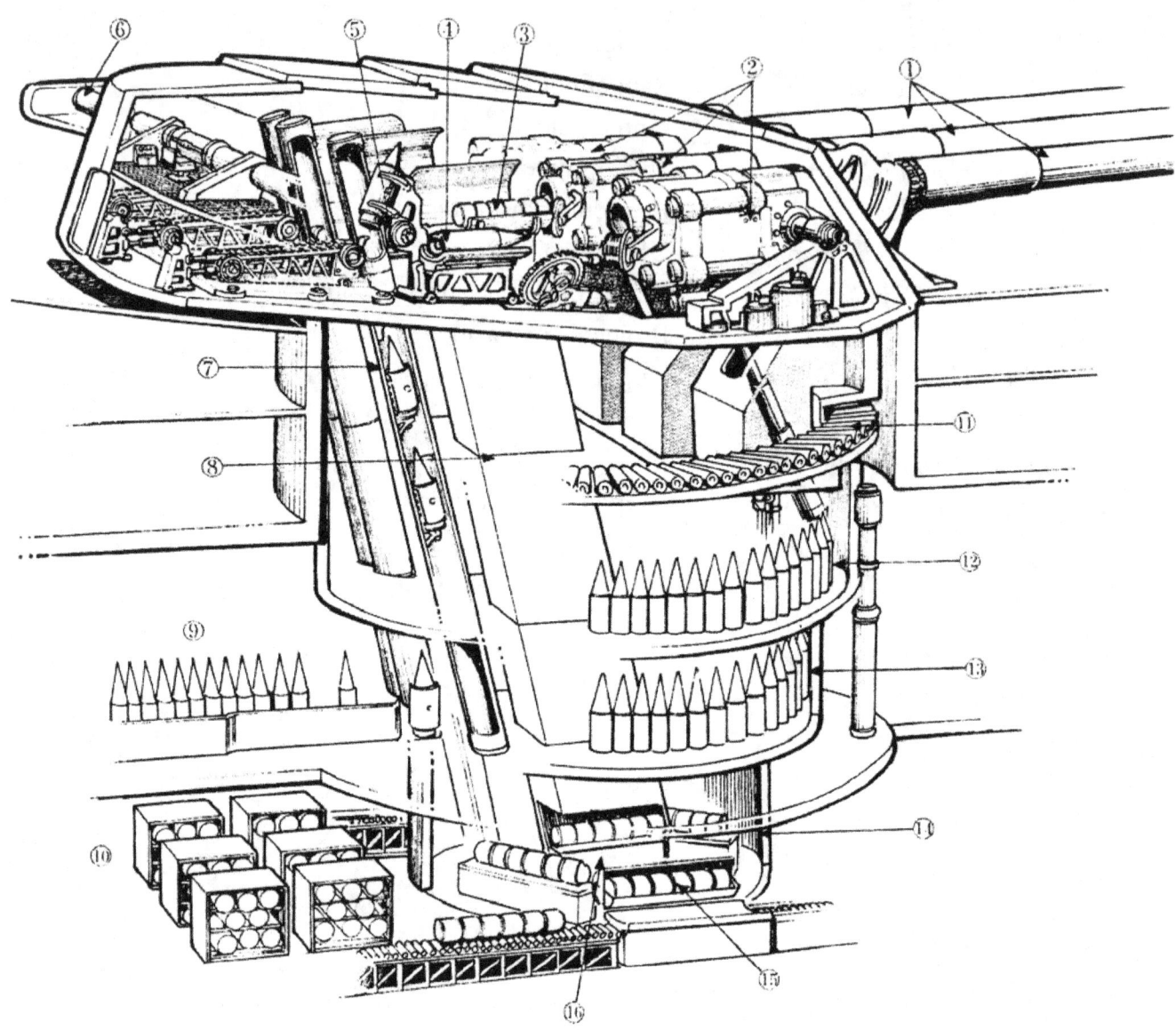

Figure 6-7: Type 94 45-cal 46-cm main gun triple turret (*Teikoku Kaigun: Kyū Nippon Kaigun Kanzen Gaido* via Kitamura Kunio)

Key to Figure 6-7

    (1) Gun barrels
    (2) Gun cradles
    (3) Powder bags
    (4) Shell
    (5) Shell tilting bucket
    (6) 15-m rangefinder
    (7) Shell hoist
    (8) Powder hoist
    (9) Shell transport (by "push-pull" gear)
    (10) Upper powder (cordite) magazine
    (11) Roller path
    (12) Upper shell magazine
    (13) Lower shell magazine
    (14) Ring bulkhead
    (15) Revolving flashtight scuttle
    (16) Powder (cordite) transfer bogie

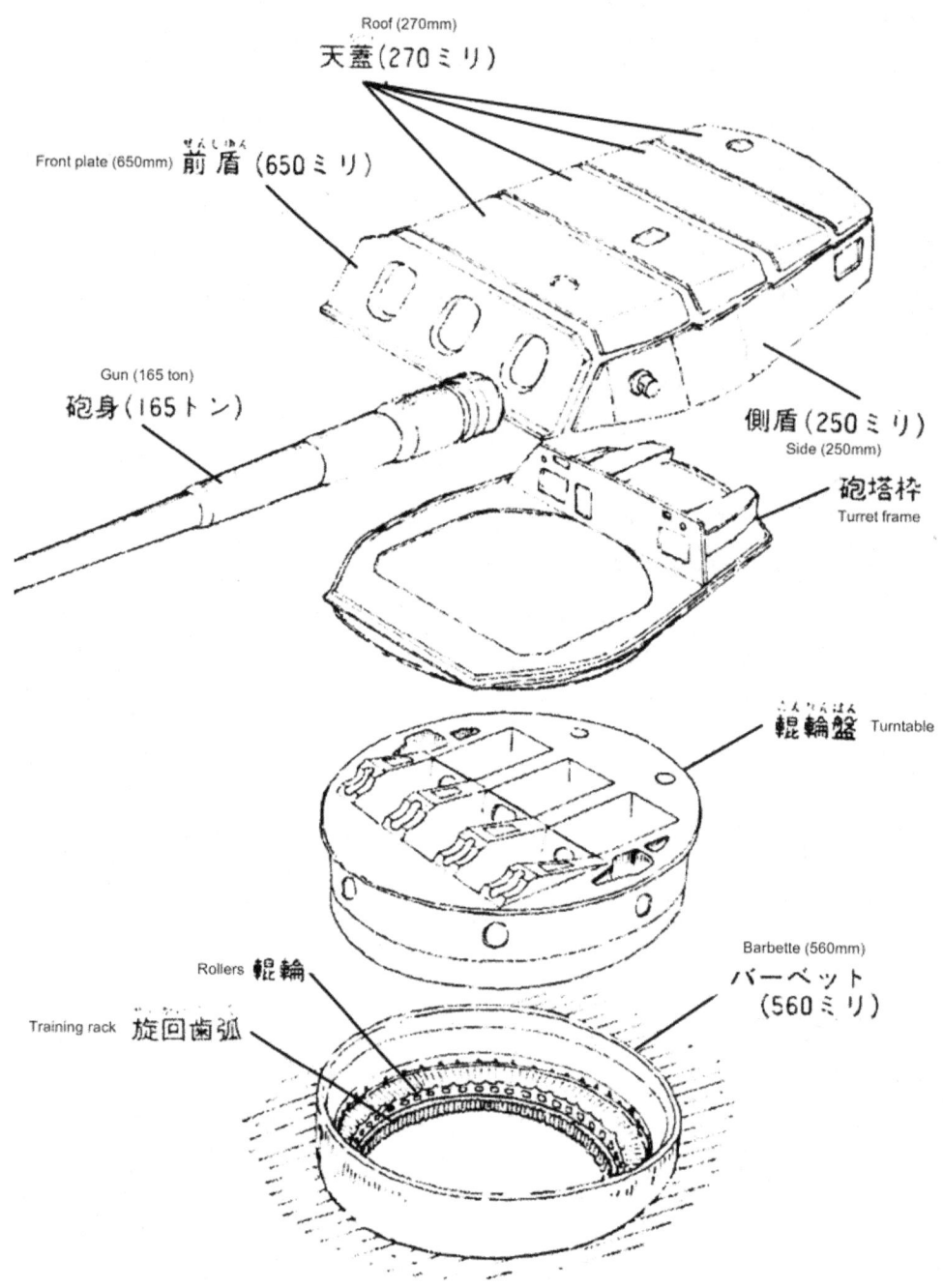

Figure 6-8: Principal parts of the revolving structure of the main gun turret. Note again that the front plate was actually 660 mm and not 650 mm (*Nihon no Meikan* via Kitamura Kunio)

Photo 6-1: Part of the revolving structure for one of *Yamato*'s 46-cm triple turrets during assembly on 3 June 1940 (Kure Maritime Museum)

Photo 6-2: Turntable of one of *Yamato*'s 46-cm triple turrets on 3 June 1940. Note the trunnions brackets and gun pits (Kure Maritime Museum)

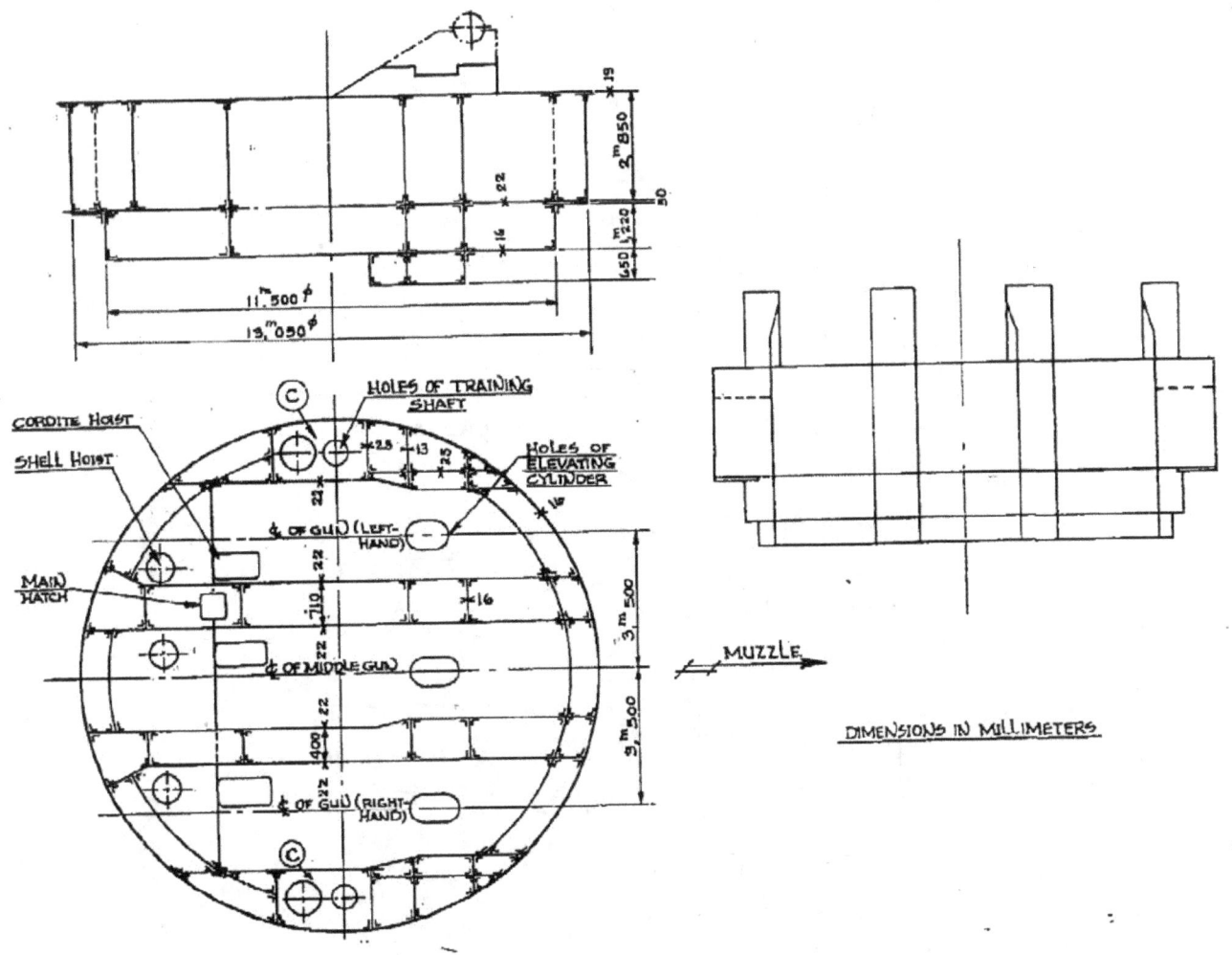

Figure 6-9: Turret turntable (US Naval Technical Mission to Japan, Report O-45 (N))

The turntable, figure 6-9, was an entirely riveted, fabricated structure using high-tensile (HT) steel plates of 16 to 22-mm thicknesses. The upper roller path was fixed to the turntable; the lower one, figure 6-9 (left), was machined and connected to the ring support. At the forward upper part of the turntable there were four trunnion brackets, figure 6-9 (right), to support the cradles by the trunnion bearings. The brackets were made of cast steel and riveted to the 22-mm thick plates of the turntable.

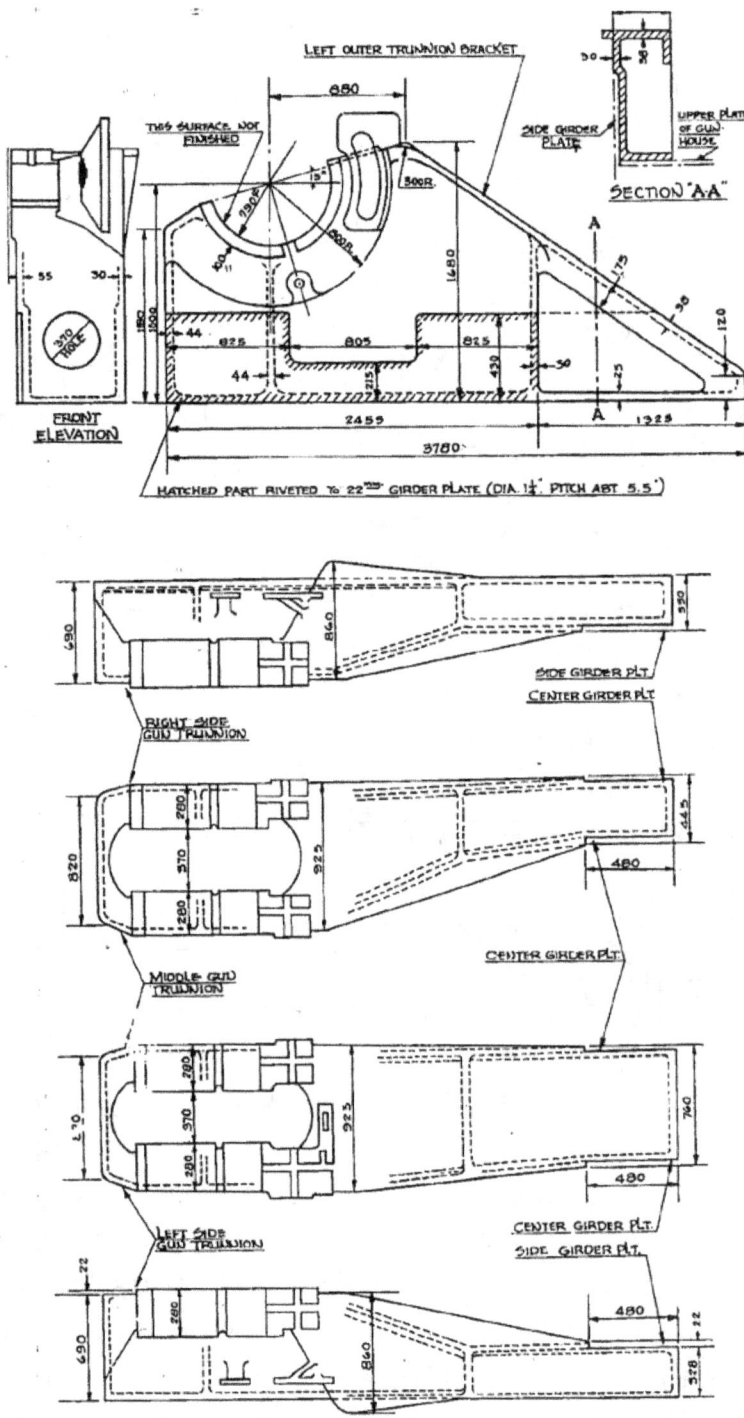

Figure 6-10: Trunnion brackets (US Naval Technical Mission to Japan, Report O-45 (N))

Photo 6-3: Nearly completed turntable for *Shinano* (US Naval Technical Mission to Japan, Report O-45 (N))

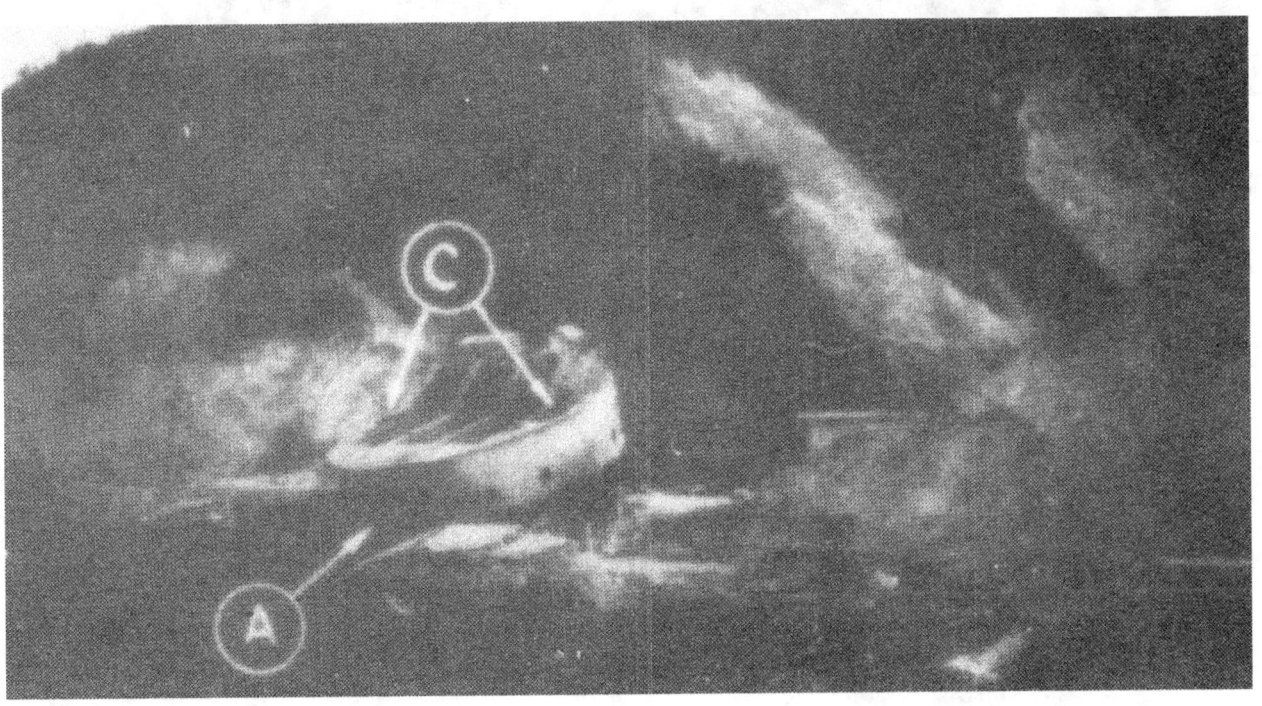

Photo 6-4: Nearly completed turntable for *Shinano*. A typhoon had swept away the supports causing it to tilt (US Naval Technical Mission to Japan, Report O-45 (N))

Photo 6-5: 46-cm turntable for *Shinano*–semi-complete. Note the trunnions brackets and gun pits (US Naval Technical Mission to Japan, Report O-45 (N))

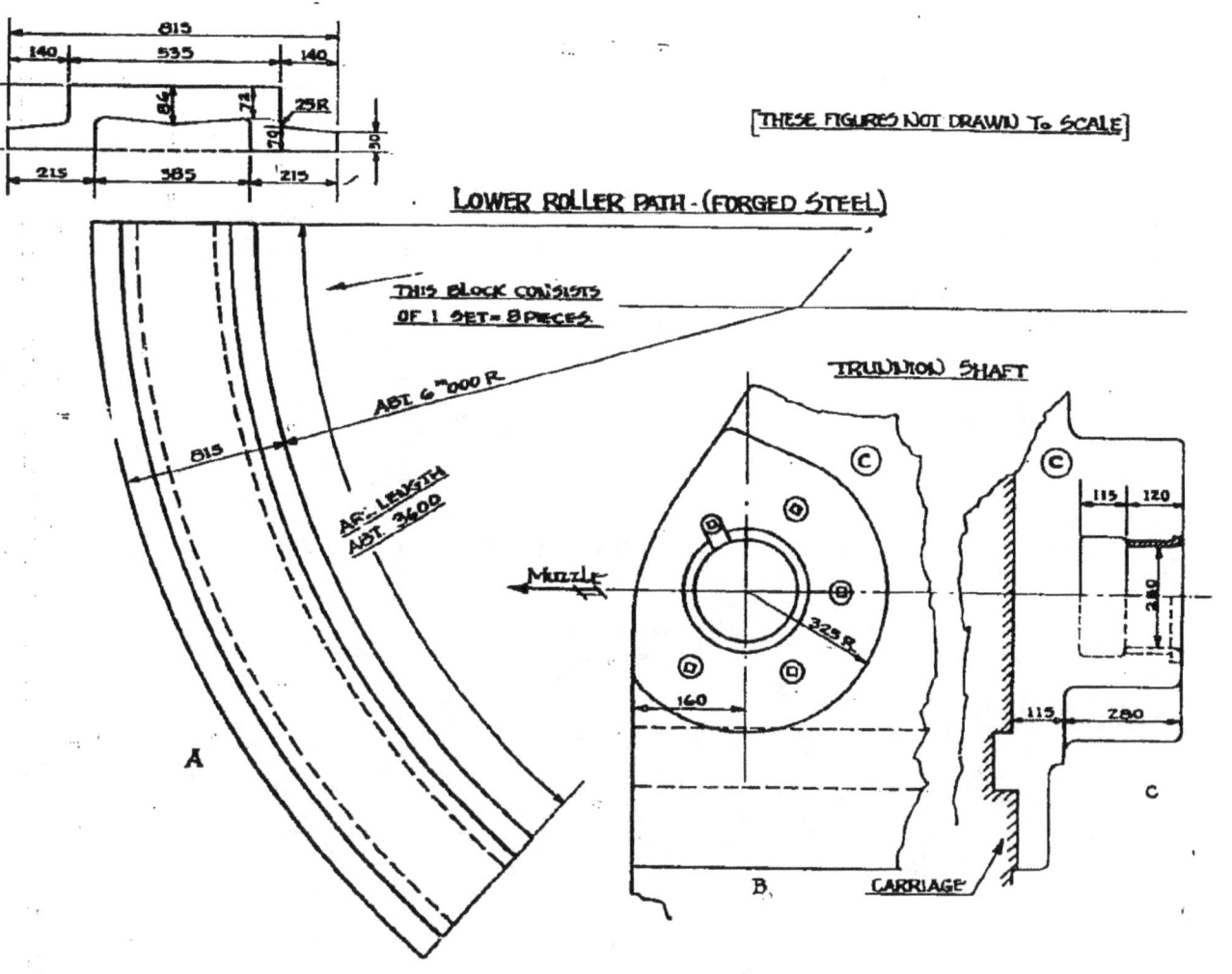

Figure 6-11: Lower roller path and trunnions shaft (US Naval Technical Mission to Japan, Report O-45 (N))

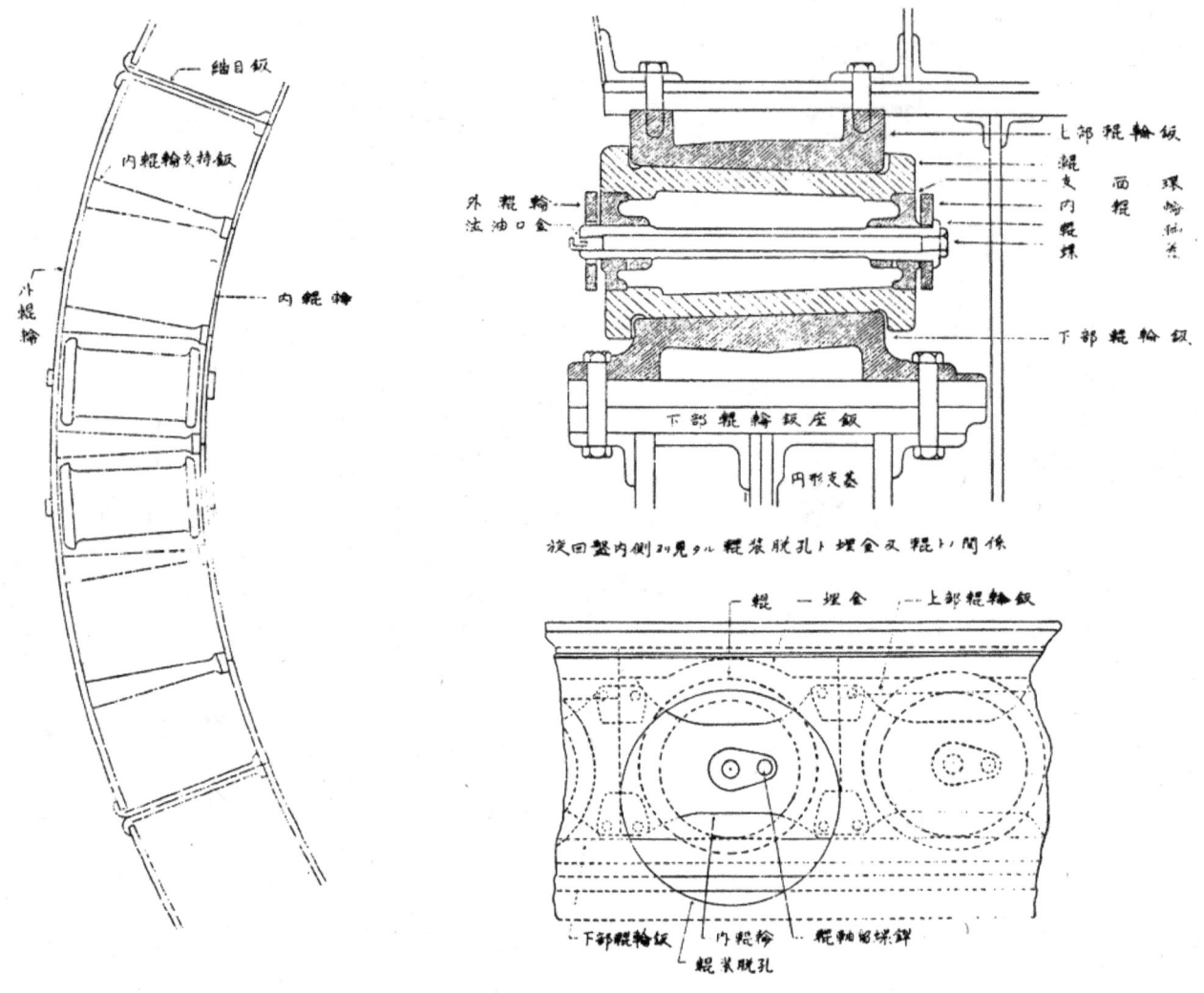

Figure 6-12: Roller path and turret roller (*Kessen Senkan* Yamato *no Zenbō*)

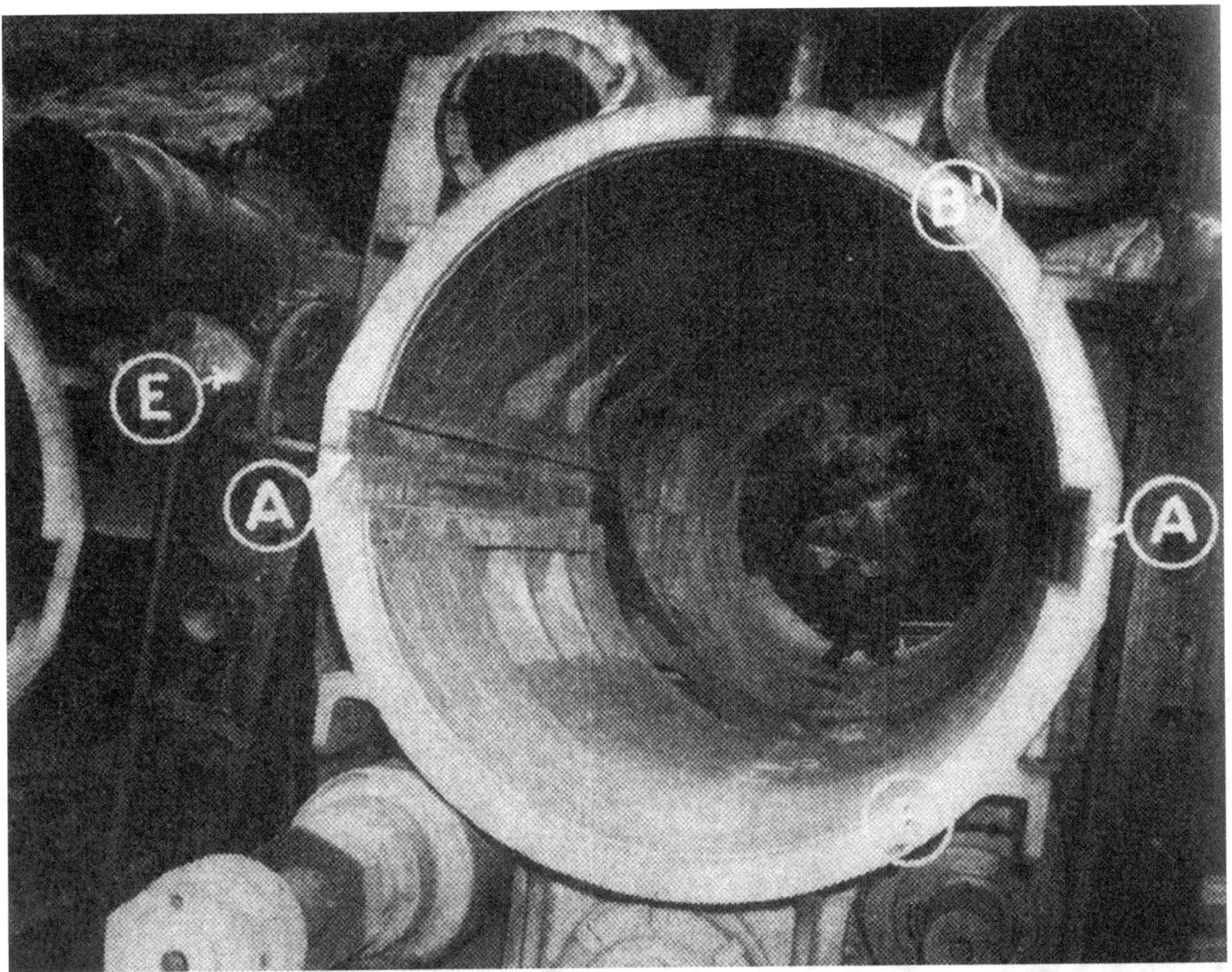

Photo 6-6: 46-cm slide for *Shinano* (US Naval Technical Mission to Japan, Report O-45 (N))

The guns were held by the cradle and slide, figures 6-10 and photo 6-6, consisting of two semi-cylindrical steel castings (B) and (B') and joined at (A, A) in photo 6-6, the centreline of the key ways for the gun keys by two large side plates (C in photo 6-7). A splinter plate (A in photo 6-7) and a light copper chase protection plate (P in photo 6-7) were fitted to the front of the cradle.

Photo 6-7: 46-cm slide for *Shinano* (US Naval Technical Mission to Japan, Report O-45 (N))

Photo 6-8: 46-cm slides for *Shinano* (US Naval Technical Mission to Japan, Report O-45 (N))

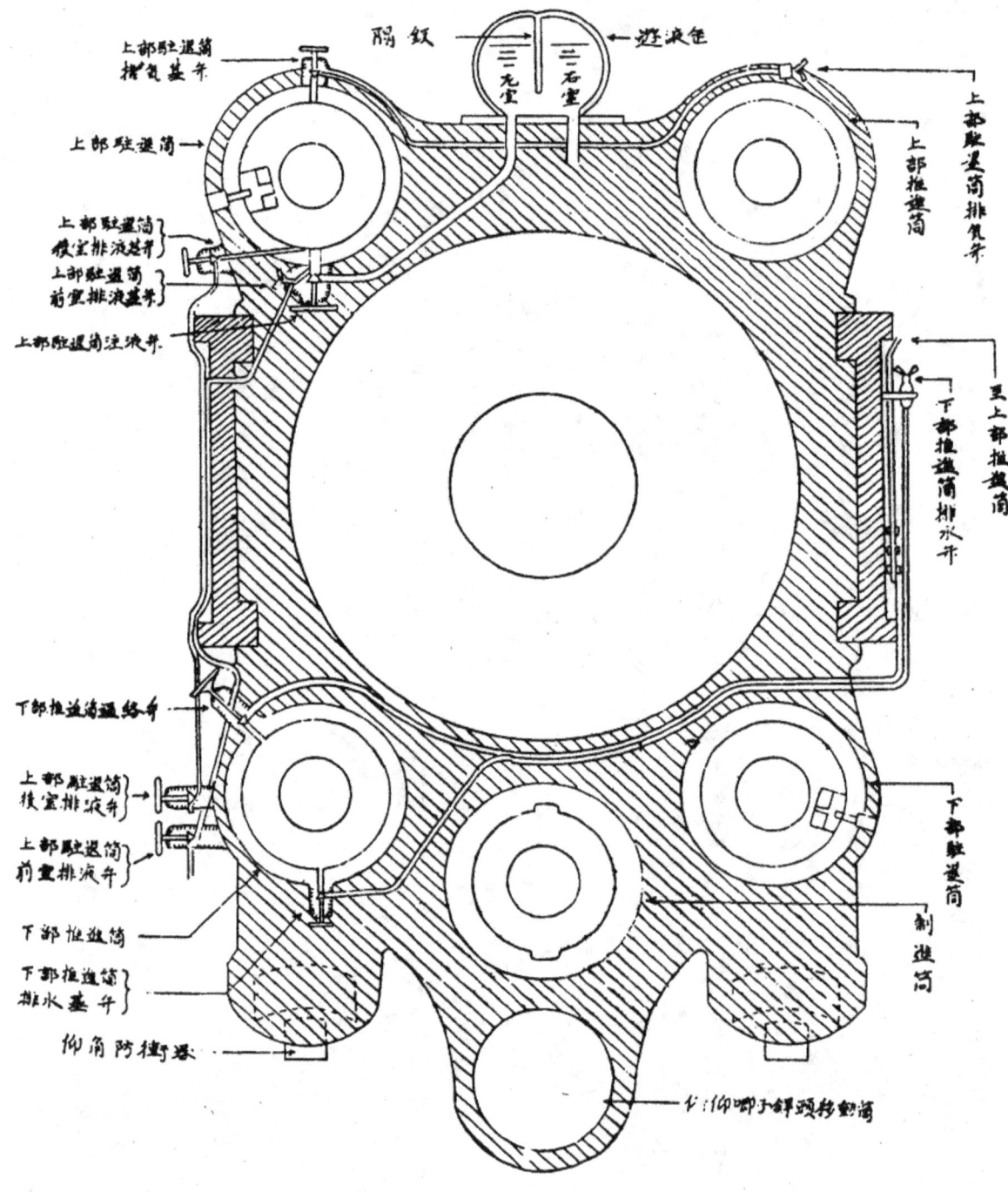

Figure 6-13: 46-cm slides showing the four recoil cylinders (one in each corner) and the run-out cylinder (between the two lower recoil cylinders) (*Kessen Senkan Yamato no Zenbō*)

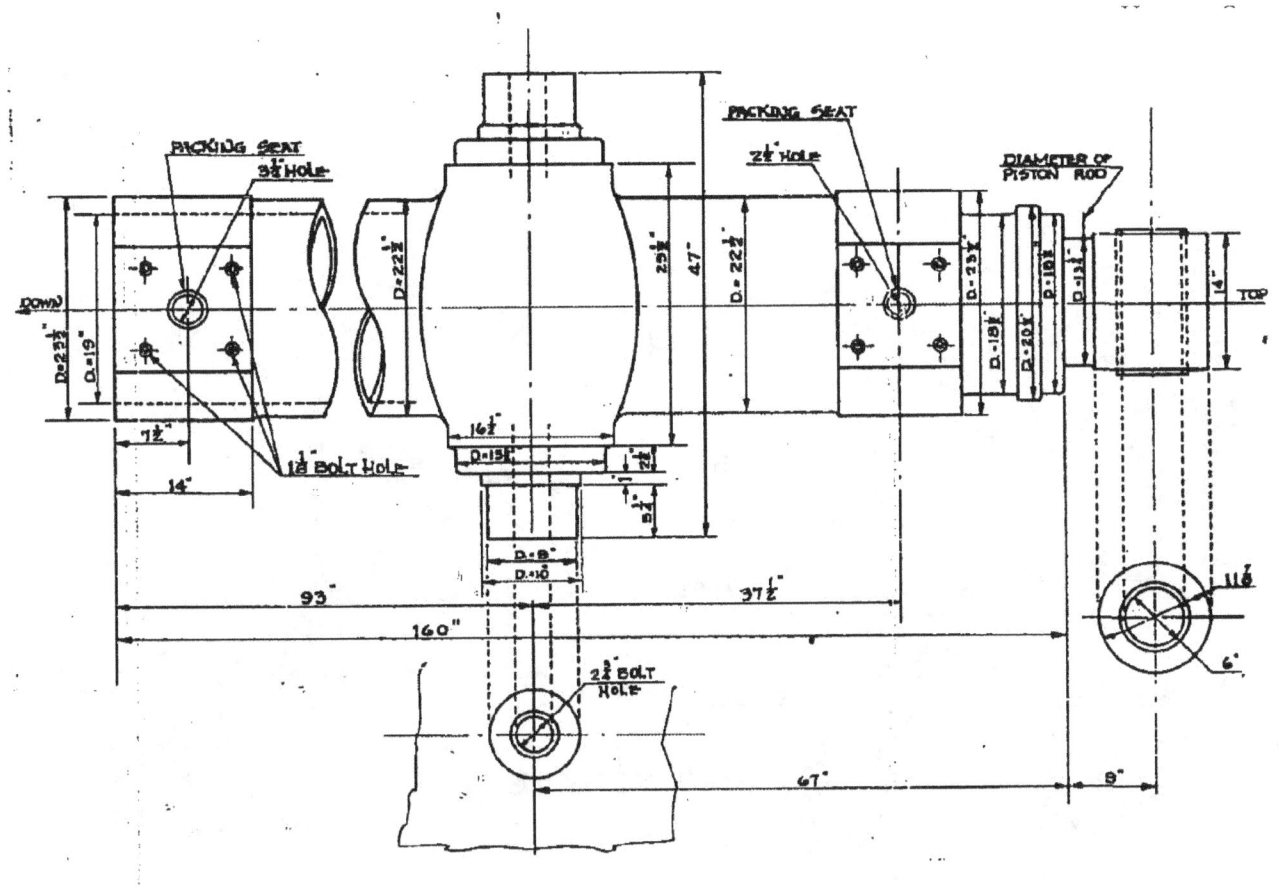

Figure 6-14: Elevating cylinder (US Naval Technical Mission to Japan, Report O-45 (N))

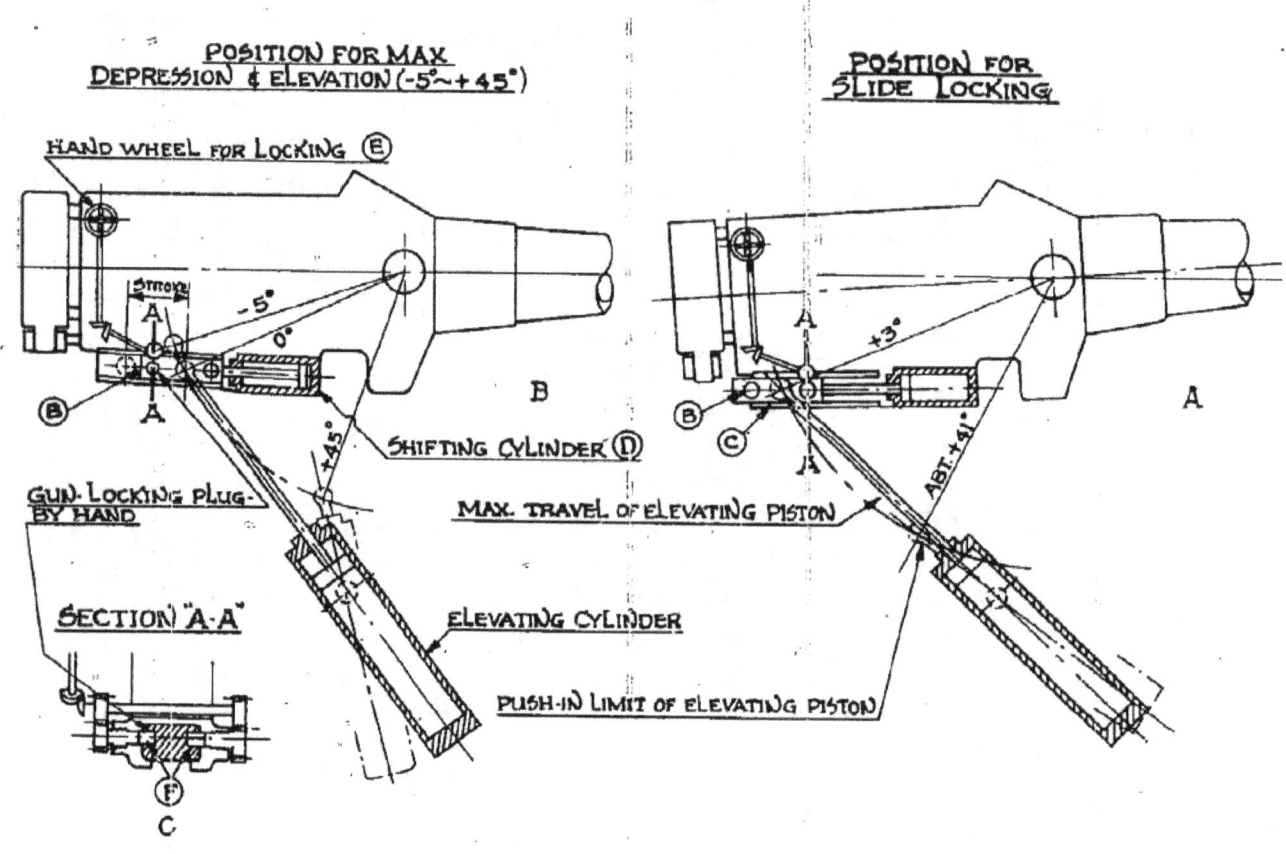

Figure 6-15: Elevating gear (US Naval Technical Mission to Japan, Report O-45 (N))

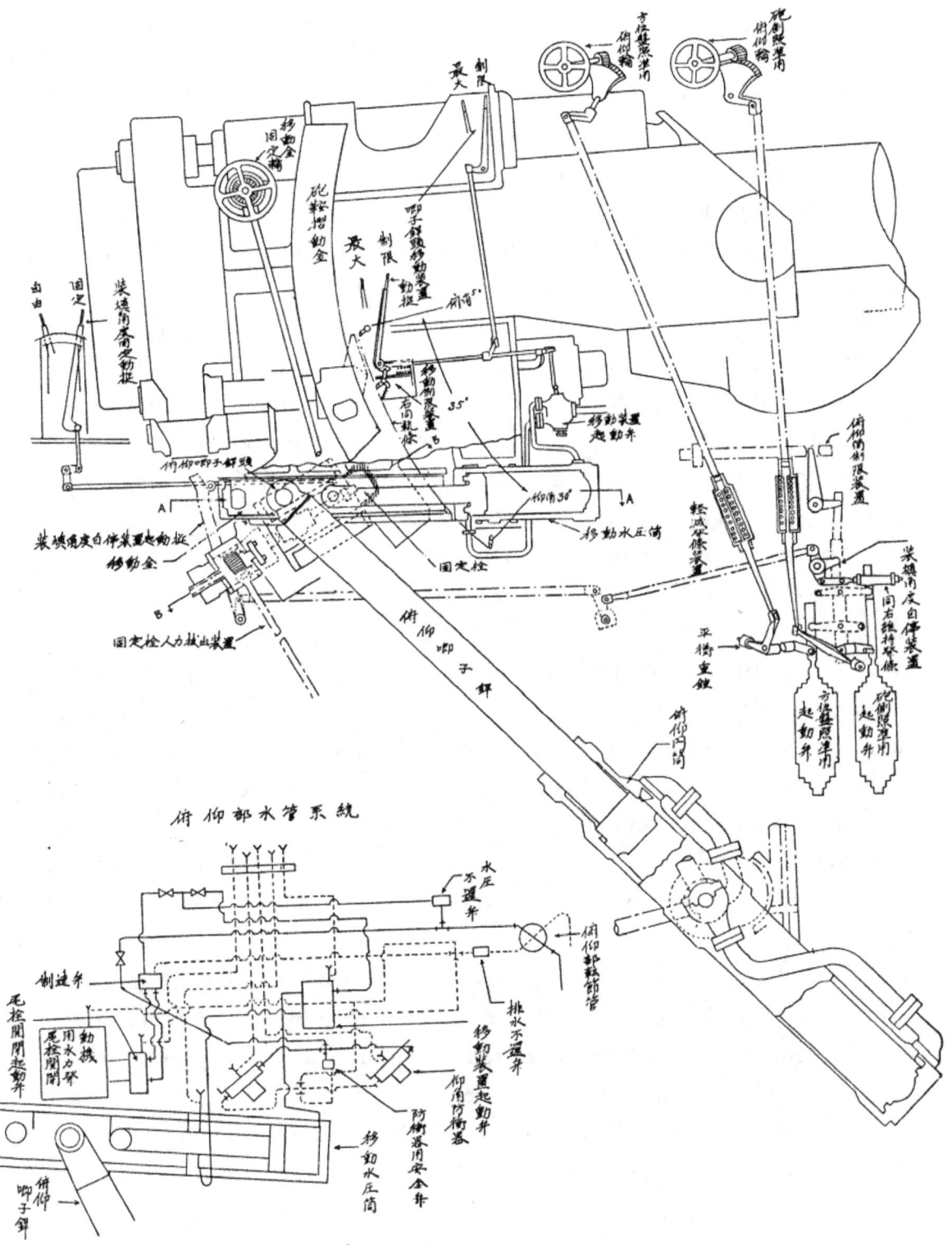

Figure 6-16: Elevating gear (*Kessen Senkan* Yamato *no Zenbō*)

When firing the guns recoiled and were run-out inside the cradle and slide and they were elevated or depressed around the trunnion shaft, figure 6-11 (right).

Two hydraulic recoil cylinders and two pneumatic run-out cylinders acted as the buffer mechanism during firing. Besides of them an independent run-out control cylinder was fitted. Therefore, recoil and run-out were controlled by five separate cylinders fitted in housings on top and below the cradle and slide. They were an integral part of the steel castings.

A small part of the shock generated when firing was also absorbed by the friction between the gun and the cradle and slide, but most of the force was delivered to the roller path below the turntable via the trunnion shafts and the force was finally absorbed by the hull through the ring support.[140].

The guns were elevated and depressed by a cylinder and piston type elevating gear. The cylinder is shown in figure 6-14; the principle of the elevation and depression mechanism in figure 6-15.

It was different from the past arrangement by connecting the upper end of the piston rod of the elevating cylinder to a crosshead and slipper (B in figure 6-15 A and B) running in slipper guides (C in figure 6-15 A). The slipper guides were also an integral part of the cradle and slide casting. The crosshead was connected to a piston rod and piston working on the hydraulic shifting cylinder (D in figure 6-15). A hand lever on the side of the cradle controlled the position of the piston in the cylinder, in order to vary the distance between gun trunnions and the elevating piston rod crosshead. In figure 6-15 B the elevating radius arm was minimum and permitted the guns to be fully elevated and depressed. In figure 6-15 A the radius arm was maximum and the elevation of the gun limited to 41°, the common way of using the guns. The crosshead could be locked at either end of its stroke by locking bolts shown, as F in figure 6-15 C, and was operated by a pinion and bevel gearing from a hand wheel (E in figure 6-15 B); it acted as a form of slide locking gear and kept the gun indirectly at 3° elevation during the loading operations.

The weight of the rotating structure was 2,510 tons per turret and was supported by 48 rollers shown in photo 6-9 running between the upper and

---

[140] If firing a salvo of all nine guns a tremendous reaction force was generated, which had to be absorbed by the hull. If there were weak parts in the hull they were bent or broken, so the hull was carefully inspected after trial firings to discover such parts and make reinforcements, etc.

lower roller paths, which, in turn, were supported by the ring support to make one turn of 360° in three minutes.

The principal power source for the operation of the mounts and guns was hydraulic pressure generated by a turbo-hydraulic pump. Power transmission was usually by hydraulic cylinder and piston actuating rack and pinion gears, bell cranks, hydraulic shifting cylinder, etc., which, in turn, were connected to other mechanical devices to fulfil the required operation. Swashplate engines were also used but they were limited to two functions.

The following enumeration proves that practically all operations were conducted by hydraulic pressure and electricity only was used for supporting purposes and for providing ventilation.

Table 6-1: Equipment involved in gun operations

Operation	Medium	Number	Note
Elevation & depression	Hydraulic cylinder and piston	One per gun	The connection of the piston rod to the slide via the shifting cylinder was a novel design in that it was moveable longitudinally along the slide
Training	Vertical 500-hp swashplate engine through straight-toothed pinion gears without use of worm and worm wheels	Two entirely independent engines were fitted 180° apart but only one at a time was used	Operation supported by No. 20 type Williams-Janney variable speed gears

Note: Because of the very heavy weight of the turret the past type training gear, using the worm and worm wheel drive gear, was dispensed with as (1) this gear would need too much horizontal space requiring a very large diameter of the turret, and (2) the load on the worm would be very high and severe pitting at the point of contact was feared. Therefore, a worm-less training drive driven by a 500-hp swashplate engine was designed. This system had no problems when trained at high speed but at the start of the training, reduction of training speed, and reversion of the training direction (counter movement) the load on the training engine rose considerably. Therefore, smooth movement could not be warranted only by the 500-hp engine. As a countermeasure two 100-hp electric motors and two special No. 20 type Williams-Janney variable speed gears (*seidoki*), connected in series, were fitted.

Table 6-2: Equipment used in projectile operations

Operation	Medium	Number	Note
Opening and closing of breech	Swashplate type (*shabon shiki*) hydraulic engine	One unit per gun	Breech opened automatically at the end of recoil
Projectile hoisting	Hydraulic piston and cylinder	One unit per gun	Projectiles were pushed up vertically step by step (pusher type hoist)
Propellant hoisting	Hydraulic piston and cylinder	One unit per gun	Propellant cage containing six bags was transported directly from handing room to gun house "in one stroke" (bucket type hoist)
Loading/ramming	Hydraulic piston and cylinder	One unit per gun for loading the projectile and six one-sixth propellant bags by one single rammer stroke each	
Reserve (auxiliary) projectile hoist	Hydraulic piston and cylinder	One unit per gun	Hydraulic winch. Transfer in the gun house manually by overhead travellers and chain purchase
Reserve (auxiliary) propellant hoist	Hydraulic piston and cylinder	One unit per gun	Same as above

Sources: (1) "Secret Weapons of the IJN" (*Kimitsu Heiki no Zenbō*), pp. 236–243, powder; (2) "History of Naval Gunnery" (*Kaigun Hōjutsu-shi*), pp. 112–114; (3) Unpublished manuscript "Japanese Naval Guns" by Hans Lengerer, pp. 61–104.

Note: While Japanese sources mention the mounting of one projectile and one powder reserve hoist per gun, Report O-45 (N), p. 57, of the US Naval Technical Mission to Japan, in contrast states that "Two auxiliary hoists were fitted in each turret."

Table 6-3: Principal technical data of the vertical 500-hp swashplate engine (hydraulic pump) for training.

Nominal hp	500
Water hp	503.1 at 250 rpm; 704.3 at 350 rpm
Maximum torque (kg/m)	1,441 at 70 kg/cm² pressure
Water velocity (m/s)	3.13 at port; 10.68 at delivery and supply pipes
Necessary water volume of engine	3,221 litres at 250 rpm
Piston	Ø 100 mm; stroke 149.11 mm; nos. 11
Diameter of cylinder circle (mm)	500
Pipe joints of engine	Ø 80 mm; area 50.27 cm²
Pressure pipe	Same dimensions as pipe joints
Area of fixed ports (cm²)	15.60
Inclination of swash plates	17º

Table 6-4: Principal technical data of the special No. 20 type 100-hp variable speed gear for supporting the 500-hp swashplate engine for training:

Diameter and stroke of piston	51.8 mm × 61.6 mm
Number of cylinders	11
Diameter of cylinder circle	234 mm
Tilting angle	15º
Standard and working rpm	500
Standard delivery	712 litres/min
Standard and working pressure	70.3 kg/cm²
Standard fluid hp	100
Diameter of inlet and outlet valves	80 mm
Number of replenishing valves	One
Stroke of controlling shaft	61.6 mm
Electric motor	100 hp, 220V, 370A

Source: Data supplied by Ōtani Toyokichi[141] to the US Naval Technical Mission to Japan and included in Report O-45 (N) "Hydraulic Pumps in Japanese Naval Ordnance". Some of these data were also used in contributions to the *Maru Magazine*.

Note: Valve plate and casing were made of special cast iron. The pressure side of the safety valve opened at 105.5–116 kg/cm², the oil supply side at

---

[141] Ōtani Toyokichi (1889–?) was a civilian engineer and from the age of 17 (1906) he worked in Kure N.Y. After the termination of the Pacific War he worked for the US Naval Technical Mission to Japan (until 1947).

14.1 kg/cm². The variable speed gear was known as "Special No. 20 type oil pressure controller."

Photo 6-9: Roller path of *Yamato*'s no 2 turret photographed 3 June 1940 (Authors' collections)

For the movement of the rotating structure one hydraulic pump of 500 hp was necessary and each turret had two units fitted 180° apart into each side of the turntable, of which only one unit was used at a time with the other one in reserve in case of failure in operation. The hydraulic pumps (engines) are shown in photo 6-10.

Photo 6-10: Training engines (US Naval Technical Mission to Japan, Report O-45 (N))

Instead of a normal worm and worm wheel driven training gear a wormless training drive was designed for saving space and avoiding too high a load on the worm due to the large weight.

The wormless training drive is shown as figure 6-17 A and B. The hydraulic motor drove the inner member (A in figure 6-17 A and B) of a coaster gear through a core clutch at (CC in figure 6-17 A and B). The inner member (A in figure 6-17 A and B) drove the outer member (B in figure 6-17 A and B) frictionally through three "flattened" rollers (D in figure 6-17 B)[142] B (outer member or drum)[143] in figure 6-17 A and B was keyed to the first of a train of straight-toothed pinion ending in the training pinion (figure 6-18), which drove the turret at 2°/s via the training rack (figure 6-19).

The dimensions of the training pinion and rack are stated in figures 6-18 and 6-19. For stopping and reversing the direction a worm gear and friction type brake was used, as shown as figure 6-20.

The arrangement of the two-storied projectile and propellant supply rooms and their adjacent compartments, particularly the shell and the two powder magazines for #1 and #2 turrets are shown in figures 6-21 to 6-26.

A more detailed view of the projectile supply (handing) rooms and powder magazines are provided in figures 6-27–30.

At the projectile magazine and the supply rooms the vertically arranged projectiles were stowed on twin skids and between heavy girders and they were moved stepwise by the hydraulic piston connected to a "push-pull" gear as shown in figure 6-31 and photo 6-11.

When projectiles had to be moved from the magazine to the lower supply room they had to be moved step by step up to the positions where the openings were located. In the fixed structure around the outside of lower projectile handing room there were three shell transfer bogies. The projectile was loaded into one of these bogies by the push-pull gear and traversed to one of the three entrances to the supply room. In this position the bogie was locked to the rotating structure and the projectile pulled out of it by the end hook of a "push-pull" gear in the supply room. The bogie is shown in figures 6-33–34 and photo 6-12.

---

[142] There were a total of six "flattened" rollers–three for each direction.

[143] The driving face of the outer drum at first suffered severe scoring but this defect was overcome by forced lubricating, using a one horsepower electric pump for this purpose as well as to lubricate all the pinion teeth and bearings.

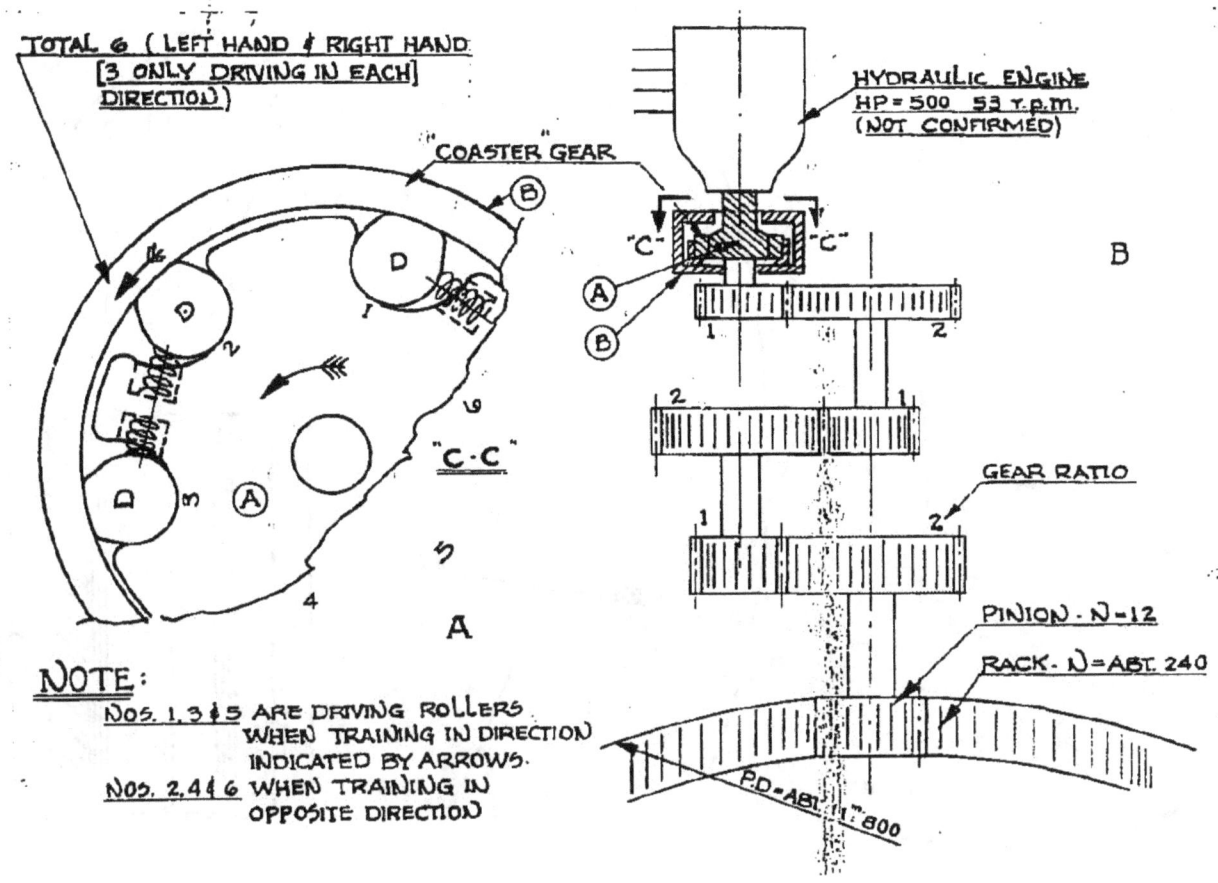

Figure 6-17: Gun turret training gear (US Naval Technical Mission to Japan, Report O-45 (N))

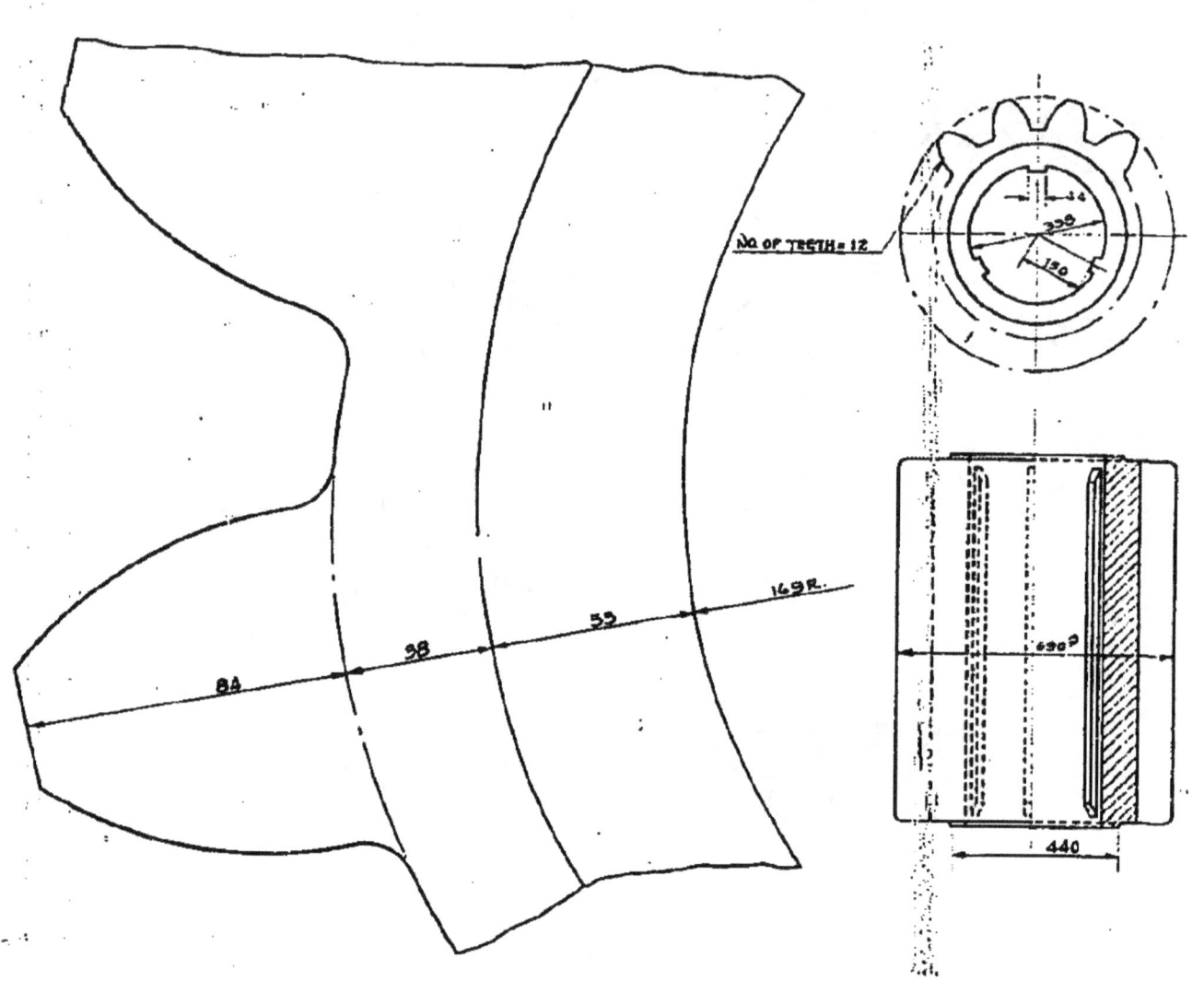

Figure 6-18: Gun turret training pinion–steel (dimensions in mm) (US Naval Technical Mission to Japan, Report O-45 (N))

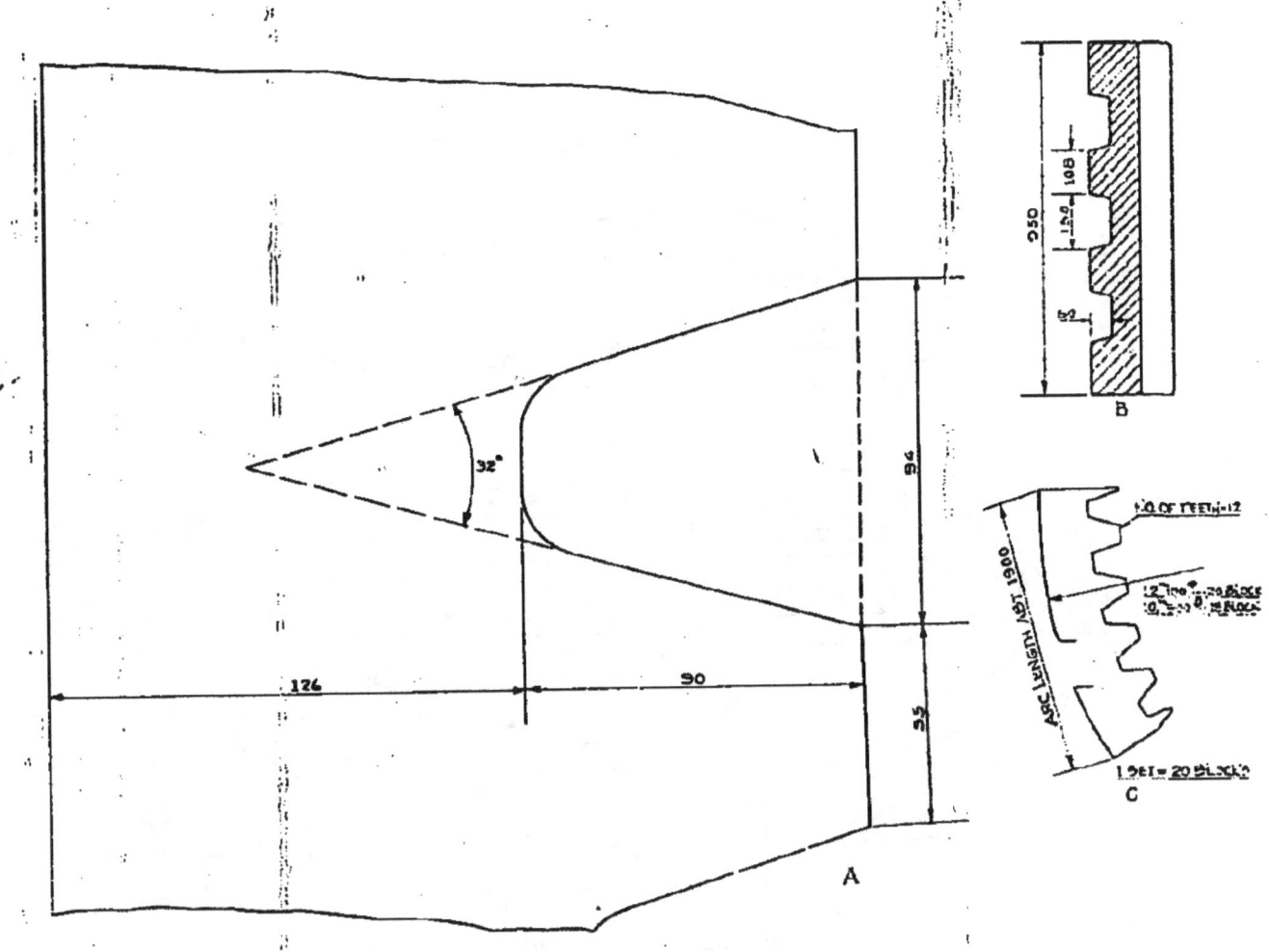

Figure 6-19: Gun turret training rack (dimensions in mm) (US Naval Technical Mission to Japan, Report O-45 (N))

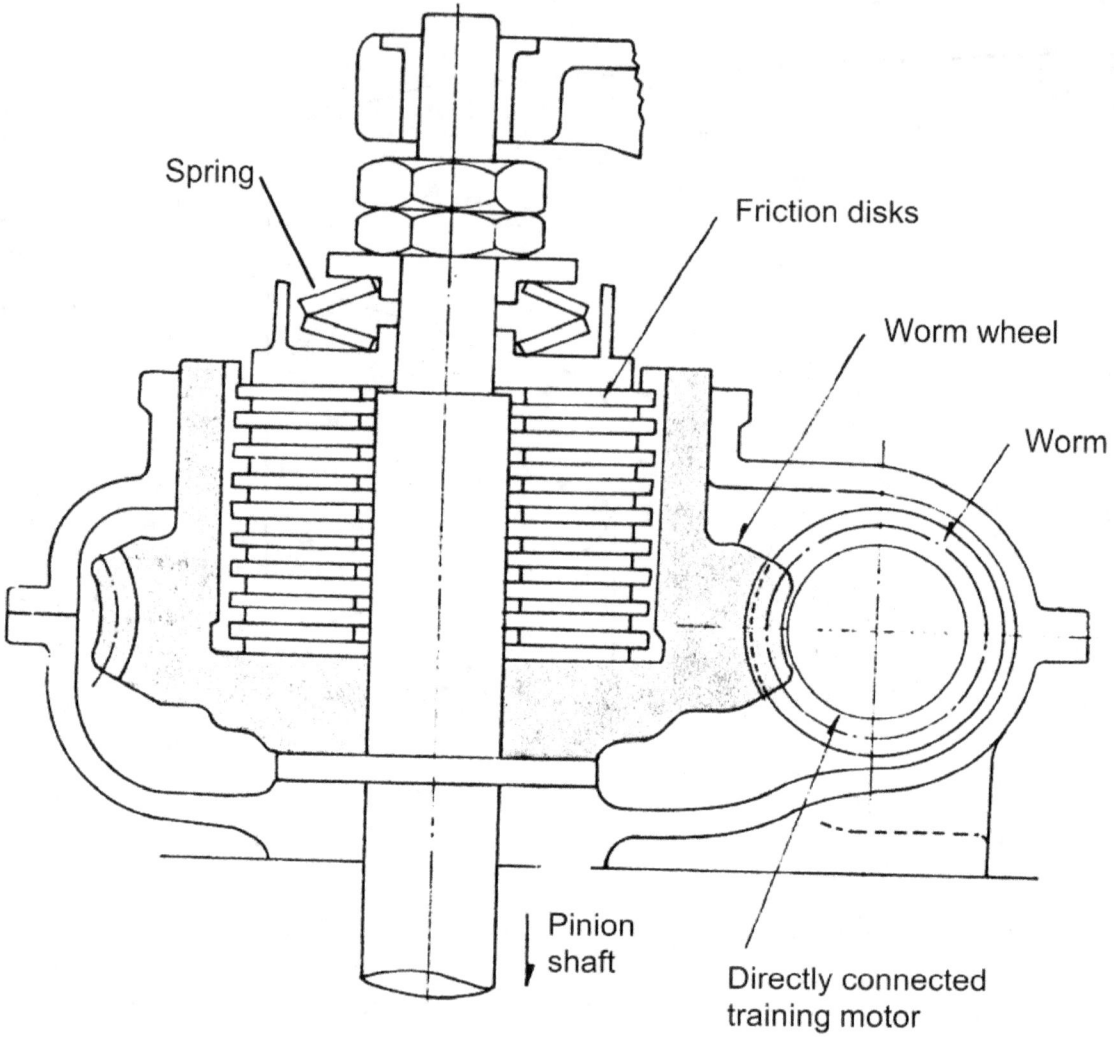

Figure 6-20: Friction coupling (*Maru*, #400, by permission of Ushioshobō-Kōjinsha Co., Ltd.)

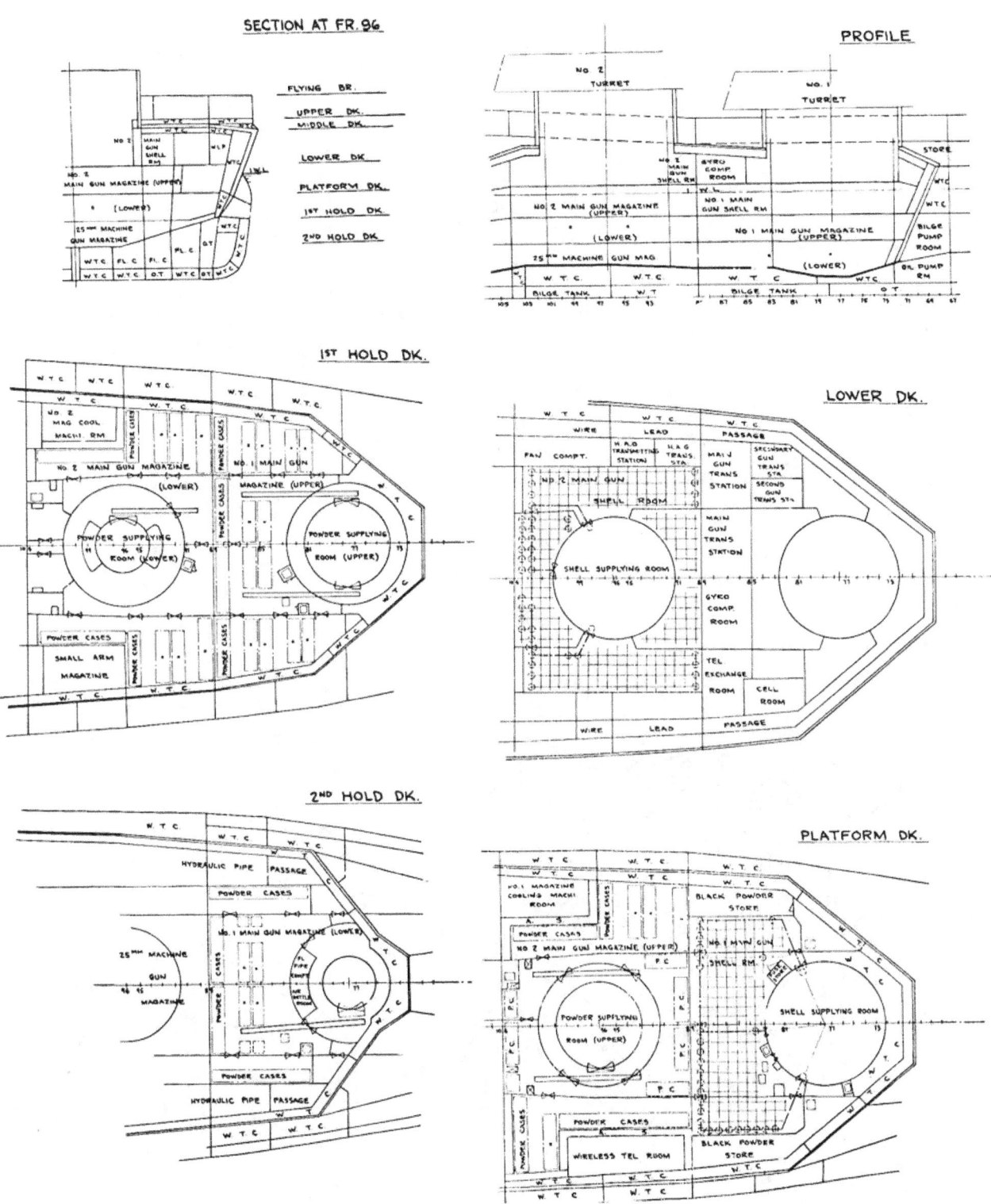

Figures 6-21–26: Arrangement of magazines and shell rooms (US Naval Technical Mission to Japan, Report O-45 (N))

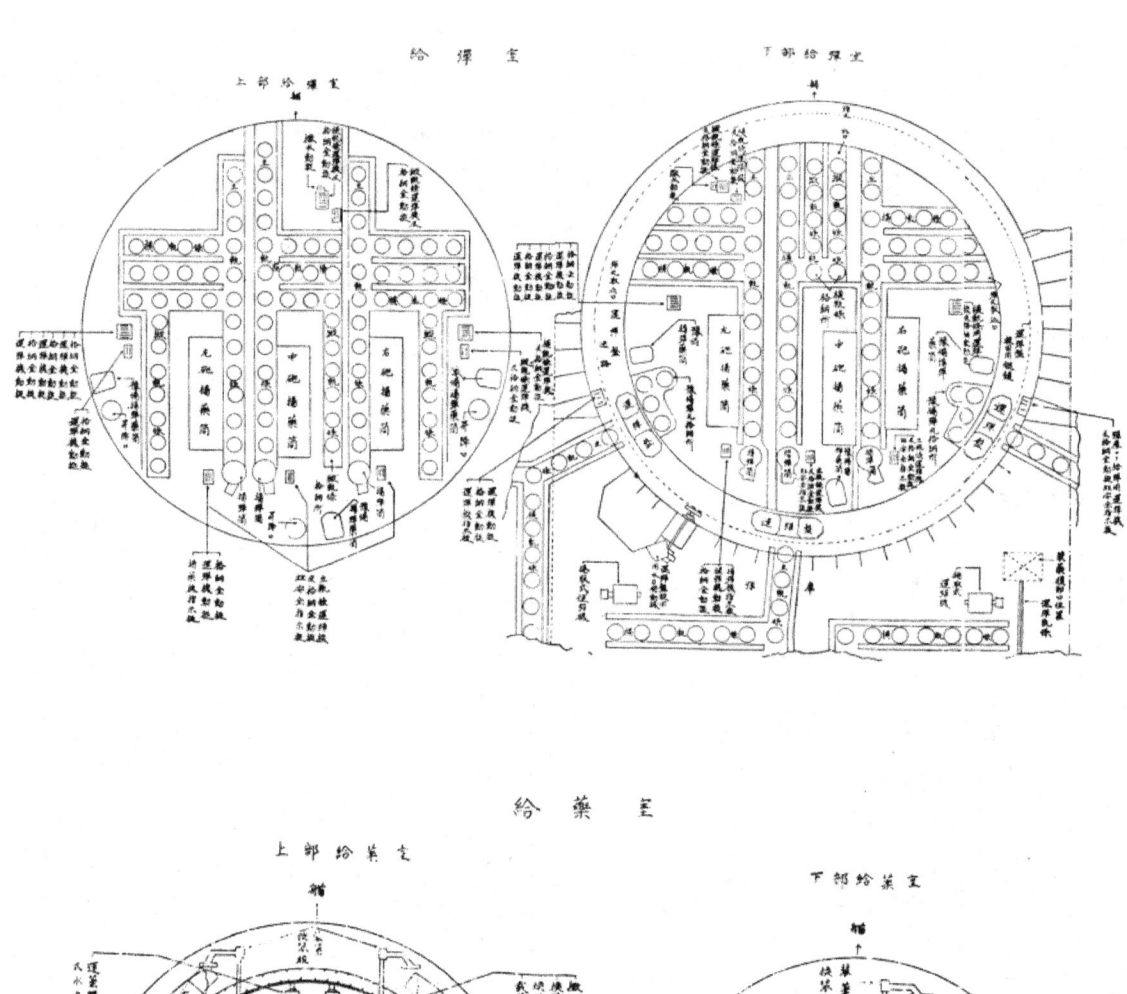
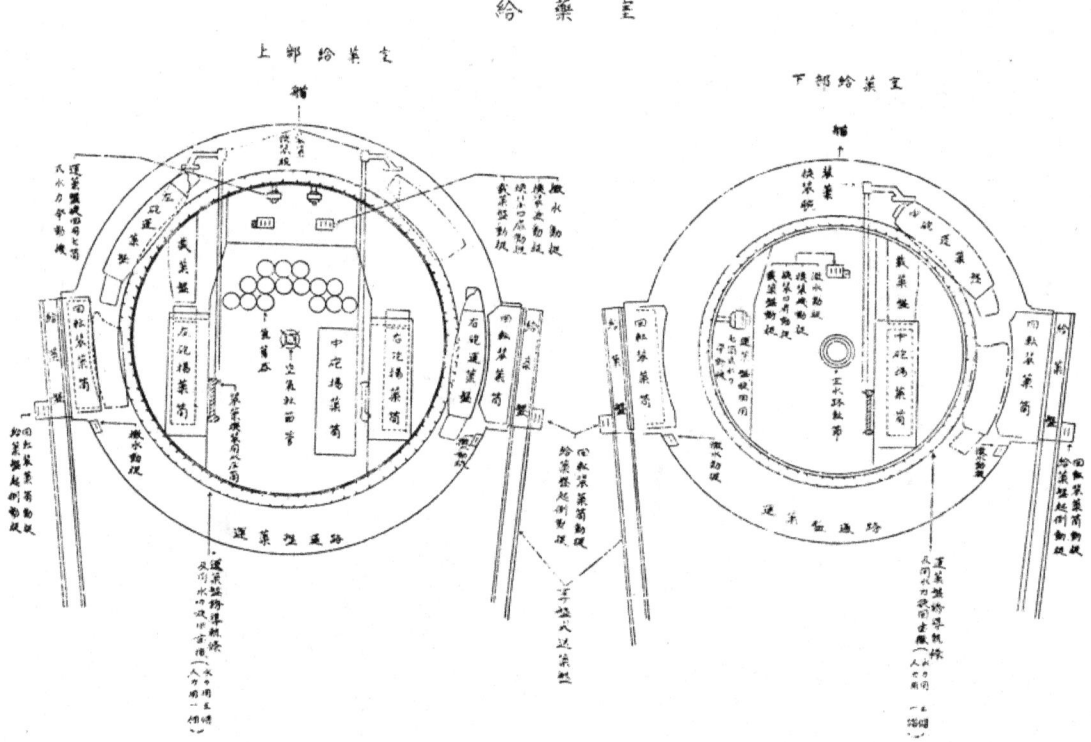

Figures 6-27–30: Lower (top left) and upper (top right) projectile supply rooms. Lower (bottom left) and upper powder supply rooms (*Kessen Senkan* Yamato *no Zenbō*)

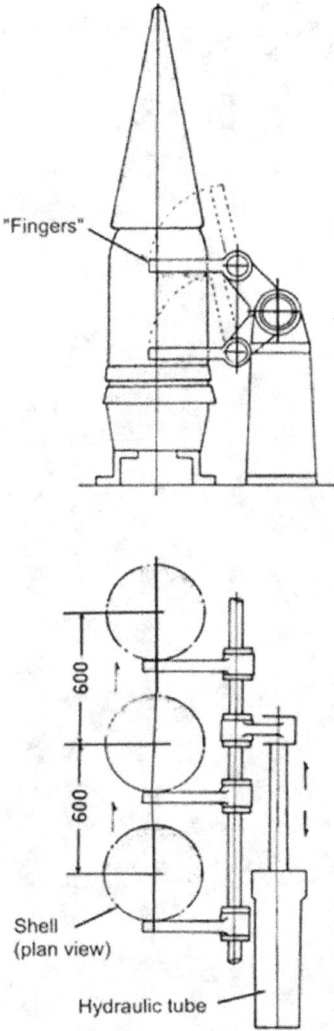

Figure 6-31: In the shell magazine and in the shell supply room the vertically stowed shells were moved stepwise on twin skids and between heavy girders by a hydraulic cylinder and piston, connected to a rod to which levers and "fingers" were fixed (the whole mechanism was referred to as "push-pull" gear by the investigators of the Allied forces). The hydraulic piston moved one step forward (600 mm) and the fingers caused the shells to move the same distance. After that the fingers moved upwards to free themselves from the shells and the piston moved backwards 600 mm. Then the fingers were lowered to again place themselves behind a shell and the next step was executed (*Maru*, #400, by permission of Ushioshobō-Kōjinsha Co., Ltd.)

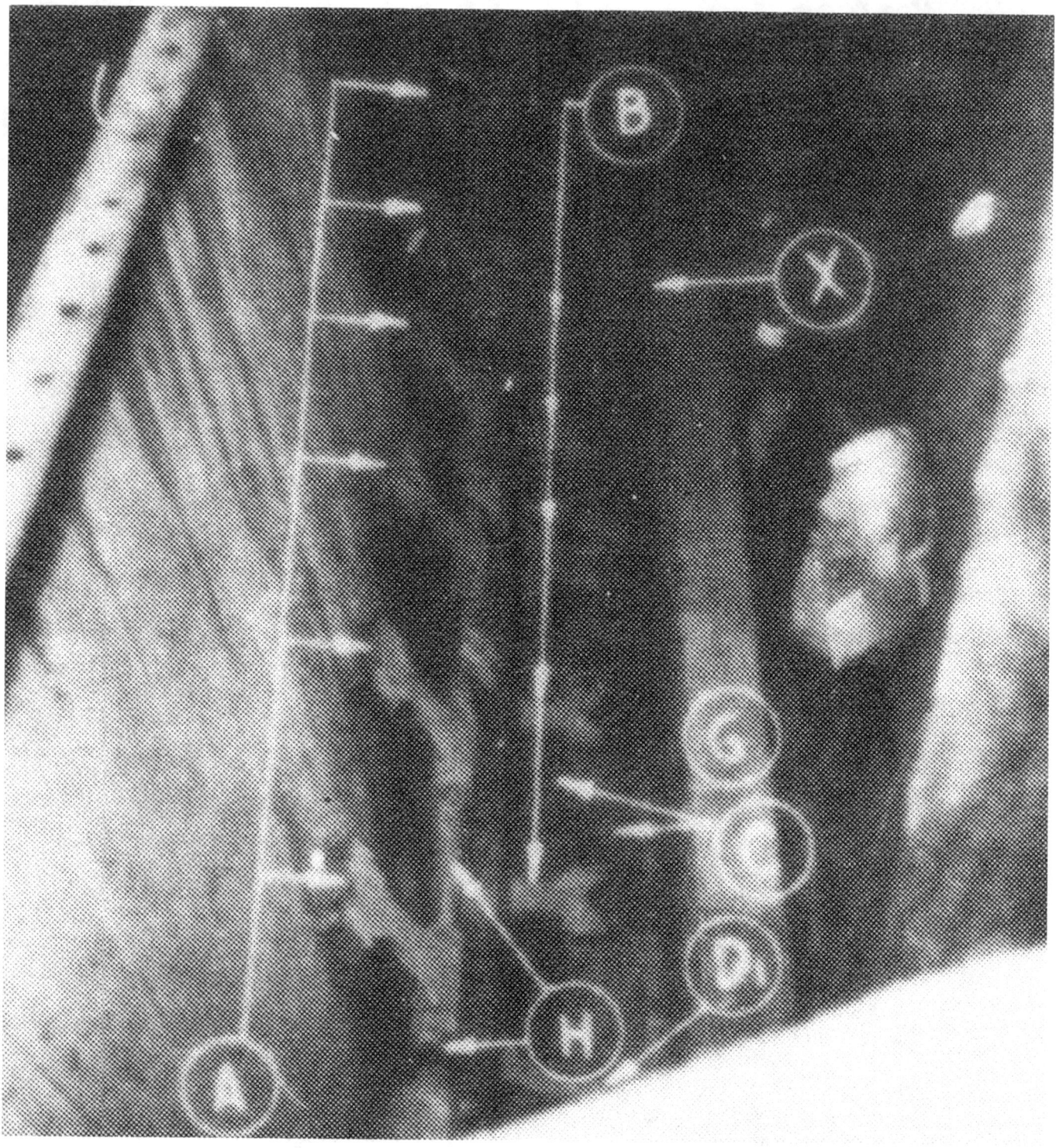

Photo 6-11: Shell "push-pull" and gear shell handing room (US Naval Technical Mission to Japan, Report O-45 (N))

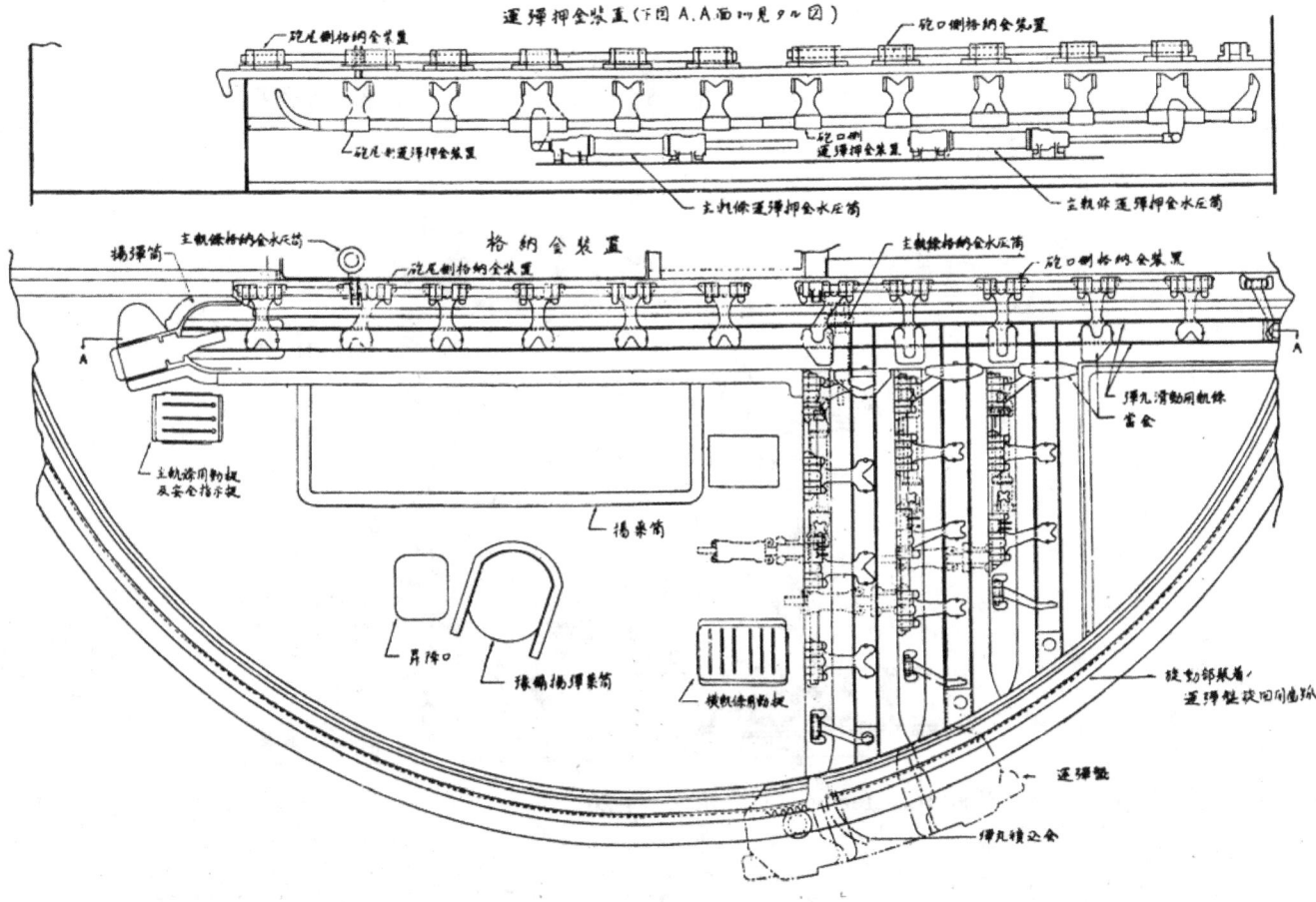

Figure 6-32: Shell "push-pull" and gear projectile supply room (*Kessen Senkan Yamato no Zenbō*)

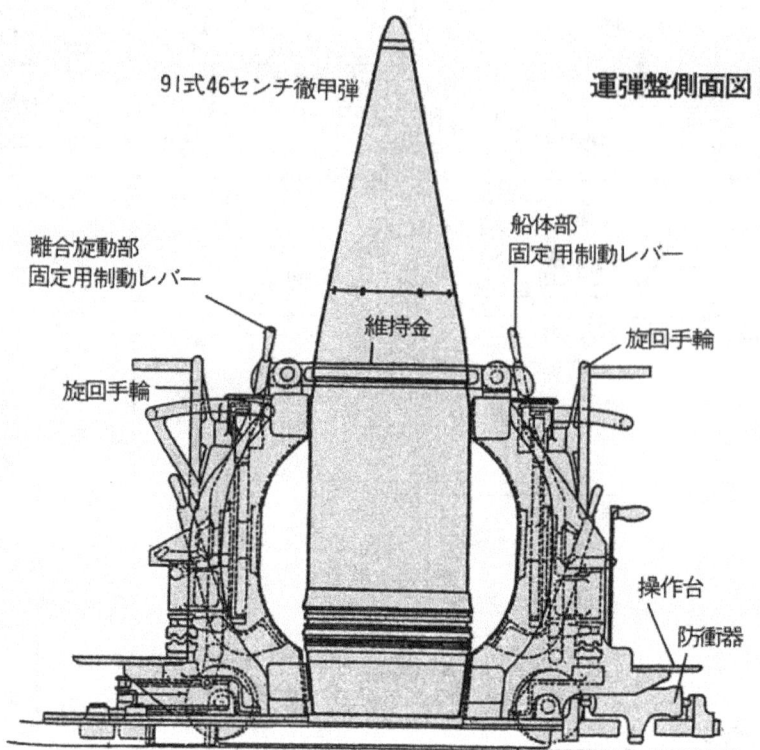

Figure 6-33: Shell transfer bogie (Gakken, #20)

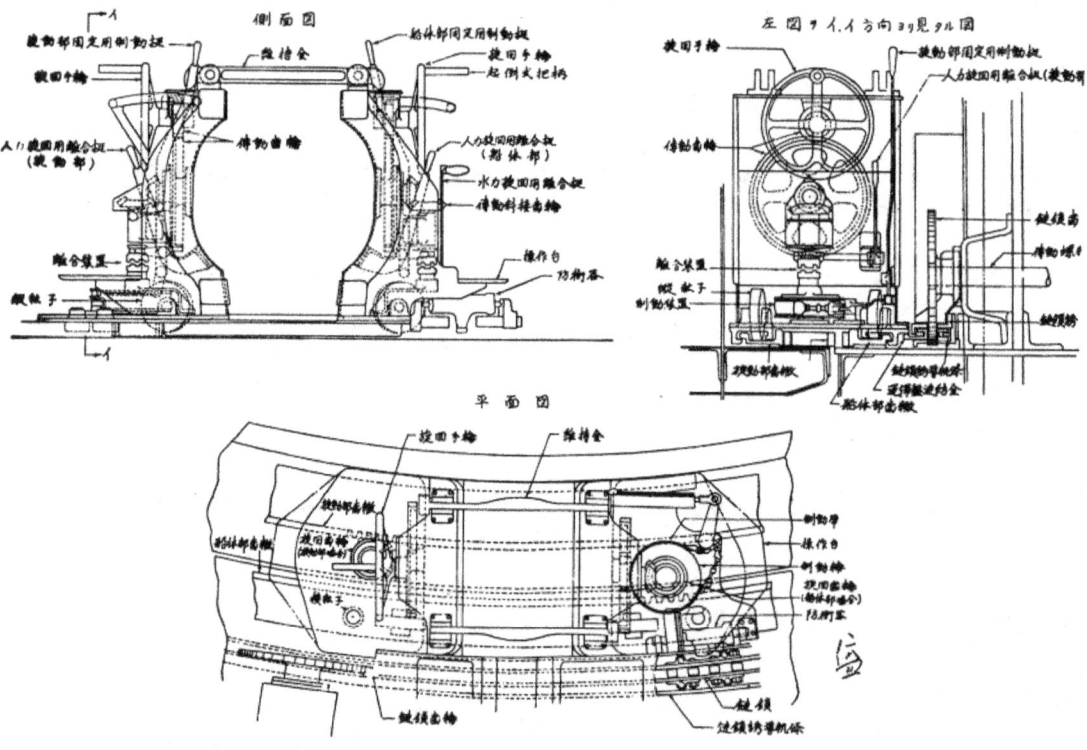

Figure 6-34: Shell transfer bogie (*Kessen Senkan* Yamato *no Zenbō*)

Photo 6-12: Shell transfer bogie (US Naval Technical Mission to Japan, Report O-45 (N))

The projectile hoists were of simple pusher type and all three carried to the bottom of the lower supply room. There was an entrance to each hoist both in the upper and lower supply rooms. The projectiles were pushed by the 'push-pull' gear directly into the hoists through suitably shaped openings, and toppled onto a platform sloped at about 5° below the horizontal, to bring them in line with the hoist, which was raked at 5° from the vertical. The shell on entering the hoist depressed a spring-loaded crank, projecting above the platform. This crank was connected to anti-rolling stops at the sides of the hoist entrance, which were thus closed, to prevent the projectile from falling out of the hoist. Each hoist was fitted with a single set of lifting pawls in the back and fixed retaining pawls at the front. The piston of the lifting cylinder was fitted with a rack extension, which was connected through a 2:1 ratio pinion gear to a rack fitted to the lifting pawls connecting rod. The stroke of the piston was about 1.3 m, thus the pawls moved approximately 2.6 m. There were four lifting pawls, which were all operated at the same time, i.e. there were four projectiles in each hoist and they moved stepwise by each stroke up to the gun house.

The three fixed pawls were all interconnected and were pushed into or pulled out of the hoist by bell crank and rod gearing, operated by a roll running in a cam groove on the side of the rack extension of the piston rod.

The principle of the pusher type hoist is shown in figures 6-35–36.

Figures 6-35 and 6-36 show the projectile hoist tube (*yōdan-tō*) within which the projectile was pushed up to the gun house from the supply room. The shell, which was shifted to the projectile hoist tube from the supply room, was pushed up step by step by means of the hydraulic piston of the lifting (hoisting) cylinder, fitted with a rack extension and pinion gear connected to the lifting pawls' connecting rod. At the uppermost part of the projectile hoist was a "U"-shaped shell tilting bucket (*kansō-tō*).

In the gun house the top pawl lifted the projectile into a "U"-shaped tilting bucket and a spring-operated pawl returned it into the bucket when the pusher hoist started its downward stroke. The bucket was tilted down to 8° above the horizontal by a hydraulically operated rack, crank and connecting rod, which is shown in figure 6-37 (left).

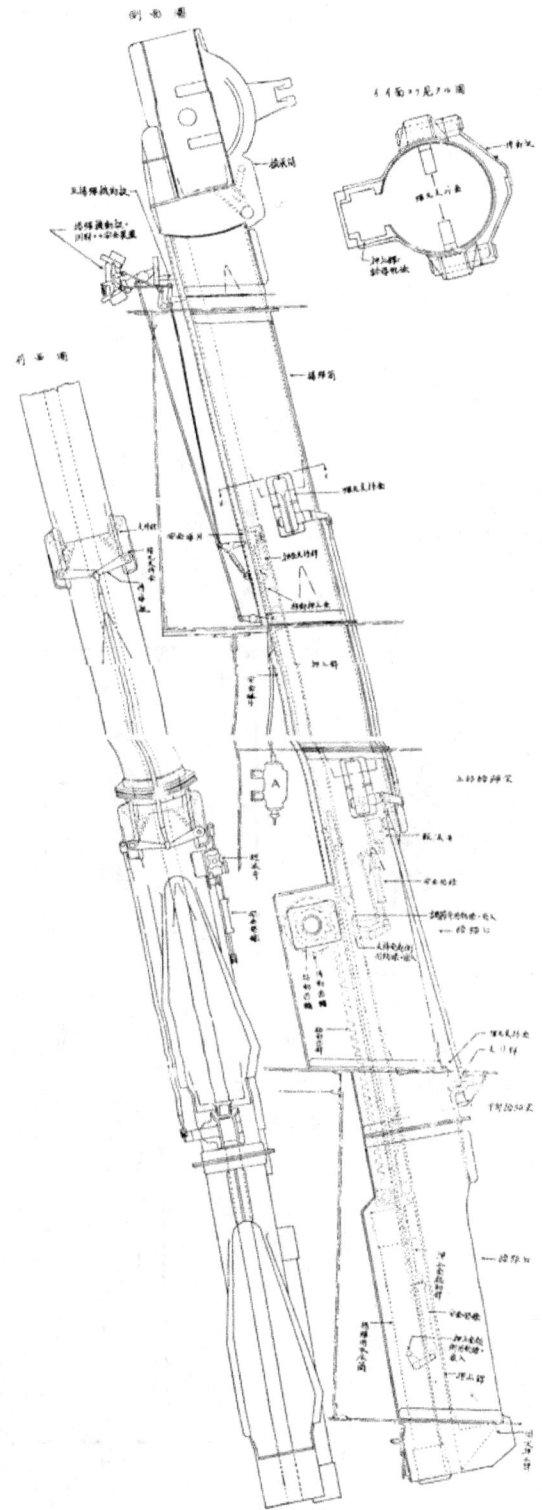

Figure 6-35: Projectile hoist (*Kessen Senkan* Yamato *no Zenbō*)

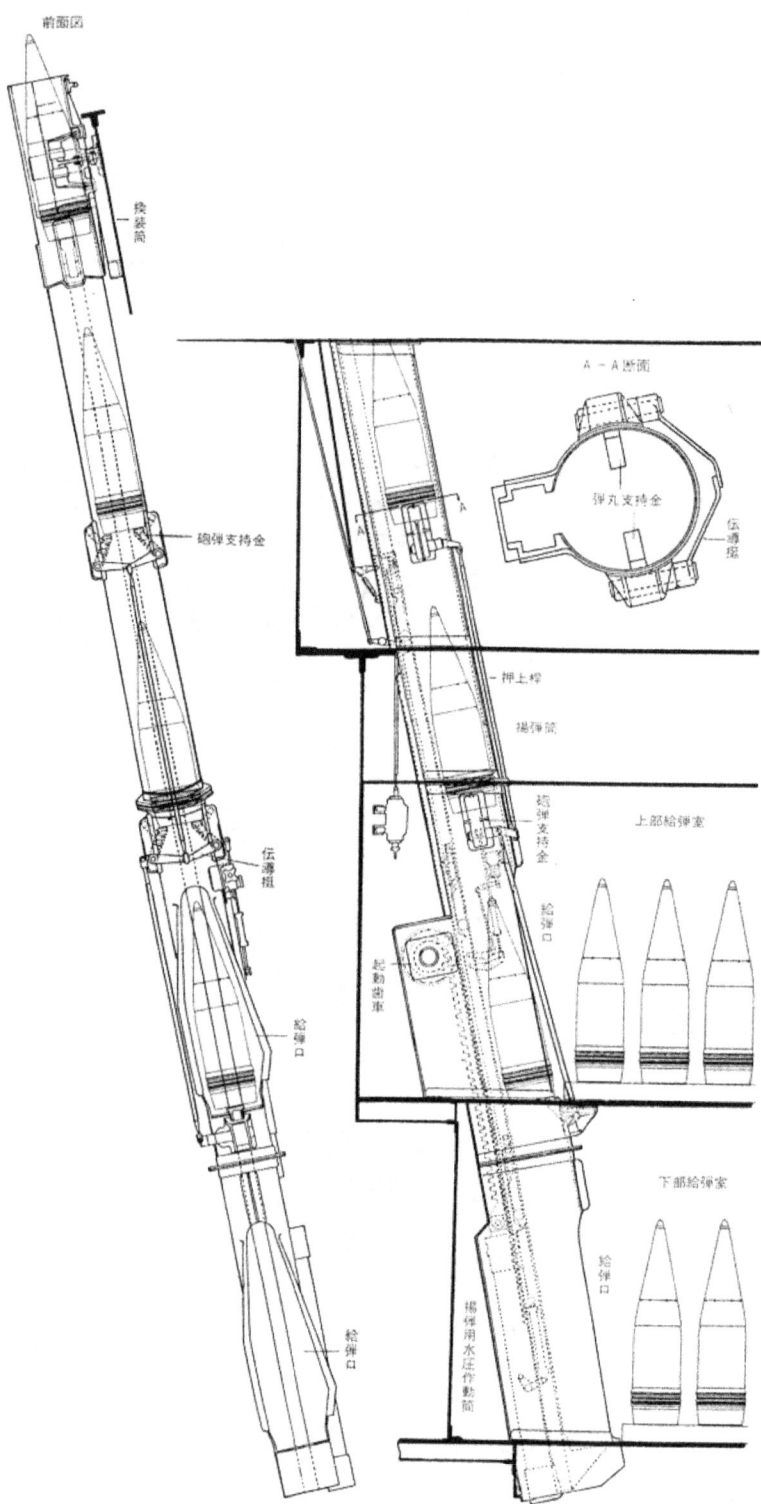

Figure 6-36: Projectile hoist (Gakken, #11)

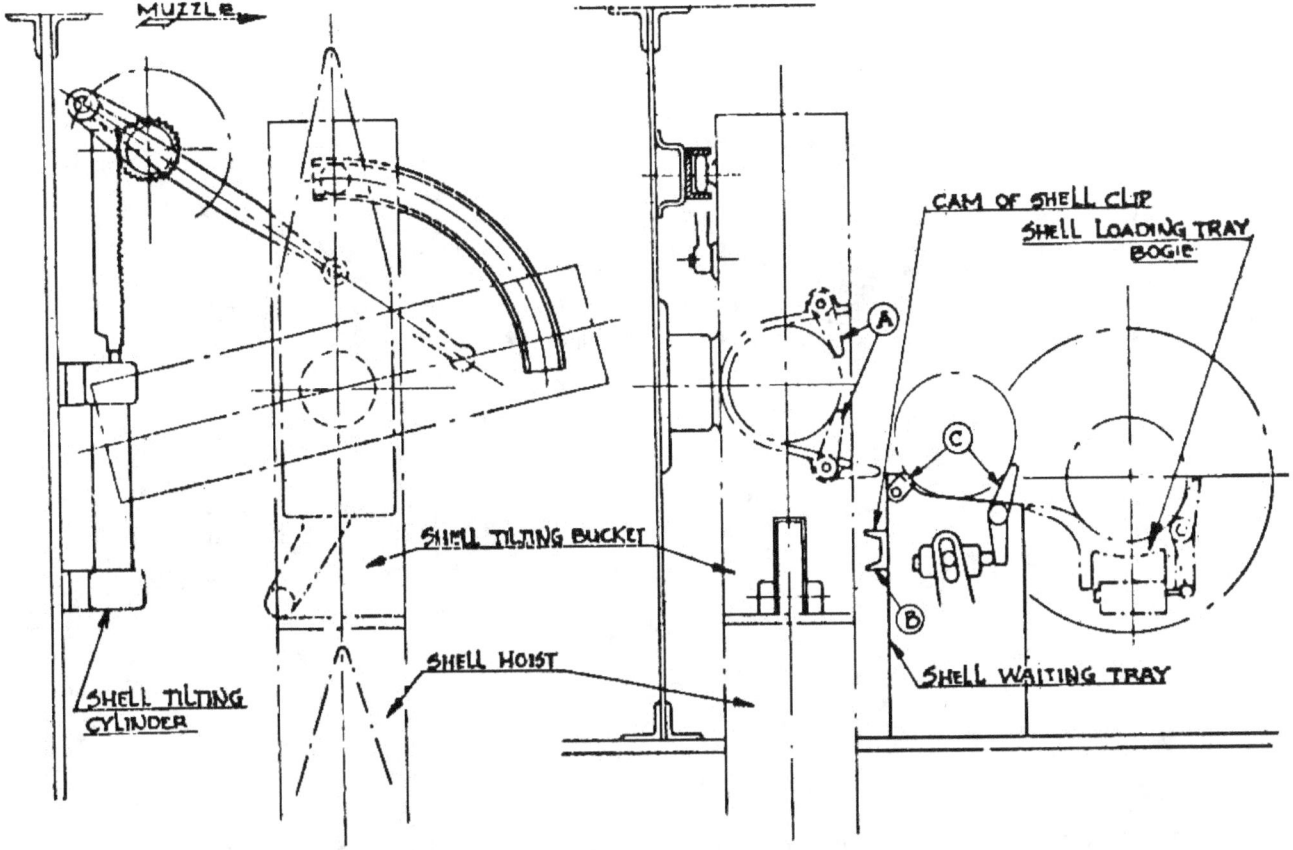

Figure 6-37: Gun turret shell transfer in gun house (US Naval Technical Mission to Japan, Report O-45 (N))

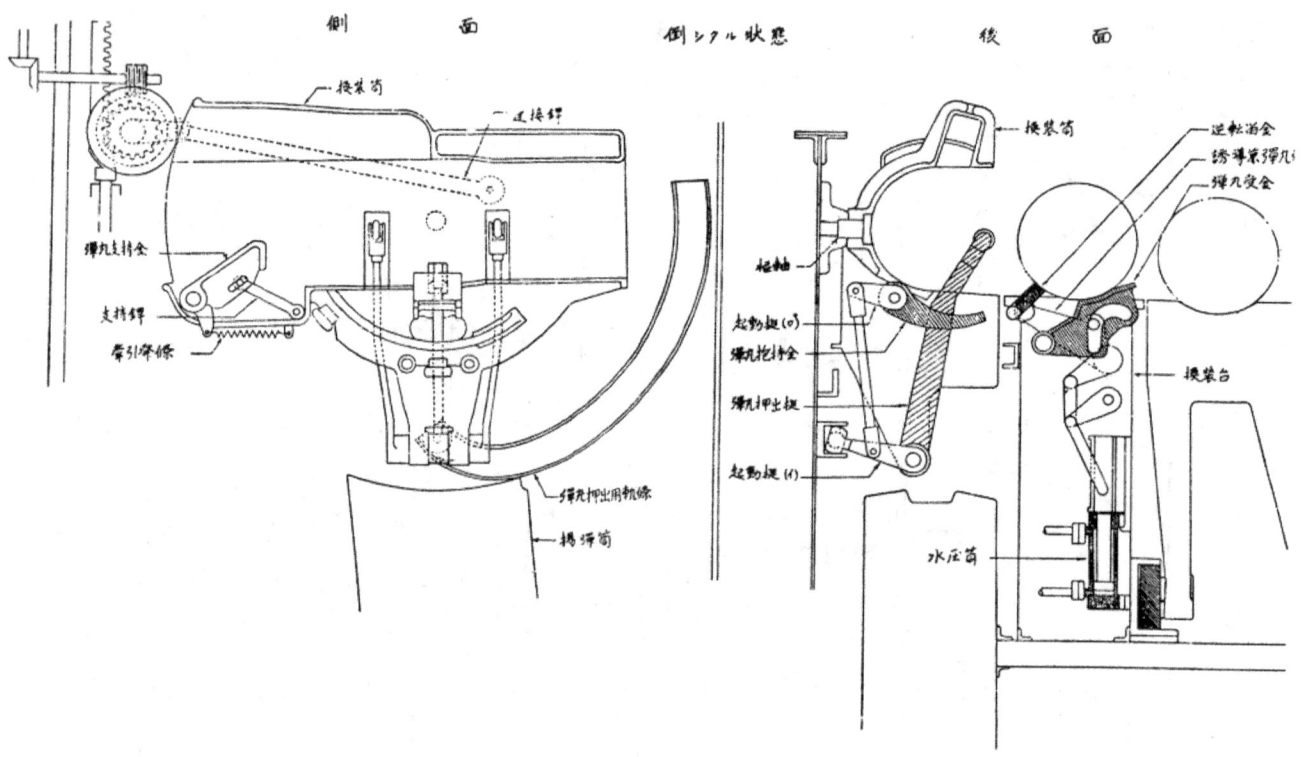

Figure 6-38: Gun turret shell transfer in gun house (*Kessen Senkan* Yamato *no Zenbō*)

The projectile was prevented from falling out of the side of the bucket by retaining clips (A in figure 6-37). These clips were opened by link gearing and a roller working in the cam rail (B in figure 6-37) on the side of the waiting tray (*kansōdai*), thus allowing the projectile to roll out of the bucket onto the waiting tray, where it was held by stops (C in figure 6-37) until it was rolled onto the projectile loading tray (*sōtenban*) of the combined projectile loading bogie and rammer (*hōdan sōtenki*), as shown in figure 6-37.

The combined loading bogie and rammer (*sōtenki*) is shown in figures 6-40 and 6-41 and photo 6-13. It was fitted on four wheels running in rails parallel to the bore of the gun. As it moved forward towards the gun the front wheels ran down a ramp to position B in figure 6-40, thus bringing the bogie and shell from 8° above the horizontal to 3°, the loading angle of the gun. A breech tread protecting tray (C) was fitted on the bolt (E) in figure 6-40. Power for moving the bogie and for ramming was supplied through telescopic pipes along the sides of the bogie. A buffer stop (D) limited the forward movement of the bogie and caused the opening of anti-rolling grips to free the projectile preparatory for ramming. The rammer was a normal chain type rammer driven through a shock absorbing mechanism (C) in figure 6-40, by pinion, rack and hydraulic piston. Hydraulic buffer stops were fitted at each end of the rammer. The rammer stroke was so powerful that the projectile bridged the about 3.5 m distance by passing through the powder room (larger bore) until its rotating bands were pressed into the lands.

After finishing loading the combined shell loading bogie and rammer returned to the original position, to make room for the propellant rammer and charge container to swing into line with the bore underneath the receiving tray (A) in figure 6-40.

The propellant was stowed in canisters in racks as shown in figure 6-43. Each canister contained two one-sixth charges, each weighting 60 kg.

After removal from their canisters in the magazine (B in figure 6-44) the bags were manhandled onto the propellant roller chute (C in figure 6-44) and were then pushed manually over the rollers of the chute into the revolving flashtight scuttle (D in figure 6-44), which was long enough to hold six bags (360 kg in total) end to end. The scuttle was revolved by means of a hydraulic cylinder and piston fitted with a rack, which engaged a pinion at the centre of rotation of the scuttle. A mechanical interlock prevented the rotation of the scuttle until the propellant transfer bogie (E in figure 6-44) was in line with the scuttle and locked to the ship.

The propellant transfer bogie is shown in photos 6-14 and 6-15 and it consisted mainly of the carriage (A), the pivoting tray (B), the hand wheel and the gear train (C). The function is briefly illustrated in figure 6-45.

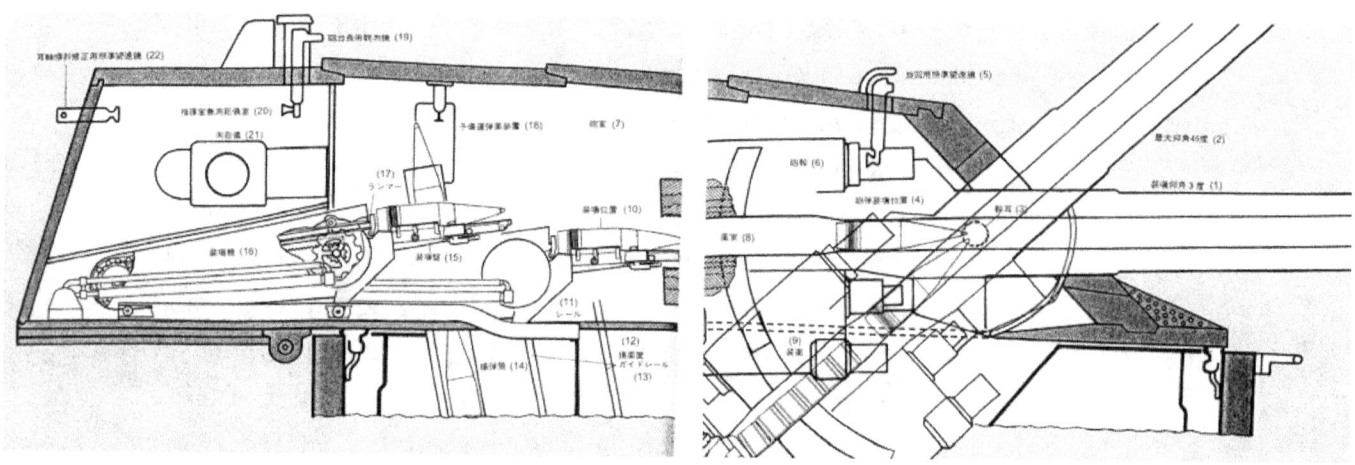

Figure 6-39: Loading procedure (Gakken, #11)

(1) Loading angle 3°
(2) Maximum elevation angle 45°
(3) Trunnion
(4) Loaded position of projectile
(5) Trainer's targeting periscope (*shōjun bōenkyō*)
(6) Cradle
(7) Gun house
(8) Powder room
(9) Powder bags
(10) Loading position
(11) Rail
(12) Powder hoisting container
(13) Guide rails
(14) Shell hoist (tube)
(15) Loading tray
(16) Rammer (*sōtenki*)
(17) Rammer
(18) Reserve shell and powder transport equipment

(19) Periscope for chief of turret

(20) Control room for range measurement

(21) Rangefinder

(22) Binoculars for trunnions tilting corrector

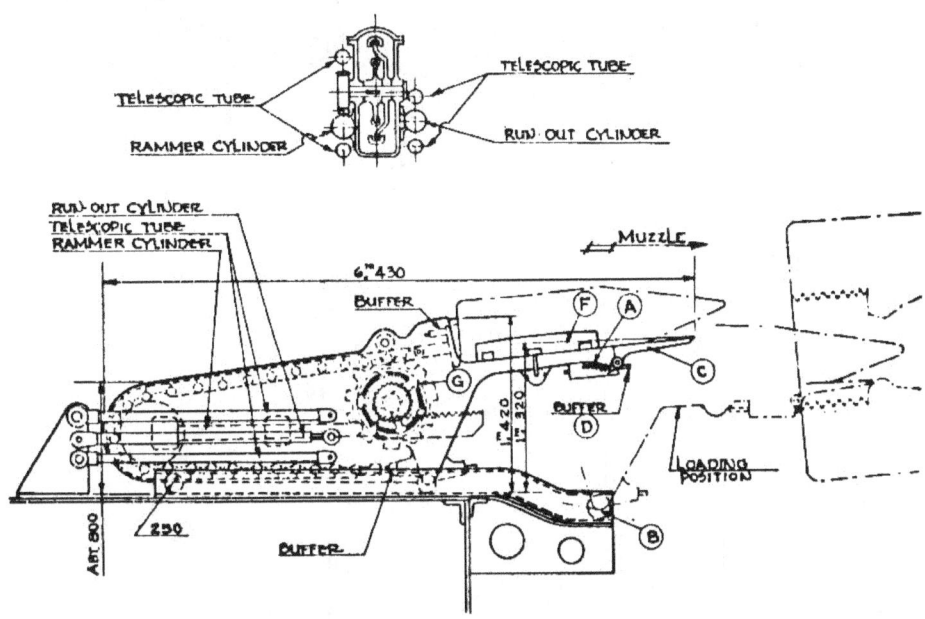

Figure 6-40: Gun turret shell rammer in gun house (US Naval Technical Mission to Japan, Report O-45 (N))

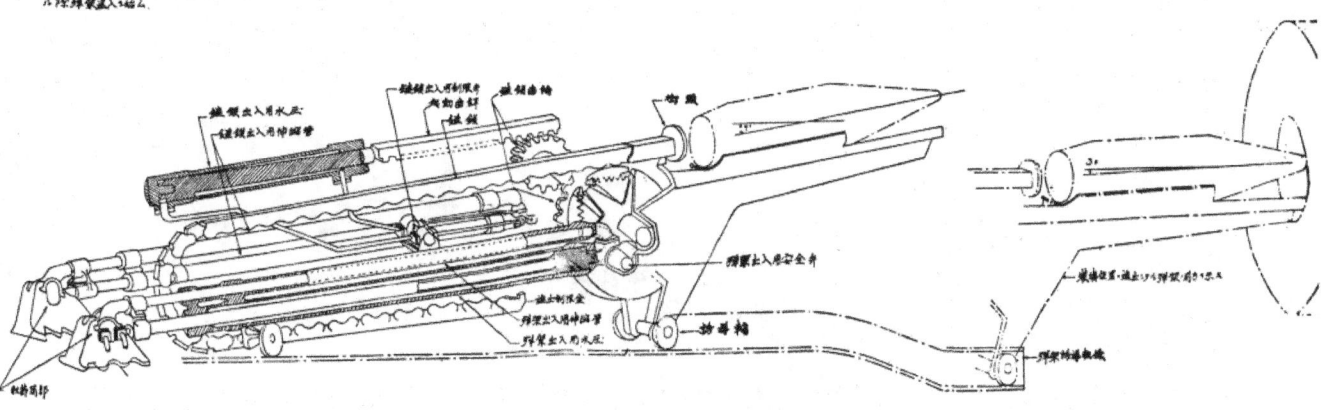

Figure 6-41: Gun turret shell rammer in gun house (*Kessen Senkan* Yamato *no Zenbō*)

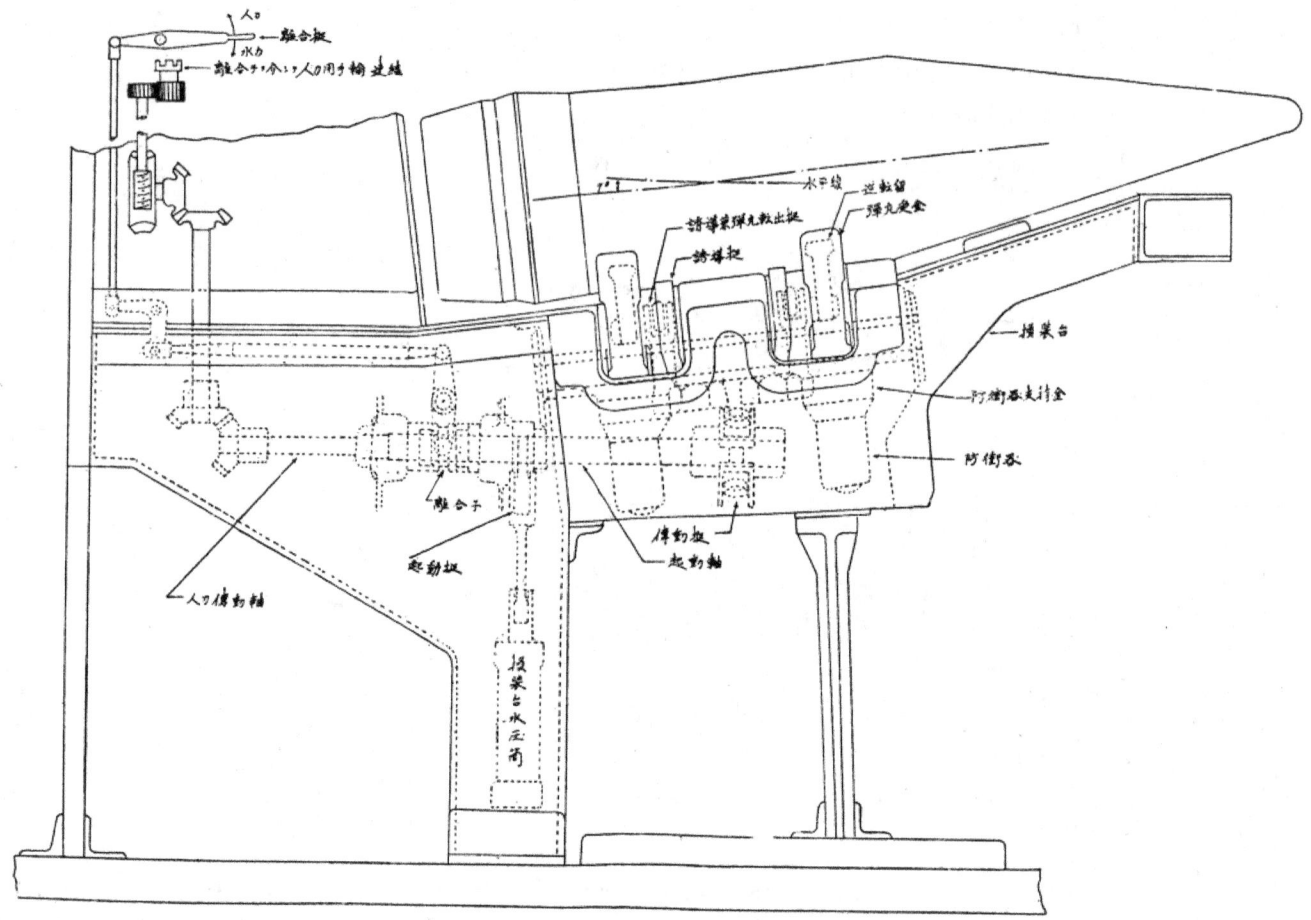

Figure 6-42: Tilting tube (*kansō-tō*) (*Kessen Senkan* Yamato *no Zenbō*)

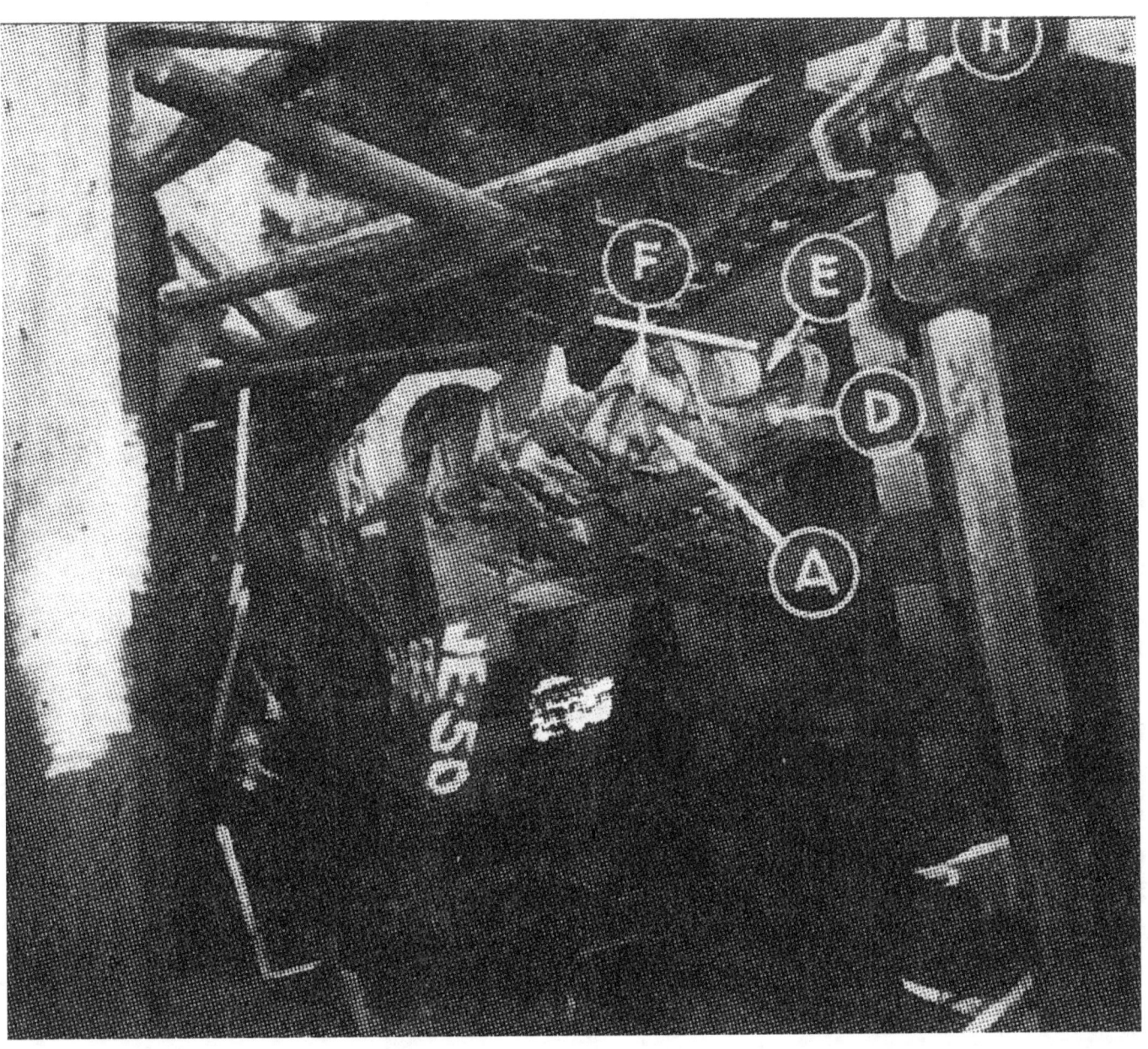

Photo 6-13: Gun house bogie and shell rammer–final design (US Naval Technical Mission to Japan, Report O-45 (N))

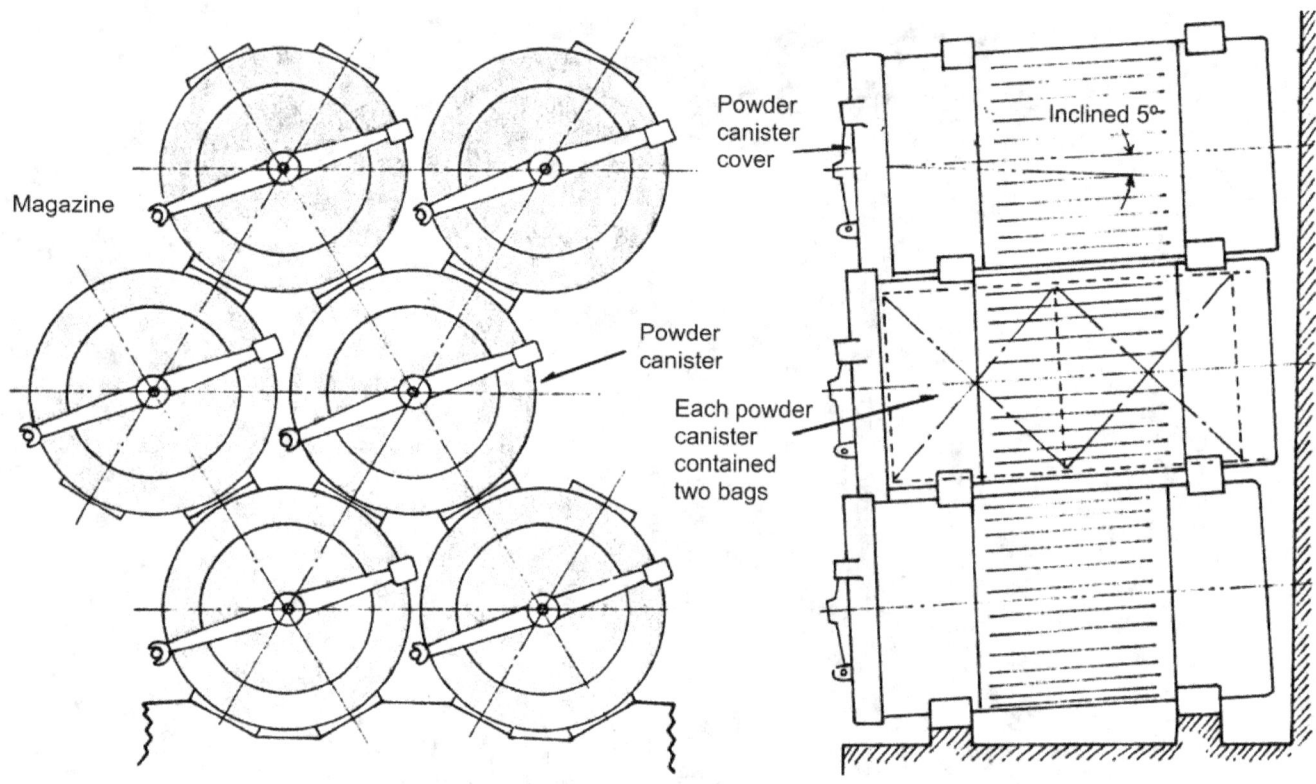

Figure 6-43: Stowage of powder canisters in the magazine (*Maru*, #400, by permission of Ushioshobō-Kōjinsha Co., Ltd.)

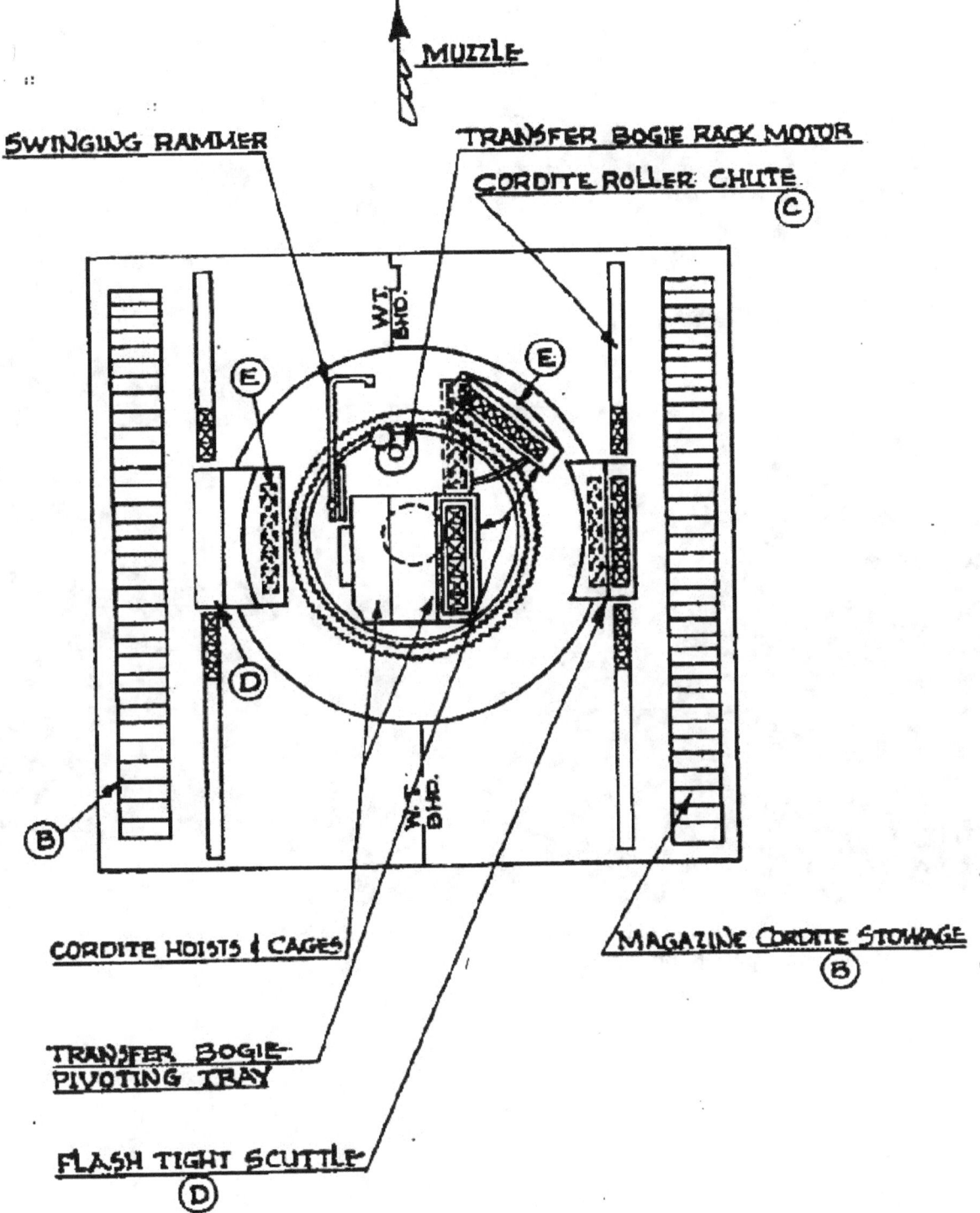

Figure 6-44: Plan of magazine and upper cordite handing room (US Naval Technical Mission to Japan, Report O-45 (N))

Photo 6-14: Cordite bogie (trial design) in handing room (US Naval Technical Mission to Japan, Report O-45 (N))

Photo 6-15: Cordite bogie (trial design) in handing room (US Naval Technical Mission to Japan, Report O-45 (N))

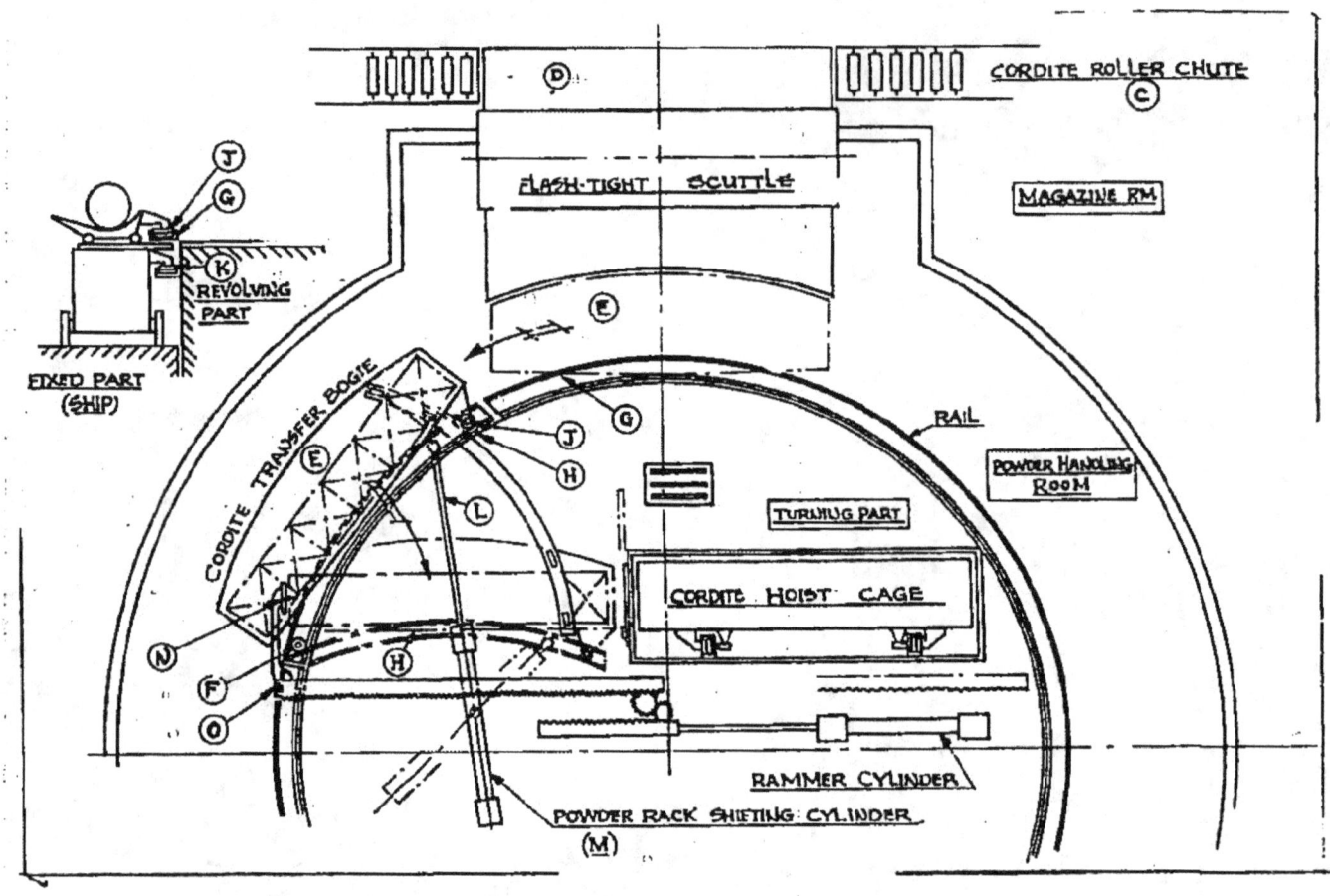

Figure 6-45: Type 94 46-cm gun turret powder handing gear (US Naval Technical Mission to Japan, Report O-45 (N))

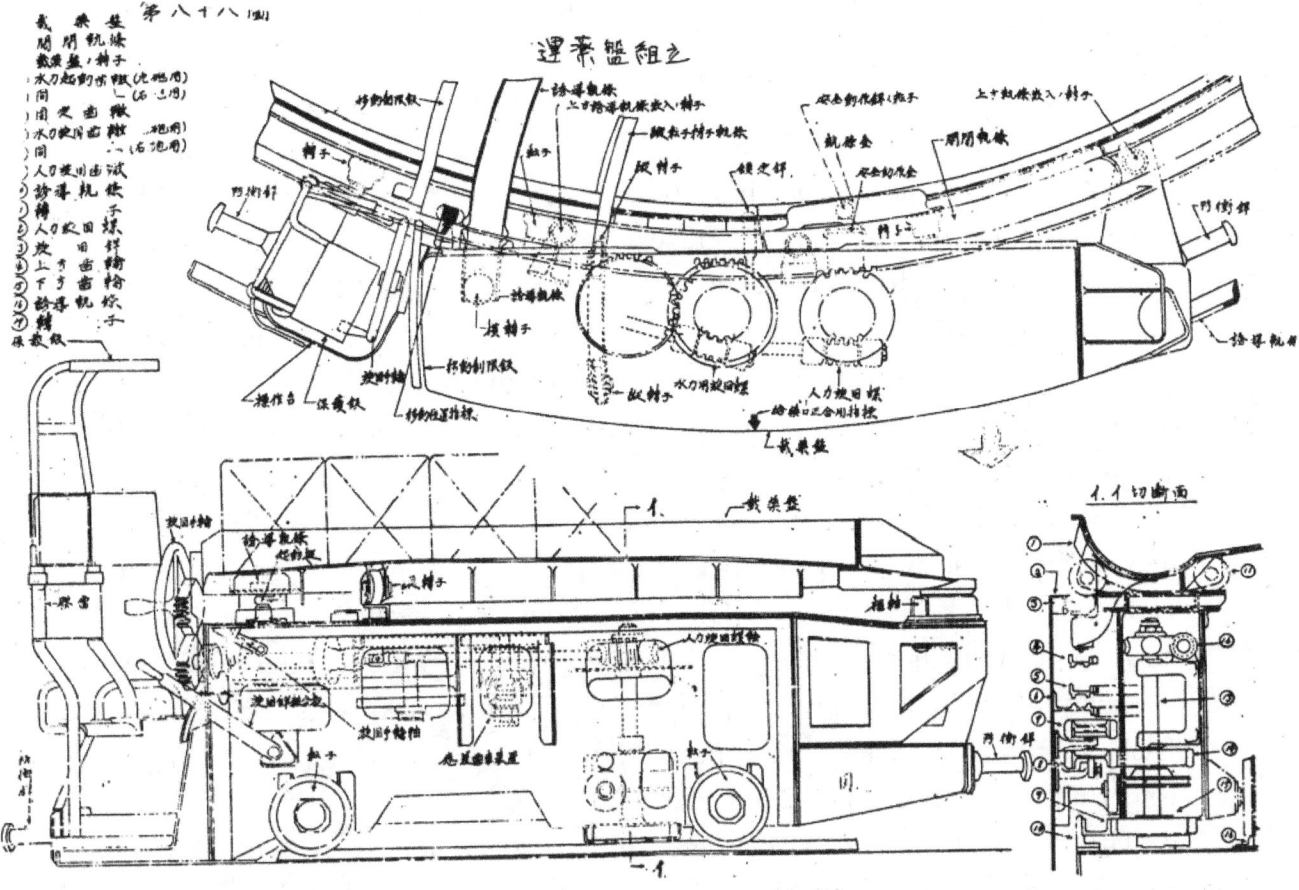

Figure 6-46: Carriage (*Kessen Senkan* Yamato *no Zenbō*)

The carriage was a girder structure mounted on wheels, so angled to each other that the carriage could be moved on a circular path on the fixed deck of the propellant supply rooms around the revolving structure of the turret. After taking over the propellant charge from the flashtight scuttle, as shown in figure 6-46, the pinion (F in photo 6-15) meshed with a circular rack on the fixed structure and was used for traversing the bogie from the scuttle to the position in line with the entrance to the propellant hoist. On reaching the loading position the bogie came up against a buffer stop, and was de-clutched from the driving racks and clutched to the revolving structure. Actuating some mechanism the pivoting tray on top of the bogie (E in figure 6-45) was made to swing until the charges were in line with the flash door of the propellant hoist and hence ready for ramming into the propellant cage inside of the hoist. The rammer was of the piston, rack and pinion type and was housed in a casing. The head (N in figure 6-45) was able to rotate vertically, around O in figure 6-45, and when the charge was ready for loading, the rammer head was brought into position and was withdrawn after ramming. At the same time the flash door was closed and the propellant hoist interlock in the gun house freed to permit the raise of the cage into the gun house.

The cordite hoist was a flashtight trunk, 2.87 m long and 0.94 m wide (interior dimensions), running straight from the propellant supply rooms to the gun house (about 17 m in #1 turret). The hoist was fitted with guide rails to take one propellant cage. An anti-flash door was fitted in the hoist just above the turntable floor and it was opened automatically by the cage on its passage up or down.

The cage was lifted by a hydraulic cylinder and piston fitted with a rack extension, driving a train of pinions connected to a wire-winch drum. The propellant cage and the rammer are shown in figures 6-48–50.

Photo 6-16: General view of upper and lower cordite handing room revolving structure of trial 46-cm mount (US Naval Technical Mission to Japan, Report O-45 (N))

(A) Cordite bogie guide rails
(B) Cordite bogie traversing rack
(C) Roller path for vertical spring guide rollers
(D) Control levers for flash doors and cordite rammer
(E) Bed plates for swinging rammer
(F) Anti-flash door (right gun cordite hoist)
(G) Anti-flash door (entrance to centre gun cordite hoist)
(H) Bottom of upper C.H.R. revolving structure
(I) Blast vent trunk

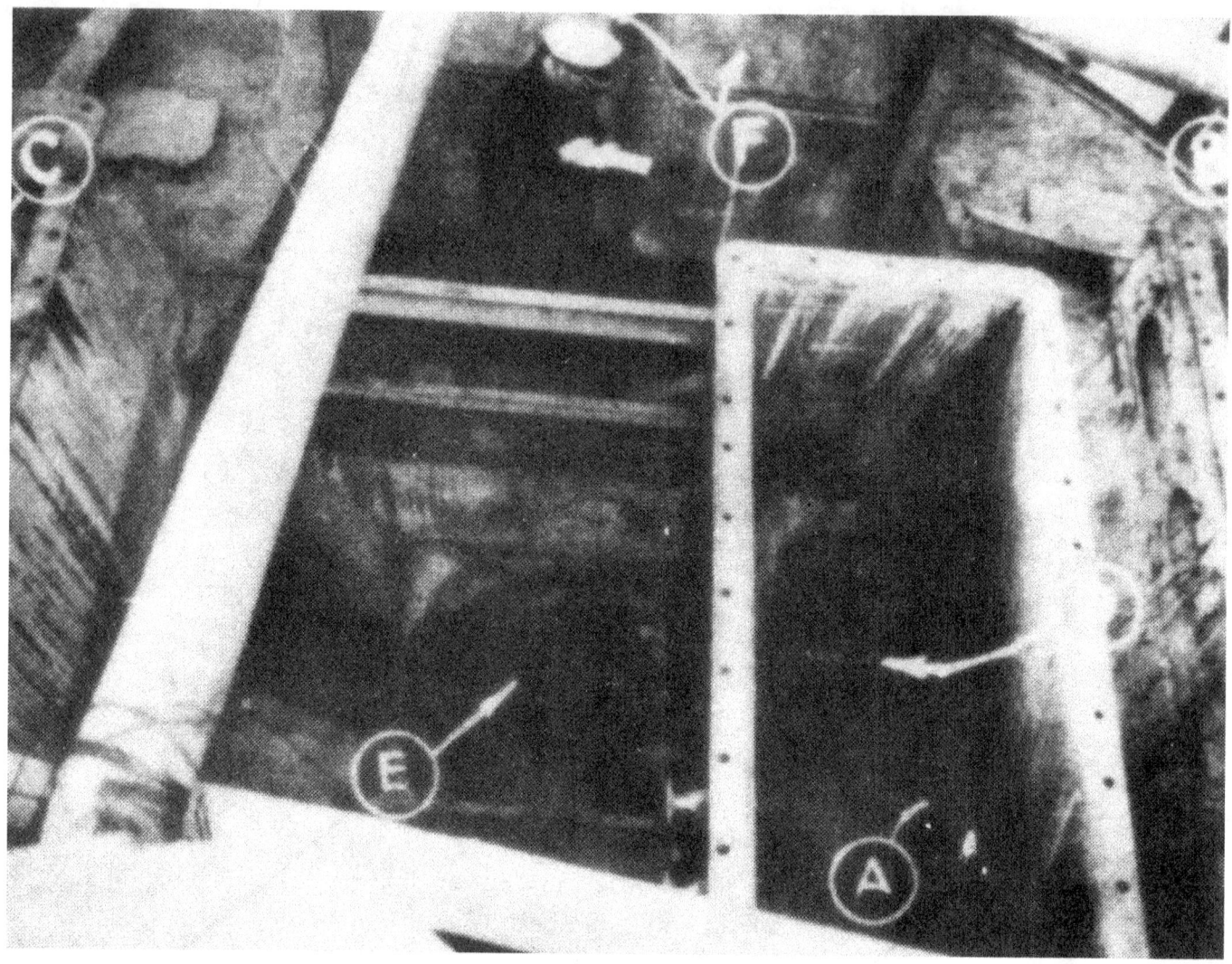

Photo 6-17: Plan view of upper cordite handing room of trial mount (US Naval Technical Mission to Japan, Report O-45 (N))

    (A) Centre cordite hoist trunk showing flash door (D) at lower C.H.R. level
    (B) Right cordite hoist trunk
    (C) Left cordite hoist trunk
    (D) Hole for securing centre pivot
    (E) Blast-vent doors

Photo 6-18: Lower cordite handing room–trial design (US Naval Technical Mission to Japan, Report O-45 (N))

    (A) Guide vent for cordite traversing bogie
    (B) Bogie traversing rack
    (C) Roller path for vertical spring guide rollers
    (D) Control levers for flash doors, cordite rammer
    (E) Bed plates for rammer
    (F) Rail for pivot tray roller
    (G) Anti-flash door
    (H) Inspection

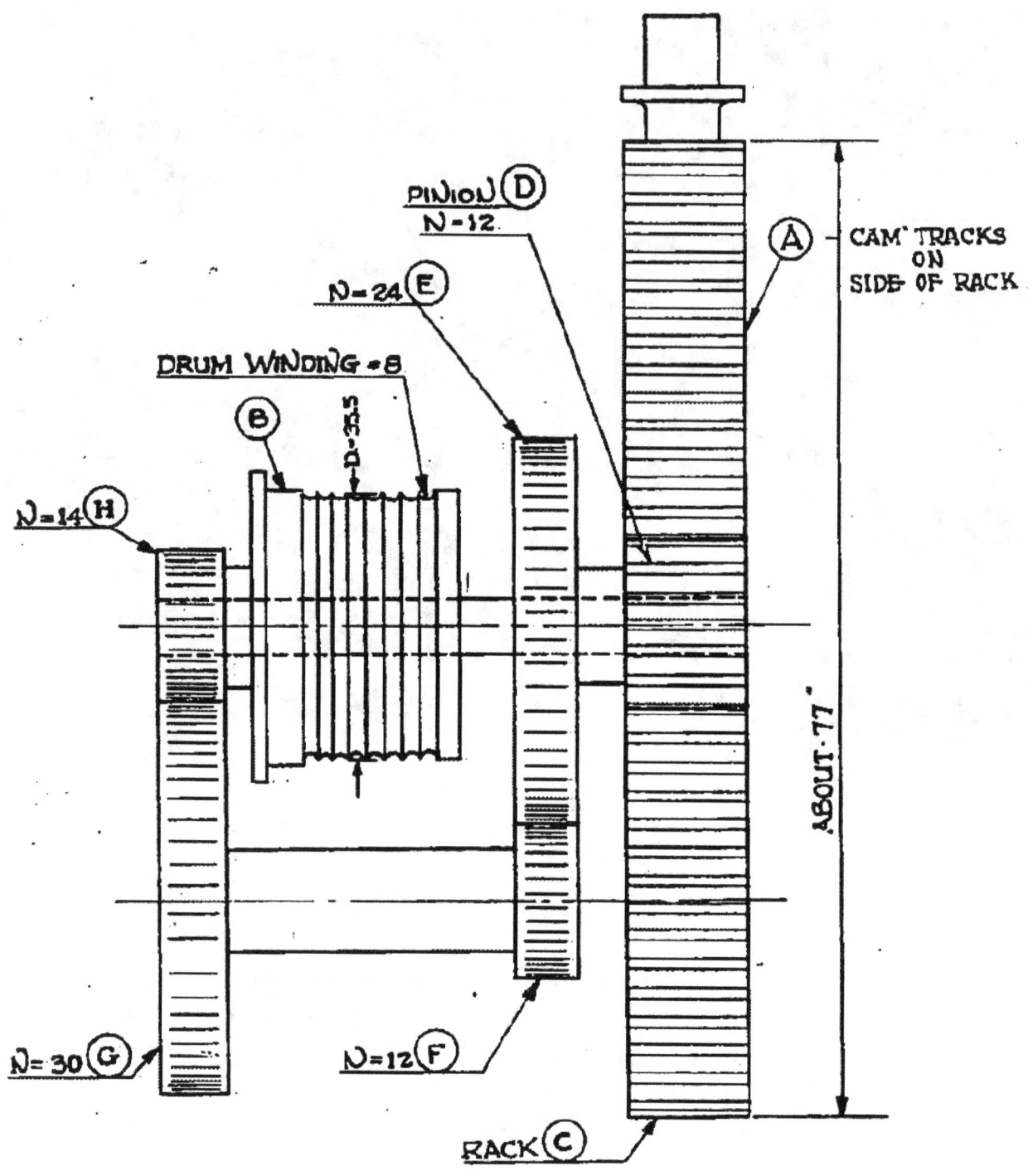

Figure 6-47: Gun turret powder hoisting winch (US Naval Technical Mission to Japan, Report O-45 (N))

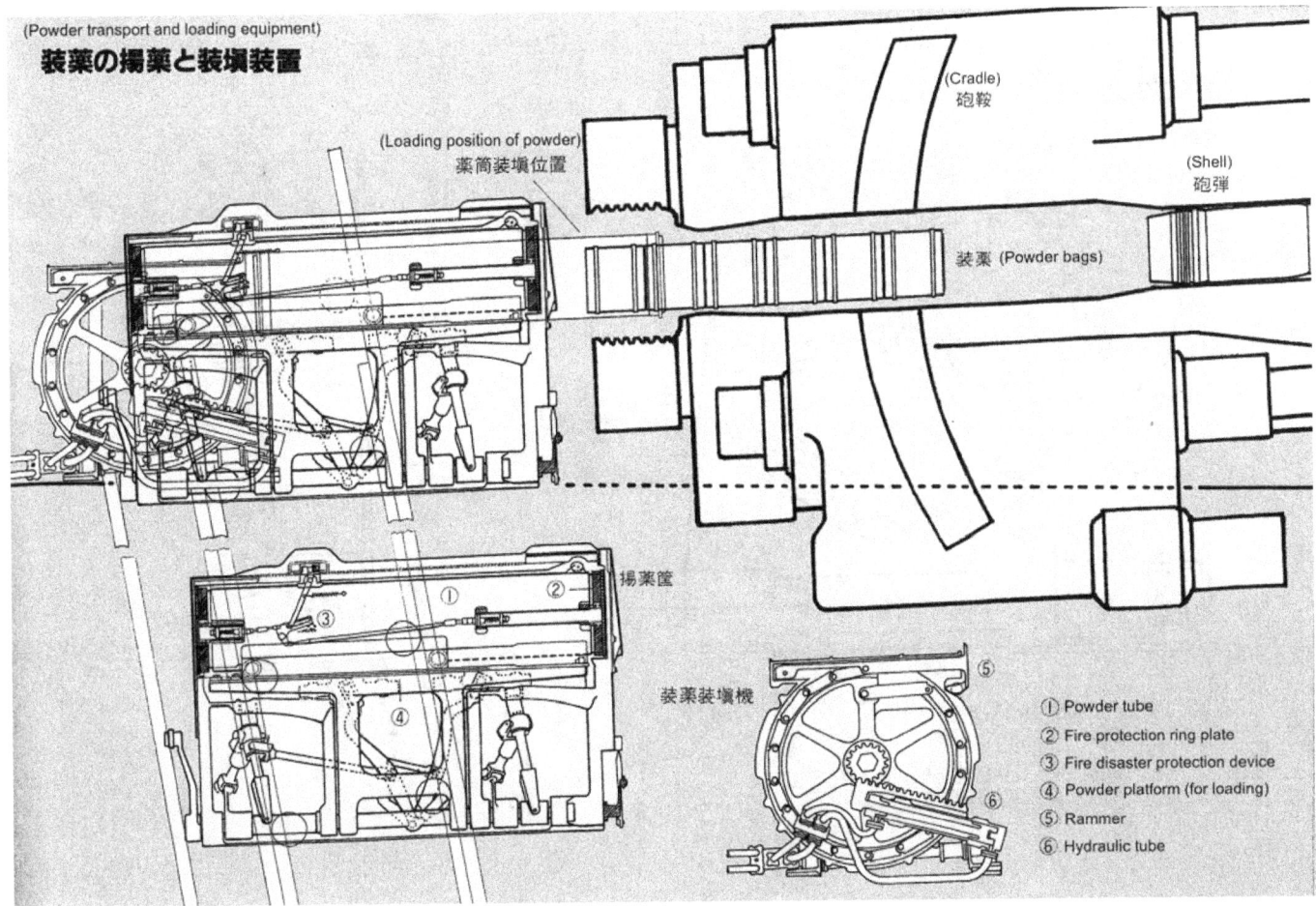

Figure 6-48: Loading procedure of the propellant bags (Gakken, #11)

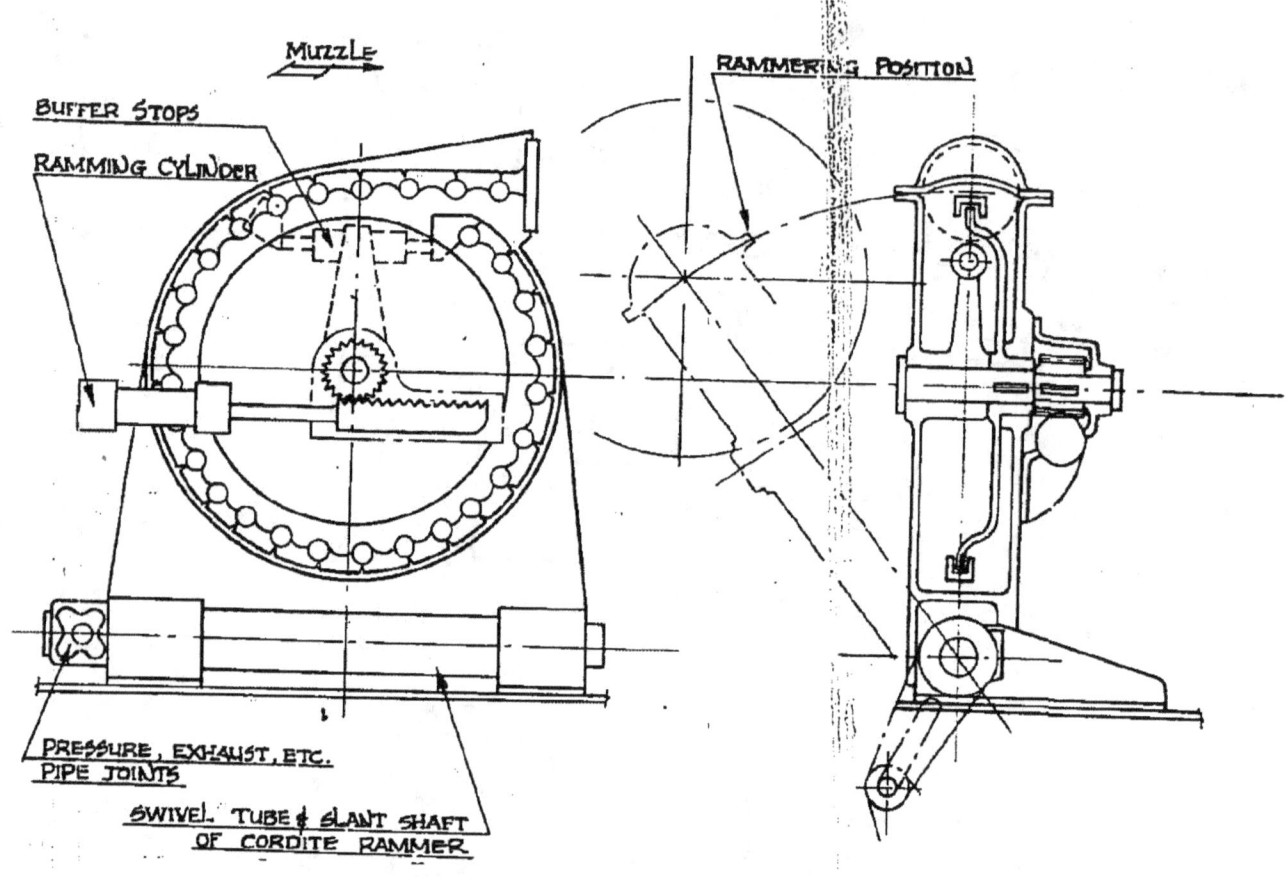

Figure 6-49: Gun turret cordite rammer in gun house (US Naval Technical Mission to Japan, Report O-45 (N))

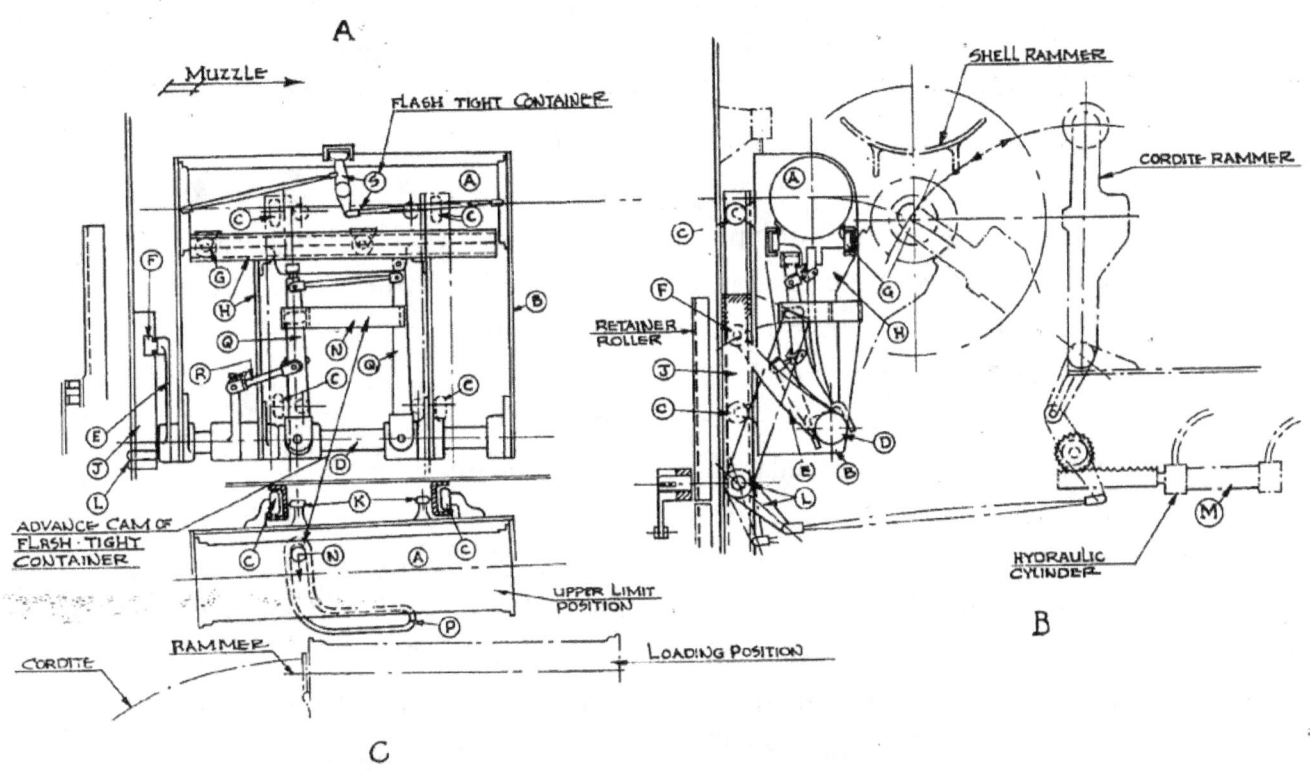

Figure 6-50: Gun turret cordite cage (US Naval Technical Mission to Japan, Report O-45 (N))

The cylindrical flashtight charge container (A in figure 6-50 A to C) contained six propellant bags and was carried in the upper part of an open framework (B in 6-50 A and B), which was mounted on wheels (C in A to C) running in suitable guide rails in the hoist trunk. The container (A) was also mounted on wheels (G in 6-50 A and B) running in rails formed in the top of the carriage (H in same), which was keyed to the shaft (D in same) and coupled to bearings at the bottom of the frame (B in same). When the cage approached the top of the hoist a hydraulic-mechanical system brought the container in line with the bore of the gun, moved the container forward relative to the carriage, opened the flashtight doors on both ends of the container, actuated the propellant rammer (a conventional chain type worked by hydraulic piston and rack) to swing and bring its head in line with the bore. The movement was controlled by the hydraulic cylinder (M in figure 6-50 B) that also controlled the swinging of the propellant container. After finishing loading the breech was closed and the gun was ready for firing.

For the various operations described above mainly hydraulic pressure was used. For certain functions, such as the ejection of gases and half-burnt remains of propellant inside the barrel after firing, operation of the two 100-hp electric motors supporting the training engines, ventilation and communication high-pressure air and electric cables, respectively, were necessary. Therefore, hydraulic pipes, high-pressure (HP) air pipes and electric cables had to be led into the turret. Before the *Yamato* class, manganese bronze was used for hydraulic pressure pipes in most capital ships, while for the exhaust pipes copper was applied, but this class required a larger diameter of the pipes so that steel pipes with copper liner were utilised. The central pivot with two pressure and two exhaust parts is shown in Figure 6-51. It was secured to the triple bottom and the pressure was taken from the centre stalk to the external revolving structure attached to the lower propellant supply room and thence to the distributing panels in the lower projectile supply room. This arrangement permitted to take in the hydraulic pressure irrespective of the training of the turret and to return the used water into the hydraulic water tank. Hydraulic pipes, starting valves, handling levers, meters, etc. were placed at every required part.

Electric cables and HP air (the blast air pipe) were led in the centre of this pivot and after passing the training part the former came to the outside of the fixed part through four holes (B in figure 6-52) and were then led into the revolving structure at the underside of the upper propellant supply room (C in figure 6-52) via five sleeves for a height of about 3 m.

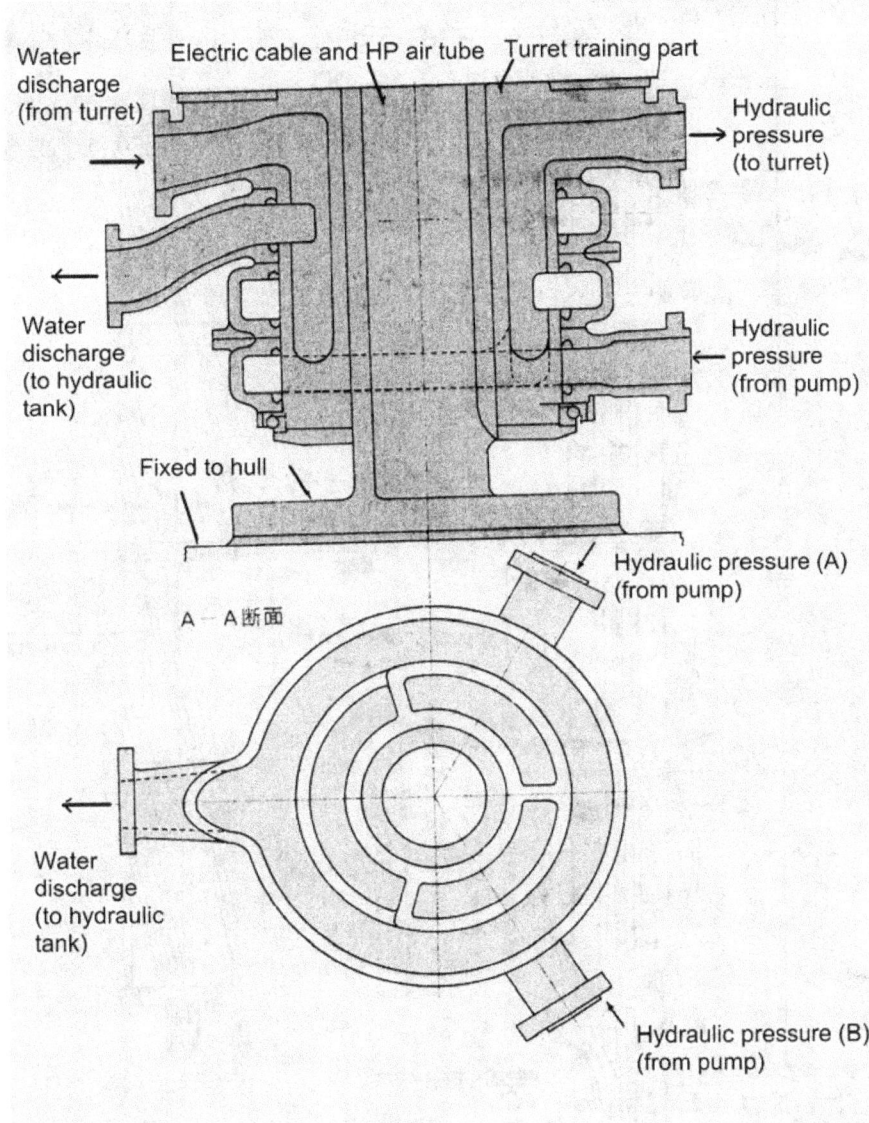

Figure 6-51: Central axis tube for hydraulic water in the centre pivot. This tube always took in hydraulic pressure irrespective of the training of the turret and the discharged water was returned to the hydraulic water tank. This system resembled that used in the past capital ships. Note that HP air and electric cables also were led in (*Maru*, #400, by permission of Ushioshobō-Kōjinsha Co., Ltd.)

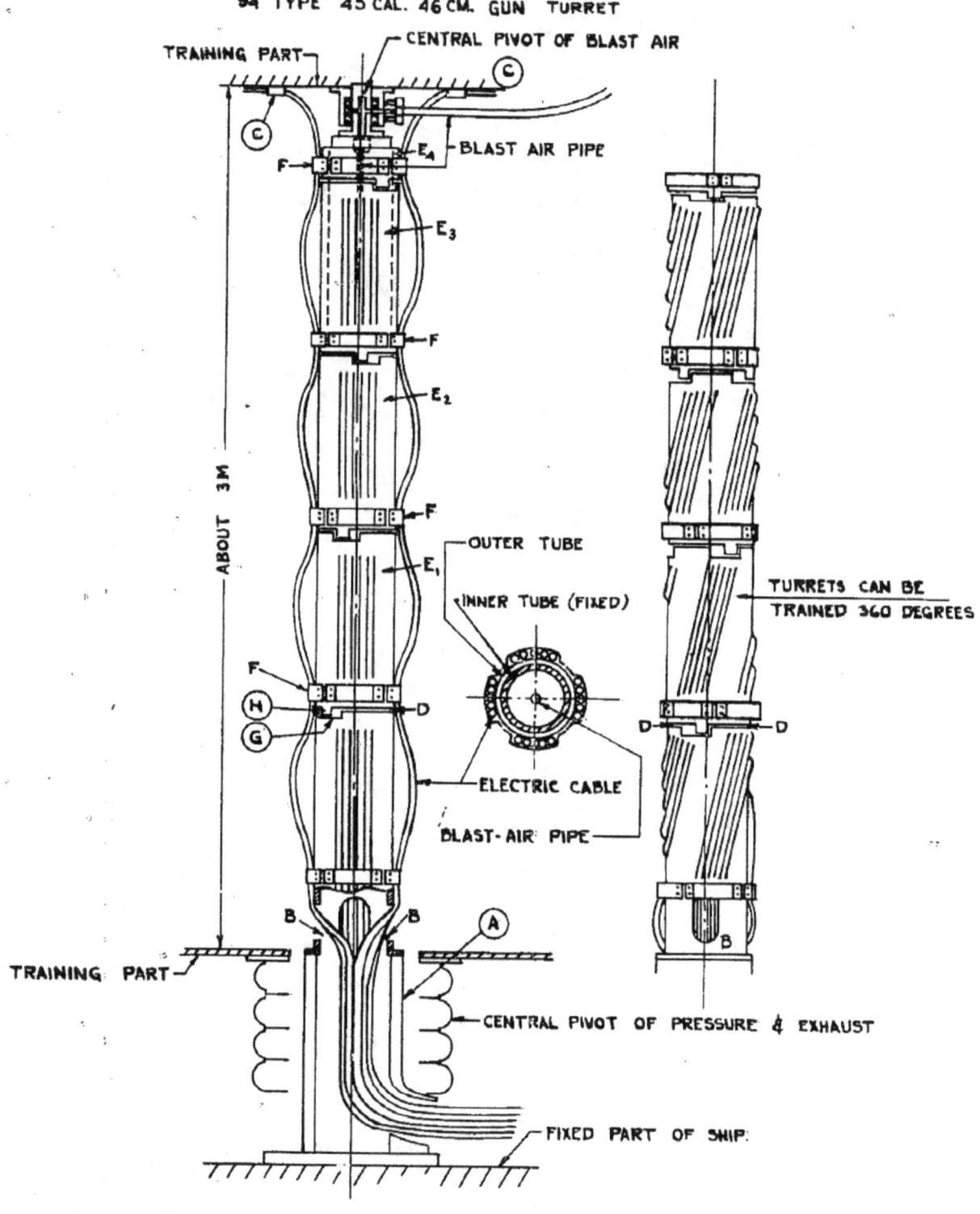

Figure 6-52: Cable lead-in gear (US Naval Technical Mission to Japan, Report O-45 (N))

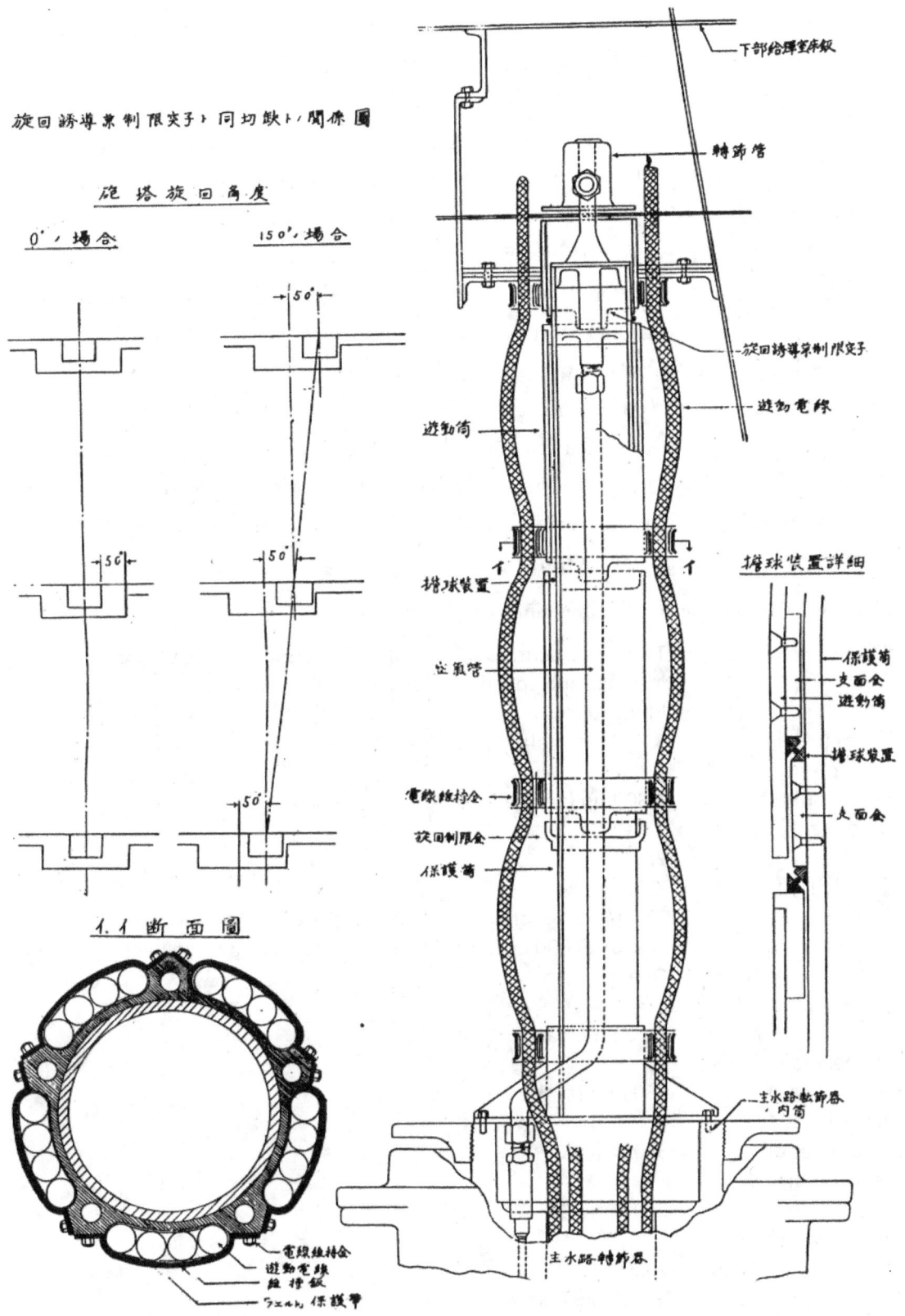

Figure 6-53: Cable lead-in gear (*Kessen Senkan* Yamato *no Zenbō*)

Four of the five sleeves were revolving when the turret was trained, as shown in figure 6-52 (right) to allow a training of 360°.

The blast air pipe was led into the centre of the sleeves to near the underside of the lower propellant supply room where it was connected to the HP air centre pivot. It was then led away into the revolving structure, as shown in figure 6-52.

Four Brown Boveri turbine pumps placed below the protective deck generated hydraulic power, which was considered a safe and simple power source for the movement of the various turret mechanisms. Three pumps operated the three turrets and one was in stand-by position. The standard pressure was 70 kg/cm², and the medium water blended with glycerine. Turbine pumps were used for the first time (older battleships had four to five 450-hp DE crankshaft type steam engines), after experiments in the converted battleship *Hiei*, and were derived from a purchased Brown Boveri 700-hp turbine pump, which is shown in figure 6-54.

Table 6-5. Brown Boveri type turbo pump of the *Yamato* class

Type	Two-stage centrifugal impeller type pump with pressure increase and speed acceleration at the inlet and HP oil lubrication
Rpm (of turbine and pump)	3,700 (normal); 4,000 (overload)
Power of the turbine	4,800-hp (normal); 5,000-hp (overload)
Water HP	2,850
Efficiency ratio	75%
Steam pressure	25 kg/cm² before chest; approx. 21 kg/cm² at chest
Weight of turbine	approx. 9,000 kg (including bed and auxiliary machines)
Number of pumps per turbine	One
Number of impellers per pump	Three (two at the first stage)
Diameter of impellers	450 mm (at the first stage)
Diameter of suction pipe	380 mm × 2
Diameter of pressure pipe	260 mm × 1
Working pressure	70.3 kg/cm²
Delivery pressure	Vacuum 580 mm
Pumping capacity	1,100 m³/h
Total weight	approx. 20,000 kg (main turbine, pump, bed)

Table 6-6. Technical data of the Brown Boveri turbine pump

Condition	Unit	Standard power	Overload power
Capacity	litres/s	75	106
Pressure	kg/cm²	70	70
Rpm	1/min	4,400	4,400
Steam pressure	kg/cm²	13	13
Vacuum	kg/cm²	0.1	0.1
Steam consumption	kg/h	6,800	6,800
Power	Hp	700	990

Between the turrets and pumps a so-called ring main was formed by placing several two-stage centrifugal pumps, shown in figure 6-55, to deliver hydraulic pressure through the pipes of 260 mm in diameter,[144] as described above.

In case of failure of a projectile or propellant hoist supply was possible by two auxiliary hoists fitted in each turret. Hoisting was by hydraulic winches as used for the main propellant hoists. As shown in figure 6-56 both projectiles and propellant bags were transported vertically in containers.

In the gun house the old transfer method by overhead travellers and chain purchase was used.

The magazines, supply rooms and propellant hoists were fitted with the usual sprinkler system for firefighting. In case of emergency the magazines could be completely flooded in 15 minutes. Remote control valves situated in a cabinet in the lower propellant supply room hydraulically operated the flooding valves for the magazines.

---

[144] To give an idea of the dimensions–note the diameter of 380 mm of the two suction pipes from the hydraulic water tank.

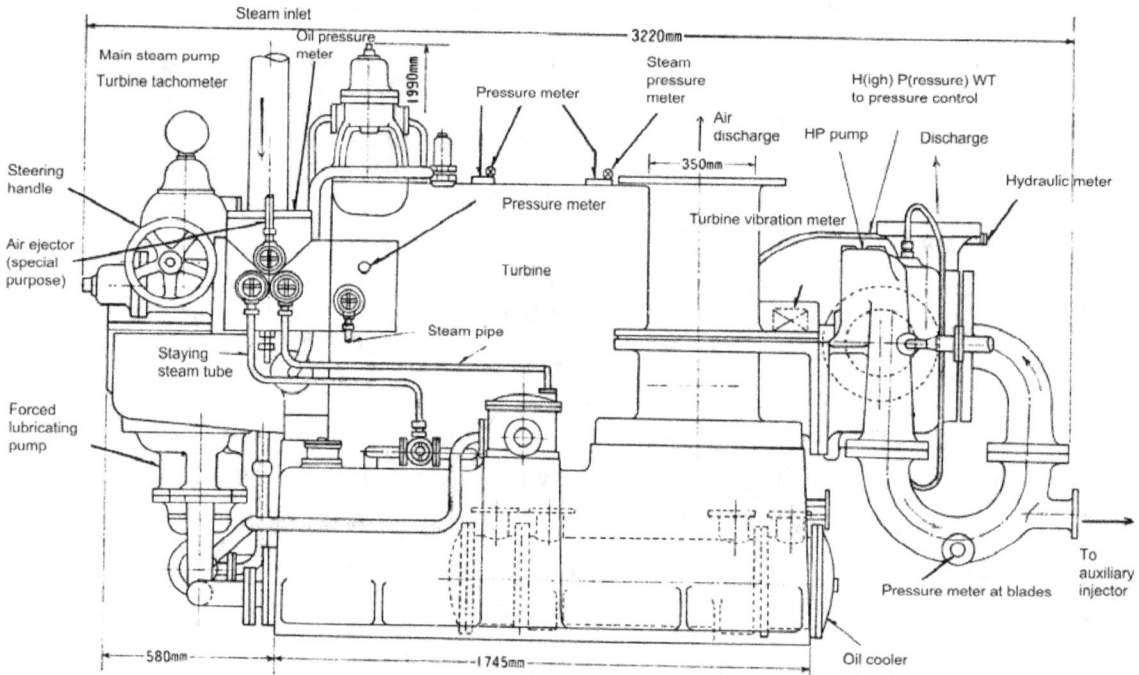

Figure 6-54: 700-hp Brown Boveri turbo pump. Note that according to *Kaigun Hōjutsu-shi*, p. 114, the First Division of the Navy Technical Department bought this turbine from Brown Boveri Co. of Switzerland in 1925 in preparation for the *Kongō* replacement ship. It was of about half the weight and volume compared with the British Armstrong type steam reciprocating pump. After investigation the turbine and pump were taken as models to produce one 400-ton (1,040-hp) turbo pump in Hiro N.Y. This pump was fitted on the battleship *Hiei* during her conversion, after the termination of the arms limitation treaty system, to inspect the properties of the turbo pump in the 36-cm twin gun turret. After confirmation of the intended purpose the Fifth Division of the Navy Technical Department and Hiro N.Y. Engine Experimental Division designed the turbo-hydraulic pump for the *Yamato* class "by independent design" (but actually on the basis of the Swiss design, with several revisions). The arrangement in *Hiei* below the protective deck, ring main with "between pumps" and "urgency lines", spare pump, etc. served as a model for the *Yamato* class. Four pumps for three triple turrets were fitted. The piping permitted the use in any combination for all three turrets. In Report O-53 (N) "Hydraulic Pumps in Japanese Naval Ordnance", p. 7, the use of "conventional, combined speed and pressure, oil operated governors" and the apparently very satisfactory operation is pointed out by "very little trouble was experienced in keeping a steady delivery pressure when changing suddenly from 'no load' to 'full load' condition" (*Maru*, #400, by permission of Ushioshobō-Kōjinsha Co., Ltd.)

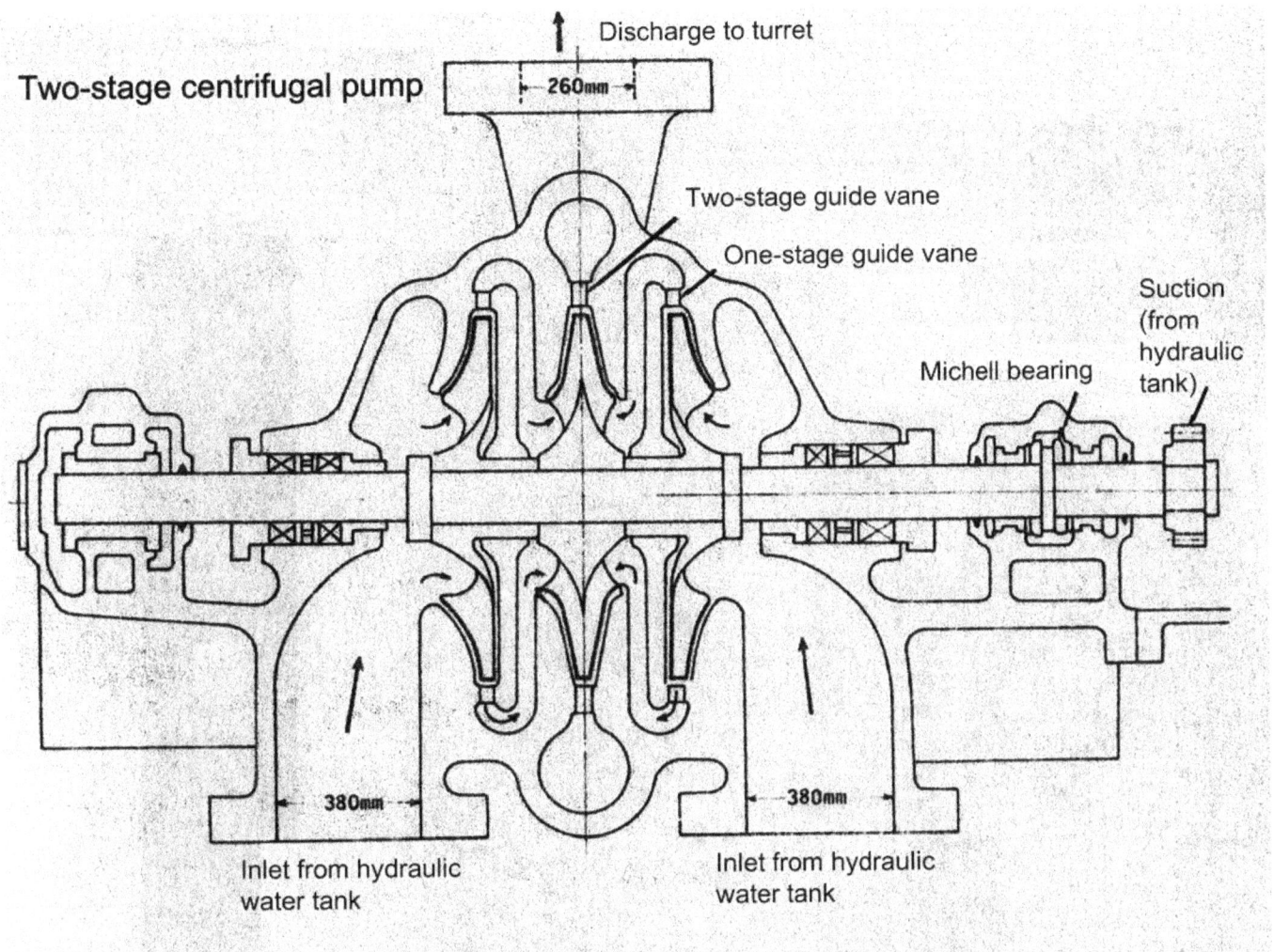

Figure 6-55: Two-stage centrifugal pump. Between the turret and the turbo pump there were several pumps, called ring main. Among them the pipes of 260 mm in diameter (as shown in the figure) were included and they delivered the hydraulic pressure necessary for the operation of the turret. The used water was returned to the hydraulic water tank. In case of disorder in one part of the ring main the circuit could be changed to maintain the supply and avoid the breakdown of the power source. Owing to the large diameter steel pipes with copper liners were used as hydraulic pipes (in the capital ships before the *Yamato* class, generally, manganese bronze had been used for the hydraulic pressure pipes outside the turrets and copper for the discharge water pipes) (*Maru*, #400, by permission of Ushioshobō-Kōjinsha Co., Ltd.)

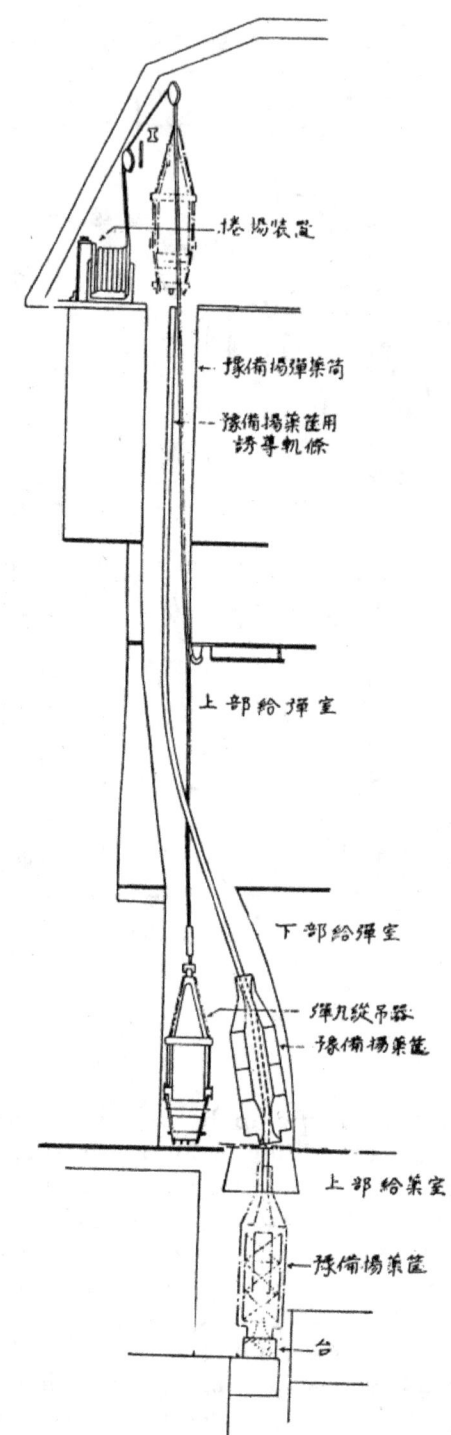

Figure 6-56: Auxiliary hoist (*Kessen Senkan* Yamato *no Zenbō*)

Part II–Operational Section

Nimble Books LLC

Chapter 7–Operational Histories

These tabular records of movement are principally adapted (with permission) by Lars Ahlberg from the originals written by Robert Hackett and Sander Kingsepp.[145]

Commanding Officers

Yamato

Number	Date	Rank	Name	Notes
	1941-09-05	Captain	Miyazato Shūtoku	Chief fitting-out officer
	1941-10-15	Rear-admiral		Promoted
1	1941-11-01	Captain	Takayanagi Gihachi	Chief fitting-out officer
	1941-12-16			Commanding officer
	1942-05-01	Rear-admiral		Promoted
2	1942-12-17	Captain	Matsuda Chiaki	Commanding officer
	1943-05-01	Rear-admiral		Promoted
3	1943-09-07	Captain	Ōno Takeji	Commanding officer
	1943-11-01	Rear-admiral		Promoted
4	1944-01-25	Captain	Morishita Nobuei	Commanding officer
	1944-10-15	Rear-admiral		Promoted
5	1944-11-25	Captain	Aruga Kōsaku	Commanding officer
	1945-04-07	Vice-admiral		Promoted posthumously

---

[145] http://www.combinedfleet.com/senkan.htm

Photo 7-1: Takayanagi Gihachi (1891–1973)– *Yamato*'s first commanding officer (Gakken)

Photo 7-2: Matsuda Chiaki (1896–1995)–*Yamato*'s second commanding officer (*Sekai no Kansen*)

Photo 7-3: Ōno Takeji (1894–1976)–*Yamato*'s third commanding officer (Gakken)

Photo 7-4: Morishita Nobuei (1895–1960)–*Yamato*'s fourth commanding officer (Gakken)

Musashi

Number	Date	Rank	Name	Notes
1	1941-09-15	Captain	Arima Kaoru	Chief fitting-out officer
	1942-08-05			Commanding officer
	1942-11-01	Rear-admiral		Promoted
2	1943-06-09	Captain	Komura Keizō	Commanding officer
	1943-11-01	Rear-admiral		Promoted
3	1943-12-07	Captain	Asakura Bunji	Commanding officer
	1944-05-01	Rear-admiral		Promoted
4	1944-08-12	Captain	Inoguchi Toshihira	Commanding officer
	1944-10-15	Rear-admiral		Promoted
	1944-10-24	Vice-admiral		Promoted posthumously

Photo 7-5: Arima Kaoru (1893–1956)—*Musashi*'s first commanding officer (Gakken)

Photo 7-6: Komura Keizō (1896–1978)—*Musashi*'s second commanding officer (Gakken)

Photo 7-7: Asakura Bunji (1894–1966)–*Musashi*'s third commanding officer (Gakken)

Tabular Records of Movement

Yamato

Time	Noteworthy movements, events etc.
4 November 1937	Kure Naval Arsenal. The keel of Battleship No. 1 is laid down.
8 August 1940	Launched.
12 August 1941	Departs Kure for trials.
16 December 1941	Battleship No. 1 is completed and registered (commissioned) as the *Yamato* in the Kure Naval District. *Yamato* is assigned to the Combined Fleet's Battleship Division 1 with *Nagato* and *Mutsu* at Hashirajima.
21 December 1941	Departs Kure. Arrives at Hiroshima Bay, Inland Sea. Anchors W of *Nagato* at Hashirajima.
21 December 1941–10 February 1942:	Inland Sea. Final fitting-out. Deficiencies found are corrected at Kure.
12 February 1942	Departs Kure. Arrives at Hashirajima. The flag of the Combined Fleet's C-in-C Admiral Yamamoto Isoroku is transferred from *Nagato* to *Yamato*.
19 February 1942	Battleship Division 1 departs Hashirajima for training in the Iyo Nada. Returns later that day.
20–23 February 1942	The Chief of Staff of the Combined Fleet, Rear-Admiral Ugaki Matome, conducts a series of war games aboard *Yamato* to test plans for the second-stage operations. Commander Prince Takamatsu Nobuhito (brother of Emperor Hirohito) and Major Prince Tsunenori Takeda arrive aboard *Yamato* to observe the table top maneuvers.
30 March 1942	Inland Sea. Admiral Yamamoto observes while Captain Takayanagi conducts more armament trials at a range of 23 miles. They are judged a failure. Both Takayanagi and his gunnery officer are upbraided because *Yamato's* gun aimers manning the main rangefinder misread the horizontal settings.
March 1942	Inland Sea. Training and gunnery practice.
11 April 1942	Fleet Admiral Prince Fushimi Hiroyasu pays a call on *Yamato*.
April 1942	Captain Arima Kaoru, the Chief Fitting-Out Officer of *Yamato's* sister-ship *Musashi*, pays an orientation visit with members of *Musashi's* fitting-out crew.
April-May 1942	Inland Sea. Training and gunnery practice.
Early May 1942	Admiral Yamamoto conducts war games aboard *Yamato* to test plans for the Invasion of Midway.
19 May 1942	Departs Kure for battle training. The new carrier *Junyō* almost sideswipes *Yamato*.
23 May 1942	Returns to Hashirajima.
27 May 1942	*Yamato* is deemed operational.
29 May 1942	The Battle of Midway
	At 06:00, *Yamato* departs Hashirajima with the First Fleet,

Time	Noteworthy movements, events etc.
	Main Body: Battleship Division 1, light carrier *Hōshō*, seaplane/submarine tenders *Chiyoda, Nisshin*, Destroyer Squadron 3's light cruiser *Sendai*, nine destroyers, Supply Group No. 1. The Main Body remains 600 miles behind the Carrier Striking Force.
30 May 1942	The Japanese intercept, but cannot decode, a report by USS *Cuttlefish* (SS-171) returning from patrol near Saipan. Around midnight, the IJN's 6th (Submarine) Fleet at Kwajalein also reports monitoring messages exchanged by two American task groups located 170 miles NNE of Midway, moving westwards.
	Aboard *Yamato,* Admiral Yamamoto suggests that the information be relayed to the First Air Fleet's flagship, carrier *Akagi,* but senior staff officer Captain Kuroshima cautions not to break radio silence.
5 June 1942	00:15: Admiral Yamamoto orders the night engagement cancelled. 02:55: Yamamoto orders Operation MI cancelled.
9 June 1942	The Chief of Staff of the First Air Fleet, Rear-Admiral Kusaka Ryūnosuke and staff officers Captain Ōishi Tamotsu and Commander Genda Minoru arrive aboard *Yamato* from light cruiser *Nagara.*
10 June 1942	1,200 miles SE of Tōkyō. After sunset, an unidentified submarine fires two torpedoes at *Yamato* about 100 miles NNE of Minami-Torishima (Marcus Island). Yamato and the other ships in the Main Body turn to port and both torpedoes miss.
14 June 1942	At 19:00, arrives at Hashirajima.
14 July 1942	*Nagato* and *Mutsu* are reassigned to Battleship Division 2. *Yamato* remains in Battleship Division 1.
10 August 1942	Hashirajima. Admiral Yamamoto convenes a meeting aboard the Yamato with the C-in-C, First Air Fleet, Vice-Admiral Nagumo Chūichi, C-in-C, Second Fleet, Vice-Admiral Kondō Nobutake and top Combined Fleet staff officers. Yamamoto discusses his desire to exploit Mikawa's success at the Battle of Savo Island and the need to protect convoys carrying troops to recapture Guadalcanal.
17 August 1942	Yamamoto and his staff depart Kure for Truk with the Main Body: *Yamato,* escort carrier *Kasuga Maru* (later renamed *Taiyō*), Destroyer Division 7's *Akebono, Ushio* and *Sazanami*.
28 August 1942	Near Truk. Yamato is attacked by USS *Flying Fish* (SS-229). Since the ONI 41-42 "Recognition Manual" does not include the unknown *Yamato* class, she is identified as a *Kongō*-class battleship. *Flying Fish* fires four Mark 14 steam torpedoes and two hits are observed, but they are premature explosions. *Yamato* launches at least one E13A1 "Jake"

Time	Noteworthy movements, events etc.
	floatplane to counter-attack. *Flying Fish* is bombed and depth-charged by four escorts, but makes good her escape.
28 August 1942	*Yamato* makes port safely at Truk. She serves there as headquarters and flagship of the Combined Fleet.
9 September 1942	The Combined Fleet's main units on Truk are transferred to a new anchorage south of Summer (Dublon) Island.
17 October 1942	Truk. Oiler *Kenyō Maru* arrives empty. *Yamato* and *Mutsu* each transfer 4,500 tons of fuel oil to her to refuel IJN warships that are involved in the Guadalcanal operations.
1 November 1942	Aboard *Yamato,* a festive dinner is held for all skippers stationed at Truk to celebrate the IJN's victory at the Battle of Santa Cruz.
11 February 1943	After one year's service, Admiral Yamamoto's Combined Fleet flag is transferred to *Yamato's* new sister-ship *Musashi*.
8 May 1943	Departs Truk for Yokosuka.
13 May 1943	Departs Yokosuka for Kure.
21 May 1943	Drydocked for inspection and repairs.
30 May 1943	Undocked.
12 July 1943	Kure. Drydocked. A Type 21, Mod 3, air and surface search radar is installed. Twelve new (4 × 3) 25-mm AA guns are fitted on the weather deck. *Yamato's* total 25-mm AA suite is now 36 guns. Her 155-mm wing mount guns are provided with coaming armor and their barbettes with 28 mm of additional armor. *Yamato's* fuel storage is reduced and her main and auxiliary rudder controls are improved.
16 July 1943	*Yamato* is visited by the German Naval Attaché to Tōkyō, Rear-Admiral Paul Wenneker. Prior to Wenneker's arrival there are a series of debates between Vice-Admiral Nomura Naokuni, CO of the Kure Naval Base, and Rear-Admiral Matsuda, *Yamato's* CO[146], concerning security issues.

The officers are of different opinions as to Wenneker's ability to distinguish between large-calibre guns. A data sheet is given to the German prior to his visit that describes *Yamato's* main armament calibre as 40-cm, rather than the actual 46-cm. Nomura thinks that the German Admiral, a former commanding officer of the 28.3-cm gun armored ship *Deutschland/Lützow*, will not be able to tell the difference between 40 and 46-cm guns, but Matsuda is not so sure and opposes the visit.

Wenneker is invited to spend a night at the Kure Navy Club. He dons an IJN uniform. His stay aboard *Yamato* the next day

---

[146] CO = Commanding officer

Time	Noteworthy movements, events etc.
	is fairly short and the route chosen avoids the main gun turrets. The tour is less than one hour and areas below deck are not shown at all. Wenneker admires the elevator, bridge, air defense centre and the main gun director. The German attaché even starts a discussion about the best location for battleship reserve main gun directors with Matsuda.[147]
17 July 1943	Undocked.
16 August 1943	*Yamato*, loaded with troops and supplies, departs Kure with *Fusō*, *Nagato* and Destroyer Division 16's *Amatsukaze* and *Hatsukaze*. Stops at Yashima anchorage that night.
17 August 1943	*Yamato* departs Yashima via Yokosuka for Truk in a task group: Battleships *Fusō*, *Nagato*, escort carrier *Taiyō*, Cruiser Division 4's *Atago* and *Takao*, Destroyer Division 7's *Ushio*, Destroyer Division 10's *Akigumo* and *Yūgumo*, Destroyer Division 16's *Amatsukaze* and *Hatsukaze*.
23 August 1943	The task group arrives at Truk.
18 September 1943	Truk. The fleet sorties to Brown Island, Eniwetok in response to American carrier raids on Tarawa, Makin and Abemama Atolls. Vice-Admiral Ozawa Jizaburō, in tactical command, leads the fleet's first section Battleship Division 1's *Yamato* and *Nagato*, Carrier Division 1's *Shōkaku* and *Zuikaku*, (followed by *Zuihō* on 19 September), Cruiser Division 5's *Myōkō* and *Haguro*, Cruiser Division 8's *Chikuma* and *Tone*, light cruisers *Agano*, *Noshiro* and destroyers. Vice-Admiral Kurita Takao leads the second section with his Advance Force Cruiser Division 4's *Atago*, *Takao*, *Maya* and *Chōkai*.
25 September 1943	No contact is made with Task Force 15. The fleet returns to Truk.
17 October 1943	The Japanese intercept radio traffic that suggests the Americans are planning another raid on Wake Island. Admiral Koga sorties from Truk to intercept the enemy carriers with Battleship Division 1's *Yamato*, *Musashi*, *Nagato*, Battleship Division 2's *Fusō*, Battleship Division 3's *Kongō*, *Haruna*, Carrier Division 1's *Shōkaku*, *Zuikaku* and *Zuihō*, Cruiser Division 4's *Atago*, *Takao*, *Maya* and *Chōkai*, Cruiser Division 7's *Suzuya* and *Mogami*, Cruiser Division 8's *Chikuma* and *Tone*, light cruisers *Agano*, *Noshiro* and *Ōyodo* and destroyers.
19–23 October 1943	Arrives at Brown Atoll, Eniwetok.

---

[147] Wenneker's permission to visit *Yamato* was granted in response to a special request made by Adolf Hitler and Admiral Dönitz in reciprocity for a tour of the battleship *Tirpitz* the Germans provided Nomura in March 1941.

Time	Noteworthy movements, events etc.
23 October 1943	Departs Brown and sorties to a position 250 miles south of Wake. Returns after no contact is made with enemy forces.
26 October 1943	The fleet arrives back at Truk.
12 December 1943	Departs Truk with Carrier Division 1's *Shōkaku*, Destroyer Division 4's *Tanikaze* and Destroyer Division 10's *Akigumo* and *Kazagumo* covering troop transport operation "Bo-1."
13 December 1943	The American code-breakers learn *Yamato* is scheduled to arrive back at Truk on 25 December ferrying men and material.[148]
17 December 1943	Arrives at Yokosuka. Loads elements of the IJA's 1st Independent Mixed Regiment (*Dokuritsu Konsei Dai-ni Rentai*) Mixed Regiment and supplies.[149]
20 December 1943	Departs Yokosuka for Truk escorted by Destroyer Division 4's *Yamagumo* and *Tanikaze*.
25 December 1943	180 miles NE of Truk. At 04:40 (K) USS *Skate* (SS-305) is running on the surface at 10-13 N, 150-27 E. Acting on an "Ultra" *Skate* picks up *Yamato* at 27,300 yards (25,000 m), dives and tries to close, but is unsuccessful until *Yamato* turns towards the submarine. Skate passes down *Yamato's* starboard beam, turns and at 05:18 (K) fires four stern tubes from 2,200 yards (2,000 m) at 10-05N, 150-32E. At 0520, *Skate's* crew hears one explosion followed by a muffled explosion. At least one Mark 14-3A torpedo hits *Yamato* on the starboard hull near turret No. 3. The detonation rips a hole that extends some 15 feet downwards from the top of the blister and longitudinally some 75 feet between frames 151 and 173. The upper turret magazines flood through a small hole punched in the longitudinal bulkhead. The hole is caused by failure of the armor belt joint between the upper and lower side protection belts. The upper magazine for No. 3 turret floods. *Yamato* takes on about 3,000 tons of water, far more than anticipated by the designers of the side protective system.[150] The transport mission is aborted. Either *Yamagumo* or *Tanikaze,* or both, drop six depth charges, none of which comes close. After 30 minutes, the destroyers depart the

---

[148] The Americans were even warned about the radar of the escorting destroyers.

[149] Literally the Independently Organised Second Regiment. It belonged to the 51st Division and it was to be used for night battles to defend small islands against enemy assault on the Inner South Pacific Front. *Yamato* executed the first of three transports, called "Bo #1 Operation." She transported one part of the 2,894 soldiers and supplies included 7.5-cm mountain guns and 7-cm infantry guns.

[150] See also chapter 1.

Time	Noteworthy movements, events etc.
	area. Three hours later, *Skate* departs.
	At 08:15, USN codebreakers intercept and decrypt a message that reads: "From Surface Escort Unit No. 2. Torpedo attack at 04:00 the 25th, in position 10-05N, 150-32E."
	Arrives at Truk later that day. Undergoes emergency repairs by repair ship *Akashi* that also prepares a damage assessment report.
	At 1435, codebreakers decrypt a message from the CO of *Yamato* that reads "Hull damage summary resulting from torpedo attack. Details affecting armament and machinery will be submitted later. Hole from frame 163 to 170. 11 meters in diameter above the 'bilge' and 5 ½ meters below penetrating outer plates of bilge."[151]
10 January 1944	Departs Truk for Kure with Destroyer Division 4's *Michishio* and *Asagumo* and Destroyer Division 32's *Fujinami*.
11 January 1944	At 18:00, *Yamato* is spotted by USS *Halibut* (SS-232), but the submarine is unable to attack.
14 January 1944	At 23:30 USS *Batfish* (SS-310) picks up the *Yamato* group on radar, then visually, but *Batfish* is unable to close the range for an attack.
15 January 1944	At 07:10 (I) the soundman aboard USS *Sturgeon* (SS-187) picks up screw noises at 105 degrees true. Soon a battleship is sighted at about 11,000 yards at 32-24N, 133-44E. *Sturgeon*'s crew sees only one escort and no air cover, but the target is moving at about 24 knots and soon disappears.
16 January 1944	Arrives at Kure. On the 28th, *Yamato* is docked in No. 4 drydock to repair the torpedo damage to her hull and correct deficiencies in her armor belt. A sloping plate is fitted at a 45-degree angle across the lower corner of the upper void compartment between the two longitudinal inboard bulkheads. This modification, proposed to run the full length of the citadel, is installed only in Yamato in the area affected by torpedo damage.[152]

---

[151] The remainder of the message concerning flooded areas, compartments etc. is not available. An undated POW report, noted re 25 December attack: "Submarine scored two hits in mid-section of BB *Yamato*. Ship began to list immediately and slowed down considerably. However, after approximately two hours of repairs she was righted and resumed normal speed toward Truk. There were no casualties as hits were scored in provisions department. Damage could not be repaired at Truk and POW later learned that *Yamato* had returned to Japan."

[152] In the event, the measure was inadequate. A recommendation to use 5,000 tons of steel to reduce the volume of compartments beyond the citadel and so increase resistance to flooding was re-

Time	Noteworthy movements, events etc.
3 February 1944	Undocked.
25 February 1944	Kure. Battleship Division 1's *Yamato* and *Musashi* are reassigned from the First Fleet to the Second Fleet.
	Drydocked in No. 3 drydock. Two beam triple 155-mm turrets are removed and replaced by six (3 × 2) 127-mm high-angle AA mounts. Twenty-four (8 × 3) and 26 single 25-mm AA mounts are added. Shelters are also added on the upper deck for the increased AA crews. Type 13 air search and Type 22, Mod 4, surface search/gunnery (rudimentary–at best) control radars are installed and the main mast is altered. Two 150-mm searchlights are removed and later installed ashore at Kure.
	Yamato is fitted with Type 2 infrared (IR) Identification Friend-or-Foe (IFF)/signalling devices mounted midway up on each side of the bridge. It is built around a telescopic sensor that receives light-waves in the IR range and registers a readout in the radio shack. The system also includes a pair of 20-mm binoculars coaxially mounted with the transmitting IR lamp on the bridge so that another ship can use the IR detector for elementary signalling or as a formation light for station keeping.
	About this time, *Yamato* is also fitted with multiple E27 radar detectors.
18 March 1944	Undocked.
11 April 1944	Departs Kure for trials in the Iyo Nada; returns to Hashirajima that evening.
17 April 1944	Returns to Kure to load supplies.
21 April 1944	Departs Kure for Okinoshima. Loads troops.
22 April 1944	Departs Okinoshima with cruiser *Maya*, destroyers *Shimakaze*, *Yukikaze* and two other destroyers.
28 April 1944	Arrives at Manila, unloads troops and supplies, then departs.
1 May 1944	Arrives at Lingga (near Singapore).
3 May 1944	Lingga. Designated the flagship of Vice-Admiral Ugaki Matome's Battleship Division 1.
11 May 1944	Steams with Vice-Admiral Ozawa Jisaburō's Mobile Fleet from Lingga to Tawitawi.
14 May 1944	Anchors at Tawitawi.
May–June 1944	Tawitawi: *Yamato and Musashi* participate in joint gunnery drills at ranges of almost 22 miles.

jected because the extra weight would have increased displacement and draft beyond acceptable limits. See also chapter 1.

Time	Noteworthy movements, events etc.
10 June 1944	Operation *Kon,* the relief of Biak

At 16:00, departs Tawitawi for Batjan, Halmahera Island with *Musashi,* Destroyer Squadron 2's light cruiser *Noshiro* and destroyers *Okinami* and *Shimakaze.* USS *Harder* (SS-257), on station nearby, reports the *Kon* Force leaving Tawitawi.

Shortly after departure, a periscope (perhaps *Harder*'s) is sighted and a submarine alert is given. All ships quickly execute "hard left-rudder" but the *Musashi* turns too late. She closes on *Yamato* just ahead. On *Yamato*'s bridge, near panic reigns! Captain Morishita takes over the helm himself and carries out an evasive turn, but the situation remains critical. Then a lookout reports that the "ship behind us has stopped." All aboard both super-battleships are relieved that a collision between them has been avoided on the eve of battle.

12 June 1944	The US Invasion of the Marianas begins. Operation *Kon* is "postponed." Ugaki's force arrives at Batjan where they are joined by Cruiser Division 5's *Haguro* and *Myōkō* and destroyer *Asagumo.*
13 June 1944	At 22:00, Ugaki's force departs Batjan to rendezvous with the Mobile Fleet.
15 June 1944	E of Mindanao. The *Yamato* group is sighted and reported by USS *Seahorse* (SS-304).
17 June 1944	Refuels from the 1st Supply Force's oilers, then joins the Mobile Fleet. Later, the Mobile Fleet is sighted by USS *Cavalla* (SS-244) in the Philippine Sea.
19–23 June 1944	Operation *A Gō,* the Battle of the Philippine Sea

Vice-Admiral Kurita's Second Fleet steams about 100 miles ahead of Vice-Admiral Ozawa's carriers.

At 0920, *Yamato*'s lookouts spot aircraft approaching at 13,125 feet. This is the fighter unit of Air Group 601's second strike. Admiral Kurita has received no information about a friendly overflight. Cruiser *Takao* fires four star shells meaning "identify yourself", but no reply is received. The planes keep approaching.

At 16,400 yards, *Yamato* and the other ships execute a turn to port and open fire. *Yamato*'s main guns, loaded with *San Shiki dan* shells, are fired in anger for the first time—but at friendly forces! Four "Zeke's" are damaged. Another ditches. *Yamato* may have damaged some of the planes. *Musashi*'s lookouts correctly identify the planes and she is the only ship that does not open fire.

Time	Noteworthy movements, events etc.
	The Mobile Fleet's aircraft attack US Task Force 58 off Saipan but suffer overwhelming losses. *Yamato* remains undamaged and retires northward with the Mobile Fleet.
22 June 1944	The Mobile Fleet arrives at Nakagusuku, Okinawa. Refuels destroyers, then departs.
24 June 1944	The Mobile Fleet arrives at Hashirajima.
29 June–8 July 1944	Departs Hashirajima for Kure with *Musashi*. Fifteen new (five triple-mount) 25-mm AA guns are installed. The entire *hinoki* (Japanese cypress) deck is also replaced. *Yamato* loads the 106th Infantry Regiment of the IJA's 49th Division and materials aboard.
8–10 July 1944	*Yamato* departs Kure for Okinawa with Group A's Battleship Division 1's *Musashi*, Cruiser Division 4's *Atago, Takao, Maya* and *Chōkai,* Cruiser Division 7's *Kumano, Suzuya, Tone* and *Chikuma*, Destroyer Squadron 2's light cruiser *Noshiro* and destroyers. Accompanied by Group B's *Kongō, Nagato,* Cruiser Division 7's *Mogami*, Destroyer Squadron 10's light cruiser *Yahagi* and destroyers.
10 July 1944	Group A detaches from Group B. Departs Okinawa for Lingga (S of Singapore) to join the Mobile Fleet.
17 July 1944	Arrives at Lingga. Remains in the vicinity for three months conducting training with the *Musashi* and other fleet units.
18 October 1944	Black deck camouflage, intended for the night breakthrough in the San Bernardino Strait, is hastily applied to both *Yamato* and *Musashi*. The main component is soot from *Yamato*'s funnel.
18–20 October 1944	The fleet departs Lingga for Brunei Bay, Borneo to refuel.
22 October 1944	Operation *Shō Ichi Gō* (Victory 1), the Battle of Leyte Gulf
	Yamato receives Mitsubishi F1M2 "Pete" aircraft from *Nagato*. Sorties from Brunei towards Philippines with Vice-Admiral Kurita Takeo's First Mobile Striking Force, First Section, Force A (Centre Force) Battleship Division 1's *Yamato, Musashi* and *Nagato,* Cruiser Divisions 4, 5 and Destroyer Squadron 2.
23 October 1944	The Battle of the Palawan Passage
	Two American submarines attack Force A. USS *Darter* (SS-227) sinks Kurita's flagship, cruiser *Atago* and damages *Takao*. Kurita abandons ship and is picked from the water by destroyer *Kishinami*. Ten hours later, he transfers to *Yamato* and resumes command of the First Diversion Attack Force. USS *Dace* (SS-247) sinks cruiser *Maya*.
24 October 1944	The Battle of the Sibuyan Sea 0810 Three enemy scout planes are sighted, bearing 10, range 31 miles. Speed is increased to 18 knots.

Time	Noteworthy movements, events etc.
	1026 *Yamato* opens fire on enemy aircraft, using her main guns and Type 3 (*San Shiki dan*) rounds.
	1032 Attacked by two Grumman TBF Avengers from USS *Cabot* (CVL-28). No hits are scored.
	1047 From this time on, lookouts on *Yamato, Musashi, Chōkai, Noshiro* and *Kishinami* report periscope and torpedo wake sightings. Several false sightings delay the fleet reforming.
	1331 *Yamato* opens fire on aircraft from Task Group 38.3.
	1350 A Curtiss SB2C Helldiver dive-bomber from USS *Essex* (CV-9) drops two AP bombs that damage the port bow abreast of main gun turret No. 1.
	1413 Lookouts sight aircraft from *Essex* approaching. Vice-Admiral Kurita's fleet orders the force to increase speed to 22 knots.
	1430 Attacked by four Grumman F6F Hellcat fighters and 12 SB2C dive-bombers. They drop five 1000-lb AP and seven 500-lb AP bombs. The first bomb penetrates the anchor deck, demolishes the port chain locker, explodes below the waterline, blows out a side plate and holes the bow. The mess deck is wrecked. Two bombs hit turret No. 1. One blows a hole above the waterline. Another bomb penetrates through the top deck to the crews' quarters.
	Yamato ships 3,000 tons of seawater and takes on a five-degree list to port. Damage control counterfloods and reduces the list to one degree. *Yamato* is down by the bow and maintains a 2 ft, 8 in bow trim.
	Force A continues on course through the Sibuyan Sea. During the day, the Force endures raids by over 250 US carrier aircraft. *Musashi* is hit by numerous aircraft torpedoes and bombs and sinks in the Visayan Sea. *Nagato* takes two bomb hits. *Haruna* is damaged by near-misses.
	1530 Admiral Kurita orders the force to reverse course back through the Sibuyan Sea.
	1715 Force A again reverses course.
	2330 Force A enters the narrow San Bernardino Strait hours in single file.
25 October 1944	The Battle off Samar
	0335 San Bernardino Strait. Force A exits the strait and proceeds eastward.
	0400 Off Samar Island. Force A changes course due south towards Leyte Gulf.
	0523 *Yamato*'s Type 13 radar picks up enemy aircraft.
	0544 Enemy carriers sighted on the horizon, hull down, bearing 60 to port, range 23 miles. They are misidentified as

Time	Noteworthy movements, events etc.
	six fleet carriers, escorted by three cruisers and two destroyers.
0545 *Yamato* opens fire on enemy planes.
0558 Force A opens fire at escort carriers of "Taffy 3" USS *St. Lo* (CVE-63), *White Plains* (CVE-66), *Kalinin Bay* (CVE-68), *Fanshaw Bay* (CVE-70) (F), *Kitkun Bay* (CVE-71) and *Gambier Bay* (CVE-73). Carriers screened by destroyers USS *Hoel* (DD-533), *Johnston* (DD-557), *Heermann* (DD-532), destroyer escorts USS *Samuel B. Roberts* (DE-413), *Dennis* (DE-405), *Raymond* (DE-341) and *John C. Butler* (DE-339).

Both of *Yamato's* forward turrets open fire at a distance of 20 miles. Of her six forward rifles only two are initially loaded with AP shells, the remainder with Type 3s.
0606 *Yamato* continues on an easterly course, firing her 155-mm (6.1-in) secondary guns.
0651 A charging "cruiser" emerges from behind the smoke. *Yamato* engages her from a distance of more than 10 miles and scores a hit with the first salvo. The target is seen burning before it is lost sight of.
0654 The destroyer *Heermann* fires three torpedoes at *Haruna*. The torpedoes miss but head towards *Yamato* whose crew spots their tracks to starboard. *Yamato* turns away to port, steams northward for 10 miles until the torpedoes run out of fuel. Although the maneuver avoids the torpedoes, it puts *Yamato* and the force's commander, Vice-Admiral Kurita out of the battle.
0755–0910 Force A sinks *Gambier Bay*, *Hoel*, *Samuel B. Roberts* and the *Johnston*. Kurita orders all ships to head north, but at 1020 he reverses course southward and again heads towards Leyte Gulf.
1020 Kurita orders the course reversed to southward. The Force again heads towards Leyte Gulf.
1030–1320 *Chōkai*, *Chikuma* and *Suzuya* are disabled by battle damage, drop out of formation, and are subsequently lost. Force A reverses course northward and at 2100 retires through San Bernardino Strait. |
| 26 October 1944 | 08:00 Tablas Strait off Panay. Force A is attacked by about 30 Grumman TBM Avengers from the USS *Wasp* (CV-19) and *Cowpens* (CVL-25).
0834 The Force is attacked by about 50 Curtiss SB2C Helldivers and Avenger torpedo planes from USS *Hornet* (CV-12). Two bombs hit *Yamato*. The first penetrates the forecastle forward and to the right of the main breakwater, demolishing nearby crew's spaces. The second bomb causes slight damage to the side of main gun turret No. 1.
10:40 About thirty 13th Army Air Force Far Eastern Air Force |

Time	Noteworthy movements, events etc.
	B-24 Liberators of the "Long Rangers" based at Morotai attack the Japanese force. Bomb fragments wound Rear-Admiral Koyanagi Tomiji, Chief of Staff, Second Fleet and about 60 others. *Yamato* and *Nagato* open fire with their main armament using Type 3 (*San Shiki dan*) shells. Their gun crews claim several bombers shot down.
	1100 Sixty aircraft from Task Groups 38.2 and 38.4 attack the force. Light cruiser *Noshiro* is sunk.
27 October 1944	No attacks. Twenty-nine *Yamato* crewmen killed in action are buried at sea.
28 October 1944	Force A arrives at Brunei and refuels from oilers.
8 November 1944	*Yamato* sorties from Brunei to Pratas Islands, to avoid air raids, with the *Nagato*, *Haruna* and *Kongō* and escorts. *Junyō*, cruisers *Tone* and *Ashigara*, light cruiser *Kiso* and Destroyer Division 30 follow. *Junyō, Tone, Kiso and* Destroyer Division 30 detach to Manila. The remainder of the task group makes a feint through the Balabac Strait, then returns to Brunei.
11 November 1944	The *Yamato* group arrives at Brunei.
15 November 1944	Battleship Division 1 is disbanded. *Yamato* is assigned as the flagship of the Second Fleet.
16 November 1944	Departs Brunei for Kure with *Kongō*, *Nagato* and escorts.
21 November 1944	The *Yamato* group is attacked by USS *Sealion* II (SS-215). *Kongō* and destroyer *Urakaze* are sunk.
23 November 1944	Arrives at Kure.
25 November 1944	Kure. Drydocked. Begins battle damage repairs and refit. Twenty-four older 25-mm AA single mounts are removed. Twenty-seven 25-mm AA guns (9 triple mounts) are fitted in their place. *Yamato*'s final AA complement is 152 25-mm AA guns (50 triple mounts, 2 single mounts).
23 December 1944	At Kure. Vice-Admiral Itō Seiichi assumes command of the now diminutive Second Fleet.
1 January 1945	*Yamato, Haruna* and *Nagato* are assigned to the reactivated Battleship Division 1, Second Fleet.
3 January 1945	Undocked.
15 January 1945	Moves from Kure to Hashirajima.
10 February 1945	Battleship Division 1, Second Fleet is deactivated for the last time. *Yamato* is reassigned to Carrier Division 1.
March 1945	Returns to Kure.
13 March 1945	Hashirajima. Mistakenly, *Yamato* fires on 343rd Naval Air Group Kawanishi N1K2-J Shiden Kai "George" fighters on patrol from their base at nearby Matsuyama airfield.
19 March 1945	US Task Force 58 carriers make the first carrier attack on the Kure Naval Arsenal. *Yamato*, underway in the Inland Sea, sustains minor damage from a hit on the bridge by a Helldiver dive-bomber from USS *Intrepid*.
28 March 1945	Tokuyama Navy Fuel Depot, Yamaguchi Prefecture. Tanker

Time	Noteworthy movements, events etc.
	Matsushima Maru arrives from Singapore. *Yamato* takes on about 4,000 tons of fuel oil from her. *Matsushima Maru* unloads 9,279 tons of crude oil at the depot. At 17:30, that same day, the Second Fleet departs Hashirajima for Sasebo. 1800 Vice-Admiral Itō's fleet is recalled after Headquarters, Combined Fleet, receives a report about a Task Force 58 raid on airfields in southern Kyūshū.
29 March 1945	At Kure. Awaits sailing orders. *Yamato* takes aboard a full supply of ammunition: 1,170 rounds for her 18.1-in guns, 1,620 rounds for her secondary guns and 13,500 AA rounds. *Yamato* receives fuel from the destroyers *Hanazuki* and *Asashimo*. Light cruiser *Yahagi* receives fuel from destroyer *Hatsushimo*.
2 April 1945	10:00 *Yamato* departs Kure for anchorage at the Mitajiri Bight.
3 April 1945	09:18 The Second Fleet receives an order from the C-in-C Combined Fleet Admiral Toyoda Soemu alerting it about a sortie to Okinawa.
4 April 1945	Three Mitsubishi A6M "Zeke" fighters of the 332nd *Kōkūtai* from the nearby Iwakuni Air Base fly very low over *Yamato* to act as targets for gunnery training for the ship's new and untrained AA crews.
5–7 April 1945	Operation *Ten-Ichi-Gō* (Heaven Number One). See chapter 9.
31 August 1945	*Yamato* is removed from the Navy List.
May 1979	Kure. A stone monument is erected in the old naval graveyard to those who died aboard *Yamato*.
1 August 1985	A Japanese team in deep research submersible *Pisces II* locates *Yamato* 1,410 feet deep in the East China Sea. The wreck is in two pieces. Its forward section is on its starboard side, while the after section is bottom up.
24 January 2009	The Kure Chamber of Commerce and Industry announces a plan to salvage parts from *Yamato*. Panel members say they hope to at least raise the 2,780-ton main guns and the front portion of the hull. In the 1985 and 1999 surveys, a bugle, eating utensils and other artefacts were salvaged, but no ship parts. The panel says an executive committee will be formed in April to start the drive to raise funds, which it estimates will run into millions of yen.

Photo 7-8: Yamato off Hashirajima, Hiroshima Bay, on 9 February 1942 (Kure Maritime Museum)

Photo 7-9: Yamato at Truk Lagoon in 1943 (Kure Maritime Museum)

Photo 7-10: *Yamato* between the heavy cruiser *Myōkō* (right) and the auxiliary aircraft carrier *Chūyō* or *Unyō* off Truk 1943 (Kure Maritime Museum)

Photo 7-11: *Musashi* (left) and *Yamato* (right) in Truk Lagoon in September–October 1943 [Kure Maritime Museum]

Photo 7-12: *Yamato* and heavy cruiser *Tone* in the Sibuyan Sea on 24 October 1944 (Authors' collections)

Photo 7-13: *Yamato* under attack on 25 October 1944 (Authors' collections)

Photo 7-14: *Yamato* maneuvers while under air attack on 26 October 1944 (Authors' collections)

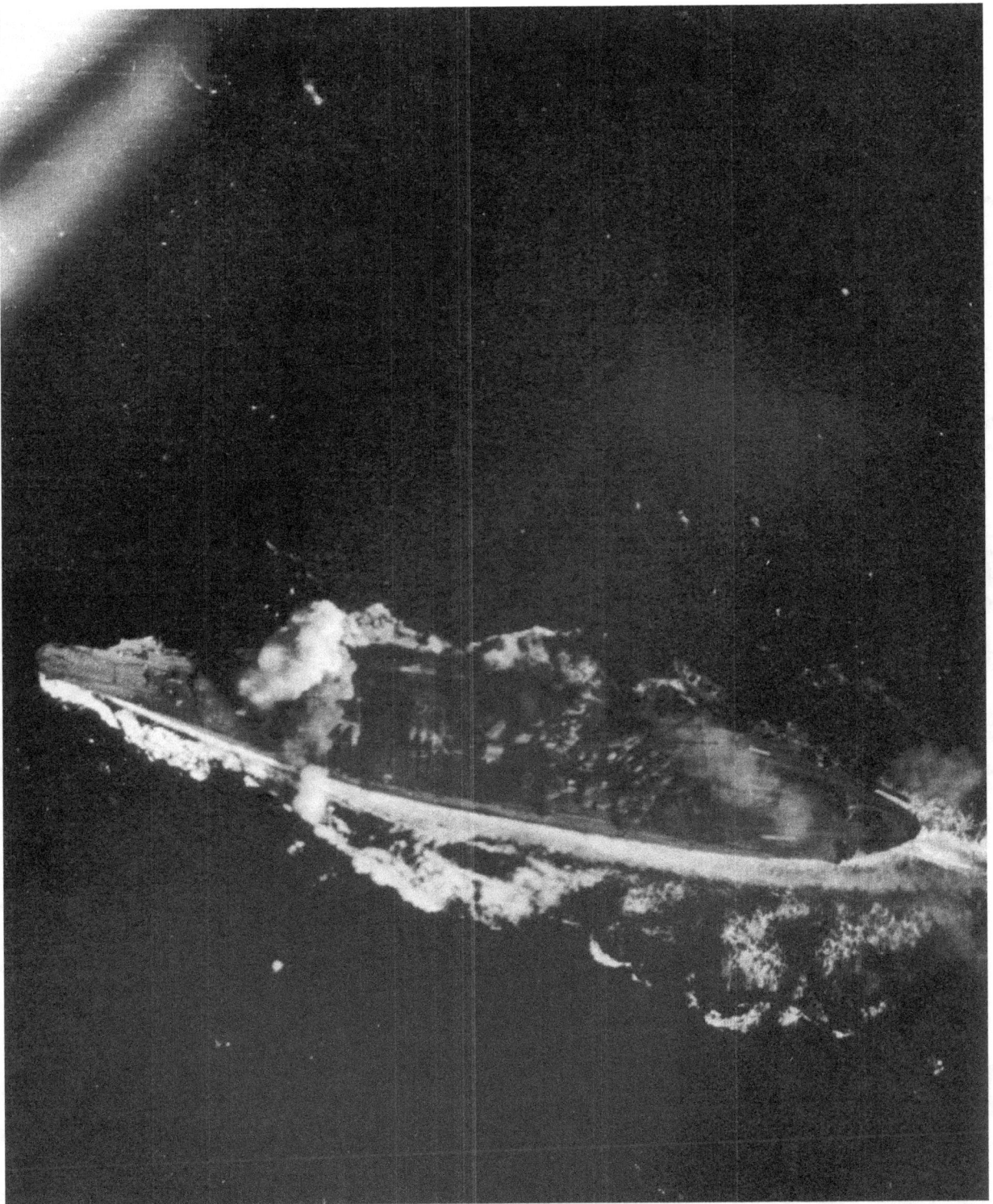

Photo 7-15: *Yamato* under attack by American Helldivers and Avenger torpedo planes on 26 October. Two bombs hit her causing slight damage (Authors' collections)

Photo 7-16: *Yamato* photographed from a USAF B-24 Liberator on 26 October 1944 (Authors' collections)

Photo 7-17: Yamato under air attack on 26 October 1944 (Authors' collections)

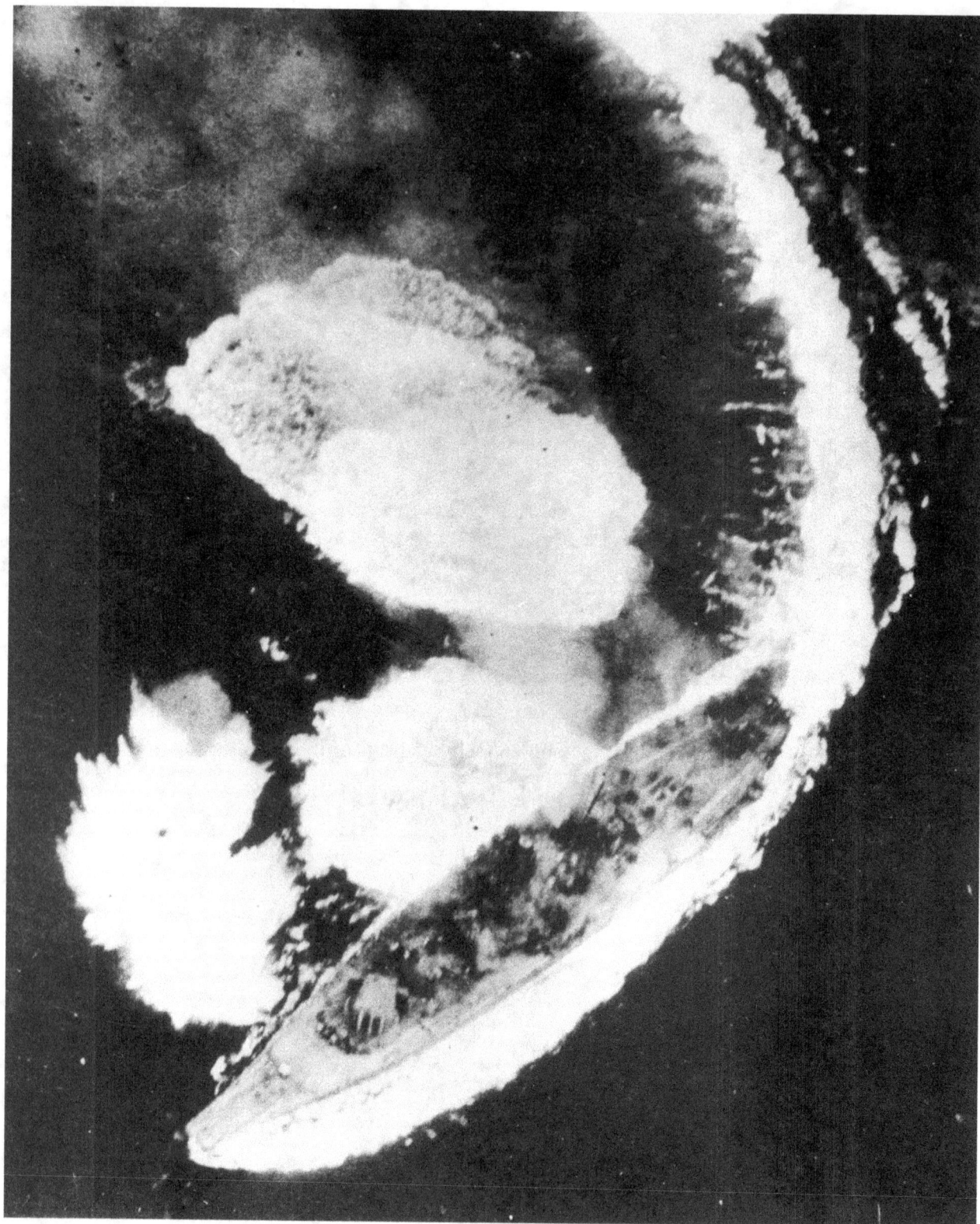

Photo 7-18: *Yamato* under air attack in the Inland Sea on 19 March 1945 (Kure Maritime Museum)

Musashi

Time	Noteworthy movements, events etc.
29 March 1938	Nagasaki. Unnamed Battleship No. 2 is laid down at Mitsubishi Shipbuilding's yard.
20 May 1938	The Sino-Japanese War
	Near Hankow, China. At dawn, six Soviet Tupolev TB-3 long-range bombers, with Chinese markings but manned by Russian crews, take off and fly to Kyūshū, Japan. The Russians overfly Fukuoka, Nagasaki and Sasebo, drop leaflets and take pictures. Over Nagasaki they photograph a battleship under construction in the No. 2 slipway. This is Battleship No. 2.
1 November 1940	Nagasaki. To maintain secrecy concerning this new class of super battleships, attendance at the launching ceremony for Battleship No. 2 is held to a few dozen top naval officials including the Chief of the Naval General Staff, Fleet Admiral Prince Hiroyasu Fushimi,[153] the C-in-C, Kure Naval District, Vice-Admiral Toyoda Soemu, Constructor Vice-Admiral Kuwabara Shigeharu and various other officials of the Navy Technical Department.
	Battleship No. 2 is launched from the No. 2 slipway. As soon as she is in the water, new freighter *Kasuga Maru* (later converted to escort carrier *Taiyō*) is towed alongside the battleship to block her silhouette from any foreign eyes.
6 October 1941	Nagasaki. At 20:00, special ammunition ship *Kashino* arrives from Kure carrying the first of nine of Battleship No. 2's Type 94 460-mm main guns and a turret. The turret and the gun are hoisted aboard the battleship's deck by a 350-ton capacity derrick. Once aboard, the turret and gun are covered with canvas to maintain secrecy.
5 August 1942	Battleship No. 2 is completed and named *Musashi*. She is registered in the Yokosuka Naval District three months late because of the requirement to be fitted as a flagship with additional communications gear. She is moved from Nagasaki to Kure for fitting-out. *Musashi* is assigned to the Combined Fleet's Battleship Division 1 with *Yamato*, *Nagato* and *Mutsu*.
10 August 1942	*Musashi* arrives at Hashirajima where she carries out additional tests, such as full speed trials and maneuvering in the Iyo Nada, mooring and aircraft launch drills.

---

[153] Cousin of Emperor Hirohito.

Time	Noteworthy movements, events etc.
3–28 September 1942	Final fitting-out at Kure. Twelve additional 25-mm guns (4 × 3) and a Type 21 radar are installed during this period.
28 September 1942	Returns to Hashirajima for trials.
October–November 1942	Training, gunnery practice in the Western Inland Sea.
December 1942	Western Inland Sea. Conducts air training exercises with carrier *Zuikaku*.
18 January 1943	Departs Kure.
22 January 1943	Arrives at Truk.
11 February 1943	Truk. Relieves her sister-ship, *Yamato*, as flagship of Admiral Yamamoto Isoroku's Combined Fleet
23 April 1943	In the evening, a flying boat arrives carrying the ashes of Yamamoto and six of his staff officers. Yamamoto's ashes are secretly transferred to the Admiral's sea cabin under the supervision of senior staff officer Captain Kuroshima Kameto.
25 April 1943	Truk. At 15:00, Admiral Koga Mineichi arrives on an Emily from Yokosuka, ostensibly for an inspection tour. It is not made public until May that Koga is the new C-in-C of the Combined Fleet.
17 May 1943	Admiral Koga sorties from Truk for Yokosuka in response to the Attu invasion with Battleship Division 1's *Musashi*, Carrier Division 2's *Junyō*, *Hiyō*, Cruiser Division 8's *Tone*, *Chikuma* and nine destroyers. *Musashi* also carries Admiral Yamamoto's ashes to Tōkyō for a state funeral.
20 May 1943	Alerted by "Ultras", USS *Sawfish* (SS-276) picks up the *Musashi* task force on radar but the submarine is unable to attack.
22 May 1943	USS *Trigger* (SS-237) sights the task force off Tōkyō Bay, but the submarine is unable to attack. The task force arrives safely. *Musashi* drops anchor at the Kisarazu Bight. That evening, a Buddhist ceremony is held aboard. Yamamoto's ashes are sent ashore the next day aboard destroyer *Yūgumo*. Carriers *Zuikaku*, *Shōkaku* and *Zuihō* and light cruisers *Agano* and *Ōyodo* join the task force at Yokosuka, Tōkyō Bay. Cruiser Division 7's *Kumano*, *Mogami* and *Suzuya* also arrives from Tokuyama. Before this powerful force can depart for a counterattack against the Aleutians, Attu falls to US forces.
9 June 1943	The battle group puts to sea.
23 June 1943	Returns to Yokosuka for overhaul and overpainting (ostensibly preparing for an inspection tour by Yokosuka Navy Yard officials).
24 June 1943	Imperial visit (*Gyōkō*) Yokosuka. Between 11:03 and 14:25, *Musashi* is visited by the Emperor and other officials. It is a top-secret event,

Time	Noteworthy movements, events etc.
	nevertheless the Imperial flag is hoisted.
	Admiral Koga hosts Hirohito and his brother (Navy Captain) Prince Takamatsu Nobuhito, Lord Keeper of the Privy Seal Marquis Kido Kōichi, Navy Minister Admiral Shimada Shigetarō, Chief of the Naval General Staff Admiral Nagano Osami, Commander of the Yokosuka Naval Base Admiral Toyoda Soemu, Commander of the Navy Technical Department (*Kampon*) Vice-Admiral Sugiyama Toshisuke, IJN Air Force Chief of Staff Admiral Tsukahara Nishizō, Minister of the Interior Matsudaira Tsuneo, Hirohito's Chief Aide-de-Camp Hasunuma Shigeru and Imperial Chamberlain, Admiral Hyakutake Saburō.
	A festive dinner is enjoyed. Later, the Emperor visits the crew's quarters and an AA defense station on the upper bridge. Most probably, the Emperor uses *Musashi*'s elevator to reach it.
25 June 1943	Departs Yokosuka for Kure.
27 June 1943	Arrives at Kure.
1 July 1943	Kure. Enters drydock. Type 22 Mod 4 radars are installed on the bridge. The Type 22 provides rudimentary fire control.
8 July 1943	Undocked.
14 July 1943	Departs Kure for trials, returns to Hashirajima that evening.
30 July 1943	Departs Kure for Yokosuka, stops at Nagahama Bight overnight.
31 July 1943	Departs Yokosuka.
5 August 1943	Arrives at Truk.
17 October 1943	The Japanese intercept radio traffic that suggests the Americans are planning another raid on Wake Island. Admiral Koga sorties from Truk to intercept the enemy carriers with Battleship Division 1's *Yamato*, *Musashi*, *Nagato*, Battleship Division 2's *Fusō*, Battleship Division 3's *Kongō*, *Haruna*, Carrier Division 1's *Shōkaku*, *Zuikaku*, *Zuihō*, Cruiser Division 4's *Atago*, *Takao*, *Maya*, *Chōkai*, Cruiser Division 7's *Suzuya*, *Mogami*, Cruiser Division 8's *Chikuma*, *Tone* and light cruisers *Agano*, *Noshiro*, *Ōyodo* and destroyers.
19 October 1943	Arrives at Brown Atoll, Eniwetok.
23 October 1943	Departs Brown and sorties to a position 250 miles S of Wake. Returns after no contact is made with enemy forces.
26 October 1943	The fleet arrives back at Truk.
4 February 1944	*Musashi* opens fire unsuccessfully on two United States Marine Corps Consolidated PB4Y-1 (B-24) Liberator photo-

Time	Noteworthy movements, events etc.
	reconnaissance planes that overfly Truk from Bougainville.[154]
10 February 1944	Departs Truk for Yokosuka with light cruiser *Ōyodo* and destroyers *Michishio* and *Tamanami*.
15 February 1944	Arrives at Yokosuka.
24 February 1944	The IJN organised the 87th AA Unit (*Bōkūtai*) to reinforce Palau. This unit was equipped with 12-cm high-angle guns and was under the command of the 9th Fleet, whose headquarters was at Hollandia, New Guinea, at that time. *Musashi* was ordered to transport men and material. Her destination should have been Truk but this base had already been ruined by air raid and bombardment on 17/18 February 1944. Since Truk lost its function as an anchorage, the IJN had to withdraw its bases. The West Caroline Air Unit was constructing an air base at Palau and 13 bombers and 13 fighters were being advanced to that new base.

Bombs, gasoline drums, trucks, ammunition, guns, machine-guns, etc. were loaded on *Musashi*. She sailed from Yokosuka escorted by *Michishio*, *Shiratsuyu* and another destroyer on 24 February 1944 and, while underway, met a strong typhoon. During the storm, *Musashi* has to reduce speed from 18 to six knots to allow her escorts to keep up. Gasoline drum-cans and even some trucks went overboard, but she was not damaged and unloaded her "freight" after entering the "beautiful island of palm trees surrounded by coral reefs", but Palau was no safer. Enemy activities against the Marshall Isl., in the Bismarck area, and radio transmission caused the C-in-C Combined Fleet, Admiral Koga, to order his ships to go north. |
25 February 1944	Battleship Division 1's *Yamato* and *Musashi* are reassigned from the First Fleet to the Second Fleet.
29 February 1944	Arrives at Palau. Remains there for one month.
29 March 1944	*Musashi* departs from Palau through the western channel.[155] American submarines are already waiting for the fleet, expecting they would rush out in surprise when the air raids begin. One of seven submarines is USS *Tunny* (SS-282) and she sights a big warship coming out of Palau. Recognising her as a battleship of the *Kongō* class, she approaches to about 1,800 m and releases six torpedoes, when the ship is zigzagging together with four destroyers. At 17:26 the destroyer

---

[154] The photographic "take" from this mission is processed by the Office of Naval Intelligence (ONI) at Pearl. The photo-interpreters and ship designers who review the huge battleship in the photos conclude that she must displace at least 60,000 tons and carry 18-in guns.

[155] Carrier-based aircraft attacked Palau on 30 and also 31 March, so *Musashi* departed just in time. By the way, on 31st Koga's aircraft disappeared without a trace and the CF lost its second C-in-C.

Time	Noteworthy movements, events etc.
	Harusame detects an enemy submarine and carries out a depth charge attack. In view of this situation, *Musashi* changes to a more northerly course at 17:34, concluding it would be more favorable. But her sonar detects a suspicious sound 90° to port at 17:43. The rudder is turned full a starboard and full speed ahead is ordered to evade by turning to starboard. However, three torpedo wakes 100° to port, distance about 2,000 m are sighted at 17:44. The centre torpedo is trailing large bubbles and is slightly delayed. Course is reversed by laying the helm full a port. Thirty seconds later the inner of the three torpedoes, which was closest to the ship, hit to port, about 6 m below the waterline at F27. A water column as high as 15 m rose up and flames coming out from the hawse pipe were seen. Seven men, stationed in the hydrophone room are killed, eleven more wounded. Both (in fact five) other torpedoes were evaded by turning urgently to port. At 17:46 the destroyer *Isokaze* carries out a depth charge attack in the vicinity of the point of launch.
	At 17:47.20 damage of the hull was discovered but no list was noted. At 17:56 the forward anchor windlass room is flooded. Upon receiving *Isokaze*'s report on sighting an enemy periscope at 18:14, the helm is put full a starboard to evade. About 20 minutes later, screening ships of the main force are sighted carrying out depth charge attacks. At 18:30 immersion is reported but *Musashi* completes emergency repair measures and shoring and ascertained that no impediment to cruising exists. *Musashi* ships 3,000 tons of water. Destroyer Division 17's *Urakaze* and *Isokaze* remain on the spot and counterattack *Tunny* dropping 38 depth charges, but their efforts are unsuccessful.
	Anticipating another air raid, Koga's staff forbids her to return to Palau after being hit. As soon as the damaged sections are shored up, *Musashi* departs that night for Kure with Destroyer Division 4's *Michishio*, Destroyer Division 27's *Shiratsuyu* and Destroyer Division 32's *Fujinami*.
2 April 1944	At 06:00, USN codebreakers intercept and decrypt a message that reads: "*Musashi* BB was torpedoed on the 29th, hit at frame No. 12 to frames No. 40. Central shafts ----- cannot use ----- not clear, otherwise no damage. Request arrangements be made for immediate inspection and repair upon entering port."
3 April 1944	*Musashi* arrives at Kure.
10 April 1944	Enters Kure drydock No. 4. Repairs are made to the hull. Two beam triple 6.1-in turrets are removed, each is replaced by three triple-mount 25-mm. AA guns. 21 more triple and 25

Time	Noteworthy movements, events etc.
	single 25-mm guns are added. *Musashi*'s 150-cm searchlights Nos. 7 and 8 are removed to make room for the single mounts. The searchlights are later reinstalled for use by Sasebo's AA batteries. *Musashi*'s final AA suite is one hundred-thirty 25-mm AA guns (35 × 3, 25 × 1). A Type 13 radar and a new Type 22 radar set are fitted. Depth-charge rails are also installed on the fantail.
22 April 1944	Undocked.
22–27 April 1944	Kure. Additional supplies are taken aboard.
10 May 1944	Departs Saiki for Okinawa. *Musashi* joins Carrier Division 2's *Hiyō*, *Junyō* and *Ryūhō* and Carrier Division 3's *Zuihō*, *Chiyoda*, *Chitose* and destroyers *Akishimo*, *Michishio*, *Shigure* and *Tamanami* and heads for Okinawa.
12 May 1944	Arrives at Nakagusuku Bay, Okinawa. Departs for the Mobile Fleet operating base at Tawitawi.
16 May 1944	Arrives at the Tawitawi anchorage, Sulu Sea.
16 May–10 June 1944	Tawitawi. In Vice-Admiral Ozawa Jisaburō's Mobile Fleet with Vice-Admiral Ugaki Matome's Battleship Division 1's *Yamato* and *Musashi*. *Musashi* and *Yamato* participate in joint gunnery drills at ranges of almost 22 miles.
10 June 1944	Operation *Kon*, the Relief of Biak At 16:00, departs Tawitawi for Batjan, Halmahera Island with *Yamato*, Destroyer Squadron 2's light cruiser *Noshiro* and destroyers *Okinami* and *Shimakaze*. USS *Harder* (SS-257), on station nearby, reports the *Kon* force leaving Tawitawi. Shortly after departure, as a result of a submarine alert and the subsequent maneuvering, *Musashi* nearly rams *Yamato*.
12 June 1944	The US invasion of Marianas begins. Operation *Kon* is "postponed". Ugaki's force arrives at Batjan where they are joined by Cruiser Division 5's *Haguro* and *Myōkō* and destroyer *Asagumo*.
13 June 1944	At 22:00, Ugaki's force departs Batjan to rendezvous with the Mobile Fleet.
15 June 1944	Ugaki's force is reported east of Mindanao by USS *Seahorse* (SS-304).
16 June 1944	Joins the Mobile Fleet. At 20:00 hours, USS *Cavalla* (SS-244) sights the Mobile Fleet in the Philippine Sea.
19 June 1944	Operation *A Gō*, the Battle of the Philippine Sea. The IJN suffers an overwhelming defeat.
22 June 1944	*Musashi* retires to Nakagusuku Bay, Okinawa to refuel the destroyer escort, then departs for Japan.
24 June 1944	Arrives at Hashirajima.
9 July 1944	Departs Kure for Okinawa with Group A's *Yamato*, Cruiser

Time	Noteworthy movements, events etc.
	Divisions 4, 7, Destroyer Squadron 2 and Group B's *Kongō*, *Nagato*, cruiser *Mogami* and Destroyer Squadron 10.
10 July 1944	Group A detaches from Group B. Departs Okinawa.
17 July 1944	Arrives at Lingga (near Singapore) to join the Mobile Fleet.
September 1944	Captain Inoguchi orders paint from the Singapore Naval Arsenal. The paint furnished is possibly from former Royal Navy stocks. Within a day, *Musashi*'s sides receive a new, dark coat.
18 October 1944	Black deck camouflage intended for the night breakthrough in the San Bernardino Strait is hastily applied to both *Musashi* and *Yamato*. The main component is soot from *Musashi*'s funnel.
18–20 October 1944	Departs Lingga for Brunei Bay, Borneo–Operation *Shō Ichi Gō* (Victory 1), the Battle of Leyte Gulf: Sorties from Brunei towards the Philippines with Vice-Admiral Kurita Takeo's First Mobile Striking Force, Force A (Centre Force): Battleship Division 1's *Yamato*, *Musashi*, *Nagato*, Cruiser Divisions 4, 5, Destroyer Squadron 2.
23 October 1944	The Battle of the Palawan Passage Two American submarines attack Force A. *Maya*'s surviving crewmen are picked up by destroyer *Akishimo* and are transferred to *Musashi* that afternoon.
24 October 1944	The Battle of the Sibuyan Sea. See chapter 8.
25 October 1944	At 02:30, USN codebreakers intercept and decrypt a message that reads: "Completed *Musashi*–BB rescue operations at 02:15 on the 25th. Following numbers of personnel rescued: *Hamakaze*: Executive officer and 800 men (of which 30 were officers). *Isokaze*: 30 officers and 410 men. Escorts arrive Coron at 17:30."[156] Later, *Musashi*'s survivors are taken to Manila then to Corregidor Island. Many are then sent home, about 200 on carrier *Junyō* and some on *Yamato*. 420 are transported from Manila to the homeland aboard *Manju Maru* (ex-*Santos Maru*). On 25 November *Manju Maru* is torpedoed in Luzon Strait by USS *Atule* (SS-403) and sinks. 300 *Musashi* survivors perish and the 120 survivors are transported to Takao (Formosa). They are incorporated into the Guard Division and remain on Formosa until the end of the war. 300 of the remaining 620 survivors are divided between IJN

---

[156] Based on this intercept, it appears *Kiyoshimo* rescued 136 officers and men.

Time	Noteworthy movements, events etc.
	units defending Cavite Naval Base, Fort Drum in Manila Bay, Clark Field, the Caraballo Mountains and the Cabaruan Hills. The remaining survivors are incorporated into the Special Naval Landing Force of Rear-Admiral Iwabuchi Sanji's 31st Naval Base Force and most are killed defending Manila. *Musashi*'s CO Rear-Admiral Inoguchi was promoted to vice-admiral posthumously.
31 August 1945	Removed from Navy List.

Photo 7-19: Probably *Musashi* photographed from the heavy cruiser *Atago* in August 1942 (Authors' collections)

Photo 7-20: *Yamato* (left) and *Musashi* (right) off Moen (Harushima), Truk Lagoon, in May 1943. Moen, with the 360-m high Tonoken and 240-m high Witpwon, is in the background (Kure Maritime Museum)

Photo 7-21: The Emperor's (*Shōwa tennō*) visit to the *Musashi* at Kure on 24 June 1943. The Emperor is seated in the middle (number 9). Admiral Nagano Osami is number 6 from the left, Prince Takamatsu number 8, Admiral Shimada Shigetarō number 11, Admiral Koga Mineichi number 12 and Vice-Admiral Fukuda Keiji is seated 3rd from the right (Author's collections)

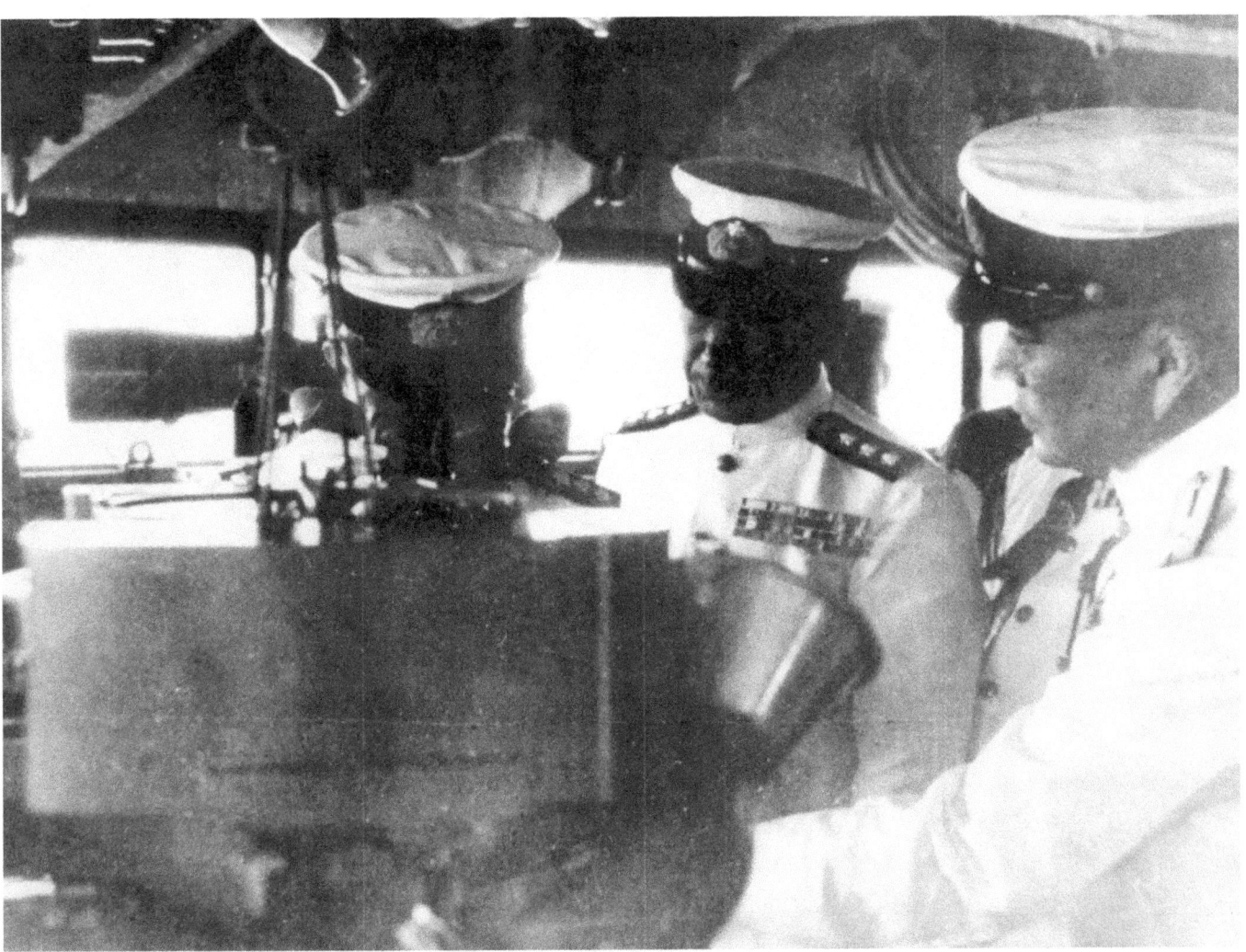

Photo 7-22: *Shōwa tennō* (left), Admiral Koga Mineichi and staff officer Doi Kazuo on *Musashi* in June 1943 (Kure Maritime Museum)

NIMBLE BOOKS LLC

Chapter 8–Loss of the *Musashi*

Operations Plan, Training and Alert

The Naval General Staff expected that the enemy would begin the attack on the Philippines in mid November 1944 and the operational planning for this area was established on 21 July 1944 (IGHQ[157] Directive #431). On 26 July (IGHQ Directive #453) it was divided into four operation plans (depending upon enemy operations) called *Shō 1* to *Shō 4*. The *Shō 1* operation would be executed if the enemy advanced to attack the Philippine Islands. The Combined Fleet issued the outline of the *Shō Gō* operation on 1 August (CFOpOrd[158] #83).[159]

The principal force was the First Diversion Attack Force (*Dai Ichi Yūgekitai*–1st YB) composed of: (1) 1st Force commanded by Vice-Admiral Kurita Takeo, the Commander-in-Chief (C-in-C) of the 2nd Fleet (1st Night Battle Force), (2) 2nd Force commanded by Vice-Admiral Suzuki Yoshio, the commander of Battleship Division 3 (2nd Night Battle Force), (3) #3 Force commanded by Vice-Admiral Nishimura Shōji, the commander of Battleship Division 2 (3rd Night Battle Force).[160] The battleship *Musashi* was assigned to Battleship Division 1 (1st *Sentai*) belonging to the 1st Night Battle Force composed of: (1) 1st *Sentai* (battleships *Yamato*, *Musashi*, *Nagato*), (2) 4th *Sentai* (heavy cruisers *Atago*, *Takao*, *Chōkai*, *Maya*), (3) 2nd Destroyer Squadron (light cruiser *Noshiro*, 9 destroyers).[161]

---

[157] Imperial General Headquarters.

[158] Combined Fleet Operational Order.

[159] The main source for this chapter is Vol. 56 of the official *Senshi Sōsho* series, "Battle of the Philippines", part 2. Written permission to use all data and illustrations was obtained from the Historical Branch of the Japanese Maritime Self Defence Force.

[160] The 1st YB came under the direct command of the C-in-C of the Combined Fleet at the command station at Higoshi on 21 October (CFDesOpOrd #367). Until that time it was under the command of Vice-Admiral Ozawa Jisaburō, the commander of the task force.

[161] This description is restricted to essential data considered necessary to understand the background of her loss.

The 2nd Fleet, including *Musashi*, had practised war training at Lingga anchorage south of Singapore for *Shō Gō Sakusen* since July and the fitting of radar was hurried.

On 17 October 1944 an advance party of the US Army landed on Suluan Island near Leyte Bay. The Japanese watching post reported the approach of warships etc. at 08:00 and the C-in-C of the Combined Fleet alerted the forces for Shō 1 at 08:09. On 18th its execution was ordered.

Departure of the 1st YB

The Kurita Fleet departed Lingga anchorage on 18th at 01:00 and entered Brunei Bay on 20th at 12:00 and fuelled. On 21st the 1st YB was ordered by the C-in-C of the Combined Fleet to pass through the San Bernardino Strait and arrive at Tacloban early in the morning on 25th to destroy the enemy landing force. The 1st and 2nd Night Battle Forces were ordered to take the western side of Palawan Island to north. It was the most dangerous route from the viewpoint of submarine attacks.

Photo 8-1: Vice-Admiral Kurita Takeo (1889–1977) Commander-in-Chief of the 2nd Fleet (Authors' collections)

After hasty fuelling the 1st and 2nd Night Battle Forces departed Brunei on 22nd at 08:05 and made a zigzag course at 18 knots as a precaution against submarine attacks. After sunset the zigzag movement was stopped and speed was reduced to 16 knots, to head straightforward to Palawan Strait. On 23rd at 04:55 speed was increased to 18 knots and zigzag movement was begun, but it was in vain and the force lost two heavy cruisers (*Atago* and *Maya*) by torpedo attacks from the American submarines early in the morning, and *Musashi* rescued sailors from *Maya*. The heavy cruiser *Takao* was damaged by two torpedo hits (her two sisters had each received four hits) and became immobilised. Vice-Admiral Kurita was aboard his flagship the heavy cruiser *Atago* and the flag of the 2nd Fleet was transferred to the battleship *Yamato* at 16:30, after a temporary stay aboard the destroyer *Kishinami* that had rescued him.

On 24th the force rounded the southern part of Mindoro Island and advanced into the Sibuyan Sea, where the circle formation was taken at 07:47. The fleet came into the enemy carrier plane zone and expected air attacks, while, in contrast, neither Japanese carrier nor land-based aircraft provided air escort.[162]

Consecutive Air Attacks and the Loss of the Musashi

According to the "Detailed Battle Report #4" of the Battleship *Musashi* (*Gunkan* Musashi *Sentō Shōhō Dai Yon Gō*) published by the War History Division of the Defense Research Institute of the Japanese Defense Ministry (*Bōeichō Bōeikenshūjo Senshibu*) and the description of the naval operation "Operation Victory #1" (*Shō Gō Sakusen Dai Ichi Gō*) in Vol. 56 of *Senshi Sōsho* she was attacked by a total of 161 aircraft, recorded as attacking in five waves[163] even though the American carriers launched only four strikes. She received a total of 20 torpedo hits (of which two were duds), 17 bomb hits and 18 (+?) near misses and sank about four hours after the last attack had ended.[164].

---

[162] At that time the carrier forces (3rd Fleet), with a small number of aircraft, departed the Inland Sea and advanced to the South as a bait force (*otori butai*). The Philippine-based air forces searched for the enemy carriers in order to execute kamikaze attacks. Vice-Admiral Ugaki Matome asked several times for planes to provide air escort, but in vain.

[163] *Kaigun Zōsen Gijutsu Gaiyō* ("Outline of Warship Construction Techniques"), vol. 1, and Matsumoto Kitarō divide it into six waves, but this is identical with five waves for waves 3/1 and 3/2 in the five-waves-version are separated in the six-waves-version.

[164] While the reported bomb hits mainly coincide there are remarkable differences as for the number of torpedo hits. For example: The summarised report of Captain Katō Kenkichi, *Musashi*'s execu-

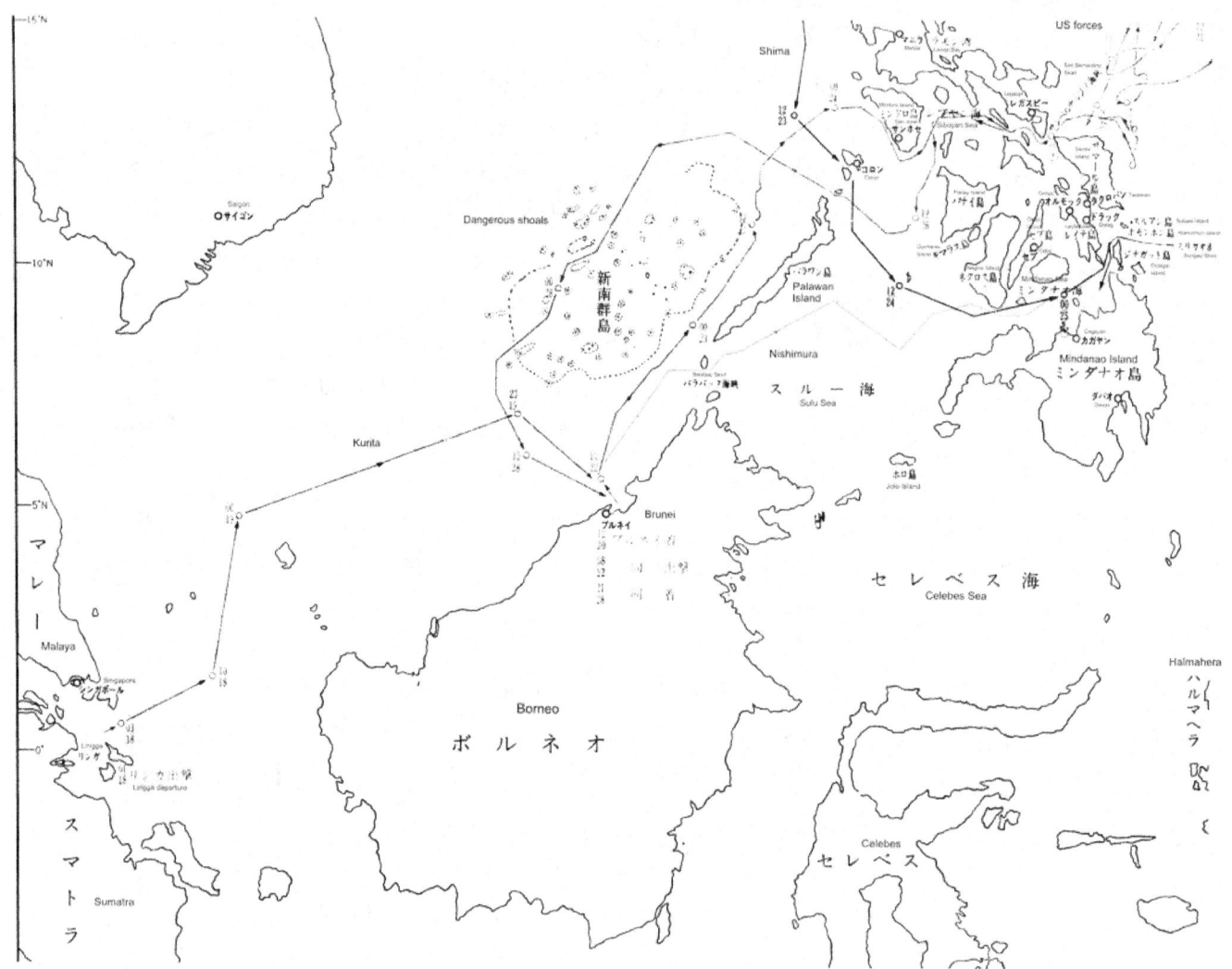

Map 8-1: Track chart of IJN forces during the Battle for Leyte Gulf (Adapted from *Senshi Sōsho*)

---

tive officer, who gathered the information from survivors after sinking, lists 23 hits. Signal man Hosoya Shirō, who accompanied Katō and was in an lookout station during the battle, reported 25 hits to port and five more to starboard. But 25 hits would have caused her to capsize in a much shorter time as is shown by the case of *Musashi*'s sister *Yamato*. Therefore, this report must be considered unreliable. Also, in contrast to the official document Hosoya states that the firing of 46-cm Type 3 incendiary projectiles against aircraft was only from the fourth attack on and not the second one, because the gunnery officer rejected firing on the grounds that the main guns should not be fired before *Musashi* rushed into Leyte Bay.

Photo 8-2: *Musashi*, heavy cruiser *Mogami* (closest), heavy cruiser *Chōkai* (right) and *Yamato* at Brunei on 21 October 1944 (Authors' collections)

Photo 8-3: *Musashi*, heavy cruiser *Mogami* (closest) and battleship *Yamashiro* at Brunei on 21 October 1944 (Authors' collections)

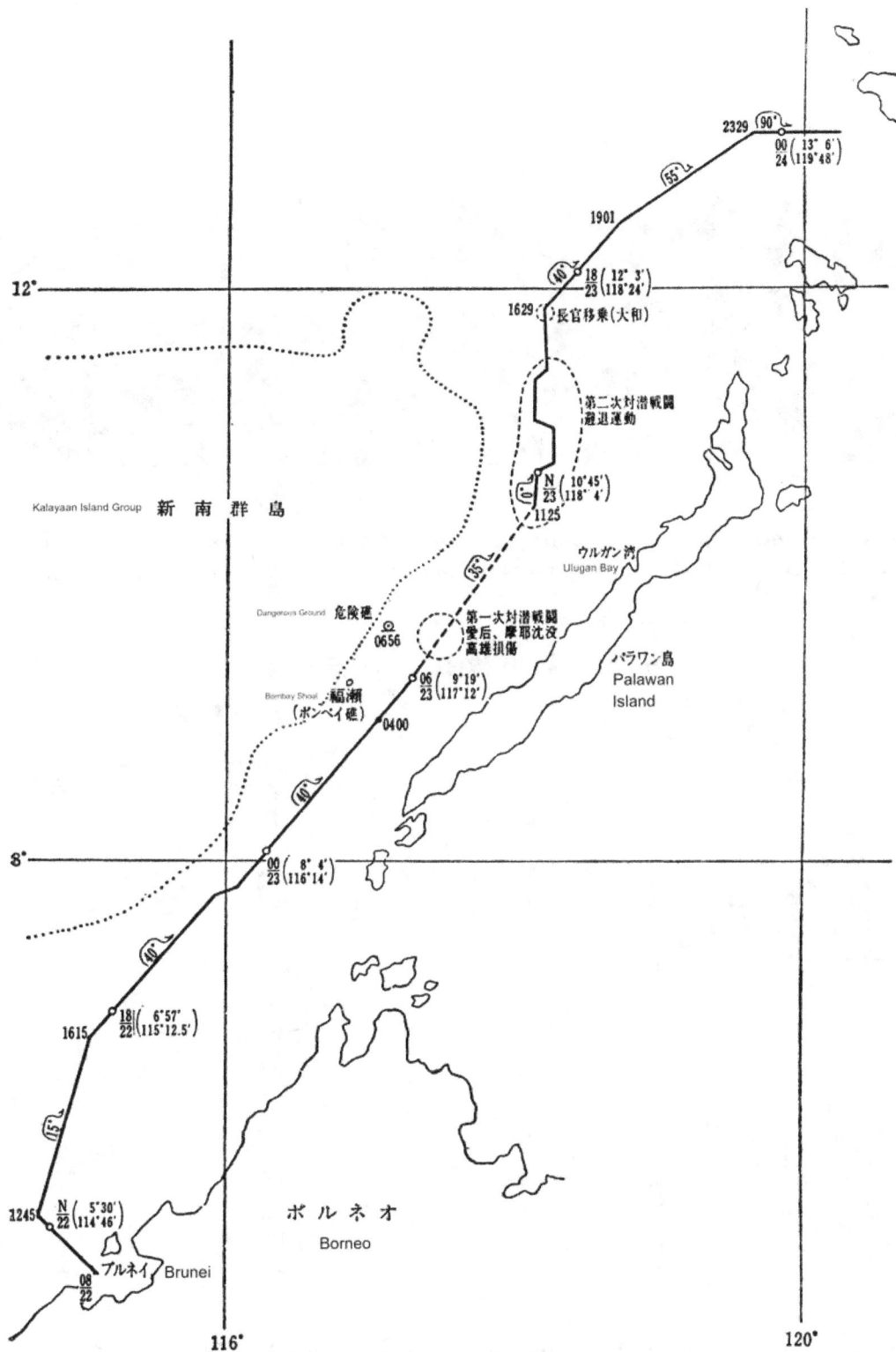

Map 8-2: Movements of the 1st YB on 22–23 October 1944. USS *Darter*'s and USS *Dace*'s attacks in the Palawan Passage are marked with a dotted circle. As noted in *Yamato*'s *sentō shōhō* (Adapted from *Senshi Sōsho*)

Photo 8-4: *Fusō, Musashi, Mogami, Yamashiro, Chōkai* and *Yamato* depart Brunei on 21 October 1944. This photo was taken from the destroyer *Isokaze* (Authors' collections)

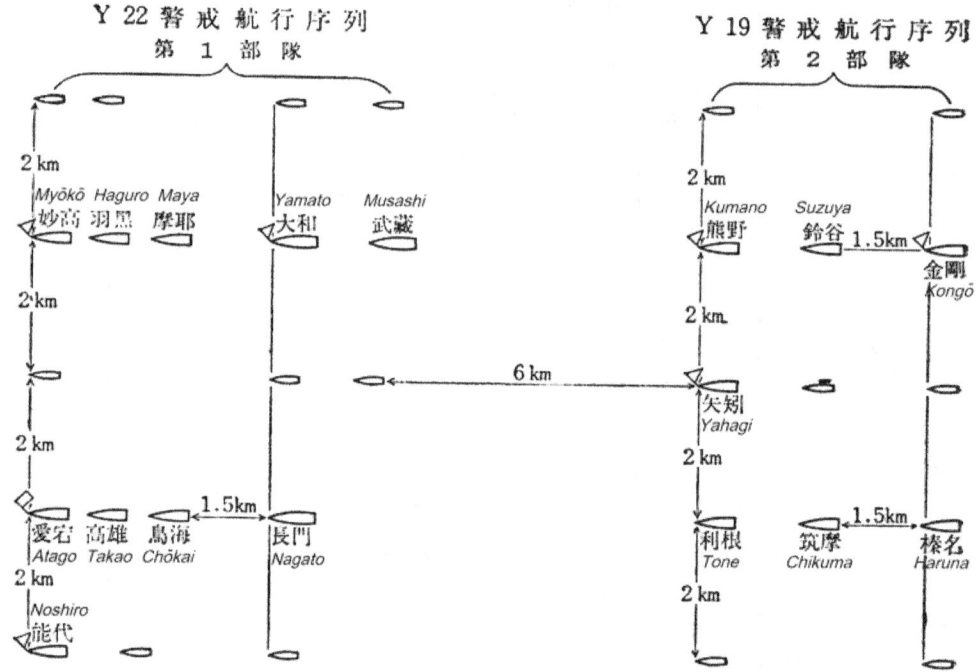

Map 8-3: The 1st YB in #1 Alert Cruising Formation (*Dai Ichi Keikai Kōkō Joretsu*). 1st *Butai* in Y 22 Alert Cruising Formation and 2nd *Butai* in Y 19 Alert Cruising Formation. As noted in the 1st YB's *sentō shōhō* (Adapted from *Senshi Sōsho*)

Photo 8-5: *Musashi* departs Brunei at 08:30–09:00 on 22 October 1944 (Authors' collections)

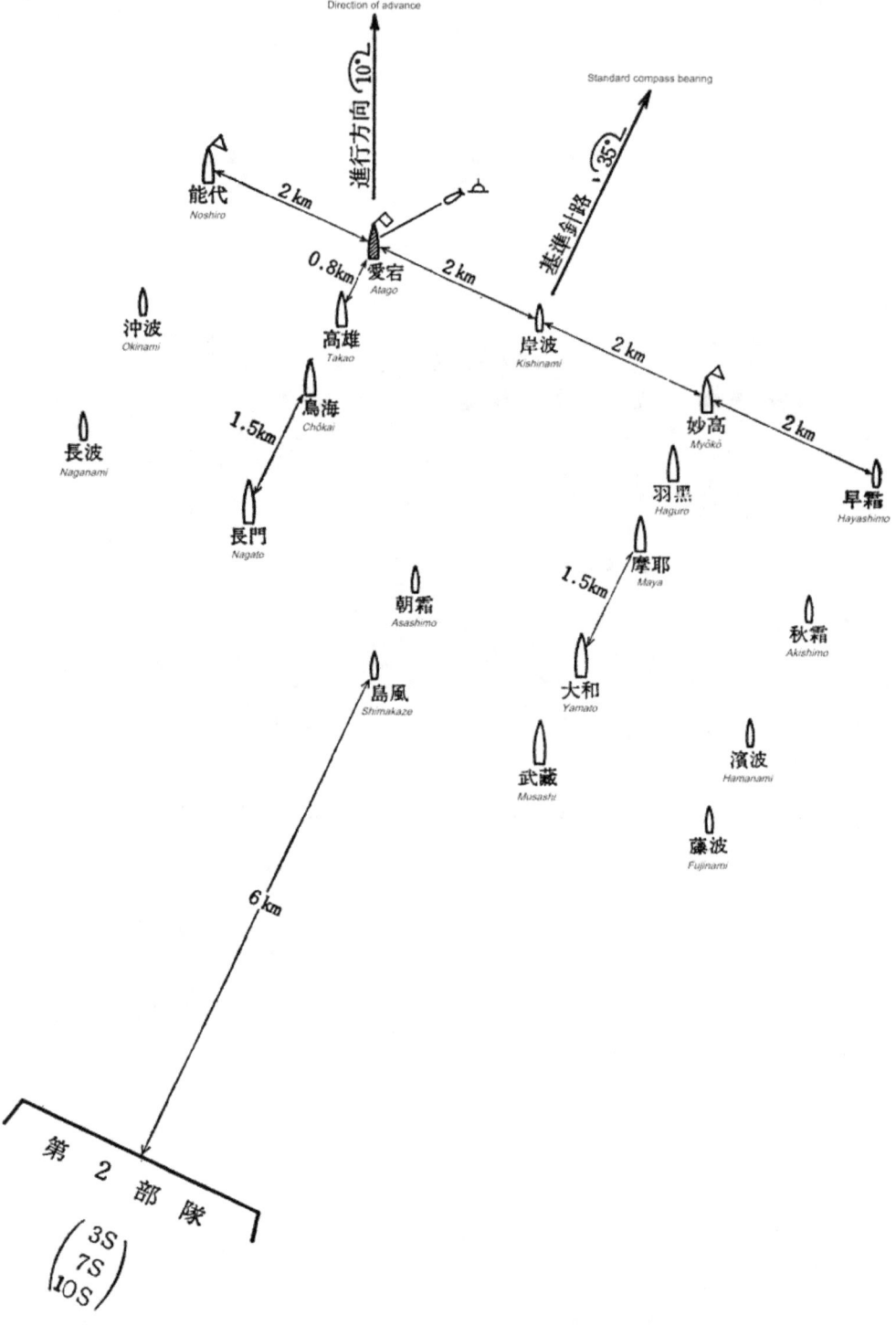

Map 8-4: Formation at the time of *Atago*'s loss on 23 October. As noted in *Atago*'s *sentō shōhō* (Adapted from *Senshi Sōsho*)

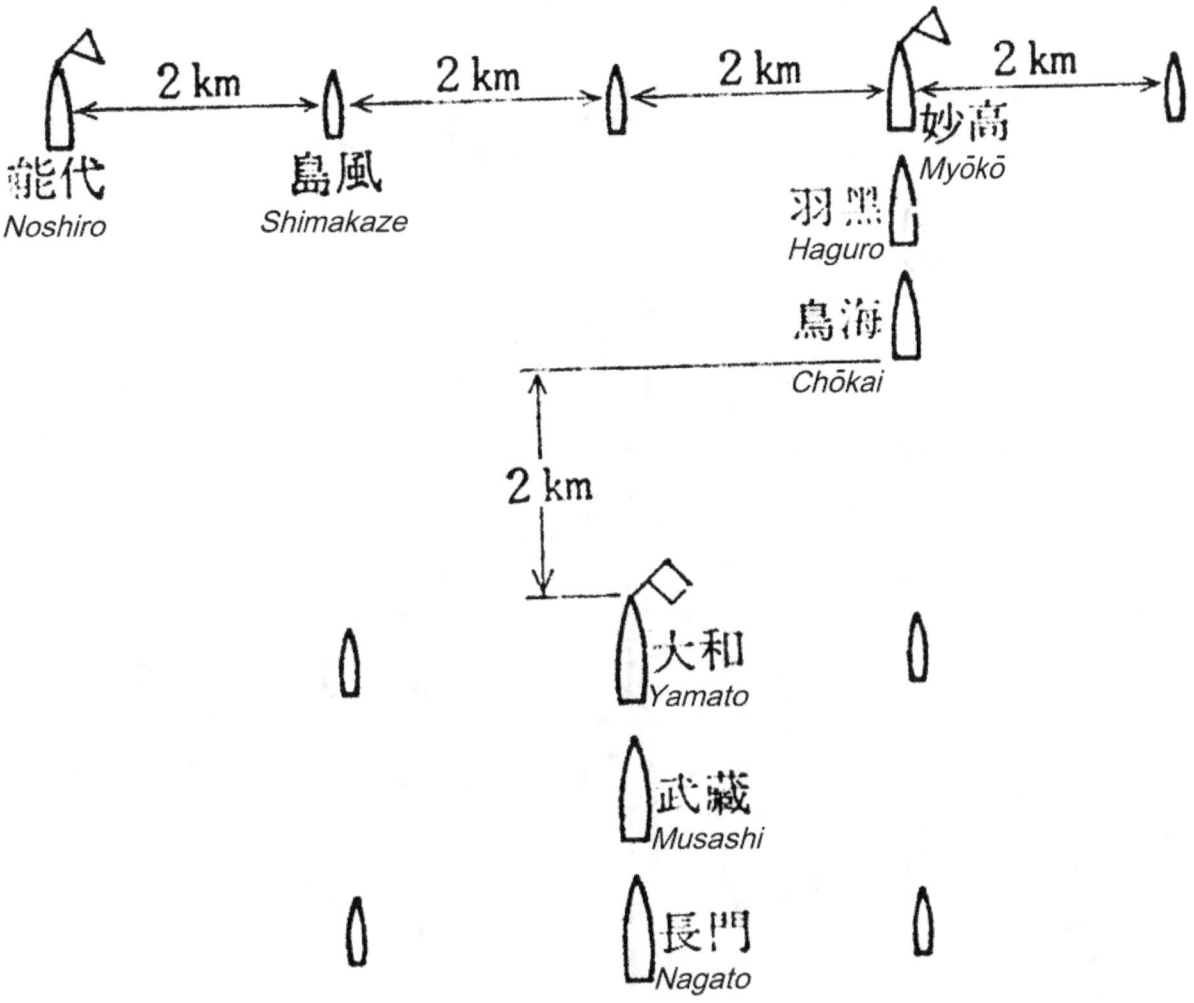

Map 8-5: Y 23 Alert Cruising Formation (*Y 23 Keikai Kōkō Joretsu*) on 23 October 1944. As noted in the 1st YB's *sentō shōhō* (Adapted from *Senshi Sōsho*)

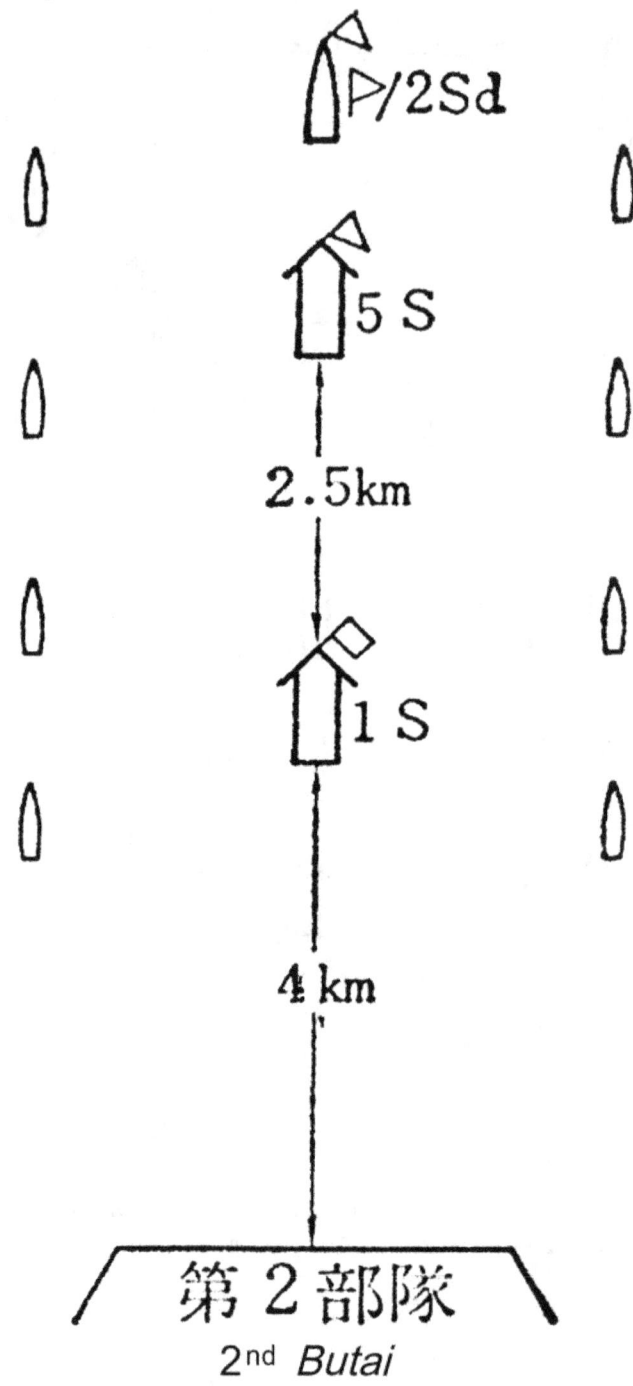

Map 8-6: Y 24 Alert Cruising Formation (*Y 24 Keikai Kōkō Joretsu*). As noted in *Yamato*'s *sentō shōhō* (Adapted from *Senshi Sōsho*)

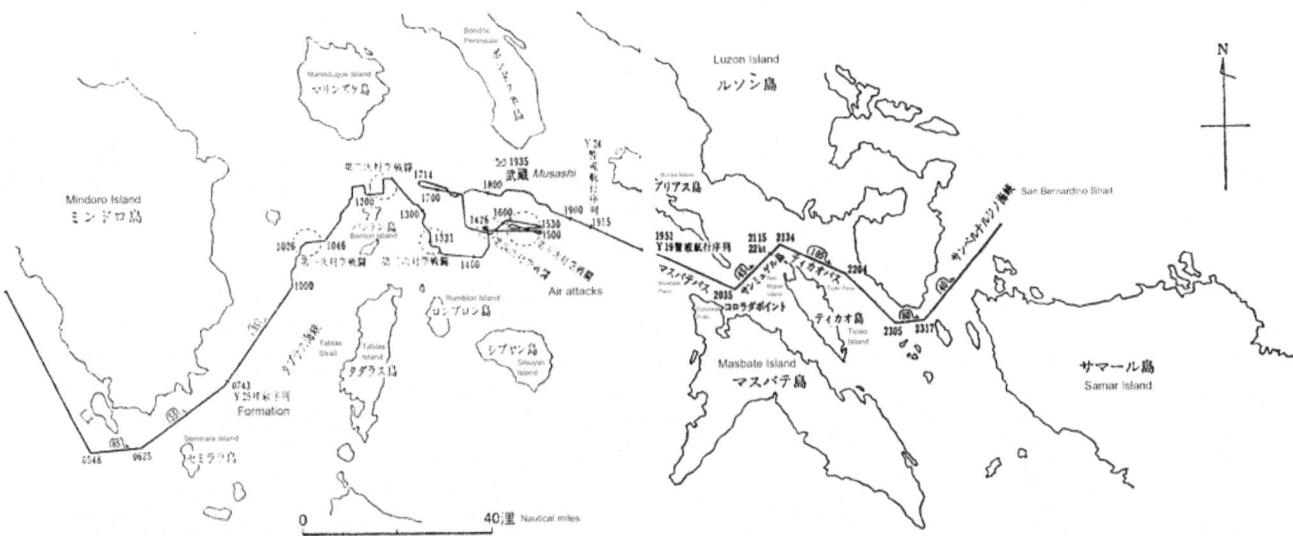

Map 8-7: The 1st YB's movements on 24 October 1944. It should be observed that Vice-Admiral Kurita reversed course for a while after the loss of the *Musashi* but he soon continued the advance. His "turn" became a much discussed affair. Movements as noted in the 1st YB's, 1st *Sentai*'s and *Yamato*'s *sentō shōhō* (Adapted from *Senshi Sōsho*)

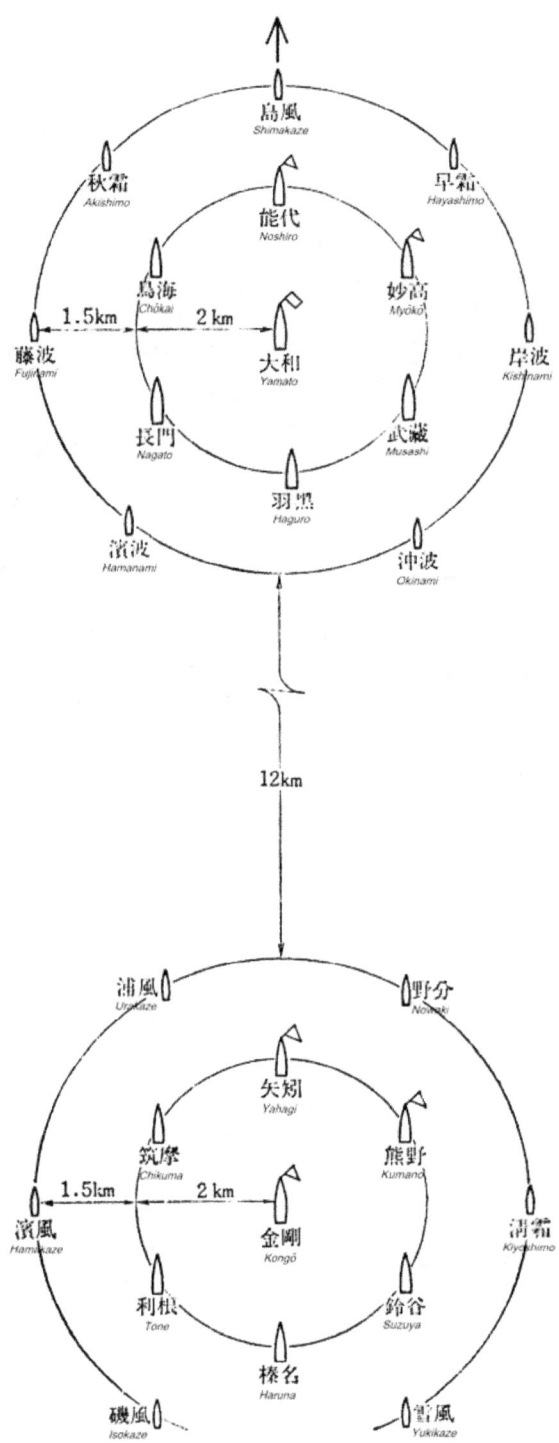

Map 8-8: The 1st YB steaming in AA formation, "circle formation". Formations Y 25 (top) and B 3 (bottom), respectively. As noted in *Yamato*'s and the 7th *Sentai*'s *sentō shōhō* (Adapted from *Senshi Sōsho*)

Photo 8-6: *Yamato*, *Musashi*, battleship *Nagato* and heavy cruiser *Haguro* on 24 October 1944 (Authors' collections)

The following description is based primarily upon the detailed battle report, being the only existing official document and also the only one describing the damage caused by the hits. As for the attack times, number of attackers, ammunition consumption and personnel losses, Vol. 56 has been the main source. While the latter data are not included in Report S-06-2 the hits and damage generally coincide with the Japanese official war history. But after all, there are uncertainties and the description may sometimes be wrong. On the other hand, it is thought as reliable as possible in view of the lack of documents and the well-known differences of eyewitness reports.

First Attack from 10:29 to 10:40

The first attack was executed by bombers and torpedo planes from 10:29 to 10:40. The bombers scored one hit on the roof of #1 main gun turret at F70[165] with a small bomb causing no damage. But she was bracketed by near misses on starboard F20 and F145 and port F25 and F145. Splinters penetrated the hull plating and water immersed into several bow compartments through holes, particularly two small tanks in the vicinity of F20 were flooded. It is important to note that flooding into the bow watertight compartments began with the first attack.

One torpedo hit to starboard at F130, in way of #11 boiler room, and two passed under her bottom at F140 and F150, both from starboard to port. By the shock of the torpedo detonation rivets in the longitudinal bulkheads on the sides of #7 and #11 boiler rooms sprung loose and these rooms had a small water immersion. The forward main gun fire director atop the bridge jammed and became incapable to train. The watertight compartments in the vicinity of the hit and outside the vital part were flooded and *Musashi* listed about 5.5° (read from inclinometers) to starboard, thus indicating considerable leakage. The list was at first corrected to 3° and then 1° to starboard by counterflooding.[166]

---

[165] Frame 70.

[166] Vice-Admiral Ugaki noted in his diary: "I thought then that this wouldn't be too bad" (p. 489) and the crew's reaction was only "mosquito bite."

Second Attack from 12:07 till 12:15

After the first attack the fleet formation was rearranged and from 10:53 zigzag advancement began. More than one hour after that the second wave concentrated the attacks on the big two. While *Yamato* was successful in evading all bombs and torpedoes, her sister *Musashi* received more damage. Within eight minutes she was hit by two bombs and three torpedoes, all to port, and also suffered five near misses.

One bomb hit the forecastle deck at port F15, beam. It passed down and cut through the port outside shell above the waterline. The bomb did not detonate and damage to the crew's space was negligible. Also, there was no flooding. The second bomb struck at port F138 forward of #4 high-angle gun. It penetrated the uppermost and upper deck before detonating at the middle (armor) deck at #10 crew's space. The damage was bigger than expected. Fire broke out and flames reached the #2 engine room (port inboard)[167] and also #10 and #12 boiler rooms, damaging steam pipes etc. The #2 engine room was filled with steam, was abandoned and never manned again. From this time on *Musashi* only operated with three-shafts. The revolutions of the three operable shafts were increased and formation speed (decreased in the attack) was maintained with little effort.

Splinters from the five near misses (four to starboard, between F50 and F60, and one to port, at F70 and, hence, all outside the protected vital area) penetrated the outside plating and a small immersion of water contributed to the increase of the list.

The torpedoes hit at F80 in way of #1 main gun turret, F110 at the forward bulkhead of the forward port outboard boiler room and F145, close to the bulkhead separating the port outboard engine room and the port #2 hydraulic machinery room.[168] The latter room was flooded and minor leakage into the engine room was also reported.

The list after this attack was 5° to port (it had been 1° to starboard) but it was corrected to 1° port by counterflooding starboard voids. Flooding of

---

[167] The chief engineer who was in the port inboard engine room control station moved to the starboard inboard engine room.

[168] While Vice-Admiral Ugaki noted these torpedo hits in his diary he again neglected the bomb hits, as in the case of the first attack. Even though he later mentions some bomb hits it was always the torpedo hits he counted. This is interesting in view of the conclusions drawn by the US Naval Technical Mission to Japan.

compartments in the fore ship continued and her trim changed by two meters to 1 m bow from 1 m stern before fighting.

Third Attack from 13:31 to 13:50

After the second air attack the 1st YB arrived in the Sibuyan Sea at 12:18 and reduced speed to 18 knots bearing 150°. After about 30 minutes radar detected the approaching 3rd wave and order was given to increase speed to 24 knots. But it had quickly to be changed to 22 knots considering the speed of the three-shafted *Musashi*. In spite of this *Musashi* was forced to decrease speed and she gradually fell back.

This attack may be divided into two waves, which attacked immediately one after another. During this attack *Musashi* received four bomb hits and at least three near misses and was damaged by five torpedo hits, of which one must be considered very doubtful. Three torpedoes passed under the bottom. At the end of this attack the bow was down to above the middle deck, speed dropped to about 16 knots and damage neared a critical degree.

First Wave

Two near misses at F180 caused little damage, but fragments from a near miss at the stern damaged the post of the aircraft crane.

One torpedo hit at starboard F60, forward of the protected vital part, flooded several large store rooms, destroyed the sounding room and filled the forward sick-bay with carbon monoxide, poisoning many crew members, particularly of the damage control party.

The trim by the bow increased to about 2 m or a little more.

Second Wave

Four bombs hit at F45, port (near to #1 staircase), F65, port, F70, port, and F135, starboard (near the galley's business office). The first bomb detonated in a crew's space after penetrating three decks, but there was no fire and only small damage. The second bomb penetrated two decks before detonating and brought about the same result as the first one. Damage by the third bomb, that detonated slightly forward of the sloping armor bulkhead, was still more minor. The fourth bomb detonated upon impact, destroyed the galley office and knocked out some 25-mm machine-guns. However, damage to the structures in the vicinity of these hits was generally superficial and no bomb started fires or caused flooding, quite different from the situation of torpedo hits.

The torpedo hits at both sides of F70 caused the flooding of many store rooms, and in company with the former hit at starboard F60 the fore part up to the middle deck was almost completely flooded from about F54 back to the forward transverse bulkhead of the armored citadel. The trim by the bow increased further and became 4 m. The torpedo hit at starboard F138 caused instant flooding of the starboard hydraulic machinery room, and it is said that the urgent fortifications, made by the damage control party after the hit during the first attack, were destroyed, the electric wire passage separated etc. The location of the fourth hit is differently recorded, either to starboard at F110 (S-06-2 and Matsumoto) or F130 (Naitō etc.). The members of the Allied investigation team denied the confirmation of a hit at F110 because there was no flooding of the starboard forward boiler room and too small an increase of list, while the Japanese take it for granted.

The list after the end of the attack was about 2° to starboard (it had been 1° to port) and was corrected to 1° to starboard by counterflooding port voids, but after that almost all watertight compartments were flooded. List did not provide any problem but the previously stated trim by the bow became a serious matter. She settled towards the bow and speed was reduced to about 16 knots, so that she gradually dropped out of formation.

Fourth Attack from 14:26–14:40

The fourth attack was made by about 20 dive bombers (SB2C) and torpedo bombers (TBF) but miraculously no damage was inflicted and not even near misses were recorded.

At that time *Musashi* was behind the main force and not supported by other ships in the defense against attackers. When the planes turned away she was located on the port side of the 2nd Fleet. The distance increased, i.e. *Musashi* fell further back, and the heavy cruiser *Tone* approached her for assistance. Then Vice-Admiral Kurita ordered *Musashi* to return to Manila via San Jose escorted by the destroyer *Kiyoshimo*.

Fifth Attack from 15:15–15:30

Most of the aircraft of the fifth wave concentrated upon the small group composed of the already heavily damaged *Musashi*, the heavy cruiser *Tone* and the destroyer *Kiyoshimo*. It was a most vicious attack, and she received ten bomb and eleven torpedo hits (of which two were duds) within some minutes. The torpedo hits were fatal.

One bomb hit the right side of the air defense station on top of the fore mast (tower bridge), penetrated the deck and detonated in the upper bridge, causing great destruction within the bridge and the operations room. The chief navigator, the anti-aircraft commander and a further five senior officers were killed; others, including the commanding officer Rear-Admiral Inoguchi Toshihira, were wounded.[169]

Three bombs hit to port near F105 and F115 and on the beam of F120 and detonated on the uppermost deck. #2 and #4 25-mm single machine-guns and #2 shielded triple machine-gun, #1 radio room, telephone room, and the information centre were destroyed and superstructures damaged.[170]

Two bombs hit close together to starboard at F115 and detonated on impact with the uppermost deck. #1 and #3 25-mm single machine-guns and #1 shielded triple machine-gun were destroyed and the front wall of the entrance to #7 boiler room was damaged. Damage to topside structures was great.[171]

One bomb struck at F 127, beam, centreline inside of the central stand-by room for AA personnel and destroyed it together with the backside of the fore mast from the AA deck down to the uppermost deck.[172]

One more bomb struck near to F75, starboard, destroyed the wardroom and caused a crack (at places about 2 m wide) at the side of the uppermost deck from F70 to F95.[173]

Another bomb is reported to have detonated on the roof of #1 main gun turret with the same result as the bomb hit in the first attack, i.e. no damage.[174]

---

[169] Identified as F120, centreline, in S-06-2.

[170] Identified as F108, port, F115, port, and F120, port, but the point of detonation of the latter is different in S-06-2.

[171] Identified as F115, starboard, and F115, starboard, in S-06-2.

[172] Identified as F127, centreline, in S-06-2 but damage was greater than stated in the report.

[173] Identified as F79, starboard, but damage was again greater than stated in the report.

[174] Identified as F75, starboard, in S-06-2.

One bomb detonated on the uppermost deck near F62, port and added to the damage of the uppermost and flying deck caused by the third attack.[175]

Most noteworthy again is the fact that no bomb penetrated the protective deck or caused damage below it. Also, damage to hull sides above the waterline was small while superstructures were totally destroyed in some areas. However, such damage was more or less superficial for a ship like *Musashi*.

Five torpedoes hit on the port side near F40, F60, F75 and starboard F80 and F105, and caused the great expansion of the already existing damage in these areas. The flooding in the fore part increased and the bow settled much deeper. Among the hits, that near to F75 hit in way of #1 main gun turret magazines and caused the flooding of the magazines on the two lower levels.[176] The hit near F105, starboard, detonated in way of the high-angle guns magazines, which were flooded rapidly on two levels.

One torpedo detonated near F125, port, causing the immediate flooding of #8 boiler room through rivet holes and cracks in the outer wall. #12 boiler room flooded slowly.[177]

Three torpedoes hit near F140, port, but only one detonated and increased the pressure upon the lower armor. The warheads of the not detonated ones are reported to have entered the 25-mm ammunition magazine to port and caused its flooding.

One torpedo struck near F145, port, flooding the port outboard #4 engine room within four minutes. The sidewall of this room had already been buckled by a hit received in the second attack and was now destroyed. In addition, there appeared a hole near the lower part of the water supply pump to #2 engine room through which water immersed. After that *Musashi* was steered by only two shafts.[178]

---

[175] Identified identically in S-06-2.

[176] The investigation team of the US Naval Technical Mission to Japan assessed only the hit at F75, port, as certain and also dismissed Captain Katō's opinion that this torpedo hit in the same area as one torpedo in the third attack, which in turn had also not been assessed. The hits at about F40 and F60, port, and F80, starboard, were assessed as possible hits (the reason may have been the settling of the bow). That on F105, starboard, was also assessed as certain.

[177] This hit was assessed as certain.

[178] Assessed as a certain hit, but the foregoing one (second attack) was denied on the grounds that the chief engineer discovered no signs of damage inboard. The investigation party's criterion for assessment of a "certain hit" was the depth of the hit and the subsequent inboard flooding. Assuming that no torpedo was set shallower than about 1.20 m (like the submarine torpedo that struck *Yamato* in

One torpedo detonated near F165, port, and caused the immersion into the projectile magazine of #3 main gun. The ventilation duct was destroyed and the ammunition handlers stood in water up to their knees. The middle part of the left sidewall of #6 high-angle gun magazine was destroyed and water immersed into the magazine and its adjacent rooms. The port shaft room also began to leak.[179]

<u>The End</u>

Musashi listed about 10° to port after the fifth attack but her heel could be corrected to about 6° by counterflooding. The trim forward was alarming with the freeboard forward reduced to 2 m, from 6 m earlier,[180] and the bow continued to settle. Seawater swept over the bow onto the flying deck and speed slowed down to 6 knots, not sufficient for steering. Only the two starboard engine rooms and seven boiler rooms were still in operation.

December 1943) they concluded that "all hits other than duds should have caused some inboard flooding" (p. 21). The authors consider this criterion, particularly the conclusion, questionable and believe that the official report is more correct.

[179] Assessed as a possible hit in S-06-2.

[180] Her freeboard forward was 10 m and this means that her draught had increased by 8 m.

Photo 8-7: *Musashi* taking evasive actions on 24 October 1944 (Authors' collections)

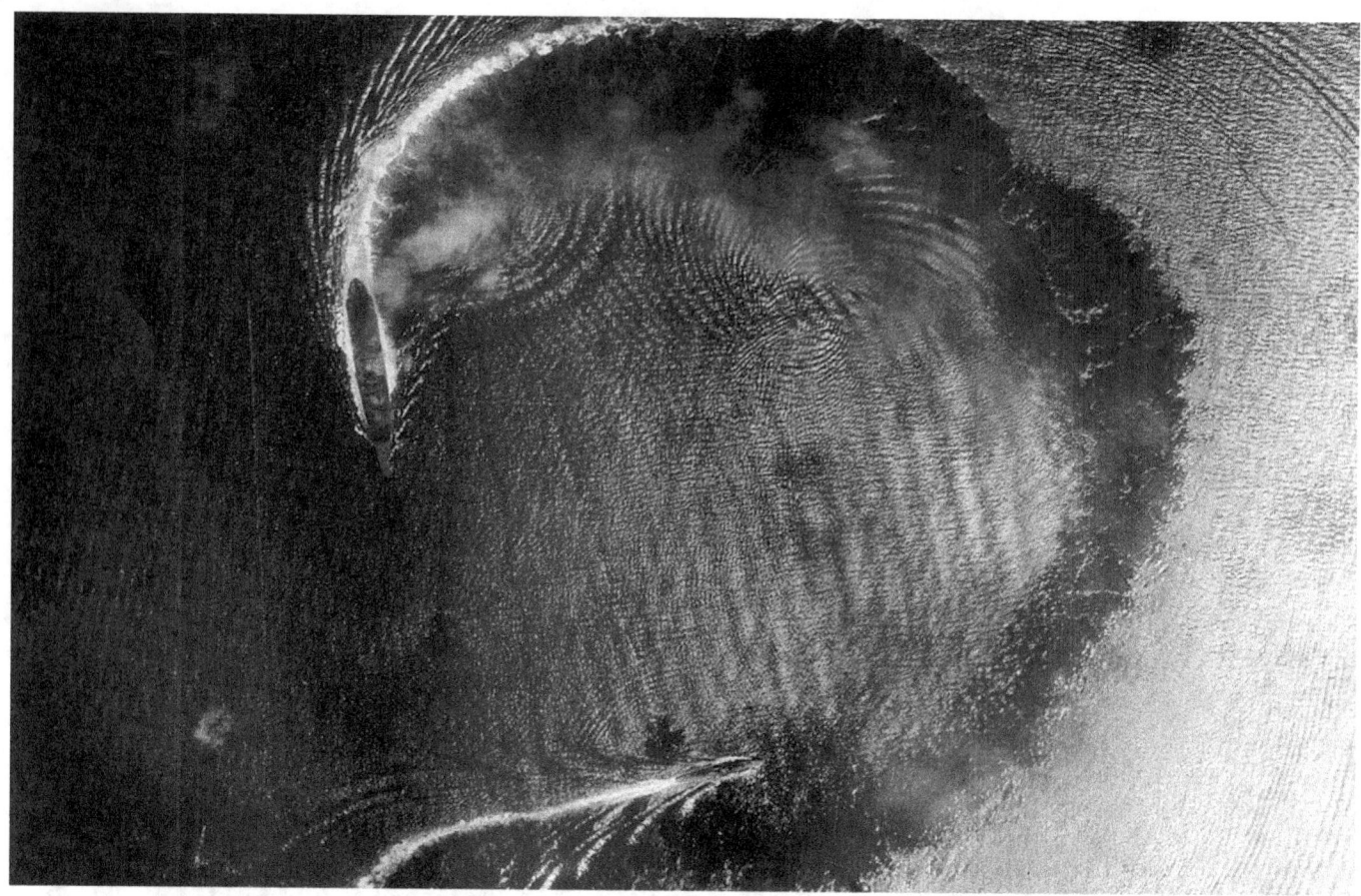

Photo 8-8: *Musashi* and the destroyer *Okinami* maneuvers heavily on 24 October 1944 (Authors' collections)

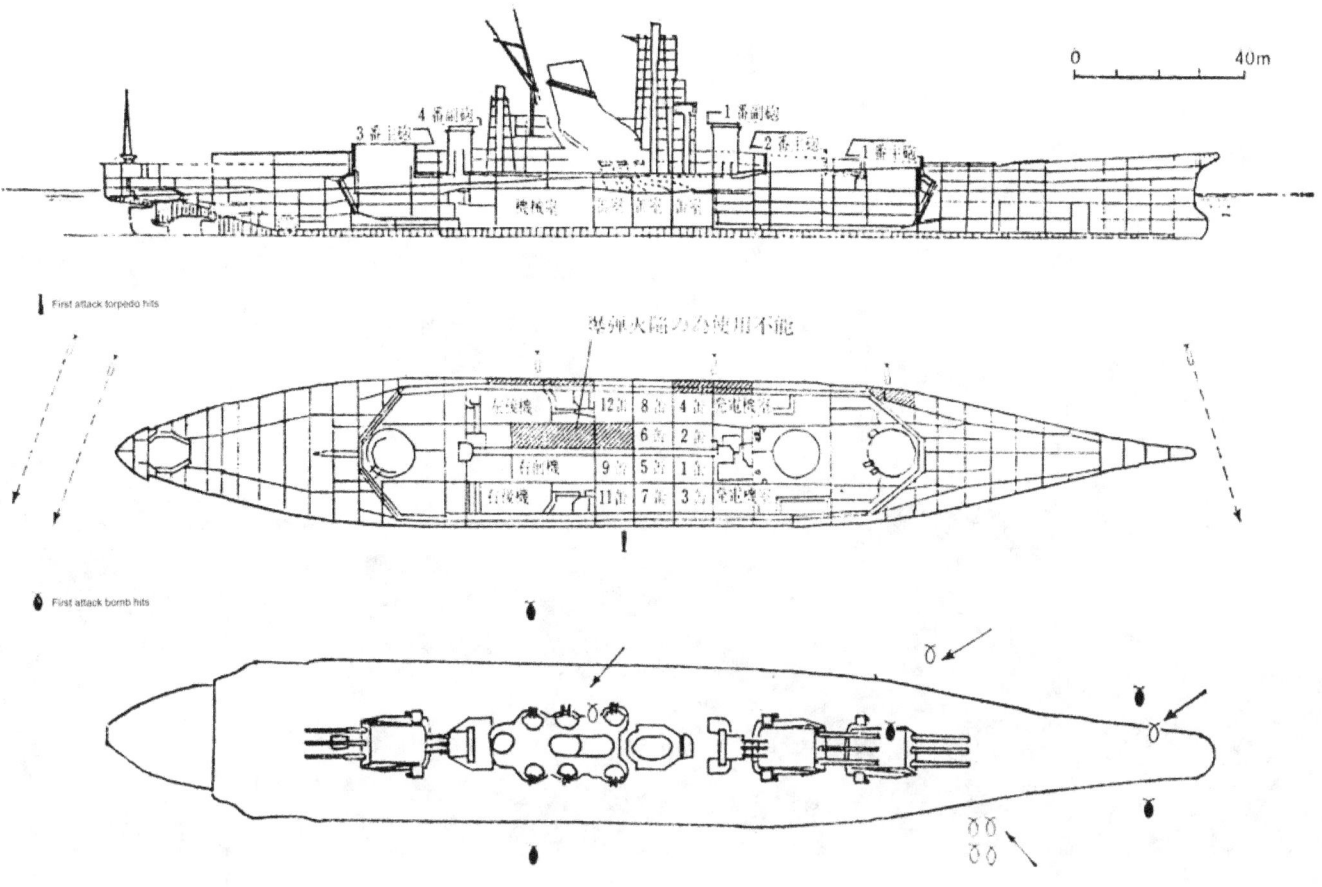

Figure 8-1: Hits on *Musashi* during the second air attack (Adapted from *Senshi Sōsho*)

Photo 8-9: *Musashi* and the destroyer *Kiyoshimo* in the Sibuyan Sea on 24 October 1944 (Authors' collections)

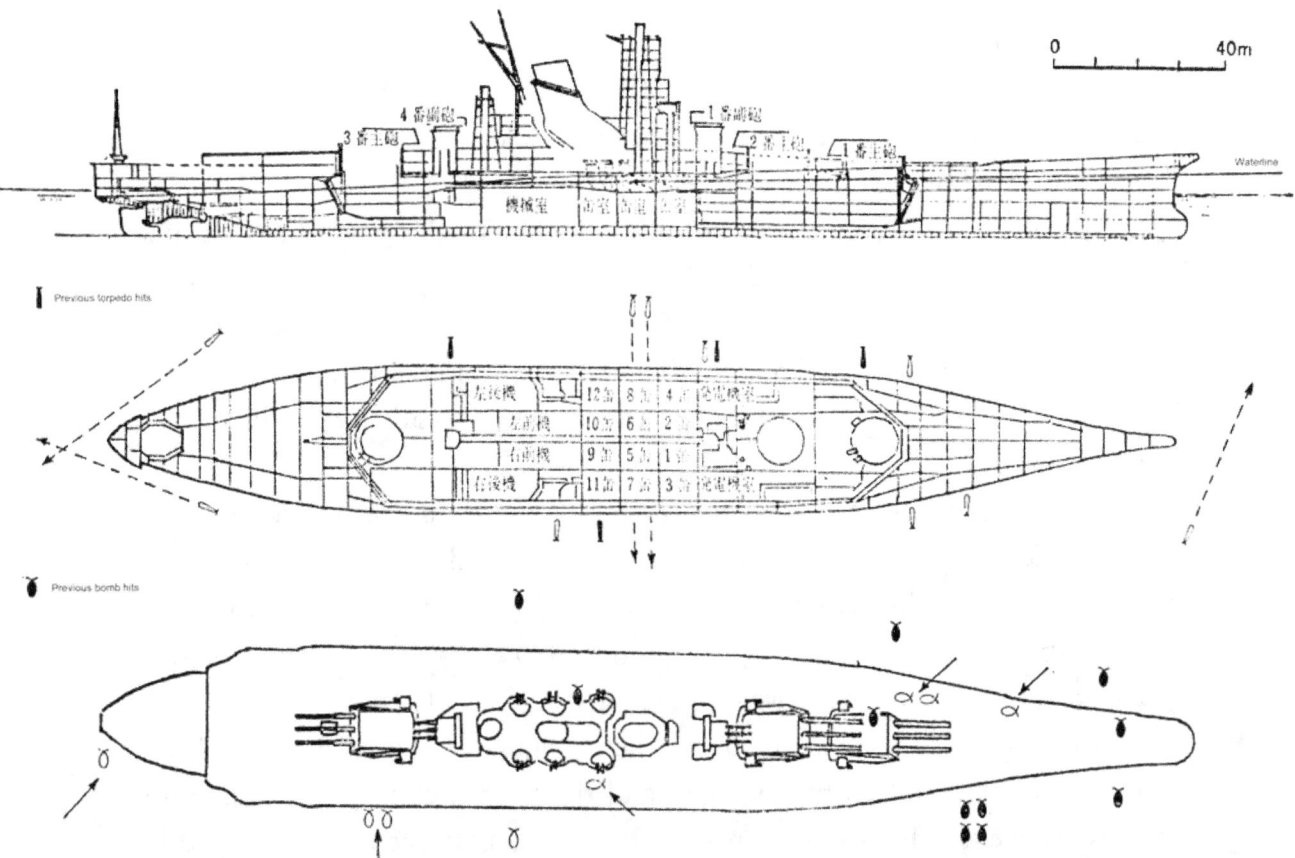

Figure 8-2: Hits on *Musashi* during the third air attack (Adapted from *Senshi Sōsho*)

In order to correct the continuously increasing trim and list, the flooding of large storerooms on the starboard quarter was ordered, but the attempt failed. While there are reports about technical shortcomings such as lack of pumps etc., Matsumoto, p. 319, points out that the damage control system lost its function and list began to again increase.

At 15:30 the 1st YB turned about and Vice-Admiral Ugaki noted (p. 490): "… we passed by our partner *Musashi*, whose miserable position was a sorrowful sight. All available compartments for pumping-in had been filled with water, and she listed about 10° to port. Though the Imperial crest was seen, her bow was already under, with the lowest part of the weather deck in front of the fore turret barely out of water …"

Recognising that the fatally damaged ship could not make it back to San Jose, he ordered to signal to *Musashi* his advise as division commander (he commanded Battleship Division 1) to ground the bow temporarily on a shoal of a nearby island to repair the damage (pp. 490–491). But *Musashi* could no longer make speed. Damage was investigated and an effort was made to prevent flooding. But list and trim by the bow gradually increased so much that heavy items were shifted to starboard and the port anchor was dropped into the sea. However, the listing increased further, so that even the starboard living compartments were flooded. In this way, every effort to balance the ship was in vain. On the other hand, preparations were made to tow her by destroyers at port stern in response to Vice-Admiral Ugaki's advice, but nothing materialised.

Meanwhile Vice-Admiral Kurita had received the strict order of the Combined Fleet to proceed ahead and the main force turned about and passed by *Musashi* for the second time. At 18:00 Vice-Admiral Ugaki, who noticed little change in her situation, asked her commanding officer if she could not move by herself. After about 15 minutes she gave the signal: "Only the starboard inboard shaft moves. Rudder steering is possible." It was the last communication with the commanding officer of *Musashi*. The main force with her sister *Yamato* and the heavy cruiser *Tone*,[181] which so far had escorted the damaged battleship, turned to east and headed for Leyte Gulf. Only the destroyer *Kiyoshimo* stood by.

---

[181] Her commanding officer recognised that he was unable to do anything about the *Musashi* and was ordered to return to the original group.

Photo 8-10: Vice-Admiral Ugaki Matome (1890–1945) (*Sekai no Kansen*)

Photo 8-11: *Musashi* photographed at approx. 18:00 on 24 October 1944 by Lieutenant Shiraishi Tōbei, torpedo officer of the destroyer *Isokaze* (Authors' collections)

The last minutes of the battleship *Musashi* are described in her battle report as unsuccessful measures to correct the progressing heel, further settling of the bow, preparation for her abandoning and sinking: "… List increased 10° to port and therefore #3, #7 and #11 boiler rooms were flooded, but it was not so effective. Then #3 engine room was also flooded. But the list increased to 12° to port [and continued] … After confirming the further settling of the bow,[182] the crew was ordered to prepare for abandoning ship … Flags were

---

[182] In S-06-2, p. 21, this is described: "The bow continued to settle, indicative of progressive flooding forward, despite damage control efforts to establish flooding boundaries. The list continued to increase slowly. By 1800 all power was lost, and by 1900 the situation was hopeless. Although list still was not more than 12° to 15° port, the flying (forecastle) deck forward was submerged back to No. 1 turret."

lowered … List came to about 30°[183] and all hands abandoned ship … list increased rapidly and she capsized[184] when two consecutive explosions took place. Sank 19:35."

The personnel losses amounted to 1,023 dead, including her commanding officer, Rear-Admiral Inoguchi Toshihira, and missing.

The battleship *Musashi* sank at 13°07'N/122°32'E at a water depth of about 800 m.[185]

Some Quotations from Rear-Admiral Inoguchi's Last Letter[186]

I can hardly find words to apologise for losing this ship, due to my unworthiness, a ship given great expectations not only by the navy but also by the whole nation. *Only a little consolation for me is to see that this ship absorbed most of the enemy attacks in this battle, and as a result little damage was inflicted upon the other ships.*[187]

Another thing for which I could not be excused in this battle was that the power of the antiaircraft firing was not fully displayed. *Every ship seemed to be poor* … It seemed that they fired excessively, thus inviting a disadvantage of losing targets. Also, cases of firing at long range and firing at running-away targets were many …

It was a tremendous blow that the main fire director of the main guns was put out of action at the beginning of the battle. That the *main director could easily be put out of order by a slight shock should receive attention in the future planning of structure.*

Enemy aerial torpedoes were not so powerful, but they released them at a point to make certain hits and yet at a high altitude … *Today's fatal damages were from torpedo hits* … Once the ship started turning it was, needless to say, difficult to control. Even so, we evaded at least five. Better to say that they were evaded unintentionally in the course of action.

I think machine guns must be more powerful. In spite of machine gun hits, enemy planes did not fall easily. *Some hits could not cripple planes.* The ene-

---

[183] In S-06-2, p. 21, this situation is described: "At about 1920 the list began increasing at an alarming rate. At 1930 it was greater than 30° and the rate was increasing. At 1935 a sharp lurch to port occurred and MUSASHI turned bottom-side up. She slid under, bow first."

[184] According to the already mentioned Hosoya Shirō, the list of *Musashi* stopped at about 45° for the time being and it took time until she rolled over. He ran to the bow and jumped into the sea. Soon the capsized ship raised her stern high and then quickly disappeared into sea. Two explosions took place, and the brilliant red light spread at the bottom.

[185] The destroyer *Kiyoshimo*, "the stand-by destroyer [that] signalled that *Musashi* suddenly heeled over and sank at 1937" (Ugaki, p. 491), reported 12°48'N/122°41.5'E and water depth about 1,350 m.

[186] Printed in Vice-Admiral Ugaki's diary (pp. 523–524), and (in abbreviated form) in *Build the Musashi!* by Yoshimura Akira, p. 175.

[187] Authors' italics.

my was very tenacious in his attacks. Under an unfavorable situation, not a few waited until the situation improved … When the ship was made unable to move, they seem to have made attacks in a steadier manner. I want to continue efforts until the last moment, but it seems to be hopeless at this moment …

Table 8-1: Summary of torpedo and bomb hits and bomb near misses

# of attack	Time	Torpedo hits Port	Starboard	Bomb hits Port	Starboard	Near misses Port	Starboard
1	10:29–10:40		1 × F130	F76 (roof # 1 main gun turret)		1 × F20 1 × F145	1 × F25 1 × F145
2	12:07–12:15	1 × F80 1 × F110 1 × F145		1 × F15 1 × F138		1 × F70	4 × F50–F60
3/1	13:31–		1 × F60				2 × F180 1 × stern
3/2	13:50	1 × F70	1 × F70 1 × F130 1 × F138	1 × F45 1 × F65 1 × F70	1 × F135	Unknown	Unknown
4	14:26–14:40	----	----	----	----	----	----
5	15:15–15:30	1 × F40 1 × F60 1 × F75 1 × F125 1 × F140* 1 × F145 1 × F165	1 × F80 1 × F105	1 × F62 1 × F105 1 × F115 1 × F120	1 × F68 1 × F75 2 × F115** 1 × F120 1 × F127	2 × F130–F140	4 × F130–F140
Total		11 (*13)	7	10	7	5	13
Grand total		18 (*20)		17		18	

Notes:

* Japanese reports calculate three hits of which two were duds. However, as pointed out in S-06-2, p. 20, "while identifying a dud torpedo hit in the midst of a heavy air attack offers grounds for speculations …" it must be acknowledged that these duds could hardly have any destructive effect and their counting appears very doubtful.

** One bomb hit the foremast (bridge).

Torpedo hits: A total of ten torpedoes were reported passing either the bow (2), or the stern (4), or below the bottom (4).

Table 8-2: Summary of the number of attackers, counted as shot down (uncertain), and ammunition consumed

Attack #	Time	# of attacking aircraft	# of aircraft shot down	Ammunition consumption		
				Main guns	Secondary guns	HAGs
1	10:29–10:40	17	3 (1)	----	48	160
2	12:07–12:15	16	7	9	17	217
3/1	13:31–	13	4 (1)	13	43	294
3/2	13:50	20	5 (3)	15	37	116
4	14:26–14:40	approx. 20	5	7	----	118
5	15:15–15:30	75	6 (10)	10	58	412
Total		approx. 161	30 (15)	54	203	1,317

Note:

A total of 125,000 25-mm bullets were consumed but the amount per attack is unknown. Note also the sudden increase of the ammunition consumption during the last attack. This indicates that the losses among the high-angle guns' handlers were much less than for the 25-mm machine-gun crews, for it is reported that one-third to one-half was killed or wounded after the third attack.

Table 8-3: Summary of the number of planes launched by the US aircraft carriers on 24 October 1944

#	Take-off	Attack	Hellcat	Helldiver	Avenger	Total	CV
1	approx. 09:10	approx. 10:26	21	12	12	45	*Intrepid, Cabot*
2	approx. 10:46	approx. 12:45	19	12	11	42	*Intrepid, Cabot*
3	approx. 10:50	approx. 13:30	16	20	32	68	*Essex, Lexington*
4	approx. 13:15	approx. 14:15	42	33	21	96	*Essex, Lexington, Intrepid, Cabot*
Total			98	77	76	251	

Notes:

(1) Time differences between Japanese and American data gradually become bigger. The number of the attacking planes registered as #5 attack in the Japanese records indicates #4 attack by the American counting, but time differs with about one hour.

(2) American losses were 18 planes shot down, ten planes were lost in reconnaissance flights, combat air patrols etc. and two more were lost operationally, making a total of 30.

(3) The battleship *Musashi* was sunk and the following ships were damaged: (1) The heavy cruiser *Myōkō* was torpedoed and returned to Brunei without escort, (2) the battleship *Yamato* was damaged by two bomb hits and one near miss, the battleship *Nagato* was damaged by two bomb hits, (3) the battleship *Haruna*, the light cruiser *Yahagi* and the destroyer *Kiyoshimo* were damaged by near misses.

Personnel Losses

Table 8-4: Officers (including warrant officers)

Rank	At sortie	Survived	Dead	Unknown
Officer	37	23	7	7
Reserve officer	9	5	2	2
Special duty officer	33	19	6	8
Warrant officer	33	26	1	6
Total	112	73	16	23
BB *Nagato* crew	1	1	0	0
CA *Maya* crew	approx. 40		2	1
CF command staff	3	3	0	0
Others	21		0	0

Table 8-5: Petty officers, sailors, hired men

Rank	At sortie	Survived	Dead	Unknown
Deck	1,634	908	173	553
Flier	2	1	1	0
Repair	19	14	2	3
Engine	458	288	25	145
Carpenter	69	33	15	21
Medical assistant	18	16	2	0
Accountant	79	38	14	27

Rank	At sortie	Survived	Dead	Unknown
Hired men	8	5	0	3
Total	2,287	1,303	232	752
BB *Nagato* crew	8	8	0	0
CA *Maya* crew	approx. 780		70	43
CF command	3	3	0	0

Note:

One part of *Musashi*'s crew left on board the destroyer *Shimakaze*.

Source: Senshi Sōsho.

Photo 8-12: Inoguchi Toshihira (1896–1944)—*Musashi*'s last commanding officer (Gakken)

Recognition of Defects and Proposed Countermeasures[188]

The loss of the battleship *Musashi* was fully investigated in order to work out countermeasures to improve her sister *Yamato*. The weak points of this class were recognised and Tech. Captain Makino Shigeru of the Fourth Division of the Navy Technical Department reported the results of a technical analysis to the Chief of the Shipbuilding Division of the Kure Navy Yard on 31 December 1944.[189]

To state some important items:

(1) Protection against projectiles was very good and was no theme until now. But the ships are not sufficiently protected against bombs and torpedoes. The parts not protected directly are voluminous and when several torpedoes detonated here the amount of immersed water became very big, resulting in a larger heel than expected.

(2) The capacity of the flooding and counterflooding system is insufficient to correct heel and trim. The damage by near misses caused more flooding to make the list more prominent. At the same time the flooding of the engine rooms and the boiler rooms did not work so well. The training in this case was not done. After the large list, the air release pipes of oil tanks and other parts sometimes caused flooding. Even protected parts received water beyond imagination. At the immersion G[190] comes down, GM[191] becomes bigger and this relation makes the regaining of balance more difficult.

(3) Four torpedo hits at one side means the immersion of about 10,000 tons of water, causing a list of about 18°. The calculated correction angle is 10°, but was actually only 6°. Namely, 60% of the calculated value was attained.[192]

(4) The backside of the upper armor moves by the pressure of the torpedo hit and the splinter bulkhead is easily broken.[193] Immersion at the lower

---

[188] *Kaigun Zōsen Gijutsu Gaiyō*, vol. 1, pp. 183–198; Matsumoto, pp. 319–325.

[189] The analysis covered all ship classes participating in the Philippine Sea battle and Tech. Lieutenant Fukui Shizuo, working in the same division, documented the content.

[190] Centre of gravity.

[191] Metacentric height.

[192] Note that the calculations of the damage control system stopped after three assumed hits on the same side.

[193] Already recognised when *Yamato* was hit by a torpedo in 1943.

armor did not stop at the bulkhead and reached boiler rooms and engine rooms. Therefore, the longitudinal bulkheads along the (armored) hull sides should be strengthened to the degree of the splinter bulkhead.

(5) The bulkhead inside the longitudinal one, along the hull sides, was considered to prevent water coming in but about 2,000 tons of water came in to cause a 4° list (vital part). The splinter bulkhead also permitted immersion of about 5,000 tons of water to cause about a 7° list.

The proposed countermeasures reveal these recognitions and can be divided into three sections, as follows:

Reinforcement of the Underwater Protection

- Fitting of two longitudinal bulkheads inside the hull over the whole length of the armored citadel, to prevent the immersion of water into the vital part. At the same time abolishment of the (useless) triangle shaped bulkhead fitted in *Yamato* after the torpedo hit in 1943. Of the newly fitted bulkheads, that next to the armor should have the reinforced splinter protection.[194]
- Reinforcement of the lower armor and prevention of delivering the shock generated by an underwater detonation to the inner longitudinal bulkhead by the movement of the armor.
- The watertightness of the manholes of the electric wires and the hydraulic pressure pipes passages was insufficient by using wing nuts. The nuts were loosened by the shock and they must be replaced by bolts etc.

Countermeasures to Limit Flooding

- The indirectly protected large compartments, particularly those forward and aft, outside the vital part should be subdivided more meticulously to reduce the range of flooding.
- The plate thicknesses should be increased at certain positions.

---

[194] *Yamato* had some improvements at the upper magazines after completion but not at the lower ones and *Musashi* had none at all. Besides of the upper magazines, Matsumoto also lists the black powder magazines, the wireless rooms and the cooler rooms as protected by "the splinter bulkhead between important parts and hull side armor."

- Double plates, like the double bottom, should be fitted at the sides of the indirectly protected parts to minimise flooding.
- The structure of the ladder trunks should be heightened and reinforced. Many trunks at the fore ends aft had the upper end at the middle deck, and when flooding reached this deck traffic to the lower compartments ended and flooding of the lower compartments was occurred through the openings. Therefore, the height should be increased to the upper deck in order to enable traffic and reduce flooding. The structure should also be reinforced because it was often broken by the shock with the subsequent loss of watertightness.
- The air release pipes of the fuel tanks and the damage control system broke rather often and it is likely that tanks flooded through them. Therefore the tops on the exposed deck should have a convenient splinter protection.
- The ventilation trunks above the honeycomb armor at the middle deck should have the splinter protection structure up to the upper deck.
- The ventilation system of the protective compartments should be made independent for each compartment in order to prevent the expansion of the flooding through ventilation trunks.
- The ventilation system should be revised both as for the type of ventilators and independence of the rooms. Ventilation ducts should also be reinforced, like traffic trunks, where necessary.
- The lower living compartments should be abolished.
- The size of the traffic trunks to small compartments should be reduced to that of manholes.
- Multi-porous ebonite and empty oil cans should be filled into empty compartments and the bulges in order to improve reserve buoyancy and maintain buoyancy.[195]

---

[195] In his *Kansen Nōto* Makino Shigeru mentions an episode that took place on 8 August 1940 when *Yamato* was launched. Among the top members of the fitting-out committee (the later crew) was also Commander Mayuzumi Haruo, "an outstanding gunnery authority" and future executive officer. Considering the extremely concentrated protection and the large unprotected (indirectly protected) parts forward and aft, he proposed to fill buoyancy material into empty watertight compartments to restrict immersion, and referred to the example of the target ship *Settsu*. But its realisation would require the addition of considerable weight and also man-days and it was rejected without much study. Makino remembers that the proposal was submitted to the "central organisation" (Navy Ministry) but it was

Expansion of the Damage Control System

As stated before, the calculation of the stability in riddled condition was 18°, and it was planned that the flooding of a total of 3,823 tons of water would correct a list of 13.8°. For a ship of the size of the *Yamato* class it was clearly insufficient. Therefore, a radical increase of this system was planned. The principal items were as follows:

- All compartments inside the bulges should be used for the correction of list.
- The compartments forward and aft below the hold deck should be fitted for the correction of trim.
- Fuel tanks located at the sides should be refitted to charging and discharging compartments, and so used if not filled with oil (correction of heeling).
- The shifting of fuel from forward to after tanks, and vice versa, should be expanded (trim correction).
- The damage control system in the boiler rooms and engine rooms should be radically improved.

Conclusion

As pointed out in Makino's report and recognised in the proposed countermeasures; the battleships of the *Yamato* class had some weak points. The connection of the upper and lower armor and the excessive collective protection, which was allotted to reduce weight, invited the cracking of bulkheads of the watertight compartments due to torpedo and bomb hits and brought about the expansion of the flooding. Therefore, one cannot but agree that the loss of *Musashi* could not be prevented, technically.

On the other hand it must be acknowledged that she received and also resisted for some time extreme damage, more than expected and more than she was designed for.

The direct protection of the vital part was almost complete, but unfortunately only "almost," and was only as strong as its weakest part. The design of the indirect protection was not made considering such air attacks and the cal-

---

not admitted. He refers to the problem of weight, which prevented even important bulkheads to be made stronger to prevent (or avoid expansion of) immersion (pp.170–173).

culation of the damage control system stopped after considering three torpedo hits at one side. Therefore, it was not suited to correct larger heeling angles than 18° in riddled condition to 4.2°, and the Achilles heel of this system was the correction of trim.

Matsumoto estimates the amount of the immersed water immediately after the fifth air attack as about 35,000 tons (p. 323). The reserve buoyancy in undamaged condition was calculated as 57,450 tons, so that even in this condition about 22,000 tons reserve buoyancy should have been left. Of course, superstructures were destroyed and water had immersed into a few parts of the vital part and rooms inside had been flooded, so actual buoyancy must have been much reduced. But even if the loss of buoyancy was beyond imagination, some reserve buoyancy must have been left when she came to the point of no return and sank. In other words, the stability of the *Yamato* class proved better than expected and the same can be said for the damage control system. But no unsinkable ship can be built and in view of her damage she was sure to sink.

The authors would like to finish this consideration with some citations from S-06-2 "Reports Of Damage To Japanese Warships-Article 2: Yamato (BB), Musashi (BB), Taiho (CV), Shinano (CV)":

(1) Under the circumstances, and considering that warship design as a science in the Japanese Navy dates back only to the last years of World War I, the boldness of the design of the YAMATO class is impressive.

(2) Damage control performance was reasonably good in MUSASHI's case.

(3) The 16 bomb hits ... none of which penetrated deeply, again demonstrate the fact that bombs, even in large numbers, can not do sinking damage unless they are capable of penetrating below the waterline in case of hits, or well below the surface in case of close near misses, prior to detonation.

(4) The absence of fire is noteworthy.

(5) She went down by the bow, capsizing when the forward flying (US forecastle) deck was submerged.

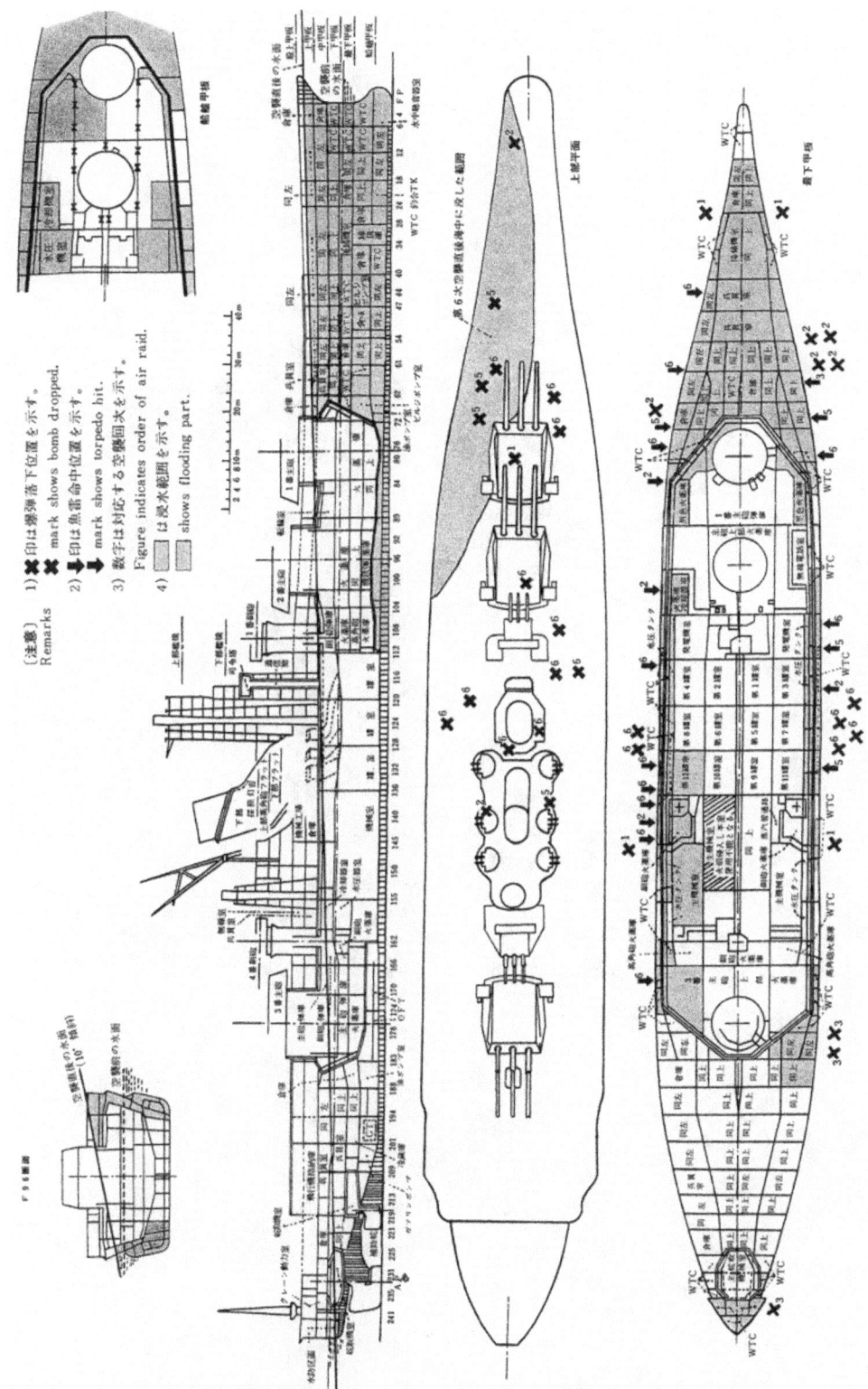

Figure 8-3: Damage to the *Musashi* (*Senkan* Yamato • Musashi *Sekkei to Kenzō*)

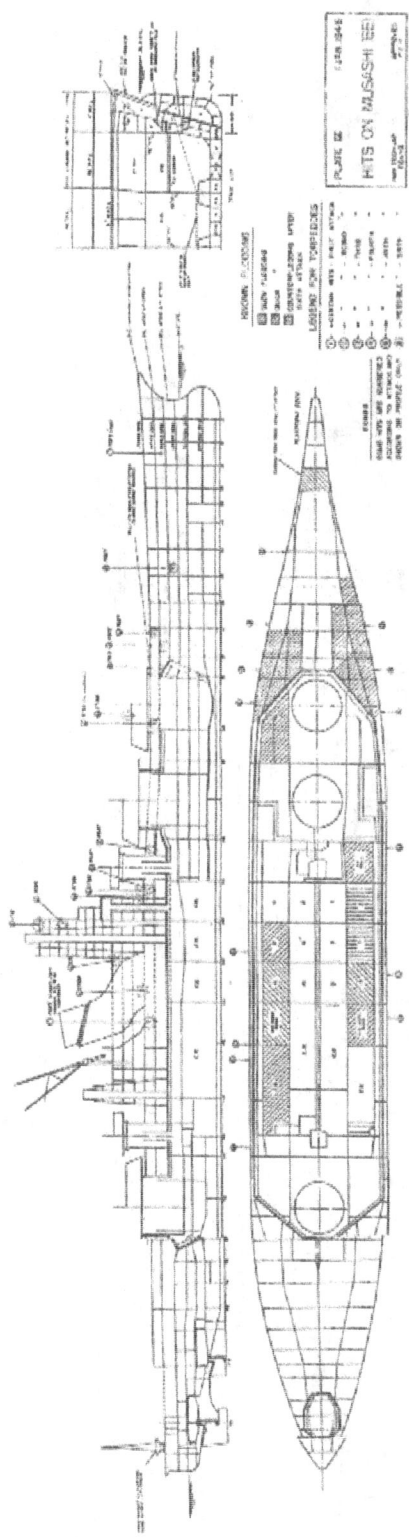

Figure 8-4: Hits on *Musashi* (US Naval Technical Mission to Japan, Report S-06-2)

CHAPTER 9–LOSS OF THE *YAMATO*

Introduction

In contrast to the loss of the battleship *Musashi* the loss of her sister *Yamato* was not investigated and the collection of the reports of survivors can be assumed to be incomplete. Recollections long years after the termination of the war have generally to be considered cautiously. It seems that uncertainties caused the author of the official war history to repeat the data given in *Yamato*'s detailed action report [one part summarised in source (8) below]. The authors have followed these data due to the lack of reliable data and in doing so may have repeated errors.[196]

To draw general conclusions, often with reference to the torpedo damage of both battleships before their loss, and the loss of *Musashi* can be recognised as a method applicable in view of the almost identical construction, provided that the differences with regard to the position of the hits and subsequent nature of the damages are sufficiently considered. In the end, however, the consideration is more or less estimation.

In the authors' opinion the last operation of the battleship *Yamato* cannot be reflected upon detached from the other ships united into the IJN's last organised surface warship special attack group, departing with the certainty not to return. Consequently, the following outline refers to the whole force. With regard to the arrangement the authors have followed the official history with some omissions and additions. Written permission to use all data and illustra-

---

[196] The principal sources were (1) *Senshi Sōsho*, vol. 17, *Okinawa Hōmen Kaigun Sakusen* (Naval Operations in the Okinawa Area), pp. 620–652 and enclosure 3; (2) Yoshida Mitsuru (translated by Richard H. Minear): *Requiem for Battleship Yamato*; (3) Matsumoto Kitarō: *Design and Construction of the Yamato and Musashi*; (4) Makino Shigeru & Fukui Shizuo (Ed.): *Kaigun Zōsen Gijutsu Gaiyō* (Outline of Naval Shipbuilding Technique), vol. I; (5) Samuel Eliot Morison: *History of United States Naval Operations in World War II*, vol. 14, *Victory in the Pacific 1945*, pp. 199–209; (6) Russell Spurr: *A Glorious Way To Die–The Kamikaze Mission of the Battleship Yamato, April 1945*; (7) Hara Tameichi: *Japanese Destroyer Captain*, pp. 271–304; (8) United States Strategic Bombing Survey (USSBS) (Pacific) Naval Analysis Division: *The Campaigns of the Pacific War*, pp. 324–338; (9) US Naval Technical Mission to Japan: Reports of Damage to Japanese Warships–Article 2 (S-06-2) *Yamato, Musashi, Taiho, Shinano*; (10) *Kaigun Hōjutsushi*.

tions was obtained from the Historical Branch of the Japanese Maritime Self Defense Force.

Summary

Defeated in Operation Victory 1 (*Shō Ichi Gō Sakusen*) the larger part of the 2nd Fleet returned to the homeland (Inland Sea). The 2nd Fleet had lost the principal power of the heavy cruisers and had also only three battleships, namely *Yamato*, *Nagato* and *Haruna*. This means that the 2nd Fleet could no longer be considered a balanced tactical unit and could not operate as such. The shortage of fuel caused a serious situation and hampered training and other movements. At the end of March 1945 only the battleship *Yamato*, the light cruiser *Yahagi* and nine destroyers were stationed at Hashirajima as the 2nd Fleet when the enemy attack of Okinawa was approaching.

After the completion of the occupation of Iwō-jima the Allied forces were en-route for the landing on Okinawa, a vital area in the concept of the *Ten* (Heaven) Operation Plan then in effect for Japan's inner defenses. Preceded by strikes of carrier-based aircraft on Kyūshū, Shikoku and Western Honshū on 18 and 19 March[197], then, from 23rd, directed against Okinawa and supported by surface bombardment etc., the amphibian assault on Okinawa began on 1 April.

Before that, the Combined Fleet, considering the last effective mission of the surface force, ordered (1) on 26 March in the afternoon the start of *Ten 1 Gō Sakusen*, (2) the advance of the *Yamato* force (*Yamato butai*) to Sasebo from the Inland Sea in order to lure the enemy Task Force in the vicinity of Okinawa into attack range of the Japanese land-based air force and provide the chance to attack them. However, this action became unnecessary by the attack of the US task force on 28 March and the advance was stopped.

At the day of the landing the US Army occupied the North and Central airfields so that the attack of the Japanese mainland by large bombers taking off from Okinawa could be expected in the near future. However, during the first five days the American invaders found both the defense by the defenders on Okinawa and the expected air counterattacks surprisingly light but on 6 April

---

[197] E.g. attack of the warships in Kure port. Almost all (of the few remaining) big units suffered damages of different degrees.

No. 1 *Kikusui* (Floating Chrysanthemum) Operation[198] was put in effect and "struck with a fury never before encountered."[199]

Fearing that the chance for the counterattack would pass forever, if the days passed without reaction, the Combined Fleet had on 5 April ordered an all-out attack of the air force for the next day. Because the Okinawa Operation was considered a decisive battle, the Combined Fleet decided the execution of a special attack operation utilising all available surface warships (*suijō-heiryoku*) and in the afternoon on 5 April ordered the composition of the Surface Special Attack Force, with the battleship *Yamato*, the light cruiser *Yahagi* and destroyer divisions 41, 17 and 21, a total of ten ships, and the execution of the Okinawa Assault Attack Operation. This was in conformity with the Total Attack Plan of the 32nd Army for the re-occupation of the North and Central airfields in co-operation with the air, sea and land forces on 7 April. The HQ of the 2nd Fleet had expected such a mission. However, the chance to survive the advance to the south, lasting one day and one night, was estimated to be very small.

In the evening of 5 April the cadets who had boarded *Yamato* and *Yahagi* three days earlier were ordered to disembark the ships. Fuel for a one-way mission should only be supplied but the logistics officer at the Tokuyama Fuel Depot did not obey his orders and fuelled them sufficiently for a return journey. But it was in vain and, as stated above, it was doubted from the beginning of the planning whether the force would actually have a chance to break through to Okinawa under the enemy air supremacy.

The US Naval Intelligence even knew the time the ships were to supply at Tokuyama, they also knew the time of departure and the track etc. for cryptologists read most of the Japanese radio traffic.[200] Before the 1st YB (*Dai Ichi Yūgekitai*) departed as the Special Attack Force, Vice-Admiral Marc A. Mitscher, commanding Task Force 58, had ordered its destruction through massive attacks of his carrier-based planes.

---

[198] A total of ten major organised *Kikusui* (*Kamikaze*) operations were executed between 6/7 April and 21/22 June 1945 with decreasing effect. All were part of the *Ten Gō Sakusen*.

[199] USSBS (Pacific) Naval Analysis Division: *The Campaigns of the Pacific War*, p. 325.

[200] See, e.g., John Prados *Combined Fleet Decoded*, p. 711, pointing out 5 and 6 April as "key dates for radio intelligence." On the same page a German naval attaché report, dated 29 March, is cited wherein the greatly divided opinion of naval officers on the success of such an operation is stated. With regard to the *Yamato* force the reading of pp. 706–715 is recommended.

American submarines were informed and waited for the force that departed Tokuyama at 15:20 on 6 April and had begun the advance southwards at 18:00. Two of them (*Hackleback* and *Threadfin*) located the ships with their radars while proceeding south through the Bungo Strait (first contact at 17:45) and reported positions etc. but they lost contact in the late evening.

In the morning on 7 April Zeros provided direct escort but they soon had to retire, to be included in the all-out attack on the US task force. Therefore, the *Yamato* force had to proceed south without air cover. Immediately after the Japanese fighters retired US reconnaissance planes watched and reported the force.

On that day contact had been regained. First at 08:22 by an *Essex* plane of an air search group at 31°22'N/129°14'E bearing 300°, speed 12 (actually 22) knots. From about 10:00 the force was shadowed by flying boats based at Kerama Rettō, occupied in preparation for the landing on Okinawa, for five hours. A plan was drawn up to receive the 1st YB by six US battleships, seven heavy cruisers and 21 destroyers in an area between the approaching Japanese and Okinawa, should they escape destruction by the air raids.

A total of 386 aircraft (180 fighters, 75 dive bombers and 131 torpedo bombers took-off in two waves from the US aircraft carriers.[201] 280 planes took-off at 10:00 as the first wave and attacked and sank first the destroyer *Asashimo*, that had fallen behind due to engine trouble. Then the planes concentrated on the battleship *Yamato* and the light cruiser *Yahagi* and by a series of co-ordinated attacks both ships were sunk; the battleship capsizing at 14:23 after ten torpedo and six bomb hits and sending up a fireball about 300 m and smoke more than 1,000 m after blowing-up by induced detonations. The smoke, signalling the death of the IJN's last hope, was observed by coast-watchers at Kyūshū.

Before that, the light cruiser *Yahagi* had gone down at 14:05, after seven torpedo and twelve bomb hits, and the destroyer *Hamakaze*'s hull had broken in two and sunk at 12:48, after one bomb and one torpedo hit.

Neither the main guns (firing Type 3 incendiary projectiles) nor the high-angle guns and AA machine-guns could effectively be used against the planes

---

[201] Actually three but the 53 planes which took-off from the aircraft carrier *Hancock* failed to find the enemy and are excluded here. The principal damages were attained by the first wave consisting of 280 planes, among them 98 torpedo bombers, for once again the torpedo proved its destructive power (see "Loss of the *Musashi*").

attacking between the clouds from near distances. The extraordinary meagre result of the AA defense was even below the very low expectations presented during a conference about this item after the air raid of the US task force on 19 March. Outdated fire control systems and ammunition (only time fuses; no proximity fuses) and insufficient power of the close-range AA machine-guns, besides of mechanical defects, hampered the efficiency of the Japanese AA defenses all through the Pacific War.

After strafing the swimming Japanese and killing hundreds the last American planes departed about 14:45 and the remaining three destroyers began to rescue survivors. The commanding officer of the 41 Destroyer Division took over command temporarily and reported the result, whereupon the halting of the operation and the return to Sasebo by the Combined Fleet was ordered at 16:39.

The destroyer *Kasumi* was sunk at 16:57, after the crew had been taken off, and the last ship lost of the 1st YB was the destroyer *Isokaze*, scuttled at 22:40 after personnel transfer. The AA destroyer *Fuyuzuki* and the destroyers *Hatsushimo* and *Yukikaze* entered Sasebo port in the morning of the next day, the AA destroyer *Suzutsuki*, lacking a portion of the forecastle and navigating stern first, arrived at 14:30 and entered #7 dry-dock to prevent sinking.

The destroyer *Hatsushimo* was the only undamaged ship and "lucky *Yukikaze*'s" damages were very small, but it may be considered a particular irony that *Hatsushimo* sank on 30 July by a mine at Maizuru port.

By the decision of Admiral Toyoda Soemu, then C-in-C of the (few remnants of the) Combined Fleet, 3,721 men,[202] one battleship, one light cruiser and four destroyers were sacrificed in the execution of a hopeless operation only because the surface forces should "save face" before the air and ground forces. His excuse after the war that the situation required this decision is not understandable even though very often used by politicians and military and other "leaders"–even today.

---

[202] Numbers differ according to source but the authors have taken the official ones as stated in *Senshi Sōsho*, vol. 17, p. 644.

Reorganization of the Combined Fleet after October 1944

After the catastrophic defeat in the Battles for the Leyte Gulf (Philippine Sea Battles) the surface forces of the Combined Fleet were reorganised on 15 November 1944. The Carrier Fleet (*Kidō Kantai*–Mobile Fleet) and the 3rd Fleet were abolished and the 1st Division (Battleship Division) was dissolved. The battleship *Yamato* became the flagship of the 2nd Fleet. She departed Brunei (Borneo) on 16th and entered Kure on 24th.

The 2nd Destroyer Squadron (*Dai Ni Suiraisentai*) remained in the Lingga area for training. The organisation of the 5th Fleet was changed on 5 February 1945 and the 2nd Destroyer Squadron was placed under the operational command of the C-in-C of the 10th Area Fleet. Five days later the organisation was revised again and the 2nd Destroyer Squadron again came under the operational command of the commanding officer of the 4th Carrier Division (*Dai Yon Kōkūsentai*) and was assigned to the Northern (*Kita*) Operation Group to participate in the Fast Homeland Circulating Operation (*Kinkyū Naichi Kansō Sakusen*), for the transport of vital raw and important war materials from the South to the homeland. At the same time these ships,[203] still in southern waters, was to remain in the Inland Sea and prepare for the homeland defense. The ships departed Lingga Roads on 6 February, were loaded at Singapore from 7th to 9th and departed Seletar on 10th. Despite two submarine attacks[204] on 13th they safely entered Kure on 20th. Here the 2nd Destroyer Squadron was again assigned to the 2nd Fleet and in company with this the flagship was changed from the destroyer *Kasumi* to the light cruiser *Yahagi*. After that the ships prepared for further operations and undertook individual training with either Kure or Hashirajima as bases.

The organisation of the 2nd Fleet on 1 March 1945 was as follows:

Second Fleet (C-in-C 2nd Fleet Vice-Admiral Itō Seiichi, who also directly commanded the 1st Carrier Division)

---

[203] The battleship-carriers *Ise* and *Hyūga*, the light cruiser *Ōyodo*, forming the 4th Carrier Division, and the destroyers *Kasumi*, *Asashimo* and *Hatsushimo* of the 2nd Destroyer Squadron.

[204] The Americans knew of the operation beforehand by deciphering most of the radio traffic. A total 25 US submarines were ordered to attack the force but only two of them managed to fire spreads of torpedoes, but all torpedoes missed.

- 1st Carrier Division (*Kōkūsentai*): Battleship *Yamato* (flag), aircraft carrier *Amagi*, aircraft carrier *Katsuragi*, aircraft carrier *Shinano*[205], auxiliary aircraft carrier *Junyō*
- 2nd Destroyer Squadron (*Suiraisentai*): Light cruiser *Yahagi* (flag)
    - 7th Destroyer Division: Destroyers *Hibiki*, *Kasumi*
    - 17th Destroyer Division: Destroyers *Isokaze*, *Yukikaze*, *Hamakaze*
    - 21st Destroyer Division: Destroyers *Asashimo*, *Hatsushimo*
    - 41st destroyer Division: Destroyers *Fuyuzuki*, *Suzutsuki* (Commanding officer Rear-Admiral Komura Keizō)

The Combined Fleet estimated on 17 March that the US forces intended to execute a new operation and had begun preparations for it. In order to prepare a counterattack the HQ of the Combined Fleet ordered the operational principles and details by issuing Dispatch Operation Order[206] #564A. The order for the Surface Force (*Kaijō-butai*) was as follows:

(1) No. 1 Assault Force [*Dai Ichi Yūgeki-butai*] should patrol intensively, stand-by in the Western Inland Sea, and prepare for departure after receiving the Special Order [*Tokurei*].
(2) If the air operation is advantageous, the No. 1 Assault Force should depart depending upon the Special Order and destroy the enemy Attack Force [*Kōryaku-butai*].

On 17 March the ships of the 7th, 17th and 41st Destroyer Divisions assembled at Kure, Otsushima etc. in expectation of the attack of the enemy task force. The 2nd Fleet, stationed at Hashirajima, was attacked by about 70 carrier-based aircraft (*kanjōki*) on 19th, which mainly concentrated upon the battleship *Yamato*. But both the damages and the battle results, i.e. planes shot down by high-angle guns and machine-guns, were small. An investigation conference was held afterwards and the participants concluded that no AA defense could

---

[205] Sunk on 29 November 1944. *Shinano* is stated on p. 621 of *Senshi Sōsho*, vol. 17. According to other sources the light carrier *Ryūhō* was also assigned to the 1st Carrier Division. According to *The Imperial Japanese Navy in World War II* (Japanese Monograph #116). p. 4, the 1st Carrier Division was established on 1 January 1945 and was deactivated on 20 April 1945. *Amagi*, *Junyō* and *Ryūhō* became 4th class reserve ships, *Katsuragi* and *Shinano* were assigned to the Combined Fleet, as was *Yamato*, also resting on the bottom of the sea like *Shinano* when this organisational reform was executed.

[206] Sometimes abbreviated DesOpOrd.

be expected from the destroyers, except the AA destroyers (*bōkū kuchikukan*) of the *Akizuki* class. Also, the use of Type 3 projectiles (a particular shrapnel shell which distributed hundreds of incendiary fragments from the point of explosion–funnel-shaped to forward) and the high-angle gunfire of the battleship *Yamato* did not bring about satisfactory results. Therefore, the defense of the surface force against future air attacks was considered very uncertain. The conference ended without finding any effective countermeasure except the conclusions that (1) a ring formation with a radius of 1,500 to 2,000 m was better suited for AA defense and (2) the ships should carry out still more intensive training in this respect.

Depending on these conclusions main emphasis of the training was put upon defense against air attacks. The night battle drill, radar-directed firing (*densoku shageki*), radar-directed torpedo launching (*densoku hassha*), utilisation of the "double-depth-torpedo" (*nijū shindo gyorai*)[207] and anti-submarine weapons measures, particularly the use of hydrophone and sonar, were considered important. But the fuel, allocated to the 2nd Fleet for training and the 'usual' (stand-by) time, permitted the battleship to navigate for only five days and nights and even only two days and nights for the destroyers, provided that the average speed did not exceed 12 knots. Therefore, training and drill were severely restricted and much existed only on paper. Also, most of the ships of the 2nd Destroyer Squadron required improvements, repair and maintenance of the hull, machinery and weapons, but the works were either not begun or stopped. All in all, it was a very dissatisfactory condition and it was hard to find a commanding officer that did not find fault with the condition of his ship or complement, or both.

Bait Operation of the No. 1 Assault Force

Nine days after the large air attack on the warships in the Kure area the HQ of the Combined Fleet ordered the activation of the "Heaven Operation" (*Ten Gō Sakusen hatsudō*) on 26th. The purpose of this operation was to lure the enemy task force, operating in the vicinity of Okinawa since several days, into the operational radius of the Japanese land-based aircraft, which were to inflict hard blows upon the enemy by destroying as many aircraft carriers as possible.

---

[207] A torpedo initially approaching at deep depth but taking a hitting depth in the vicinity of the target.

The HQ of the Combined Fleet considered the transfer of the No. 1 Assault Force (1st YB) to the south a sufficient bait to cause the US task force to advance and approach Kyūshū and ordered the 1st YB to navigate to Sasebo. The Combined Fleet Dispatch Operation Order #581 of 26 March said that the 1st YB (1st Carrier Division [only the battleship *Yamato*], 2nd Destroyer Squadron, 31st Division and 11th Destroyer Squadron [only the ships which could navigate at full power]) should finish the preparation for departure and take a stand-by position in the Western Inland Sea. Some hours later Combined Fleet DesOpOrd #583 of 26 March ordered the 1st YB to depart on 28th after 12:00, depending on the decision of the commanding officer, and advance to Sasebo via the Bungo Strait with the main body and via the Shimonoseki Strait with a branch force and stay there in stand-by condition.

Owing to these orders the 1st YB accelerated or stopped the previously mentioned works and quickly turned to the preparation for the sortie. On 28th the HQ of the Combined Fleet's DesOpOrd #589 decided the forces that had to proceed to Sasebo as the battleship *Yamato*, the 2nd Destroyer Squadron (one part lacking) and the 31st Division (one part lacking). On the same day, at 17:30, the C-in-C of the 2nd Fleet departed Kure with the battleship *Yamato*, the 2nd Destroyer Squadron (the light cruiser *Yahagi* and nine destroyers) and the 31st Division (three destroyers). But from about 17:00 US carrier-based aircraft attacked the southern part of Kyūshū and Amami-Ōshima. Therefore, the approach of the US task force to Kyūshū became obvious and it was no longer necessary to lure them into the action range of the Japanese planes stationed at the bases located in these areas. In this situation, the advance of the 1st YB to Sasebo was postponed by DesOpOrd #590 (Secret #281939) of the HQ of the Combined Fleet, received on 28th in the evening and Shubō-nada[208] was determined as the new stand-by position.[209] Thus, the force advanced to Kagoshima Bay and anchored off Kabutojima (in Hiroshima Bay) before continuing the navigation to Mitajiri on 29th at 03:30.

---

[208] More often written Suō-nada.

[209] Lieutenant-Commander Mikami Sakuo, then staff officer in the HQ of the Combined Fleet, remembered about the course of this operation after the war: "The HQ of the Combined Fleet assumed that the advance of the 1st YB to Sasebo would not only lure the US task force but make easier also an attack operation of the 1st YB to destroy the remnants of the task force should the air operation develop favourable for us. But the 1st YB did not simply agree with the intention of the HQ of the Combined Fleet because the Inland Sea was more advantageous than Sasebo for evasive manoeuvres in case of air and also submarine attacks. Therefore, the sortie was postponed until this date."

The use of the 1st YB as bait was agreed by the chief of the First Division (Operation) of the Naval General Staff but Vice-admiral Ugaki Matome, C-in-C of the 5th Air Fleet since 10 February 1945, noted in his "War Diary" (*Sensōroku*)[210] under the date of 27 March:

> ... Based upon a Combined Fleet order, the First Attack Force is going to leave the Inland Sea at noon tomorrow and head for Sasebo. Its object of stimulating the destruction of the enemy remnants can be somewhat appreciated, but its favourite trick of trying to lure the enemy task force out by sailing south off the east of Kyūshū so as to let the First Attack Force hit the enemy task force is laughable. I was already ordered at the Biak Operation to lure the enemy to the Palao area in order to provide a good opportunity for the success of the A Operation. Also, after the Seabattle of the Philippines the damaged fleet was to penetrate into the Sulu Sea in order to draw the attention of the enemy planes upon it and facilitate the execution of the Leyte Transport Operation. The former was not executed and the purpose of the latter was not attained. The enemy does not change his planning lightly. Furthermore, the superiority of the enemy is too big to be tempted or lured by the advance of the First Attack Force. When we thought they bit the bait, it was only a coincidence. The stand-by position of the First Attack Force in the Inland Sea is suited now as before particularly in view of the present lack of fuel...

At that time the Combined Fleet's estimate of the enemy situation was stated in the Combined Fleet Secret #301345 dated 30 March, 12:00, as follows:

(1) The main body of the enemy task force operates east of Kyūshū with the probable intention to totally destroy our defense forces together with the base air forces stationed in the Kyūshū and Shikoku areas.

(2) The main body of the enemy attack forces is standing-by in the SE sea area of Okinawa; the preparations for the landing operation are completed and it is very probable that the landing will begin within a few days.

Deliberations about the Operation of the Surface Force and the Course of the Special Attack

As stated before, the operation of the surface force of the Combined Fleet, the 1st YB, was earmarked to, at first, destroy the US task force, provided that the air operation developed favorably.

---

[210] An English translation of the first part can be found in *Fading Victory*, p. 563.

After that the Combined Fleet planned to use this force as a bait in order to lure the US task force, which had successively attacked and controlled the area of the Southwest Islands, into the operational range of the base air forces. The Combined Fleet considered Sasebo a suitable stand-by position and ordered the advance of the 1st YB to this naval port. According to the views of the Combined Fleet it was located nearer to Okinawa and had a higher safety coefficient against air attacks.[211] But this operation lost its *raison d'être* due to the active attacks of the enemy task force on bases in Kyūshū and elsewhere and was abandoned. In this situation the Okinawa Assault Operation (*Okinawa Totsunyū Sakusen*) was planned as the third operation.

The landing of the US forces on Okinawa began on 1 April and in the evening the airfield area had been occupied. In order to blockade the use of the airfields by US planes the Imperial General HQ and the Taiwan Area Army demanded the 32nd Army, in charge of the defense of Okinawa, to carry out a very strong and resolute counterattack. In order to assist and support the general attack of the 32nd Army, whose start had been set to 7 April, the C-in-C of the Combined Fleet, Admiral Toyoda Soemu, decided the execution of an air attack on 6 April and at the same time the composition of a Surface Special Attack Force (*Kaijō Tokkōtai*) by the 1st YB, which should assault Okinawa at dawn on 8 April to complete the annihilation of the US Attack Force.

About the Assault Operation (*Totsunyū Sakusen*) of the 1st YB (popularly known as the *Yamato* Force) contrary arguments and also strong critique existed, not only at the time of the decision but also after the termination of the war. In his "The Last of the Imperial Navy" (*Saigo no Teikoku Kaigun*) the former Admiral Toyoda states that at that time the Navy believed to be obliged to take every possible measure that offered the slightest chance of execution, because the fall of Okinawa was tantamount to the beginning of the decisive homeland battle. As a method to use effectively the then still available battleship *Yamato* the organisation of the Surface Special Attack Force was planned in order to carry out the assault operation to the landing area at Okinawa. One cruiser and eight destroyers should escort the battleship *Yamato*. Due to lack of fuel the last drop of heavy oil was pumped into the ship but if cruising at high speed the fuel would only be sufficient for a one-way journey. "Not to

---

[211] While the geographical situation was incontestable, the opinion of the 2nd Fleet was contrary in view of the air attacks as described above.

come back" was not said but they were to return only if the fuel permitted it. The fuel stored in Japan was insufficient to fuel the ships so completely that they could return. Admiral Toyoda points out that he estimated the success chance as less than 50 percent and believed a 50:50 exchange difficult to attain "but I never thought of an absolute zero chance even thought the success of this operation would be like a wonder." He justifies his decision with the explanation that the then very urgent situation did not permit to passively observe the annihilation of the air and ground forces while still operable forces were available and continues that the decision for this operation, which meant the sacrifice of many lives for a hopeless operation, was "painful but even if the chance of success is flimsy one is forced to take the chance and to do what one can do. Therefore, the execution of this operation was decided. The decision was very hard for me … There is no excuse for me except to state that I had to handle like that in that situation."

He explains that the main causes of the defeat in the war had been the lack of air forces and … the friction in the co-operation of the land-based air forces (*kichi kōkūbutai*) and the surface forces (*suijō-butai*) … and continues, referring again to the *Ten Gō* Operation, "that the reason why we were unable to carry out AA protection sufficiently was the too generous concentration of the air force upon the enemy task force, that is the tactical ideology about the common operation was underdeveloped and brought about a decisive weakness."[212] The next statement makes almost certain that the calculation of a flimsy chance based solely upon the principle "hope", for Admiral Toyoda explains: "But if the weather would be so bad as to prevent or remarkably restrict aircraft operations, the Special Attack Force … had passed through Ōsumi Strait and assaulted Okinawa after one day and night. However, the weather was not as bad as to hinder the operation of the aircraft. On the other hand, the war situation was so urgent that we could not argue if to wait for the worsening of the weather. Most of the officers held the opinion … [to sortie] as soon as possible …"

The chief of staff of the Combined Fleet, Vice-Admiral Kusaka Ryūnosuke, left the HQ of the Combined Fleet at Shikaya and went to the HQ of the 2nd

---

[212] One has to note that the Army and Navy air forces assigned to the defense of Okinawa were placed under the command of Admiral Toyoda as C-in-C of the Combined Fleet in order to increase the their effectiveness.

Fleet to explain the operation. He was accompanied by the staff officer Mikami Sakuo who after the termination of the war remembered this assault operation: "I believe that an assault operation bringing the main guns of battleships into action can be very effective if the time is suitable. Immediately after the defeat of the task force at the *A Gō* Operation [Battle for the Mariana Islands] it was proposed to order the battleship force to assault Saipan and to use them as grounded gun platforms for the attack of the enemy with the main guns and the support of the land battle forces. However, this risky operation was not executed ... "[213] He continues that after the beginning of the Okinawa Operation Captain Kami Shigenori of the staff of the Combined Fleet often demanded the operation of the battleships "but I persuaded him ... to wait for a better chance. When I was at Shikaya he called at me and reported about the decision ... of the C-in-C of the Combined Fleet of the assault operation of the battleship *Yamato* and demanded to be dispatched to the battleship *Yamato* in order to explain the operation ..."

Vice-Admiral Kusaka Ryūnosuke describes in his "Combined Fleet" (*Rengō Kantai*): "The operation method, operation time and stand-by position of the remaining force, namely the 2nd Fleet, was a big headache for us. One part [of the staff] ... argued to use the force as quickly as possible. However, I thought all the time that if this operation has to be executed eventually, it should not be absurd ... But the assault operation was decided when I was absent."

Rear-Admiral Tomioka Sadatoshi, then chief of the First Division of the Naval General Staff, explained about this operation by stating that the IJN was decidedly determined to use all available forces for the Okinawa Operation, considering it to be the last decisive battle. He continued that the naval air forces have been used as Special Attack Force so far, but the surface force still survives and pointed out that "Now, in the fight for life or death of the Imperial country the call became louder why this forces are not

---

[213] This idea was proposed to Rear-Admiral Nakazawa Tasuku, then chief of the Operation Bureau of the Naval General Staff, by Captain Kami, then working in the Education Department (*Kyōiku Kyoku*) of the Navy Ministry. He wanted to become the commanding officer of a battleship in order to participate in the operation. Nakazawa remembered in 1965 that he rejected Kami's proposal for the reason of almost insurmountable difficulties of the navigation and that even in case of the penetration to Saipan the machinery, hydraulic pressure, electric etc. of the battleship had to be fully operable in order to carry out the main gun bombardment.

brought into action ... When this draft was submitted to the Naval General Staff I opposed the explanation by stating that I do agree if *Yamato* is despatched to the S of Kyūshū in order to lure the enemy task force and hit them hard, but I do not agree if she is to make the assault attack to Okinawa. Especially, we do not have the necessary fuel. The decisive battle at the homeland is not desirable but if it cannot be avoided eventually we should have some fuel for the warships. However, without my knowledge, Vice-chief Ozawa[214] agreed to the proposal that the fuel should be sufficient only for one way."

The then Vice-chief of the Naval General Staff, Vice-Admiral Ozawa, declared his agreement to the one-way operation[215] when the planning of the Surface Attack Force was submitted from the Combined Fleet by stating that "if the C-in-C of the Combined Fleet believes in the necessity of the execution of this operation then that's all right. The chief of the Naval General Staff was also present and heard my answer. The execution of this operation was a matter of course in view of the general situation at that time and even from today's viewpoint. The biggest responsibility was in my hands ..."

The staff officer of the Combined Fleet, Commander Mikami Sakuo, who was then in charge of the operation of the Surface Special Attack Force, remembered after the war that the surface force could not become an unused giant. It had still to be a thorn in the flesh of the attacking and advancing US Navy so that the operation had to be absolutely useful. When Vice-Admiral Itō Seiichi became C-in-C of the 2nd Fleet I visited him and he told me at that opportunity: "The surface force may not be operated insignificantly and clumsily. It is an unbalanced fleet and at the operation planning deep considerations should be made how to bring the whole power into action. E.g. the underwater high-speed submarines will soon be completed and they should be used in company with the air force." Commander Mikami continued that he made deep deliberations about the operation after the talk with Vice-Admiral Itō and then referred to the unsuccessful operation course before the decision of the Special Attack Mission:

---

[214] Vice-Admiral Ozawa Jisaburō, long-time commanding officer of the Mobile Force.

[215] The statement that the battleship *Yamato* had fuel only sufficient for one way was repeated in Japanese and Western literature about the Pacific War for many years but, as will be explained later, the chief of the Tokuyama Fuel Depot supplied sufficient fuel for a return cruise–contrary to his orders.

The Combined Fleet had no chance because the enemy task force did not advance into the operational range of the land-based air force in the Kyūshū area. In order to lure it to an area S of Kyūshū and to use the surface force effectively, the advance to Sasebo was planned and it was believed that the sortie of this unit and the entering of Sasebo port would be sufficient to lure the enemy task force. Because Sasebo was located comparatively close to Okinawa the execution of the operation in that area was advantageous. In case of air attacks this place also offered topographical advantages because high mountains surround it. We conferred with the HQ of the 2nd Fleet with these facts in mind. But the HQ did not agree at once and referred to avoiding the air attack, potential danger by enemy submarines at the time of departure from Sasebo port, mine danger in the shallow East China Sea. The HQ maintained that the force could also operate advantageously from the position in the Inland Sea. In this way the advance to Sasebo was delayed until it was too late ... However, until 5 April the organisation of the Surface Special Attack Force was almost no theme. When I was at Shikaya together with the chief of staff Kusaka I was surprised to hear about the Surface Special Attack Force by telephone from Hiyoshi[216] ... In response to his wish I accompanied chief of staff Kusaka to the 2nd Fleet in order to explain the operation. But the C-in-C Itō was not convinced after the explanation.[217] Of course, such a daring planning, which could not be called an operation, cannot be agreed upon. Finally, it was explained that it should be only the beginning of the total special attack of one hundred millions people and after that the HQ of the 2nd Fleet agreed, 'Well, in that case we do agree!' I proposed to stay aboard *Yamato* in order to participate in the operation because I would no longer be needed if the 1st YB would be sent as Special Attack Force. But it was rejected by the senior staff of the 2nd Fleet, Yamamoto,[218] stating: 'Even without you we should execute this operation well'. Therefore, I departed the ship ...

The previously mentioned staff officer Captain Kami Shigenori proposed to the vice-chief of the staff of the Combined Fleet, Captain Takada Toshitane, to be moved to the staff of the 2nd Fleet in order to participate in the operation, but he was persuaded by the latter and had to give in.[219].

In the end, the exact course until the decision to use the 1st YB as Special Attack Force cannot be reconstructed but by the statement of the former C-in-C of the Combined Fleet Toyoda in his "The Last of the Imperial Navy" as

---

[216] Combined Fleet headquarters. Hiyoshi is located halfway between Tōkyō and Yokohama.
[217] For Vice-Admiral Itō's 'resistance' see also Yoshida, op. cit., pp. 12–13, 36–38.
[218] Rear-Admiral Yamamoto Yūji.
[219] Takada remembered that when an aircraft with Kami aboard made a crash landing in Tsugaru Strait after the war Kami did not make any effort to rescue himself.

well as his special message on the occasion of the sortie of the Special Attack Force[220] it becomes almost exact. This may probably be understood that Admiral Toyoda decided the Special Attack solely by himself without being influenced from outside.[221]

Preparation of the Surface Special Attack Force

On 5 April, in the afternoon, the 1st YB received the Combined Fleet DesOpOrd #603 (Secret #051359) by which the preparation for the operation as Surface Special Attack Force was ordered:

> The 1st YB [*Yamato*, the 2nd Desron (*Yahagi* and six destroyers)] should as Surface Special Attack Force penetrate into the Okinawa anchorages and carry out a special attack upon targets at dawn of 8 April. The preparations for the sortie should be finished quickly.

Successively the C-in-C of Kure Naval Station (Kure *Chinjufu*) was ordered to guard the Special Attack Force by sweeping the not yet swept operational area of the 1st YB (Western part of the Inland Sea and Bungo Strait) with assigned warships and aircraft until the evening of 6 April, and the execution of anti-submarine warfare (ASW) in the Bungo Strait. In company with this Vice-Admiral Itō Seiichi, the C-in-C of the 1st YB, was ordered to also compose a sweeping force consisting of four destroyers of the 31st Division, which was to guard the Surface Special Attack Force against submarines and air attacks to the sea area S of Kyūshū. The C-in-C of the General Escort Force (*Kaigun Goei Sōtai Chōkan*) was ordered to reconnoitre the sea area SE of Kyūshū with assigned planes and execute "guarding against submarines," that is ASW. The HQ of the Combined Fleet issued all orders.

About one hour after the order of the preparation for the sortie the 1st YB received the Combined Fleet DesOpOrd #611 (Secret #051500), which read:

---

[220] "... a Special Attack Force was composed on purpose and the assault operation of unrivalled bravery ordered so that the power of the Imperial Navy was concentrated upon this one action in order that the brilliant tradition of the Imperial Navy's Surface Force may be exalted and our glory handed down to posterity ... thereby establishing firmly an eternal basis for the empire ..."

[221] An often repeated version which identifies the chief of the Naval General Staff, Admiral Oikawa Koshirō, as the true responsible person is stated in Ugaki Matome's *Fading Victory*, p. 575. See also Spurr, p. 87, with other wording.

(1) The Imperial Navy Force [*Teikoku Kaigun Butai*] and the Sixth Area Army [*Roku Kō Gun*] should attack with all power and annihilate the warships in the vicinity of Okinawa after X day [after 6 April].

(2) The Army the 8th Air Division [*Rikugun Dai Hachi Hikō Shidan*] should co-operate and attack. The 32nd Army should begin the general attack on 7th with the intention to annihilate the enemy land forces.

(3) The Surface Special Attack Force should depart Bungo Strait at dawn of Y-1 day and penetrate into the sea W of Okinawa at dawn of Y day and attack and annihilate the enemy surface warships and transport group. Y day will be 8 April.

After receiving this order the 1st YB reported the opinion about the composition of the forces, time of departure and route whereupon the HQ of the Combined Fleet corrected one part of the previous order and issued the following DesOpOrd #611 (Secret #060751) on 6 April:

(1) The forces of the 1st YB as decided in DesOpOrd #603 are changed and the force should be composed of *Yamato* and the 2nd Destroyer Squadron [*Yahagi* and eight destroyers].

(2) The departure of the Surface Special Attack Force should be decided by the commanding officer of the 1st YB.

In response to this order the Surface Special Attack Force for the assault attack was composed as follows:[222]

Second Fleet, C-in-C Vice-Admiral Itō Seiichi**

Fleet flagship battleship *Yamato***, CO*[223] Captain Aruga Kōsaku** (under direct command of Vice-Admiral Itō Seiichi**)

Second Destroyer Flotilla (2 dg), CO Rear-Admiral Komura Keizō (all ships of 2 dg under his command)
    Flagship light cruiser *Yahagi***, CO Captain Hara Tameichi

---

[222] *Senshi Sōsho*, vol. 17, p. 628, Hara Tameichi *Japanese Destroyer Captain*, p. 274, and Sakamoto Seiki & Fukukawa Hideki *Nihon Kaigun Hensei Jiten* ("Japanese Navy Organization Dictionary"), pp. 533–534.

[223] * = Commanding officer.

17th Destroyer Division, CO Captain Shintani Kiichi
>Destroyer *Isokaze*** (flag), CO Commander Maeda Saneo
>Destroyer *Hamakaze***, CO Commander Maekawa Kazue
>Destroyer *Yukikaze*, CO Commander Terauchi Masamichi

21st Destroyer Division, CO Captain Kotaki Hisao**[224]
>Destroyer *Asashimo*** (flag), CO Commander Sugihara Yoshirō**
>Destroyer *Kasumi***, CO Lieutenant-Commander Matsumoto Shōhei
>Destroyer *Hatsushimo*, CO Lieutenant-Commander Sakawa Masazō

41st Destroyer Division, CO Captain Yoshida Masayoshi
>AA destroyer *Fuyuzuki* (flag), CO Commander Yamana Hirō
>AA destroyer *Suzutsuki*, CO Commander Hirayama Toshio

On 5 April, from 16:47 till 21:10, Vice-Admiral Itō ordered the ships by signal to successively supply fuel and load or re-store torpedoes and ammunition. Fresh water and provisions were also to be supplemented, if necessary.[225] This work lasted the whole night.

When the ships departed the fuel storage was as follows: Battleship *Yamato* 4,000 tons[226] (full load was 6,300 tons); light cruiser *Yahagi* 1,250 tons; AA destroyers *Fuyuzuki* and *Suzutsuki* each 900 tons; destroyers *Isokaze*, *Hamakaze*

---

[224] ** = Sunk or killed in action (KIA).

[225] In Hara, op. cit., p. 280–281, is said that all nonessential supplies were off-loaded from the light cruiser *Yahagi* and this is also true for all other ships.

[226] In April 1945, immediately after the staff of the General Escort Command (*Kaiyō Goei Sōtai*) had obtained 7,000 tons of fuel oil for one-month operations of the ASW forces, the staff of the Combined Fleet informed that 4,000 tons were needed for the Surface Suicide Attack Force (*Suijō Tokkōbutai*) "in order that the brilliant tradition of the Imperial Navy's surface forces may be exalted and our glory handed down to prosperity …" In a fine contribution titled "Strategy of the Imperial Japanese Navy in the Shōwa Era" (*Nihon Kaigun no Senryaku-shisō o Toi to*) and published in *Sekai no Kansen* 8/2005, pp. 84–89, Sakonjo Naotoshi criticises "The Surface Special Attack Force whose annihilation was certain was still more important than the urgent necessary material transport to Japan." He continues his critique with the IJN's adherence to the pre-war strategic conception (gradual reduction operation, quick showdown, obsession to attack enemy large warships and to neglect ASW and merchant warfare) by reference to Vice-Admiral Mikawa's force in the First Solomon Seabattle (7–8 August 1942), Vice-Admiral Kurita's force at Leyte (23–26 October 1944) etc. and points out grave strategical errors.

and *Asashimo* each 599 tons; destroyer *Yukikaze* 588 tons; destroyer *Kasumi* 540 tons; destroyer *Hatsushimo* 500 tons.

In addition, *Fuyuzuki* and *Suzutsuki* received two torpedoes each from their sister *Hanazuki* and ammunition was re-stored to the battleship *Yamato* from the 31st Division, which also transferred AA ammunition to the 2nd Destroyer Squadron.

While these works were in progress, the 2nd Destroyer Squadron held an operation conference aboard the light cruiser *Yahagi* from 20:00 onwards.[227]

On 6 April at 06:00 the major part of the 1st YB anchored outside Tokuyama port. As the day before nonessential items and secret documents were landed and the ensign candidates, who had boarded the ships on 2 April for practical exercises, were ordered to disembark, an order most of them obeyed reluctantly after their common request to stay aboard had been rejected in unison.[228]

Before that, at 13:00, an operation conference with officers from the commanding officers of the destroyers and upwards was held aboard the battleship *Yamato*. After an address by the chief of staff of the 2nd Fleet, the chief of staff of the Combined Fleet explained the operation followed by a directive

---

[227] This is the official version but according to Hara, op. cit., p. 280, it was a farewell party.

[228] In *Senshi Sōsho*, vol. 17 pp. 629–631 the reasons are explained very detailed and further data may be found in Hara, op. cit., pp. 278–279. In short: 77 cadets graduated from the Naval College (74th class) on 30 March and boarded the battleship *Yamato* (49) and the light cruiser *Yahagi* (28), anchored off Mitajiri, on 2 April and were introduced into the routines aboard by graduates of the 73rd and 72nd classes. The departure of the *Yamato* Special Attack Force became certain on 5 April and the preparation of the departure began immediately after 15:00 by the order of Vice-Admiral Itō. The destroyers *Asashimo* and *Hanazuki* came alongside the battleship *Yamato* and started the fuel transfer. The cadets observed the procedure by order but at 17:30 they were ordered to prepare for disembarking. Appeals to stay aboard and participate in the mission were rejected on the grounds that they did not even know the ship, were useless during the certain death mission but were useful for the country, if alive. The proposal for disembarking to Vice-Admiral Itō was made by Captain Aruga and the chief of staff of the 2nd Fleet, Rear-Admiral Morishita Nobuei, and Itō agreed. At the same time he ordered them to board other ships of the 2nd Fleet such as the aircraft carriers *Amagi* and *Katsuragi* on 6 April. Then, on 10 and 12 April the move to other ships was officially ordered. In this way, 49 cadets of *Yamato* and 28 of *Yahagi* were saved and 'contributed to the rise of Japan after the unconditional surrender'. In company with the cadets more than ten seriously ill men (unable for service) and also more than ten "replacement sailors" from Kure disembarked. For *Yahagi* see Hara, op. cit., p. 279 where only 22 cadets are mentioned, but the authors have used the official figures in *Senshi Sōsho*, vol. 17, p. 631.

from the C-in-C of the 2nd Fleet and ending with a toast (*kanpai*).[229] After the war Rear-Admiral Komura remembered:

... The chief of staff Combined Fleet [Vice-Admiral Kusaka Ryūnosuke] visited the battleship *Yamato* and there were conferences of the commanding officers repeatedly. We believed to confer about the operation, deliberated and discussed our opinions but [from the conference with Vice-Admiral Kusaka] we returned without expressing our opinion because it was a Special Attack Mission (*Tokkō*). Vice-Admiral Kusaka pointed out the wish of the Combined Fleet to offer the 1st YB a way to die gloriously "heralding the deaths of one hundred billions Japanese who prefer death to surrender"[230] and I have a strong recollection of this explanation. Afterwards, the feeling was a 'precursor of one hundred billions of total special attacks' explains everything; there is no room for opposition or diverging opinions. Today one may think how the war condition will be after the one hundred thousand total special attacks. Theoretically this imagination is curious but not at that time [nobody did think about consequences] and it was accepted unanimously [without opposition] ...

Estimation of the Enemy and Own Situation at the Time of the Departure

At that time the 1st YB estimated the enemy situation and the own forces in the Detailed Battle Report (*Kaijō Tokkōtai Sentō Shōhō*) as follows:

1) The enemy forces at Okinawa and vicinity
    a) The forces of the landed army
       On 4th, 09:00, North, centre of airfield, front-line reinforced by three divisions. According to the information of the army about 300

---

[229] Excerpts of the informal briefing and the serious critique immediately before this conference may be found in Hara, op. cit., pp. 275–278. Note also the remarks to Captain (Rear-Admiral) Morishita Nobuei, former commanding officer of the battleship *Yamato*. The formal briefing aboard the battleship *Yamato* is not described but Hara ends (p. 278) with Vice-Admiral Itō's remark that "in view of the extraordinary nature of this mission commanding officers will remove from their ships all cadets, the sick ... and others who are considered unfit ..."

[230] In other words: Japan's whole population was to be transformed into special attack warriors and 100,000,000 Japanese should die as heroes by the execution of the "total special attack" taking the 1st YB as a model. Yoshida, op. cit., p 38, states that Vice-Admiral Itō, who "expressed vigorous opposition to the concept of Operation *Ten'ichigō*" (p. 12) because of (1) lack of air power, (2) inferior power, (3) time of the sortie (p. 13) "was won over at last only after receiving the final word—"you are being requested to die gloriously, heralding ...". This is in conformity with Rear-Admiral Komura's statement. See also Hara, op. cit., pp. 275–278.

men landed on Keiseshima on 5ᵗʰ and are installing a heavy gun.[231] Another heavy gun exists on Kamiyama Isl.

    b) Enemy surface forces

        On 6ᵗʰ 09:00–12:00 off Kadena: one to three battleship, seven to twelve cruisers, five to seven destroyers, 130 transports. At the same time off Naha: one battleship, zero to five cruisers, three to four destroyers.

        On 5ᵗʰ, afternoon, near Nakagusuku Bay: one battleship, four cruisers, 33 destroyers. On 3ʳᵈ 12:00 till 4ᵗʰ in the morning at Kerama Island chain: two aircraft carriers, one battleship, 30 cruisers or destroyers.

        On 6ᵗʰ the following ships were moving: one aircraft carrier, three auxiliary aircraft carriers, six battleships, six cruisers, 12 destroyers, 51 transports.

    c) The airfield was occupied; one part of the aircraft takeoff and are landing, but the field is not fully operable.

2) Movement of enemy task force
    a) Two to three groups operate in the vicinity of Okinawa main island.
    b) One to two groups operate in the area 100 nm S of Kyūshū (counterattack against our planes taking-off from the Kyūshū area for attack).
    c) One group operates E or SE of Ishigakijima (Suppression of our forces on Taiwan, Ishigakijima, Miyakojima).

3) Our forces at Okinawa are concentrated in the South in order to carry out the general attack on 8ᵗʰ in response to the 1 *Kikusui* Operation and the 1ˢᵗ YB Assault Operation.

4) Our land-based air force

    Ten Gō Operation was activated with the 5ᵗʰ Air Fleet under the command of the C-in-C of the Combined Fleet as main force and all operable forces of the 3ʳᵈ Air Fleet and 10ᵗʰ Air Fleet should be concentrated in the southern part of Kyūshū.

    The air forces under the command of the General Escort Command should be concentrated in the western and southern parts of Kyūshū.

    The 6ᵗʰ Air Fleet should be dispatched to the SW part of Kyūshū and the SW islands.

    Also, one air flotilla (reinforced by one part of the 13ᵗʰ Air Fleet) should be dispatched to Taiwan.

    Should the enemy forces attack the SW Islands again on 6 April the complete annihilation of the enemy is expected by the *Kikusui* Operation.

    The co-operation of the 8ᵗʰ Army Air Division is intended.

---

[231] According to Spurr, op. cit., p. 52, it was a 155-mm gun.

5) The C-in-C of the Combined Fleet should advance to the 2nd Operations Centre (Shikaya) on 6th at 16:30 and take over the general command of this operation.

The Operations Plan of the 1st YB

Basing upon the respective orders of the Combined Fleet and the own estimate of the situation the staff of the 1st YB worked out the following operation plan (1st YB #3):

In accordance with DesOpOrd #607 the 1st YB should penetrate into the western sea area of Okinawa at dawn of Y day (8 April) in order to attack and annihilate the enemy surface warships and transport groups in company with the air forces and the forces stationed in the Okinawa area.

The operational procedure, except the following one, follows the details of the No. 1 Heaven Operation (*Ten Ichi Gō Sakusen*) of the 1st YB.

Table 9-1: #1 Composition of the 1st YB

All forces operated under the command of the C-in-C 2nd Fleet.

Force	CO	Forces	Main Task
Main Body	C-in-C 2nd Fleet	Yamato	Annihilation of the enemy surface warships and transports
Guard Unit	CO 2nd Destroyer Squadron	2nd Destroyer Squadron (*Yahagi*, 8 destroyers)	
Sweeping Unit	CO 31st Division	31st Division (3 destroyers)	ASW and AA defense

Note: This composition should be maintained until an official order is given

Table 9-2: #2 Composition of the 1st YB

All forces operated under the command of the C-in-C 2nd Fleet.

Force	CO	Forces	Main Task
1st Force (1 Ng)	C-in-C 2nd Fleet	Yamato, 41st Destroyer Division	Annihilation of the enemy surface warships and transports
2nd Force (2 Ng)	CO 2nd Destroyer Squadron	2nd Destroyer Squadron (41st Destroyer Division lacking)	

Note: This composition should be taken if the day or night battle with the enemy surface forces is considered a principal attack method

2) Essentials to the Advance and Approach of the Enemy
 a) The 1st YB should sortie Bungo Suidō (Strait) on Y-2 day 18:00, pass through Ōsumi Kaikyō [Van Diemen Strait] during the night of Y-2 day and advance westwards of the SW islands and penetrate into the western sea area

of Okinawa on Y day 04:00. After passing through Ōsumi Kaikyō the Sweeping Unit (*Zenro Sōtōtai*) should separate depending on the order and return to the western part of the Inland Sea.

b) Until passing through Ōsumi Kaikyō the area should mainly be guarded against submarines, after that strict guarding against submarines and aircraft should be made.

c) Reconnaissance seaplanes (*Suijō teisatsuki*) The HQ reconnaissance seaplane should guard the fleet against submarines on Y-2 day and Y-1 day with Saiki as base. The reconnaissance plane of *Yahagi* should be catapulted on Y-1 day according to the order to reconnoitre mainly the sea area west of Okinawa.

3. Battle Details.

Whether the force will make the day or night total attack in company with other forces or quickly approach the enemy and execute the deadly special attack as the principal battle method, the battle details depend upon the battle tactics of the 1st YB.

4. Advance Course

Should no other order be given the #2 course will be taken as shown in the accompanying chart.

Items Particularly Considered in Working Out the Operations Plan

1. The enemy task forces are located in the vicinity of Amami-Ōshima and E of Okinawa presently. Therefore the assault operation can be executed from the NW area of the E sea (*Tōkai*). The penetration time is decided to be dawn of the 8th. Therefore, the 1st YB should pass through Bungo Strait after sunset and pass the Ōsumi Channel at dawn of 7th. The enemy attack is expected to take place in the E sea.

2. If a powerful enemy task force appears the 1st YB should retire to the N without keeping to the planning and carry out the assault after the successful attack of our air forces.

3. The search for the enemy as well as ASW will be executed by the base air force and the General Escort Command. However, the command reconnaissance planes of the 2nd Fleet[232] (*Dai Ni Kantai shireibu suitei*) will be utilised for ASW and the plane of *Yahagi* for the reconnaissance before the assault.

4. The character of the Special Surface Attack Force should be shown and the battle fought until the last projectile has been fired, never thinking of returning alive.

---

[232] The planes carried on the battleship *Yamato*.

5. An explanation of the chief of the Naval General Staff[233] about the Heaven Operation, Surface Special Attack Operation (*Ten Gō Sakusen Kaijō Tokkōbutai Sakusen*) is added.

---

[233] In this 1st YB Secret #1 the general character of the operation was explained, the preparation of a draft for the day and night battle was required and much was written about technical aspects, which should be given attention. Explanations about the execution of a gun battle, torpedo battle, AA defense, gunfight against submarines (!), ASW and communications were given and items requiring strict observation pointed out.

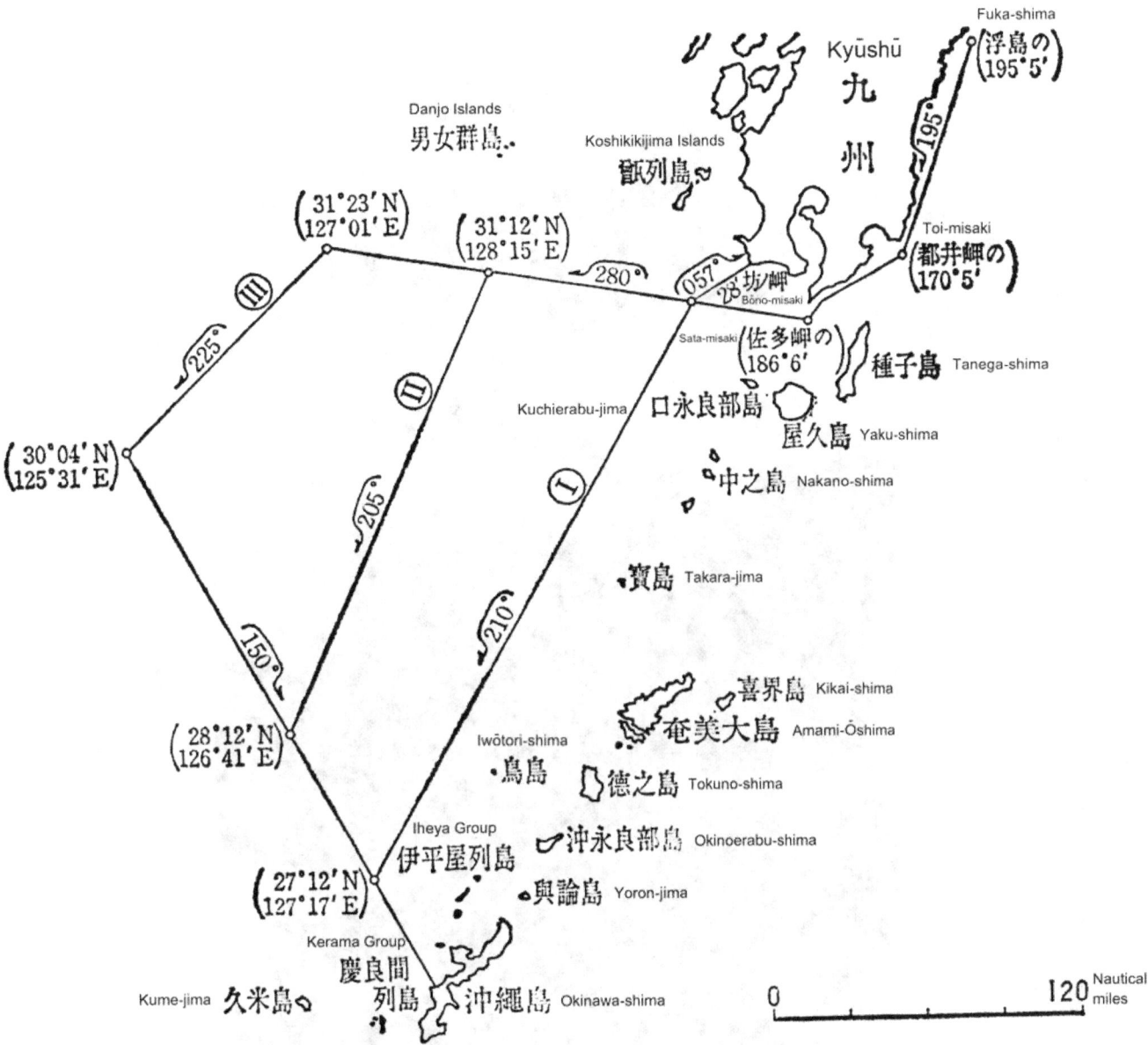

Map 9-1: Possible courses for the advance to Okinawa (Adapted from *Senshi Sōsho*)

Photo 9-1: The Commander-in-Chief of the Combined Fleet Admiral Toyoda Soemu (1885–1957) (Authors' collections)

Photo 9-2: Second Fleet, Commander-in-Chief Vice-Admiral Itō Seiichi (1890–1945) (Kure Maritime Museum)

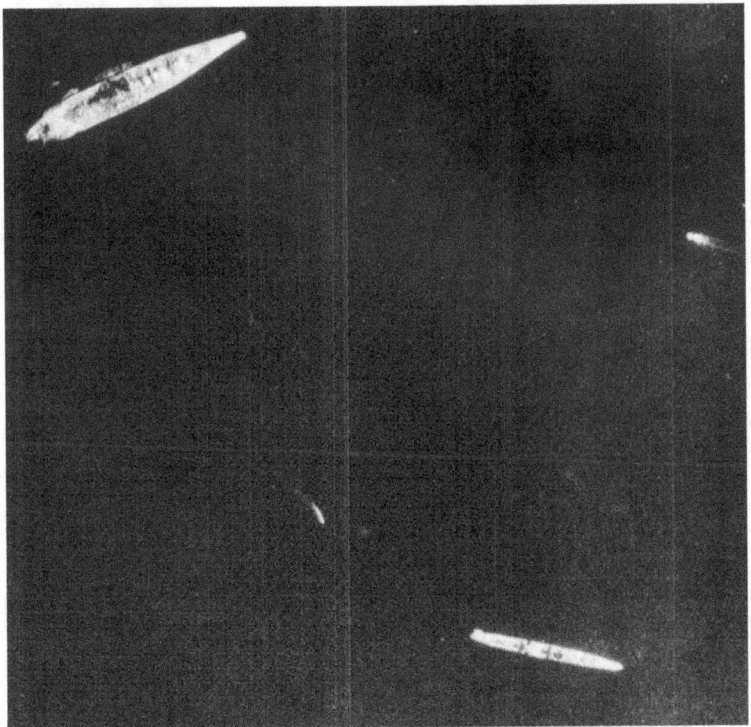

Photo 9-3: *Yamato* and light cruiser *Yahagi* at Tokuyama at approx. 10:00 on 6 April 1945 (Authors' collections)

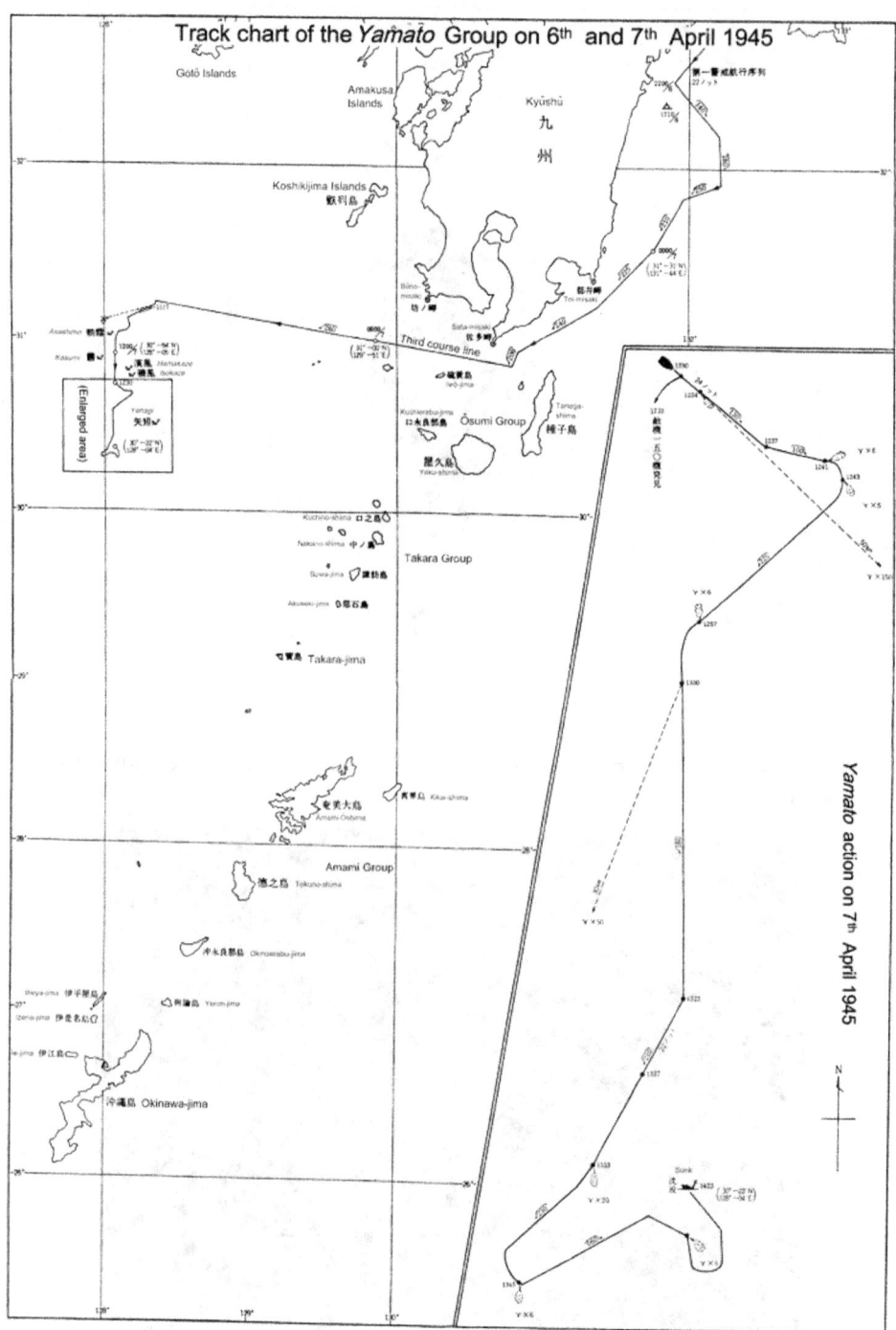

Map 9-2: Track chart of the *Yamato* Group 6–7 April 1945 plus detail of her final movements (Adapted from *Senshi Sōsho*)

The Sortie

The Special Attack Force[234] and the Sweeping Force[235] departed Tokuyama on 6 April at 15:20. The sky was cloudy, amount of clouds was 8 and the SE wind blew with 10.5 m/s. The speed was increased to 20 knots at 16:10 and Vice-Admiral Itō's message on the occasion of the departure was signalled to every ship. Before or after that the special message of the C-in-C of the Combined Fleet, Admiral Toyoda, which was sent to all forces on the 6th (Combined Fleet Secret #060001),[236] was read:

> The Imperial Navy is mounting a general offensive against the enemy at Okinawa by mustering in concert with the Army all of Japan's air, sea and ground strength.
>
> The fate of our Empire truly rests upon this one action. I have called for the organisation of a Surface Special Attack Force for an assault operation of unrivalled bravery, so that the power of the Imperial Navy may be felt in this one action in order that the brilliant tradition of the Imperial Navy's surface forces may be exalted and our glory handed down to posterity. Each unit, regardless of whether or not it is a Special Attack Force, will harden its resolve to fight gloriously to the death to completely destroy the enemy fleet, thereby establishing firmly an eternal foundation for the Empire.[237]

The 31st Division separated at 16:20 and afterwards the 2nd Destroyer Squadron carried out attack exercises against the battleship *Yamato*, or quick formation changes from 16:30 to 17:00 (!)[238] Owing to the lack of fuel training could only be executed stationary usually and the laying of the guns was seldom executed in order to save the fuel for the operation of hydraulic pumps etc. Therefore, the crews lacked training and these exercises should supplement this and also heighten their fighting spirit.

---

[234] Battleship *Yamato*, light cruiser *Yahagi*, 41st Destroyer Division (*Fuyuzuki, Suzutsuki*), 17th Destroyer Division (*Isokaze, Hamakaze, Yukikaze*), 21st Destroyer Division (*Asashimo, Kasumi, Hatsushimo*).

[235] 31st Division (*Hanazuki*), 43rd Destroyer Division (*Kaya, Maki*).

[236] An abbreviated and different worded version is given in Hara, op. cit., p. 284 and a longer one in Spurr, op. cit., p. 120. See also the whole text but different wording in Yoshida, op. cit., pp. 31–32.

[237] Vice-Admiral Itō's message read still more histrionic. Referring to mysticism at first he appealed to every man to fight determinedly and smash down the enemy by showing the peculiarity of the Surface Special Attack.

[238] *Senshi Sōsho*, vol. 17, p. 635. The reference to a training lasting half an hour in the official history tells more about the real training situation of the IJN than a lengthy description. This should be seen in company with the previously mentioned fuel rations for training before a sortie.

At about 16:45 a B-29 was sighted and the 1st YB took a deception course for some time to render more difficult a report about the true course.[239]

Near the course of the 1st YB in the Bungo Strait more than two ASW patrol planes were continuously in the air from about 17:00 to 20:00, and also six warships cruised in the Strait to guard the 1st YB and attack submarines. At 18:00 the 1st YB, marching at 22 knots, came to the western part of the Strait and had passed it at 19:50. 30 minutes after entering this part, the reconnaissance plane of the Saiki Air Group discovered an apparently hostile submarine bearing 105°, distance 10 nm off Hotojima and attacked it. According to the information transmitted till that time two enemy submarines operated at the outlet of the Bungo Strait and one more was reported in Hyūga-nada. In order to avoid the enemy submarine operating in the Hyūga-nada, the 1st YB deviated largely from the planned course to port and took bearing 140°. At 19:50 the formation was changed to #1 Alert Cruising Formation (*Dai Ichi Keikai Kōkō Joretsu*) and from 20:00 onwards zigzag movement was begun.

The destroyer *Isokaze* detected what seemed to be an enemy submarine at about 20:20. The light cruiser *Yahagi* located it at bearing 50°, distance 7km and intercepted radio waves of 4235kc with sensibility 5. Also, two white waves were recognised at the receiving bearing. The 1st YB changed the course to 180° at 21:00 and at about 21:30 the *Yahagi* intercepted an operation special urgent message of a submarine to Submarine Base Guam. The sensitivity was extremely high and according to a later report of the Ōwada Communication Unit (Ōwada *Tsūshintai*) the submarine was located approx. 30 nm E off Toimisaki. It had most probably discovered the 1st YB and shadowed it nearby.[240] At 22:00 the course was changed to 225° and the 1st YB advanced again to S practising "*seidō undo*."[241]

On 7 April at 02:00 the 1st YB came to the Ōsumi Channel, reduced speed to 16 knots and reduced the distances between the ships to R = 1 km and B =

---

[239] The 1st YB had been daily reconnoitred by B-29s since March and the deception course was in vain because the American naval intelligence had deciphered the orders of the HQ of the Combined Fleet to the 1st YB and other forces and Vice-Admiral Marc A. Mitscher, commanding Task Force 58 (the Fast Carrier Force) had already ordered to destroy the 1st YB long before the sortie.

[240] According to Morison, op. cit., p. 203 it was USS *Hackleback*. For more details about the three US submarines in Bungo Strait (*Threadfin*, *Hackleback* and *Silversides*) readers should refer to Spurr, op. cit., p. 177–186, and to Clay Blair *Silent Victory: The U.S. Submarine War against Japan*, pp. 829–832.

[241] All ships are changing the bearing simultaneously at determined positions. See Hara, op. cit., p. 286, criticising the zigzag ring formation.

0.5 km.[242] At 03:45 course 280° was taken and at about 06:00 the passage of the Ōsumi Channel was finished and the 1st YB took #3 Alert Cruising Formation.

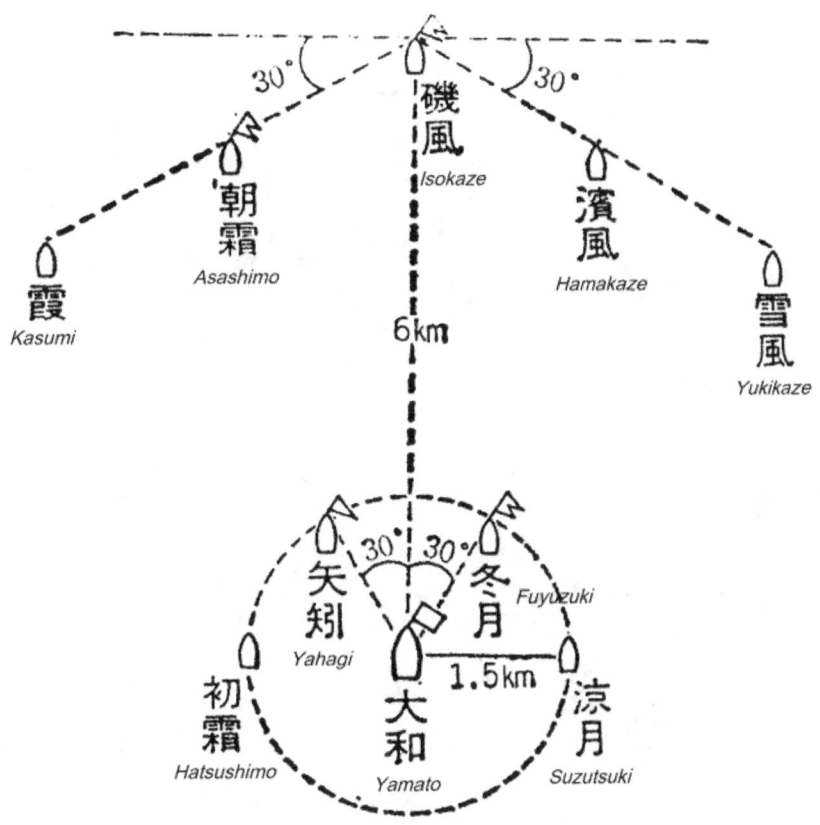

Map 9-3: The *Yamato* Group in No. 1 Alert Cruising Formation (Adapted from *Senshi Sōsho*)

---

[242] In *Senshi Sōsho*, vol. 17, p. 636, the term "*kinshuku jinkei*" is used, meaning a "shrunken formation."

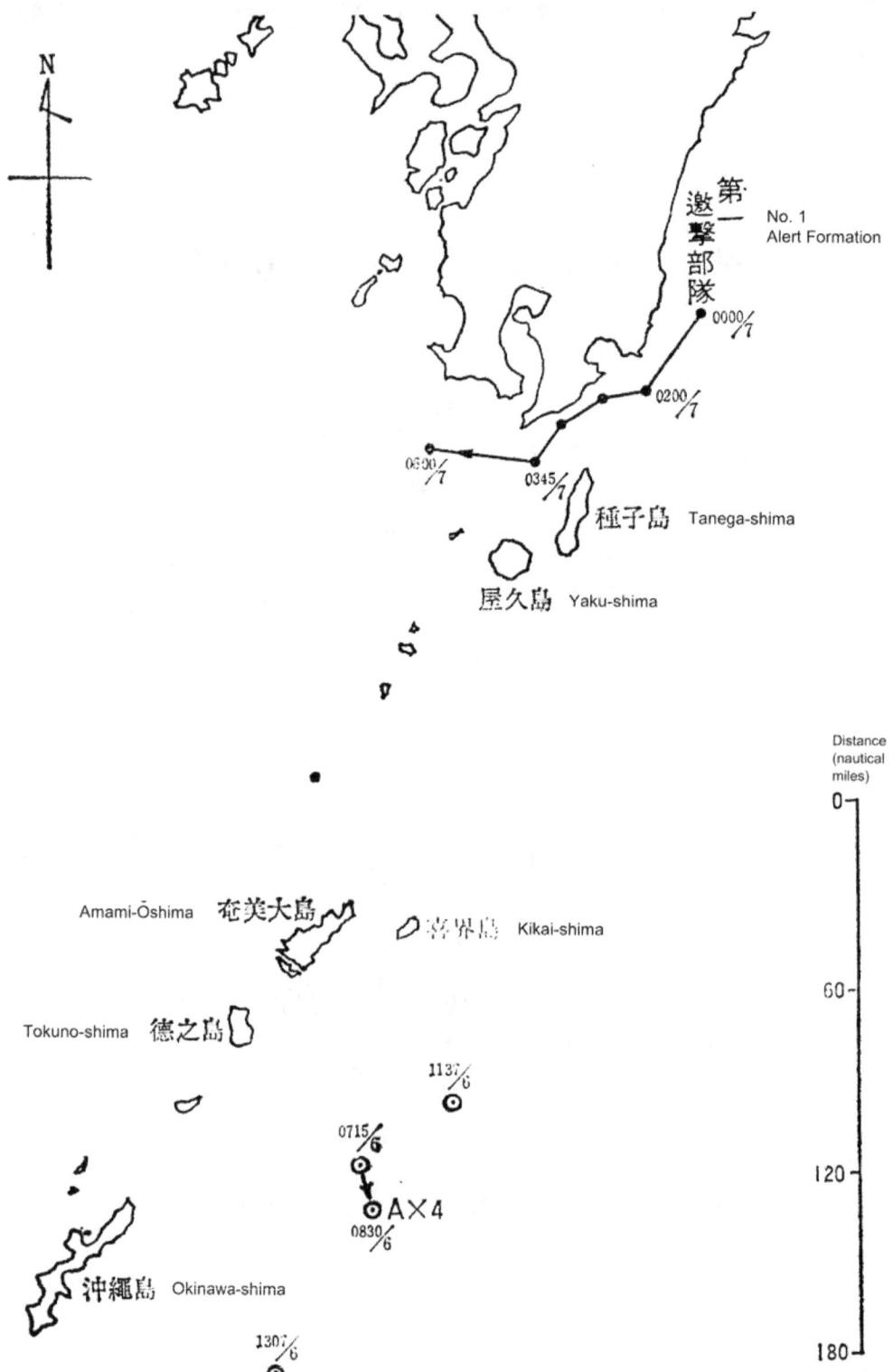

Map 9-4: Track chart of the *Yamato* Group until 06:00 on 7 April and reported positions of US task forces on 6 April (Adapted from *Senshi Sōsho*)

No. 3 Alert Cruising Formation

Distance = 1,500m

Map 9-5: The *Yamato* Group in No. 3 Alert Cruising Formation (Adapted from *Senshi Sōsho*)

Since the beginning of 7 April the 1st YB knew by radio from the HQ of the Combined Fleet that No. 1 *Kikusui* Operation on 6 April had been successful. The damage to the US task forces was very big and several ships, among them also some aircraft carriers, had been sunk.[243] Also, during the passage of the Ōsumi Channel, at about 04:00, the 1st YB was informed that on 7th between 06:00 and 10:00 fighters of the 203rd Air Group would provide direct escort over the force.[244]

In *Senshi Sōsho*, vol. 17, there is a map (no. 59) showing the information about the positions of the US task forces, received by the 1st YB until the time when it had passed the Ōsumi Channel (at about 06:00). See map 9-4.

At 06:00 one reconnaissance plane was catapulted from *Yamato* as direct escort against submarines[245] and from 06:15 the air search radar observed the air space against enemy planes, while hydrophones and sonar searched for submarines below the surface. From 06:30 till 10:00 between five and ten fighters escorted the 1st YB, as announced in the information received about two hours earlier.

The destroyer *Asashimo* reported engine trouble at 06:57 and was forced to reduce speed to 12 knots. Afterwards the destroyer dropped back gradually and came out of sight at about 11:00.

The morning was again cloudy with the amount of clouds 10, compared with 8 on the former day, but the wind force was still light. The 1st YB advanced to the west with standard course 280°, but even the low cloud height

---

[243] The claims were totally exaggerated. According to Radio Tōkyō two battleships and three cruisers had been sunk in company with 57 smaller warships. A further 61 ships, among them five aircraft carriers, were badly damaged. Actual losses were three destroyers, one LST (landing ship tank) and two ammunition ships sunk and many more ships damaged but among them the light aircraft carrier *San Jacinto* (CVL-30) was the only aircraft carrier suffering from near misses of kamikazes. A complete list may be found in Robert J. Cressman's *The Official Chronology of the U.S. Navy in World War II*, pp. 309–310.

[244] According to Prados, op. cit., p. 712, this radio was also intercepted and translated and J(oint) I(ntelligence) C(enter) P(acific) O(cean) A(rea) commented the escort by fighters from 06:00 to 10:00: "They quit too soon." See next page for the retreat of the fighters and the appearance of the American flying boats and also Ugaki, op. cit., p. 574, "... but an enemy flying boat shadowed the force after our fighters left the scene."

[245] Between about 07:00 and 08:30 there were mostly two own seaplanes over the force and for this purpose the CL *Yahagi*'s #1 plane was catapulted at 08:15 for direct protection against submarines and returned after 09:00.

of 1,000 to 2,000 m could not offer the protection the planners had hoped for.[246]

At about 08:30 an attack of US carrier-based aircraft on the bases in South Kyūshū was reported and at 08:40, when the ships were bearing 260°, distance 60nm off Bōno-misaki lighthouse, seven carrier-based F6Fs circled the 1st YB once and withdrew without attacking.[247]

In this situation and in view of the reported distance to the US task force the staff of the 1st YB estimated that "the probability of serious enemy air attacks is not big." A fateful error in judgement!

This estimate of the situation was based upon "facts" known until approx. 09:00 and read:

1. Situation
   a) The enemy task force is composed of only one unit and the position at 08:10 was reported as bearing about 175°, distance 250 nm to the 1st YB.
   b) The enemy task force approached early in the morning and carried out a small attack upon bases in South Kyūshū.
   c) The enemy carrier-based aircraft discovered us but turned away after shadowing for a short period of time. They were probably at the limit of the reconnaissance area or evaded our fighters air-borne for counterattack.
   d) There is still no report about the take-off of our air groups for the attack of the enemy task force but it is expected to come soon.
2. Estimation
   Serious air attacks from the aforementioned task force should not be expected.

About one hour later (approx. 10:00) the 1st YB received a telegram that had been issued at 08:42 and by which the take-off of the 721st Air Group for the attack of the 1st group of the US task force had been ordered. After that information about the 2nd group, 3rd group and eventually also the 4th group of the US task force came in quick succession. At about this time the 1st YB should have recognised the true strength of the enemy forces, particularly the large number of aircraft carriers, and the serious error in judgement. But the

---

[246] Also, Vice-Admiral Ugaki noted in his War Diary (*Fading Victory*), p. 574, under the date of 7 April 1945 referring to the Surface Special Attack Force "... So I feared it might be attacked later today. The only consolation was that the weather was gradually worsening from the west, so I thought it might be able to evade enemy attacks due to foul weather ..."

[247] Morison, op. cit., p. 203, states that an *Essex* plane discovered the *Yamato* group at 08:23 and reported the enemy course as 300°, speed 12 knots (actually 22 knots), at 08:32.

aforementioned estimation that serious air attacks were improbable was obviously also held after the reports of three more "groups" and instead of retiring to N, and avoid the enemy attack until the successful attack of the own air force had been carried out, as stated in #2 of the "Items Particularly Considered in Working Out the Operation Plan," the 1st YB continued to head for Okinawa and chose the path of certain destruction.

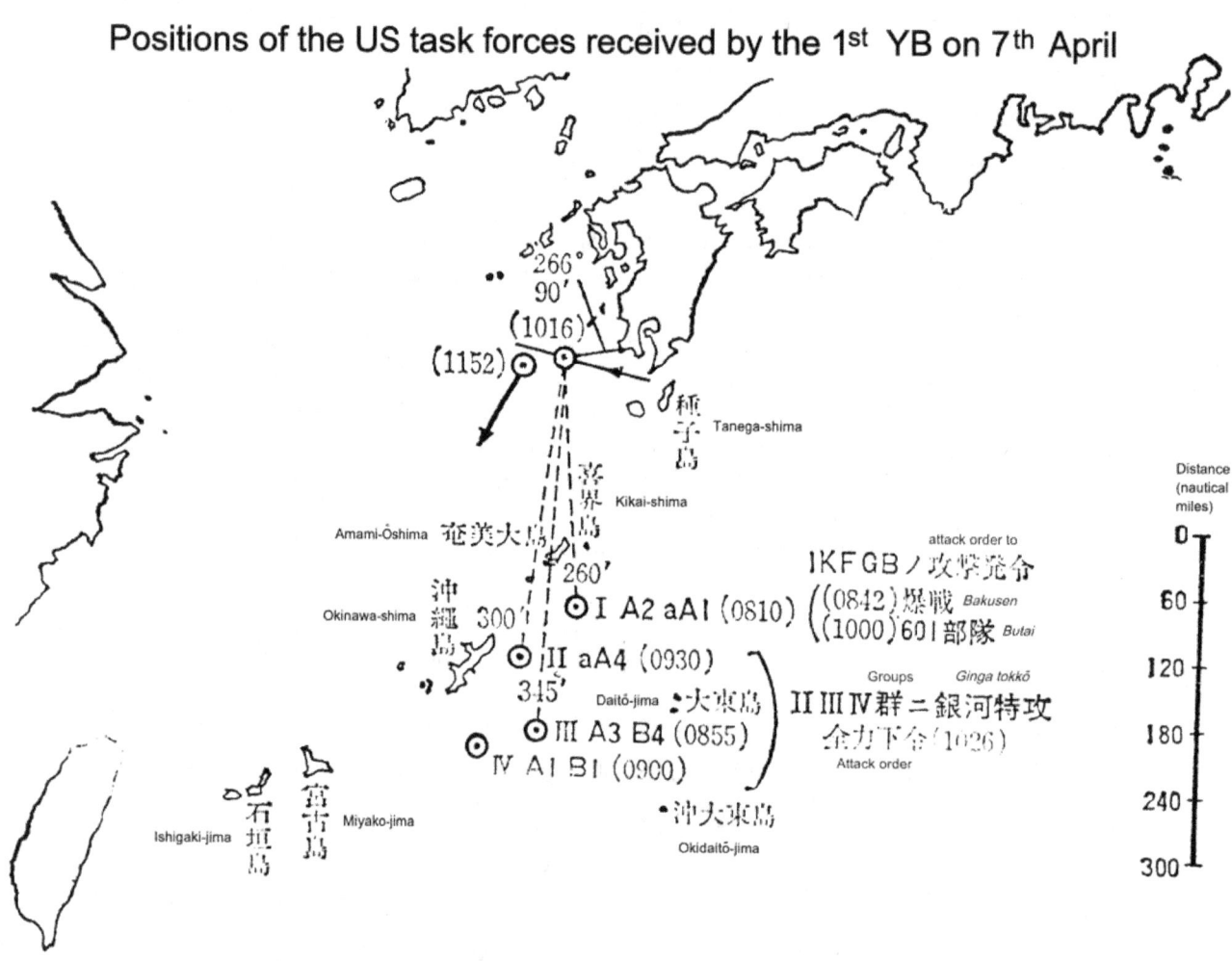

Map 9-6: Positions of the US task forces as reported by own aircraft and received by the 1st YB on 7 April (Adapted from *Senshi Sōsho*)

The Anti-Aircraft Battle of the 1ˢᵗ YB

At about 10:00 the direct escort of Zero fighters withdrew. Shortly afterwards, at 10:16, two enemy PBM flying boats were discovered bearing 230°, distance 45 km off the *Yamato*, whose position was then bearing 266°, distance 90 nm off Bōno-misaki lighthouse. The battleship intercepted an urgent operation message of the US planes and jammed the transmitting. At 10:17 the 46-cm main guns commenced fire, using Type 3 incendiary projectiles, but ceased after one salvo for the flying boats opened range and continued the shadowing at a distance outside the main gun range. At 10:22 a simultaneous turn to starboard of 320° was executed and then at 10:44 to port 160°, in order to make more difficult the estimation of the course for the PBMs. At the same time the light cruiser *Yahagi* jammed the transmitting of radio messages from the "Charlies."

At 11:07 a large enemy aircraft unit at bearing 180° was shown on the screen of the *Yamato*'s #13 radar,[248] and all ships were informed that the first wave of the enemy carrier-based aircraft approached the 1ˢᵗ YB. At 11:14 eight F6Fs were discovered but the planes hid themselves in the clouds and kept contact. The *Yamato* and the *Yahagi* commenced AA firing. At 11:16 the 1ˢᵗ YB increased speed to 24 knots and took course 200° but changed to 270° at 11:18 and to 205° at 11:30, and again reduced speed to 20 knots at 11:35. During this time the radar screen showed the approach of "more than two enemy aircraft formations" at a distance of about 70 km.[249]

The weather conditions were almost the same as in the morning: cloudy, amount of clouds 10, drizzle, height of clouds 1,000 to 2,000 m, wind from S with 12 m/s. At 11:30 the 1st YB was informed that the 2nd, 3rd and 4th groups of the US task force were attacked by the full strength of the Ginga special attack bombers of the 706th and 762nd Air Groups. This meant that all four groups of the enemy task force were the targets of special attacks.

---

[248] This 2 m-wave-radar had a peak power of 10 kW and a large aircraft unit could be discovered at ranges of 100 km, occasionally also up to 120 km. The chief artillery officer of the *Yamato*'s secondary guns, Lieutenant-Commander Shimizu Yoshito, remembered after the war that he recognised the great range of 80 to 100 km that the radar could discover the enemy, but his "I remember that both targets did neither approach nor move" cannot be true while in contrast his statement that the 1ˢᵗ YB took the formation against air attack due to the discovery of the enemy by radar is correct.

[249] The targets referred to by Shimizu Yoshito.

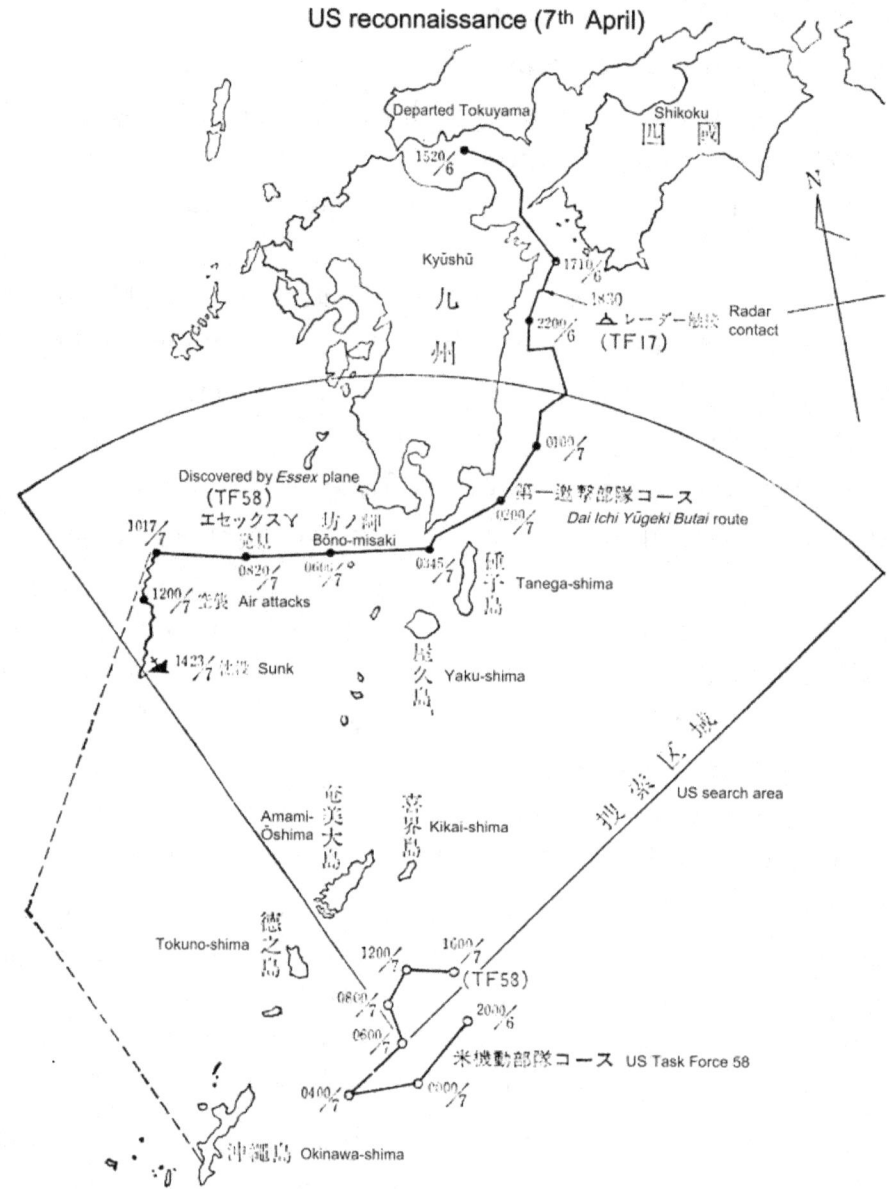

Map 9-7: US (Task Force 58) reconnaissance on 7 April and discovery of the *Yamato* Group (Adapted from *Senshi Sōsho*)

In this situation serious air attacks were still considered improbable despite the discovery of more than two large enemy plane formations, because of the weather conditions (drizzle) and the big distance between the 1st YB and the US task force. The estimation of the situation at 11:40 was almost the same as before in this respect and read:

1. The attack of enemy carrier-based aircraft is certain. However, because of the weather condition and the situation of the enemy[250] the number of planes will not be large.[251]
2. We are very much interested to know the result of our first attack.[252]

At 11:45 zigzag movement was resumed and at 11:52 the 1st YB radioed "F4U 8, F6F 10 circling nearby, not yet attacking, position bearing 250°, distance 105 nm off Bōno-misaki lighthouse, course 205°, speed 18 knots, 11:45."

The First Victim of the Air Attack

The destroyer *Asashimo* that had disappeared from view at about 11:00 reported at 11:59 that the engine troubles would presumably be remedied at 13:00. The 1st YB judged this information as completion of the engine repairs. But at 12:08 the destroyer reported the sighting of carrier-based planes bearing 130° and two minutes later it radioed "We are fighting against enemy aircraft." The destroyer *Fuyuzuki* confirmed smoke and gunfire at bearing 30°. Then, at 12:21, *Asashimo* reported more than 30 enemy aircraft at bearing 90° and this was the last report heard by the 1st YB from her. The destroyer sank immediately after the attack with, apparently, the whole complement.

The First Air Attack upon the Yamato

The *Yamato* confirmed the presence of the Ōshima-Transport Group at 12:22 in bearing 250° and distance 45 km and also the large tracking plane, followed by the report about the sighting of 20 enemy carrier-based planes. Ten minutes later about 150 enemy planes were sighted from *Yamato* in bearing 130°, distance 50 km and identified as SB2C dive-bombers, F6F fighters, F4U Corsair fighters and TBM torpedo bombers. Two minutes later zigzagging was stopped, speed increased to 24 knots and the AA fight began. The first wave was recognised as "about 200 planes mainly attacking the battleship

---

[250] This must have referred to the execution of special attacks against the whole US task force.

[251] The report from Kikaitō (Kikai-shima, Nansei Shotō) mentioned about 150 carrier-based aircraft flying over the island to NW at about 10:50 and another report about another big air attack unit passing Kikaitō to N at about 11:30 was received by the 1st YB only after the beginning of the air attacks. But even if the reports were received in time it would have been too late to evade.

[252] The attack of the 1st group of the enemy task force by the 721st Air Group.

Yamato and the light cruiser *Yahagi* from all directions between 12:40 and 13:00."

According to the *Yamato*'s DAR Vice-Admiral Itō sent a radio message at 12:35 informing about the fighting against more than 100 enemy carrier-based aircraft, and at 12:40 all ships turned to port and pursued a 100° course.[253] At the same time several SB2Cs began diving in bearing 90°. One plane was shot down but others continued and at 12:41 independent evasive maneuvers at maximum battle speed were ordered and the battleship tried to evade. However, it was in vain and two medium sized bombs hit her near the after mast. The after main gun fire control room (*shageki shikisho*), #2 secondary gun[254] and the #13 radar (the antennae and the radar room), which had discovered the approaching enemy planes when they were about 100 km distant, were destroyed.

At 12:43 five TBMs headed for her from port bearing 70°, distance 7,000 m. *Yamato* turned independently to port to evade the torpedoes but immediately afterwards three tracks were noted bearing 90°, distance 1,000 m and at 12:45 one torpedo hit to port forward. At 12:57 several SB2Cs went into dives from starboard aft. *Yamato* began to turn, shot down one of the planes and could evade the bombs. At 13:00, when the air attack had ceased and the planes turned back, course was set to 180°.

Thus the first attack ended for *Yamato* with two bomb and one torpedo hits.[255]

---

[253] Before that, at 12:37, independent evasive manoeuvres to port and course 100° had been ordered.

[254] Note that the former #2 and #3 secondary guns had been replaced by 12.7 cm high-angle guns and the former #4 secondary gun had become #2.

[255] It may be pointed out that the Action Record of the 2nd Destroyer Squadron erroneously states that three torpedoes and two bombs hit *Yamato*. Report S-06-2, also considers the first attack of dive-bombers and torpedo planes as a single attack (p. 11). It states four bomb hits in the vicinity of no. 3 turret and two or three torpedo hits on the port side (p. 12) with reference to data given by the chief of staff, executive officer and the assistant gunnery officer (p. 11).

Photo 9-4: A bomb hits *Yamato* during her final battle on 7 April 1945 (Kure Maritime Museum)

The First Air Attack upon the Second Destroyer Squadron

At 12:45 the destroyer *Hamakaze* was hit by a bomb that detonated aft to starboard and damaged both propellers. Navigation became impossible. One plane was shot down. Two minutes later, at 12:47, the immobilised destroyer was hit by a torpedo–starting fires. At 12:48 she broke in two and both halves sank at 30°47'N/128°08'E, presumably the second destroyer loss of the 1st YB.

Before that, the *Yahagi*, the second main target, suffered bomb and torpedo hits and navigation became impossible.

At the time of *Hamakaze*'s sinking two rockets hit the AA destroyer *Fuyuzuki* but fortunately both were duds so damage was slight. Her luck continued and at 13:05 one torpedo passed below her bottom.

At 13:08 the AA destroyer *Suzutsuki* was hit by one bomb forward. The detonation started fires but these could fortunately be extinguished rather quickly.

The Second Air Attack and the Loss of the Yamato

As stated earlier, the *Yamato* set course 180° at 13:00, but two minutes later a new target of 50 aircraft (the second wave) was sighted bearing 200°, distance 30 km. In the short lull between the attacks of the first and second waves Vice-Admiral Itō's staff evaluated the situation on the basis of *Yamato*'s damages (The damages caused by the two bomb hits and the torpedo detonation were slight for a ship like *Yamato* and did not impair her fighting ability.) and some officers considered that the advance to Okinawa was still probable despite the approach of the next attackers:

1. The present damages of *Yamato* do not impair her fighting capabilities.
2. Should the damages increase a change of the assault attack time will be necessary.
3. In order to confirm the condition of damaged ships, particularly that of the flagship of the 2nd Destroyer Squadron, *Yahagi*, we take course for them.[256]

At 13:19 the fleet flagship signalled "Speed 12 knots!" and at 13:22 all ships made a simultaneous turn to starboard to 210° and increased speed to 22 knots at 13:27, because the attack of the second wave had begun. Before that, at 13:25, the *Yamato* had signalled to the destroyer *Hatsushimo* that she should take over communications.[257]

The attack of the second wave[258] lasted from about 13:30 to about 14:20. At 13:33 20 TBMs headed for *Yamato* bearing starboard 60°, distance 4,000 m and the battleship turned individually to port to evade, but at 13:34 six torpedo tracks bearing 50° to port, distance 2,000 m were observed, of which three hit her to port amidships at 13:37. The auxiliary steering gear was damaged and the auxiliary rudder blocked to starboard at an unknown angle. Because of the concentration of the attacks to the port side (the first torpedo had also hit her to port) *Yamato* listed 7° to 8° to port, and in order to correct her list 3,000 tons of salt water were counter-flooded in the starboard compartments. By this she almost returned to even keel.

---

[256] At that time the distance between the main body and the light cruiser *Yahagi* was about 20 km.

[257] This order must have been given in anticipation that *Yamato* would again become the main target.

[258] Actually the third attack wave the US aircraft carriers had started.

Photo 9-5: *Yamato* on 7 April 1945 (Authors' collections)

At 13:40 a simultaneous turn to starboard to 230° was executed and one minute later four torpedo tracks to port bearing 60°, distance 7,000 m were discovered. *Yamato* attempted to evade by making an individual turn to port and shot down one torpedo bomber about 500 m from the bow. But two torpedoes hit to port amidships at 13:44 and increased the number of portside hits to six. At 13:45 the auxiliary rudder could be fixed to the centreline and standard course was changed to 205°. At the same time several SB2Cs went into dive from the starboard bow direction and she attempted evasion by turning to starboard individually. During this maneuver two dive-bombers were reported to have been shot down and no bomb hit. While this was going on her list to port increased gradually and became 15° at about 14:00. The two hits at 13:44 had opened new compartments for immersion and the concentration of torpedo hits to the port side proved much more effective and dangerous than the almost equal division of hits to both sides in case of her sister *Musashi*. But still a speed of 18 knots was maintained.

Photo 9-6: Aruga Kōsaku (1897–1945)–*Yamato*'s last commanding officer (Authors' collections)

At 14:00 several SB2Cs dove on her from starboard bow and she turned to starboard to evade them. But the maneuver was not successful and she was hit by three medium-sized bombs to port amidships at 14:02, bringing the total of bomb hits to five. During this time her list to port increased further and since the damage control and additional compartments on the starboard side had already been flooded completely, Captain Aruga decided to flood the starboard engine rooms and boiler rooms, as they were the biggest compartments, in order to correct the list. However, this hope was in vain and was only sufficient to correct the list temporarily.[259] While this was underway one torpedo track was sighted bearing 60° to starboard, distance 800 m at 14:05. She attempted to evade by a hard turn to port but was hit starboard amidships at 14:07, thus increasing the number of hits to seven. At 14:10 four more torpedo tracks were noted bearing 60° to port, distance 1,000 m. She turned to port immediately but two torpedoes hit to port, one amidships and the other aft at 14:12.

After that she set course on 0 and tried to withdraw northwards. Her actual speed was down to 12 knots because only the port side turbine sets and boilers were in operation—the corresponding rooms to starboard had been flooded to counter the rapidly increasing port list, as stated before. The torpedo that had struck to starboard brought about a counter-flooding effect but when the new course was set she was listing 6° to port.[260]

---

[259] Report S-06-2, p. 16, points out "… Counterflooding of outboard engineering spaces is an extreme measure and inadvisable except under the most adverse circumstances. It can scarcely be classed as a routine operation." In criticising the damage control system the investigators stated–after pointing out that with a list in the order of 16° the outboard voids could be filled only to about 55 per cent capacity by flooding from the sea–"… there was no damage control pumping system of adequate capacity provided for completely filling the outboard voids in case of large angles of list. Thus, even though the ships [*Yamato* and *Shinano*] were not seriously damaged, there was no ready means of removing lists as large as 16°–18°, other than by flooding outboard engineering spaces". The conclusions that having in the underwater protection system "… outboard layers filled with liquid (either salt water ballast or fuel oil) to limit initial angles of list would have been far preferable." and that a larger capacity pumping system for damage control "… also would have been a distinct asset …" cannot but be agreed with. On the other hand, viewed from the design of the underwater protection system—counterflooding capacity sufficient to right the ship after hits by three torpedoes on one side, provided that the underwater protection system was not damaged, the counterflooding system responded to the design but the underwater protection system did not.

[260] According to S-06-2, p. 13, "All three officers agreed that the starboard hit flooded No. 7 fireroom [boiler room] rather quickly, the torpedo having struck in the vicinity of frame 125. None of them knew of any other damage on the starboard side, …"

Photo 9-7: *Yamato* during her final battle (Authors' collections)

At 14:15 one torpedo track was observed bearing 90° to port, distance 1,000m and two minutes later the torpedo hit the port side amidships, despite an evasive turn to port. It was the last of ten recorded torpedo hits of which nine were located on the port side and only one to starboard. The concentration from amidships to aft sealed her fate and after the tenth hit the list increased rapidly and reached 20° at 14:20. She capsized at 14:23[261] and immediately after showing her bottom above the water surface inducted detonations blew up the forward and after turrets and she sank at position 30°22'N/128°04'E. Vice-Admiral Itō Seiichi, Captain Aruga Kōsaku as well as 2,498 officers, petty officers and ratings shared their fate with the battleship *Yamato*.[262]

---

[261] The time given in the DAR of the 2nd Destroyer Squadron (14:17) is considered an error.

[262] The order to abandon ship was given at about 14:10 after the executive officer, Captain Nomura Jirō, had recognised at 14:05 that *Yamato*'s list could not be corrected and she was in an acute state of sinking. At that time Vice-Admiral Itō rose to his feet, looked in the eyes of every man on the bridge, shook hands and answered every bow before going to his rest room one deck below, while the list of *Yamato* still increased. After entering the cabin he closed the door from inside and it was never opened again. Captain Aruga tied himself to the binnacle located at the centre of the AA defense sta-

tion (*bōkū shikisho*). The chief navigation officer, Commander Shigeki Shirō, and his assistant, Sub-Lieutenant Hanada Taisuke, bound themselves to the mother binnacle on the navigation bridge. The assistant gunnery officer, Lieutenant Hattori Shinrokurō, went to the wardroom where the portraits of His Imperial Majesty's hung, locked the door from the inside and sacrificed his life. The cipher officer (*angōshi*) took the cryptographic aids and all military secret documents with him in the cipher room, located below the bridge, locked the door and rose barricades to protect the documents from falling into enemy hands and went down with the ship.

Most of the crew became victims of enemy bombs, torpedoes and machine-gun bullets either on the ship or in the water. The underwater detonations of *Yamato* also contributed to the enormous number of losses. Except for the latter reason most of the crews of the other ships shared the same fate.

The AA destroyer *Fuyuzuki* had been called to come alongside to take over *Yamato*'s crew but it was impossible to approach her; the destroyer would have been dragged down when the IJN's pride capsized.

Personnel losses according to Morison, op. cit., pp. 308–309. *Senshi Sōsho*, vol. 17, states 2,740 (including HQ of the 2nd Fleet?) killed in action and 117 wounded on pp. 648–649. Total personnel losses are given as 3,665 by Morison and 3,721 by *Senshi Sōsho*. The losses of the individual ships are given in the "damage sketches" on pp. 648–649.

Photo 9-8: The end at 14:23 on 7 April 1945 (Kure Maritime Museum)

The following table lists the torpedo and bomb hits as stated in the official history with reference to *Yamato*'s DAR but the DAR is often in striking contrast to the data given in S-06-2 and *Interrogation of Japanese Officials*:

Time	No.	Torpedo	No.	Bomb	Note
12:41		-----	1–	2	Medium-sized (250-kg) struck near the

			2		after (main) mast
12:45	1	1			On port side forward
13:37	2–4	3			On port side amidships
13:44	5–6	2			On port side amidships
14:02				3–5	3	Medium-sized (250-kg) hit to port amidships
14:07	7	1			On starboard side amidships
14:12	8–9	2			One on the port side amidships and one aft
14:17	10	1			On port side amidships

Notes:

(1) The sketch on p. 648 of *Senshi Sōsho*, vol. 17, illustrating the position of the hits shows the torpedo that struck to starboard as the no. 4 hit, while both the DAR and TROM state it as no. 7.

(2) The same sketch shows six bomb hits (corresponding e.g. to S-06-2) but depending on DAR, TROM and description only five were received.

(3) Matsumoto, op. cit., deals with the loss of *Yamato* on pp. 327–333 on the basis of the publication of Captain Nomura's report, published in the press on 12 April 1946, giving the number of attacking American planes as about 1,000 attaining hits of 12 torpedoes, seven large bombs and countless small ones and also an unrecorded number of near misses. Therefore, his data–still in 1961–are necessarily wrong but his conclusion that damage by bombs was not fatal and that the immersion, while sealing *Yamato*'s fate, was caused by the torpedo hits is surely correct and agreed on also in S-06-2, p. 15.

(4) The editors of *Kaigun Zōsen Gijutsu Gaiyō*, vol. 1, while dealing with the loss of *Musashi* very detailed, are vague as for *Yamato*. Even though not explained the reason may have been the widely varying data of survivors and lack of documents.

(5) Owing to such uncertainties the authors have recognised their incapability to decide what is correct and consider it estimation, at best.

(6) Matsumoto, op. cit., pp. 330–331 states in his "General Discussion on the Sinking of the *Yamato* Class Battleships" that from the viewpoint of design the following items as means to escape sinking should have been studied thoroughly: (1) Maintaining buoyancy outside the vital part (including the space below the magazines), (2) Maintaining the waterline area in the areas stated in (1), (3) Damage control system, (4) Watertightness of local parts at the side armor, (5) Structure of trunks,

small bulkheads, and floors. In the first four items shortages existed and the fifth one was weak, so that all contributed to the sinking. Finally he admits that the designers (he was in a position to know it) did not have the wide prospect of the development of the planes. While the authors do agree with his opinion about shortages (defects) and weak structures they are hesitating to accept his view in (3) because the system responded to the requirement and "shortage" was the consequence of the lack of "wide prospect of the development of planes." For some details see later.

The Second Air Attack and the Losses of the 2nd Destroyer Squadron

The first ship suffering from the attack of the second (actually the third) wave was the destroyer *Kasumi*. At 13:25 two bombs hit her and a near miss caused her to become unnavigable.

Because the light cruiser *Yahagi* had lost mobility, due to bomb and torpedo hits by planes of the first wave, Rear-Admiral Komura decided to disembark the flagship at 13:00 and ordered the destroyer *Isokaze* to come alongside. The destroyer approached, but before the execution of this maneuver the enemy second wave began the attack and afterwards every try to approach the light cruiser was prevented by the planes, which attacked the light cruiser fiercely. So the destroyer stood by the immobilised *Yahagi*. At 13:45 about 50 aircraft concentrated upon the *Yahagi* and she sank at 14:05, after having been hit by a total of 12 bombs and seven torpedoes including those received during the first attack.[263]

A near miss aft at 13:56 caused the destroyer *Isokaze* to take in water and the speed had to be reduced.

---

[263] Morison, op. cit., p. 208, states "Light cruiser *Yahagi* ... proved almost as tough as the battleship, taking 12 bomb and seven torpedo hits before going down." Truly an extraordinary big punishment for a light cruiser!

Photo 9-9: Loss of the light cruiser *Yahagi* on 7 April 1945 (Authors' collections)

Operation Stop, Rescue of Survivors and Return to Sasebo

After the battleship *Yamato* had blown up the command of the 1st YB was temporarily taken over by the commanding officer of the 41st Destroyer Division, Captain Yoshida Masayoshi.

At about 14:25 the majority of the enemy planes withdrew and at about 14:40 the last aircraft that had circled the remnants of the 1st YB opened the range.

At 14:30 the situation of the 1st YB was as follows: Battleship *Yamato* and light cruiser *Yahagi* were sunk, the fate of the destroyer *Asashimo* was unknown but most probably she was sunk. The destroyer *Hamakaze* was sunk and AA destroyer *Suzutsuki* was still burning from the bomb hit at 13:08. The destroyer *Isokaze* was underway to the N because of the immersion of water and was out of sight. Therefore, only three ships, namely the AA destroyer *Fuyuzuki* and the destroyers *Yukikaze* and *Hatsushimo*, were present. The planning of the Okinawa assault operation with these forces was nonsense; the goal could never be attained. Therefore, Captain Yoshida decided to at first rescue the survivors and to make the next decision afterwards.

Then he reported the situation of the 1st YB to the C-in-C of the Combined Fleet, Admiral Toyoda Soemu, the Navy Minister, Admiral Yonai Mitsumasa and the chief of the Naval General Staff. His message (#071445) was very much belated and only transmitted at 15:52. It read:

> Surface Special Attack Force sustained continuous attacks from large enemy carrier-based aircraft formations since 11:41. *Yamato, Yahagi, Isokaze*[264] sunk. *Hamakaze, Suzutsuki, Kasumi* immobilised. Other ships are slightly damaged. *Fuyuzuki, Hatsushimo, Yukikaze* engaged in rescuing survivors at first. Afterwards, new activity[265] will be planned.

Because of the delayed transmission there was an exchange of information between the ships and the HQ of the 17th Destroyer Division transmitted the situation report to the Navy Minister and the chief of the Naval General Staff at 15:00. The higher authorities did not share the illusion of "new activity" and Admiral Toyoda ordered a halt of the assault operation at 16:39 with DesOpOrd #616. It was received by the remnants of the 1st YB around 17:50 and read:

> 1. The assault operation of the 1st YB is stopped.

---

[264] At the time of the report *Hamakaze* was sunk and *Isokaze* was still afloat and limping away at reduced speed.

[265] Most probably the continuation of the mission as required by Commander Terauchi, commanding officer of the destroyer *Yukikaze*.

2. The commanding officer of the 1st YB should rescue the crews and then return to Sasebo.

At that time the rescue was almost finished. The destroyer *Hatsushimo* had begun with the rescue of the destroyer *Hamakaze*'s survivors at 14:50, while the AA destroyer *Fuyuzuki* and the destroyer *Yukikaze* took aboard survivors from the battleship *Yamato*. Then, *Fuyuzuki* went alongside the port side of the destroyer *Kasumi* whose crew began boarding at 16:22. It was just in time for *Kasumi* sank at 16:57 at 30°51'N/127°57'E.

At about 17:00 *Hatsushimo* began to pick up survivors from the light cruiser *Yahagi* and about 20 minutes later the other two destroyers (*Fuyuzuki* and *Yukikaze*) joined the rescue work that was ended at about 18:15, or less than half an hour after the order to stop the operation.

Rear-Admiral Komura, the commanding officer of the 2nd Destroyer Squadron, was one of the survivors and began the search for damaged ships sailing N with the three destroyers. At 18:30 *Fuyuzuki* separated to search for sister *Suzutsuki* and *Hatsushimo* and *Yukikaze* took course 265° to stand by the *Isokaze*, which had radioed her position. When the ships arrived *Isokaze* was deep in the water and almost unable to navigate. However, the distance to Sasebo was still 160 nm and this meant that the destroyer would need more than 24 hours to come to the port. At that time the situation was as follows: (1) The success of the air-borne special attack units upon the US task force was unknown, (2) a flying boat had attacked in the evening, (3) the presence of a US submarine had been confirmed by measuring, (4) an attack by enemy carrier-based aircraft the next morning could be expected as almost certain. Rear-admiral Komura concluded that the loss of *Isokaze* was unavoidable in case of the expected attack, and should the other two destroyers stand by her they would almost certainly share her fate. He ordered the scuttling of *Isokaze* after the transfer of her crew but the staff of the 17th Destroyer Division opposed him and demanded that *Yukikaze* should tow the *Isokaze*. But Rear-Admiral Komura did not change his opinion and the transfer of the crew was begun at 20:50 and after almost two hours, at 22:40, *Isokaze* was sunk by gunfire from the *Yukikaze* at 30°46.5'N/128° 9.2'E. She was the last ship of the 1st YB to be sunk on that disastrous day of 7 April. Ten minutes later *Hatsushimo* and *Yukikaze* left the spot and took course to Sasebo, speed 20 knots, entering that port on 8 April at 10:00.

The AA destroyer *Fuyuzuki*, searching for her sister *Suzutsuki*, navigated to the N near to Koshikijma and turned to the S but did not discover any trace of the damaged ship. The search was stopped on 8 April at 01:23 and the ship set course to Sasebo, entering there at 08:45. The last ship entering port, at 14:20, was *Suzutsuki*. She had steamed the entire way stern first. Steering with the propellers to avoid the breaking of the bulkhead since a torpedo hit had blown away about 6 m of her forecastle.[266] Because of the gradual increase of immersion she went into dock immediately.

The staff of the 2nd Destroyer Squadron summarised the reports and Rear-Admiral Komura sent a rough battle report of the Surface Special Attack Force to the C-in-C of the Combined Fleet, the Navy Minister and the chief of the Naval General Staff (#081530).

After referring to the outline reports about the air battle in the sea SW off Kyūshū on 7 April the confirmed shooting down of 19 US planes (without those shot down by the sunken ships) was stated and then the damages were stated:

> Damage: *Yamato*, *Isokaze*, *Kasumi* sunk. *Asashimo*: Separated due to engine trouble and navigated independently; reported fighting against enemy carrier-based aircraft about 12:40, no report since that time (probability of being sunk very big). *Suzutsuki*: badly damaged but managed to return to Sasebo under her own power; when anchored immersion increased and the forecastle sank deep so she was towed into the dock.[267]

The rescued crews of the sunken ships were stated as follows:

Table 9-3: Rescued crews

Organisation/Ship	Officers, Special Duty Officers, Warrant Officers	Petty Officers and Ratings
HQ 2nd Fleet	4 (Chief of staff, Artillery staff, Vice- chief incl.)	3
BB *Yamato*	23	246
CL *Yahagi*	37	466 (incl. HQ of 2nd Destroyer Squadron)
DD *Isokaze*	All	326
DD *Hamakaze*	12	244

---

[266] With the radio etc. out no information about her position could be given and with the fires extinguished *Fuyuzuki*'s chance to find her was very small.

[267] The loss of the destroyer *Hamakaze* is missing in the report.

| DD *Kasumi* | 15 | 307 |

Note:

Hamakaze listed as loss. See also Ugaki's "War Diary", p. 579, where a few slightly different numbers are given.

BB = Battleship; CL = Light cruiser; DD = Destroyer.

The present condition of the 1st YB was recognised as follows:

- AA destroyer *Fuyuzuki*: After 20 April fully operational.
- AA destroyer *Suzutsuki*: Stationary use for AA defense possible after 5 May; complete repair requires about three months.
- Destroyer *Yukikaze*: After 15 April fully operational.

Combat Success and Damage

The Detailed Action Record of the battleship *Yamato* lists three planes damaged and 20 planes shot down. The 2nd Destroyer Squadron reported 19 planes shot down (without those shot down by the sunken ships).[268]

---

[268] According to Morison, op. cit., p. 209, referring to the Action Report of Task Force 58, the actual losses were ten planes shot down and twelve men killed in action.

Table 9-4: Damage by ship

Name	Damage	Personnel losses Dead	Wounded	Rescued 1	2	Note
BB *Yamato*, fleet flagship	Sunk at 14:23 at 30°22'N/128°04' E after ten torpedo and six bomb hits and numerous near misses	2,760	117 (14)	23	246	C-in-C 2nd Fleet, Vice-Admiral Itō Seiichi and CO, Captain Aruga Kōsaku, killed in action
CL *Yahagi*, flagship 2nd Destroyer Squadron	Sunk at 14:05 at 30°40'N/128°03'E after seven torpedo and twelve bomb hits	446 (28)	153 (9)	37	466	CO 2nd Destroyer Squadron, Rear-Admiral Komura Keizō, and CO, Captain Hara Tameichi, rescued
DD *Asashimo*	Sunk at uncertain position and time	308 + 18	-----	-----	-----	Fell back due to engine troubles and sunk during the attack of the first US wave. Last radio signal at 12:21
DD *Hamakaze*	Sunk at position 30°°47'N/128°°08'E after one torpedo hit in #3 boiler room (time uncertain)	100 (5)	45	12	244	
DD *Kasumi*	Sunk at 16:57 at 30°51'N/127°57'E after one hit and one near miss between #1 and #2 boiler rooms; three near misses at #3 boiler room (all to starboard) and one near miss to port causing the floating of #1 magazine	17 (1)	3	15	307	Crew taken off by AADD *Fuyuzuki* at 16:22. *Kasumi* then scuttled
DD *Isokaze*	Damaged by a near miss to starboard aft and scuttled at 22:40 at 30°46.5'N/ 128°9.2'E after crew transferred to DDs *Yukikaze* and *Hatsushimo*	20	54 (2)	?	326	The near miss at 13:56 caused immersion and reduced speed. In view of an expected air attack Rear-Admiral Komura decided to scuttle her. Sunk by gun fire from DD *Yukikaze*
AADD *Fuyuzuki*	Hit by two rockets (both were duds). Roof of main gun conning station medium damage and one salt water	12 (1)	12 (2)	-----	-----	Two weeks necessary for repairs. Fully operable after 20 April

AADD *Suzutsuki*	pipe in boiler room damaged Hit by one bomb. #1 and #2 gun houses heavily damaged, fires started, forecastle up to F73 deep in water. Flooding starboard aft due to near misses	57 (1)	34	-----	-----	Returned to Sasebo stern first at full speed, but actual speed supposed to have been 9 knots. Time for repair calculated as three months
DD *Yukikaze*	Slightly damaged by near misses and strafing	3	15	-----	-----	Time for repair one week. After 15 April fully operational
DD *Hatsushimo*	No damage	-----	2	-----	-----	Only ship with no damage and no personnel losses

Notes:

(1) "1" in the column "Rescued" means "Officers, special duty officers, and warrant officers"; "2" means "Petty officers and ratings."

(2) Sinking position of the light cruiser *Yahagi* according to Cressman, op. cit., 310, but he states the same position for the sinking of the battleship *Yamato*.

(3) Adding personnel losses and the number of rescued men to *Yamato*'s complement (incl. HQ 2nd Fleet) would have been 3,143.

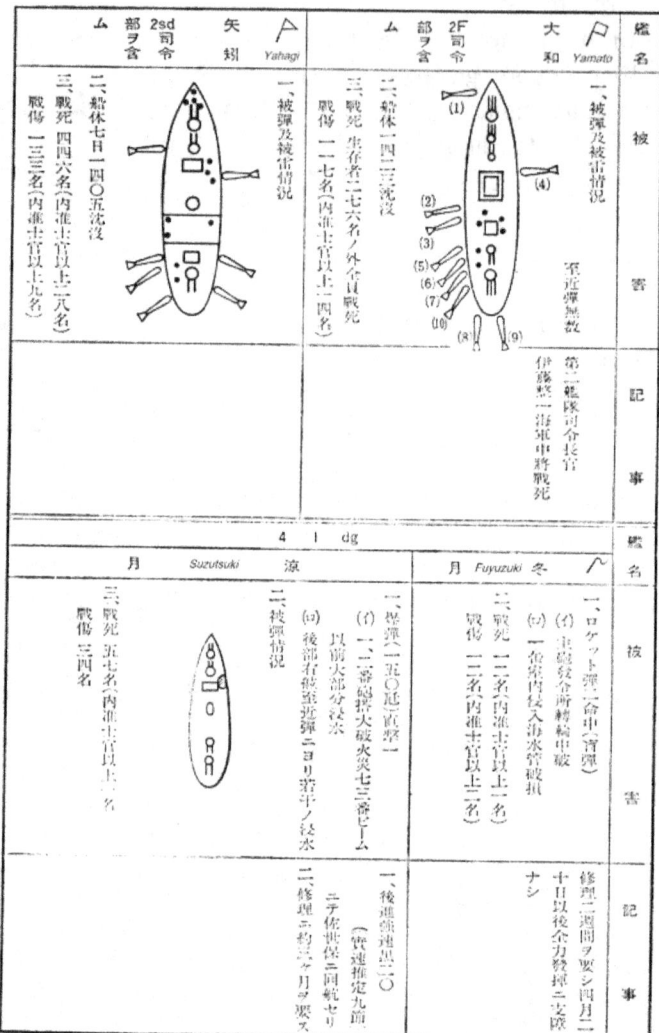

Figure 9-1: Damage as reported by *Yahagi, Yamato, Suzutsuki* and *Fuyuzuki*. See also table 9-4 (Adapted from *Senshi Sōsho*)

Key to Figure 9-1

Yahagi: I, Locations of torpedo and bomb (black points) hits. II, Sunk 7 April 1945. III, 446 killed (including 28 warrant officers and higher ranks). 133 wounded (including 9 warrant officers and higher ranks).

Yamato: I, Locations of torpedo and bomb (black points) hits. II, Sunk at 14:23. III, 2,760 killed (including command division). 117 wounded (including 14 warrant officers and higher ranks). (See also table 9-4)

Fuyuzuki: I, Hit by two rockets (both duds). (a) Salt water pipe in boiler room damaged. (b) Medium damage to roof of main gun control station. II, 12 killed (including 1 warrant officer and higher ranks). 12 wounded (including 2 warrant officers and higher ranks).

Suzutsuki: I, Hit by one bomb (*bakudan* 150-kg). (a) First and second gun houses heavily damaged, fires started, forecastle up to F73 deep in water. (b) Immersion of water due to near misses starboard aft. II, Sketch shows location of bomb hit. III, 57 killed (including 1 warrant officer and higher ranks). 34 wounded.

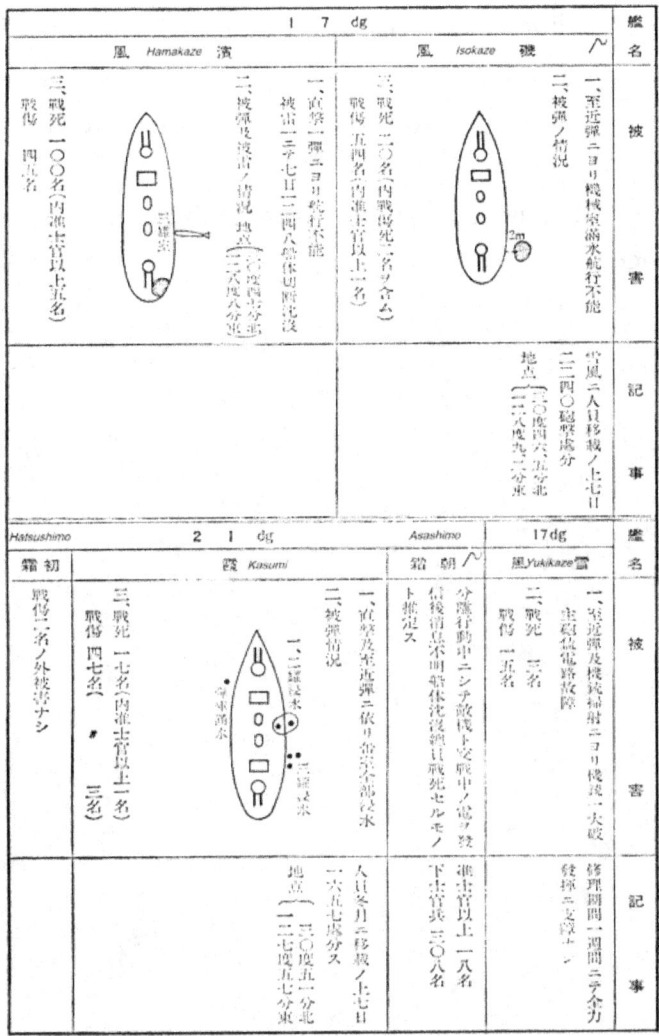

Figure 9-2: Damage as reported by *Hamakaze, Isokaze, Hatsushimo, Kasumi, Asashimo* and *Yukikaze*. See also table 9-4 (Adapted from *Senshi Sōsho*)

Key to Figure 9-2

Hamakaze: I, Immobilised due to direct hits. Hull broken by torpedo hit in #3 boiler room at 12:48 and sunk.

Isokaze: I, see table 9-4.

Hatsushimo: Except for two men wounded no losses and no damage.

Kasumi: I, Water immersion into #2 and #3 boiler rooms due to one bomb hit and several near misses.

Asashimo: Reported fighting with enemy aircraft while separated from the main force. Afterwards radio communications were interrupted. Supposedly sunk with all hands.

Yukikaze: I, Slightly damaged by near misses and strafing. Electric cables of main gun damaged.

Some Considerations on the Loss of the Yamato

In his "Design and Construction of the *Yamato* and *Musashi*" former Tech. Captain Matsumoto Kitarō describes the loss of *Yamato* on pp. 327–330 referring to the story of *Yamato*'s executive officer, Captain Nomura, printed in the Japanese press on 12 April 1946. Therefore, he repeats the attack of about 1,000 US planes in three waves and the hits on *Yamato* with seven large bombs, countless smaller ones and twelve torpedoes.[269] Other than this, the concentration of the torpedo hits to the port side, from amidships to aft, and the almost total immersion of the unprotected compartments at the stern is pointed out. He also correctly stated that, as opposed to the case of the *Musashi*, no investigation was conducted,[270] because at that time the IJN had no more organised power and had lost the eagerness to survey the extent of damage for future data. He complains that the lack of reliable records prevents a detailed survey, like in case of *Musashi*, and forces him to only "roughly state about the condition at that time." In contrast to this uncertainty, the general conclusions drawn from the sinking of these super battleships do mostly agree with the findings of the US Naval Technical Mission to Japan about the causes of the loss. In short:

(1) Even if the structure of the ship had many local defects the resistance against damage was better than could be expected by the designed resistance (three torpedo hits at one side).

(2) The damage by the bomb hits was comparatively small and the detonation pressure and splinters of near misses caused immersion. Very narrow near misses seemed to be more dangerous for the ship than hits. However, the damage caused by bomb hits and near misses was not at all fatal.

(3) Like in case of *Musashi* the torpedoes were the real enemy to these ships since they destroyed the underwater protection system and caused tremendous immersion. Despite the difficulty to sink them by

---

[269] This story was obstinately adhered to in the Japanese literature and, e.g., Yokoi Tadatoshi repeats it in part II of his "The End of the First Fleet" in *Sekai no Kansen*, 5/1967. It seems that until the publication of *Senshi Sōsho*, vol. 17, Nomura's description was considered accurate and American publications, including Morison's *Victory in the Pacific*, were ignored.

[270] See Komura's statement in 1966.

damage never thought possible at the time of the design both ships sank after all.

(4) The cause of the much quicker sinking of *Yamato* compared with *Musashi*, by fewer torpedo hits, was their concentration to one side and from amidships to aft.

To prevent sinking following such attacks Matsumoto considered the study of the following items necessary from the viewpoint of the designer:

(1) Shortage of the maintenance of buoyancy outside the vital part (including the large spaces below the magazines).

(2) Shortage of maintaining the waterline area of these parts.[271]

(3) Insufficient capacity of the damage control system.

(4) Shortage of local watertightness behind the side (belt) armor.

(5) Weak structure of trunks, bulkheads of the watertight compartments and floors.

Matsumoto admits that the designers did not have the farsightedness in designing the battleship for the future war by having the wide prospect of the development of the aircraft.

In Report S-06-2 "Reports of Damage to Japanese Warships–Article 2 Yamato (BB), Musashi (BB), Taiho (CV), Shinano (CV)" the investigation team of the USNTMtJ agrees with Matsumoto's conclusion (3) when stating that "There can be no doubt that YAMATO was sunk by torpedoes—the magazine explosion occurring after she had capsized." and neglecting bomb damages in the "discussion" about the causes of her loss, thus confirming indirectly Matsumoto's statement in (2). "The aircraft torpedoes … employed warheads containing approximately 600 pounds [271 kg] of torpex. The majority of the torpedoes … had depth settings of 18 [5.50 m] to 22 [6.10 m] feet … there is every reason to believe that such a charge would have defeated YAMATO's torpedo defense system." It is well known from earlier torpedo hits that this system was 'defeated' and it is also acknowledged by some of her designers. With reference to the damage control system, also found to be in-

---

[271] The authors have to confess to be unable to grasp the correct sense of this statement. He may refer to the immersion that occurred in both cases and caused *Musashi* to capsize, when her bows became awash (trim), and when *Yamato*'s one-sided immersion became too big (list). Items ① and ② bring about the same effect when crossing "the point of no return."

sufficient by Matsumoto (3), the investigators believed that "The reliance which the Japanese placed in counterflooding measures to control large angles of list was not substantiated in YAMATO's case. Although a moderate list could be removed quickly, as in MUSASHI's case, counterflooding capacity was limited to little more than required to right the ship when struck by three torpedoes on one side, if the torpedoes did not defeat the torpedo defense system."

This is in sharp contrast to Matsumoto's finding in (1) and also Fukuda's satisfaction with the resistance proven by both battleships. The calculations are included in Matsumoto's (third) book and the investigators confirm that the capacity was sufficient for compensating three hits on one side. The true defect of this system was the general insufficient capacity or, in other words, the insufficient number of torpedo hits upon which the design was based. There is no doubt, that both ships developed more resistance than could be expected. That the one-sided concentration of the hits in case of *Yamato* accelerated the sinking, as pointed out by Matsumoto in (4), is quite natural. However, one has to agree with the finding "With a sharp list, of the order of 16°, where the upper (US main) deck takes the water, the outboard voids could be filled only to about 55 per cent capacity by flooding from the sea–a serious deficiency in attempting to control list, by virtue of the small righting moment thus available." and also "There was no damage control pumping system of adequate capacity provided for completely filling the outboard voids in case of large angles of list."[272] Thus, even though the ships were not seriously damaged, there was no ready means of removing lists as large as 16°–18°, other than by flooding outboard engineering spaces." Another important defect, whose main cause was the protection against underwater projectiles–one gets the impression that after the development of the Type 91 AP projectile there was an obsession that the underwater protection of armored ships had to be decided by the power of this projectile and not by torpedoes–had already been pointed out by then Captain Fujimoto Kikuo in 1930 and stated by the investigators as follows: "From the standpoint of resistance to damage, it is considered that carrying outboard layers filled with liquid (either salt water ballast or fuel oil) to limit initial angles of list would have been preferable." Investiga-

---

[272] The investigators concluded: "A damage control pumping system of large capacity would have been a distinct asset on the ships of the YAMATO Class."

tions and a large number of experiments carried out by the Tech. Vice-Admiral Tokugawa Takesada etc. on protective systems of capital ships from the time of World War One to present times (1937–1941) clearly proved the superiority of the liquid layer system compared with the "underwater projectile defense system" but due to the building stop of large ships on 6 November 1941 it seems as if no final decision about the system to be applied to future ships was made.[273]

---

[273] Besides of Vice-Admiral Tokugawa's extensive reports (Mr. Hans Lengerer do have copies of three.) and the comprehensive summary of the Navy Technical Department some interesting data can also be found in Fukuda's "Outline of the Fundamental Design of Warships", p. 103ff, *Shōwa Zōsen-shi*, *Kaigun Hōjutsu-shi*, *Kaigun Suirai-shi*, Matsumoto's books and some issues of *Sekai no Kansen*, with #4/1976 and #5/1976 in particular devoted to protection.

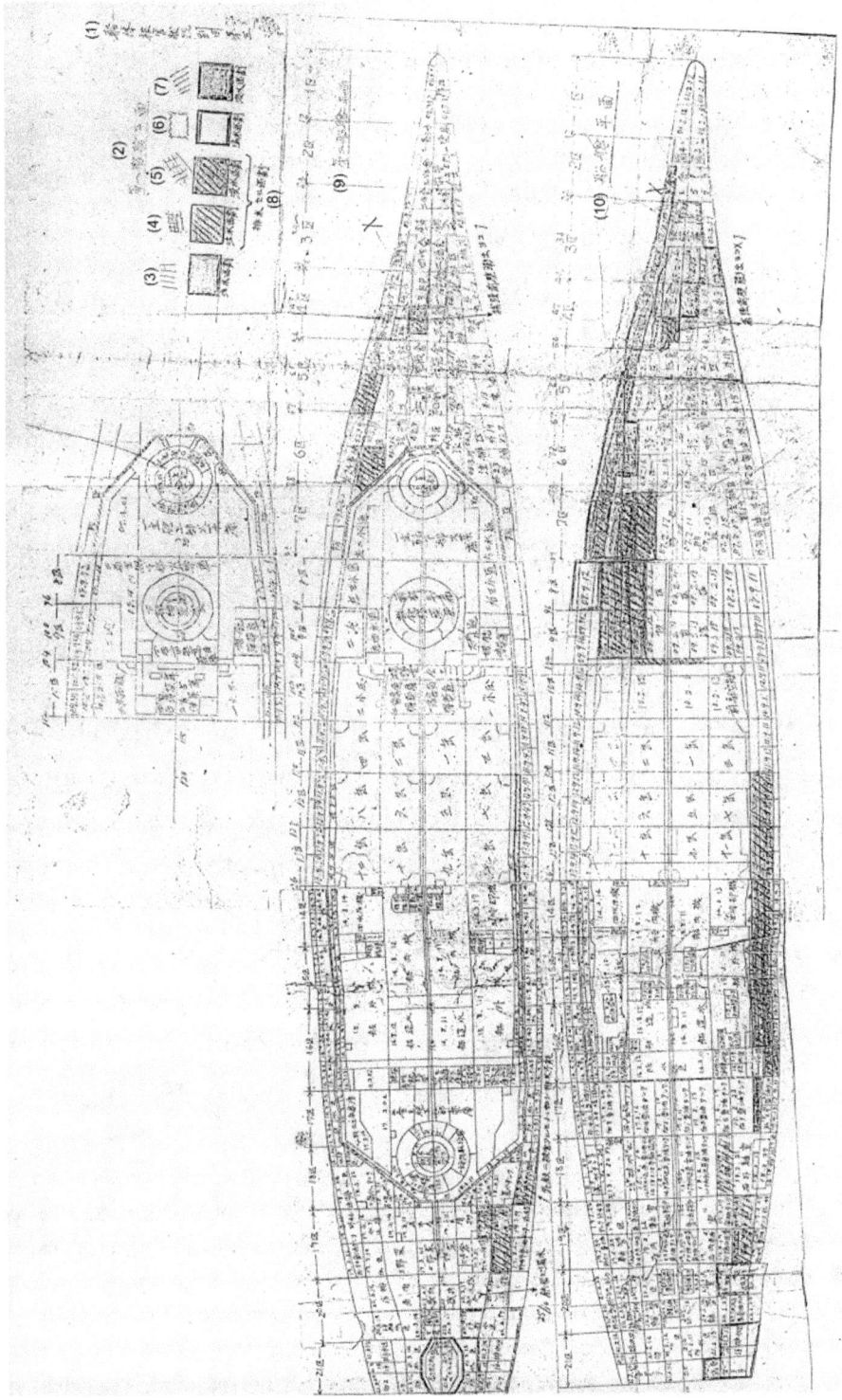

Figure 9-3: Part of the official flooding scheme of the *Yamato* (*Senkan* Yamato *Kenzō Hiroku*)

Key to Figure 9-3:
(1) Details of hull damage situation appendix figure 3
(2) 1st hold plan
(3) For stability intentionally flooded compartment
(4) For stability intentionally flooded compartment
(5) By damage flooded compartment
(6) By damage leaky compartment
(7) By damage flooded compartment
(8) Compartment later pumped dry
(9) 2nd hold plan
(10) Hold plan

Some Excerpts from the War Lessons

The DAR of the battleship *Yamato* is comparatively voluminous so that its rendering is outside the scope of this description. But picking up some statements under the headline "War Lessons" may be of some interest.

For instance, as for the operational use the close co-operation of the surface force as Special Attack Force with the base air forces was pointed out as absolutely necessary. Air supremacy, or at least control of the air, should be attained and the weather condition be used advantageously etc. Every possible measure should be taken in order to avoid that the Special Attack Force would become an easy prey to the enemy's aircraft, either before or after the assault.[274] With regard to the AA defense the effectiveness of the angle-speed fire control system (*kaku sokudo shōjunki*) of the 25-mm machine-guns was pointed out and it was added that the number of enemy aircraft, whose shoot-

---

[274] More or less a repetition of the basic principles that should have been applied to the present mission, but they were illusory in view of the true condition of the IJN at that time. The records of the air special attack forces were tremendously exaggerated, air control could never be expected and even under the most favourable weather conditions a 50:50 chance was only seen by Admiral Toyoda. US Naval Intelligence intercepted and translated the operation orders and knew almost everything about the mission. The orders for the interception and destruction of the *Yamato* Force had been issued about 15 hours before the sortie, and should foul weather prevent air attacks the US surface ships were powerful enough to stop it. The Surface Special Force had never a chance of success and after its almost total destruction the IJN surface forces actually ceased to exist because lack of fuel, carrier-based aircraft and pilots etc. made the surviving units almost immobilised.

ing down could be confirmed, would not be many in the future either because of bad sight, turning and listing of the ships etc. "but the accuracy of the line of fire and the concentration of this fire control system is very good compared with the former fire control system."

The absolute necessity of using a parallax angle correction device (*shūchū kaku shūsei sochi*) in case of large distances between the machine-gun and the "following-the-movement" fire control system (*jūdō shiki shōjun sōchi kijū*) was also mentioned.

Structural defects and the reinforcement of the machine-gun carriage were referred to in order to secure the easy training of the machine-gun in case of sharp turns of the ship causing considerable list and the training in case of slight damage was also to be secured by the reinforcements.

Evasive maneuvers of the ship to avoid bomb attacks should be carried out depending on the speed without considering the negative influence upon the gunfire. The authors pointed out that this lesson had been recognised unequivocally already in previous battles.[275]

In evaluating the enemy battle tactics the authors of the battleship *Yamato*'s DAR did not recognise any new tactics but they pointed out that co-ordinated attacks of fighters, dive bombers and torpedo planes had become still better compared with the Philippine Sea battle. They recognised the improved fire protection of the enemy planes by pointing out that many aircraft had been hit by 25-mm projectiles, which started fires, but these were soon extinguished[276] with the consequence that the plane did not crash.

On 23 August 1966 the commanding officer of the 2nd Destroyer Squadron, former Rear-Admiral Komura Keizō, recalled the Special Attack Opera-

---

[275] One might be inclined to take this as a confession of the relative ineffectiveness of the high-angle guns and AA machine-guns.

[276] The US planes were fitted with CO_2 fire extinguishers, self-sealing tanks, armor protection for the pilot etc. Japanese planes lacked such fittings and equipment and until the termination of the war only few plane types were so fitted (late in 1944) but without attaining the effectiveness of the US equipment. US planes often returned to their bases with 50 to more than 100 recorded hits, while Japanese planes burned after only a few hits and crashed. The lack of these common fittings and equipment in US aircraft contributed remarkably to the loss of many Japanese planes in combination with the VT fuse and sophisticated (radar-directed) fire control system.

tion and because his statement may represent the opinion of the executive side some excerpts may be of interest:[277]

> The thought whether the sortie of the 1st YB as Special Attack Force was an assault operation with Okinawa as target or was a bait to lure the enemy task force was based upon considerations before the start of the assault operation. At that time the staff often dealt with these questions and it may probably so have been stated in the DAR of the 1st YB that the operational goal was still questionable even after the start of the assault operation. But I did not have any doubts about our task and thought that the operation had to be executed without further deliberations after the visit of the chief of staff of the Combined Fleet [Vice-Admiral Kusaka] with the 1st YB and his explanation that it was a special attack [Tokkō].
>
> Only the execution of the operation should perhaps be criticised. Advancing straight a way after the determination of the time of sortie and arrival of the order, the destruction of the force on the way was unavoidable. But with the annihilation of such a force a corresponding success should be attained.
>
> The operation of the destroyer squadron is principally the night battle. An assault after dawn is senseless. The advance to Okinawa is not impossible provided that a sufficiently wide detour is made and the weather conditions are considered. If such plans are worked out one should take a period of about one month for research, preparation of the weapons, training of the crews and strive for conformity between the central organs [the Naval General Staff and the Navy Minister] and the operative force.[278]

---

[277] The official DAR repeated mainly the opinions stated in the battleship *Yamato*'s DAR and it criticised the highest command organisation for the sacrifice of the whole force, but it did not point out openly the blunders made during the planning and execution of the operation.

[278] This sentence makes obvious the existence of (grave?) discrepancies between the central organ (the Naval General Staff) and the 2nd Fleet about the operational use of the latter. It must be regarded as almost certain that Rear-Admiral Komura referred to the intention of the HQ of the 2nd Fleet to ask the central organ for the disbanding of the fleet. Two days before issuing the operation order for the Surface Special Attack Force a conference of the 2nd Destroyer Squadron was held on 3 April 15:00 about the operative use of the 2nd fleet. Estimating their own situation and the situation of the enemy it was concluded that air operations would scarcely develop advantageously for Japan. Should in this situation the assault operation of the surface force be planned as the last resort, its destruction *en route* to the operational target was almost sure. The conclusion was to disband the surface force, to land the complements as well as weapons and ammunition for the defence of the country and to use the ships as floating batteries and for "operations" in the Inland Sea. The HQ of the 2nd Fleet shared this conclusion and Vice-Admiral Itō decided to submit this proposal to the HQ of the Combined Fleet and the central authorities on the following day (confirmed by Rear-admiral Komura's statement on 18 July 1966). But on that day (4 April) the 2nd Fleet received DesOpOrd #601 of the Combined Fleet about the No. 1 *Kikusui* Operation (Principal Particulars of the Total Air Attack–*Kōkū sō kōgeki yōryō*) so that the submission of the proposal was postponed. On 5 April the *Tokkō*-operation of the 1st YB was ordered and the proposal about the disbanding of the 2nd Fleet was never officially submitted (as for informal channels the situation was different).

> The advance to Sasebo [to function as bait for the US Task Force 58] was ordered suddenly, the use as Surface Special Attack Force was also ordered surprisingly and there was no directive in between. In this way no successful operation can be planned. There was also no time to communicate between the air and the naval forces. Of course, basing upon the facts and experiences of the past air support (escort) was not expected. Such an unfounded operation cannot produce any fighting spirit.
>
> After the sortie half a day earlier than planned there was no time to choose the approach route; the 1st YB was forced to take the predetermined route.
>
> After the return to Sasebo the Vice-chief of staff of the Combined Fleet, Rear-Admiral Yano Shikazō,[279] visited me and asked to be forgiven that *Yahagi* had not been fitted with radar.[280] Other than this there was no visit from the central organisation and I do not remember of an investigation about the operation.[281] The flag of the 2nd Destroyer Squadron was hauled down and I visited the Naval General Staff at Tōkyō on 20 April and also reported to the C-in-C of the Combined Fleet …

On 30 July 1945 Vice-Admiral Ozawa Jisaburō, then C-in-C of the Combined Fleet, issued a citation (Combined Fleet Secret Citation #114) "to the main part of the 1st YB" commending the "incomparable heroic assault operation" again,[282] referring also to the "tradition of the Imperial Navy" and ending with the "confirmation" of the "outstanding achievement."

In addition, the achievement of the commanding officer of the *Yamato*, Captain Aruga Kōsaku, was proclaimed in a separate citation (Combined Fleet #193).

On 3 May 1945 Vice-Admiral Itō was promoted admiral, posthumously, and Captain Aruga received a rare double promotion, posthumously, to vice-admiral on the request of Admiral Toyoda.

To cite Hara, op. cit., p. 304, "What was the great war result?" He refers to the damage of the aircraft carrier USS *Hancock* (CV-19), the battleship USS

---

[279] A staff officer of the Naval General Staff accompanied him but Rear-Admiral Komura did obviously not remember his name.

[280] No details are stated but he may have referred to the installation of fire control radar, a modification of #22 radar.

[281] This may be understandable in view of the then state of the IJN for any investigation would have been of only academic value.

[282] See Hara, op. cit., p. 304, for the citation of Admiral Toyoda, which was handed over to Rear-Admiral Komura when he returned to Sasebo aboard the destroyer *Hatsushimo* on 8 April, praising the "gallant self-sacrifice which enabled the Special Attack planes to achieve a great war result."

Maryland (BB-46) and the destroyer USS *Bennett* (DD-473)[283] at a cost of almost 100 planes and then lists the tremendous losses of the 2nd Fleet (Special Attack Force), the American side gained with incredible low personnel and material losses. On the other hand, one might agree with the criticism of some Americans that the 386 carrier-based planes which took off to attack the *Yamato* unit should have been sufficient to annihilate the total force.

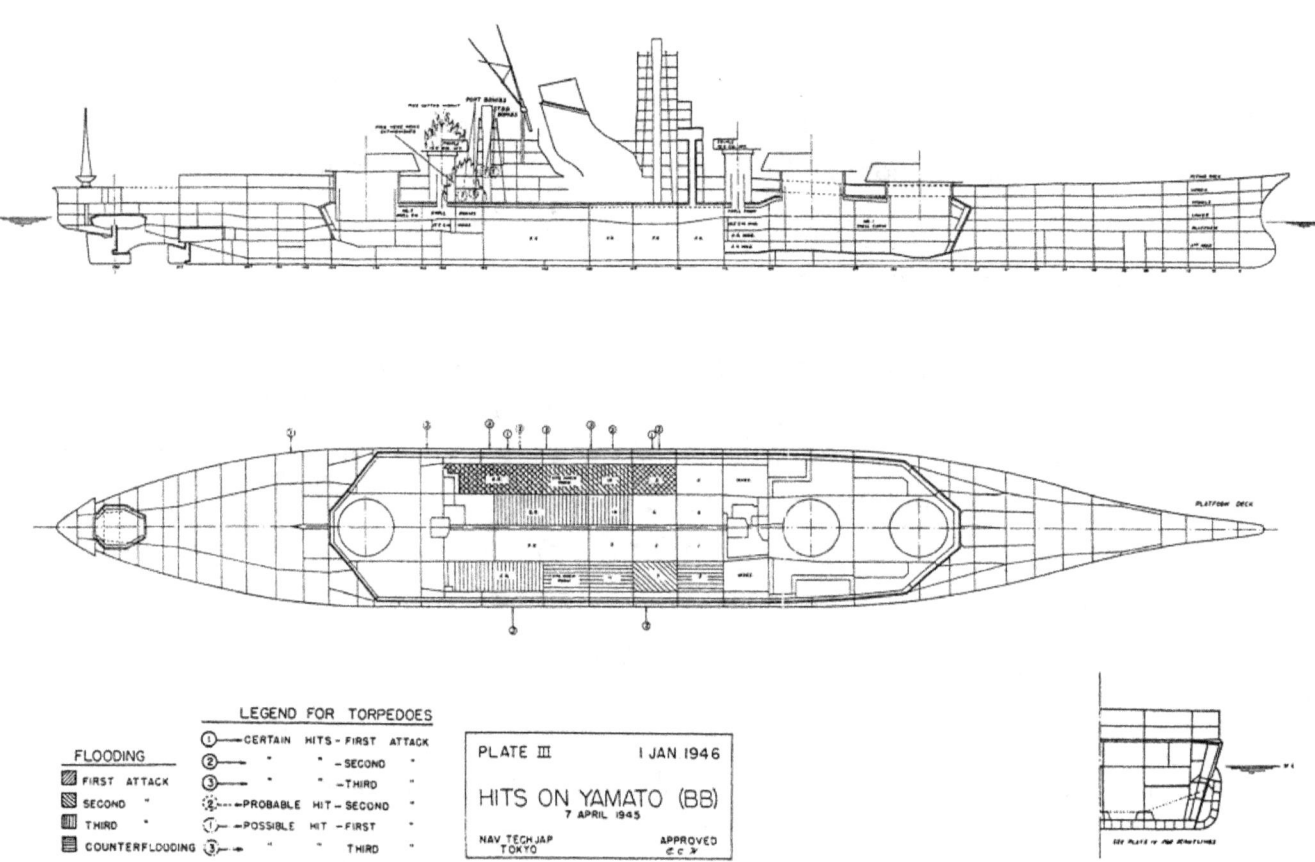

Figure 9-4: Hits on *Yamato* (US Naval Technical Mission to Japan, Report S-06-2)

---

[283] Also damaged by Kamikazes on 7 April were the destroyer USS *Longshaw* (DD-559) and the destroyer escort USS *Wesson* (DE-184).

Part III–Subsequent Planning Section

CHAPTER 10–INCOMPLETE SISTERS AND THE NEVER-BUILT SUPER *YAMATO* CLASS

When the Naval General Staff worked out the tactical requirements for the *Yamato* class, the possession of two ships was at first considered sufficient. Both were included in the Third Naval Armament Replenishment Programme of 1937 (which passed the 70th Diet session opened on 26 December 1936) and was popularly known as the *Maru San Keikaku*. However, in view of the resumption of battleship building by the US Navy and the Royal Navy, after the termination of the arms limitation treaty system, the possession of a further two ships was recognised as being necessary. They were included in the Fourth Fleet Completion Programme of 1939 with the intention to be built as identical sisters bearing the temporary names #110 warship and #111 warship. This programme passed the 74th Diet session (opened on 26 December 1938) and was popularly known as the *Maru Yon Keikaku*.

But the US Navy accelerated the naval race. In June 1940 the Third Vinson-Trammel Act (the 11 percent Naval Expansion Bill) was adopted followed in July by the so-called Stark Planning (the Two-Ocean Fleet Act). The latter permitted the building of a further four battleships of the *Iowa* class (BB-63 to BB-66) and five *Montana*s (BB-67 to BB-71). In addition the budget for building six battle cruisers (unofficial classification) of the *Alaska* class (CB-1 to CB-6) passed.

In summary: Between 1937 and 1940 the budgets for building 17 battleships and six battle cruisers with a total of 23 capital ships passed.

The IJN reacted upon the 11 percent Naval Expansion Bill with the planning of the Fifth Naval Armament Replenishment Programme, popularly known as the *Maru Go Keikaku*. It included three battleships with the temporary names #797 warship, #798 warship and #799 warship. Among them the first one was of a modified *Yamato* type, still armed with 46-cm main guns, and recognised as *Kai* #110 warship. The other two ships were to be armed with 51-cm main guns and were said to have been tentatively classified as the Super

Yamato class. To oppose the American new type battle cruisers two ultra cruisers (battle cruisers) armed with 30-cm (actually 12" = 30.48 cm) main guns were also included.

The Two-Ocean Fleet Act forced the IJN to take countermeasures. The Naval General Staff planned the Sixth Naval Armament Replenishment Programme, popularly known as the *Maru Roku Keikaku*, almost in parallel with the Fifth ... Programme but this planning could only be realized superficially, at best. When the content of both programmes was submitted formally to the navy minister on the 21 September 1941 the Sixth ... Programme included four Super *Yamato* class battleships armed with 51-cm main guns and four ultra cruisers.

The answer of the navy minister pointed out that utmost efforts would be paid in view of the opening of the war to execute both programmes, but nothing definitive could be said about the Sixth ... Programme. In the very hectic situation immediately before the beginning of the Pacific War there was not the slightest chance of realization and the Naval Affairs Division of the Navy Ministry admitted that the postponement of the beginning of the Fifth ... Programme was almost unavoidable at that time.[285]

---

[284] The late Rear-Admiral Takasu Kōichi supposed that the building of four *Yamato* class battleships had been planned in the first draft of the Fifth ... Programme, but it was reduced to three when, in the course of the revisions, two super (ultra) type cruisers were included after the building of "large cruisers" by the US Navy became known.

[285] It should have started at the beginning of FY 1942 (1 April) but was postponed (at that time two years were calculated, at least). It was totally revised three months later.

After the beginning of the Pacific War the war lessons required the revision of the shipbuilding policy. The defeat at Midway caused a complete revision of the Fifth Naval Armament Replenishment Programme into the *Kai Maru Go Keikaku*, with the Urgent Aircraft Carrier Reinforcement Programme in the centre and the abolishment of the battleships. When in 1943 the Wartime Warship Replenishment Programme was adopted, the *Maru Roku Keikaku* (with a total of 197 warships displacing approx. 800,000 tons standard) disappeared automatically without the design of a single ship being completed. Among the ships whose building was permitted by the modified *Maru Go Keikaku* only a small percentage was completed. In other words: As predicted long before the beginning of the Pacific War, Japan could not but loose a naval race against the United States of America. The American shipbuilding capacity was about five-times as large as the Japanese one and the industrial, economical and financial power enabled the USA to out-build Japan, who also suffered from lack of raw material, in all products.

#110 and #111 Warships (Nos. 3 and 4 Yamato Class Battleships)

Battleships #110 and #111 were to be built as sister ships according to the design of the *Yamato* and *Musashi* and were to compose one battleship division. However, some improvements were attempted in response to the appearance of a new weapon, improvement of flagship facilities and cruising range.

(1) *Reinforcement of the ship's bottom protection.* When World War II began in Europe the very sensitive magnetic mine was used, against which the IJN had no countermeasure. As protection against this mine the reinforcement of the ship's bottom in the range of the machinery spaces, particularly the engine rooms, and ammunition magazines was considered as necessary. Above the double bottom, consisting of two layers of 25.4-mm thick DS plates, another DS layer of 12.7-mm thickness was stretched to make a triple bottom. In areas lacking the space to fit this plate, the double bottom was reinforced. According to calculations and experiments the detonation of a mine with a charge of 300 kg at 2.5 m distance to the bottom would not cause any leakage.

(2) *Reduction of armor thickness to compensate the weight increase by the partial triple bottom and reinforced double bottom.* The protection against the magnetic

mine required an increase of the weight by approx. 600 tons. On the other hand, several armor thicknesses had some "reserve" which could be used to compensate the weight increase by the strengthening of the ship's bottom protection. Consequently, the thickness of the belt armor was reduced to 400 mm from 410 mm, that of the protective (middle) deck to 190 mm from 200 mm and the barbettes of the main guns to 540 mm from 560 mm.

(3) *Reinforcement of the protection of the secondary gun turrets against bombs.* The weight saved by the aforementioned reductions exceeded the required approx. 600 tons and also permitted the reinforcement of the protection of the secondary gun turrets against bombs. The 25.4-mm thick plates of the turrets provided only splinter protection and the barbettes above the weather deck also had insufficient protection. However, the design of the reinforcement is uncertain.

(4) *Improvement of the flagship facilities.* The revision of the flagship facilities as flagship of the Combined Fleet caused changes in the fleet operation room, which, in turn, affected the nearby command centres in the foremast.

(5) *Reduction of the fuel storage.* New calculations had shown a remarkable excess of the required range so a reduction of the fuel storage was intended.

(6) *Planned reinforcement of the anti-aircraft defense.* Instead of the 40-cal Type 89 12.7-cm twin high-angle guns the most modern and much more efficient 60-cal Type 98 10-cm twin high-angle guns should be mounted. But this planning had to be given up because of the insufficient production of this gun.

#110 warship (later *Shinano*) was laid down in the #6 building dock of the Yokosuka Navy Yard on 4 May 1940. The building progress was rather slow because the dock was expanded in parallel with construction work. When the Pacific War began, her construction as a battleship was stopped. But at the same time it was decided to complete her into launching condition so that she could be able to leave the dock. For this purpose the completion up to the middle deck, partly also to the upper deck, was considered as being necessary.[286] However, at a conference in June 1942 her conversion into an aircraft carrier was decided and she became one of the aircraft carriers of the Urgent Aircraft Carrier Reinforcement Programme.[287]

The construction of #111 warship started on 7 November 1940 in Kure Navy Yard and progressed quickly. When the double bottom was completed, it was to be reinforced as described before. For this reason construction was temporarily halted and the construction of other ships were favored depending upon the requirements. Construction was cancelled as soon as the Pacific War was begun. In March 1942 the disintegration of the double bottom was decided and after dismantling the material was used for the construction of pontoons and *Sharan* type freighters.[288]

#797 Warship (Modified Yamato Class)

The major modifications incorporated in the rough design of #797 warship, planned to be built in Yokosuka Navy Yard, were as follows:

(1) *Reinforcement of the ship's bottom protection.* The reinforcement was in the range as described above.

(2) *Reinforcement of the underwater protection.* Mounting of longitudinal bulkheads along the unprotected sides forward and aft of the vital part to limit immersion resulting from a torpedo hit. (It is uncertain whether or not the thickness of the bulkheads in these parts was increased since the very long unprotected areas had been recognised as a seriously weak point of the *Yamato* class.)

(3) *Reinforcement of the AA defense.* The secondary guns were abolished to mount as many as possible of the 60-cal Type 98 10-cm twin high-angle guns and Type 96 25-mm triple machine-guns (Some sources state the number of the 10-cm high-angle guns as ten but even this

---

[286] In 1937 the US Navy decided to build two battleships of the *North Carolina* class (BB-55 & BB-56) and in 1938 four battleships of the *South Dakota* class (BB-57 to BB-60) followed. In 1939 the Second Vinson-Trammel Act included two battleships of the *Iowa* class (BB-61 & BB-62). Even though the latter two battleships had not much effect upon the Fourth Naval Armament Completion Programme the new building of six American battleships was more than sufficient to prove that the IJN needed more battleships of the *Yamato* class to oppose the

[287] The aircraft carrier *Shinano* will be dealt with in another volume.

[288] A particular Japanese type of ship corresponding to an open lighter according to the classification of the US Navy in World War II.

number is uncertain.). As for the 25-mm machine-guns the authors have found no numbers in the sources consulted. To control these weapons the increase of the high-angle gun fire control system and machine-gun directors was intended. The air defense control stations on top of the foremast and the main mast and the air watch stations were revised in response to the increased numbers of these weapons.

(4) The rooms of the commanding headquarters were shifted forward to make them rather more spacious.

#798 & #799 Warships (Super Yamato Class)

#798 & #799 warships were to mount 51-cm guns and were known as the Super *Yamato* class. The background for selecting this calibre was the thought that the USN would become aware of the 46-cm calibre of the main guns of the *Yamato* class when these ships would operate in the war theatre, at the latest. It was supposed that the USN would begin to build battleships mounting the same calibre. To oppose them, the IJN wanted to have superior battleships mounting 51-cm guns. This would ensure Japanese superiority in firepower for a period of at least five years.

The fundamental design number of the Super *Yamato* class was A 150. At the early design stage the armament should consist of eight 45-cal 51-cm guns, mounted in four twin turrets in superimposed style forward and aft. The standard displacement was calculated as 85,000 tons. The Naval General Staff wanted the ships to have a speed of 30 knots, but in this case the displacement would go up to at least 90,000 tons and approach 100,000 tons. Therefore, the speed was reduced to 27 knots, like *Yamato* class.

The protection had to be designed to resist the impact of the same calibre projectiles. Thus the armor thicknesses exceeded considerably that of the *Yamato* class, so that two layers had to be used because the production technique did not permit the production of plates up to 800 mm thickness.

The completed ships necessitated a dry dock for the cleaning of the ships' bottom but at that time there was no dock capable of such big ships. In addition, modernization and changes of port facilities etc. would become necessary. In view of these obstacles the Naval General Staff agreed to a revision of the design to mount six 45-cal 51-cm guns in three twin turrets on the principal dimensions, hull shape, structure and general arrangement of the *Yamato* class. The propulsion plant was also similar.

Two of the three twin main gun turrets were to be mounted superimposed forward of the tower mast; the third one aft. What deserves attention is the fact that the twin turrets were to be replaceable with the 46-cm triple turret of *Yamato* class, indicating the same idea as in case of the 15.5-cm triple and 20.3-cm twin turrets and, if not better prepared, the creation of still more serious difficulties than in the *Mogami* class. Should the mounting of six 51-cm guns in place of nine 46-cm guns on the *Yamato* class have been intended, the increase of the hull strength in the vicinity of the turrets to absorb the increased forces when at firing the main guns might have been solved, but only by the addition of considerable weight.

The storage of the projectiles and propellant powder bags, whose shape was changed and number increased to eight bags of 60 kg each,[289] was a little different in the magazines compared with the *Yamato* class. The transportation method had also to be revised. A wooden model in actual size was test produced and inspected. It ended with the decision of the transportation method (mechanically operated) but left the revision of the magazine structure (which also required more space than in the *Yamato* class) as a theme for a later discussion.

Even though neither a 45-cal 51-cm gun, temporarily called A Gun (*Kō Hō*) without any calibre specification, nor a turret was completed due to the building stop of large ships on 6 December 1941 it may still be of interest to provide some additional data.

Captain Yanagimoto Ryūsaku[290] became chief of the Third Section of the Second Division of the Naval General Staff, headed by then Rear-Admiral Takagi Takeo, on 15 November 1939. After keeping this post for almost a year he proposed to investigate the building of battleships mounting 20" guns following the *Yamato* class. At that time there was a rumour that the secret of mounting 18" guns had already been leaked to the USA.

---

[289] This means that in total 480 kg of propellant powder were necessary to fire one shell.

[290] He was a gunnery specialist and had been the chief gunnery officers of the battleship *Hiei*'s secondary guns before being dispatched to Britain for two years. His talent was considered outstanding, his efforts were regarded as extreme and he was much respected in navy circles. He became the commanding officer of the aircraft carrier *Sōryū* on 6 October 1941 (until that time he was in the Naval General Staff) and participated in all operations of the First Air Fleet until sharing his fate with his ship at the Battle for Midway on 4 June 1942.

In October 1940 he visited Rear-Admiral Shimizu Fumio, the chief designer of guns in the First Division of the Navy Technical Department, and questioned him about the possibility to produce 20" guns. After explaining the likelihood that the USN already were aware of the building of battleships mounting 18" guns, he expressed his belief that the production of guns of a still larger calibre would cause the impression that Japan could not be defeated and would prevent the outbreak of a war with the USA.

According to the late Rear-Admiral Takasu Kōichi, the Navy Technical Department had already begun to investigate the production of the 51-cm gun in June 1939 when the design of the 18" gun was completed. The background was the requirement of the Naval General Staff to mount this gun even earlier. Therefore, Captain Yanagimoto's "question" was no surprise but accelerated the rough design of the 45-cal 51-cm gun on the basis of the actual data of the 45-cal 46-cm gun of the *Yamato* class, for which, in turn, the trial production of the 48-cm (18.9") gun had provided useful data.[291] When the outline of the *Maru Go Keikaku* was planned the design of the 85,000-ton battleship mounting four twin turrets was begun in 1940 and had already been dealt with in the Higher Technical Conference in early 1941. In June 1941 this topic was again a theme of the Higher Technical Conference. One of the results was the order of a trial production of two barrels, one gun carriage, ammunition transport system etc. placed with Kure Navy Yard by the Navy Technical Department.

When the building planning of the 51-cm-gunned battleships was stopped by the start of the Pacific War the Gunnery Division, barrel factory, of Kure Navy Yard had completed the #1 barrel to the stage of fitting the breech. The second barrel was completed up to 4 A, requiring the fitting of 5 A and 5 B

---

[291] In *Senshi Sōsho*, vol. 31, pp. 489–90, parts of the recollections of the designer of large calibre guns in the Navy Technical Department and the chief of the Fundamental Design Section of the First Division of the Navy Technical Department as of July 1968 and 13 December 1967, respectively, are included. Depending hereupon the fundamental designs of 18" and 20" guns were practised until 1930 without any particular purpose (although supposedly for mounting on battleships) and efforts were directed upon the triple 18" mount. After the completion of the first 18" gun in March 1938 and the satisfactory result of the trial firing at Kamegakubi the design of the 20" gun was accelerated. It was scheduled to mount this gun after the fifth ship (of the *Yamato* class). The trial production of this gun began in 1940 but trial firing did not take place.

tubes only. The gun carriage and their fittings were close to completion. However, they were left as they were and were not assembled.

For the trial production of the *Kō Hō* the Gunnery Division had to execute several modifications such as:

(1) Increase of the floor area of the heat-hardening factory.
(2) Installation of a 250-ton crane in the heat-hardening factory.
(3) Increase of the depth of the tank for the heat treatment of the gun barrel.
(4) Fitting of new equipment for hanging (gun barrel).
(5) Improvement of several machine tools and equipment.
(6) Building of a carrier boat for 350 tons.

The next tables provide some details of the weights and dimensions of the 45-cal 51-cm gun. The comparison with the 46-cm gun of the *Yamato* class shows remarkable differences by the apparently modest increase of the calibre of 5 cm.

Table 10-1. Comparison of tube weights (in tons) 45-cal 51-cm gun and 45-cal 46-cm gun

Tube	Ingot	Stage of heat treatment	Machining	Finished	45-cal 46-cm gun; finished
1 A	157	64.2	41.0	21.7	15.9
2 A	157	75.6	47.6	30.0	22.5
3 A	177	79.5	53.6	33.7	24.7
4 B	123	53.8	28.5	18.3	13.4
5 A	157	69.4	42.1	26.0	19.0
5 B	157	66.8	40.5	28.9	21.2
Total	928	409.3	253.3	158.6	116.7

Note: The weight of the wire and attachments are not included.

Table 10-2: Comparison of tube weights and finished weights (in tons) of the 45-cal 51-cm gun and the 45-cal 46-cm gun

Gun	Ingot	At heat treatment	Finished	Percentage
45-cal 46-cm / 51-cm gun	725 / 985	417 /?	166 / 227	100 / 136.75
Tubes of 46-cm / 51-cm gun	680 / 928	354 / 409	116.7 / 158.6	100 / 135.90

Table 10-3: Length of the tubes of the 45-cal 51-cm gun

Tube	Crude machining (m)	Finished (m)	Total length of gun barrel
1 A	25.720	23.050	
2 A	24.890	23.047	
3 A	14.190	12.330	23.560 meters (46-cm = 21.130)
4 B	14.390	13.280	
5 A	6.340	5.240	
5 B	10.550	9.360	

Table 10-4: Specifications of chemical properties of the steel used for gun production (quantities are in percentages)

Carbon (C)	Nickel (Ni)	Chrome (Cr)	Copper (Cu)	Silicium (Si)	Phosphorus (P)	Sulphur (S)
0.3	3.5	1.0	0.45–0.85	0.05–0.3	< 0.035	< 0.035

Table 10-5: Specification of the physical properties of the aforementioned steel.

Tensile strength	Elastic limit	Elongation	Contradiction	Impact test
66.14–81.89 kg/cm²	47.25 kg/cm²	> 16%	> 30%	2.765 kgm

In *Kaigun Hōjutsu-shi*, p. 63, after referring to experiences made in Britain, France and Germany during stays in the principal weapon factories (Armstrong, Vickers, Schneider & Cie., Krupp) in the 1920s and 1930s, it is claimed that the specifications as given above were not inferior to those of the European navies.

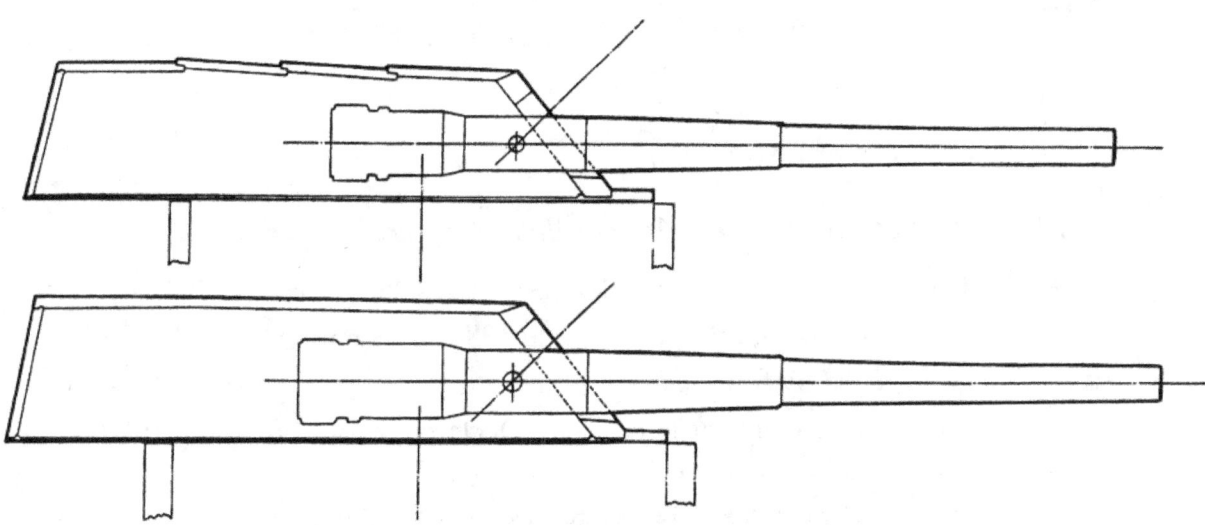

Figure 10-1: Comparison of the 46-cm 45-calibre gun (top) and the 50.8-cm 45-calibre gun (*Sekai no Kansen*)

The weight of a twin turret was calculated as 2,780 tons (the 46-cm triple turret of the *Yamato* class weighed 2,560 tons). The weight of the training part was 216 tons; the diameter was 13.0 m, that of the roller path was 12.0 m (The 46-cm triple turret was 12.274 m.). The diameter of the barbette was 15.040 m. The height from the base plate to the trunnions was 6.00 m.

The thickness of the front shield of the gun house was 800 mm, thus requiring the application of two armor plates (double layer), while the thickness of the roof plate of 295 mm permitted the production in one layer.

The weight of the AP projectile was 1,950 kg (A 46-cm AP shell weighed 1,460 kg.), the length was 1.535 m (without windshield)[293] and the diameter at the (rotating) bands was 531 mm. For the production of these projectiles the Gunnery Division, projectile factory, of Kure Navy Yard had to design the necessary equipment for the heat treatment, particularly the hardening process (heating furnace, annealing furnace, melting bath, etc.)

Figure 10-2: Super *Yamato* (Gakken)

Super Heavy (A Class) Cruiser (Actually Battle Cruiser)

In 1940 the USA ordered the *Alaska* class as "large cruisers" but these 27,500-ton heavy cruisers, armed with nine 12" (30.48-cm) guns in three triple turrets and propelled by four geared turbine sets developing 150,000 shp to attain 33 knots were actually battle cruisers. Declared as opponents of the Ger-

---

[293] The length of a 46-cm AP projectile with windshield was 1.9835 m and it is supposed that the total length of the 51-cm AP projectile would have been in the range of 2.10 m, provided that the same angle for the windshield as in the 46-cm AP shell (23° 30') was used.

man 11" (28-cm) *Admiral Graf Spee* class armorclads, the IJN recognised the American ships as a threat to the IJN's heavy cruisers and the need arose to produce a counterpart capable of opposing this new type.

The necessity to have a super large cruiser had apparently already been recognised the year before, but for quite a different reason. After the formation of the Second Fleet as a night battle force in 1930 the number of heavy cruisers assigned to the fleet increased gradually following the completion of these ships. They participated in very hard exercises and considerable results were expected by their action, particularly after the adoption of the oxygen-propelled Type 93 61-cm torpedo. A 10,000-ton heavy cruiser was considered insufficient to serve as a flagship for this large force, judging from various factors ranging from visibility to communication facilities and including also components regarding seaworthiness and military characteristics.

In the Naval General Staff Commander Inoue Ken'ichi, the top member under Captain Yanagimoto, collected the opinions of the Naval Gunnery School (*Kaigun Hōjutsu Gakkō*), the Naval Underwater Weapon School (*Kaigun Suirai Gakkō*), the Higher Naval College (*Kaigun Daigakkō*), the Combined Fleet (*Rengō Kantai*), etc. and studied the various data. He concluded that the construction of a super large cruiser displacing 20,000 to 25,000 tons was necessary to lead the heavy cruisers in the night battle that was to precede the decisive battle of the main forces.

After informing his chief about his conclusion, Yanagimoto decided to propose the building of such a ship and this proposal was made to the navy minister and the Navy Technical Department in August 1940. Rough calculations of the Navy Technical Department showed that a ship armed with six 14" (35.56-cm) in three twin mounts, a speed of 35 knots and with a protection against the own gun calibre guns, in order to out-perform the American super-heavy cruiser, would displace about 40,000 tons. This initial design was recognised as excessively large. By reducing the calibre of the main gun but increasing the number and reducing the speed, a decrease of the displacement to about 32,000 tonnes (35,000 tonnes trial displacement) could be realized. The Naval General Staff agreed with the mounting of nine 50-cal 12" (30.48-cm) guns in three triple turrets and the reduction of the speed to 33–32 knots. However, this project was cancelled.

The new 12" gun was temporarily called "Trial B Gun" and the Naval General Staff made the request for its design to the First Division of the Navy Technical Department at the same time as the *Kō Hō*. According to *Shōwa*

Zōsen-shi, vol. 1, p. 536, the trial production of the 50-cal 30-cm gun and the design of the turret were progressing at the beginning of the Pacific War—when everything was cancelled. This source gives the weight of this triple turret as 1,000 tons, including 350 tons of armor, and thus it was almost equal to the twin 41-cm of the battleships of the *Nagato* class. Unfortunately, no data of the *Otsu Hō* are given and according to the late Rear-Admiral Takasu Kōichi no documents referring to the rough design have been found.

In his *Gunkan Kihon Keikaku Shiryō*, p. 157, Fukuda Keiji gives the weight of the triple turret as 1,012 tons and the weight of the projectile (supposed to be AP) as 355 kg.

Terazaki Takaji, who also contributed to *Kaigun Hōjutsu-shi*, gives no technical data of this gun in a fine contribution entitled "Unfinished *Kō* Gun & *Otsu* Gun of the Japanese Navy," nor have anything been found in Mayuzumi Haruo's book about naval gunnery.

Therefore, lack of sources forces the authors to bring to an end this story about both unfinished guns with a very disappointing result, at least as far as the new 30-cm gun is concerned.

The 18.1" guns carried by the *Yamato* class thus remain the culmination and peak of the rifled gun technique in Japan. Considering the fact that the construction of heavy guns (whose calibre exceeded 8") in Japan only began in the 1910s, based upon the techniques of the Armstrong and Vickers Companies, it is quite understandable that Japanese designers and constructors took great pride in producing, within roughly 20 years, a locally constructed gun that was the prerequisite for the realization of the "outranging" strategy and, hence, the most important item of the conception of the *Yamato* class.

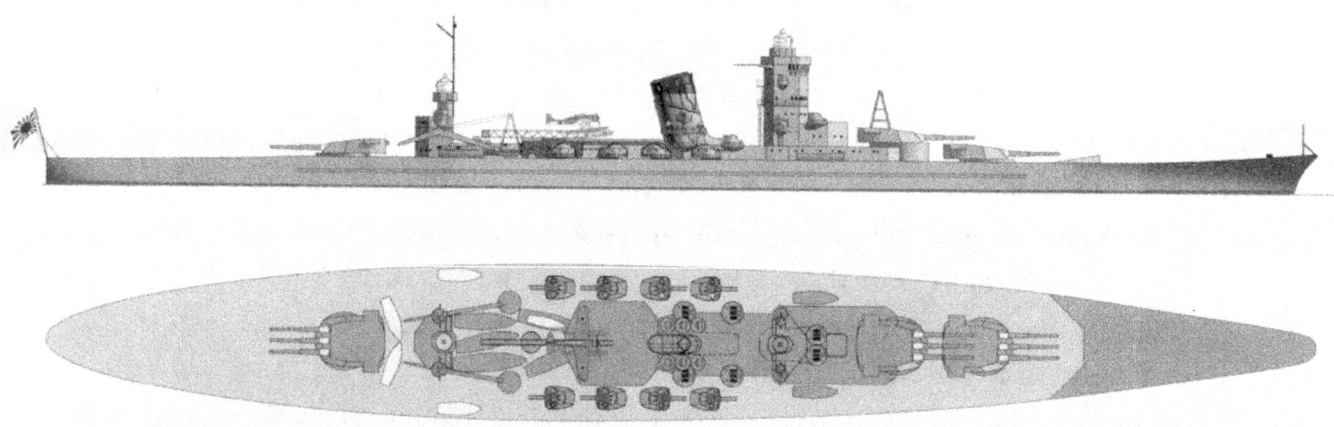

Figure 10-3: Artist's impression of the unfinished super large cruiser armed with nine 12" guns (Gakken)

Select Bibliography

Books

Agawa Hiroyuki. *The Reluctant Admiral: Yamamoto and the Imperial Navy.* Tōkyō: Kōdansha, 1979.

Asada Sadao. *From Mahan to Pearl Harbor: The Imperial Japanese Navy and the United States.* Annapolis: Naval Institute Press, 2006.

Blair, Jr., Clay. *Silent Victory: The U.S. Submarine War against Japan.* Philadelphia: J. B. Lippincott Company, 1975.

Bōeichō Bōeikenshūjo Senshibu. *Senshi Sōsho* (Military History Series), volumes 17 and 56 (of 102). Tōkyō: Asagumo Shimbusha, 1966–1980.

Cressman, Robert J. *The Official Chronology of the U.S. Navy in World War II.* Annapolis: Naval Institute Press, 1999.

Fukada Masao. *Gunkan Meka Kaihatsu Monogatari (Story of the Development of Warship Mechanisms).* Tōkyō: Kōjinsha, 1988.

Fukuda Keiji. *Gunkan Kihon Keikaku Shiryō (Outline of the Fundamental Design of Warships).* Tōkyō: Konnichi no Wadai-sha, 1989.

Fukui Shizuo. *Nihon no Gunkan: Waga Zōkan Gijutsu no Hattatsu to Kantei no Hensen (Japanese Warships: Development and Transition of Naval Engineering).* Tōkyō: Shuppan Kyōdōsha, 1956.

Fukui Shizuo. *Shashin-shū Nihon no Gunkan (Pictorial: Fighting Ships of the Imperial Japanese Navy).* Tōkyō: KK Bestsellers, 1970.

Fukui Shizuo. *Kaigun Kantei-shi (Japanese Naval Vessels Illustrated, 1869–1945),* volume 1: *Senkan • Jun-yōsenkan (Battleships & Battle Cruisers).* Tōkyō: KK Bestsellers, 1974.

Fukui Shizuo et al. *Rengō Kantai Fujōsu (Combined Fleet at Sea).* Tōkyō: KK Bestsellers, 1983.

Fukui Shizuo et al. *Fukui Shizuo Chosaku-shū: Gunkan Nanajū-go Nen Kaisō-ki (The Collection of the Works of Fukui Shizuo: Seventy-five Years of Warship History Reflection),* volumes 1, 2 and 6 (of 12). Tōkyō: Kōjinsha, 1992–2003.

Fukui Shizuo et al. *Shashin Nihon Kaigun Zen Kantei-shi (Japanese Naval Vessels 1869–1945: Fukui Shizuo Collection),* 2 volumes. Tōkyō: KK Bestsellers, 1994.

Gakken. *Nihon Kaigun Nyūmon (The Imperial Japanese Navy).* Tōkyō: Gakken, 2007.

Hara Katsuhiro. *Senkan Yamato Kenzō Hiroku (All about super-battleship Yamato).* Tōkyō: KK Bestsellers, 1999.

Hara Katsuhiro. *Kessen Senkan Yamato no Zenbō (The Complete Story of the Decisive Battle of the Yamato)*. Tōkyō: Ariadne Military, 2004.

Hara Katsuhiro. *Senkan Yamato Eien nare! (Battleship Yamato Forever!)* Tōkyō: KK Bestsellers, 2005.

Hara Tameichi. *Japanese Destroyer Captain*. New York: Ballantine Books, 1961.

Hodges, Peter. *The Big Gun: Battleship Main Armament 1860–1945*. London: Conway Maritime Press, 1981.

Ishibashi Takao. *Senkan • Jun-yōsenkan (Battleships & Battle Cruisers)*. Tōkyō: Namiki Shobō, 2007.

Izumi Kōzō. *Nihon no Senkan (Japanese Battleships)*. Tōkyō: Grand Prix, 2001.

Kaigun Hōjutsu-shi Kankōkai. *Kaigun Hōjutsu-shi (History of Naval Gunnery)*. Tōkyō: Kaigun Hōjutsu-shi Kankōkai, 1975.

Kaigun Suirai-shi Kankōkai. *Kaigun Suirai-shi (History of Underwater Weapons of the Navy)*. Tōkyō: Shinkōsha, 1979.

Kure-shi Kaiji Rekishi Kagakukan. *Senkan Yamato • Musashi (Battleships Yamato & Musashi)*. Tōkyō: Daiyamondosha, 2005.

Makino Shigeru, Fukui Shizuo et al. *Kaigun Zōsen Gijutsu Gaiyō (Outline of Naval Shipbuilding Technique), volumes 1, 5 and 7 (of 7–handwritten)*. 1948–1954.

Makino Shigeru. *Kansen Nōto (Warship Notes)*. Tōkyō: Shuppan Kyōdōsha, 1987.

Maruzen Co. *Gunkan Meka (Warship Mechanisms), volume 1: Nihon no Senkan (Japanese Battleships)*. Tōkyō: Maruzen Co., 1980.

Matsumoto Kitarō & Chihaya Masataka. *Senkan Yamato • Musashi Sekkei to Kenzō (Design and Construction of the Yamato and Musashi)*. Tōkyō: Hobaku Shoten, 1952.

Mayuzumi Haruo. *Kanpō Shageki no Rekishi (History of Naval Guns and Fire Control Systems)*. Tōkyō: Hara Shobō, 1977.

Morison, Samuel E. *History of United States Naval Operations in World War II, 14 volumes*. Boston: Little, Brown & Company, 1947–1962.

Naitō Hatsuho et al. *Senkan Musashi Kenzō Kiroku: Yamato Gata Senkan no Zenbō (The Construction of the Musashi: A Portrait of the Yamato-Class Battleships)*. Tōkyō: Atene Shobō, 1994.

Nihon Zōsen Gakkai. *Shōwa Zōsen-shi (History of Ship Construction in the Shōwa Era), volume 1 (of 2)*. Tōkyō: Hara Shobō, 1977.

Niwata Shōzō. *Kenkan Hiwa (Secret Stories about Warships)*. Tōkyō: Senpaku Gijutsu Kyōkai, 1961.

Niwata Shōzō. *Senkan Yamato o Wasureruna (Do Not Forget the Battleship Yamato)*. Tōkyō: Kyū Nippon Kaigun Kantei Kenshō Shuppan-kai, 1979.

Nomura Minoru. *Teikoku Kaigun: Kyū Nippon Kaigun Kanzen Gaido (The Imperial Navy: Complete Guide to the Old Japanese Navy)*. Tōkyō: Shōeisha, 1995.

Padfield, Peter. *Guns at Sea*. London: Hugh Evelyn, 1973.

Prados, John. *Combined Fleet Decoded: The Secret History of American Intelligence and the Japanese Navy in World War II*. New York: Random House, 1995.

Sakamoto Seiki & Fukukawa Hideki. *Nihon Kaigun Hensei Jiten (Japanese Navy Organization Dictionary)*. Tōkyō: Fuyō Shobō Shuppan, 2003.

Schmalenbach, Paul. *Die Geschichte der deutschen Schiffsartillerie*. Herford: Koehlers Verlagsgesellschaft, 1968.

Shiga Fujio et al. *Kimitsu Heiki no Zenbō (Secret Weapons of the IJN)*. Tōkyō: Kōyōsha, 1952.

Spurr, Russell. *A Glorious Way To Die: The Kamikaze Mission of the Battleship Yamato, April 1945*. Annapolis: Naval Institute Press, 1981.

Ugaki Matome. *Sensōroku (War Diary)*. Tōkyō: Nippon Shuppan Kyōdō, 1953.

Ugaki Matome. *Fading Victory: The Diary of Admiral Matome Ugaki 1941–1945*. Pittsburgh: University of Pittsburgh, 1991.

U.S. Strategic Bombing Survey. *Interrogations of Japanese Officials*. Washington: U.S. Strategic Bombing Survey, 1946.

U.S. Strategic Bombing Survey. *The Campaigns of the Pacific War*. Washington: U.S. Strategic Bombing Survey, 1946.

Yamamoto Yoshihide et al. *Nihon Kaigun Kansai Heiki Daizukan (All about Japanese Naval Shipboard Weapons)*. Tōkyō: KK Bestsellers, 2002.

Yoshida Mitsuru. *Requiem for Battleship Yamato*. Seattle: University of Washington Press, 1985.

Yoshimura Akira. Build the Musashi! The Birth and Death of the World's Greatest Battleship. Tōkyō: Kōdansha, 1991.

PERIODICALS

Contributions to the History of Imperial Japanese Warships. Birkenhard: Hans Lengerer.

Maru (Circle). Tōkyō: Ushio Shobō.

Nihon no Meikan (Japanese Warship Names). Tōkyō: Kōbunsha.

Sekai no Kansen (Ships of the World). Tōkyō: Kaijinsha Co.

Taiheiyō Senshi Shirīzu (Pacific War History Series). Tōkyō: Gakken.
Umi to Sora (Sea and Sky). Kōbe: Jishūkai.
Warship. London: Conway Maritime Press.
Warship International. Toledo: International Naval Research Organisation.

DOCUMENTS

Military History Section Headquarters, Army Forces Far East. *The Japanese Monographs*. Tōkyō: Military History Section Headquarters, Army Forces Far East, 1945–1960.

U.S. Naval History Division. *Reports of the U.S. Naval Technical Mission to Japan*. Washington: U.S. Naval History Division, 1945–1946.

INTERNET

Nishida Hiroshi. *Imperial Japanese Navy*. http://homepage2.nifty.com/nishidah/index.htm

Postlude photo: Yamato at Hashirajima in 1943 (Kure Maritime Museum)

ALSO FROM NIMBLE BOOKS:

The World Wonder'd: What Really Happened Off Samar by Robert Lundgren. ISBN 978-1608880461.

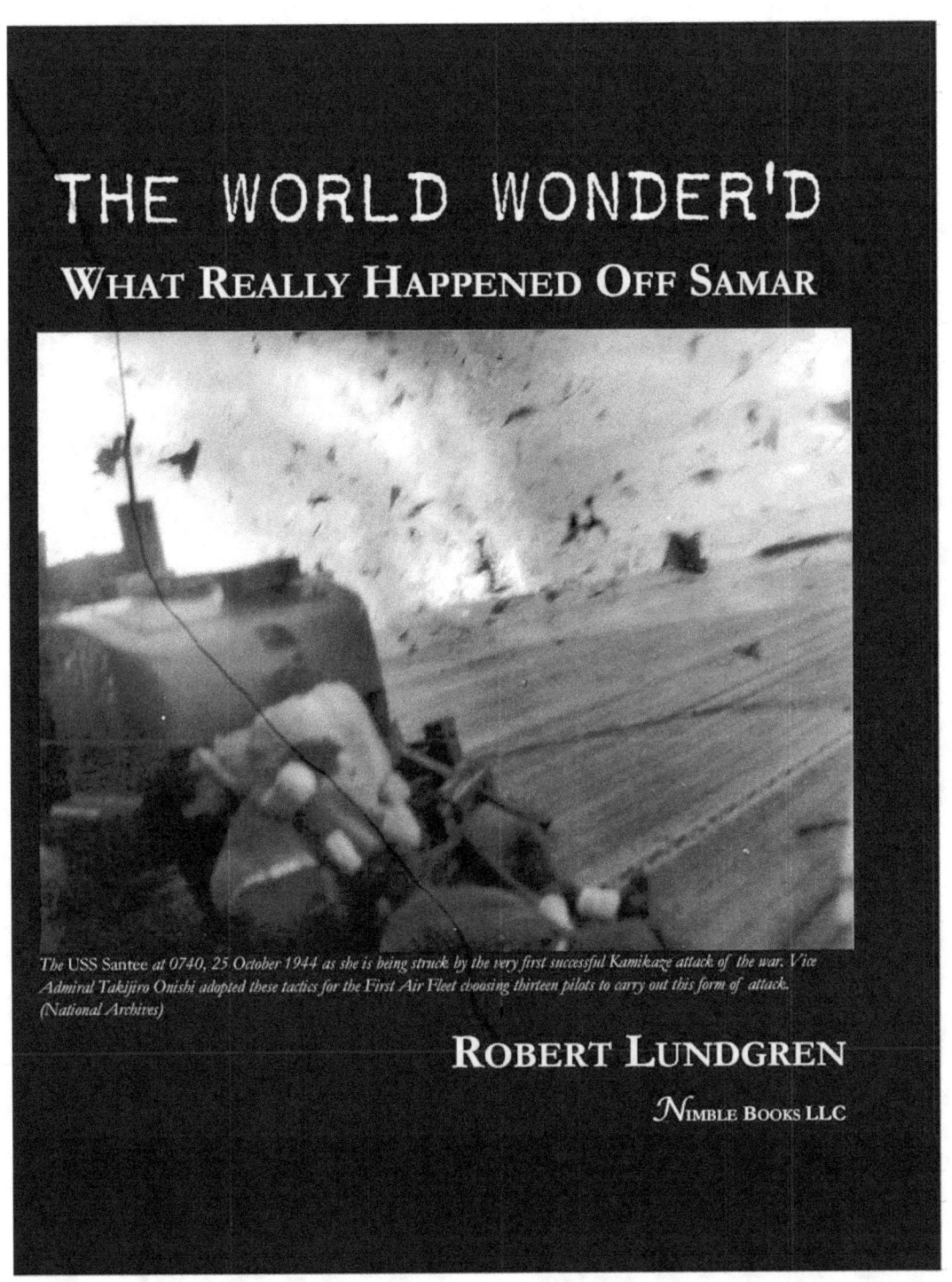

www.ingramcontent.com/pod-product-compliance
Lightning Source LLC
Chambersburg PA
CBHW080934020526
44116CB00034B/2595